# Voyaging Under Power

## FOURTH EDITION

# Voyaging Under Power

## FOURTH EDITION

By Captain Robert P. Beebe

Revised by Denis D. Umstot

**International Marine / McGraw-Hill**

Camden, Maine • New York • Chicago • San Francisco • Lisbon • London • Madrid • Mexico City •
Milan • New Delhi • San Juan • Seoul • Singapore • Sydney • Toronto

1 2 3 4 5 6 7 8 9 10 11 12 13 14 15 FGR/FGR 1 9 8 7 6 5 4 3
ISBN 978-0-07-176733-0
MHID 0-07-176733-9
Ebook (four color) ISBN 0-07-176747-9

**Library of Congress Cataloging-in-Publication Data is available from the Library of Congress.**

All photos courtesy the author unless noted otherwise. Art credits/permissions are found at the captions and in the endnotes. Photo on page i, *Avatar*, off New Zealand (Steve Dashew); on page ii, *Teka III*, in Icy Straits, Alaska (Peter Geerlof).

International Marine/McGraw-Hill books are available at special quantity discounts to use as premiums and sales promotions or for use in corporate training programs. To contact a representative, please e-mail us at bulksales@mcgraw-hill.com.

This book is printed on acid-free paper.

Questions regarding the content of this book should be addressed to
www.internationalmarine.com
Questions regarding the ordering of this book should be addressed to
The McGraw-Hill Companies
Customer Service Department
P.O. Box 547
Blacklick, OH 43004
Retail customers: 1-800-262-4729
Bookstores: 1-800-722-4726

NOTICE: Repairing, modifying, and maintaining your boat can expose you to potentially dangerous situations and substances. References to brand names does not indicate endorsement of or guarantee the safety of using these products. In using this book, the reader releases the author, publisher, and distributor from liability for any loss or injury, including death, allegedly caused, in whole or in part, by relying on information contained in this book.

*To Mary, my life and cruising partner who made this lifestyle enjoyable and possible. And to all those voyagers out there who shared their experiences about their sea adventures.*

# Contents

# Chapter Thirteen. Proven Passagemakers of the Past     235

# Chapter Fourteen. Voyage Preparation and Planning     259

# Chapter Fifteen. Crossing Oceans     269

# Appendices

# Foreword

## Bill Parlatore

When my wife, Laurene, and I started *PassageMaker, The Trawler & Ocean Motorboat Magazine* in 1995, it was chiefly because we had interest in these boats, but could find little information about them. Our many questions were largely unanswered because there were few passagemakers with experience to share. Around the same time, Jim Leishman was updating the earlier edition of Beebe's classic, *Voyaging Under Power*. That third edition was a fresh look at the concept of cruising long distances under power and included the worldly experiences of Jim and Suzy Sink on *Salvation II*, a Nordhavn 46 that Leishman's company PAE built to demonstrate that a production powerboat could be safely voyaged around the world.

But past editions of this book represented, in my opinion, a single voice, a single point of view. Back then few people had voyaged long distances in powerboats and anyone interested in pursuing this lifestyle generally lacked hard information on how to go about it. But that didn't tarnish the dream potential of the book. Readers of *Voyaging Under Power* could buy into the dream, and many did. One of those readers was Denis Umstot.

As we grew *PassageMaker Magazine*, I became passionate about adding practical information to fill in the gaps, publishing various people's preparations and voyaging experiences—material that gave others confidence to pursue their own dreams. Most passagemaking couples were happy to share the details, techniques, and skills that came from voyaging offshore.

When I first met Denis and Mary they were deeply involved in restoring *Teka III* on which they intended to see the world, up close and personal. Like many others who wanted to pursue the passagemaking lifestyle, they figuratively inched along, gaining experience on each trip, finding what worked, and what needed modification. By the time they stopped to visit us in Annapolis, Maryland, on their way to cross the Atlantic to Europe, they had sorted it all out.

It is a process that is both fulfilling and inspiring.

And therein lies the reason I am confident that Denis's new edition of *Voyaging Under Power* is a tour de force. It is significantly more than a freshening up of the earlier editions.

To best describe why this is such a valuable work unlike anything done before, I offer one word: community.

The biggest change in passagemaking, and what Denis captures so well, is the growing community of people out there cruising the world. No single voice represents what it is, how it is done, and why it is so wonderful. Many men and women experience this lifestyle and freely offer their advice about living the dream. There are lessons to be learned by anyone venturing offshore—with so many passagemakers having now successfully crossed oceans there is a virtual wealth of information about long-distance voyaging.

The heroic exploits of early pioneers has been largely displaced by ordinary people living the dream in safety and comfort. Not every distance cruiser yearns to complete a circumnavigation—many are satisfied simply to do a transatlantic or cross the Pacific. Others just want the capability of a passagemaking vessel since coastal cruising can be challenging in many parts of the world.

There were a decidedly small number of suitable passagemaking boats and their courageous crews at sea in 1995. Today it is a much larger community, and a truly global one at that. (When the Sinks crossed the Atlantic there were but a handful of Nordhavn sisterships; today the Nordhavn fleet numbers almost 500 boats. And there are many other vessel choices out there, both production and custom, as you will read in this edition of *Voyaging Under Power*.)

What is so great about this community of cruisers is our willingness to learn about, and readily share, our collective experiences. No two passages are alike, and no two boats and crew experiences are the same, even when experienced together. There are too many variables: crew personalities, presence and condition of onboard equipment, vessel characteristics in a seaway, food, and, of course, wind and weather. Sometimes life is so good the passage is boringly calm and uneventful, all systems work well, individuals become a team, and the seas are flat calm. Write a book, live in paradise, all systems go.

Other times, well—thoughts of selling the boat and buying a pig farm far from the sea. (Yes, that was their sentiment.) But that feeling passes quickly as tomorrow is another day....

Querying one cruiser to get his or her ideas on the right boat and its systems may not reveal your silver bullet, but it adds to your knowledge base. An experienced cruiser with an older boat, for instance, especially on a relatively small budget, has a vastly different concept of voyaging and its priorities than another starting out with a shiny new boat, and perhaps more money than experience. Each may be valid, but it is prudent to hear both cruisers address and answer the same question.

Denis has masterfully compiled a rich body of knowledge in this new edition, interweaving many voyagers' experiences, opinions, and recommendations on the many subjects that encompass passage-making. To this he adds the wealth of his own experience gained while traveling thousands of miles aboard *Teka III*. As a result, the reader of the fourth edition of *Voyaging Under Power* has a vast amount of information from which to form his or her own ideas, or make one's lists about what is needed to cruise long distances in powerboats. The chapters offer not one perspective, but many perspectives. The people who contributed to this book are the major players, if you will, within our community—they speak from experience and know what they are talking about.

The level of detail here is practical and useful. I am reminded of one ocean crossing I went on some years back. The owner, a nice fellow eager to learn the ropes of a competent world cruiser, pulled me aside into the engine room before we departed. He told me he read my articles over the years and my fairly consistent message to go into the engine room hourly when underway offshore. He said that while it made sense to him, what exactly was he supposed to do when he went into the engine room? This book will help enlighten those with such questions.

Advances in technology have dramatically changed the passagemaking seascape. We now have utterly reliable propulsion systems, stabilization solutions, and navigation equipment. Even anchors have come a long way. Satellite communications and watermakers are commonplace, and comfort is an essential priority. Modern electronics improve and weather routing gets better and more accurate with each passing year—today a family can safely cruise without the many unknowns that once made such adventure a risky proposition.

While Denis makes a fine argument for doing more with less—which I happen to agree with—it is also true that others can get away from it all bringing every piece of technology with them as well. Denis includes these varying perspectives throughout the book. It is refreshing and informative to see what works for successful cruisers.

The list of contributors shows the quality of experience in the pages of this fourth edition of *Voyaging Under Power*. Anyone wanting to join, or at least understand the elements of the long-distance passagemaking lifestyle will find a great deal of knowledge that is realistic, useful, and timely. Denis has done a superb job at pulling this all together and I salute him for the result. I know the cruising community will as well.

I am sure you will keep *Voyaging Under Power, Fourth Edition*, on your pilothouse bookshelf (or its electronic equivalent) for years to come.

Annapolis, Maryland
October, 2012

# Preface to the Fourth Edition

## Denis Umstot

*Twenty years from now you will be more disappointed by the things that you
didn't do than by the ones you did do. So throw off the bowlines. Sail away from
the safe harbor. Catch the trade winds in your sails. Explore. Dream. Discover.*
*Mark Twain*

I had no intention of writing another book. Before
we started our life as voyagers, I taught management in various universities in the United States and
Hong Kong.* I had to write academic papers and text-
books to maintain my status in academia. When I
retired from that life, I told my wife that I was through
with writing. Well, I was dead wrong. My wife and
partner, Mary Umstot, began her writing career about
the time I was retiring from mine. She has written
13 articles for *Passagemaker Magazine* (a few with my
assistance or perspective). As a result of our involve-
ment with Bill and Laurene Parlatore, *PassageMaker
Magazine*, and Trawler Fest, we have been lucky to be
meet many of the leaders in this field.

Our voyaging life started out slowly and gradually
developed into major passages, including two Atlantic crossings. We started out with a Hershine 37',
Taiwan trawler, which we owned for about 10 years

and cruised the Pacific Northwest from our home in
Gig Harbor, Washington. After my retirement, we
sold the boat and went looking for something more
seaworthy. At that time we were thinking of Alaska
and the Queen Charlotte Islands. While searching for
this boat, we discovered Bob Beebe's *Voyaging Under
Power*. Reading this book opened entirely new horizons for me—imagine, a boat that could cross oceans!
(I had dreamed of world cruising in a sailboat since
adolescence. Alas, my bride did not share my love of
sailing—she hated heeling!)

We looked at several affordable passagemakers,
but each had some major fault. One had the master
stateroom combined with the galley. Another big,
steel European boat had heavy waterproof doors,
making it look more like a submarine than a yacht.
Then in 1996 we were visiting our son in San Diego,
when we saw an advertisement for a Beebe Passagemaker, called *Teka III*. This was the boat for us! It had
some quirks that we learned to love, like an entrance to
the owner's stateroom via the covered aft deck. It also
had a very large covered area behind the pilothouse
that has turned out to be one of the best things about
the boat. In addition, it had a legendary Gardner
engine that looked very businesslike and bulletproof.
The boat was already 15 years old so we spent a lot of

---

*I also spent 20 years in the United States Air Force, part of the
time in various logistics jobs, and the remainder as a Profes-
sor of Management at the Air Force Institute of Technology.
I have a Ph.D., courtesy of the USAF, from the University of
Washington. My additional academic teaching and research
positions were at the University of Washington, the Air Force
Academy, the University of Puget Sound, and the Chinese
University of Hong Kong.

time and money repairing, replacing, and improving systems, but the hull was strong and seaworthy. The boat had already crossed the Atlantic four times with the original owner.

This began our odyssey with *Teka III*. We took her up the Pacific Coast to Canada and then to Alaska. Then we decided to experience the Sea of Cortez and Central America. It was an easy decision to transit the Panama Canal into the Caribbean, where we found new places to explore. We finally wound up cruising the Intracoastal Waterway from Florida to Maine. Sometime during these voyages, we decided we would take the boat to Europe. Crossing an ocean for the first time is anxiety producing, but the rewards could be great. Mary was not sure about this ocean-crossing business, but decided she could jump ship in Bermuda if she did not like the experience. However, she was hooked! She did not want to miss one moment of the adventure. She has been aboard every one of *Teka III*'s over 60,000 nautical miles. She wrote a book about our cruising experiences, *Voyaging to the Mediterranean Under Power*. You will get a chance to read a few excerpts later in the book.

When Mary was publishing her book, Bill Parlatore put her in touch with his friends at International

Denis and Mary Umstot aboard *Teka III*.

Marine. They asked Mary if she would be interested in doing the revision of *Voyaging Under Power*. Mary said she didn't feel competent to handle the technical parts of the book, but recommended me for the job. I was reluctant. I had been through the process of publishing a book before and knew I would have to make a major time and energy commitment. On the other hand, I felt that I had learned a lot over the years of cruising, much of it the hard way. I felt an urge to share my experiences. Thus began this revision of Captain Beebe's seminal work. I feel honored to continue his legacy.

One of the advantages of this edition over earlier ones is the wealth of cruising experience that is now available. Thanks to the Internet and numerous websites and blogs, it is much easier to gather the experience of others. This edition is full of the experiences, good and bad, of experienced voyagers. There are also many more boats to choose from, both new and used. Systems are complex and sometimes difficult to understand. Choosing the right boat, especially if you are on a budget, is a major task.

I have tried to balance the coverage for various boat builders and designers—there are many paths to successful voyaging. Nordhavn gets a good deal of coverage simply because they have more boats out there cruising so there are more tales to tell. You may tire of my now 30-year old boat, but it would still be my first choice (with perhaps one exception, not to be disclosed), even if I were rich enough to afford any boat out there. I hope you will see that you can still go cruising on a relatively modest budget and with a relatively small investment.

My general philosophy of voyaging seems close to Captain Beebe's—crossing oceans to exotic, interesting, and beautiful places, in comfort, with a minimum of problems and expense. Boats that are overly complex may cause a great deal of angst rather than joy. It is no fun to spend most of your time fixing problems. I have never envied the mega yachts, with crew and engineers needed full time just to keep the boat operating. For me, that is not what cruising is all about.

The Mark Twain quote at the beginning has been cited by many passagemakers and is so true. There is a wonderful world out there if you just make up your mind to do it. If you wait too long, success may be elusive or your health may fail.

## CHAPTER ONE

# Robert Beebe: An Introduction

## Jim Leishman

Born in 1909 and raised as an "Army brat" (his own description), Robert Beebe was introduced to his lifelong passion as a young child. His interest and love for all things nautical began with his experiences in a dugout canoe given to him by his father, the commanding officer of a garrison on the island of Zamboanga in the Philippines.

Recalling his childhood, Captain Robert Beebe states:

*I don't think one day passed that we were not out on those marvelous, clear, tropical waters right in front of our quarters. I have never forgotten those days and have been a tropics buff ever since, and a boat nut as well. In a dugout canoe my brother and I, together with some of the neighboring kids, fought more pirates, found more buried treasure, and raised more mysterious shores than any kid today possibly could in the present-day outboard-driven dinks.*

Throughout adolescence, Beebe's experience and skill grew, and he began to develop an appreciation for the technical aspects of the various sailing dinghies and small cruisers he had sailed aboard. He studied the few periodicals of the day and paid particular attention to the "How to Build" articles by William Atkin that appeared in *Motorboating*. As he neared completion of his primary school education, aviation caught his interest, and he was faced with a decision: whether to study aeronautical engineering at MIT or enter the Naval Academy at Annapolis. In the end, his lifelong love of the water drew him to Navy service and Annapolis, where the Academy offered plenty of opportunities to hone his already keen sailing skills, along with a degree in aeronautical engineering.

Graduating in 1931 and becoming a naval aviator in 1933, Beebe spent his first fleet tour in the San Diego/Long Beach area. It was there on the West Coast that he began to think of an oceangoing cruising sailboat for himself and his new bride. When it became apparent to the Beebes that his next tour of duty would be in the Hawaiian Islands, they searched for a vessel capable of crossing the Pacific

Captain Robert Beebe, 1909–1988.

Figure 1–1. Philippine canoe Robert Beebe owned as a boy.

and suitable for cruising the islands. They located a partially completed 30-footer that seemed perfectly suited for the voyage. Beebe later related:

> We inspected the boat. She was set up in her own building shed in what is now Newport Beach. The hull was practically complete, and all the material for her rigging and interior was present. All the workmanship was beautiful, all fastenings the best, lead keel, bronze hardware, and so on. She was an Atkin design, number 311, and had never been given a name. She was one of his double-enders. Many vessels of this size go to Hawaii every year, but in 1936 we didn't get much encouragement.
>
> The problem was getting her done in time. We checked everywhere and had several builders in to give us an estimate, more of time than money. We reluctantly had to conclude there was practically no chance for us to get her in time for a proper shakedown and passage before I had to report to Hawaii. We let her go. I've often wished since then we had been a little bolder. She was really an exceptional vessel. The next year a member of the services did sail out for duty in Hawaii—(then) Colonel George S. Patton, U.S. Army, arrived in an Alden schooner.

Stationed at Pearl Harbor in 1936, Beebe found himself piloting the biplane flying boats of the era over the waters west of Hawaii. The Pearl Harbor Yacht Club had a fleet of eight Herreshoff S-class sloops, two of which belonged to the commanding officers of the air station and navy yard. Beebe became sailing officer, responsible for all maintenance of the two vessels, which allowed him to participate in almost every one of the weekly races. What he learned from competitive sailing in the rugged conditions around the island of Oahu would be formative: "I developed a profound admiration for the Herreshoff S and, by extension, a liking for heavy keelboats in general."

His continuing desire to own a cruiser with live-aboard accommodations was as strong as ever, and his experience with the S boats caused him to develop his own ideas about a suitable design. "I started sketching my own ideas, and it was soon apparent I didn't know beans about how to go about it."

Beebe ordered a copy of a newly published book called *Yacht Designing and Planning*, by Howard I. Chapelle.

> I must have read through that book a half-dozen times. It certainly changed my life. Where formerly I had been content to sail in what I could find without much thought as to whether the boats were really good or not, now the fundamentals explained in Chapelle's book led my thoughts to how things could be improved, the advantages of certain shapes, and the influence of various factors.

Beebe continued to develop his own rough sketches, and when time permitted he read the published works of other designers. He began to correspond with William Atkin about his ideas. When his tour of duty in Hawaii ended, he returned to Annapolis for postgraduate studies, where he developed a friendship with his mentor, Howard Chapelle. Chapelle's sharpie designs greatly appealed to Beebe for sailing in shallow Chesapeake waters, and after a visit with the designer in Ipswich, Massachusetts, Beebe returned to Annapolis with a set of Chapelle plans in hand.

He commissioned a local Annapolis yard to build a 34-foot sharpie, christened *Sara Reid* after his mother.

Beebe sailed his new ketch every chance he got and was so impressed by her performance that he wrote numerous articles about her, the first of which appeared in the August 1939 issue of *Yachting*. The next 40 years saw many articles by Robert Beebe in the most popular boating magazines, and not all of a purely technical nature. Beebe developed the skills of an excellent storyteller, and his adventures gave him a constant supply of new material. He tells of a particular experience aboard the *Sara Reid* that undoubtedly influenced his lifework:

> Working to windward once in the company of a 40-foot ketch, we were in the center of the bay (Chesapeake) with a south wind of 22 knots blowing against an outgoing tide. Naturally we could not hold the ketch under those conditions. We started our borrowed 2-horsepower outboard and ran it at half speed. The *Sara Reid* caught and passed the ketch both pointing and footing—the best illustration I have ever seen of the effect of a bit of power in windward work.

1939 marked the beginning of World War II, and Beebe found himself called to Florida as a training officer, producing much-needed carrier pilots. He found time to sail the *Sara Reid* south, and it was while sailing aboard his agile sharpie on the north end of Biscayne Bay on a beautiful winter's day that Beebe learned of the attack on Pearl Harbor. There was no time now to think of yachting.

With his accumulated experience and training, Beebe was given command of an air squadron in the Pacific. But then the unexpected happened:

> Well, we did go West, and I did get command of a dive bombing squadron. Unfortunately, just as our air group was ready to proceed to the South Pacific, I had to be hospitalized for some necessary surgery. My squadron went off and left me, and by the time I returned to duty, I was sent to the USS Saratoga as a ship's officer, where I became navigator of this aircraft carrier, one of the world's largest ships, and served in her the rest of the war.

> Regardless of how I might have felt at losing my squadron, from the point of view of yacht design, no job could have been better. The navigator's duties, while extremely important, were not overwhelmed with the details of a department with hundreds of men. He did have some free time. In addition, he had at hand an excellent source of drafting paper because so many of the ship's charts were made obsolete by later ones, a process that went on with amazing speed as we probed deeper into the South Pacific. In addition, while the ship was underway, which was most of the time, the navigator was on the bridge and in his charthouse. This kept him out of such mundane distractions as bridge games in the wardroom and encouraged industry. The result was the production of a good bit of work in several fields.

It was this sequence of events that likely sealed Beebe's fate—becoming a designer/authority whose expertise would ultimately equal those for whom he had such great respect.

At the war's end, Beebe had amassed a considerable amount of design work on cruising sailboats, particularly sharpies similar to *Sara Reid*. Beebe's now close friend Howard Chapelle admitted that he could not justify working on the sharpies for clients

**Figure 1–2.** Aircraft carrier USS *Saratoga*, Beebe's wartime ship.

who were so value-conscious that they were unwilling or unable to pay a reasonable designer's fee. Beebe, considering himself an amateur and with a primary income paying his bills, took referral work of this type from Chapelle for a number of years.

Robert Beebe proved to be a very modest man. Even in 1980 he continued to refer to himself as an *amateur*, but note how he qualified the term and considered it an important ingredient in his success in the field of long-range seagoing motorboats:

> Certainly I have sold plans from time to time since the earliest days of learning the art. But at no time have I been under any compulsion to try to make designing my principal source of income. I think this is the key. A professional yacht designer is anyone who intends to make designing his primary source of income. He may fail, of course, but if he does have this intention, he is under certain constraints that do not affect the amateur. He must, for instance, seek out the most active and popular field of design of his day and try to carve a niche there. Recently this field has been the so-called cruiser-racer sailing vessel. And here he must work in the restrictions of the rules in vogue, regardless of his own ideas. However much he may wish to experiment and advance the art, he must judge his work not on whether it is, in fact, a new breakthrough, but on what is saleable. An amateur does not labor under any of these restraints. He is free to go where his interest leads him.

Beebe's experience and enthusiasm for sail and his extensive design work in the field were all a solid foundation for his developing concept of passagemaking in specially designed motorboats. The thought process could not have evolved without the sailing experience and possibly the "amateur" association with naval architecture. It should be remembered that in the late 1950s when Beebe was developing his *Passagemaker* concept, long-range cruising in small motorboats was almost unheard of.

Let's move now to Robert Beebe's introduction to his vessel *Passagemaker* and some of the history that led up to her design.

## CHAPTER TWO

# Historical Background of Power Voyaging

## Robert Beebe, 1974

It was the last day. As I came on deck for the 0400–0800 watch, a faint light in the east showed the horizon clear, with brilliant stars overhead. There would be a good fix on this, our landfall day.

Sipping a mug of coffee while waiting for sight time, I had much to think about: the years of research and theorizing, the days and weeks of drawing plans, the months of watching the vessel grow in the builder's yard—a vessel whose highly unusual makeup we hoped would prove my theories—the sea trials, the first miles of our cruise, the ports we visited, the weather. Everything. Now, just ahead lay Rhodes, one of the fabled islands of Greece.

My thoughts went back even further: to World War II. Like so many other armchair long-cruise planners, I found myself transported to the South Pacific under circumstances that had never entered my wildest dreams. There, as navigator of the aircraft carrier *Saratoga*, I observed firsthand the conditions small cruising boats would meet after the war. It was this experience that first turned me toward a vessel distinctly different from traditional long-range types. Now, as we neared Rhodes, the work begun on the bridge of the old *Saratoga* had passed from dream to reality, and the reality was carrying me and my crew northward across the Mediterranean on this clear, calm morning toward the castle of the Knights Hospitalers.

The yacht *Passagemaker* was about to complete her first voyage in six weeks *to the day* we had made the passage to Greece from Singapore. Almost six thousand miles of calms, brisk breezes, and gales lay astern. And through it all, our ocean-crossing motorboat had chugged steadily along, averaging exactly her designed passage speed of 7.5 knots.

I knew now that crossing oceans in owner-operated small craft in the 40- to 50-foot range, under power alone and using crews by no means made up of rough-and-tough seamen, worked well. I had also learned what I'd only suspected before: that a very good case could be made for the power approach over sail for all long voyages.

To generations of seamen brought up on tales of long voyages in small sailing craft, such statements must sound like heresy. Some years ago, I too would have counted myself among those seamen. But certain experiences, certain selective reading with a critical eye, and certain designing in new directions had finally convinced me that it was possible on long voyages to do better. It is the evolution of the theory, its testing with *Passagemaker*, what we learned, and what can be recommended for the future that this book is all about.

This book, then, is about voyaging under power as contrasted with voyaging under sail. While a vast literature exists about deep-sea cruising under sail, there is little in print about long-range power voyaging. Of course, many of the problems encountered at sea are similar in both cases. But the power approach does differ from sail in several important ways that need consideration. To cite just one example: the naval architecture rules that govern the speed and range of a long-range motorboat are quite rigid and must be thoroughly understood before selecting such a craft or operating it to the limits of its ability. On the other hand, the sailing cruiser, with its "free" propulsion power, is largely independent of these rules.

Of course, I have nothing against cruising under sail. The long sailing cruises I have made have all been great fun. But, there are certain conditions and certain groups of sailors for whom the power approach has definite advantages. It is for those sailors this book is written.

It was the search for a retirement boat that led me to consider power as an alternative to sail. The more I looked into it, the more interesting it became, until the years spent pursuing the matter finally led to the building of our 50-foot *Passagemaker*. Some sixty thousand miles of deep-water cruising in her, including three ocean crossings, a round-trip to Hawaii, and two East Coast–West Coast passages taught me much that can be safely passed on to those who share this interest. Of course, during those years I exchanged experiences with the few others who had background in this narrow field, considered the features of other ocean-crossing motorboats, and studied the work of other designers.

One of the first things I undertook when I decided to embark on the design of a long-range motorboat was research in the history of the boat type. It is a scanty field, but useful lessons can be learned from what material is available.

## Early Atlantic Crossings

There were two early small-boat voyages across the Atlantic under power; both were made to demonstrate the reliability of the internal combustion engines then coming into use in boats. The first voyage was by the *Abiel Abbot Low*, using a kerosene engine. In 1902, she crossed from New York to Falmouth, England, in thirty-eight days. The second voyage was by the motorboat *Detroit* in 1912. She used a gasoline engine to cross from New York to Queenstown (now Cobh), Ireland, in twenty-eight days. What lessons have we learned from these two pioneer efforts?

My first impression after reading the logs of the *Low* and the *Detroit* was that the voyages were excellent examples of what *not* to do. With due regard for the guts of the crews, it is clear that the designers and builders had a lot to learn. This is understandable, of course, because no one had attempted such a voyage. Possibly more important, the men involved in these projects had their major training in sail.

It must have been this sail background, for instance, that produced the astonishing layout of *Detroit*. She was 35 feet long with a 9-foot beam and a 4-foot 6-inch draft. She was double-ended and resembled a lifeboat in that she had high shelters bow and stern. Amidships she was lowsided, and in the center of this deck space was the steering station—a stand-up wheel with no shelter whatsoever. The watchstander was supposed to stand there with no handholds and steer the vessel while waves washed across the deck from either side. Fantastic! Here was a station well laid out for the watch to keep an eye on the sails—but no sails!

Figure 2–1. The *Tordenskjold*, built in 1911 in Seattle, was one of the early long-range motorboats. It was designed for halibut fishing in the waters off Alaska. This boat and many like her are still fishing there one hundred years later. (Puget Sound Maritime Historical Society)

Understandably enough, this feature caused a good deal of discontent among the crew of four when *Detroit* entered the open Atlantic. However, the engine performed flawlessly, and *Detroit* arrived in Queenstown in good order.

The *Low* was not well laid out for the crossing, either. She was 38 feet long with a 34-foot waterline, 9-foot beam, and 3-foot 8-inch draft, double-ended, with a trunk cabin forward and cockpit aft. Instead of providing some shelter by putting the wheel against the trunk cabin forward, it was placed aft as on a sailing vessel and was wide open to the elements.

*Low*'s principal problem was crew trouble. Her skipper, having been hired to make this engine-demonstrating voyage, chose to take his 16-year-old son as his only crew; then he tried to do everything himself. With no relief from the tyranny of continuous steering, he soon became exhausted. This produced all sorts of crises. *Low* also had unfortunate luck with

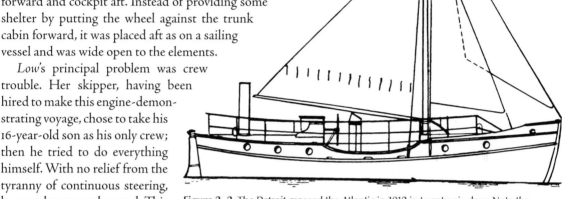

**Figure 2–2.** The *Detroit* crossed the Atlantic in 1912 in twenty-six days. Note the steering arrangement and the low side amidships.

weather, spending a good deal of time hove-to or riding to a sea anchor. When this was compounded by her copper fuel tanks springing numerous leaks due to the pounding of heavy seas, by kerosene getting into everything below decks, and by a constant battle to bail as much oil as possible back into the tanks, her crew was reduced almost to survival conditions. But they toughed it out and made it. The engine ran perfectly all the way.

Nobody felt impelled to follow in the wake of these two vessels, and the way these voyages tested

to the limit the endurance of hardened professional seamen makes this reluctance understandable.

Commencing in 1912, annual motorboat "races" were held from the United States to Bermuda. They died after three runs from lack of entries. I do not think the designs of the vessels that participated show any developments of particular interest to us today.

***Arielle*'s 1937 Atlantic crossing.** It was not until 1937 that the next crossing of the North Atlantic by a small motorboat took place. This voyage is of great interest because it was the first in a craft incorporating features found in modern ocean-crossing motorboats. The voyage was made by a Frenchman named Marin-Marie, who was the official marine painter to the French government. Marin-Marie had been a small-boat sailor all his life. In 1933, he built a double-ended cutter and sailed it singlehandedly across the Atlantic from France to New York. He enjoyed this adventure so much that he wondered how the voyage would go under power.

**Figure 2–3.** The *Abiel Abbot Low*, the first motorboat across the Atlantic. She crossed in thirty-eight days in 1902.

He certainly did a good job of researching the project and made up a specification designed to correct the flaws of earlier boats and to add features permitted by modern developments. His book, *Wind Aloft, Wind Alow* is maddeningly vague about details, but it appears that his *Arielle* was about 42 feet 6 inches long and drew 4 feet 6 inches. She was equipped with a 75-horsepower, 4-cylinder diesel and carried 1,500 gallons of fuel, a steadying and emergency propulsion rig, an enclosed steering station, a primitive form of photoelectric autopilot, and a vane steering gear that antedated by many years the models popular today on sailing cruisers. In fact, I think the only thing missing from *Arielle's* equipment was some method of stabilizing against rolling. She did use her steadying rig for this purpose, but it was ineffective for the usual reasons (see Chapter 8).

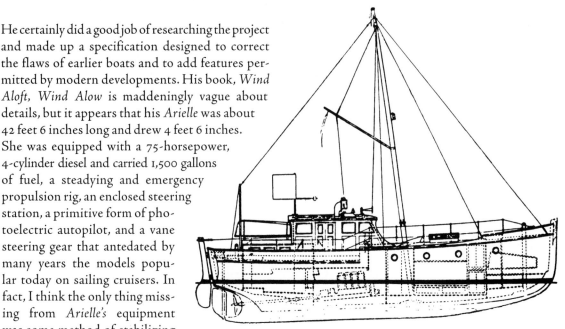

Figure 2–4. *Arielle*, profile. Note the covered steering station, steadying rig, and general air of competence in this excellently planned 43-footer.

In spite of dire predictions of disaster, to the point that the elders of the Club de Yachts de France considered having Marin-Marie restrained legally from such a foolish venture, *Arielle* left New York on July 22, 1937, and arrived in Le Havre, France, nineteen days later, essentially with nothing to report—the way any well-conducted cruise should end.

Figure 2–5. *Arielle* at sea—a photo taken from the deck of a steamer. Despite her seamanlike crossing in 1937, the feat was met by a "devastating silence."

Marin-Marie's voyage was met with devastating silence on both sides of the Atlantic. The fact that a yacht of *Arielle's* size, under the command of a well-known yachtsman, had crossed the Atlantic to now cruise the fascinating waters of Europe, and had done so in less time and for less money than would have been required to prepare the boat and ship it across (and probably arrived in much better shape than if she had been shipped), didn't seem to make *any* impression. Marin-Marie and *Arielle* were far ahead of their time, and I want to pay tribute here to their successful pioneering effort.

**Eckero's 1939 east-to-west crossing.** In 1939, the first [small-boat] crossing of the Atlantic from east to west was made in a 31-foot motorboat named *Eckero*. One might say this voyage presaged things to come: *Eckero* was not designed for the voyage; nor was she specially fitted; nor was her crew trying to prove anything.

*Eckero's* owner was Uno Ekblom, who lived on the Aland Islands in the

Baltic. In 1939 he decided to visit the United States, but for some reason he couldn't get a visa—no visa, no steamship ticket. Not one to let such a detail upset his plans, Ekblom decided to go anyway, in the motorboat *Eckero* that he had designed and built for himself ten years previously. She was 31 feet long with a beam of 9 feet 10 inches and had a single-cylinder diesel of 10 horsepower—like thousands of fishing vessels in the Baltic.

Ekblom got together a crew of two friends, gave the diesel a factory overhaul, fitted a small steadying rig, and left on May 3, 1939.

The friends stopped in Copenhagen, Denmark, and Göteborg, Sweden; had their worst weather of the trip in the North Sea; and arrived in Rotterdam, Holland, on May 28. They then motored to Dover, Southampton, and Falmouth, England, while following Ekblom's rule of spending only one night in a port—a rule he observed scrupulously to the end of the voyage. On June 9, they left Falmouth, bound for Horta in the Azores, and arrived at the end of a passage of 1,260 miles in nine-and-a-half days. After a day in port, they were off for Bermuda, 1,800 miles away. They entered St. George on July 7, refueled, and left the following day. When they arrived in New York on July 13, they had covered no fewer than 3,725 miles in thirty-four days, with only two in-port days.

All these details are from Humphrey Barton's book, *Atlantic Adventurers.* Barton called this ". . . an amazing distance to cover in 34 days." He then went on to say, "I believe this to be the most outstanding voyage that has ever been carried out by a small motorboat and great credit is due to Uno Ekblom and his crew for their seamanship and endurance. Nor must the little diesel engine which served them so faithfully be forgotten. It must have run like a clock."

I certainly agree with Barton that credit was due to the ship, her crew, and her engine, but not necessarily with his comment that the performance was "amazing." Perhaps it seems so to a long-time sailor with several Atlantic crossings under sail to his credit. But the fact is that judging her voyage by the technical yardsticks to be developed later in Chapter 6, *Eckero* didn't do too well. Her time underway—if compared with standards that seem reasonable—should have been twenty-four to twenty-six days, not thirty-four.

What conclusions can we draw from these voyages? In the first place, they made such demands on the endurance of their crews that these enterprises obviously were not suitable for inexperienced seamen or their families. The greatest complaint was about rolling. A reliable and consistent means of reducing rolling appears to be the prime factor necessary for popular participation in long-distance power voyaging. Crew comfort is a must. Such absurdities as exclusively outside steering stations, absence of steering assistance, and hulls too small to carry the required load and still provide decent room for the crew reduce this sort of voyage to the stunt level. Single-handed ocean passages prove nothing; not many people are interested in such feats.

On the other hand, the perfect record of the engines involved shows that this part of power passagemaking is a solid base on which to build. By correcting the objectionable features noted, a vessel of unique qualities can be produced with capabilities for a new sort of cruising.

Aside from the pioneering efforts that concentrated on crossing the Atlantic, a major portion of the development of true seagoing motorboats has taken place on the west coast of the United States. This development was dictated by the characteristics of the area. From San Francisco northward, the year-round

**Figure 2–6.** *Eckero,* the first small powerboat to cross the Atlantic from east to west. She crossed in 1939 in 34 days.

weather off the coast is, on average, worse than that of any other area except the high latitudes of the Southern Ocean. This coastal area not only has winter storms but also is bedeviled in summer by very strong winds caused by differences between pressure over the cold ocean waters and pressure over the hot interior valleys. The worst gale *Passagemaker* ever encountered, for instance, was off Cape Mendocino, California, in the middle of August. It was not a storm, just a gradient wind.

Yet fishing vessels operate off the coast and in the Gulf of Alaska all year-round, so it is possible for well-found craft to cruise these waters. In the postwar years, it gradually became clear that a type of vessel was required that was not an advertised stock item.

The early examples were modified fishing boats. Designed first by Seattle designers Edwin Monk and William Garden, a type of boat began to evolve that was lighter and more economical than a true fishing boat, yet offered adequate seaworthiness. At first, these fishing boats were commonly called "northwest cruisers," although this term has about died out today.

As more and more of these boats were built, their reputation gradually became widespread and led to the sudden proliferation of vessels that today are called "trawlers." There will be a good deal said on that subject later.

This was the background, then, for the design of *Passagemaker*. In Chapter 3, we explore the development of the *Passagemaker* concept and the design, building, and testing of the vessel herself.

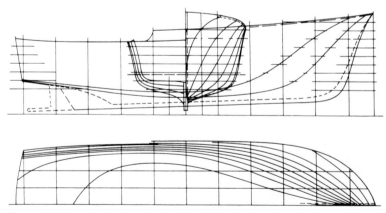

**Figure 2–7.** Lines of a "northwest cruiser" by William Garden, showing the evolution of the early fisherman-shaped cruisers to a lighter model. (Retraced by R.P.B.)

# Other Historic Voyages Under Power
*Denis Umstot*

In addition to the history Beebe has provided in this chapter, other voyages have been significant in the history of power voyaging. Although there isn't enough space in this book to cover every circumnavigation or every significant voyage, I have summarized some of the more interesting ones in the rest of the chapter.

### *Speejacks*: The First Power Yacht to Circumnavigate, 1921–1922

Albert and Jeanne Gowen from Chicago built the yacht *Speejacks* and adapted it for an around-the-world trip. The boat was 98 feet long, had a 17-foot beam and 6-foot draft, displacing about 64 tons. Power was two 250 hp gasoline engines. Cruising at 8 knots, she had a range of about 2,000 nautical miles on 3,000 gallons of gasoline. She had wireless telephony, fans and radiators, a portable Victrola, two machine guns, and lots of spare parts. The Gowens hired a professional captain and crew to navigate and operate the boat. They left New York on August 21, 1921, bound for Miami, Jamaica, and the Panama Canal.

Because it could not carry enough fuel to make it from Panama to Tahiti, *Speejacks* was towed by the steamer, *Eastern Queen*, for twenty-two days (4,400 miles) to within a few hundred miles of the South Sea Islands. The Gowens ran a 10-inch manila rope around the boat and then attached it to a 6-inch tow rope. The ride was not comfortable, being described as 1-2-3, jerk; 1-2-3, jerk, continuously. Their route took them from Tahiti to Samoa and Fiji, then onward to New Zealand in the height of the hurricane season in January. They were warned not to go, but departed, anyway—they had to maintain their schedule. They did not linger in New Zealand, but headed straight to Sydney, Australia. In Brisbane, they hired a newspaper reporter, Dale Collins, to go along on the rest of the voyage and write their story. The result was his *Sea-Tracks of the Speejacks: Round the World*.

They had great luck in avoiding hurricanes in the Caribbean, typhoons in the Pacific, as well as cyclones in the Indian Ocean. However, they did encounter a few stretches of difficult weather. Between Papeete and Pago Pago they encountered a storm with "winds approaching hurricane force" and mountainous seas. Here is the way they described it in their article for *International Yachtsman*:

**Figure 2–8.** *Speejacks,* the first power yacht to circumnavigate in 1921–1922, was 98 feet long and powered by twin 250 hp gasoline engines. *Speejacks* is shown here entering the harbor of Sydney, Australia. (Collins)

> *Great seas buffeted her hither and thither, and all hands crouched on the hatch in the shelter of the wheelhouse while the deck ran green (a thing which happened seldom) and the dinghy slung on davits touched the waves with each roll. It would have been impossible for her to go a degree further, you would have said, without rolling right over.*

In those days there were no stabilizers to prevent rolling. Jeanne Gowen described *Speejacks* as being like a cork in the bathtub, "bobbling up and down, backward, forward." The Gowens played a mealtime game called "the pursuit of a bean," chasing their food as it slid around or fell off the table. There was also no autopilot. Hand steering was the only method—no wonder they had a crew! Watches were two hours on and six hours off, day after day. An additional problem was that supplies of gasoline were not always available. They sometimes had to be prepositioned, a logistical problem of the first degree.

From Australia the Gowens went to New Guinea, Bali, and Singapore. After their first attempt to depart from Singapore into the teeth of the southwest monsoon they had to delay for a change of seasons. They categorized the monsoon-driven seas as "Himalayan," making it impossible to make progress. When the monsoons changed to the more friendly northeast direction, they headed nonstop for the

Seychelles Islands, 3,100 miles away. They left with 6,200 gallons of fuel (3,200 in tanks and 300 cases lashed on deck). They arrived with 1,000 gallons in reserve. They then proceeded up the Red Sea to Egypt and into the Mediterranean. Their final route was via the Canaries and Cape Verdes to Puerto Rico, then on to New York, arriving on December 11, 1922—478 days later.

Although there were no mechanical problems with the engines, *Speejacks'* steering cables and chains failed twice, and the emergency tiller had to be installed. Once she lost steering in a gale at the entrance to the Red Sea, causing considerable apprehension for everyone until *Speejacks* was successfully repaired.

The Gowens' trip covered more than 34,000 miles. They burned 73,000 gallons of gasoline (.46 miles per gallon). Gas prices ranged from 31 cents to $1.24. Photographers who were along to shoot a movie shot 93,000 feet of film. (Keep a lookout for the movie on the Internet; it might yet become available.)

### *Westward:* First Motor Yacht to Circumnavigate Entirely on Its Own Power, 1970–1976

In 1968, Don and Ann Gumpertz bought *Westward,* an 86-foot wooden yacht, custom-built in 1924 for accommodating the rich and famous on fishing trips up the Canadian coast and Alaska. Don did a major renovation in Seattle to prepare the boat for a circumnavigation under power, installing two 500-gallon water tanks, rewiring everything, installing modern marine heads, revising and replacing much of the paneling, and replanking nearly half the hull. He also installed Pacific Sea stabilizer fins, two 12 KW diesel generators, and a 30 gph watermaker. *Westward* was built strongly: the planks are 2 3/4" Douglas fir; the ribs are 8" × 8" on 18" centers; the decks are 2" thick; the beam is 18.5 feet; and the draft is 9 feet.

Don kept the original engines: 110 hp, 4-cylinder Atlas Imperial Heavy Duty diesels (see Figure 2–10). The engines turn a very slow 325 revolutions per minute. Fuel burn is approximately 8 gph at 8–10 knots, which is quite good even by modern standards. Range is 3,000 miles at 9 knots. The difficult part about this engine, other than the availability of parts, is that it requires 200 oiling points to be serviced every two hours.

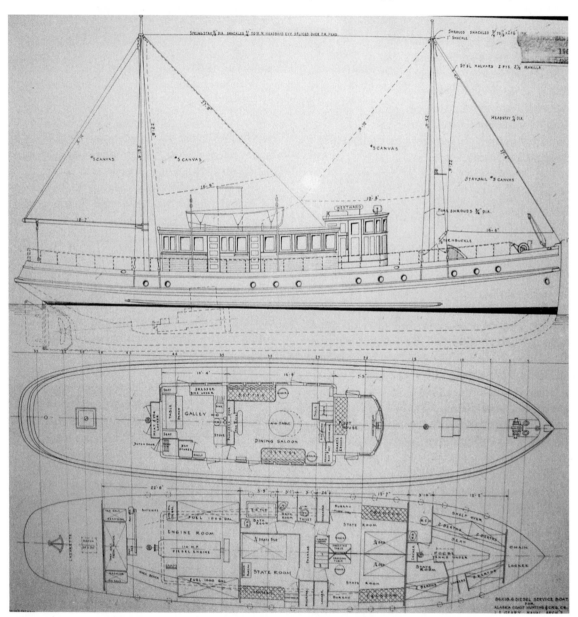

**Figure 2–9.** *Westward* was originally built as perhaps the first Alaskan charter boat in 1924.

Don and Ann Gumpertz departed on November 7, 1970, from Los Angeles, California, serving as the escort vessel for the Los Angeles to Mazatlan race. They travelled on a nontraditional route from west to east. They traversed the Panama Canal and proceeded along the coast of South America and then up the Leeward and Windward Islands to the eastern United States. Their route took them to the Bahamas, Bermuda, Azores, and into the Mediterranean. Leaving the Med, they travelled south along the west coast of Africa, rounding the Cape of Good Hope and then travelling up the eastern side of Africa as far as Kenya. They then headed across the Indian Ocean to Sri Lanka, Singapore, and Indonesia, eventually making their way through the islands to Hawaii and then directly back to Los Angeles on March 6, 1976.

Because Don and Ann's voyage preceded satellite navigation systems, they relied on sextant and radio direction finders as navigation aids. Don was a professional electronics man, so he installed a 2,000-watt ham radio system on the boat with directional antennas. It was their single most valuable item for keeping in touch with the world. Ham radio nets also provided a great social network in each new port they entered. For example, in South Africa they were met at the dock and feted to barbecues and tours of the wine country.

Ann made a courtesy flag for each of the countries they visited. An onboard sewing machine and lots of colorful flag material were her raw materials. She made more than 40 flags for the trip.

Don and Ann found that clearing in and out of ports was time-consuming and often required bribes to speed the clearance. Fees were numerous and inflated. In Mombasa, Kenya, they were handed a bill of $2,500 for two weeks of moorage! In addition, security was a problem, particularly in Africa. They were boarded by thieves during the night and lost $800 worth of boat gear, including the all-important toolbox. Spanish customs presented very difficult problems clearing a shipment of an 800-pound crate of boat parts, charts, and radio equipment.

The worst seas were off the coast of Colombia as they were heading for Aruba. Don said that "the winds blow for a couple thousand miles without interruption and kick up a sea that is almost square-edged. We'd cruise off the end, into a 30-foot hole, crash, sail on a bit, then crash again."

### Westward's Next Adventure: Circumnavigating the Pacific in 2007–2008

Hugh and Teresa Reilly purchased Westward in 1993. Hugh supervised a major restoration in 2005–2006, including stem and bow renewal, replanking, guard (rub rail) renewal, Atlas engine overhaul (including automatic oiling system), Naiad stabilizers, new electronics, auxiliary sails, and other improvements. The Reillys made their way from Seattle, Washington, to La Paz, Mexico, where they began their Pacific crossing in June 2007. Westward was now 83 years old! They visited French Polynesia, Fiji, and many other South Pacific islands. They made their way up the islands to Japan and Korea and then to Alaska and back to Seattle. Their voyage covered 21,500 nautical

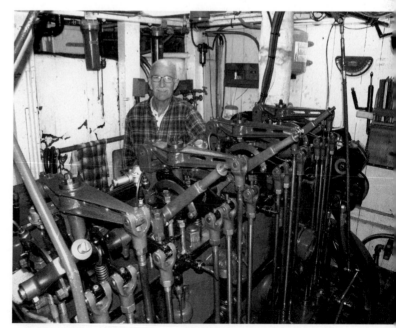

**Figure 2–10.** Hugh Reilly purchased Westward in 1993; here he shows off the 1924 Atlas engine. It is still purring along.

miles. The following log excerpts give glimpses of the trip that seemed particularly interesting:

*June 2007 Crossing the Pacific: The sails & sheets are strained, but the rigs indifferent & the cleats are holding; the mighty Atlas is loafing—stack temps in the mid-500s @ 250 RPM (a power-stroke every 1/8th second)! Moving this ancient, 250,000 lb sled at 8 knots on a beam-reach with a steady 10 deg. heel, burning only 0.6 gal/mile, is a sight to behold and an experience to remember! Oh boy, whatta ride!*

*March 2008 Nearing Japan: As we neared the coasts of Japan, South Korea & China, the passage brought evidence, in the form of steadily increasing numbers of massive ships laden with ores, oils, LNG & grains, of the industrial might of Asia. In our last six hours approaching the Kushimoto entrance, we tracked more than 100 deep-water ships and coastal freighters & fishing vessels on our radar & AIS (Automatic Information System)! With all this traffic, Japan is a ship-watcher's heaven; but for our modern electronics and the professionalism & courtesy of the mariners here, it would be a navigator's hell!*

*May 2008 Japan to Pusan, Korea: Following recent weeks of daylight-only navigation in Japan's*

*busy coastal & inland waters, it was a demanding run—a moon-less night of thunder-storms & dense steamer traffic, illuminated by brilliant lightning and fleets of fishing boats, both Japanese & Korean, often fishing squid with bright incandescent fishing lights which easily evidenced their presence but blinded us to other traffic. It was an important night for vigilance and for radar & AIS navigation!*

*July 2008 Alaska: The scenery all the way has been spectacular; rugged, snow-capped peaks plunging steeply into deep bays rich with stunning geology & life of all varieties—whales, bears, otter, eagles, foxes, gulls, salmon, wildflowers. We've enjoyed an abundance of fresh halibut from these rich waters; a fish for dinner has been near-assured, with just a little effort, at each of our anchorages.*

## Larry Briggs' Circumnavigations, Beginning in 1977

Most circumnavigators are satisfied to complete only one voyage around the world, but Larry Briggs has done four and is partway around on what may be his fifth! He is about as salty as a yachtsman can be. He began cruising on sailing vessels to the South Pacific in the 1960s, then bought a 30' steel fishing boat in Seattle and took it from San Francisco to Honolulu. His next boat was a motorsailer that he also brought to Hawaii and used for charter.

**Champion: The first circumnavigation with a small trawler yacht, 1977–1980.** Larry set out on his first circumnavigation on *Champion*, a 53' Lapworth design built in Hong Kong by Cheoy Lee with teak planking in 1959. *Champion* (originally named *Feng Shui*) is an unusual yacht design: its engine, a Detroit 6-71, is located in the bow rather than the more typical amidships or stern location. The fuel capacity of 2,400 gallons gave the vessel substantial passagemaking range, although the 2-cycle 6-71 diesel may be less efficient than most modern 4-cycle diesels. This voyage appears to be the first circumnavigation of a trawler-type boat

Figure 2–11. *Westward* in 2007, anchored at Hanavave Bay, Fatul Hiva, French Polynesia. (Hugh Reilly)

**Figure 2–12.** *Champion,* a 53-foot Lapworth design built in Hong Kong by Cheoy Lee, is the first known small trawler to circumnavigate. Note the paravane stabilizers used to minimize rolling. (Larry Briggs)

small enough to be handled by the owner without a professional crew. The general route for this three-year voyage was San Diego (California), Hawaii, Tahiti, Pago Pago, New Zealand, Eastern Australia, Indonesia, Singapore, Malaysia, Sri Lanka, Suez Canal, Mediterranean, Canaries, Caribbean, Costa Rica, and Mexico.

*Neptune's Chariot.* Larry commissioned this 75', 18' beam, canoe-stern yacht designed by Paul Kotzebue and built by Knight & Carver in San Diego in 1981. Larry wanted really long range without stopping, so they designed her to hold 10,000 gallons of fuel with a range of 17,000 miles at 8 knots. Larry departed San Diego in October 1981, heading to Cabo San Lucas, Honolulu, Manila, Singapore (where he finished the interior of *Neptune's Chariot*), and then nonstop to the Suez, through the Mediterranean to Florida, where he spent some time before completing this circumnavigation to the west coast of the United States in 1984. In 2009 Larry

repurchased this boat and after quite a bit of refitting he set out in 2010 on yet another possible circumnavigation, *his fifth,* on *Neptune's Chariot*—when halfway around the world in Malaysia in 2012, he sold *Neptune's Chariot.*

**Chartwell's Circumnavigations.** Larry went around the world twice in *Chartwell,* a 55' Cheoy Lee LRC (Long Range Cruiser), powered by a single Cummins 855M2 engine. His first voyage in this boat was from 1998 to 2003. The second circumnavigation went through the central Pacific islands and Indonesia, skipping New Zealand and Australia this time around. He had a long stay on the island of Langkawi, off the coast of Malaysia. Then he was off to the Maldives, Camores, Tanzania, South Africa, and Brazil before settling in

**Figure 2–13.** *Neptune's Chariot* is a 75' Kotzebue design built in San Diego by Knight & Carver in 1981. Larry loved the extreme range of this boat with 10,000 gallons of fuel. He used active fin stabilizers on this boat. (Larry Briggs)

Figure 2–14. *Chartwell*, a 55' Cheoy Lee LRC, took Larry Briggs on two circumnavigations. Paravane stabilizers were used. (Larry Briggs)

the area. They then headed across the infrequently traveled part of the South Pacific to Fernandez Island, Easter Island, Pitcairn Island, and the Gambier Islands. When they reached French Polynesia, they followed the more normal cruising route through such exotically named places as Moorea, Bora Bora, Suwarrow, and Tonga. They spent fourteen months in New Zealand; then on to Tasmania, spending nine months exploring Australia. They then set off on a 3,365 nautical mile leg from Freemantle to Mauritius. They motored on to Reunion, South Africa, and Namibia. Their final leg, completed in February 2011 back to the Canaries, was via St. Helena and the Ascension Islands. From there, they retraced their route to the Mediterranean and then crossed the Atlantic again, returning to New England.

Scott and Mary have shared their stories of the trip on the voyage of *Egret* website sponsored by Nordhavn and in *PassageMaker Magazine*. Some of their adventures will be related in other chapters in the book.

Trinidad, where he sold *Chartwell* and repurchased *Neptune's Chariot*. In 2012, he sold *Neptune's Chariot* and repurchased *Chartwell*. If you are confused, so is your author—it seems to be an unusual case of musical "boat" chairs. He is planning to head off into the Pacific again.

### *Egret's* Circumnavigation: The Southern Capes

Scott and Mary Flanders, aboard *Egret*, their Nordhavn 46, completed their circumnavigation in an unusual way—around the Southern Capes, including Cape Horn; Cape of Good Hope; and the southern capes of New Zealand, Tasmania, and Australia. Most circumnavigators take the route closer to the equator, where the seas are calmer and weather is warmer. Scott and Mary even considered a trip to Antarctica, but had to abort when the logistics of permits and insurance became insurmountable.

Scott and Mary departed Las Palmas in the Canary Islands in September 2006. Their route took them first to Brazil and Argentina. They really enjoyed the "deep south" of South America and spent fifteen months exploring

Figure 2–15. *Egret* in the South Pacific. (Nordhavn/Scott and Mary Flanders)

## CHAPTER THREE

# Evolving the *Passagemaker* Concept

## Robert Beebe

Imentioned in Chapter 2 that the first idea of such a boat came to me during World War II when I was the navigator of a large aircraft carrier in the Pacific. Years before, like so many small-craft sailors, I had built up a library of cruising tales—from Joshua Slocum on. During prewar duty in the Pacific, there had been ample opportunity to keep an eye on the activities of the comparatively few long-range sail cruisers at sea in those days. So I was reasonably well aware of their problems, and my developing designer's eye noted how few of these vessels seemed suited to their intended work.

As the war ended, and we cruised through waters hitherto forbidden to small craft, it became apparent to me that the cruising routes would differ sharply from the "standard track" so often described in cruising yarns: from Panama to the Galapagos, the Marquesas, Tahiti, and on.

For one thing, cruising among the islands that the United States occupied during the war leads one into areas having long periods of little or no wind, so considerable range under power would be useful. As I sketched and designed boats on the backs of old charts (as time allowed), my idea of a postwar cruiser gradually evolved into a long, slim hull of 54-foot length overall (LOA), easily driven under power, with fuel for 1,500 miles, and carrying a three-masted-schooner rig. It was interesting to see L. Francis Herreshoff's ideas of a postwar cruiser published later in *Rudder*. He had come to the same conclusion I had, producing the 55-foot *Marco Polo*, another three-masted, long, slim vessel. While comparison of our vessels ended there, I found it nice to be in such distinguished company.

Nothing came of all this at the time except the publication of my thoughts on "Postwar Pacific Cruising" in *Rudder* for August and September of 1946. The case for more range under power was stated as follows:

*The chief difference from cruises of the past is that the voyager may venture into waters where for long periods there is hardly any wind at all. He will also make passages that do not lie entirely within the trade wind belt. It would seem therefore that good power is essential, coupled with cruising range well above what we are accustomed to. Whether this is to be achieved by a large craft or one that achieves range from being easily driven is a matter of opinion. Personally I favor the latter, as it ties in with my ideas of a small crew and easily handled sail plan. Draft is not a problem unless one wishes to explore off the beaten track, away from islands that have been used for war purposes.*

*To my mind the editor of* Rudder *has done the prospective cruising sailor a great service by bringing forth Herreshoff's* Marco Polo. *Not only is this model a good sailing machine, adapted in every way to the use for which it is intended, but its basic design is ideally suited to the conditions to be met in a Pacific cruise. It also permits a new type of cruise, one that will fill the needs of the sailor who, however much he may dream of spending months lying under the shade of a palm, watching sarong-clad native girls dance for his amusement, must limit his cruise to a definite time and get back to the old grind, where he may happily accumulate enough of the wherewithal to go cruising again.*

This statement made in 1946 was my first step away from the conventional sailing cruiser, a step that, it will be seen, was subject to further modification. In particular, the last sentence contains the germ of an idea that was destined to grow, the idea of concentrating on passagemaking.

In 1957, I jumped at the chance to be navigator of the first Herreshoff 55-footer to be completed—Joe Newcomb's *Talaria*—on a November trip from New York to the Bahamas. This rugged trip under winter conditions raised certain questions about the concept evolved during the war, and was more grist for the mill—a mill now shifting into high gear as my retirement from 30 years of Navy service drew closer.

In 1959, three years before *Passagemaker* was designed, I wrote a story about the subject, mainly as an exercise in lining up my thoughts on what I was trying to do. The editor who requested the story had not published it by the time I knew *Passagemaker* would be built, so I asked that the manuscript be returned to me, promising the editor a report on the finished boat and its performance at a later date. Now that *Passagemaker* has proved all the story's points—and more—the story has become something of an historical document, a statement of basic principles. The early developmental work that led to the concept on which *Passagemaker* was built can be illustrated by excerpts from this story.

## The Story of the *Passagemaker* Concept

At the suggestion of the editor, I wrote the story in the form of a conversation among three friends at a yacht club. The characters were Tubby Watson, a dedicated ocean-racing man; Don Moore (Beebe) an experienced amateur yacht designer; and Bob Reid, a "dedicated boat nut from way back who had also done some designing." Here's a condensation of the article:

Tubby Watson walked out onto the yacht club porch in company with Don Moore. Moore was a tall, spare man with the look of the sea about him. Under his arm he carried a roll of blueprints. Moore had recently moved to the West Coast and

was thinking about a retirement boat that would not only be suitable for local cruising but also something more. Tubby had invited him to bring his plans over to the club.

Moore said, "Suppose I give you a little background first. I find it helps. When I moved to the West Coast and found I had more time for cruising, I started thinking about all the places I hadn't covered: parts of the East Coast, the Bahamas, Great Lakes, and so on. And out here, British Columbia and Mexico. The question was how to do it?"

"Why not fly there and charter?" offered Tubby.

"That has its points, of course. But I've owned boats all my life and would feel lost without something to putter around on and fix up. My first idea was a trailered cruiser, so you could make the long jumps by car. This is probably the cheapest way, and the boat is reasonably able. But it would be nice to have a genuine liveaboard boat when you got there. So I looked into the problems of making the trips by water."

"That's quite a project," Bob Reid said, "going from here east by boat."

"Most people think so," Moore responded. "But the more I worked on it, the more I began to see you could do a good deal to cut it down to size. The problem, of course, is making the passages. In fact, I call the final result a 'Passagemaker.'"

"It seems to me," Reid said, "there are a lot of boats that could qualify as Passagemakers."

"Actually, there aren't," Don replied. "Let's really look at passagemaking for a minute. Of course, many people do make long passages. But the general idea seems to be to take a well-found sailboat of some sort and start out. They get there, of course; but what most of them are really doing is *ocean cruising*. I'm not interested in that—I've been to sea. What I like to do is go to a nice area like Puget Sound and poke around from port to port. The quicker I get there, the more time I'll have for cruising. Speed and dispatch is what I want. By speed, I mean to keep *average speed* as high as possible. And by *dispatch* I mean to meet some sort of *schedule*. It is much easier to find a crew if they can be told with reasonable certainty when they will get home—"

"You mean if their wives can know—" interrupted Tubby.

"That's right! Why not face it?" replied Moore. "All these considerations *do* affect the basic idea. If you read accounts of 'voyaging' with a critical eye, you will soon pick up hints that it's possible to do better . . ."

(*This exchange was the first use of "Passagemaker," the word I coined to describe the type of yacht that was evolving from my thoughts on the subject.*)

The group went on to discuss Moore's idea that any of the boats should be capable of singlehanded operation. Tubby didn't think much of doing that, so Moore explained that with a crew, you can "singlehand" by turns, so to speak; that is, run with a one-man watch. (*This remains a fundamental point.*) Tubby then suggested that Moore needed a long-range diesel motorboat.

"I considered that, of course," said Don. "The fact that so many of them are being built out here is a tribute to the good sense of some yachtsmen. The trouble is they are too expensive for me. I ran through a preliminary design of one to see how it would go in the 50-foot size. Here is the sketch I drew. She is about as 'houseboaty' as you can get and still be really seaworthy. And she has a feature I like—lots of unobstructed deck space."

"Looks nice. Too bad you couldn't swing it," Reid said.

"Well, what we are doing here is facing facts, and that's one of them. But the interesting thing about these boats is the performance you can get out of them."

The group next had a thorough discussion of the significance of "hull speed," "speed/length ratio," and range. (*Because all these technical matters are thoroughly explored in Chapter 6, we will hold them until later.*)

Moore said, "Now let's look at the sailing cruiser. She shows up worst of all: she is not adapted to singlehanding, she can't guarantee speed or dispatch, and she must have a full watchstanding crew of experienced sailors before she can leave the dock."

Tubby demurred. "It's not as bad as all that!"

"Well, let's go back to the concept. In the passage to and from the East Coast, the leg from Acapulco to Panama is particularly well known for its calms and light airs. This is where the ordinary cruiser falls down on the job. You end up wishing you had a motorboat with more fuel than the auxiliary can carry so you can meet your schedule. In fact, it was considering this aspect that first turned my ideas toward what I call a 'motor-all-the-time boat.'"

"What sort of a craft is that?" Reid inquired.

"The original idea came from a designer friend of mine," Moore answered. "He pointed out that when considering ocean racers, having something less than 5 horsepower available continuously for propulsion and using only a simple rig of two or three lower sails, you could lick the best of the lot carrying their load of spinnakers, jibs, genoas, mizzen staysails, and the rest—and do it a lot cheaper."

"The Race Committee wouldn't like it," Reid offered.

"The Jib Tenders Union would *never* allow anything like that," said Tubby with quiet confidence.

"Of course, it's not a practical proposition," Don answered, "and my friend hasn't done anything with it. But the principle involved looks good for what I've already called a 'Passagemaker'— where you want an assured average speed. Basically the question was this: Would it be possible to shrink the seagoing motorboat down closer to the size and shape and accommodations

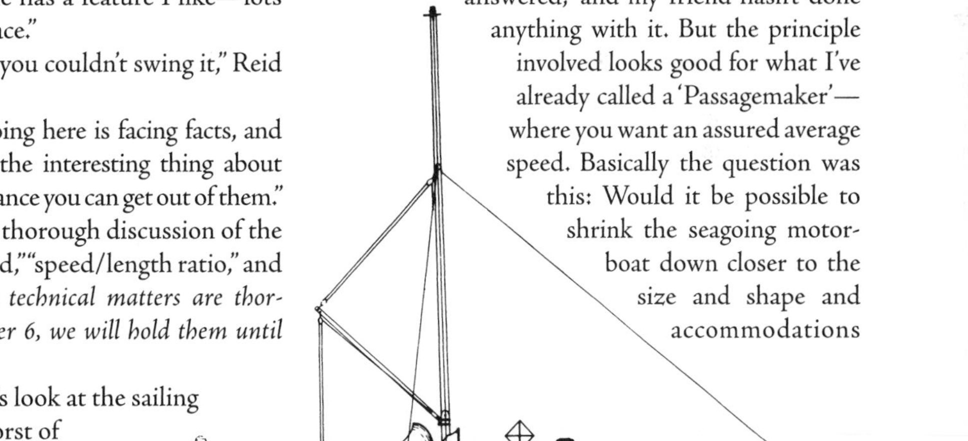

Figure 3–1. Profile, Beebe Design 50—a 52-foot "oceangoing motorboat," sketched in 1959.

of the sailing cruiser, with a great reduction in cost, and still get the performance desired?" He looked around the table. "Well, it turns out that you can. And then I put a rig on her suitable to the sailing you would do while cruising singlehanded."

"So you settled on a motorsailer," said Tubby.

"No, *sir!*" said Don Moore emphatically. "I don't consider my boat a motorsailer. To me, a motorsailer is something different. It has a rather large rig and is expected to use sail alone whenever the wind is at all favorable. Most of them do not carry much fuel, though more than the ordinary auxiliary, of course. And they usually compromise on propeller/hull efficiency in an attempt to provide a reasonable sailing potential. I guess you could call my boat a 'motorboat with rig.'"

"Aren't you quibbling a bit?"

"Not really. What I am referring to is the underwater body—it is wholly dedicated to efficiency under power. It is a matter of prismatic coefficient."

*(This discussion reflected a tremendous amount of research and calculation. It is, of course, no great trick to take a large, burdensome hull, load it up with fuel, and achieve a very long range. What was not readily apparent in the beginning, from the available technical data, was whether this "shrinking down" process was feasible. If you don't want to be burdened with a large, heavy vessel, or your budget won't build it, shrinking down must be the answer. I recall vividly the sense of discovery and pleasure I felt when I finally found I could have Moore honestly say, "Well, it turns out that you can." There are many technical matters involved— matters such as stability when fuel is almost gone, for instance. A good deal of the research done appears again in Chapter 6 in the discussion of "displacement/ length ratio.")*

The three men spoke at length of the significance of the "prismatic coefficient" *(another topic covered in Chapter 6)*. Moore explained that he was trying to achieve the required range with the least fuel possible. This led to a discussion of what the range should be.

"What range are we talking about?" Reid asked.

"In the San Diego–Key West voyage, with stops at Acapulco and Panama, the longest leg is 1,400 miles. But returning from the East Coast, you might want to head out to sea from Acapulco on the starboard tack and power-sail up the old sailing-ship route to California. It's rather hard to pin down, but I decided a 2,400-mile 'still-water' range would be about right and stuck to that. That would be useful coming back from Honolulu, too."

"What size boat do you need to achieve that?" Reid asked.

"I worked her up in several sizes," said Moore. "The ideal would be 48 feet overall, with a 42-foot 6-inch waterline, and a 27,000-pound displacement—with 600 gallons of diesel fuel. Here are the lines of that boat. She actually weighs about half of that 50-foot motorboat I showed you and costs a great deal less to build. She has the correct prismatic coefficient for a speed of 8 knots and will do the 2,400 miles at that speed, using about 30 horsepower. A lot of people won't believe that, but it's true. If you back off on the speed, the range takes a tremendous jump. For instance, she could make San Diego–Panama nonstop at 7 knots without stopping in Acapulco for some of that good Mexican beer."

"No nonstop for me," Tubby said fervently.

"It doesn't appeal to me, either," said Moore, "but I can think of several trips where the extra range would be useful. Unfortunately this 48-footer proved too expensive, too, so I settled for a final design that is 40 feet 6 inches long, 36 feet on the waterline, and some 20,000 pounds displacement. She will make the 2,400 miles at 6 knots on 300 gallons of fuel. For shorter passages, she will do 1,400 miles at 7 knots and 900 at 8."

*(This discussion was the end result of a great deal of work that finally made it apparent that the project— designing specifically to make the desired passage— could be accomplished and made sense.)*

Moore pointed out that his vessel could go from San Diego to Key West in 28 days, with 4 days off— 2 each in Acapulco and Panama. Thus, a cruise to the desired area on the East Coast and return could be accomplished in less than a year.

*(I still believe that a 2,400-mile range is a figure that makes a lot of sense. But, as we'll see in Chapter 6, range figures must always be qualified by the speed that the operator expects to use.)*

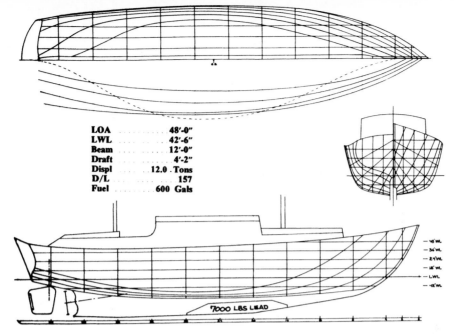

| LOA | 48'-0" |
| LWL | 42'-6" |
| Beam | 12'-0" |
| Draft | 4'-2" |
| Displ | 12.0 Tons |
| D/L | 157 |
| Fuel | 600 Gals |

7000 LBS LEAD

**Figure 3–2.** Lines, Beebe Design 53—a 48-footer using the *Presto* midsection. This was the first of Beebe's designs called a "Passagemaker."

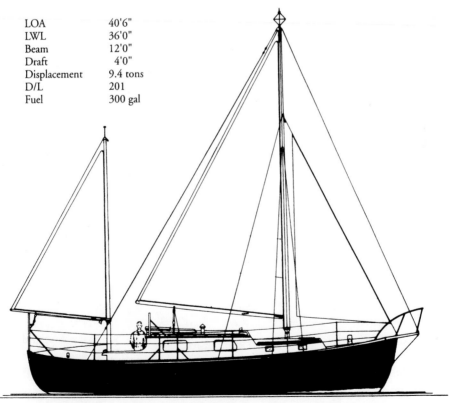

| LOA | 40'6" |
| LWL | 36'0" |
| Beam | 12'0" |
| Draft | 4'0" |
| Displacement | 9.4 tons |
| D/L | 201 |
| Fuel | 300 gal |

**Figure 3–3.** Profile, Beebe Design 57—a sailing Passagemaker of 40 feet LOA. This is the design Don Moore was having built in the story told in this chapter.

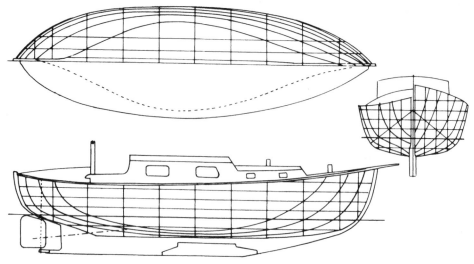

**Figure 3–4.** Lines for Beebe Design 57.

Moore then explained why it was impractical to design a boat that would do what he wanted and also be capable of Tubby's ocean racing. Moore did mention that if the big propeller were removed, sailing performance might be surprising.

"Aha!" exclaimed Tubby. "So you do want to race her!"

"Well, no," replied Moore, "I don't think my budget would stand two or three spinnakers, genoas, and all the rest. But someone might want to outfit my design with racing sails and try it. I was all through with the design before I suddenly realized that she should do very well in some of these West Coast downwind races, like the ones to Honolulu and Acapulco."

"Why do you say that?" Reid inquired.

"Because any race off the wind, with no windward work, should go to the boat that needs the least push to exceed the speed required to win on her own rating. The instant the first boat finishes, every following boat has an average speed it must exceed to place first on corrected time. The less

actual horsepower a boat needs to attain that speed, the more chance she has that prevailing conditions will provide it. As I concentrated on this, I saw that my design should have an advantage over the round-the-buoy racers with their emphasis on windward ability. Here are two pictures of a model test I made (*Figures 3–5 and 3–6*). This one is at her hull speed of 8 knots, while this one shows her being overdriven to a speed-length ratio of about 1.6. She has a good deal less wave hollow amidships than most Cruising Club of America (CCA)–type cruiser/racers under these conditions, yet she weighs about the same."

**Figure 3–5.** Model test of Design 57 showing her being towed at her hull speed of 8 knots.

**Figure 3–6.** Model test of Design 57 showing her being overdriven to a speed/length ratio of about 1.6 (10.19 knots). Note minimal wave hollow amidships.

**Figure 3–7.** A CCA rule–type ocean racer. Note how the overdriven hull has developed an extreme wave hollow amidships. (Rosenfeld)

Moore's photos showed graphically the effect of prismatic coefficient on efficiency under power. The friends then moved on to discuss the interior of the vessel.

(*In the design's accommodation, I had the chance to emphasize features that I felt, from research in long-range cruising tables, needed a new direction. As can be seen from her accommodation plan, she is laid out for singlehanded convenience, though she has bunks for four. The Root berths in the main cabin can be replaced with an ordinary transom berth/settee for local cruising.*)

"Now, how about her cabin?"

"The main cabin is very carefully designed for the work to be done in it. It is as high as it is because all the space below the waterline is taken up by tanks. Everything in this area is dedicated to singlehanded convenience. Personally, I think it is a great advance over anything that has been used for this kind of cruising

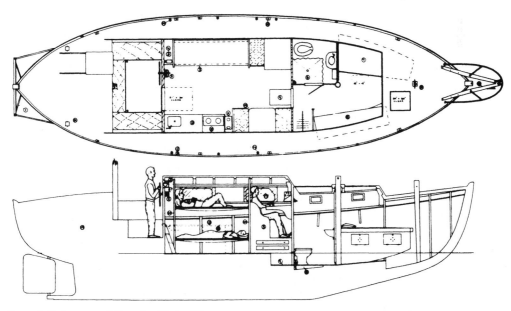

**Figure 3–8.** Accommodation plan, Design 57.

before. For instance, the skipper's bunk is up in line with the ports so he can look out while resting."

"The officers of the deck are a bunch of drunks. They stand their watches in their bunks!" chortled Tubby.

"*Mister* Watson!" Don said with mock severity. "You know very well I never touch the stuff underway. But seriously, I fail to understand why *not one* singlehander has ever done this. If you read the cruise accounts, you will be struck by how many times the skippers leap from below to see what's going on. If they could just open one eye for a look around, many vague dangers would evaporate."

"How about the cockpit?" Tubby asked. "Isn't it a bit unusual?"

"Yes, it is," Moore answered. "But I made a cruise years ago in a Francis Herreshoff yacht, the *Marco Polo* type, that had one like this. That spoiled me—I never want to go very far to sea again in a conventional cockpit cruiser where you sit way aft on deck without any shelter. The deep, standing-room, athwart ships cockpit—with seats all around—was just wonderful. In this case, the wheel is on the forward bulkhead at stand-up height as you only use it for maneuvering."

"How do you mean?" asked Tubby.

"Why, she uses an autopilot, of course," said Don. "This is basic to the concept and one of the great advantages of an engine-running-all-the-time vessel—you always have power for it. That's what makes a singlehanded passage not only feasible but also enjoyable. Your crew steers all day and never talks back, never gripes about the chow, never gets seasick. Steering a motorboat day after day can be a terrible bore."

The three men finished their discussion with an examination of Moore's boat's proposed delivery trip. She was being built in Europe, and an interesting point developed when Don said he intended to go to the Canary Islands about September 1 and then cross the Atlantic via the Cape Verde Islands.

"Why, that's right in the middle of hurricane season," protested Tubby.

"That's right. But I can't sit around the Canary Islands until the middle of November like the sailing cruisers do before starting for the West Indies, and my 'Passagemaker' doesn't have to. We'll start out

from the Cape Verdes, trying to get in a little trade wind running with twin staysails and self-steering, but continually slanting south toward the Equator. Then, when we get down to latitude 5 or 6 degrees north, we'll head due west, getting what help we can from the winds, but prepared to go all the way under power. There's never been a hurricane recorded that far south.

"We'll stop at Port-of-Spain in Trinidad for fuel and some rum; then head west along the coast of South America, still south of the hurricane belt, to Panama. From there to Acapulco, I'm sure we will use a lot of power. After a couple of days ashore, we'll be off on the last leg. We'll head directly for Cabo San Lucas, the southern tip of Baja, California. When the wind comes ahead, I'll put her on the starboard tack with power and head out to sea. As the wind shifts around, we'll gradually come to a more northerly course and end up where the clippers used to, about 600 miles west of San Francisco. Then it's due east on a reach till she slides under the Golden Gate Bridge, and there we are! How about it, Tubby, want to come along? I'll make a real cruising man of you yet."

"I'd sure like to. Maybe I could make at least one leg of it—or two."

"Your ideas are very interesting, Don," Bob Reid said. "It will be fun to watch how she works out. As far as I can see, you have everything you need for your 'Passagemaker.' Count me in with Tubby for part of your voyage, if you can. I'll do my best to make it."

"I'll do that, Bob," replied Moore, rolling up his prints. "You and Tubby will be hearing from me one of these days. Keep your seabags packed!"

They sat for a few minutes, thinking about Don Moore's story. Bob saw Tubby had a faraway look in his eye, a look that said he was running through the trades with Don—blue water and a fair wind, with the 'Passagemaker' chugging quietly along. Finally he sighed and looked around for a waiter.

"George," he said, "bring me the check—."

That was the end of the story. Looking back on it now, from the actual years of operating at sea that followed it, I can see that it extended the ideas first expressed in the 1946 *Rudder* article to encompass the requirement that range under power should be complete; that is, fuel for continuous motoring for any contemplated passage should be carried. Not only is that necessary for speed and dispatch, but it also permits the continuous use of the autopilot. The "APE," as Carleton Mitchell calls it (for *autopilot extraordinaire*), is not simply a convenience for the crew, it is also a necessity. It permits the use of a one-man watch, makes it possible to use inexperienced watchstanders, and, by taking the most onerous task off the crew's shoulders, contributes a great deal to establishing passagemaking as a relaxed and pleasurable way to cross oceans.

The boats discussed in the story were full-sail vessels that could be used for sail cruising upon reaching their destinations, after exchanging their passage propellers for two-bladed sailing types. It is obvious now, though it was not then, that placing increasing emphasis on power would bring great changes to the status of the sailing rig, as will be seen.

This story was the origin of my use of the terms *Passagemaker* and the *Passagemaker concept*, the words I coined to differentiate my type from other classes of yachts. (The correct version of this word when applied to voyaging is *passagemaker* or *passagemaking*.) In fact, the whole discussion was pointed toward why the vessels discussed could not be classified as any existing type, but were really a new concept.

Before then, the terms "motor-all-the-time boat" or "motorboat with rig" were used when I had to describe this craft, one that could not properly be called a motorsailer.

In fact, what to call long-range motor cruisers still causes trouble today. In his book *Sea Sense*, Richard Henderson calls *Passagemaker* a "modified MFV Type," which she certainly is not. The term "trawler yacht" started out to mean just that—a yacht patterned after a fishing trawler. Today, "trawler yacht" is used to describe boats that never in one's wildest dreams could be called true trawlers.

Let me set down here what I conceive *my* Passagemakers to be now:

1. She may carry sail or not, but in any case must carry at least enough fuel for an Atlantic crossing under power. The quantities of fuel and speeds involved are discussed in Chapter 6.

2. Her layout and equipment must be primarily for the comfort and efficiency of the crew on long passages. In-port convenience must, as Robert Beebe said, be secondary. For some items that bear on this, see Chapter 4.

3. Her seaworthiness, glass areas, above water/below water areas ratio (A/B), ballast, and other factors must clearly mark her as capable of making long voyages in deep water in the proper seasons for each area. These factors are discussed in Chapter 6.

In retrospect, it is surprising but quite true that the designs I worked on were considered solely in the light of their suitability to make the San Diego–Key West passage. It was not until the work was near completion that it occurred to me to think, "If it will do that, why not extend your ambition to cross the Atlantic and cruise the Mediterranean? Or the South Seas? Or around the world?"

This was the prospect before me while I labored on the last of the series of designs. When this vessel was built and launched to test my ideas, she could hardly be called anything else but *Passagemaker*. How she was designed and built and how she worked out comes next, in Chapter 4.

## CHAPTER FOUR

# *Passagemaker*: Designing, Building, and Testing—and the Lessons Learned

## Robert Beebe

The design for the boat that was finally built and christened *Passagemaker* was drawn in a hectic six-week period beginning in January 1962. Innumerable sketches and six designs taken through the lines and layout stages preceded her. Each one of these provided something for the next—it is surprising how much can be learned from a design that is never built. When *Passagemaker's* turn came, she went together with ease, involving only the combining of concepts that had previously been tested and refined on paper.

By now, the original concept had been expanded. Due to a drastic change in my personal situation, it became desirable to have a vessel that not only filled the requirements of the Passagemaker concept discussed in Chapter 3, but also had room for full-time living and working aboard. Sketching with this in mind, I soon realized that the 50-foot size was best to fill this specification along with the basic Passagemaker concept—especially as the contemplated vessel would have no "double-decking"—a term that will become familiar later.

Figures 4–1 through 4–3 show what *Passagemaker* looked like. Later we will discuss what we learned from her.

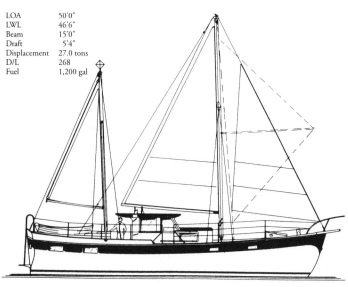

| LOA | 50'0" |
| LWL | 46'6" |
| Beam | 15'0" |
| Draft | 5'4" |
| Displacement | 27.0 tons |
| D/L | 268 |
| Fuel | 1,200 gal |

**Figures 4–1A and B.** Left: *Passagemaker* cruising in British Columbia. Right: Profile of *Passagemaker*, Beebe Design 67.

The lines show a hull of moderate deadrise with constant deadrise aft and a perfectly straight run. The quarter-beam buttock aft is literally straight. And thereby hangs a tale. Howard Chapelle, designer and marine historian, has helped me extensively over the years by criticizing my designs and admonishing me when I needed it. One day at the Smithsonian Institution, I showed the plans for *Passagemaker* to Howard.

Looking at the lines, he nodded and said, "Not bad." Then, pointing at the quarter-beam buttock aft, he added, "But that should be straighter."

That gave me the opening I was looking for. "Damn it, Howard," I said, "I *knew* you would say that. That line was drawn with the straightest straightedge I could find!"

He merely answered, "Humpf."

The high stern was needed to preserve the room inside the stern cabin by providing the last 7 feet with an area where the sole could be raised. The bow was the same height as the stern, which is unusual and made her look a bit like a dhow. The entire hull shows the influence of my previous sailing experience. *PM* (my abbreviation of her name) certainly ran nicely, with no wake to speak of, at her ocean-crossing speed of 7.5 knots. When completely built, she was somewhat overweight, and the significance of this will be discussed in Chapter 6 as an example of the technicalities of the business. The long keel and skeg with large rudder made her run before a gale as if on rails, and effectively handled the broaching problem so often exhibited by ordinary motorboats.

The arrangement shows the big stern cabin that was originally wide open—a combined drafting office and social center. Forward of this was the cockpit, on the same level as the pilothouse. It was designed to ensure the single watchstander a secure place to go outside and observe—something that has to be done as it is impossible to keep the pilothouse windows salt-free all the time. The pilothouse was kept small, but had all the required space, including a chart table and a raised settee with a good view all around. Forward of this and down three steps was the combined galley/dinette. The six-person dinette was raised 18 inches to put diners' eyes at the level of the ports while eating—a much appreciated feature. The space under it provided 21 bins for canned goods—stores for six people for 60 days. Forward of this was the owner's quarters, with head and shower. In the stern a convertible sofa made two berths, with a third on top of the drafting table. In this way, there were four berths for the passage-making crew, which was the number we had on the first voyage from Singapore to Greece. Later, a pipe berth was fitted up forward, increasing crew berths to five—until the aft cabin was further modified as described under "What We Learned."

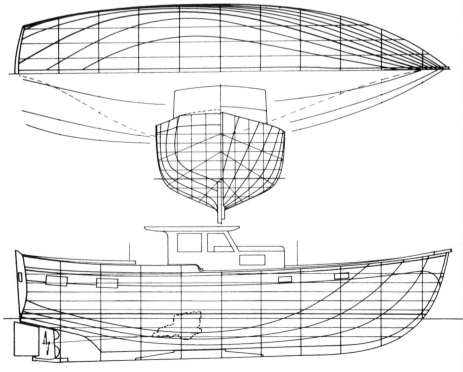

**Figure 4–2.** Lines of *Passagemaker.*

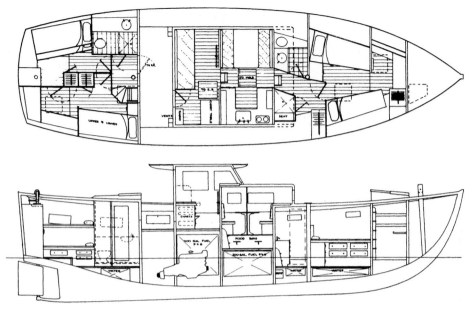

**Figure 4–3.** Accommodation plan of *Passagemaker*.

The profile (Figure 4–1B) shows the rig. It was quite short. Originally I had planned to have a much taller mainsail so I could attempt to sail in fair winds—motorsailer fashion—with the aid of a Hyde feathering propeller. But when the Hyde people told me they did not approve of their propeller being used in this manner—that is, on what was essentially a motor-all-the-time-boat—the rig was reduced and considered as emergency propulsion only. At that time, there was no other feathering propeller I would trust. It would have been hopeless to try to sail well with her 32-inch, 3-bladed prop. We did have plans to carry and rig all the gear necessary to remove the prop at sea, but never did it. The mizzen was wholly dedicated to carrying the stabilizing rig, and its bit of sail was rarely used.

The single Ford 330, 6-cylinder diesel, a Thornycroft conversion with heavy flywheel (a must with Fords) and capacity for 1,200 U.S. gallons of fuel was selected to take us the required 2,400 miles. Due to doubts raised in researching the problems of attaining maximum range—let alone estimating it—I made allowances everywhere I could to ensure we got the range desired. These included drawing the hull to the prismatic coefficient suited to a speed of 7.5 knots; providing an oversize propeller for greatest efficiency at cruising speed—but without the ability to use all the power the engine could provide; and providing an excess of fuel over what was theoretically necessary. As a result of these precautions, she attained a range well in excess of that desired, showing a reserve on a run from San Diego to Panama without fueling of some 400 miles, for an all-gone range of 3,200 miles.

## Building *Passagemaker*

My research on the building problem showed that the family budget could stand the cost if she were built abroad of wood and with very simple equipment. The plans were sent out for bids, and a contract for the construction was ultimately awarded to John I. Thornycroft & Sons of Singapore. Work commenced in July 1962.

I spoke of being able to swing the cost if the boat were built abroad. I planned to take advantage of all the money-saving possibilities of such a project. There are a number of steps involved that can lead to the greatest possible economy. Not everyone will be able to take advantage of all these, but here is how they worked for me:

1. The construction bid itself was lower than those from yards in the United States.

2. I designed her myself and avoided that cost.

3. I went to Singapore and superintended the job. Not only did I live more cheaply than at home, but I also feel some form of supervision is essential on a foreign contract. It is impossible to draw the details of everything, and if any solutions are left to the yard, differences in building practice are bound to make you unhappy over some of them.

4. The vessel came home under her own power. This is a saving in two ways. First, you save the considerable freight bill, which includes many hidden expenses. Second, you save on duty since the boat is second-hand on arrival. *Passagemaker* arrived in the U.S. 17 months after completion. The duty was reduced by 20 percent, that reduction covering the expenses of the trip. And we had a fine cruise in the bargain.

Experience since 1963 shows steadily rising building costs in the Orient, reducing the differential in bid costs. But it still appears possible to save money if the boat comes home under her own power. One thing more: supervising is not easy. I worked seven days a week all during the seven months I was there.

Thornycroft did an excellent job on the boat, using teak planking over triple-laminated chengal frames and plywood decking

**Figures 4–4, 4–5, and 4–6.** Three views of *Passagemaker* during construction at the yard of John I. Thornycroft & Sons, Singapore.

topped by Cascover sheathing. With spruce spars and English sails, and now properly christened *Passagemaker*, she lay alongside the Thornycroft pier ready to go—tanks full of fuel, provisions stowed, and crew aboard—on March 18, 1963, eight and a half months after construction began.

**Figure 4–7.** *Passagemaker* at Thornycroft's fitting-out dock, with flags flying in celebration of the christening.

**Figure 4–8.** *Passagemaker* during her sea trials in Singapore harbor. The stabilizer poles are swung out for the first time, but the stabilizers are not in the water.

## *Passagemaker's* Cruising

I mentioned earlier that Marin-Marie's voyage in *Arielle* resulted in his crossing the Atlantic with essentially nothing to report; this is the way it was with *Passagemaker*. Although we passed through the fringes of two hurricanes and had some gales, we always made our ETAs, suffered no damage we couldn't fix, and had the engine start when the switch was turned on and run until we stopped it.

When we left the builder's yard in Singapore on March 18, 1963, none of the crew knew what to expect. Two of us, Captain Ralph Arndt, USN, Ret., and myself, had considerable sailing experience; Colonel Everett Bibb, USA, Ret., had extensive coastal motorboat experience; Congdon Curts, my old friend from service in Alaska, was the only man qualified as a novice. But the vessel and the ideas behind it were wholly untried. At that time, [Beebe believed that] no other vessel could even attempt what we were trying to do.

Any anxieties we may have felt turned out to be completely groundless. *Passagemaker* soon showed she would do all we expected and more. The log of that first voyage essentially went like this: We hurried our departure because the boat was late being completed, as is usual with yacht builders. We feared the beginning of the southwest monsoon in the Indian Ocean that would have effectively barred our way to Aden. We finished storing supplies late one night and left at dawn the next day. The three days spent running up the flat-calm Strait of Malacca were used to shake things down, get the rigging in shape, and so on before entering the Bay of Bengal, headed for Ceylon [now Sri Lanka]. In the bay, we found favorable winds, the remnants of the northeast monsoon, and made excellent time to Colombo, arriving before dawn on the seventh day. We had to jill around for several hours before we were able to enter port.

After a stay of four days, we were off on the 2,200-mile passage to Aden. We touched the southern tip of India at Cape Comorin to get a good navigational departure, then headed for Minicoy Island and the passage through the Maldive Island reefs. From there, it was a straight shot to Cape Guardafui, the northeast tip of Somaliland, and another run of 400 miles to Aden. That section took 12 days—in a flat calm most of the way. We were lucky—the southwest monsoon must have set in just a few days after we passed this critical point.

After three days in Aden, we left for Suez, experiencing the usual blow from the south at the south end of the Red Sea and from the north at the north end. In the middle it was quite nice. Bucking the norther at the north end convinced us that we rated some time off, so we stopped for two days at Endeavour Harbour on Tawilla Island at the entrance to the Gulf of Suez. At the canal, they were kind and efficient, and we started through at the stern of a convoy the next morning and made the usual one-night stopover at Ismailia. The next afternoon, we let our pilot off with a running jump to the dock in Port Said and headed out into the Mediterranean for Rhodes, taking care to pour a libation to Poseidon as we entered his domain. The *Meltemi* from Russia to Egypt was blowing pretty hard, and we had to buck it most of the way. It took us four days, but we finally arrived in Rhodes—in a flat calm.

In a total elapsed time of six weeks, we made some 6,000 miles to Greece, averaging underway *exactly* our designed ocean-crossing speed of 7.5 knots. We knew then that in *Passagemaker* we had something. And subsequent cruising in her has shown how right we were. There we were, 42 days from Singapore, ready for cruising in the fascinating waters of the Mediterranean. It's difficult to determine the records of sailing vessels that have made the same trip, but we had certainly arrived ahead of any of them by a matter of months! Our record was achieved not only by keeping up a high average speed but also because the crew was rested and relaxed enough to be ready to leave port again in a matter of days. That was the start of our kind of passagemaking.

For the rest of the summer, we cruised in Greece and Yugoslavia. The next spring we cruised to Malta and Italy; then we moved eastward along the Riviera to the mouth of the Rhone River. There we prepared

**Figure 4–9.** *Passagemaker* at anchor in Endeavour Harbour, Tawilla Island, at the entrance to the Gulf of Suez, where we took a well-earned rest.

to test another of *Passagemaker*'s features: her capability to go into the French canals (see Chapter 16). With her masts down and her engine turning at the maximum permitted rpm for a speed of about 9.4 knots, our vessel went up the Rhone to Lyon in two days. This was followed by an idyllic meander through France to Strasbourg on the Rhine River, then down the Rhine and across the North Sea to England for some work at the Thornycroft plant, which lies three locks up the Thames River past London.

On departure day from London, we dropped down the Thames in the middle of the night to catch the tide, put up our masts in the Medway, went to Plymouth for fuel and supplies, and crossed the Atlantic via the Azores and Bermuda to Newport, Rhode Island, in 21 steaming days.

Singlehanded, I then took her down the Inland Waterway to Miami. With a new crew, we went from Miami through the Bahamas to Panama and then up the coast to San Diego, California, in 29 days—not bad, considering that we took three days off to cruise in the Bahamas. (How well I recall my earlier concern about this east-west passage in the planning and theory-stage years!) After San Diego, a crew of two took *Passagemaker* up the coast to her home port of Monterey to end a delivery cruise of some 21 months that had been fun all the way.

After that, *Passagemaker* made a cruise to Hawaii and returned via the Pacific Northwest. She also made a trip to the Pacific Northwest straight up the coast, nonstop, in seven days—our most rugged cruise.

Figure 4–10. *Passagemaker's* dinghy was patterned after the Herreshoff Columbia model, and sized to fit the raised poop deck. Here she takes a capacity "liberty party" ashore at Delos, Greece.

In 1967, she went east to Expo '67 in Montreal and was stored on the East Coast preparatory to sailing to Europe the following summer. Some months later, a gentleman who had made a long cruise with me bought her, on the condition I would help him take her to Europe in 1969, which I did.

It was a wrench to let her go, but I felt I had learned all I could from her and wanted to take the next step. *PM* happily cruised in Europe from April to October for the next five years, covering beautiful cruising grounds from Norway to Turkey. (Umstot's note: *Passagemaker* was still cruising the Caribbean in 2011.)

## What We Learned

The lessons learned comprise such a big file that I can give only the conclusions here. But believe me, there is much data to support every point, even if some of the conclusions sound dogmatic. So here is a list of the major items, emphasizing those that affected future design:

**Layout.** The highly specialized and personal layout of *Passagemaker* would not be anyone else's cup of tea. As a matter of fact, it did not work out and was never used for its designed purpose. We finally converted the stern cabin into two double cabins with a head. While this layout was highly satisfactory at sea, it was not a success in port.

The reason for this layout failure was that I had been so concerned about *Passagemaker's* seaworthiness and ability to perform at sea to the required concept that other facets of the whole boat problem were neglected or ignored. For instance, to keep her above water/ below water areas ratio as low as possible, she was not "double-decked." This concentration on performance contributed to making her a seagoing machine. I would be hard put to find some feature of her performance at sea that could be changed to advantage.

But in port, her lack of lounge space, except the galley/dinette area and the pilothouse settee, was a distinct drawback to her having any wide appeal. The fact is, such a large and expensive vessel does not make sense unless she is used the greater part of the year. This leads to the requirement that such a vessel should have good in-port living space for the owner and his wife, with all the amenities of a shore apartment if they can be fitted in. When you get right down to it, such a vessel is most suitable for a retired couple who use it as a home afloat. The problem is to combine living space with the necessary seaworthiness for ocean voyaging. I believe now that a better balance of such qualities is feasible.

I mentioned "double-decking" previously. It means to have one full-headroom compartment under another full-headroom compartment. *Passagemaker* was not double-decked, nor is such a popular model as the Grand Banks 42. As an example of double-decking, the Grand Banks 50 takes it about as far as you can go. It is clear the amount of double-decking largely determines how much living space a vessel can have.

**Cockpit.** At sea, *Passagemaker's* cockpit—4 feet deep—was one of her best features. It enabled the watchstander to go outside to observe all around while remaining securely *in* the boat, with no possibility of falling overboard. This is a very serious problem on the seagoing motorboat. We found that the single watchstander was alone much of the time, day as well as night. The consequences of someone falling overboard while alone, with the ship running on autopilot, are not pleasant to contemplate. On *Passagemaker* there was only one absolute rule: the watchstander was not allowed to go on deck without someone watching him. The captain was always available for this duty. But the 4-foot-long cockpit, subtracted from the overall length, certainly hurt the accommodations. In subsequent designs, I have felt it necessary to dispense with this feature.

With a pilothouse placed on deck where the watchstander can gain access to the side of the vessel, I feel it is necessary that the rails should be not less than 4 feet high and solid in any area the watchstander is permitted to go. The presence of sailing racer–inspired, 30-inch-high lifelines on seagoing powerboats is shocking. They make sense on a sailing vessel because higher ones interfere with sails, the crew wears safety harnesses, and there is more than one watchstander on deck. But for the single watchstander of the oceangoing motorboat they certainly are not adequate, being a height only sufficient to trip you overboard. On *Passagemaker*, the lifeline stanchions forward were 40 inches high, and on the raised afterdeck they were 30 inches high. It was surprising how much difference the 10 inches made in the feeling of security.

**Sailing rig.** This feature is hard to justify by the facts of our cruising. It is not a good emergency propulsion system for this reason: if the engine should fail, sail would get you somewhere, but the chances of its being where you wanted to go are pretty slim. Consequently, your cruise would be ruined, while an alternative power system would allow the cruise to continue. In addition, an efficient sailing rig is expensive—*more* so than another diesel engine.

Sail has two things to recommend it. It gives the crew something to do and is fun from this point of

Figure 4–11. Beebe, left, talks with Dr. James Kergen in British Columbia. Note the deep cockpit, so useful at sea.

Figure 4–12. Aboard *Passagemaker*. Beebe, left, with Dr. John Gratiot at Mykonos Island, Greece. Note the lifelines that are 40 inches high forward and 30 inches high aft. They are slack, preparatory to launching the dinghy.

view. (But with an assured speed of 7.5 to 8 knots, it is surprising how often the wind is so far ahead that the sails won't draw.) And sail gives the vessel the aspect of a motorsailer, making it more acceptable to proceed at hull speed or below without embarrassment when passed by faster coastal motorboats. I'm not being facetious here: I am convinced this

**Figure 4–13.** *Passagemaker* spreads her downwind running sails by backing down for the photographer. Note the wake at the bow. (Norris D. Hoyt)

is the real reason for the existence of the so-called "motorsailer." I have never seen one with its sails up in coastal waters. This is certainly a legitimate reason, but an expensive one. For vessels with sail, I now recommend they *also* have alternate engine-driven emergency drive.

**Stabilizing rig.** *Passagemaker's* rig, the West Coast antiroll stabilizer familiarly called "flopperstopper" (F/S; see Chapter 8), changed the whole aspect of our cruising in ways we could not imagine before we started. For one thing, it made ocean crossing by motorboat an activity that could be thoroughly enjoyed by persons without any seagoing experience. This aspect turned out to be such a vital contribution to the success of our Passagemaker concept that there is a whole chapter devoted to it later. Now I'm sure it is a *required feature* of the ocean-crossing motorboat, so important that in the larger and more expensive vessels an alternative means of stabilizing should be provided.

**Freeboard.** The bow was too low. We found that the measure of

speed possible against the sea depended very much on the height of the bow. When encountering seas from ahead, it is mandatory that you slow down until green water does not come over the bow. If you do not, you will eventually damage the vessel. We often wished our bow was higher by a foot or so, as it could have been without aesthetic damage to the profile.

**Stern.** Some people expressed concern about our broad stern in a following sea, a concern I did not share, feeling that the shape under water, not above, was the criterion. I was pleased to observe that in gales from astern we never had more than a foot or two of water over the stern platform.

**Steering comfort.** *Passagemaker* was built with a sprocket on the wheel to provide eventually for an outside steering station. This was never installed as we felt no need for it, piloting around docks and through the canals from inside with no difficulty. While the flying bridge has its points in local cruising of the weekend variety, one must remember that the tropical sun cannot be faced day in and day out on a long voyage. In *Passagemaker*, the watchstander could go outside as much as he pleased when there were others on deck.

**Handholds.** Although our stabilizing gear cut rolling by two-thirds, which made ordinary rolling around 5 to 10 degrees at most, we found that *Passagemaker's* pipe handholds in the galley were one of her best features. At the corner of each counter and at the inboard edge of the dinette table there were brass pipes to the overhead. They were constantly in

**Figure 4–14.** Beebe's stepdaughter, Gael Donovan, in *Passagemaker's* galley. She is holding two of the galley handholds, and the third one is visible.

use as handgrips, particularly by the cook in passing hot plates to the table, which could be reached with one hand while the other securely held a pipe.

If handholds were so useful in the intimately related galley and dinette of *Passagemaker*, it's clear that a greater separation between galley and dining table with no handholds would be quite dangerous. If a person loses his balance and starts to move across the ship, this movement must be stopped before it can accelerate to the point of injury. That is the reason why, in the days of trans-Atlantic passenger steamers, storm-wracked ships used to reach port with extraordinary numbers of injured passengers. Yachts with wide saloons must be careful about this.

**Propeller.** *Passagemaker* was fitted with an oversize prop. That is, she could not turn up the maximum permitted rpm for continuous duty. The reason for this was to get her long-range speed of 7.5 knots at a lower rpm, 1,750, which placed the engine at its most efficient fuel-consumption rate. While this provided a percent or two of better range, I feel now it would have been better to use the conventional prop for maximum continuous horsepower at maximum continuous rpm. You would then not have to worry about overloading the engine and would have a somewhat higher top speed and be allowed a higher local cruising speed.

**Equipment.** While simplicity of equipment is an ideal given much lip service, oceangoing motorboats are often found with amazing amounts of equipment for amazing amounts of money. This is discouraging to those with small budgets.

It doesn't have to be that way; *Passagemaker* proved it. We left Singapore with hardly more equipment than one would expect to find on a 30-foot sloop making the same voyage. We did have an autopilot—but this is a necessity on an oceangoing motorboat. We had a compass, a sextant, a radio for time ticks, a small radio direction finder (RDF), a 100-foot depth-sounder, a two-burner Primus stove, hand pumps for water, and a box for ice—when we could get it. That was the lot. And we had a ball all the way, ate very well, and were able to fix any small item that went wrong.

We did *not* have radar, a radio transmitter, a watermaker, hot water, gas ovens, air conditioning,

a pressure water system, or any of the multitudes of items so often installed today; and we never missed them. I recommend this approach, though I think it is pretty much a lost cause today. Basically, you must be sure you have an answer to the question, "What will I do when that quits?" Not *if* but *when*, as it will. For instance, there is the incredible story of the all-electric yacht that went to the South Seas where its *single* generator gave up the ghost. They couldn't even flush the heads. End of story—and end of cruise.

Of course, I have no objection to owners installing as much equipment as their budgets can stand. It makes sense to provide space for the later installation of equipment by building in everything possible in the construction phase. But you don't really *need* this stuff. Get underway without it and enjoy the cruise. Once you convince yourself that warm beer is just as good as cold, refrigeration is a waste of time and money, in my opinion—but not that of my wife!

**Night vision.** One thing I completely forgot to provide for was night vision in the pilothouse. If a light was on in the galley, the watchstander couldn't see a thing. And the galley was the only space available for the navigator to work up his evening stars. In Ceylon [now Sri Lanka] we tried to fix this with a hatch cover and curtain. This helped, but a real light lock with a door is a necessity. This problem should be well up on the list in the design stage.

**Fuel tanks.** *Passagemaker*'s fuel tanks were fitted with a draw-off sump that trapped all contamination. We opened a tank after five years to see how it was doing. It was perfectly clean and free of corrosion. I feel, then, that it is permissible to build tanks without clean-out plates if a sump is used. This gets rid of a potential leak source.

**Guardrail.** *Passagemaker* had a guardrail 6 inches wide outside, with full-length scarfed and glued timbers. It was considered an external sheer clamp. Inside, the frames were blocked and, with the internal clamp, there was a solid 12 inches of timber at the sheer. Knocking around ports overseas as we did, with no yacht-type moorage to speak of, we were *very* glad we had this rail. It took some incredible knocks with aplomb. It also furnished a dividend we

**Figure 4–15.** *Passagemaker* arriving at the dock in Monterey, California, in 1964, at the end of her passage three-quarters of the way around the world, proudly flying the flags of the 18 nations she visited.

didn't anticipate. The 6-inch, flat-top surface of the rail made a convenient and safe place to run around outside the lifelines when setting fenders, lines, and so on. I recommend the arrangement. Most American yachts are flimsy in this department.

**Noise.** In the planning stages, I was concerned about the possible effect of noise and vibration on the crew over long stretches. Some information on this subject indicated that noise alone can cause cumulative fatigue if the level is high enough. Consequently, as much as possible was done to suppress noise. Two inches of fiberglass insulation was used both in the engine room and in the overheads. The entire vessel from end to end inside also had acoustic tile on the overhead. The aft bulkhead of the engine room, which opened on the aft living spaces, was also heavily insulated.

No fatigue from this source was evident. In fact, the steady noise of the engine soon became a part of life and was ignored. The comment often made by sailing men that noise would drive us crazy turned out to be wishful thinking on their part.

I believe the acoustic tile did more to suppress noise than anything else as it stopped reflection back and forth from sole to overhead, a potent source of noise. In addition, the insulation and tile kept the interior of the boat cool on the hottest days.

**Hot salt water.** Something I thought up and tried out proved to be the most popular and appreciated feature on the ship. This was to have hot salt water from the engine cooling system piped into the galley to furnish an unlimited supply of very hot water for rinsing plates and pots when the engine was running. The cooks and cleanup crew really missed it when the engine was shut down in port. To avoid unbalancing the engine cooling system, the water ran all the time. A two-way valve either dumped it into the sink drain or turned it into the faucet. As an added dividend, the temperature and volume of the running water gave the watchstander a quick check on the cooling system.

**Summary.** Finally we (and by "we" I mean all the people who cruised aboard *Passagemaker*) discovered how much fun even long passages could be in a vessel that made no demands on one's endurance nor required skills developed over years of experience under sail. Well, we achieved [our goals] and it does make for a different sort of cruising. On our voyage to Hawaii and return we went out in 12 days and returned in 13. By contrast, a sailing vessel that at speeds comparable to ours should have come back in 16 days left about the same date—and took 70 days!

## CHAPTER FIVE

# The Philosophy of Power Passagemaking

## Beebe's Philosophy of Power Passagemaking

Captain Beebe's philosophy can be summed up in this paragraph from the previous editions:

*So much for Passagemaker and what we learned from her cruising. It was a revelation to me. In my career at sea I have handled ships from El Toro dinghies to 80,000-ton aircraft carriers, and cruised in sail in all rigs from 26 to 55 feet. But none of this prepared me for how our long voyages in Passage-maker turned out to be so relaxing, such a delight to people who had never been to sea before, such an impressive demonstration that the world's cruising grounds were indeed available with "speed and dis-patch." It is this side of our concept that has made me such a missionary on the subject.*

More recently, Steve and Linda Dashew also support Beebe's experience. They are famous for their extensive cruising and racing under sail and for their Deerfoot line of sailboats. Their power-boat, *Windhorse*, an 83-foot long, narrow, and fast passagemaker resulted in a new line of boats that will be discussed in later chapters. In describing their experience with oceangoing powerboats, they state "the bottom line is that this boat is by far the most comfortable aboard which we have ever voyaged. In all sea states—from confused head seas to large crossing swells on the beam—the motion is significantly less than anything we have experienced in the past".

Given that Beebe had spent much of his life on the water, he did not find his time at sea to be as delightful as many others have described—he wanted to make a fast and comfortable passage to his cruising grounds. In our voyages in *Teka III*, we have found wonder in the sea voyages themselves: the rise of the moon appearing on the Sea of Cortez that looks much like a giant ship with floodlights, the shimmer of the moonlight on long ocean rollers, the delight in schools of dolphins as far as the eye can see, flying fish skimming the waves, the bright phos-phorescence trail we leave in the water at night, the countless beautiful sunsets, the fish we fight and eat along the way, and the star-filled night skies. Even the periods of rough seas are memorable—seeing large waves with breaking tips approach from the stern and simply roll under the boat is both scary and exhilarating. And the thrill and satisfaction of sighting land after weeks at sea cannot be adequately described. Thus, we found the passages themselves to be very rewarding experiences.

In earlier editions of this book, Captain Beebe illustrated his philosophy by including two stories of transatlantic passagemaking. I have also included two voyages: one describing the Sinks' voyage, related by Jim Leishman, and one of our own experience cross-ing from the Canaries to Antigua. We also include a new section in this chapter that highlights the keys to successful voyaging under power. These ideas are an outgrowth of a Trawler Fest seminar presented by Denis and Mary Umstot, and Christi and Eric Grab.

## Keys to Enjoyable Voyaging Under Power

**Compatible people.** Living in relatively small quarters puts some strain on relationships. It is helpful if both parties agree on the cruising lifestyle before buying an expensive boat and making the commitment to travel extensively. If only one party is dreaming of the cruising life, it is probably better if the couple gets some experience such as chartering a power yacht for several weeks or living in an RV for a season. Shared decision making is also important, both in the strategic plan such as voyaging to the Mediterranean or cruising around the world, and the tactical plans such as when to leave and what the next port will be. One way to satisfy differing needs of each partner is a cruising plan that involves laying up the boat for several months and traveling back home to take care of medical issues, social connections, grandchildren, and other needs.

**Experience and competence.** Although some voyagers have started with little or no experience and succeeded, many others have failed or have not fulfilled their cruising dreams. Cruising and boating experience under either power or sail is very important. You don't want to be studying the "how to" books during a storm at sea. Most people get experience by owning smaller boats and gradually moving up in size, range, and capability. If your circumstances don't permit this approach, and you both want to go cruising, start with coastal cruising such as trips to Alaska or the Bahamas. You will gain experience rapidly with this type of approach and find that at the end of a year or two you are ready to take off for an ocean passage.

**A seakindly boat.** Beebe's philosophy of "comfort at sea" requires a boat that will be comfortable in most any sea condition. In later chapters, we will discuss some of the design and stabilization decisions that can make the boat more comfortable at sea and at anchor. Too much motion at sea can wear down any crew and can also be quite dangerous because decision making is affected. Many examples exist of boats (mostly sailing vessels) that have been abandoned, sometimes with loss of lives, because of crew exhaustion—only to find that the boat eventually floated to land months later.

**Weather avoidance.** When passages are made in good weather, they are delightful, relaxing, and fun. If a voyage is made against the prevailing winds and currents, it can be extremely uncomfortable, slow, and frustrating. When we were voyaging in the Mediterranean, we seriously contemplated going the rest of the way around the word in an easterly direction, in opposition to the monsoon winds and other prevailing winds. The more we studied the pilot charts (which show average wind directions and forces along with tropical storm tracks), it was obvious that we would be bucking the wind much of the time or going during a season of possible tropical storms. We decided that the trip in that direction would not be much fun and presented some weather risks we were not willing to take. (See Chapter 18 for weather issues involved in passagemaking.)

**Simple, easy-to-fix systems.** There are two prevailing views about this topic. One view I definitely share with Beebe is that simple, easy-to-fix, reliable systems are a must for enjoyable voyaging. The other view is that all the comforts of a luxury home should be available on your boat and that somehow, with modern communications and transport systems, anything that breaks can be fixed at the next port. The ultimate boat for this point of view would have spacious accommodations; a large galley; all-electric appliances; full-time air conditioning; a full array of interconnected electronic instruments; and satellite telephone, Internet, and TV. In addition, some boats have such complex and automatic mechanical systems that some breakdown is almost guaranteed during a long voyage. It is difficult to accumulate the knowledge and experience to fix many of these modern complex systems, and expertise in foreign ports may be nonexistent. Many of these "luxury boats" find that a great deal of their passage time is spent fixing things, or trying to figure out how to get along without some piece of equipment. The "simple boat," on the other hand, will be much less likely to have equipment failures and much more likely to be fixable by the boat owner or at least a mechanic in some foreign port.

## Voyaging Approaches

Other major decisions regarding voyaging fall into at least three categories: choice of area for cruising, speed of cruising, and approach to destinations. In addition the cruiser has the choice of a "go-it-alone" approach or joining the cruising community consisting of all boats transiting the same areas.

**Choice of cruising area.** Much of this book is aimed at transoceanic cruising to distant ports and islands; however, one might also cruise closer to home, say on a great-circle route, or down the Caribbean islands to Trinidad, or to the Sea of Cortez in Mexico. Cruising closer to home and avoiding long ocean passages minimizes the risk from weather and makes solving mechanical problems easier. For the newcomer to voyaging, it may be a good choice to begin here and then expand to more far-away places.

**Speed of cruising.** Voyaging under power gives the option to reach distant ports in relatively short times. You may often go on the shortest route regardless of trade winds and at a very steady rate of 6–8 knots, 24/7. People who take limited time off (such as one year) from their jobs often find themselves pressured to accomplish great distances in short periods of time. If your time and budget do not allow more leisurely cruising, this approach may be the best choice. However, fast trips miss a lot.

**Approach to destinations.** One of the joys of cruising is having your home and "stuff" with you rather than just a suitcase. You can go slow and savor the locations for as long as you wish, given constraints of storm seasons and visa restrictions. We spent more than 10 years on our voyage to the Mediterranean and back. Heidi and Wolfgang Hass have accomplished two circumnavigations on their Nordhavn 46, *Kanaloa.* Here is how they view their cruising schedule:

> *Our minimum stay is about 14 days, said Heidi. If you only stay five days, by the time those five days are up you've cleaned the boat, done the laundry, done the grocery shopping, and then it's time to go—you've never even seen the area or met the locals. So we often stay a month or two. We are out to enjoy other countries and the people who live there, and to do some sightseeing. Rushing around the world is not on our agenda. We like to relax and rent cars and drive around. Even if we've been there before, we always find something new, something we haven't seen before.*

**Joining the cruising community.** For many, one of the major pleasures of cruising is that you are part of a unique group of adventurous people who have much in common with you. In most cruising destinations you will find other voyagers, mostly on sailing vessels, but ever more commonly on motor vessels. We have always felt welcome and at home in this diverse cruising community. We found that a great ice breaker was to go around to the anchored

**Figure 5–1.** *Kanaloa,* owned by Heidi and Wolfgang Hass, anchored off Moorea. They are on their third circumnavigation aboard their Nordhavn 46. (Heidi and Wolfgang Hass)

# Famed Sailor, Carleton Mitchell, Switched from Sail to Power

The race was a six-day nightmare of groping through fog, hunting for the flicker of a breeze, and battling howling gales of 60 knots that heeled over the big ocean racers, ripped sails, snapped rudders, and forced sailors to lash themselves to their craft. But fair weather or foul, the short, stubby yawl out of Annapolis was the master of the Atlantic, clipping off miles with the regularity of an ocean liner. When the fleet of 135 boats finished the 635-mile thrash from Newport to Bermuda last week, the overall winner, for an unprecedented third straight time, was *Finisterre*, owned and skippered by a shrewd, affable, literary-minded salt named Carleton Mitchell. (*Time*, July 4, 1960)

Carleton Mitchell, who also wrote four books on sailing, spells out why he converted from sail to power. This passage gives insight into his philosophy of cruising:

*What dark, unfathomed depths of the ocean lie ahead of the windjammer contemplating the transition to–ugh–a motor boat? Ever since I made my own escape from what I only half facetiously call "the tyranny of sail." For me living and cruising aboard a displacement vessel driven by docile slaves under hatches has been much like cruising the sailing craft I have owned except there is more room, less dependence on others, and a new-found leisure making it possible to enjoy more of what I think of as the fringe benefits of cruising: scuba diving, poking into gunk-holes, ham radio, reading, listen-ing to music, lolling in the sun, whomping up meals in a spacious galley, or simply taking it easy, even when underway, while the autopilot does the work and the soporific hum of the engines brings into focus thoughts which never seem to take form ashore. Thus, as I have tried to say reassuringly to others, the transition can be considered a way of life, instead of only a time of life. (Motor Boating and Sailing, November 1979)*

[Carleton Mitchell, who won the Bermuda Cup for the third time in 1960, died in 2007 at the age of 96.]

Figure 5–2. Carleton Mitchell's boat, *Coyaba*, in 1976. (Mystic Seaport)

boats in our dinghy and invite them over for "sun-downers." In most places, this means sharing snacks and drinks around sundown, often with each boat bringing something to contribute. We had the advantage of a very large covered aft deck area; many people could come aboard and not feel crowded, and yet the inside of the boat need not be open to every-one. These get-togethers usually led to additional social engagements and sometimes lifetime friend-ships. They were also useful for finding out about the local area and its attractions, shopping, and so on. One could usually find out information about other desirable places to go or anchor as well. Those cruis-ers who elect to "go it alone" and do not mingle with the cruising community miss a great deal. Whenever we see a megayacht with its crew and owner aboard, we always feel a bit sorry that they are so isolated from this wonderful community.

# Two Voyages Under Power

What follows are two successful power passagemaking journeys. The first is the 1990 transatlantic portion of *Salvation II*'s circumnavigation, written by Jim Leishman. This account may provide inspiration to the ambitious yet inexperienced enthusiast. The second is written by Mary Umstot and tells of our passage on *Teka III* from the Canaries to Antigua in 2005. Later in the book, you will hear from other voyagers about their passages, both successful and difficult. This section provides a little preliminary insight into what it is like to cross oceans in a power boat.

## Transatlantic Aboard Salvation II

*Jim Leishman*

Jim and Susy Sink, a retired couple from Houston, had a dream of owning a boat and going cruising. The Sinks' preparation for this adventure actually began with the dream's conception almost thirty years ago. While they were not able to gain experience aboard yachts at sea, they spent thousands of hours reading of others' travels. Their library also contained dozens of technical volumes and references, including the original edition of this book. Jim became convinced that a proper motor yacht, designed within the parameters outlined by Robert Beebe, would best suit their needs.

They selected a Nordhavn 46, and I found myself northbound as both delivery captain and teacher aboard *Salvation II* headed for the Pacific Northwest. Jim was aboard from Dana Point, California, northward; and Susan boarded in Coos Bay, Oregon, and continued on with us to Bellingham, Washington, where the delivery crew departed. The three of us spent the next three days reviewing the

**Figure 5–3.** Jim and Susy Sink. (*PassageMaker Magazine*)

basic operation and the handling of their new home. I must admit that upon bidding these eager but very inexperienced owners a fond farewell, I had concerns about their ability to fulfill the ambitious cruising plans to which they had committed themselves. As it turned out, they were fine.

The Sinks gained experience by cruising to Alaska; then continuing south to Mexico, Costa Rica, and the Panama Canal; finally winding up in Maine for the early summer. From there they completed the great circle route down the Mississippi to Houston. Thus, they gained considerable experience in handling the boat in many different conditions. They were ready to try circumnavigating the world!

Jim and Susy asked if I'd assist in the transatlantic leg from Florida to London via Bermuda and the Azores. I agreed but made it perfectly clear that any number of business commitments might force me to cancel prior to departure. As the weeks went by, things seemed to fall into place to allow me to firm up the commitment. Jim finally advised me that he would cancel the voyage without my help (I don't believe he would have), and I formally signed on to the crew list.

Hank Schuette, who assisted in the original Dana Point-Bellingham delivery aboard *Salvation II*, was also asked to join us in Florida for our May 15th departure. With four aboard, loads of food, and 938 gallons of clean fuel, we headed east across the Gulf Stream for the south end of Great Abaco Island. There we would pass through the Bahamas and turn northeast for Bermuda and the wide Atlantic.

At the beginning of any long voyage, everyone aboard feels some apprehension. After many thousands of miles aboard *Salvation II*, Jim and Susy trusted her completely. I, too, knew the boat well enough to have absolute confidence in her capability, but Hank had only our word that this was no ordinary motorboat.

Hank is a long-time member of the San Diego Yacht Club and has thousands of miles of offshore experience—mostly under sail. A dozen or so years earlier I had sold Hank a new 49-foot ketch—the largest in a line of sailboats he had owned—which he used extensively between San Francisco and Acapulco, Mexico. After nine years he sold it to take delivery of a popular new production 49-footer, a commodious motor yacht with the above-water shape of an offshore cruiser and the underbody of a standard semidisplacement coastal cruiser. He kept the powerboat less than two years, replacing it with a 38-foot sailboat. His inability to gain confidence in the motor yacht's offshore ability was the reason for its sale.

An ex-Marine jet-fighter pilot, Hank doesn't scare easily. A year before this trip, he and I sailed one of our Mason 53s in the Transpacific Yacht Race, and he wouldn't hesitate to cross an ocean in his small sailboat, but the motion and behavior of his previous motor yacht when offshore had left him apprehensive about powerboats. His experience running up the West Coast aboard *Salvation II* almost two years earlier offered only delightful summer conditions with no gales or significant weather to test the vessel's capability, and I had to assure him that, unlike his previous motorboat, this little ship had the capability to handle almost anything the Atlantic would likely throw our way. The *Pilot Chart* of the North Atlantic for the month of May showed we could expect about 15 knots of breeze from the east, which is exactly what we experienced. We all settled down for this 925-mile first leg and anticipated a little uncomfortable going with the wind and sea on our nose. As we closed on Bermuda we expected the wind to shift more to the south and offer some assistance.

Early on the fourth day, the wind began to freshen and shift more to the northeast. The weather faxes showed a fast-developing low-pressure system brewing to the southeast of Bermuda, and soon gale warnings were issued for the entire area. Bermuda was only 300 miles ahead, but the low was building strength and moving to the northwest—directly across our path.

During the evening we made radio contact with *South Bound I* (an amateur weather forecaster in Bermuda) and were warned that this fast-developing storm was building in intensity and headed in our direction. Our weather briefer, Herb, somberly suggested we turn to the southwest (almost a 180-degree turn) and try to run across the storm's path and into its southern quadrant, where wind speeds would be less. Concerned and plagued with a poor SSB [single-sideband radio] connection, we inquired as to the anticipated strength of the storm and learned that wind speeds of around 40 knots were anticipated, but with considerably stronger winds likely. Since we had already seen gusts to 50 mph on our anemometer (a mph-calibrated home unit), we decided to press onward directly toward Bermuda. Our boat was performing perfectly, experiencing little difficulty, maintaining headway of about 5.5 knots, and still steering under autopilot. We had taken the precaution of installing our port-side storm plates on the saloon windows, and we spent the night riding out the storm in relative comfort. It didn't take Hank long to figure out that this motorboat was "an entirely different kettle of fish" from his previous 49-footer, and he expressed his confidence in the vessel's ability to handle seas significantly worse than what we were encountering.

Figure 5–4. Installing saloon window storm panels in building seas near Bermuda. *Salvation II*'s asymmetrical saloon makes this an awkward job on the port side.

Dawn broke and the Force 8 conditions continued with a steady barometer. By midday we were picking up Bermuda on the radar, and by 1900 we had passed the first channel market at the entrance to St. George. Interestingly, we had come in just behind a 100-foot-plus motor yacht, the *William I*. Dockside conversations with her captain revealed that they had experienced the same conditions we had, but the larger vessel did not fare as well. The semidisplacement design was not well suited to open-ocean conditions, and storm damage to her forward saloon windows and some to her interior forced her to heave-to for repairs. When underway again, her progress into the rough seas was very difficult, and despite her great horsepower she could not maintain the speed of *Salvation II*. Hank boasted to the captain that we rode out the gale in T-shirts and stocking feet and never had to alter course or reduce speed. We were quite proud of our able little ship.

There was little time to enjoy Bermuda as our stay was only about 40 hours. Two dinners ashore, an oil change, fueling, light provisioning, and a little touring of St. George by foot were all we had time for. I was sorry that we could spend so little time in such a pleasant place; Bermuda offers beautiful beaches, perfect weather, friendly people, and a tremendously interesting history.

I promised myself I'd return, but we were all anxious to get underway. We departed under bright sunny skies and with an exceptional weather forecast. The gale that roughed us up coming into Bermuda had dissipated and moved to the northwest, and we were finally seeing the overdue development of a high-pressure system around the Azores—commonly referred to as the Azores High. This was a relief as the area had been plagued by constant gales prior to our Fort Lauderdale departure and throughout the first leg of our voyage. This high-pressure system is a necessary ingredient to a pleasant transatlantic crossing, and we were happy to see it forming.

This second leg—sailing a great-circle course—calculated out at just under 1,800 nautical miles. The Nordhavn's range graphs show this to be an easy undertaking, but considering the possibility of a long duration of adverse weather and potentially unfavorable currents, we decided on a very conservative approach. Departing Bermuda with a maximum load (1,072 gallons) of diesel aboard, the initial governor setting allowed 1,650 rpm, which propelled the heavily laden *Salvation II* along at a leisurely 6.5 knots with a fuel burn of 2 gallons per hour. As we progressed and burned fuel, the speed would increase, but at this initial speed we were guaranteed a calm-water range in excess of 3,200 miles.

A "How-Goes-It" fuel curve was developed for this leg of the trip, and we decided upon a target fuel reserve of 20 percent at our arrival in Horta on the Island of Faial. In retrospect, Beebe's recommended 10 percent reserve was probably sufficient, but we were taking no chances. By the beginning of our sixth day our speed had increased to about 7 knots, and with 873 miles to go and 747 gallons remaining, our fuel curve indicated that we would have a reserve of about 1,000 miles, or 55 percent—well above our target.

The beautiful weather that greeted us on the east side of Bermuda somehow got better each day: air temperatures in the low 80s by day and the 70s at

**Figure 5–5.** *Salvation II* taking on fuel in Bermuda in preparation for the next leg of her transatlantic passage—1,800 miles to the Azores.

night, low humidity, and a breeze going from light to absolute calm. For two days the ocean looked like undulating glass, without a zephyr-induced ripple to be found. The sea surface mirrored the sky with such duplication of color that it was difficult to make out the horizon. We all agreed that we had never seen a more beautiful combination of sky and sea.

The water temperature was 78 degrees, and Hank and I decided to go for a swim. In the absolute middle of the Atlantic Ocean, in over 15,000 feet of water, we left the security of the ship and dove into the deep. We actually justified the stop to shut down and check the engine fluids, and after five minutes in a 110-degree engine room, the dive from the boat deck into the cool, blue Atlantic was one of the high points of the trip.

Fair weather continued with some wind filling in, but hardly enough to drive a sailboat. I paid particular attention to this as the Atlantic Rally for Cruisers (ARC) fleet was gathered in Bermuda and scheduled to depart the day after we left, also bound for the Azores. Without a deckload of diesel-filled jerry jugs, the usual 17-to-24-day passage considered normal for cruising sailboats in the 45-foot range would be wishful thinking in these windless conditions. *Salvation II*'s effortless and economical 170-mile days were looking pretty good. Most years, sailing vessels need to go quite a distance north from Bermuda to reach the westerly winds that will give them a good sail to the Azores. In contrast, a motor vessel can take a great circle route in spite of the calms created by the Bermuda high.

As we closed on the Portuguese island chain, we increased engine rpm to 1,925, and our daily distance made good increased to more than 180 nautical miles with a fuel burn of about 3.4 gph. *Salvation II* is equipped with KoopNautic hydraulically activated stabilizing fins (see more on this topic in Chapter 8), and while they extract a cruising-speed penalty of about three-eighths of a knot, the added comfort is well worth the price. On our tenth day at sea we sighted the 7,700-foot peak of the island of Pico, the highest peak in the Azores and, in fact, in all of Portuguese territory. Soon we began to see the closer but lower island of Faial on radar. We arrived in the harbor of Horta just before dawn with 350 gallons

of diesel remaining—representing more than 1,000 miles of reserve range (almost 60 percent) running at 155-mile days.

Like Bermuda, Horta proved to be a delightful place worthy of weeks of exploration. At 38 degrees north latitude, the climate is not really tropical, but still warm and comfortable with little humidity. The terrain is mountainous, and the town has great character, reminding me of Avalon on the Island of Catalina off the California coast. Whitewashed, red-tile-roofed buildings line well-kept narrow streets rising from a quaint but primarily commercial waterfront. An interesting feature of the harbor area is the extensive but tasteful graffiti on the surfaces of the seawalls and surrounding rocks and concrete walkways. Yachts from around the world leave behind bright and carefully painted murals indicating the ship's name, hailing port, date, and sometimes, crew names. This mural has become a tradition in Horta and is encouraged but controlled by the Portuguese government. The quality of the artwork must be guaranteed, and a background of white paint is required.

After far too little time, but with full fuel tanks, fresh fruits and vegetables, and a case of excellent Azorean wine, *Salvation II* departed Horta and took up a course direct for England, steering around the islands of Sao Jorge and Terceira. Only 1,300 miles remained, but we had to climb over 12 degrees of latitude, and those last seven days proved the toughest of the trip. Air and water temperatures dropped as we cleared the Azores, and the barometer began to fall. Weather faxes indicated numerous lows descending from the Arctic and far North Atlantic, and soon *Salvation II*, with storm plates in place, was again running into rough and uncomfortable weather. We endured two Force 7 gales with some discomfort but little reduction in speed. We progressed confidently and on schedule, arriving in Falmouth, England, at dawn on June 13. Following a brief champagne celebration and after clearing customs, Hank and I bid Jim and Susy farewell, and boarded a train for London and home.

It had been a pleasant, relaxing, and quick trip without incident. While we were prepared to deal with significant mechanical breakdowns, our only problem was an autopilot motor. With more than

**Figure 5–6.** *Salvation II* arrives in Falmouth, England, with a happy, rested, and relaxed crew.

3,000 miles on the little DC motor, we anticipated its possible failure and carried a replacement. We made the change in a matter of minutes, and the off-duty watch never knew of the problem. *Salvation II* required no service in Falmouth other than an oil change and departed two days after her arrival to continue on with her summer's cruising. We had crossed the Atlantic burning a volume of diesel fuel that cost little more than four one-way airline tickets over the same route—economy class. But without question, we had traveled first class.

[The Sinks completed their circumnavigation in 1995—the first Nordhavn to circle the globe. They logged 50,446 nautical miles.]

## Heading for Antigua, Almost 3,000 Miles Away

*Mary Umstot*

[The following story, abridged from Mary's book, *Voyaging to the Mediterranean Under Power*, describes our passage back to the Caribbean after cruising the Med for a number of years. Our return voyage started from Rota, Spain, where we made a comfortable passage to the Canary Islands in October.]

*Teka III* left Las Palmas about 10 A.M. on Sunday, December 4, 2005 with four people on board, including our son David and a cruising friend, Marvin Day. We calculated a 16-day/night journey to English Harbour, Antigua, on the Caribbean side. There is no place to anchor in the ocean, so we go 24/7 until we reach our destination. Daughter Dawn and son-in-law Larry made an "on-line tracking

system" on our website for interested people to follow along and "see" us at sea. Each day at noon, Denis sent an e-mail to her via the single-sideband radio (SSB) with our latitude and longitude position, plus other information—e.g., the weather, fishing reports, or mammal sightings. She looked forward to being a kingpin in our operation. After all, if her brother could be "crew," she could be "operation central." Both good positions filled by capable people.

Many sailboats went south to Cape Verdes, a seven-day trip, to rest, refuel, and break up the crossing into smaller parts instead of one big leap. They also needed to get far enough south to find the trade winds since none carried enough fuel to make the passage under power. Only three powerboats made the crossing: *Pamacea* (a Moonen 65), *Suprr* (a Nordhavn 46), and *Teka III* (a Knight & Carver 52), all starting from the Canaries. All three were passagemakers, specially designed as long-range trawlers that could carry enough diesel fuel for the trip. In fact, we still had almost half a tank on arrival in the Caribbean, having started with about 2,000 gallons. Altogether I think there were 50 boats heading west at about the same time frame, but we never made visual contact with any one of them. Plotting them on the paper charts let us know just how close we might be to each other, but that's about all.

Our days were full. Along with the ability to pick up ten weather faxes a day over the SSB and computer setup, we had four radio times for check-ins with other cruisers. Our informal 50-vessel "Atlantic Crossing" Cruisers' Net met twice a day (breakfast time and dinner time) over the SSB. In addition, we kept up with the other powerboats at scheduled times each day, also by SSB. I started tracking on the paper chart—about 25 boats nearby at first, which filtered down to 6 over time, as people spread out. It became a game to see who would be in the Caribbean first. Some were headed to Barbados; others, like us, were headed to Antigua. When sailboats did not have wind, they conserved fuel by just drifting or used their engines to keep on target. As a powerboat, we could run our engine 24/7, giving us a bit of an advantage. We heard some sail boaters announce over the VHF they were going swimming while "becalmed." It sounded like fun until one person reported seeing a shark. That report sort of dashed our desires for a swim.

Each morning on the net, boaters exchanged weather information gleaned from many sources; reported positions and conditions; and shared information, good or bad. Good: how many fish caught? Bad: how many got away! One boat hit a sleeping whale and headed to Cape Verdes to check for damage. Another one got a fishing net caught on the prop, but released it easily.

On Day 2 out of Las Palmas, we tried the new sails David had brought with him from San Diego. Denis had been concerned about potential problems with the rudder or prop putting us out of commission in the middle of the ocean crossing and, with Marvin's help, had designed sails just for *Teka III*. A sailmaker in Texas produced them and shipped them to David. The day we pulled them out of the bag we had 10-knot winds behind us. With the sails in a wing-on-wing position, engine in neutral but autopilot still engaged, the boat moved forward at 2.8 knots. That's quite good, considering the flopper-stopper weights were in the water, which at normal cruising speed causes a half knot loss of speed. The setup looked like Christmas Angel wings! Feeling so good about the initial test, Denis really wanted to try the system again when the winds increased to 20 knots, but we didn't do it. Maybe we should have, just to see the outcome.

After successfully trying our sails, we watched as Tropical Storm Epsilon appeared in the picture. Weather faxes showed it forming midocean, but not traveling the usual way—west toward the Caribbean. It seemed to be unable to definitely set a course. It moved west, stalled, moved slightly east again, all the while churning up the sea. If it decided to move east on a grand scale, instead of the expected westward pattern, headlines in African newspapers could have read, "Tropical storm ravages western Africa, going the wrong way!" Our weather router wondered if it would start west and hook around to the east toward us as we travelled west. With that in mind, we dropped our course farther south and kept an eye on it!

Winds at first were from northeast at 10–12 knots, increasing to 18–20 knots from the north that evening, with 8-foot waves from the northwest. The next day, the wind shifted to east-southeast at 9–15 knots, with waves of 6 feet. Two days later, Epsilon had stalled enough that a cold front overtook it, dissolving the potential for a bigger storm. Our waves increased to 14 feet, and the winds increased to 25 knots in advance of the cold front. The fifth day, the winds changed to northwest, topping at 15 knots, yet

**Figure 5–7.** *Teka III* sailing for the first time ever, making 2.8 knots with her emergency "come home" sails mounted on the paravane poles. Mary and I are happy they work so well.

**Figure 5–8.** The beauty of the sunset through a squall—a few days more to Antigua.

the seas refused to lay down, so we slowed during the night for a more comfortable ride. The long, relatively comfortable ocean swells of between 9 and 14 feet on the beam finally calmed the next day. After that we had a mixture of weather from almost slick calms to minor tropical squalls.

At the halfway point we celebrated not only that event but also Marvin's sixty-fourth birthday with turkey, dressing, mashed potatoes, gravy, cranberry sauce, and a glass of wine. For dessert we had coca-cola cake (made from scratch!).

Fresh fish constituted the main meal each day. For the first half of the trip, we couldn't seem to keep up with the catch of the day, an abundance of mahi-mahi (also called dolphin fish on the East coast). What we could not eat, we froze, until we just had to give up fishing for a while. By the time we started fishing again, something had happened to the luck. Larger fish took the lures and broke the lines, disappointing the fishermen. But the excitement of the fight kept the blood running! David had one fish on that took off with his line so fast he had a hard time holding the rod, until the line broke. At another time we had a billfish on, and when he jumped out of the water, the line broke. The fishing did keep us entertained, involved,

and fed. Sunrises and sunsets are spectacular at sea, and we saw many. Moonrise and moonset of the full moon are spectacular as well. The moon rose late on Saturday, December 17, off the stern. With it came a "moonbow" off the bow, the first we had ever seen—and it was simply amazing.

Equally awesome were the mammals that crossed our paths. Dolphin, Pantropical Striped ones and Atlantic Spotted ones, came several times to play around the boat. One morning about 9:20, David walked by me in the pilothouse and pointed off the bow. There, two fins in line with each other showing out of the water became a mama and a baby whale. They swam at the surface for a minute, dove, surfaced once more, and then we never saw them again. I said, "Is the mother showing us off to the baby, or the baby to us?" Another time a pygmy killer whale surfaced and "blew" not too far off the starboard bow. Both times we made identifications with our dolphin and whale book, compliments of the Whale Museum at Lanzarote, in the Gran Canaries.

In addition, a meteor filled the sky about 5 one morning. What a burnout! Only Denis witnessed it since it happened on his night watch. Too bad for the rest of us.

**Figure 5–9.** Land ho! After 17 days and nights, Antigua appears on the horizon.

Three hours before reaching Antigua we could see it as the day started to fade. By the time we arrived at the entrance it had turned quite dark—no moon! We entered English Harbour carefully as the entrance lights, marking rocks on one side and shoaling water on the other, were not working. Two range markers, positioned on shore for further guidance in entering, weren't working either. Using our radar and a light from *Suprr*, already in the anchorage, to line up on the channel, we cleared the entrance and gasped as we saw boats anchored all over the place—not only in the appropriate anchoring field but also right in the channel. We needed help, so were happy when our friends on *Suprr* showed the way by shining their spotlight at us.

We had a comfortable passage and no one got seasick. There were no mechanical problems. The weather was great and the seas mostly comfortable, but it was nice to have made it back to land.

In the next three chapters we explore boat design, stability, and roll reduction—essential knowledge for choosing a safe and seakindly ocean-crossing vessel. Selecting the right boat and equipment makes the difference between an enjoyable voyaging experience and one that could be most unpleasant.

## CHAPTER SIX

# Beebe on the Technicalities of the Seagoing Motorboat

In turning now from what *Passagemaker* proved to applying this experience to future vessels, the first step needs to be a solid grounding in the technical side of the business. The figures and how they are arrived at are not difficult—but they do require some study.

Technical calculations are important because small, long-range motorboats must press every factor that affects performance if they are to achieve the desired results. It is one thing to design a racing sailboat and hope it will make a shambles of the opposition—all sorts of "ifs" can affect that. It is quite another thing to say, "I want a motorboat to take my wife and me, with a crew of friends, across the Atlantic. A range under power of 2,400 miles at a speed/length ratio of 1.2 is about right." Here there is only one measure of success—that the vessel *does* achieve your goal.

It is the whys and wherefores of those figures that concern us here. If your vessel is an original design, the naval architect will gladly discuss these matters with you. If you are interested in an existing boat, knowledge of the factors involved in performance will give you a gauge of whether such a vessel will fill your needs, whether it will do what its builder says it will.

A case in my files is an example of the confusion caused by the advertisements for motorboats billed as "seagoing," or "trawlers," or "go-anywhere boats." A husband and wife bought a popular brand of 42-foot "trawler" with the expectation of cruising in the South Seas, an expectation amply reinforced by the salesman who sold them the boat. It was my sad duty after much work on their project to tell them their

vessel could not possibly do the job, and no feasible modification would help.

A wider understanding of the technicalities has become even more necessary because of the recent great increase in the number of designs for what are called "trawlers." What is needed is a summary of the naval architecture rules involved in the selection of *any* seagoing motorboat. The rules are not complicated when compared to designing an ocean-racing yawl. But they must not be ignored! What follows is as simple an exposition as I can make, but it does take studying. My advice to a prospective owner is to approach salespeople and advertising with your calculator in hand—ignoring Madison Avenue blurbs—and check out their figures against what is said here. If the figures are not made available, demand them. If you don't know how to make the necessary calculations, learn; you will certainly need this ability later to run your long-range cruiser.

A further consequence of the expansion of interest in seagoing motorboats is that they come in such a range of sizes and performance characteristics that one term can hardly be used to cover all types. For our purposes here, let's call vessels "ocean-crossers" if their performance is roughly comparable to *Passagemaker*'s. Of course, this does not mean they are useful solely for ocean crossing. Rather, they have the range and seaworthiness to do it, have the equipment and comfort at sea to make such a cruise safe and enjoyable, and are ready to cross an ocean if the owner is. You can see such characteristics are also desirable for shorter cruises. Let's apply "trawler" to lighter vessels with some seagoing capability, but with neither the equipment nor the range to qualify for full status as ocean-crossers. And we will use "seagoing motorboat" to cover all types when such a general term is needed.

There is one thing more that needs to be said about "trawler." Because we are going to use the term here to designate a class of motorboats that has sprung up lately—a class that has solid virtues in itself—we must first understand that the majority of today's "trawler yachts" have not even a nodding acquaintance with a real seagoing fishing trawler. Such statements as one printed in a recent article on "trawler-yacht design," saying ". . . designers went to work and developed a type of hull that had none of the faults of the commercial trawler yet retained all the desirable features and the general trawler look," are pure nonsense. Don't misunderstand me. There is nothing wrong with these yachts if they meet your needs. But just because they are called "trawlers," don't imagine that the seaworthiness of the true trawler has rubbed off on them.

Now, naval architects judge hulls mostly by using *coefficients* or *ratios*. There are many of these, but we will limit ourselves to four. They are:

Displacement/length ratio (D/L)
Speed/length ratio (S/L)
Above water/below water area ratio (A/B)
Prismatic coefficient (PC)

And we might add one I invented. It is called the *trawler/truth ratio (T/T)*. A trawler is and always has been a fishing vessel designed to tow a *trawl* (or net) that is pulled along the bottom to trap fish. To do this, she needs a husky hull with a good grip on the water and aperture space for a large, slow-turning propeller. She is expected to work the sea, winter and summer, and some of the best trawling grounds have the worst weather. Hence the seaworthiness of the North Sea and Icelandic sea trawlers made "trawler" the symbol of seaworthiness; that is, until Madison Avenue got hold of the term. Thus the need for this T/T ratio—how near to a true trawler is the boat? There are yachts that would score quite high because they were patterned after true trawlers. But today we see advertised as "trawlers" designs that would score, if one were charitable, 1 or 2 percent.

## Displacement/Length Ratio

Let's first consider the common way of comparing relative *heft*, or weight, in boats. This is important because a relatively heavier boat must have more volume underwater to provide that weight. Hence she has more space for accommodations, fuel, stores, and the like.

What we use to measure this is called the *displacement/length ratio (D/L)*. This is the displacement *in long tons* (2,240 pounds) divided by the *cube* of the *length at waterline (LWL)*, divided by 100. The division by 100 is merely to keep the number small.

$$D/L = \frac{D}{\left(\dfrac{LWL}{100}\right)^2}$$

The ratio is useful for this reason: if you take a certain yacht and make a second model of it, *twice as big* but with the same lines exactly, its D/L will remain the same, although the bigger vessel will weigh *eight times as much*. But if you take another vessel that is not the same shape or the same length, comparing its D/L to the first model's will tell you whether the new model is relatively heavier (greater D/L) or lighter (lower D/L). It is also, from experience, a good way to separate the men from the boys, so to speak. For instance, checking the D/Ls of coastal motorboats that are designed to use considerable power to attain quite respectable speeds in local cruising, you find their D/Ls range from, say, 160 to 220. Of course, these types are not expected to cross oceans.

So, taking the ocean-crossers first, what D/L should they have? This question is open to argument. But I have had certain experiences in this matter that are a good basis for my thoughts on the subject. First, let's define what we are talking about in relation to space required for crew, fuel, stores, and so forth—a space requirement that must eventually be reflected, in part, by cubic feet under water—which, of course, is displacement.

Take my client who wanted to go to the South Seas in his 42-foot "trawler." To make that cruise, in my opinion he needed a vessel with a range of at least 2,400 miles under power; permanent bunks for five or six; 60 days' supplies; and, ideally, full-time live-aboard space for owner and wife. The vessel he purchased did not meet any of these requirements and could not be modified to have them—the cubic space simply was not there. In other words, her D/L of 230 was too small.

My own *Passagemaker*'s design was supposed to be on the light side compared to the heavy diesel motorboats of the 1950s and 1960s, which were mostly fishing boat models. The idea behind her relative lightness was economy in construction and powering. The lines were drawn with a D/L ratio of 230. But when she was built and loaded, ready to go with all the gear required for long-range cruising, we found her draft had increased, so her D/L rose to 270. There was some overweight in construction, but most of this increase was in disposable load. Obviously, she should have been built to a D/L of 270 to begin with.

This and other data led me to the following conclusions: a satisfactory ocean-crossing vessel—a vessel to meet the requirements of the gentleman who wanted to go to the South Seas—cannot have a D/L less than 270 in the 50-foot overall size, and a bit more is desirable. A specialized vessel such as a long, slim aluminum yacht could prove me wrong. But for a conventional hull, carrying good accommodations for living on board and not stinting on equipment, supplies, and ballast, this rule is a good guide.

The shorter a vessel, the larger its D/L should be. In fact, you *must* increase the D/L in smaller vessels to carry the load. I see in two of my recent designs that the 50-footer has a D/L of 300, while the 42-footer has a D/L of 375. There is no particular rule here—the proportions just look right to me. Contrast the D/L of my 42-footer with that of the 42-foot "trawler" discussed previously. Their respective displacements are 24 tons and 15 tons—a difference of 9 tons! This essentially shows a difference in the requirements to which the boats were drawn, for I am sure the *designer* of the light 42-footer did not expect his boat to head for the South Seas.

If your demands for range, accommodations, and seaworthiness are less than those of a well-equipped ocean-crosser, you may find a "trawler type" acceptable. In the 40-to-43-foot size, their D/Ls run from 156 to 230, the difference largely concentrated in the amount of fuel they carry. Naturally these D/Ls seem low to me, but I admit to limited experience with the type. My suggestion would be to investigate these craft very thoroughly as to motion at sea and storage area, in addition to tests to be described later. Keep in mind there is a great deal of difference between a vessel fresh from the builder's yard and one fully loaded for a long cruise. I have not seen a long-range cruiser yet that did not fill every nook and cranny with stores and spares. There was absolutely no vacant space under the cabin soles of *Passagemaker*, for instance.

We have talked about low limits on D/L to emphasize the importance of enough cubic capacity to carry the loads the cruiser requires. What about high limits?

The highs, of course, would be the true fishing trawlers. Studying the three volumes of *Fishing Boats of the World* (published by the F.A.O. branch of the United Nations and absolute gold mines of information applicable to long-range motorboats), we find the D/Ls running from 450 for a 40-foot waterline, to 400 for 50 feet, and 350 for 60 feet. Yachts that have some relation to true trawlers in their design, say a T/T ratio of 80 percent or more, run somewhat less—about 20 percent. This makes sense because a yacht does not have the load problems of a fishing boat. The yacht essentially does not vary its "payload," while the trawler has to handle loads from zero to several tons. For this reason, it is not at all good practice to slavishly copy a fishing boat model for a yacht.

The suggested figures for D/L must not be taken too rigidly, especially those given in relation to length overall. As the waterline length is cubed, slight variations can have a good deal of effect. In addition, the varying weights of fuel and stores are constantly changing a vessel's D/L. One must check for just what condition the displacement figures are given. Our suggested figures are for all-up weights, ready to depart on that long cruise.

## Speed/Length Ratio

So much for displacement, or heft, and for the D/L ratio. We will talk more about D/L after we take up the *speed/length ratio (S/L)*, as the two become quite intertwined when you talk about power, range, and speed.

The S/L ratio is the speed of the vessel in knots, divided by the square root of the waterline length in feet:

$$S/L = \frac{V\ knots}{\sqrt{(LWL)}}$$

This is a very important ratio and has a powerful effect in many ways. At the same time, let me define *hull speed*. Strictly speaking, this is the speed at which the hull makes a wave as long as its waterline. It is an S/L of 1.34. If you find salesmen using S/L ratios of 1.4 or even 1.5 as hull speed, or telling you their pride and joy has a hull speed of *x* knots that is clearly *over* an S/L of 1.34, you have an excellent indication that they don't know what they are talking about. And if a salesman does the unspeakable and gives you speeds in *statute* miles per hour, laugh in his face and walk out! You are surely being conned.

To appreciate the importance of the S/L ratio, look at a typical speed/power/range curve. The curve in Figure 6–1 was made for a 50-footer and is based on one of the estimating formulas used by naval architects. In practice, it seems to be a bit on the conservative side in the area that is useful, from S/L 1.0 up. Below that it becomes too optimistic as the formula used would produce zero power at zero speed, where, as a practical matter, at around S/L 0.6 your engine would be idling and you couldn't go any slower.

Although the ordinate is shaft horsepower at the engine, what

we are really interested in here is gallons per hour so it can be combined with speed to give range, as the curve shows. A consumption of 0.06 gallons per horsepower per hour is a good average figure to use here.

Note how the horsepower required starts out relatively low at the slow-speed end and curves up rapidly to an S/L of about 1.2, where it becomes a straight line that continues on up. Marked on the curve are the S/L ratios from 0.8 to 1.2 and the hull speed of 1.34. So this curve can represent the relative

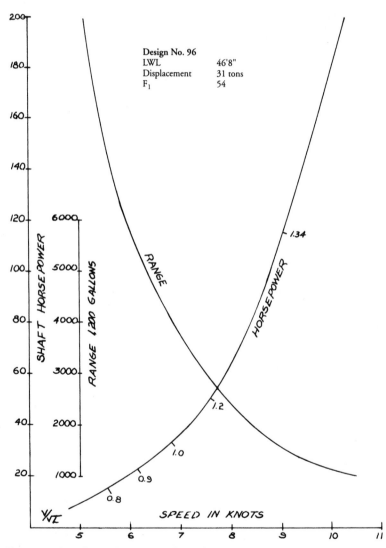

**Figure 6–1.** Speed/power/range curve for Beebe Design 96.

changes for any craft by using S/L ratios instead of speed in knots. In fact, when discussing the performance of seagoing motorboats, it is better to speak in terms of S/L ratios than in knots, so differences in size will not affect the results. We can also say that this curve illustrates the *cost of speed*. For instance, in this particular craft, doubling the horsepower from 100 to 200 will produce 1.7 knots more speed.

The region between S/L ratios 1.1 and 1.2 encompasses the practical speeds for long-range voyaging under power in small craft and hence is of greatest interest to us. Note that for this particular vessel the range is 2,800 miles at 1.1 S/L and 2,200 miles at 1.2. Thus, she can do the Bermuda–Azores run of 1,850 miles easily at 8.25 knots, or S/L 1.2. But to cover the 2,240 miles to Honolulu, she would have to slow to 8 knots—with a 200-mile reserve. And let us say you are running at an S/L ratio of 1.15. If you start to worry about fuel, dropping the speed to 1.0 will produce *50 percent more range on what remains!* In other words—and this is important—small changes in speed make large changes in fuel consumption. In fact, the whole secret of the long-range boat is that it goes slowly, using small S/L ratios. It has to; there is just no way to lick this.

The type of curve shown, taken from mathematics, is useful for planning a boat of a certain weight, but as soon as possible, the new craft should be actually tested carrying the weights with which she will start a cruise—to develop a curve that is more useful. In fact, the careful skipper will add his experience to his curve as he goes along. Salespeople of stock boats must also be ready to furnish such a verified curve.

The simplest way to check cruising ranges is to use a calibrated standpipe that will allow accurate measuring of fuel used while the vessel is running a measured mile.

## Above Water/Below Water Ratio

The third ratio we will consider is the ratio of area of the side view of the vessel *above* water to the *below* water (A/B). That is:

$$\frac{Area\ Above\ Water}{Area\ Below\ Water}$$

# How Fast Can a Displacement Vessel Go?

## Denis Umstot

In this chapter, Captain Beebe indicates that the hull speed for displacement boats is S/L 1.34. Dave Gerr, noted naval architect, author, and teacher, says this constant only works for relatively heavy boats with a D/L ratio of 340 or higher. Longer, lighter hulls are able to exceed this ratio. For example, if *Passagemaker* had been held to a D/L of 230, its true hull speed would be about 1.52 rather than 1.34. When the true D/L turned out to be 270, she still had a hull speed of about 1.42.

In Chapters 7 and 12, the ocean-crossing catamarans of Malcolm Tennant are highlighted. These catamarans are quite capable of cruising at 20 knots, well above the 1.34 hull speed, and they are true displacement hulls. How can this be? It turns out that the S/L ratio was mathematically derived from wave characteristics: length, period, and speed. It seems these lower D/L craft can reach higher speeds by piercing through their bow waves, although these higher speeds do require more power. This is in contrast to a planning hull that rides on top of the waves and requires a whole lot more power.

Dave Gerr uses the example of his 57-foot voyaging motor cruiser, *Imagine* (details for this boat are presented in Chapter 12 as one of our selected designs). This boat has a displacement of 60,780 pounds; her waterline is 50.7 feet; and she is powered by a single CAT 3306B, rated at 290 BHP. The D/L ratio is 208, and the maximum hull S/L ratio is 1.57. The speed with this engine horsepower is figured at 11.08 knots. Actual sea trials showed a speed of 11.05 knots. This boat would not be able to cross oceans at this speed, but would be capable of using this 11-knot pace for coastal cruising and shorter passages, provided that the owners were not concerned about consuming extra fuel.

To get the full benefit of higher-speed displacement boats, the objective must be stated during the design phase so that bottom contours (buttock angles) are correctly designed and that a compatible engine is specified. In addition, since weight is a factor here, the boat should be designed as light as practical. For example, heavy additions, such as granite countertops, should be avoided. (See the endnote on page 404 for more details on this subject.)

Obviously, the smaller this ratio the better. Thus fishing trawlers may get as low as 1.0 to 1.5. It is difficult to get below 2.0 in a yacht because of the pressure for more and better accommodations. And it is this demand for more space and comfort that has gradually pushed up this ratio in contemporary

# The A/B Ratio: Myth or Reality?

## Denis Umstot

Respected and experienced yacht designer, Stephen Seaton, has called the A/B ratio (area *Above* water compared to the area *Below* water) a myth that is fundamentally useless. It is not used by most designers to describe their boats and it cannot be used to estimate a vessel's stability. He says that "Yes, in general too much above the waterline and not enough below is bad, BUT to put numbers to this ratio is just wrong." Michael Kasten, also a well-known yacht designer, says that the A/B ratio is a gross oversimplification of the factors that should be considered for stability and sea keeping. However, recent requirements for ISO stability ratings (see Michael Kasten's article in Appendix B) call for analysis of windage effects that may closely approximate the A/B ratio.

In the next chapter we will discuss factors which *are* critical for stability and sea keeping. While the A/B ratio does not do justice to stability analysis, it does give us clues to these critical dimensions of boat design. Perhaps Beebe wanted to emphasize that tall boats (with a high A/B) ratio would possibly have a higher center of gravity and likely be less stable. Higher boats also have more side surface for impact of wind and waves. In addition, if the pilot house is up high on the superstructure, the boat may be much more uncomfortable in seaway. After you read the next chapter, I think you will agree that there is much more to stability than this ratio. However oversimplified, it may at least give a quick rule of thumb for evaluating competitive designs.

yachts, with an accompanying loss of seaworthiness. Several vessels that meet my ideas of being qualified as ocean-crossers range from 2.1 to 2.6. In the light "trawler" group, this ratio tends to run higher. It has to, of course, with less hull under water. In one case it ranges as high as 4.6, which scares me, particularly as a large part of this increased area is usually glass, and thin glass at that. Steps that can be taken to hold the

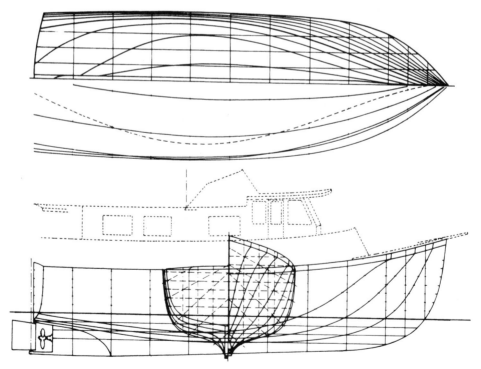

**Figure 6–2.** Lines of Beebe Design 88, 50' *Mona Mona*. Beebe thought this design's A/B ratio was poor and restricted its passage to the easiest Atlantic crossing routes. It crossed the Atlantic and cruised the Mediterranean successfully.

# The Ideal Passagemaker Design

## Michael Kasten

A power vessel has the advantage [over sailing vessels] of being able to eliminate much of the keel, reducing wetted surface area and therefore surface friction drag. A power vessel keel will preserve only what is needed to carry the vessel's structure, to house the propeller, and to carry the rudder. Since there are no sails, a power vessel requires less beam. With less beam, a power vessel can optimize flow characteristics around the boat (less beam = less drag).

Surface friction drag is the dominant drag component at slow speeds below S/L 1.0 or so (depending on vessel shape, smoothness, fouling, etc.). Ordinarily, at speeds above S/L 1.1, wavemaking begins to dominate, becoming much the greater drag component at these hull speeds. At speed, a vessel's underwater hull shape has the most effect on wavemaking, and therefore on drag. Whatever one can do to reduce wavemaking is ordinarily beneficial.

As Howard Chapelle[*] observed, [analyzing] vessels built well before this

[*]Chapelle, Howard I., *Search for Speed under Sail: 1700-1855*. W.W. Norton, 1967.

century, the features of a relatively fast displacement hull are:

- A fine entry, provided that it is not so fine as to create a hollow forward which would tend to create a secondary bow wave at the "shoulder." This is why a chine should ordinarily be kept either entirely above or entirely below the water's "under-way" wave contour on a displacement vessel.
- An easy shape to the forward buttock lines.
- A balanced shape to the hull diagonals, in other words, symmetry fore and aft.
- A long, fine run, having straight or nearly straight buttock lines at a low angle of intersection to the surface as they approach the surface. It is a benefit to have a counter stern, which contributes waterline length at speed.

The idea is to part the water with as little fuss as possible, move through it easily, then leave it behind as gracefully as possible having created the smallest possible wave pattern. In other words, changing the momentum of the water

abruptly with an un-graceful shape is a [great] disadvantage in terms of resistance and [even] more so at speed. Thus, if a boat is shaped so that she is slender; pushes up as small a bow wave as possible; does not have a marked "shoulder" in the forward waterlines which would then encourage a secondary bow wave; and does not pull along a big stern wave, we will have done the best job in terms of reducing resistance under power.

The ideal passagemaker will therefore have a long waterline; an easy entry without creating a hollow forward; there will not be a "shoulder" forward where, for example, a chine may cross the waterline; there will be as long and straight a run as possible; and the boat will not be overly wide or tall.

The net result of these characteristics will be a vessel that is more spacious due to her length; gentler in terms of rolling accelerations; and one that will reach her destinations more quickly and efficiently. In other words, the boat will not only travel faster, but will do so at less cost and in greater comfort.

---

line after such increases are greater beam and conversion of the largest possible proportion of the side area to watertight-integrity portions of the hull.

## Prismatic Coefficient

The last item for us to consider is the *prismatic coefficient* (PC). This must be calculated from the lines and is not ordinarily available from salesmen. But it is well worth inquiring about the PC of any vessel you are considering.

The prismatic coefficient compares the actual volume of the hull below the waterline in cubic feet to what the volume would be if the body were a *prism* composed of the largest section from the lines carried the full length of the waterline. In effect, it is an expression of how much you sharpen the ends.

Tank-testing of hull models has shown that for each S/L ratio there is an ideal PC. That is, at each

S/L a vessel designed with the correct PC will need less power to make that S/L than a vessel with an incorrect PC. It so happens that the correct PC varies most widely from one S/L to another in the very range we are interested in, S/Ls from 1.0 to 1.34, and on into the area where the light types try to drive past hull speed for local cruising, say to S/L 1.6. The accompanying table, from D. Phillips-Birt's *Naval Architecture of Small Craft*, shows this clearly.

| Prismatic Coefficient Relationship to Speed/Length Ratio | | | | | |
|------|------|------|------|------|------|
| S/L | PC | S/L | PC | S/L | PC |
| 1.0 | 0.53 | 1.4 | 0.64 | 1.8 | 0.70 |
| 1.1 | 0.54 | 1.5 | 0.66 | 1.9 | 0.70 |
| 1.2 | 0.58 | 1.6 | 0.68 | 2.0 | 0.70 |
| 1.3 | 0.62 | 1.7 | 0.69 | | |

After S/L 2.0, dynamic lift becomes a major factor and the hull becomes a *planing* hull. Nobody is going to go very far at sea in such a vessel. As Bill Garden said once in an article on this type of boat, "A planing hull can't carry enough fuel to get out of sight."

In heavy seagoing motorboats, the effect of the PC can be dramatic. The British Fisheries Board actually built three 62-foot waterline coastal fishing boats of exactly the same length and displacement but differing PCs. The results, also from *Naval Architecture of Small Craft*, are shown in the accompanying table.

| Power Requirements for Three 62-foot Boats with Differing Prismatic Coefficients | |
| --- | --- |
| **PC** | **Hp Required for S/L 1.14, 9 Knots** |
| 0.645 | 123 (Many fishing boats have this PC.) |
| 0.612 | 105 |
| 0.537 | 75 (This is the correct PC.) |

We should not be too hard on the fishermen. The requirements of the trade may demand a larger than ideal PC. But yacht builders do not have this excuse for choosing the wrong PC.

If you are interested in maximum range with minimum fuel, there is no question that you should have a vessel with the PC set for the desired cruising speed. If you desire to cruise somewhat faster in local cruising, however, a compromise position might be better. You would use a little more fuel but have a hull shape designed for a slightly higher speed.

If the PC of a vessel you are interested in is more suited to higher speeds, say from an S/L of 1.5 to 1.9, this suggests that the hull is really better suited to local use than to long-range cruising. We might say then the PC indicates the designer's (not the advertiser's) intentions and is worth checking.

## True Trawler versus Light Trawler Yachts

So much for the four formulas that have the most effect on seagoing motorboats. We will look later at how to apply them to specific design problems. But first let's go further into the differences between the *true* trawler yacht and the lighter types we are calling "trawlers" for convenience, the name having been preempted by this type. [Note: George Buehler calls true trawler yachts "troller yachts" to distinguish them from the coastal trawler types. He takes the name from the Northwest salmon troller fishing boats that share most characteristics with Beebe's true trawler yachts.]

Long-range passage-making essentially is aimed at reaching the desired cruising ground *with dispatch* so you have time to enjoy the local area. Once there, there is no problem of range or fuel availability (we hope!) so you can run at any speed you wish. On *Passagemaker* we habitually ran at [maximum] hull speed [S/L 1.34] in local cruising. This was 9.1 knots on a 46-foot waterline. Would it be possible to do better—that is, cruise even faster locally and still have a vessel seaworthy enough for ocean passages?

A true trawler yacht is so heavy there is no question of driving her over hull speed. It simply wouldn't make sense to carry the machinery to do it. Their owners must therefore content themselves with thinking, when faster boats pass them, how their fuel bill is peanuts compared to the types that drink up hundreds of gallons per day. The hull offers enough room to be a real home afloat and the solid feel that makes for comfort at sea. This type's domain is the open sea, and if they are not used there, but stick to local cruising or coastal waters, they don't make much sense. In addition, a real trawler would, at 50 feet, have draft of around 7 feet. This is excessive in many cruising grounds, particularly on the east coast of North America. It was this draft problem, for instance, that turned me away from considering one for myself.

### Light Trawlers

On the other hand, the light "trawlers" have their own advantages and drawbacks. One of their chief virtues is their ability to run somewhat over hull speed. Now, hull speed is pretty low by U.S. standards. It takes enormous increases in waterline length to get displacement hull speed up to the speeds ordinary coastal motorboats can achieve. In fact, to have a

12-knot hull speed takes a waterline length of some 80 feet! Yet 12 knots is an ordinary top speed for coastal motorboats. Is there a way to lick this?

What the designers of the light "trawlers" have done is to compromise between the heavy, extremely seaworthy *true* trawler on the one hand and the coastal type on the other—so light everyone would agree it should not go to sea. In effect, they have opted for a lower trawler/truth ratio. They say it is possible to design a hull that can exceed hull speed by a certain amount and still retain the basic seaworthiness required at sea. The steps in this process lead to lightness (relative lightness, that is) to hold down power demands and a flat stern aft to avoid squatting at higher speeds. They contend that the resulting hull form has ample seaworthiness for any reasonable cruising and cite impressive statistics to prove it. They also say that most clients who buy this type will not actually make long trips, but will be content with coastal cruising and island hopping, and be happy to have a vessel for this purpose that is clearly superior in seaworthiness to the ordinary motorboat. All of this is perfectly true, and it is not the designers who write those ads that imply these craft are fit to "go anywhere." Our quarrel is really with the advertisers and salesmen who produce the unhappy situation of our gentleman who wanted to take his 42-footer to the South Seas.

Obviously, the further above hull speed a light "trawler" is driven, the closer she will approach the coastal motorboat in lightness and use of large amounts of horsepower. So claims in this matter must be approached with a *really* critical eye. Taking the advertisements of seven yachts that are touted as "trawlers" or "go-anywhere boats," yet also claim they "cruise" at *x* knots *over* hull speed, we find they range from S/L 1.44 to 1.67, with D/Ls from 156 to 234. As "cruising speed" has no definition in naval architecture, it really would be better to check their claimed maximum speed to see how much over hull speed they are being driven.

At the same time, these vessels claim ranges from 900 to 1,500 miles. While boats with these ranges may be sufficient for many skippers' needs, it is surprising to see them advertised as go-anywhere-your-heart-desires boats when they can't even cross the smallest ocean, the Atlantic. But nothing is impossible in the advertising world, apparently. And a little slide-rule [calculator!] work shows they achieve these ranges not at their "cruising speed" but right down at S/L ratios around 1.1, where we would expect to find them. To improve these ranges you would have to add fuel capacity. And, as I found out working over the 42-footer for the gentleman who wanted to go to the South Seas, there isn't any safe place to put it; the space just isn't there.

All of these craft have the broad, flat stern necessary to exceed an S/L of 1.6. Characteristically, this type of hull steers badly with seas from the quarter or aft. As the true long-range motorboat *seeks out* these conditions, keeping the wind aft as much as possible, this point is important. I recall a client who really went into this motor passagemaking business, including a long trip with me, and who was talking about being able to run over hull speed locally. He took the opportunity to make a delivery trip from San Francisco to Puget Sound as crew on a fine, custom-built, twin-screw, flat-stern yacht. Off Cape Mendocino they had a gale from astern and had a wild night, handing the throttles continuously to keep her from broaching. He came home and said to me, "Forget it. From now on I'm a hull-speed boy."

Now it will be noted that this yacht made it, even if it was uncomfortable. And, in fact, the problem with this boat was not hull shape per se but was connected with her being twin screw with small spade rudders behind each prop. These perform well at normal smooth-water speeds. But when you slow way down, they don't have enough area to take command properly. A single-propeller craft with deep skeg and large rudder would not have this trouble. So it's possible to avoid this steering problem.

Another problem with "trawlers" is they do not carry any ballast. Now I may be supercautious, but to me, whether a seagoing yacht carries some ballast is what distinguishes the true seagoer from a vessel that is not really serious about it. My *Passagemaker* (46-foot LWL, D/L 270) carried 5,000 pounds of lead on her keel, with more inside. I doubt if we needed it 98 percent of the time, and we paid good money to carry it around. But believe me, when we got into gales and the fringes of the two hurricanes we managed to find, we were delighted to have it aboard. A quotation from L. Francis Herreshoff's *Common Sense of Yacht Design* captures this even more graphically:

*It is, though, interesting to note that several designers at various times have thought they had discovered the secret of designing a V-bottom launch that went smoothly in a seaway, and this reminds me of an incident that happened to Bill Hand about 1915. Mr. Hand was one of the early big game fishermen to use high-speed gasoline launches for that purpose. Well, one fall he was fishing for tuna somewhere southeast of Block Island. It was probably pretty rough and probably Mr. Hand was quite proud of the good weather his V-bottom launch was making of it when all of a sudden it became very much rougher (which it can do suddenly in that region). To make a short story of it, Mr. Hand finally got back to New Bedford okay, but after that he made a specialty of designing heavy auxiliary schooners much after the fashion of Gloucestermen, and this is the type he subsequently used himself for fishing southeast of Block Island, and, gentle reader, I am under the impression you will do the same thing after you have really been caught out in the same kind of weather.*

## Beebe's Conclusions

Now that we have reviewed all this material, what have we got? All of my recommendations are arguable. Naval architects are by no means in agreement on the levels of the figures I have given. So in your quest for a vessel that meets your needs, you can expect to hear rebuttals of what is offered here. But with your slide-rule [OK, calculator!] in hand and a knowledge of the basics, you are much better armed to check what they say.

**Range.** One of the first things to check is range. You simply have to decide for yourself what range you require. A realistic decision on how your boat

will actually be used, not how you would like to use it, is the first step. Then the cruises you expect to take must be checked for their maximum legs. In this connection the capabilities of the seagoing motorboat can be exploited to improve on conventional ways of doing things. For instance, instead of departing from Miami direct against wind and current to the Virgins, it would be much easier on the crew and the vessel to go north far enough to get out of the trades, then go east until you can head south to your destination. It even appears attractive (if you plan to spend the winter cruising the Islands) to make your first hop a passage east, then south clear to Grenada to cruise up the entire island chain.

**Size and displacement.** A decision on size and relative heft is next. Size is much influenced by one's budget. Any naval architect will tell you any vessel would be better if longer. But size has to stop somewhere. The number of persons to be carried is also a factor. With comfortable full-time accommodations for owner and wife, I do not believe it is possible to have more than four permanent bunks until the length reaches 46 feet, or even better, 48 feet. Long passages can be made with a crew of four, of course, but we found it easier with five or six.

If your vessel is to be an original design, the designer would now be in a position to come up with preliminary sketches and a speed/power/range curve like that shown in Figure 6–1. If you are investigating stock boats, the seller should be able to produce this curve together with certification that the vessel has been tested and will do what the curve says. If he does not have it, walk out.

Some designers make this curve at full load and half load of fuel and water. I prefer to make the curve for *full load only*. This gives you a safety factor in range from the vessel becoming lighter as she goes along. My own experience with this type of curve has shown a 10 percent reserve is ample to take care of adverse conditions, provided you are running at S/Ls from 1.1 to 1.2. If you are thinking about stretching range to the limit for some unusual passage by running at S/L 1.0 or even 0.9, you need a larger reserve as you haven't got the leeway to slow down—you would be too close to running the engine at idle. The curve should show the fuel rate used.

**An example: range to Europe.** Consider a vessel designed to cross the Atlantic and cruise in Europe. I would recommend for this a range of 2,200 miles at S/L 1.2. The longest leg is 1,850 miles from Bermuda to the Azores going east. This track can be used both ways. Returning by this route in the fall, however, you are squeezed between the hurricane season and the winter storms. It would be more fun and more comfortable to return over the usual track of sailing vessels. They leave Gibraltar for the Canary Islands not later than the end of September, go to Las Palmas to drink the excellent local wines until November 15 [or later], then take off like a flock of ducks for Barbados [or Antigua], 2,800 miles downwind, and spend the winter in the Caribbean. You can see in the curve we used as an example that a vessel that can do 2,200 miles at S/L 1.2 can do the 2,800 miles at 1.1. And if you get nervous, say at the two-thirds distance mark, you can drop the S/L to 1.0 and gain another 300 miles of range, as the curve shows. This is the sort of figuring you do for range.

**Cruising and top speed.** Analyzing the ads for the "trawlers," you can sort out the "cruising speed" and the "range" figures with the aid of the curve. Usually you will find "cruising speed" is well above the speed required to achieve the range claimed; that is, the boat will not actually "cruise" the "range." This is acceptable as long as you understand it.

Regarding statements of top speed, check the curve to see if top speed requires more horsepower than the maximum continuous rating of the engine. If it does, forget it. Diesels ordinarily have three ratings: block, which means engine block only, without any accessories, not even a water pump; maximum intermittent rating, which means for one hour only—a rather useless exercise; and maximum continuous rating—the only one worth considering in a boat. It is a sad thing, really, to see manufacturers advertising diesels as 120 hp when this is the useless block rating and the engine has a continuous rating of 102 hp. It didn't used to be this way before Madison Avenue got into the act.

If the top speed is within the continuous rating of the engine, think about it a bit. Take a 46-foot waterline boat, about 50 feet overall. If it has a top speed of 12 knots, it would be running at an S/L of 1.77. This is pretty high and requires a flat stern and a low D/L, not to mention lots of horsepower. Would you be willing to settle for 10 knots instead? This lowers S/L to 1.48. With this small excess over 1.34 you can have a reasonably high-deadrise, parallel-in-the-aft-sections, flat-run hull that steers like it was on rails with the seas aft, carries fuel for more than 2,800 miles at S/L 1.1, and has a D/L of 270. I know this is so because it describes my own boat. We didn't get *Passagemaker* up to 10 knots because her oversize prop (for range) limited her to using 85 hp. With this she reached an S/L of 1.4, or 9.4 knots—which means she could have done 10 knots on 98 hp.

**Speed and modest range.** If your range demands are more modest, say from 800 to 1,500 miles, and you really want to cruise faster in local waters than S/L 1.48, I would certainly recommend the lighter types, particularly for their first-cost economy and lower running expenses, provided consideration is given to two items not ordinarily considered in stock boats: first, remember their motion at sea—with their smaller T/T ratios—will be worse than in the heavier boats and certainly demand some type of stabilization to make satisfactory long voyages; and second, if it is a twin-engine type with spade rudders, adding a large central rudder will correct steering faults exhibited by these types when running off slowly before a sea.

**A/B ratio.** As for the above water/below water ratio, this is pretty much a lost cause today. I can only say again and again, *hold it down*. But perhaps it would be better to urge prospective owners to consider what they will do when each large window is broken. What is their second line of defense? I have seen some light "trawlers" that were very well equipped for this contingency and others where this danger had not been given a thought.

Certainly areas of operation limitation should be considered. For instance, in one of my designs destined for full-time living afloat in the Mediterranean and double-decked full length for an A/B ratio of 3.0, I have recommended—and the owner has agreed—that the boat be limited to cruising areas south of the Bermuda-Azores-Lisbon line. She has too much glass for me to be happy if she ventures into the North Atlantic.

That's the way it goes: speed/length ratio, displacement/length ratio, and so on. Figures, figures, figures. But those pesky figures are operating all the time you are out there cruising. And it behooves the careful owner to know what they are and what influence they have.

# CHAPTER SEVEN

# Seaworthiness and Seakindliness: Stability and Other Design Concepts

We move now from the figures and ratios to explore other design characteristics that ensure the safest and most comfortable boat for extended sea voyages. In this chapter, we will consider *seaworthiness*: characteristics that make boats safe enough to survive extreme sea conditions. In this and the next chapter we also explore *seakindliness*: the characteristics of a boat that create easy motion, regardless of sea direction. George Buehler, designer of the popular Diesel Duck line of boats, says the boat should look happy in the water and ride smoothly without jerkiness. A third concept is *habitability*: a comfort level for the crew that allows space, headroom, and comfort from the boat's rolling and other acceleration forces. Of course, these three design objectives interact to create the final concept.

Motor yacht design historically has been more of an art than a science. Boats have evolved over the years from fishing boats and sailing craft. Only recently have designers and naval architects been able to scientifically test their concepts with computers and tank testing. Designers and builders have been reluctant to share data on the seaworthiness of their boats. All designs are claimed to be seaworthy and sometimes seakindly. All are very habitable because marketing demands it, especially when at the dock or at anchor. However, at sea, some boats lose some of their habitability because they are not optimized for these conditions. For example, forward or aft staterooms may become very uncomfortable during rough seas.

Interest in seaworthiness and stability for small craft accelerated in 1979 after the fleet of Fastnet sailing vessels collided with an intense low-pressure storm with near hurricane winds and high, breaking seas. Of the 300 boats entered, only 85 finished—24 were sunk or abandoned, 190 were damaged, and 15 lives were lost. Forty-eight percent of the fleet reported that on one or more occasions they were knocked down to horizontal (a 90-degree heel). An exhaustive analysis of this disaster found that boat size was an important design factor in this survival situation, but not the only one. Hull form and displacement and weight distribution are also critical. (There are numerous accounts of this catastrophe; I relied upon Marchaj and Van Dorn as cited in the endnote.)

**Figure 7–1.** A fishing boat in rough seas. (Philip Stephen/ bluegreenpictures.com)

While all these boats were sailing vessels, many of the resulting analyses have been applied to power vessels. Motor vessels can also be included in other alarming statistics. We have all heard about the sinkings in Alaska, but we normally sluff it off by saying "I wouldn't go there in those conditions, so it won't happen to me." However, in one three-year period in the 1950s, when tuna fishing was at its peak, Van Dorn reports that 75 fishing vessels were lost, not in the wilds off Alaska, but in the warmer Pacific and Atlantic waters frequented by ocean voyagers (see endnote for the source). In the mid-1960s, the 66-foot steel Romsdal *Peregrine* left Mexico heading for the south Pacific, encountered an early-season hurricane near Acupulco, and was never heard from again. The crew of six was lost. In recent years, voyagers in passagemaking yachts have been both skillful and lucky not to be caught in vessel-threatening conditions that can result in loss of the boat or life, or perhaps their boats were seaworthy enough to survive.

## Stability

*Stability* is the ability of the boat to return to its initial upright position after being hit by some outside force, such as a breaking wave or a hurricane-force gust of wind. Waves, wind, sharp turns, free water/fuel in tanks or bilges, or vessel loading will affect the vessel's ability to recover back to its original upright position. Two main forces act together to determine stability: *gravity* and *buoyancy*.

### A Stable Boat

**Center of gravity (CG).** CG is the combined center of all the weights of the boat acting downward toward the sea. We are all familiar with the center of gravity for vehicles. A tall truck will turn over much easier than a low sports car, simply because its center of gravity is a lot higher in relation to its width. In boats, the concept is similar; the center of gravity must be low enough that the vessel will not turn over or capsize under severe sea conditions. Designers use the weights of engine, transmission, hull structures, machinery, tanks, and equipment, and their location on the boat, to determine the center of gravity. Some of this is scientifically calculated; and others are based on experience with similar types of hulls. Usually the CG is located slightly aft of the center of the waterline, fore and aft. Its height will depend on the items listed previously plus the pilothouse and other above-water structures. If the CG is higher than desired, then ballast is added low in the boat to lower the position. Every vessel will have both a vertical center of gravity (VCG), related to roll; and a horizontal center of gravity, related to pitch. They combine to create the total vessel's center of gravity—its CG.

**Center of buoyancy (CB).** CB is the combined center of all the forces of buoyancy acting upward toward the hull. The volume and shape below the waterline are used to find the boat's center of buoyancy. When the boat is upright, the CB will be directly below the CG. If the boat is heeled over at some angle, the CB will change to port or starboard at an angle of heel that will depend on the shape of the hull. On a newly launched boat, an inclining experiment is normally done (by a competent expert) to make sure that calculations are correct and to determine whether additional ballast is

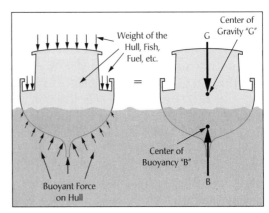

**Figure 7–3.** Center of gravity (G) and center of buoyancy (B). (Adapted from SNAME)

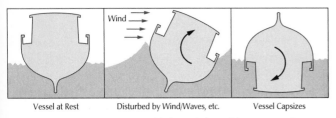

Vessel at Rest          Disturbed by Wind/Waves, etc.          Vessel Capsizes

**Figure 7–2.** An unstable boat. (Adapted from SNAME)

needed. This process is accomplished by placing a known weight near the gunnels amidships so that it heels over and then measuring the angle of heel. Various mathematical calculations allow the designer to create a stability curve (see Figure 7–6) showing the *righting force* at various angles of heel.

**Righting forces and the metacenter.** The horizontal distance between the center of gravity and the center of buoyancy at a given angle of heel shows how much righting force the hull contains. A small distance shows low force, and a large distance shows high force. While one would think that a higher force is desirable, that is not necessarily true. If the righting force is too strong, the hull will be snappy and not at all comfortable at sea. If the force is too low, the boat will roll more slowly, but may be reluctant to right itself. The distance between the center of gravity and the *metacenter* (see Figure 7–4) is designated as GM. This distance is a measure of the amount of *reserve stability* of the boat. It is possible for a boat owner to significantly change the designed GM by adding such equipment as a heavyweight dinghy with a large outboard and fuel tanks to an upper deck. Another frequent alteration is building an enclosed pilothouse in place of the flying bridge. Before proceeding with such modifications—or when considering the purchase of a boat that has had such modifications—a qualified expert should evaluate the effects on stability.

Another consideration for passagemakers—which often carry 2,000 or more gallons of fuel, plus 600 gallons of water—is that as these liquids are consumed during a voyage, the CG rises, and the GM declines. The boat designer should have allowed for this situation, but it is still good to recognize that the boat's stability will have declined. There is not much you can do to rectify this problem. If you have large water tanks and a watermaker, you can keep them full toward the later parts of the voyage. Ships can take on saltwater ballast,

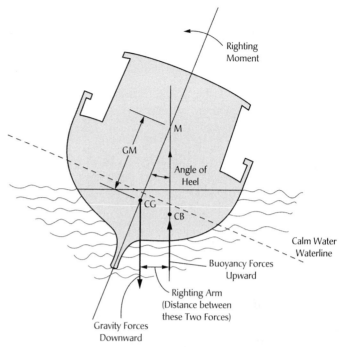

**Figure 7–4.** Summary of stability forces acting on a boat. The bold upward arrow represents buoyancy; the bold downward arrow represents gravity; the CG is the center of gravity, while the CB is the center of buoyancy. The righting arm (also called the CZ) is the distance between these two bold arrows when heeled. The farther apart, the more righting arm. The metacenter, or M, is derived by passing a line vertical to the water from the CB to a line vertical to the boat's hull. The GM is then determined by the distance from the CG to the metacenter.

but most yachts are not designed to make use of this technique.

**Stability curves.** The righting forces can be plotted with the angle of heel to determine the stability curve for the boat. As shown in Figures 7–6 and 7–7, the boat is perfectly stable in an upright position at 0 degrees heel. Righting forces then continue to increase as the boat heels to about 60°. By the time it passes the midpoint on the curve at about 70° heel, the rail will be underwater, and recovery will be increasingly difficult. Once the boat reaches 90° heel, the *righting arm* is zero, and it will most likely capsize and become stable in an upside-down position. The point where the righting arm reaches zero is called the *angle of vanishing stability* (AVS) (although it seems like it should be called the *angle of no stability*). While the curve in Figure 7–6 shows a 90° point where stability is lost,

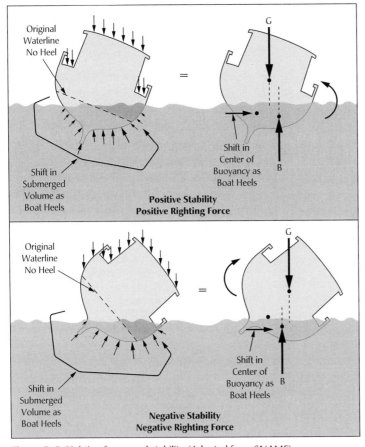

**Figure 7–5.** Righting forces and stability. (Adapted from SNAME)

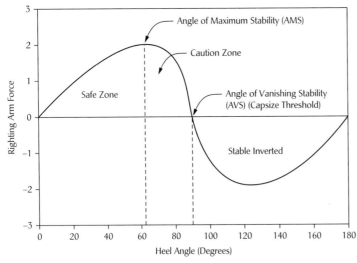

**Figure 7–6.** Hypothetical stability curve for a 50-foot trawler yacht.

examination of stability curves for small fishing boats that are roughly comparable to smaller passagemaking yachts have zero righting force at as little as 50° heel, with maximum righting force at about 25°! Stability curves are normally plotted under two loading conditions: (1) fully loaded with crew, fuel, and water; and (2) arrival loading, generally considered to be only 10% of fuel and water. Boats are generally more stable when fully loaded, provided their freeboard is high enough and places where water can downflood into the hull are protected.

Stability is affected by many forces, including loading of the boat. Heavier loading may increase stability and the angle of vanishing stability. Powerboats flooded up to their waterline will normally experience a greatly diminished angle of vanishing stability, perhaps as low as 30° heel. Transverse hull sections (cross-section views of the hull from forward or aft; for example, Figures 7–3, 7–4, 7–5, and 7–7 all show one transverse hull section) can influence stability as well. Increased beam results in increased righting force at small heel angles, providing more initial stiffness and resistance to roll. Increased freeboard will result in a higher CG that will reduce righting at low angles and increase it at large angles because it takes longer for the rail to go underwater. Softening bilges (making bilges more rounded and less sharp) increases the range of positive stability—the boat can heel to greater angles without capsizing. Wide-beamed boats, usually with harder chines, have higher stability at first, but may capsize at much lower heel angles and then stay inverted because their center of gravity

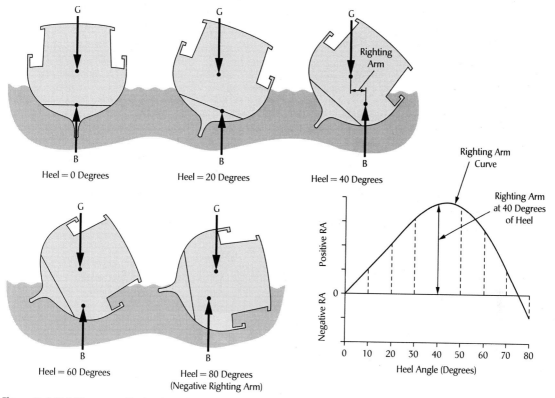

Figure 7–7. Stability curve with visuals to showing effects of various heel angles. (Adpated from SNAME)

is often near deck level. Flare increases righting force, and tumble home (reverse flare) will decrease it. Boats that are not fully decked over may be particularly apt to remain inverted if capsized.

**Example of an actual stability curve.** I would have loved to provide examples of stability curves for a number of modern passagemakers; however, this information is not easily obtainable. If you are considering the purchase of a boat, you might want to demand such a stability curve. Figure 7–8 shows a stability curve for Steve and Linda Dashew's 83′ *Windhorse*. Note that the righting arm reaches a maximum at 60° and slowly declines to the angle of vanishing stability just beyond 140°. Even after a rollover, the boat has little negative force to hold it upside down and is quite likely to come quickly to an

upright position. Stability is enhanced by a series of ballast tanks that can be adjusted for maximum stability under all conditions—something few boats have and quite expensive to incorporate into the hull design.

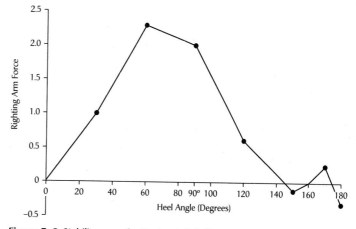

Figure 7–8. Stability curve for Dashew's *Windhorse*. (Steve Dashew)

# International Organization for Standardization (ISO) Design Categories for Recreational Boats

Many oceangoing boats are rated according to the ISO's design category described in the following sections (see Appendix B for more detailed analysis of these categories). Ocean-crossing boats should meet Category A requirements. Not all boats have been rated because the requirement is only for boats sold in the European Union or other countries using the ISO rating. Some manufacturers and most designers do not apply for a design category. The designer or manufacturer tests the vessel and submits data to an independent agency that varies by country. Basically, the builders or designers provide the data for the rating—if they follow the requirements for testing, computation, and reporting, the boat will meet the appropriate rating. There is no U.S. government requirement for any type of stability certification for pleasure boats. Many sailing race organizers, such as the Cruising Club of America, do have requirements, but they are not directly tied to the ISO ratings. However, there are some requirements for commercial vessels and fishing boats.

## Design Category A

Category A boats are designed for significant voyages, such as crossing oceans or in unsheltered waters for several hundred miles. They are expected to survive winds up to 55 knots and significant seas up to 23 feet. These conditions would be equivalent to Beaufort Scale 10, Storm Conditions: very high waves, overhanging wave crests with foam blowing in dense white patches with the wind, the sea takes on a whiter look, and visibility is adversely affected. Approximate wave heights are a maximum of 29 feet.

## Design Category B

These boats are designed for shorter offshore conditions encountered when immediate shelter may not be available. They are expected to survive winds of 41 knots and significant seas of up to 13 feet. These conditions can also exist on inland seas. This rating maximum is equivalent to Beaufort Scale 8, Gale Conditions: moderately high waves with greater wave length, edges of crests breaking into spindrift, and foam blowing well-defined streaks with the wind. Approximate wave heights are a maximum of 18 feet.

## Design Categories C and D are for sheltered water boats.
How is the category determined? Appendix B, written by yacht designer Michael Kasten, explains the definitions and evaluation criteria in more detail.

---

**Some hypothetical comparisons.** Because we are short of data from existing passagemakers, I have provided hypothetical examples based on three different boats. Trawler A, a typical passagemaker of 50 ft. length overall (LOA), shows a relatively slow curve for the righting arm force, predicting a slow, gentle, seakindly roll (see Figure 7–9). It also has a fairly weak righting arm force that might portend problems if the boat were caught in a stormy circumstance that reduced its already marginal performance, such as rolling on top of a wave crest. In addition, the rapid drop off in righting arm after the 70° maximum may indicate this boat has an aft cockpit that may flood at about this point, resulting in a steep downward rush toward possible capsize. Thus Trawler A, while seakindly, seems to have less ultimate seaworthiness.

Trawler B, of about the same size, shows a much stronger righting force and a much steeper initial slope. This boat may have a quick, almost jerky roll period. Perhaps the curve represents a boat with harder chines, rather than a rounded bottom. Or the vessel may have a lot of ballast down low that creates a stronger, quicker righting force. Or its beam may be quite wide. The maximum righting force happens just before 40°; then it declines slowly before vanishing at close to 90°. Because of its increased reserve for righting, it is probably a more seaworthy boat, although certainly less seakindly. Sometimes, the unkindly ride of these boats is improved by putting more weight up high in the boat, thus lengthening the roll period, but decreasing positive stability.

The dotted curve shows a catamaran of about 35'. It shows a very steep righting arm force maxing out at only 6°! This is caused by the catamaran's wide beam. There are strong forces toward stability that continue until capsize at about 90°. Cats don't really roll like monohulls; they follow the wave form. When a large wave reaches the steep 60° angle, the cat will heel at that angle, even though it is relatively flat riding on the wave itself. However, the heaving action of a wave on the windward hull can reduce its safe zone considerably and could result in much poorer performance than is implied in the stability chart. Strong rotational energy, such as a large breaking wave, can rapidly push a cat to the point of no return.

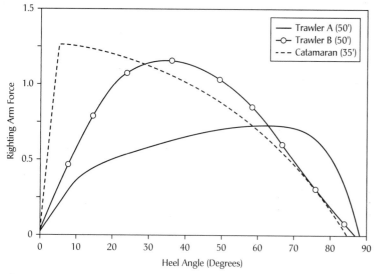

**Figure 7–9.** Comparison of hypothetical stability curves for two 50' trawlers and a 35' catamaran.

If we could compare stability data on oceangoing motor yachts, we might be able to make boats safer and buying decisions more rational. We would, of course, have to use criteria that are comparable, meaning that measurement must be standardized. The ISO standards are far from ideal, but they are perhaps a beginning for making comparisons.

## What Makes a Boat Self-Righting in Extreme Conditions?

Steve Dashew, Stephen Seaton, and Michael Kasten, all established yacht designers, design at least some of their boats to be self-righting, with stability close to 180°. The wheelhouse or pilothouse buoyancy must be considered in the stability curve to get this result. It adds considerable buoyancy below the water and makes the boat unstable in an inverted position, speeding its return to upright position. To return upright, the boat must have a strong and watertight wheelhouse, with windows and doors capable of resisting the forces of the water and sea. In addition, all hatches must be watertight, strong, and secured. Engine room vents should be designed for this event. Experts use the term *downflooding* to describe opportunities for water to make its way into the hull through various hatches, doors, ports, vents, or holes. Many smaller passagemakers might

be able to survive a rollover if the seas rolled the boat back upright fast enough to prevent serious downflooding—the real enemy here. How fast is fast enough? That would take some serious calculations by an expert to determine the speed of downflooding based on size and locations of hull openings.

**Deckhouse strength.** Most boats constructed of fiberglass have cabins built of relatively lightweight, cored fiberglass. The idea is to keep the weight down on the upper decks. Older hulls often used plywood decks and wheelhouses, covered by fiberglass. Whether any of these structures are strong enough to survive a rollover is open to question. One recent experience, related by Jim Lieshman at Nordhavn, occurred when one of their motorsailers was dropped upside down while offloading from the ship. According to Lieshman, it suffered no major damage to the wheelhouse or windows; however, it did sink, so this is difficult to verify. Some of the steel or aluminum boats have strong deckhouses and may have a greater chance of surviving the forces created by breaking waves and green water. According to Ralph Naranjo, the U.S. Coast Guard, in developing its 47-foot motor lifeboat, spent a lot of time evaluating storm force pressures on the hull and designing it to resist these forces.

**Windows, ports, hatches, and doors.** A broken window, a hatch that is swept away, or a door that opens while submerged would result in rapid flooding and then sinking of the boat with little chance of recovery. This is one of the more serious concerns for many passagemaking motor yachts, especially those with large windows with great views—that's one of the admired design features of trawlers. However, there are huge stresses on these windows and their frames when hit by a breaking wave, let alone if submerged. Storm windows made of Lexan can provide some protection and added strength. We have them on *Teka III* and install them over the most vulnerable ports before departing. They are available as an option on most oceangoing boats. However, the main wheelhouse window coverings are only installed if we are threatened by a major storm. Luckily, we have been able to avoid such storms and have never installed them in many years of voyaging.

**Engine room vents.** Some of the most vulnerable areas are the engine room vents. Many passagemaking yachts have vents located near the side of the boat, perhaps 6 feet above the water. A truly self-righting boat would have vents above the deckhouse with tubes leading to the engine room to prevent water entry. Dashew's FPB 64, covered in Chapter 12, has an automatically closing door in the air passageway leading from above deck to the engine room.

**Cockpit and side decks.** A large cockpit aft can adversely affect self-righting because the free surface water remaining will continue the vessel's instability. Likewise, large bulwarks that trap water can be a threat to stability and to the return to an upright position because they may act as dampeners to prevent rolling back upright. A boat designed without bulwarks should have better ultimate stability.

**Do we need self-righting?** It depends on your cruising plans and the risks you plan to take. If you want to cruise the waters of Antarctica, you might want to consider a boat that could survive the extreme conditions you might find there. If you want to cruise during the tropical storm season in the South Pacific or Caribbean, such extreme designs also seem appropriate. For most of us, we will not see these extreme conditions. In fact, in voyage planning, we should take care to avoid such stormy areas. A boat that can survive a 70-to-80-degree heel without capsizing is probably all we will ever need. I don't know what the most extreme heel we have encountered is—I think around 30 degrees (with paravanes in the water). Even this amount of heel would be extremely unusual for *Teka III*.

## Motions and Stability in a Seaway

While the static stability curves discussed are good predictors of ultimate stability in sea conditions, they are not perfect. Many different forces are at work at sea, including wave size and shape, wind, flow resistance, boat speed, rudder control, propeller thrust, stabilizers, etc. If forces are applied directly to the center of gravity at the waterline, the boat will move bodily by sliding sideways or surfing down a wave. If the force is applied off center, she will rotate as indicated by rolling or pitching. In really rough sea conditions, ocean waves are usually chaotic with random patterns that never exactly repeat themselves. The boat constantly strives to return to an equilibrium condition. It will be *rolling, pitching, yawing* and *surging, heaving* and *swaying*—all at once—as illustrated in Figure 7–10. How a vessel responds to these motions affects its ultimate stability and seakindliness. The higher the magnitude and speed of accelerations around these various axes, the more uncomfortable, and perhaps more dangerous, the ride.

**Roll and pitch oscillations.** Every boat has its own roll and pitch oscillation period depending on her shape, load displacement, and weight distribution throughout the boat. Dampening forces that cause the roll to reduce with each cycle are determined

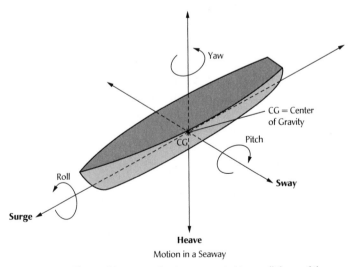

Figure 7–10. Effects of the sea on boat movement. At sea, all three of these axes will affect comfort and stability. The closer you are to the intersection of these three axes, the more comfortable the ride.

by the shape of the hull, length of the righting arm, underwater appendages such as keels and bilge keels, sail configuration (if any), and active or passive stabilizing systems. If the dampening forces are not sufficient, the boat might act like a car without shock absorbers; it would just keep on rolling when energized with a very slow decline over time. However, there is a danger here if the pattern of the waves causes a near–synchronous rolling pattern with that of the boat. The added force can result in a vessel's capsize, even in less than storm conditions. Let's say we have a 50-ton passagemaker with a roll oscillation period of 6 seconds. If we encounter 8-foot waves with a 6-second period on the beam, we would have a dangerous synchronous situation that could result in capsize if our stabilizers did not dampen the roll. On the other hand, if these 8-foot waves had a 15-second period, they should present no problem for us unless they are breaking. To resolve synchronous roll problems, the boat should alter course at once to change the roll characteristics, perhaps by heading up- or downwind a bit on the quarter. Rough water boat handling will be discussed more fully in Chapter 18.

Pitch oscillations are usually less of a problem but they can cause the boat to bury its bow or even pitchpole if allowed to continue without course change or speed change. Normally, the boat starts taking spray or green water over the bow, and the skipper immediately slows down or takes other action to minimize this problem.

## Hull Shape and Weight

**Underwater shape of the hull.** In Chapter 6, Robert Beebe discussed the prismatic coefficient that primarily relates to how the boat moves slowly through the water. In this section, we will further consider the hull shape's effects on stability and seakindliness. Longer, heavier boats generally have slower roll periods that make them more comfortable. They are less vulnerable to high accelerations, which means they are less tiring at sea, and the crew will be less likely to get motion sickness. Boats with large, flatter areas amidships or aft, whether displacement or planning hulls, are more subject to surge forces whether going into or with the waves. Although they can carry more fuel, they may be

## Evaluating an Existing Vessel's Stability

### Roger Long

So, you show up for sea trials to evaluate a potential vessel purchase and it's dead flat calm. There are still things you can learn, at least to help you decide if you should try coming back another time.

Loosen the dock lines and put one foot on the rail and one on the dock or stand where you can push on a piling. If you look closely, you will be able to see even quite a large vessel respond to your weight or pushing. By pushing or leaning as you see the vessel move, you will be able to set up a good roll. I've gotten vessels as large as 100 feet rolling all by myself enough that people started looking around to see what was going on.

Once the boat is rolling, stop pushing and use a stopwatch to time the roll all the way from one side, over to the other, and back. Look for the point where the rail or some other reference point moving against the background stops and changes direction.

A roll period around 4 seconds indicates a vessel that will be resonant in waves usually found in winds of 10 to 15 knots. Roll periods 6 seconds or greater mean that maximum rolling will generally occur with winds in the 20-to-25-knot range. Roll periods more than 8 seconds indicate a vessel for which stability should be fully evaluated from the safety standpoint.

The behavior of the boat as you let the boat roll on its own will tell you the degree of damping. A hull with low damping will continue rolling for a considerable number of rolls after you let it go. The highly damped hull will be hard to get rolling and will settle down quickly.

Knowing the roll period is also useful on sea trials since it will generally be easier in relatively calm conditions to determine the vessel's pitching period as it goes through the wakes of other vessels. If the vessel's pitching and rolling periods are very close, there is the potential for rolling motions to become coupled to pitching motions in rough water. This will produce increased rolling and an uncomfortable corkscrewing motion. Vessels with closely matched pitching and rolling periods should be carefully evaluated in rough water before committing to purchase.

less comfortable. Heavier boats usually have deeper drafts that help rudder and stabilizers to reach below the surface turbulence of the wave, resulting in better control.

**Beam and stability.** The beamier the boat, the higher the initial stability, but she may be more likely to capsize (although as we have already discussed,

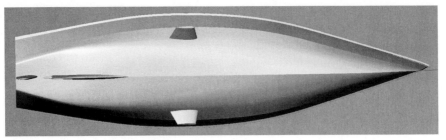

**Figure 7–11.** Fish-eye view of Dashew's FPB64. Note the slim canoe shape with very sharp entry; the symmetry bow and stern and the flatter area near the stern may provide some lift and increased speed. The stern view of this boat shown in Chapter 12 shows more rounded bilges at the stern than this computer view. Dashew's design is long and slim in comparison to the Krogen 52 shown in Figure 7–12. (Steve Dashew)

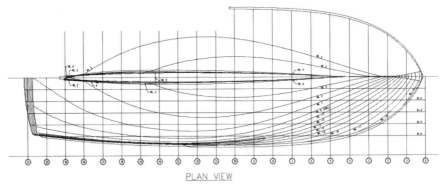

PLAN VIEW

**Figure 7–12.** Plan view of a Krogen 52. Note the smooth underwater lines, wider beam, good match bow, and stern lines. (Kadey-Krogen Yachts)

many factors influence this potential outcome). Marchaj reports that tank tests of capsizing based on various hull configurations using waves generated to simulate 13–15 foot crests on 33 foot hulls showed that a wider beam was much more likely to be related to capsize than a narrower beam. The wider model rolled to a higher heel angle as it rose to the breaking crest of the wave. On impact, the leeward deck dipped into the unbroken wave face. It then completely rolled over and became more stable inverted. It took another breaking wave to right it—an event that might not come for a long time in real sea conditions. The narrow boat was knocked down by the same-size waves, but did not capsize—it appeared to absorb the breaking crest by slipping sideways ahead of the wave.

Steve Dashew observes that "Modern, relatively light keelboats, with high freeboard, will skid on their topsides when knocked down due to being overpowered [by a breaking wave]. When a wave crest wallops your topsides it imparts energy to start the heeling process. If the boat is heavy with a deep hull or keel, immersed surfaces and inertia of the mass tends to hold the boat in place, allowing more energy from the wave to be transferred to the topsides. If the boat skids off to leeward with wave impact, then the wave crest cannot impart the same force to the hull. The boat slips away from the wave, absorbing less energy over a longer period. Think of this like a boxer rolling away from a punch, taking the sting out of it as it were. The ability to skid is a primary safety factor in dangerous seas."

The testing tank results confirm Dashew's assertion that it is better to dissipate the wave force by skidding; however, they found that higher center of gravity, higher freeboard, larger lateral keel area, and higher roll inertia did not result in more frequent capsizes. Of course, these results are from controlled tank tests and may not reflect the real world. My own experience in *Teka III*, our 52-foot, 16 foot-beam trawler is that it will skid off a steep wave when needed in spite of its nearly 50 tons and 6 foot draft with a large full keel. I have not tried this with a large plunging breaker to see what would happen in those conditions (and I hope to avoid that test). It could be that the paravane stabilizers, discussed in the next chapter, may have helped in this process by keeping the hull more upright. Rounded bilges may also make skidding easier than hard chines or sharp underwater hull changes.

**Which stern shape is best?** There is no general agreement that any one stern shape is better for ocean-crossing vessels. One would think that a double-ended design would be ideal for running in rough seas downwind because it would split and reduce any wave forces attempting to broach or pitchpole the boat. However, a canoe stern with its gently sloping aft deck may be even better because it provides a lot of reserve buoyancy to fend off breaking seas or large steep waves. The shape that appears to offer the most problem is the large relatively flat stern seen on most modern passagemaking yachts. Michael Kasten recommends that the stern be reduced to half or two-thirds of the midsection waterline beam's distance and have a rake of 30 to 45 degrees. My experience with one of these flat-stern boats is that it is underwater shape that matters most. The boat needs enough buoyancy in the stern to rise to the wave without being violently thrown upward, and it needs the lines that allow the faster-moving wave to smoothly pass by the hull— not push it along. When running before 12–14 foot waves in the Caribbean, we found the ride on *Teka III* was thrilling, but uneventful (Figure 7–13). The illustration of the bottom profile of the Krogen 52 (Figure 7–12) shows how the underwater lines result in smooth water passage around the hull, even though this boat has a relatively flat stern.

**Figure 7–13.** Large waves directly on the stern of *Teka III* in the Caribbean looked dangerous, but we rode them easily.

## Free Surface and Stability

Free-surface effects occur when movement of the boat causes liquid, such as water or fuel, to shift from one side of the tank or boat to the other, causing a decline in stability and reducing the metacentric height.

**Tank management.** When fuel or water tanks are only partially full, or when there is water in the bilges, the liquids can shift in the direction of the boat's heel and decrease her stability. With a tank that is relatively wide athwartships, the righting arm will be decreased, causing reduced stability. Any tank that has significant area across the beam can affect stability unless it is fully separated with dividers (*baffles*) to prevent the liquid from moving to the side. Even with baffles, any extended heel allows water to shift to the downward side of the tank. Another free surface problem can arise if cross-connected starboard and port fuel or water tanks have their valves opened so that fuel or water can gradually move to one side of the boat, thus decreasing stability. Partially full tanks also reduce stability, with the worst condition being 50% level.

According to Michael Kasten, the question of which tanks to empty first is more complex than it seems, primarily because of the shape of the tanks themselves. Tall, relatively narrow (atwarthships) tanks will not appreciably affect stability at low angles of heel, say up to 30 degrees. However, as the angle of heel increases, the tall narrow tanks eventually become a liability to stability. At around 80 degrees, the liquid shifts to the top of the tank—a bad situation.

Further, if you have two unconnected wing tanks (side or outboard tanks) that are tall and relatively narrow, they may reduce accelerations and provide a more comfortable ride. If the center tanks are not particularly wide and are located lower than the outboard tanks, the lower center of gravity should be beneficial, but the ride may degrade. I empty the wing tanks first on *Teka III* because my bilge tanks are a couple of feet lower than the side tanks and are not particularly wide. (I have not been able to discern any differences in seakindliness after emptying the wing tanks.)

Because either full or empty tanks do not present a free-surface problem, it is a good idea to completely empty one set of tanks before beginning to use the next set of tanks. If you only need some fraction of your total fuel capacity, always fill some tanks completely and leave the others empty. If the boat has a watermaker, it can be used to keep water tanks full during passages.

**Leaks and flooding.** Leaks should be resolved and water pumped immediately because stability can be affected quite rapidly, creating a dangerous situation. If large seas come aboard and are not immediately shed because of high *bulwarks* (upper sides of the boat without decking over them) or insufficient scuppers or drain holes, this has an immediate effect of raising the center of gravity, lowering freeboard, and causing free-surface effects—all onerous and possibly fatal results for the vessel's stability. A flooded cockpit is slow to empty, even if self-bailing, thus making it one of the most vulnerable spots on a passagemaker. A flooded deckhouse can result in rapid loss of stability for similar reasons. The boat may roll over on her side and not recover because of the weight of water in the wheelhouse. Most oceangoing yachts have wheelhouses that would not contain the water up high—it would make its way down to the bilge if the boat remained upright long enough. However, even though the problem would be lessened, there would still be a major free-surface stability problem. Downflooding rapidly decreases stability and makes capsize or sinking more probable.

## Catamaran Stability and Design

Catamarans behave differently from monohulls, and while we focus mostly on single-hull vessels here, a brief discussion about catamaran design and stability will be useful for many readers. Much of the information on this topic comes from Malcolm Tennant, a major force in ocean-crossing catamaran design who died in an unfortunate non-boating accident in 2008.

All long-range catamarans are displacement hulls, not planing hulls. These catamarans are not limited in S/L ratios as are monohulls (1.34 times the square root of the waterline length for most heavier boats)—they typically have an S/L of 3.25 or more. These catamarans are not dynamically supported as are monohulls; instead they run flat and level in displacement mode with little wake. Tennant-designed 58' displacement catamarans speed along at 30 knots with minimal horsepower.

Power cats are not just sailing cats with large engines; they require altered designs to prevent a squatting, bow up position. Increased buoyancy aft is achieved by designing a "bustle" with a vertical trailing edge. This innovation evolved into a canoe stern beneath the water, providing increased buoyancy, and allowed a finer entry at the bow, thus less resistance.

Seaworthiness characteristics are a prime consideration in choosing a power-cruising catamaran. Catamarans do not roll; they sit on the surface of the wave much like a raft. They have great resistance to roll and massive roll dampening because of the two hulls mounted so far apart. Pitching motion is comfortable, and there is little yaw due to shallow draft. Cats surf easily downwind; although large, strong rudders are needed to resist the forces of high-speed surfing. If the seas get too big, a drogue or sea anchor may be needed to slow the boat and keep it perpendicular to the seas. While cats do not roll as vigorously as single hulls, many people think their motion is jerky, quick, and uncomfortable.

While catamarans are stable and resist rolling if they do hit the point of vanishing stability, they will usually become stable in an inverted position (refer to Figure 7–9). A monohull that passes its point of

# Catamaran *Chrysalis* at Sea

### Mike Petersen

We have been in rough seas. We took *Chrysalis*, a 64-foot-long, 24-foot beam catamaran, into the Gulf Stream with 15- to 20-knot northerlies, for a sea trial shortly after launch. The seas were predicted to be 8 feet at 6 seconds. With the *stacking* [steep, close-together waves], it was a pretty intense ride. We also took some green water on top of the pilothouse coming up the Red Sea.

Basically the ride of the cat is very stable. Our main problem is that we get too lazy and leave drinks lying around and cupboards unlatched. The jerkiness you're talking about is only in certain beam seas, but after you get the waves at least a 45-degree angle off of beam, you start to notice a massive difference. I think that's because the hulls are so narrow, and if you can take half of the wave on one hull and the other half on the other hull at basically the same time, you eliminate the jerk and a lot of the roll. If you take straight ahead as 0 degrees, anything from 135 degrees to 225 degrees is an excellent ride. As we were going down the Red Sea, we had 8' seas at about 210 degrees. The wind was howling. When we got to the anchorage at about 6 am, the sun was coming up and only then did we fully realize how rough the seas were. We had several sailboats following us and they were all pretty beat up when they arrived. From 20 deg. to 70 deg. and 290 deg. to about 340 deg. the ride is excellent up to 6 feet at 6 seconds. From 340 to 20 the ride is great up to 4 feet at 6 sec. After that the nacelle will start to come into play. Slamming starts at maybe 6 feet and 6 seconds. But the nacelle softens the slamming so you don't get the same effect that you would on [some other cats].

We have about 30,000 miles under the keels and are pretty much sold on the ride. We had a writer from *Blue Water Sailing* with us on that Red Sea leg and almost had her convinced that there was a virtue to

**Figure 7–14.** *Chrysalis*, a 64', 24' beam catamaran designed by the late Malcolm Tennant. It has a range of 2,800 nautical miles at 10 knots. Mike and Kim Petersen found the bare hull in a farmer's field in New Zealand (it had suffered fire damage), brought it to the U.S., and finished it themselves. In 2007 they took her transatlantic and back, an adventure that is recounted in Kim's book, *Charting the Unknown: Family, Fear, and One Long Boat Ride.* (Mike Petersen)

powerboats by the end. We have found that with all those miles we probably had just three or four days when we were wishing we were somewhere else.

---

vanishing stability has a chance of being rolled back upright, while a multihull does not. Catamaran designers argue that watertight compartments and designs that allow the crew to stay in the inverted hull while the storm rages result in a potentially higher survival rate than a rolled monohull. However, it is a little disconcerting to have hatches on the underside of the boat for such an emergency. If the cat has a cabin that goes all the way to its sides, the stability is improved because it is much more difficult to complete the rotation due to the cabin's buoyancy.

Another important aspect of catamaran design is the wing-deck height and design. A deck that is too low will slam when heading into a chop. Tennant used a design under the wing he calls a *girder* or *nacelle*. Looking from the bow, it looks like two arches (he compares them to McDonald's golden arches) that meet in the middle. Any waves hitting in that area have no flat surface to slam against, thus limiting any slamming force.

Catamarans are extremely sensitive to overloading. The displacement for catamarans is less than single hulls—they will not support as much weight without being overloaded; thus performance is more quickly affected by adding extra pounds. This possible shortcoming is exacerbated by the huge amount of deck and hull space. Many owners just fill it up with all the essential stuff of cruising life.

## Importance of Rudders

Rudder design is often neglected, as if any reasonable-sized rudder would work equally well. The rudder is a critical element for the boat's stability. The rudder prevents broaching. It allows positive action to avoid dangerous waves or obstacles. A poorly designed rudder results in poor autopilot control, course wandering, and poor performance in rough seas. Good course-keeping in heavy weather that does not fatigue the helmsman or autopilot is an essential part of seaworthiness, according to Marchaj. In the early 1980s, I bought a 37' twin-screw, Taiwan-built trawler yacht. During sea trials, I noted that the boat was slow to respond to its rudders. The broker said not to worry; you just use the throttles to change direction by adjusting engine rpms. I bought the boat anyway, but during my first year of ownership I had the rudders redesigned and remade for better rudder control. I have heard of modern passagemakers with the same type of problem, especially in twin-screw boats. Vessels that are unstable because of poor rudder control, possibly combined with lack of a deep keel, are called cranky or worse by their owners.

The best hull and rudder designs are passive, requiring little or no effort to keep the boat headed in a straight line, the keel and the rudder acting together to counter external forces on the boat. Don Stabbert described his experience with *Starr*, his 75' Northern Marine long-range cruiser this way:

> During sea trials I learned that the steering response was slower than I expected. Having spent many years running single-screw boats, including tugs, I had a pretty good idea how this boat should respond. And she wasn't even close.
>
> When the boat was at a dead slow and the helm was put hard over to 30 degrees, Starr's response to the rudder was so slow that we needed to give a burst of power to make her turn faster. Putting the helm over 5 degrees at a cruising speed of 8 or 9 knots brought another slow response, but when the helm was back to center the boat's heading would drift past center. It became a guessing

## Diagnosing Steering Stability

Autopilot designer and manufacturer R.M. Freeman found so many autopilot problems with commercial fishing boats due to poor rudder design, that he became an expert on rudder problem diagnosis and developing strategies to fix rudder problems. (See the endnote.)

1. Set your course manually at cruise speed. Choose a time when seas are calm and there is little or no wind.
2. Note the wheel position if possible.
3. Give the wheel about a 20% turn in either direction.
4. Bring the wheel back to its original position.
5. The boat should return to its straight run.
6. If the boat continues to turn so that the opposite rudder is needed to check the turn, then a stability problem exists.
7. Repeat the turn in the opposite direction.
8. You can also center the rudder and let the boat go on its own. If it begins to go in a gradual circle, then instability exists. If it continues straight, it is good to go.

*game to figure out just where the boat would end up pointing—not a comfortable feeling with a boat this size. (See endnote.)*

*Starr* was a boat with hull-rudder instability. Diagnosing the existence of instability is relatively easy. (See the sidebar "Diagnosing Steering Stability.") Fixing it may be more difficult. Some suggestions are given later in this chapter. Stabbert solved his rudder problem by replacing his ineffective single rudder with twin rudders (see Figure 7–22).

**Size and rudder aspect.** Generally, rudders for displacement boats are sized at 4 to 5 percent of the boat's lateral plane (the boat's underbody image as viewed from the side). Another way to size a rudder is to use Skene's method with a formula that takes into account displacement and waterline length.* Using this method, the rudder area for a 40 metric ton boat with a waterline length of 49 feet would be 9.56 square feet. Another rule of thumb:

---

*The formula is area of the rudder = 4 times the square root of (the displacement in metric tons divided by the square root of the waterline length in feet). The answer to the calculation gives rudder area in square feet.

*Rudder area = Length of waterline × draft × 0.05.* This would yield a quite different figure for a 49-foot waterline, 6 foot draft: 14.7 square feet. The aspect ratio (height divided by base or chord) should be at least 2.0. Most rudders should also be balanced, with 10 to 20 percent of the rudder ahead of the center of the rudderpost, depending on the aspect ratio and the type of rudder (flat-plate or foil-shaped rudder). See Figures 7–16 and 7–20 for a better feel for these dimensions. Both rudders are *foil rudders,* having shapes so that water flows around, roughly analogous to the wing of an airplane. (For an example of a rudder that is not balanced, see the Stephen Seaton articulated foil rudder shown in Figure 7–20.)

**Figure 7–15.** Rudder for *Teka III*, showing its foil design and end plates at the top and bottom to effectively increase its aspect ratio. This rudder works well in all seas and is quite stable. The curved fiberglass sheets above the rudder are not part of the boat's bottom; they are to deflect waves and prevent slap when anchored with the stern toward the swells.

# Michael Kasten on Rudder Design

Michael Kasten's ideal rudder on this 40' Coaster has more area down deep, where the rudder is most effective, than at the surface. He uses the familiar foil fairing, but with a flat trailing edge of at least 10%—this reduces *autopilot hunting* (moving from side to side like a snake rather than in a straight line). It allows the trailing edge to bite better. He uses end plates on at least the bottom of the rudder.

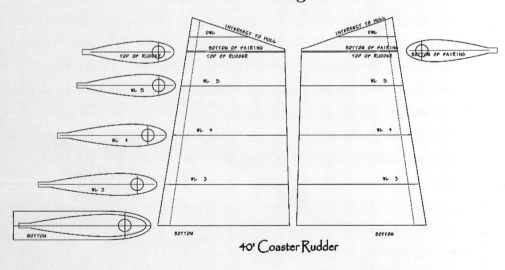

40' Coaster Rudder

Parts Scale: Full Size
Plot Scale: 3" = 1'-0"

KASTEN MARINE DESIGN, INC.
www.kastenmarine.com – michael@kastenmarine.com
Copyright 2000- Michael Kasten

**Figure 7–16.** Plans for a rudder on a 40' coaster designed by Michael Kasten. Note the increased area at the base and the fairing.

**Figure 7–17.** Rudder and propeller shaft on Dashew's FPB 64, *Windhorse*, showing an unsupported rudder with a tapered leading edge that reduces stress for this type of rudder and also reduces vibration caused by propeller blade pulses. (The lower part of this rudder is designed to break off under pressure of a major grounding, leaving enough for emergency steering.) (Steve Dashew)

## Improving Rudder Performance

**Adding end plates.** A relatively inexpensive way to improve rudder performance is to add end plates at the top and bottom of the rudder as we did on *Teka III* (see Figure 7–15). If you have a rudder made out of a flat plate, you can add the top and bottom plates and add wedges at the trailing edge of the rudder.

Two other designs are beginning to appear on voyaging boats: the articulated rudder and the dual rudder system.

**Install an articulating rudder.** The Bayview articulating rudder shown in Figures 7–18 and 7–19 provides a variable wedge shape that increases rudder force as the rudder is turned more sharply. Several brands of passagemaking yachts have installed

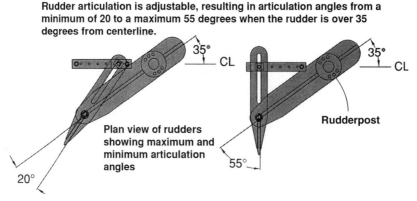

**Figure 7–18.** The Bayview Engineering articulated rudder has been installed successfully on many passagemakers. (Bayview Engineering)

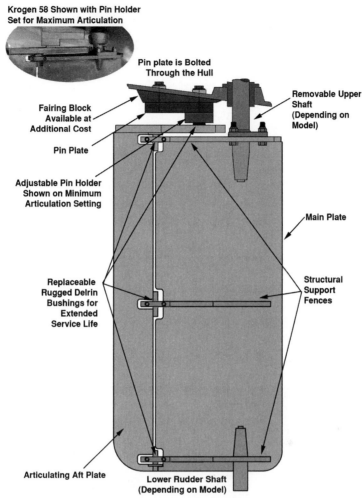

**Krogen 58 Shown with Pin Holder Set for Maximum Articulation**

Pin plate is Bolted Through the Hull

Removable Upper Shaft (Depending on Model)

Fairing Block Available at Additional Cost

Pin Plate

Adjustable Pin Holder Shown on Minimum Articulation Setting

Main Plate

Replaceable Rugged Delrin Bushings for Extended Service Life

Structural Support Fences

Articulating Aft Plate

Lower Rudder Shaft (Depending on Model)

**Figure 7–19.** The anatomy of the Bayview Engineering articulated rudder similar to the one installed on Selene 48, *Furthur.* (Bayview Engineering)

this rudder and report excellent performance. However, note that when going straight ahead the rudder is exactly the same as a non-articulating normal rudder. If there is instability in the system, this rudder may not help. An example of the installation on a Selene 48 is shown in Figure 7–19. Note that the rudder is essentially a flat-plate construction.

**Use twin rudders.** Twin rudders are another possibility where space is limited and other single rudder designs are not possible. Some twin screw boats add a third rudder amidships, so this is not

such an uncommon event—it is just unusual for a passagemaking yacht. (See Figure 7–22.)

## Bulbous Bows: How Effective?

More controversy surrounds the effectiveness and seakindliness of bulbous bows than with any other design factor. Some experts say that a bulb will reduce fuel consumption 12–15 percent and give a better ride by reducing pitching. Others think it is just marketing hype—it is better to simply build a longer boat.

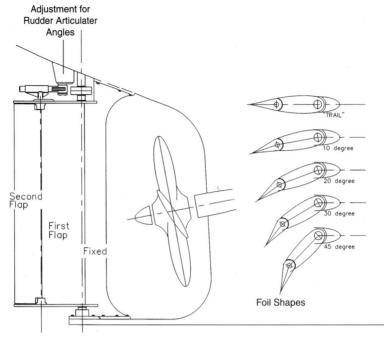

**Figure 7–20.** Stephen Seaton's articulated foil rudder. This design is reported to be very effective. Note that there is no part of the rudder forward of the rudderpost. Also the tolerance between the rudder foils is critical—only 1/32 inch. (Stephen Seaton)

**Figure 7–21.** The Seaton articulated foil rudder installed on the 63' *Ihikai*. Seaton describes his experience with this rudder: "We found out that at full speed on this boat [you] do not put the rudder hard over because you will do a 180 before you know it. We could not stall this rudder at any speed or deflection. I designed a two-speed steering system to help around the dock and it worked great; just do not turn it on at speeds over 4 knots or the boat may turn too fast." (Stephen Seaton)

**Figure 7–22.** The twin rudders on *Starr*, a 75' Northern Marine vessel, provide enough surface area to effectively control the boat. The post between the rudders is a strong support for the rudder mounting plate. It is rated at 20,000 pounds crush load. It is supported on top by a beam molded into the hull. (Don Stabbert)

Bulbous bows do work on large ships, but do they add to the capabilities of a displacement trawler?

**How does the bulb work?** The idea here is to put a pressure point ahead of the boat that creates a small bow wave and dampens or reduces the main bow wave of the boat. This reduces the resistance of the boat through the water. Bulbs seem to be most effective toward the higher end of the speed/length ratio. Patrick Bray, a Canadian yacht designer who frequently creates bulbous-bow designs, states, *"It is evident that the bulb reduces the required power throughout the range of speeds from 9 to 19 knots."* He also presents data showing a *decrease in performance* in terms of fuel consumption and range by 7% for an 8-knot yacht and an *increase* of 33% for a yacht doing 10 knots. Most full-displacement passagemakers do not cruise at 10 knots, so the savings may not exist for most boats. Bulbs are less efficient at lower speeds because they create drag. Bray's measurements show that at 10 knots, seakeeping is improved. Bow accelerations (pitching) are reduced by almost 10% and stern accelerations are reduced by 9.5%. No data was provided for 8 knots. Bray also claims that there is less water coming aboard because the bow wave is reduced, thus creating a dryer boat.

Another study done as part of the MIT Sea Grant Program, by Heliotis and Goudey, using models of 76'

New England fishing trawlers, found that at 9 knots or more there was 21.3% less resistance than a bare hull. They found that a bulb does dampen the pitch with the greatest effect at the boat's natural pitch resonance. The bulb's performance was tied to bulb shape and size and to the amount of ballast in the bulb. They recommended the use of the bulb as a ballast tank with water, not fuel as the weight, because trim was important to the bulb's effectiveness. However, they also found that "at lower speeds all bulbs were found to be detrimental due to the increase in wetted surface [and to heavier displacement of about 9%]." The efficiency improvements only happened at speeds over 8 knots.

Don Bass, Honorary Research Professor of Engineering and Mathematics at Memorial University, has also done extensive work on bulbous bows for fishing vessels. His research shows that bulbs can be quite effective for reducing pitch accelerations while fishing, although bulbous bows are very sensitive to design. He states: "Small changes in bulbous bow geometry and the way it is faired into the hull can cause some quite significant differences in vessel response. The reasons for these differences are not clear and are surprisingly too subtle to be picked up by the conventional hydrodynamic analyses."

Thus, for a bulbous bow to work, it must be properly designed and preferably tank tested. It would seem like an expensive experiment to design or add a bulb without testing to make sure it will do the job. His research confirms that bulbs, at slow speeds, are detrimental to efficiency.

The definition of slow speed where bulbs are ineffective or detrimental is not clear. Most experiments I reviewed were for larger boats with waterline lengths of 70, 90, or 110 feet. Most are also done on relatively flatter-bottomed hard chine fishing boats. How generalizable is this research to more rounded displacement yachts?

Michael Kasten provides some useful insights:

*A bow bulb must be designed for a specific service speed at which it will help reduce the amount of energy dissipated into wave making. At other speeds, it will be less effective, or will be a detriment in terms of resistance. This is why cargo vessels can make good use of a bow bulb, as they are designed* for a specific service speed. Less so a passagemaking trawler. At speeds below 0.9 times the square root of the WL length (the speed-to-length ratio, expressed in feet and knots), surface friction is the dominant component of the vessel's overall resistance. At speeds above S/L 0.9, wavemaking begins to dominate as speed increases, until at an S/L of approximately 1.34 for displacement vessels, it becomes so great as to be a limitation on further increases in speed. Because a bulb will increase wetted area, naturally it will increase resistance at speeds below S/L 0.9. The "sweet spot" in terms of speed for long range voyaging under power is usually considered to be around S/L 1.15, or approximately the speed at which the curve of wave making resistance begins to rapidly steepen. It stands to reason therefore that a bulb for a long range voyaging vessel should be designed for a service speed of between S/L 1.1 and S/L 1.2. At lesser speeds, the bulb will be a liability due to its increase in surface area friction. At speeds above its intended service speed, it will become less effective in reducing wavemaking resistance, until ultimately it becomes a liability due to its increase in surface friction.

Typically, a bulb is designed to have a sectional area that is in proportion to the vessel's mid-section area. The bulb's final diameter and in particular its length, should be determined by tank testing at the intended speed. Without tank testing, or alternatively having a substantial data base for similar applications, the bulb design would be a shot in the dark at best, and would likely be ineffective at reducing resistance.

**Problems with bulbous bows on slower displacement yachts.** The first problem follows from the data presented previously: higher fuel consumption and less range at normal cruising speeds of around 8 knots or less. Another problem, not noted in the tank studies, is bulb pounding or slamming, which can be quite spectacular and alarming. Bulb proponents say a slight change of course will rectify this problem. My own experience is it takes a course change of about 40 or 50 degrees to eliminate the pounding—not a slight change. (See the sidebar "Teka III's Nose Job.") We also experienced a much wetter ride with the bulb than without the bulb.

## Teka III's Nose Job (Bulbous Bow)

**October–November 1998:** Based on John Knight's recommendation and my decision to try the bulb, Knight & Carver, who built *Teka III* in 1981, installed a fiberglass bulbous bow. What follows are log entries concerning my experience with the bow.

**4 Dec. 1998:** South from Ensenada, California, to Cedros. Winds up to 35 knots on the stern. Seas up to 12 ft. Had a salt water leak around the rudder arm opening in the stern. Only leaking a few cups, but it's causing lots of problems with the carpet. (Later found this was caused by the bow riding higher and the stern lower, resulting in a leak where there had been none before.)

**23 Dec. 1998:** Going north in Sea of Cortez. Winds in the Canal de San Jose 25 knots with seas building from 4 feet to 7–8 feet

about 30 degrees off the nose. Bulbous bow slams into these waves with a thud! Also creates a big splash with much spray over the boat. Cannot see any difference in pitching or in fuel consumption.

**24 Dec. 1998:** Sea of Cortez. Wind from the north, 15–25. In a relatively moderate chop of 4–5 feet, still had pounding problems. Seems the bulb comes halfway out of the water and when it sinks down again the water comes around and slaps against the sides loudly. Also the bulb forces the bow wave up so that waves spurt through the hawse holes in the bow, resulting in spray and wet decks.

**1999 to 2000:** No pertinent issues as *Teka III* avoided head seas or was inland cruising on the ICW

**20 April 2001:** Ran offshore from Jacksonville, Florida, to Cape Canaveral.

Started off nice, but became rough at night with 15–20 knot winds and 5–7 foot seas directly on the bow. Bulbous bow pounded unmercifully—had to slow to 1,000 rpm and 4.6 knots to make it tolerable. Entered ICW at Cape Canaveral rather than enduring the pounding all the way to Ft. Lauderdale.

**2 Sept. 2001:** Off southern Spain we encountered 4–6 foot head seas with 15 knots plus of wind, directly on the nose. Counted the slams in one 15-minute timeframe: 14 large, boat-jarring pounds; 25 smaller, audible and felt impacts. Total 39 or 2.5 per minute. Very unpleasant.

**April 2002:** Barcelona, Spain. Removed bulbous bow. No more pounding. Speed increases by about half a knot. Much less spray.

In addition to the slamming, wet decks, and no improvement in fuel economy, other problems can happen since the basic hull design is changed. In our case, even though the bulb was submerged to about the right depth, it had too much buoyancy after installing the bulb. The designers had figured a certain amount of lead ballast to provide neutral buoyancy, but it was not sufficient. As a result, the boat was down a few inches in the stern from her designed waterline. Because it is difficult to simply add more weight in the bow, we had to live with this condition. Perhaps it exacerbated our problems described in the sidebar.

Another clue that a bulbous bow may not help for a given boat is to look at the bow wave at cruising speed. Many ocean-crossing full displacement yachts have very small bow waves at 8 knots or fewer (*Teka III* is one of them), thus the main advantage of a bulb of reducing the bow wave does not seem to apply; however, the increased resistance from additional wetted surface does apply. Although we never experienced a problem, it seems possible that the extra surface in the bow might act as a rudder and lead to broaching under severe conditions with following seas. It also makes it marginally more difficult to maneuver the boat in close quarters because the bow resists turning.

**Figure 7–23.** *Teka III*'s bulb being removed in Barcelona, Spain. The fairing at the top and the wave splitter at the stem were added in Florida to try to reduce pounding. These modifications had some effect, but pounding went on and on.

**Figure 7–24.** *Teka III* back to her original bow shape. (Mary on the bow.)

# Nordhavn and
# Bulbous Bows: 2011

## Jim Leishman

Since the material prepared in the previous edition [*Voyaging Under Power*, Third Edition in the early 1990s], we have tank-tested many more models with and without bulbous bows. In the late '90s, we even tested our Nordhavn 40 with and without the bulb. Personally I came to feel the bulb's benefit was not worth the trade offs that I described and really felt the conventional stem had benefits. In recent years, we have used bulbs on our 76 and 86 with good results. The main difference in these bulbs is that they are not cylindrical in section, but elliptical, and water does not separate from them in the same way as a cylindrical bulb and cause less noise than the older style. Contrary to what you think, the bulbs do not really slam themselves. The noise is caused by the water that separates from the bulb when the bow drops and that same water impacts the advancing topsides above the waterline in the stem area. I think the bulbs are worth considering in the larger boats, but personally I would not consider one until the boat gets into the 70-foot range; however, we did see a significant reduction in resistance during tank testing even on the Nordhavn 40.

Michael Kasten has some conclusions about using bulbous bows on passagemakers:

> It is my view that in spite of any potential reductions in resistance, placing bow bulbs on relatively small vessels cannot be encouraged due to potentially dangerous handling characteristics in following seas. This is especially so for short and fat boats that will already experience excessive yaw in following seas. In other words, here the bulb can "grip" in the trough and actually cause serious broaching.
>
> Bow bulbs may be advocated on the basis of pitch reduction. The benefits in this regard are measurable and therefore inarguable, provided the bulb is correctly designed and sized for the vessel. The benefit of using a bow bulb simply to attenuate pitch on a well-designed hull form is controversial at best. For example, on smaller craft we observe that a bow bulb can increase the likelihood of slamming in short steep seas.

All in all, this research and experience leads to the conclusion that bulbs are not very appropriate for smaller, slower designs—they offer little or no advantage for seaworthiness, seakindliness, or efficiency. It seems possible that a larger passagemaker (perhaps 65' long), with a properly designed, ballasted bulb and the fuel capacity and power to run at higher speeds may experience benefits in both efficiency and comfort from the bulbous bow.

## Final Thoughts on the Importance of Stability Information

Good stability data for use in comparing various designs is almost nonexistent. If you want to find out how capable your boat will be in extreme conditions, you need this information. If more boat buyers would demand access to stability data, it would greatly improve our knowledge and potential safety. If the designer or manufacturer will not provide stability information, you can hire a naval architect to figure the stability of your boat. It is a relatively simple process if the lines of the boat are known or can be measured because the vertical center of gravity (VCG) can be determined by an inclining measurement to determine the righting arm. Stability information on sailing vessels is routinely required for participation in races.

We passagemakers want to avoid extreme events if at all possible, but it is better to know how your boat will behave if you are caught in a severe storm than to depend on data designed to make the boat more attractive, not necessarily more seaworthy or even more seakindly. For example, yacht salespeople often remark on the great visibility of a forward pilothouse with a high-up view of the sea ahead. This helm position is a great advantage for seeing logs on the inside passage to Alaska, but it is very uncomfortable on a long ocean voyage with big seas on the stern quarter because your position is a long way from the boat's center of gravity where motion is most gentle. You feel more acceleration, which is more tiring and conducive to seasickness.

In the next chapter we deal with a central issue in stability and seakindliness: reducing roll at sea and at anchor.

# CHAPTER EIGHT

# Stabilizing Against Rolling

When Beebe wrote the first edition of this book there were few options for powerboat stabilization. He learned from commercial fishermen about the use of what he called "flopperstoppers" to reduce rolling. Since the mid-1970s, more methods have become available, including active fins, a popular, but trouble-prone method; tank stabilization, a less popular method that is only recently gaining traction; and gyros, a high-tech, high-cost alternative with promise. In addition, there are still advocates of bilge keels and sails for reducing rolling. The paravane method of stabilization is still common in boats under 60 feet and has been refined since Beebe's time to make launch and retrieval much easier. Finally, there are still boats that cross oceans with no stabilization whatsoever, enduring violent rolling as a part of the voyage.

The first part of this chapter contains, with some editing and additions, Beebe's original ideas on roll stabilization relating to paravane installation and operation. The information in the section following "Design and Operation of Flopperstoppers" is new in this edition.

## Beebe on Curing the Roll Problem

While designing *Passagemaker*, I was well aware of the infamous capability of small motorboats to roll viciously in any kind of chop. Many hours spent holding on under these conditions and studying the problem convinced me that one basic requirement of a satisfactory power-only passagemaker was

finding a method to reduce rolling as much as possible in the interests of more comfort and less fatigue. [Figure 8–2 shows that the effects of rolling, pitching, and heaving impact more than just comfort and fatigue; they also affect the capability of the crew to perform at all—the forces can be intolerable. This characteristic is known as a vessel's *seakindliness*.]

It was apparent in the beginning, and amply proved by our later experience, that rolling is one of the principal problems of power passagemaking. We must, then, devote a good deal of thought to two problems: what causes rolling and how to reduce it.

**Figure 8–1.** Nordhavn 46, *Knotyet II,* using both steadying sail and paravane stabilization in the Black Sea.

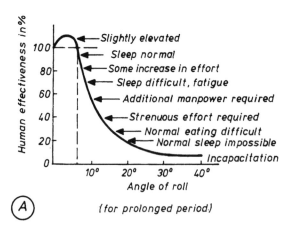

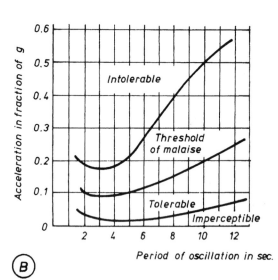

Figure 8–2. Effects of rolling and acceleration when pitching and heaving on crew capability. The maximum acceleration experienced on fishing vessels is around one g (just like the force in airplanes and spacecraft). This is ten times higher than the g-force that results in seasickness. If boat motion becomes intolerable, poor decisions result, which may even affect ultimate survival. "Habitability is more than just available space below deck." (Marchaj, see endnote.)

Briefly, the technicalities of the problems are these. Small craft do not follow the rules about rolling laid down for big ships. No combination of beam, draft, displacement, hull form, or *metacentric height* reduces the roll to a satisfactory degree until you reach quite large vessels, say over 150 feet. Do not misunderstand me. The factors named here do have an effect on the amount of roll, but the effect of variations in these

factors will not in itself reduce rolling to a degree that will be satisfactory to the crew.

The reason why small boats do not behave like ships is the concept of "forced rolling." That is, if the period of encounter with waves is greater than the natural rolling period of the ship, the ship will tend to roll in the period of the waves, not in its own period based on metacentric height. This tendency is true for small craft whenever rolling is a problem. For big ships, the reverse is true. In effect, what we call a "roll" is actually the boat trying to keep itself level with the surface of the water, as it is designed to do. But the damned sea surface keeps tilting!

In connection with "forced rolling," recent experience in this field reveals a seeming paradox: the more stable the vessel, the more it will roll when fitted with stabilizing gear comparable to that fitted on a less stable vessel. This was demonstrated when a new vessel—quite "stiff" due to hull dimensions, plus the temporary absence of appreciable amounts of topside weight—showed a roll period of 4 seconds; an older vessel of approximately the same size but with less stable lines had a period of roll of about 5.5 seconds. The geometry of their stabilizing gear, in this case the so-called flopperstoppers, was nearly the same. Tests at sea showed the stiffer vessel rolled more than the other vessel while its flopperstoppers were in use.

This paradox is easily explained. As noted previously, the "roll" in the forced-rolling situation is actually the attempt of the vessel to keep its waterline plane parallel to the water. As the boat tilts to accomplish this, the movement is opposed by the stabilizing gear, whatever it may be. With the "fish" being similar, the force available is the same. But the more stable vessel has more force generated by its shape to oppose the stabilizing force and accomplish its purpose of remaining aligned with the water's surface. Hence, it rolls to a greater degree.

While the two vessels were not tested simultaneously, persons who had sailed on both were aware of the difference. Estimates of the degree of difference varied from 25 to 40 percent. Four seconds is clearly too short a period for comfort. The usual range is 5 to 7 seconds for 40- to 50-foot vessels. Without stabilizing gear, such a vessel rolls more than a stiffer vessel, but with an easier motion. When stabilizing gear is put to use, it rolls less and still retains its easier motion.

Clearly then, period of roll is an important part of an overall evaluation and should be checked on any design you investigate. Roll is measured at the dock. With lines slack, one man can roll a 60-foot boat by either pushing up on the guardrail in time with the period or by stepping on the rail. When the vessel is rolling appreciably, time 10 over-and-back cycles and divide by 10 to give the period of roll. A vessel with a shorter period of roll is stiffer and has more initial stability.

Although the previous discussion leads to the idea that increasing the period of roll by reducing initial stability would lead to more comfort at sea while using stabilizing gear, this approach should be used with great caution because other factors are involved. In particular, coupling an easily rolled vessel with extensive topside weights can lead to catastrophic rolling due to the inertial forces involved. It was reported, for instance, that one yacht (a true trawler type) with extensive decking lost the use of its mechanical stabilizing gear in bad weather and rolled more than 70 degrees—with extensive internal damage. The trend in U.S. yachts toward increasing A/B ratio, which I inveighed against in Chapter 6, is an integral part of this problem.

What is needed is something external to the hull that reduces rolling as much as possible. Devices in use fall into two classes: passive and active. *Passive devices* essentially cause the roll to expend energy and reduce the roll by cutting down the energy left to roll the ship. They include paravanes or flopperstoppers, antiroll tanks, bilge keels, and steadying sails. *Active devices* are hydraulically driven foils or fins that move to counter rolling action. We will review all these methods, but will start with the two most popular: paravanes and active fins.

## Paravanes or Flopperstoppers (F/S)*

The advantage of flopperstoppers is that they greatly increase the lever arm, allowing a smaller surface to do

---

*Beebe used the term flopperstoppers interchangeably with paravanes. Technically flopperstoppers are designed for anchoring and paravanes for underway stabilization. Beebe's sections in this chapter will continue to use the terms as he originally wrote them. The terms "fish" and "bird" are often applied to the paravane as it moves through the water. Fishermen also use the term "stabies."

## Watch those Wakes: Fisherman Dies as Boat Capsizes in San Diego Bay

**September 12, 1990.** The *Los Angeles Times* reported that a 40–45 foot fishing boat (a lobster boat design) capsized in San Diego ship channel as it was returning from an offshore fishing trip, drowning the owner, a 64-year old man. The capsizing was apparently caused when an 80-foot luxury cabin cruiser created a large wake while traveling about 25 miles per hour, going in the same direction. The smaller boat was going only 5 mph. Harbor police divers tried to free the trapped owner, but were unsuccessful.

This incident illustrates the power of synchronous or forced rolling. A large wake is regular and steep. Its size and period can reinforce a roll that exceeds the stability for the boat, causing the boat to capsize in a stable inverted position. Changing course to meet large wakes at an angle is a prudent approach.

the job (the way they work is shown in Figure 8–3). The stabilizer, which is shaped like a delta-winged jet plane, is towed from the end of a boom projecting from the vessel's side. The stabilizer is shaped and rigged so that it dives down with little or no resistance when the boom rolls down toward it. But when the boom attempts to pull it up, it goes flat and resists the pull effectively. My research shows that the stabilizer can generate resisting forces up to 10 pounds per square inch of surface. This is no mean item in a 300-square-inch stabilizer (3,000 pounds of pressure). Until we realized what a tiger we had by the tail and beefed up our gear to handle it, we had problems aboard *Passagemaker* with our F/S rig.

In our case, the flopperstoppers reduced rolling by two-thirds, and our cruising showed this to be highly satisfactory. I think our experience established that reduction of rolling by two-thirds *on all courses and at all speeds* is a satisfactory *minimum requirement*. This two-thirds reduction brought down our rolling to less than 15 degrees most of the time, and days with only 5 to 10 degrees were common. What we had not realized was the significant manner in which this would change the whole aspect of the way we cruised.

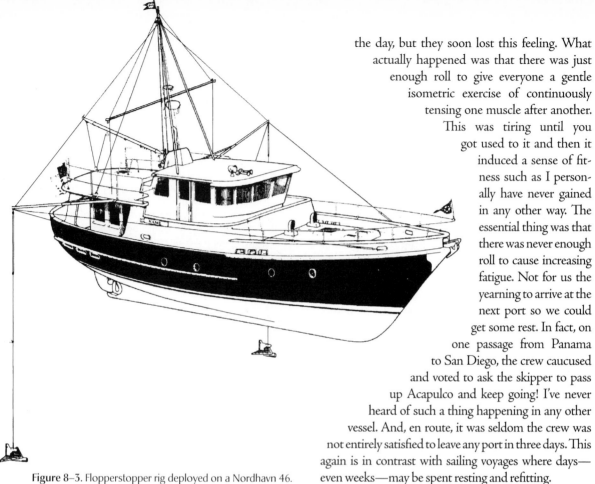

**Figure 8–3.** Flopperstopper rig deployed on a Nordhavn 46.

the day, but they soon lost this feeling. What actually happened was that there was just enough roll to give everyone a gentle isometric exercise of continuously tensing one muscle after another. This was tiring until you got used to it and then it induced a sense of fitness such as I personally have never gained in any other way. The essential thing was that there was never enough roll to cause increasing fatigue. Not for us the yearning to arrive at the next port so we could get some rest. In fact, on one passage from Panama to San Diego, the crew caucused and voted to ask the skipper to pass up Acapulco and keep going! I've never heard of such a thing happening in any other vessel. And, en route, it was seldom the crew was not entirely satisfied to leave any port in three days. This again is in contrast with sailing voyages where days—even weeks—may be spent resting and refitting.

There were two significant by-products of roll reduction. It made going to sea in *Passagemaker* a pleasure even for persons who had never been to sea before. And it reduced the fatigue factor from motion to just about zero.

Roll reduction made cruising with inexperienced persons possible because the environment produced by our stabilizing gear proved to be extremely comfortable. People cruising with us would come to the end of a long voyage and say they had never felt more fit. I finally figured out what was happening. The ship would always roll some, but the roll was not to a degree where you had to hang on, or use bunk boards, or brace yourself in a seat, or anything like that. Ordinarily, one could stand without bracing if one wished, though a hand on something was more usual. At the beginning of a voyage, people would be a bit tired at the end of

## Beebe on the Design and Operation of Flopperstoppers

As far as I know, *Passagemaker* was the first *yacht* designed to use flopperstoppers. We had to make quite a few changes in the rig before we got it to its present state, where it has been trouble free for years. Our experience produced certain rules that must be followed to achieve equivalent results:

+ The F/S rig should receive high priority in the design stage and not be tacked on as an afterthought. Remembering that the stabilizing force is the pull of the stabilizer times the length of the pole plus one-half beam, poles should be made as long as they conveniently can be within strength limits in this highly stressed column.
+ The proper position for the ends of the poles in the working position is 28 percent of LWL forward of

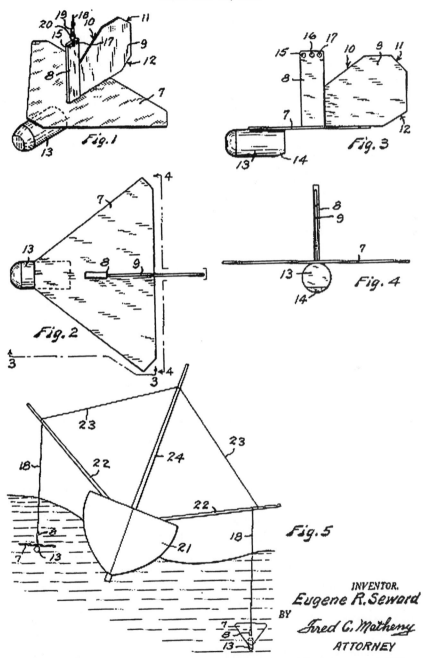

July 24, 1951          E. R. SEWARD          2,561,539

SUBMERSIBLE MARINE STABILIZER FOR BOATS

Filed Oct. 19, 1949

INVENTOR.
Eugene R. Seward
BY
Fred C. Matheny
ATTORNEY

Figure 8–4. Original patent application for submersible marine stabilizers (paravanes), 1951.
(Integrity Machining)

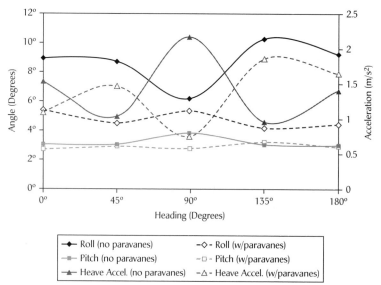

Figure 8–5. Effects of paravanes on motion. (Based on data from Akinturk, Cummings, and Bass)

the stern. In all locations appreciably forward of this point, performance grows progressively worse. If located too far forward, when the vessel pitches up, both fish will resist, causing double drag to no purpose.

- Strength of rigging must be carefully worked out. A satisfactory result ensues if the breaking strength of the tow wire is used as the load, and the rig strengths are made equal or better than this by graphical static analysis in the athwart-ships plane alone (see Figure 8–6).

- The tow wire should be as short as possible while still keeping the fish underwater. Our rig, on a 15-foot beam with 20-foot poles at 30 degrees up angle, put the fish 14 feet underwater at rest. As we skipped one only once in a gale in the Aegean, that was about right. For those who wonder what happens if a stabilizer is pulled out of the water, ours soared straight through the air like a porpoise, dove back in, and went back to work.

- A nylon spring of [at least] 7 feet should be used in the tow wire to ease the strains on the rig from jerking.

- The forward guy should be led as far forward as possible. The wire should be one size larger than the tow wire. [A fixed forestay is also practical so that the stowage of fore cables is not required.

See Figure 8–7 of Beebe's F/S design on *Teka III* completed in 1981.]

- No rigging to the stabilizer other than the tow wire is required. It is absolute nonsense to have lines "to keep the stabilizer from going aft too far" or other lines suggested by some users. [We will have more to say on additional lines in the retrieval section. Most paravane installations now use chain rather than cable for towing the fish. Chain is completely quiet, doesn't develop metal fatigue, and makes retrieval much easier.]

- The stabilizer sizes given in the Kolstrand Company bulletin on the subject work out well in practice [sizes range up to the super model made for 110' boats and weighing 170 pounds]. This company is the licensee for the most popular patented type. We used the large (48-pound) size on *PM*. All stabilizers should be ordered with the high-speed arm (see Figure 8–10). The hole used for towing should be as far forward as possible while still keeping the tow wire taut when diving. The setting is sensitive to speed. [On *Teka III* we used the third hole (8½ knots) from the front, whether going 6 knots or 8 knots. This never caused us any trouble with sensitivity.]

- Shackles located at either end of the tow wire and spring must have their pins inserted from *starboard to port*! If you don't do this, you will lose the whole assembly. The rhythmic pulling motion on each shackle causes the pin to rotate clockwise when viewed from the starboard side of the shackle. Don't learn this the hard way, as we did. [On *Teka III* we once had the shackle on the end of the pole back out despite being installed in the correct direction with double seizing wires. We changed all shackles to the bolt type with a cotter key—no more problems.]

- There is a great deal of wear at the towing lug on the pole. Parts should be well oversize. *PM*'s lugs

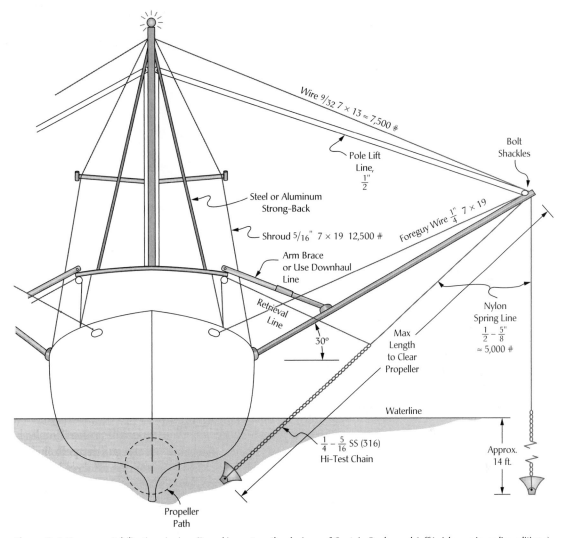

Figure 8–6. Paravane stabilization rigging. (Based in part on the designs of Captain Beebe and Jeff Leishman in earlier editions)

are now 5/8-inch steel, 2 inches wide, using shackles with 3/4-inch pins. When the hole wears egg-shaped at 7,000 miles, it can be built up with chrome-moly weld and will then be good indefinitely. Towing shackles last about 15,000 miles. Dab them with waterproof grease when you get the chance. [On *Teka III* we have not experienced this wear: the poles have gone more than 100,000 miles without replacement, although we did change to a larger diameter shackle about 50,000 miles ago.]

- A hold-down strut should be fitted to prevent the poles from flipping up if they are left out when there is no fish towing.
- Trouble with nylon towing spring lines has occurred when splices actually pulled out. Apparently, professional riggers do not appreciate how great and continuous the strains are on this spring. To my knowledge, at least four vessels have had eye splices pulled out. So make your own. A satisfactory splice must have *at least five full tucks with three half-tucks!* The whole should then be tightly

wrapped with plastic electrician's tape (which will stretch with the nylon). A marlin serving may be added, but this is mostly for appearance because the continual stretching of the splice will soon separate it—and the tape does the job.

Figure 8–9. Bolt shackles will not work loose—they should be used for all F/S connections.

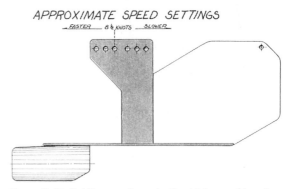

Figure 8–10. Stabilizer configured with a high-speed "arm." Speed settings for the shackle are approximate.

Figure 8–7. *Teka III* showing the permanent forestays on the paravane rig and mast supports: the poles are 25' long on a 52.5' LOA boat, made of heavy gauge steel pipes.

## Handling the Rig

*Passagemaker's* rig used a pole that was held in place by forward and aft guys, the foreguy taking the strain when operating. It was a two-man job to put the poles out because the aft guy had to have a tackle in it to adjust for the fact that the guys and the pole hinge were not in line with each other. The tackle's blocks would separate about 8 feet when the pole was lowered.

That one man could not lower the pole alone was a nuisance, particularly in some of my single-handed short trips. To fix this, the "singlehanded pole" was invented. As Figure 8–12 shows, the pole is equipped with a fixed aft guy and a strut to the pole that keeps it under control during the raising or lowering process. The foreguy is arranged to be taut in the down position and goes slack when the pole is raised. It can then either be cast loose and coiled up at the pole or held down by shock cords that take up the slack.

Figure 8–8. Swivel attachment to paravane: Canadian studies have shown that a swivel like the one shown here is absolutely essential for proper operation of the paravane.

Figure 8–11. Down under in Australia they construct their paravanes differently, using a universal joint where the paravane is connected to a rigid stainless steel pole rather than chains or cables, as described in this chapter. At the fish end, the paravane is connected using a hinge. Retrieval is easy—see the shackle and rope nearest to the fish. One simply lets it settle to the fish end, as seen in the photo, and then pulls it up. Arms swing alongside the boat when not in use. (cruisingunderpower.fastmail.net)

It is important that the rig be adjusted so the strut does not put a bend in the pole when in use, as any such stress could lead to rapid failure of this highly stressed compression member. Strut end connections that have considerable play can be useful for avoiding this problem. [On *Teka III* and some other boats we have travelled with, the poles are lowered before we leave the harbor and left down until we reach our destination. The fish are dropped as needed, usually when Mary says, "We're rolling too much!"]

### Umstot on Retrieving Paravane

In earlier versions of this book, Beebe advised using a grapnel hook to catch the fish and retrieve it. We have never used this method and have not seen it used by others. It seems pretty difficult. The problem with retrieving the fish is that if they are in the water and there is any motion at all, they will resist coming aboard with more force than a normal person can exert, so some type of winch is needed.

Nordhavn's standard installation uses dual electric winches mounted on an extended boom off the mast. A thin cable is attached to the aft vertical stabilizer of the fish and is pulled in from behind and placed into fish holders mounted on the stern. Control of the winches uses a remote so the action can be completed at deck level. This method seems elegant, but it is not without risk. Note that the fish looks much like an airplane with wings and a vertical stabilizer. This stabilizer keeps the fish going straight. If something gets caught on the cable and causes the stabilizer to be pulled in one direction or another, the fish can react erratically by jumping out of the

Figure 8–12. The author launching a paravane on *Teka III*. We slow to idle and then simply drop it in the water. We have never hit the side of the boat.

**Figure 8–13.** Paravane underway with retrieval line shown running at the waterline. This line is used to bring the paravane alongside where it can be retrieved with a dulled gaff hook (see Figure 8–16).

water or hitting the side of the boat . . . or even worse, the prop. The Nordhavn 46, *Suprr*, had this experience while crossing the Atlantic. They experienced two accidents: the first time, the fish came out of the water and into the aft cockpit, making a significant dent; the second time was on the crossing from the Canaries to Antigua when the paravane hit the prop and dented it. *Suprr* limped the rest of the way across the Atlantic at reduced speed and suffered considerable vibration. It turns out that the root cause of the problem was a bent vertical stabilizer, but this could have been related to the retrieval method, which puts strain on this part of the paravane.

Another Nordhavn retrieval method, described by Jim Leishman in the third edition, seems better to me. The key is using chain rather than cable. One quarter or 5/16 high-strength chain allows better retrieval methods. Here is Lieshman's description:

*A system that works well requires a retrieval line of about 3/8-inch diameter with a carabiner hook attached to the chain at a point slightly below the static waterline. When the vessel is running, the chain and fish stream aft, and this attachment point rises above the water. When retrieving the fish, the vessel is slowed and the retrieval line is pulled downward from a fairlead block attached to the overhead of the aft deck, bringing the tow chain alongside the gunwale. A block and tackle is then*

*lowered from the tender boom, which remains on the centerline position above and is attached to the chain with another carabiner—as far below the retrieval-line attachment as possible. A three-purchase block and tackle fitted with a cam cleat makes easy work of raising the fish clear of the water and stowing it in its transom-mounted brackets.*

Another variant of this retrieval method might be hooking the retrieval line well up the chain from

**Figure 8–14.** Paravane stabilizer (Integrity Machining)

**Figure 8–15.** Kasten's foil paravanes, fabricated from aluminium, may be twice as efficient as the older flat design shown previously. (Michael Kasten)

the fish (even near the surface), allowing the vertical stabilizer to do its thing without being disturbed. Retrieval when the fish has broken the water would be somewhat more difficult, but a blunt-tipped gaff hook could be used to grab the fish and control it while putting it in its mount. The winches would still do the heavy lifting (a large size paravane weighs 48 pounds). Regardless of the retrieval method, it seems prudent to keep the length of line for pulling the paravanes short enough so that it is impossible for the fish to hit the prop. This can be easily checked when the boat is out of the water and the paravane pole deployed.

On *Teka III*, we have a different retrieval method because we do not have the long boom with dual electric winches of the Nordhavns. We start the retrieval by lifting our poles about 60° above the water so that the paravane is about 4 feet under the water. Our poles are lifted by pole lift lines running down the mast to a hydraulic winch at deck level. Our retrieval design includes a line that is run to the chain and attached by a carabiner (much like the previous suggestion) at water level. It is loosely tethered to the boat during passages. After the pole is raised, Mary uses this line to pull the chain close to the boat where I grab it with an extra-long (12'), fixed-pole boat hook. I then walk forward on the deck bringing the fish at or near the surface. We use a dulled gaff hook about 3 feet long, with a shackle mounted in the top, to grab the fish. We have a *vang* (block and tackle) already mounted on the upper deck right above the paravane holders, which are mounted forward of the poles. Once the gaff is hooked, it's a simple matter to take in the tension and place the paravane in its holder. This retrieval method works well, but it is not possible with boats without a side deck.

**Paravanes in shallow water.** While we use the fixed mounting during long ocean crossings, we have developed a variable depth mounting for coastal cruising. One problem with fixed paravanes occurs when you have to cross a shallow bar directly from rough water. For example, we were finishing a passage from Providencia to Roatan in the Caribbean. We were running downwind in an 8–10' swell. We then had to turn a right angle to enter a shallow bar of about 10 feet of depth. Our

Figure 8–16. Retrieving a paravane. Mary swings the paravane in close, and I grab it with a dull gaff and then slip it in our side-mounted holders.

fixed paravane arrangement made this impossible, so we had to retrieve the fish in rough water—no fun at all and perhaps even dangerous.

After thought and discussions with others, we built a steel bracket that could be used to mount a winch and blocks for retrieval. We use a long braided line attached to a length of chain about 12 feet long. We can use the winch to adjust the depth of the paravane. When running in shallow water, we sometimes run the paravanes only 6 to 8 feet under the water. When we get back into deep water, we can let out some line and run them at whatever depth we want. This adjustable method also makes retrieval easier. We stop the boat and raise the poles to about 60° and then we just crank up the fish until they are above the water. We have our lines attached to the end of the chain, so we just pull the fish over to the boat where it is winched up and placed in the holder.

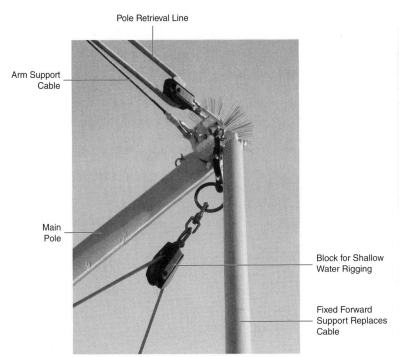

Pole Retrieval Line

Arm Support Cable

Main Pole

Block for Shallow Water Rigging

Fixed Forward Support Replaces Cable

**Figures 8–17A and 8–17B.** Left: End of pole details for adjustable flopperstopper. Top block is for pole retrieval. Cable is to fix the height of arms. Bottom block and line is for adjusting the paravane depth and for retrieval. The porcupine is for lightning dissipation. The other smaller block on edge that is almost hidden is for attaching our get–home sail halyard. The ring is attached to the pole end by a large bolt shackle. Right: A paravane holder on the side of the boat makes storage, launch, and retrieval relatively easy, but it presents an obstacle in close quarters, such as marinas and locks, and we have to remove the paravane from its holder.

## Problems with Paravanes

We have experienced few problems in our 50,000 plus miles of cruising with paravanes. Before we installed the variable depth rigging, we once dragged a paravane on the bottom. Luckily, it did not hit any obstruction—it just bumped along. Another time, we hit another boat's anchor chain while slowly maneuvering around an anchorage. It made quite a noise, but the fish just slid up on the chain and flipped over. While it got both boats' full attention, nothing was damaged. A boat off the coast of South America didn't have such good luck. It hit the anchor chain of an unlighted fishing boat at night going full cruising speed. The foreguy broke, and the main boom was bent in two.

The retrieval process discussed here can be very dangerous if attempted in rough seas. My recommendation is to heave to or anchor, and wait for the seas

to moderate before attempting to retrieve the fish in rough conditions. The swinging paravane in the movie *Perfect Storm* was strictly Hollywood fantasy, but paravanes can swing dangerously in rough conditions while out of the water.

Fouling paravanes is another threat. We "caught" a long line while cruising at full speed off Point Arena in northern California. We dragged the long line for maybe 200 feet before we stopped and studied how to remove it. I was afraid the line might foul the prop. I stationed one crewmember aft, with our long boathook to prevent any contact with the rudder and prop. Meanwhile, Mary and I raised the paravane as if we were going to retrieve it, but once it was at surface level, we dislodged the line with another boathook. It rapidly retreated to our stern after being released. Paravanes can foul on kelp or other floating debris as well. Most of the time, this does not create

**Figure 8–18.** Our shallow-water adjustment system for the paravane utilizes the winch, shown here on the port side, aft of the paravane pole, to bring in the paravane from the water or let it out to run deeper.

a problem, but if one hits a really large patch of kelp, the paravane will rise to the surface and skid along, creating drag but with no action to prevent rolling. These are rare experiences and are matched by getting lobster pots around the prop in Maine and small squid pots around the shaft in Tunisia.

Sources often note that it is dangerous to run with a single paravane in the water. We have not found this to be true. In fact, we routinely run with only one fish when on shorter hops just so we don't have to bother with pulling out two paravanes. We always put the upwind fish in the water. If it was really rough, and if you were running with the beam to the sea *and* you had the downwind paravane deployed, it could reduce stability by increasing the roll to the downwind side and possibly put the rail in the water. Whether running with a single fish in the water strains the mast and other structures is

debatable and probably depends on the strength of your rigging. Since the nature of paravanes is that only one side is loaded at a time, it seems to me stresses would not be significantly greater with only one paravane.

Research and experience shows that paravanes do reduce roll, pitch, and accelerations. One study by Akinturk, Cummings, and Bass found that both roll and pitch were reduced by about 50% (see Figure 8–5). Our experience has been that roll is much slower with paravanes deployed, and accelerations are minimized as well. They are relatively inexpensive to install and maintain compared with active fins. Reliability is excellent. However, more attention to deployment and retrieval is needed for this system—it is not nearly as easy as flipping a switch.

## Active Fin Stabilization Systems

Active fins have become the most popular stabilization method for many ocean cruisers. Fins stick below the hull like ailerons on the wings of an airplane and create forces that counter the rolling moments of the vessel. Most boats have two fins, one on each side of the boat. The fins act in unison to counter the roll. For example, a starboard roll will be counteracted by the fin moving to create lift on that side, while the fin on the port side will be pulling the vessel down on that side. The counterforce is controlled by gyros and computers to minimize roll. The fins are foils and depend on water moving relatively rapidly over their surface. As speed declines, they become less and less effective, and they have to work harder to accomplish their task. They are constantly moving to adjust to the wave forces. The lift force of fins is directly related to the square of the boat's speed. The power of the fins almost doubles from 6 to 8 knots and almost triples between 6 and 10 knots.

Fins are normally sized for the anticipated "service speed" of the vessel, typically S/L 1.15. This sizing may be good for a boat running at this speed, but consider that most ocean-crossing boats cut their speed to less than S/L 1.0 to economize on fuel and extend safe range. A fin designed for use at S/L 1.15 will not be as effective and will have to work harder, possibly causing more wear and tear and premature

Figure 8–19. Brian Rickard shows the relative size of a Naiad active fin on Dashew FPB 64. Dashew believes that the largest possible fin that fits should be installed to minimize movements needed to keep the boat from rolling. (Steve Dashew)

failure. Nordhavn 46, *Egret*, reported that on a long leg to South America, they were running so slow the fins were hitting their limits, and speed had to be increased. Perhaps fins for ocean-crossing vessels should routinely be oversized for an S/L of, say, 0.9.

One of the strongest advantages of fins is that they can be turned on with a simple switch—no complex launching or retrieval systems are needed. However, they do need to be used all the time when at sea, and they do create some drag and constant drain of engine power for the needed hydraulics.

Figures 8–20 and 8–21 show the complexity of active fin systems. Sensitive and fast data on roll velocity, angle, and acceleration are fed into a computer that translates them into signals that are passed to servos that provide direction

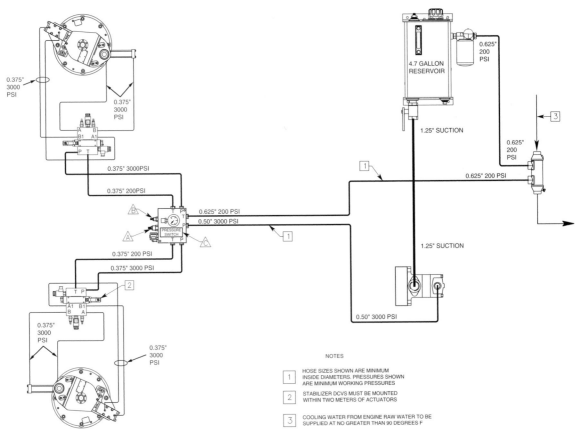

Figure 8–20. TRAC hydraulic diagram for simple active fin system. (Arcturus/TRAC)

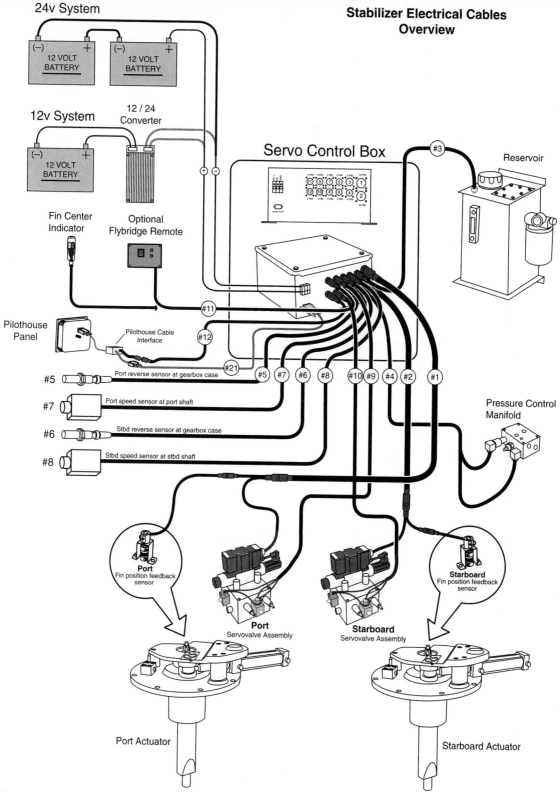

**Figure 8–21.** TRAC active fins' electrical and electronic connections. (Arcturus/TRAC)

to the fins via hydraulic systems. A complete hydraulic system with reservoir, cooling, heat exchangers, pumps, valves, and fin actuators is required. Fins move with lightning quickness—fractions of a second; some move through their entire arc of 45° in less than a second!

## Jim Leishman on Active Fin Systems

Jim's comments in the third edition are appropriate to include here:

> Robert Beebe certainly proved the value of the flopperstopper rig, not only on Passagemaker but on numerous other designs. My own experience has confirmed Beebe's conclusions, except that the F/S rig may actually work even better than he claimed when comparing it to active fin systems. I have had the opportunity to make repeated open-ocean passages on different Nordhavn 46s—identical boats except for the type of stabilizing gear selected—and encountered Force 8 conditions during two of these voyages. One vessel was equipped with Koopnautic active fins with 5-square-foot blades and the other with a flopperstopper rig using 300-square-inch Kolstrand fish on 18-foot poles. I must say that the flopperstopper rig out-performed the active fins not only in the roughest seas but in moderate conditions as well.
>
> An interesting observation of the active fin systems is their inability to deal with a "sneaker" sea or one that is completely out of rhythm with the rest. The sneaker can cause the vessel to lurch, oftentimes dislodging carelessly stowed gear or throwing a beverage can from a countertop. There's no way of anticipating the sneaker, but as soon as the gyro senses the roll, the fins are deflected and things are brought back on an even keel. On the other hand, the deployed flopperstoppers fight the sneaker the instant it hits and deeply dampen the disturbance. I've often been amazed at how rough it can be before things start falling off countertops when the flopperstoppers are in use.
>
> Criticizing the active fin system is not to say I wouldn't recommend it. To the contrary, fins are a better choice for a good many owners. The handling requirements of the flopperstopper rig should not be underestimated, with the effort required being somewhat comparable to dealing with sail aboard a sailing yacht. After thousands of miles in the Pacific and across the Atlantic with active fins, I think they work well, and I believe they are adequate for worldwide cruising.
>
> It is true that I've never had to run downwind during a severe gale with an active fin system, and it is under these conditions they may not perform well; however, my opinion differs slightly from Beebe's in that my experience with Salvation II (which now has over 30,000 miles under her keel) and her Koopnautic fins indicates that nothing more is needed. I do agree though that once active fins are selected, the only negative aspect of adding flopperstopper gear is the added cost. By contrast, if you can deal with the physical requirements of the flopperstopper gear, it would be a shame to add fins, as the added drag and vulnerability to damage will forever accompany the vessel.

## Problems with Active Fins

For a vessel that relies solely on active fins, a full set of spares and fluids is needed, and the knowledge and ability to fix things at sea is essential. Otherwise, you should rig paravanes or another backup method to cover the eventuality that the system *will* fail. (Thirty percent of the 18 boats participating in the Nordhavn Atlantic Rally 2004 experienced stabilizer problems.) What if you get in some rough water and the system goes down? This happened to the Nordhavn 40, *Uno Mas*, during the Atlantic Rally. They rolled severely and needed expert help to repair their fin system. However, if the boat has sufficient stability, survival should not be threatened; only discomfort would result.

While active fins are effective under normal conditions, they do have their weaknesses. With normal irregular beam seas, roll reduction may vary from 60 to 90 percent; however, Sellars and Martin reported in *Marine Technology* (see endnote) that they are much less effective in quartering seas and may run into difficulty in steep seas. *Kosmos*, a Nordhavn 43 with active fins and paravanes, experienced an uncomfortable ride on its passage from San Diego to the South Pacific. They experienced following seas on the quarter for much of their voyage. The ride improved considerably when paravanes were added. Unfortunately, they were worried about fuel on this extremely long passage, so they elected to suffer the motion rather than run out of fuel.

Steve D'Antonio, an expert on marine mechanical and electrical systems, points out in *PassageMaker Magazine* a rare, but particularly nasty potential problem (see endnote): most newer fin systems use an engine-driven hydraulic pump that uses a power takeoff directly from the engine or transmission. If the pump experiences a catastrophic failure caused by lack of hydraulic fluid—for instance, a large leak with loss of fluid—this could cause transmission damage or shut down the main engine. He suggests that all voyagers carry a plate and gasket designed to fit over the mounting hole once the defective pump is removed. This type of failure during the Atlantic Rally caused the Nordhavn 50, *Downtime*, to abort due to serious hydraulic leaks resulting in total failure of the fin stabilization system.

Another thing to consider with active fins is that they are exposed to encounters with rocks, sandbars, traps, nets, and so on. Almost every major accident involving an ocean powerboat has involved these types of problems. Cutters are usually installed forward of the fins to minimize impacts with kelp and light lines. Cape Horn combines dual bilge keels with active fins that provide considerable protection (see Chapter 13 for details of this boat).

Another issue with active fins is hull support. Most new designs include heavy backing blocks and numerous layers of fiberglass reinforcement. During normal operations, moving a multi-ton boat around in waves means that there are tremendous forces on fins, actuators, shafts, and mounting bolts. Aftermarket installations have to be carefully engineered to take these forces. In addition, the question arises about hitting some objects. Some fins are designed to break away without damaging the hull. Others may not give such protection.* Ideally, the stabilizer actuators would be located in small watertight compartments so that the boat would not sink in the event of a catastrophic collision. Building these compartments costs money and adds to an already very expensive boat; thus, most manufactures do not do so. In summary, perhaps the greatest disadvantage of active fins is their cost, both initial and for maintenance, and their relatively low reliability. A voyager on a budget would be prudent to select some of the less expensive methods of stabilization.

## Passive Antiroll Tanks

This concept of passive antiroll tanks (ARTs) has been around since the late 1950s and now dominates roll stabilization on larger fishing vessels. However, few voyaging powerboats have installed antiroll tanks, and many yacht designers specializing in motor yachts avoid suggesting this method of stabilization. This system works quite well, with estimated roll reduction at 54 to 69 percent, which makes them somewhat superior to paravanes. Antiroll tanks work by providing specially designed tanks on the boat that run from beam to beam with restricted flow from one side to the other. The idea is to design a tank so that the flow is 90 degrees out of phase with the roll, limiting the roll by keeping the liquid in the tank moving to minimize the roll. Designing the system requires detailed knowledge of the stability of the vessel and its roll period. The designer usually finds a place on the boat as high as possible, such as the top of the pilothouse, to locate the tank. This gives the maximum effect with the lowest amount of weight (1–2% of displacement). Tanks can be located lower on the boat at deck level or

**Figure 8–22.** *Windermere*, a Cape Horn 65, shown with bilge keels that protect the fins. (John Richards)

---

*The 42' Krogen, *Kinship*, went aground near Isla Contoy, off Mexico. Attempts at rescue resulted in the port stabilizer fin being torn off, and a 2-by-3 foot section of the hull was damaged. (See the endnote.)

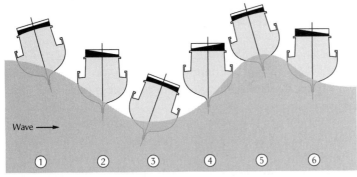

Wave ⟶

① ② ③ ④ ⑤ ⑥

**Figure 8–23.** This simplified diagram shows how the system works. The dark area above the pilothouse of the model shows the approximate position of the ART water as the boat rolls. Water flow is restricted by a series of baffles, as shown in Figure 8–27. Water in the tank does not simply rush from side to side. (Waves rarely occur in such a regular fashion, and boats are often not exactly on the beam. The true position will be determined by dampening as well.)

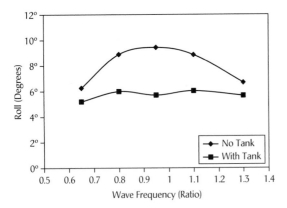

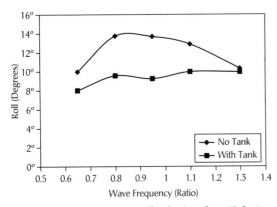

**Figures 8–24 and 8–25.** Top: Roll reductions for a 65-foot vessel in various moderate beam seas (from long ocean swells to short, wind-driven seas). The horizontal axis is the ratio of wave height to length of time between crests: an 8-foot wave with an 8-second period would be 1. Bottom: Roll reduction for a 65-foot vessel in steep beam seas. (Based on data from Dr. Don Bass, Memorial University, St. John's, Newfoundland)

below, but then they require a lot more water, hence more space and weight (up to 3.5% of displacement).

One of the strongest advantages of ART is that it works when the boat is standing still—at anchor or heaving to at sea. This is an advantage not shared by any other stabilization system except gyros. While some ARTs are retrofitted, the best time to include one is in the design phase so that it can be ideally located, and supporting structures can be sufficient to support the required weight. Tanks must be designed with a way to rapidly empty them in case the vessel lists to an unstable position and does not return from its roll. Otherwise, the water would go to the low side and threaten stability further by increasing the angle of heel. This event could be caused by an accident or major leak that allowed water into the hull. Free surface effects, discussed in the previous chapter, would exacerbate this problem.

### *Swan Song*'s Passive Antiroll Tank

When Dave Cooper and Nancy Terrell bought *Swan Song* in late 1998, they found that their "new" boat, a Roughwater 58 built in 1975 in Taiwan, had no stabilization whatsoever. Antiroll stabilization was absolutely essential because they planned to voyage to Hawaii in their renovated boat. Nancy described their process of solving this challenge:

**Figure 8–26.** *Swan Song*, a Roughwater 58, showing the antiroll tank over the pilothouse. (Nancy Terrell)

Dave's objective was to develop a design procedure for a passive tank for roll reduction in rough seas. Professor Don Bass, at the Marine Institute [of Memorial University] in St. John's, Newfoundland, had designed a tank for a friend, Bob Phillips, on Another Asylum. Dave contacted Dr. Bass, who required a lot of specific data about Swan Song. As we had no design drawings or information from the original naval architect, we had to provide the measurements. What a riot—with me aboard and Dave in our dinghy, Leda, we measured the hull, as well as the underwater hull, in one-foot vertical increments and five-foot horizontal increments. These data points, when input into Don's computer program, allowed the generation of an accurate 3-D wire-frame model of the hull surfaces. We then did a stability/inclination test with weights on the deck edge which gave us data points for SS's stability. Lastly, the roll rate and roll damping rate were determined and were also supplied, along with a nominal displacement waterline length and waterline beam.

Knowing that the tank is most effective if it is full beam of the boat, we selected a couple of possible locations for installation. Our first choice was on top of the pilot house because this would be out of the way. We gave Don the height off the water and the width available. Don's software then took all of this data and produced the dimensions of a tank in that location. We then modified these dimensions to make full use of commercially available building materials. Don, in turn, took those dimensions and modified the tank design to accommodate these materials.

Our choice of construction materials was based upon the need for a tank that is light in weight but structurally rigid and cost effective. Several composite materials were looked at that could be made into the size that was required and shipped to the BVI. Nida-Core in Stuart, Florida, won the bid. They manufactured 25mm sheets of Nida-Core bonded with 38 ounce fiberglass on both sides in 4 × 12 foot panels. This was used to fabricate the tank which, when measured, was 4′ × 12′ × 16″ high with six T-shaped baffles 18″ on either end of the tank. The empty weight of the tank is about 250 lbs.

SS's tank, as designed by Don, is filled with 1,550 lbs of sea water, which is about 6½″; this water

Figure 8–27. Swan Song's antiroll tank showing baffles needed to control water flow. (Nancy Terrell)

initially moves from a static position toward one side or the other as SS starts to roll. The baffles slow the water movement—as the boat reaches its limit on one roll it will start to roll back to the other side, like a sine wave. The water, however, is again held by the baffles, on what was the low side, so that as the roll continues it becomes the high side. (Reproduced courtesy of Nancy Terrell and All at Sea, see endnote.)

Dave has become a strong proponent of ART. He says, "Everyone is astounded by how Swan Song behaves in the water." One experienced cruiser who was aboard as a guest at anchor said he thought they were aground because the boat just wasn't rolling like all the others. Don notes that performance at sea is great, too, with most rolls being limited to 5° with an occasional 10°. The most severe roll of about 30° was caused by a breaker hitting them broadside when they were 10 hours out of Hawaii.

Once the tanks have been properly designed and the stability of the boat assured, there are few downsides to ART. As mentioned earlier, the tanks need to empty fast if the boat is listing due to damage or some other cause. In addition, other situations might warrant dumping the tank, including (1) large, steep, breaking waves on the beam; (2) water on the deck from boarding seas that is slow to clear; and (3) significant icing. Swan Song has two 4-inch diameter drains on each side to accomplish this emergency procedure.

If your boat meets the space and stability requirements for ART, it seems to be one of the cheapest, easiest, and most effective ways to tame rolling. ART is often combined with fin or bilge keels, to be discussed later. The combination of ART and paravanes would also be great. Both systems are passive and require minimum maintenance. Paravanes could be an effective backup if tank water had to be dumped.

## Bilge Keels and Fin Keels

Bilge or fin keels are not popular with most builders and designers, but there are exceptions. Yacht designer Michael Kasten notes that twin bilge keels were developed and researched for 45 years by the late Lord Riverdale. (Kasten discusses this strategy and others in an article cited in the endnotes.) Lord Riverdale's designs were mostly for sailboats and used only two keels. Powerboats normally need a center keel to protect the propeller and rudder. A three-keel design seems most appropriate.

Another yacht designer, Patrick Bray, has designed and tested a number of twin-keel boats (see the endnote). He claims twin keels have a number of advantages:

+ Reduce stern wave by capturing the wave with the keel.
+ Dampen both pitch and roll.
+ Improve directional stability.
+ Righting moment and range of stability is at least as good, if not better.
+ Enable the boat to withstand grounding without damage.
+ Allow drying out to accomplish repairs and cleaning.

According to researcher John Martin, bilge keels result in significant roll reduction in resonant waves. One study reported in *Marine Technology* found a reduction in roll from approximately 23 to 15 degrees in 10-foot seas and a reduction from 18 to 13 degrees in 7-foot seas. The key to effectiveness is the location, depth, and length of the keels. Tank tests seem to be the most economical way to verify performance. If the keels are located in the wrong position, they can cause problems in steering or increased drag. The keels never run the full length of the waterline.

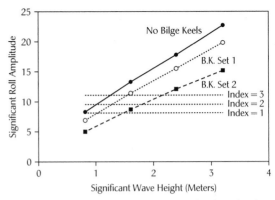

Figure 8–28. Comparative rolling of a vessel with and without bilge keels in irregular waves.

## How Well Do Fin and Bilge Keels Work in the Real World?

Since bilge keels are not common on passagemaking vessels, we do not have many anecdotal illustrations about their effectiveness. A notable exception is the new boat, *Passage of Time*, a 53' aluminum vessel designed by Michael Kasten and owned by Alan and Deborah Wagner. The boat has both twin fin keels and paravanes (see Figure 8–29). Alan's report on the effectiveness of his new keels follows.

*On the bilge keels . . . . on the way from Halifax to Boston we had about 30 hours of waves directly on the beam. Brian—the builder, who was aboard— could not believe the added stability of the keels. He always poked a little fun at the "wings" as he called them and really was more in favor of active stabilizers (that I wanted to stay away from because of reliability/complexity issues). I think the trip from Nova Scotia made him a believer. On that trip we had seas of probably 5–6 feet at times, directly on the beam—so nothing too terrible. The boat never rolled much at all, certainly nothing that even required me to "hold on" or grab for a handhold when walking.*

*The trip from Boston to Sandwich was the day that the first winter storm (without the snow) was coming up the coast. We were mostly in head-on waves of 8–10 feet, and the boat just kind of plowed right through it. As we approached Sandwich, perhaps for the last hour or so, we had some quartering*

**Figure 8–29.** The 53' Kasten-designed *Passsage of Time*, showing the fin keels (not active fins; the fins are fixed)—paravanes are yet to be added. (Alan Wagner)

**Figure 8–30.** Willard 40, *Veronica*, showing her "roll chocks." (Bob Salmons)

waves, but the boat did not roll much at all. I didn't even think to put the paravanes in the water. The next day we rode out the storm in the marina, which was nice because it was nestled down between the high banks of the Cape Cod Canal. The following day we went from Sandwich to Newport, RI. As we got south of Cape Cod, and particularly closer to Newport, we had big ocean rollers on the beam that were probably again in the 8–10 foot range. Those were fun to be in; the boat did not roll at all, but just rode up the side of the roller and down the other.

**Retrofitting a Willard 40.** There is also the experience of Bob Salmons, owner of *Veronica*, a Willard 40, a full displacement boat with a rounded bottom that is prone to serious rolling. He described his experience with adding bilge keels, or "roll chocks," as follows:

We discovered her rolling abilities early on. In a beam sea of 2 or 3 feet, she would set up a roll which got worse with every wave [synchronous rolling]. Other than holding on, it didn't bother me, but the same cannot be said of my wife and dog. I seriously considered renaming the dog "Major Chunks," but my spouse put an end to that.

In St. Charles, Virginia, I met a waterman admiring *Veronica's* lines. We got to talking boats. He allowed as she "looks to roll a mite" and I allowed she did. He suggested I stick on a pair of "roll chocks." I asked him: "what's a roll chock?" And the rest is history. "Any boatyard round here'll do it for you," he said. So I came out early in the spring to recommission and supervise the installation of roll chocks. Do they work? We took a shakedown cruise, accompanied by Goody, the yard owner, in his (shudder) Bayliner. At anchor in Onancock (that's the name of the place, really) the Willard rolled less than the Bayliner.

A couple of days later, heading for Annapolis, we got "waked" by a sportfisherman. Seriously waked. I couldn't turn to take it bow-on due to traffic, so we took a 5 ft. wake beam on. It was a total non-event. Didn't wake the dog. A couple of gentle rolls, each weaker than the last, and that was it. I said to myself, "Goody, you're an 'effing' genius."

To say the roll chocks are a success is an understatement. It is the best change I have made in the boat. 40 knots of wind on the beam, no problem. It's not as nice as balmy zephyers, but it is doable and not hazardous. No discernable change in fuel burn, turning radius, or running angle.

## Evaluating Bilge and Fin Keels

When properly designed, bilge keels can help prevent rolling, increase hull dampening, and improve dynamic stability in a seaway. They are relatively inexpensive to install and require little maintenance. They are often specified on commercial boats and small ships, and should probably be more commonly installed on passagemakers. Adverse effects can occur when the keels are not properly designed.

Steering and cavitation problems, plus increased drag, can result. However, it is usually relatively easy to modify or remove these extra keels, so the risk is lower than with most other stabilization systems. A combination of bilge keels and either antiroll tanks or paravanes seems logical and could achieve a high degree of roll reduction with high reliability and low cost.

## Sails for Reducing Roll

**Beebe's experience with steadying sails:** "Sails do a fair job when the wind is right and can even function in a dead calm when cut flat and strapped down hard amidships. But unless the rig is quite large, its effect will not match flopperstoppers. Because we had both on *Passagemaker*, we could make the comparison. The practical result was that we never used sails for steadying; the F/S gear was so much better. If there was a strong beam wind, we would use the sails to steady the roll to windward and a single flopperstopper on the windward side to steady the opposite roll. This produced good results and a slight increase in speed."

**Buehler's support for sail.** Yacht designer and author George Buehler says that steadying sails are his favorite way of reducing rolling. His idea is that sails do not slow the boat down; they may actually add some speed to motor sailing. They are also useful for getting home if your engine fails, and for anchoring or drifting at sea because an aft sail keeps the bow into the wind. He cites a "comfortable trip" down the California coast in 11-foot seas with nothing but sails for stabilization. Some of his Diesel Ducks are outfitted with sails for steadying, power assist, and come-home capability.

### Evaluating Sails for Roll Reduction

Under the right conditions, sails can help reduce roll on motorboats, much as they do on sailboats. However, when there is little or no wind or it is in the wrong direction, sails will not prevent rolling. On our last trip across the Atlantic from the Canaries to Antigua, sailing friends were desperately hoping for wind, not only to propel them but also to prevent the uncomfortable rock and roll from being becalmed. We were delighted with the light winds, even when we had 10-foot swells rolling in from the north. Our paravanes did their job.

Michael Kasten likes a sail rig, but calculates that the boat needs 1,667 square feet of sail to equal the force of 300 square-inch paravanes—an unlikely event unless designed as a true motorsailer. As we will discuss in Chapter 9 on choosing a boat, there are some other benefits of sail rigs: they can add power rather than consume it, they are great for mid-ocean get-home capability, and they are fun.

In addition, installing an effective sailing rig and outfitting it with sails, lines, blocks, winches, and so on is expensive. Additional ballast may be needed to offset the sail's forces. Masts must be installed and maintained, and they will consume space below decks. Scarce storage space will have to be devoted to storing the extra sails and equipment needed for extensive use of sails. Sailing skills and experience are also a must if the boat is to carry a significant area of sail. Storms and squalls may require reefing or removing the sails, negating their

Figure 8–31. *Peking,* a Diesel Duck 462, owned by John and Jerie Milici, with sails and paravanes deployed in the Caribbean. (Kaija Leno on *Kaija Song*)

roll-preventing power. The heel of the hull on a beam run may not be as comfortable as the gentler roll using other systems.

In conclusion, it seems that sails are not as satisfactory as other methods for roll stabilization, although some sailing capability can be very useful to prevent anchor sailing and to provide emergency get-home capability.

## Gyro Stabilization

The newest stabilization system uses gyros with fast-spinning heavyweight flywheels that exert righting forces on the boat to keep it from rolling. The system is costly, heavy (about 1,000 pounds), and requires considerable electricity to run. Seakeeper Gyros is the leader in this field, although other manufacturers also offer gyro systems. Its model 7000 gyro spins at 10,000 rpm. It demands 3,000 watts AC (190–230 volts *single phase*) for start-up and 1,500–2,000 watts operating power, depending on sea conditions. This electrical demand means serious AC generating power and may require modifications to the current system to get the specified voltage. The gyro is almost 39 inches wide by 31 inches long, meaning that it will take up quite a bit of space wherever it is mounted. Placement problems may make adding it to an existing boat more challenging; however, with new construction the space could be designed into the boat

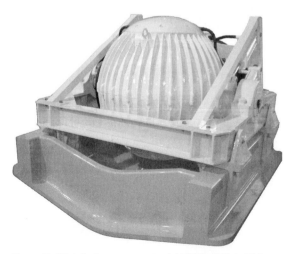

**Figure 8–32.** A Seakeeper gyro model 7000: width is 38.7 inches; it weighs about 1,000 pounds. (Seakeeper)

in the early stages. The gyro requires water cooling and a pump.

The effectiveness of gyros on ocean-crossing powerboats has yet to be tested. Most of the installations have been on large, planing, sportfishing boats or charter yachts where comfort is critical to success. The gyro system is most effective at slower speeds or stopping at sea to fight a fish. It also works great at anchor, although a source of constant electricity is needed. According to the manufacturer, the downside of gyros is that they cannot correct sustained heeling situations or instability that happens when the boat is running down sea.

We don't know much about the effectiveness of gyro systems for voyaging displacement yachts, but what we do know is that the system is expensive, power hungry, and space consuming. It requires another seawater cooling system. The maintenance and repair requirements are unknown; however, for a mechanical device spinning at such high rpm, it seems likely that regular maintenance would be required. Another gyro manufacturer, based in Australia, cautions that its gyro should not be used in big seas because overstressed gyros can "bang" excessively against their stops and cause major damage to the gyro structure. This directive seems incompatible with our voyaging powerboats unless we want stabilization primarily at anchor. (For a more detailed report on gyros, see Steve D'Antonio's article cited in the endnotes.)

## Stopping Roll at Anchor

Much of the time at anchor, we are in a quiet cove or bay with little opportunity for waves, but this is not always the case. Sometimes you are forced to anchor in exposed positions where the sea swell intrudes. Also, some anchorages have ferries or other vessels that seem to take aim at yachts and create horrendous waves. Thus, rolling at anchor can be very uncomfortable and may create resonant roll that goes on for a seemingly endless period of time. If you have an antiroll tank, it will eliminate anchor roll. Bilge keels are also somewhat effective. Gyro stabilization will eliminate the roll, but unless you are running your generator 24/7, it is not practical to keep the gyro running. Other methods to reduce roll include paravanes and true flopperstoppers.

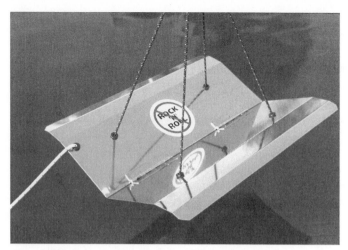

**Figure 8–33.** The Magma "Rock 'n Roll" anchoring stabilizer. (Magma Products)

**Figure 8–34.** Anchor stabilizers deployed on Dashew's *Windhorse*. (Steve Dashew)

**Using paravanes to reduce anchor rolling.** We use our paravanes to reduce rolling while at anchor with the normal fish attached. We find that leaving the fish loose at the end of the pole does not work too well—it tries to swim around erratically. This doesn't hurt anything, but it reduces effectiveness. We use our retrieval line fastened to the chain at the waterline to pull the chain closer to the boat. We then secure it to a cleat, giving the fish little room to move around. Why don't we use stabilizers that are designed to work at anchor? It is simply too much trouble to pull in the fish, remove the shackles, and replace the fish with an anchor stabilizer. We would then have to do it all over again when we leave the anchorage.

**Using specially designed flopper-stoppers to reduce anchor roll.** For those boats that do not use paravane stabilization underway and that need roll stabilization at anchor, there are several models of anchor stabilizers available commercially. The primary drawback here is that you need a long pole, say 15–20 feet minimum, on each side to get maximum roll dampening. The rigging does not need to be as strong as normal paravane systems, but it still takes some engineering to make and install properly. The stabilizers may cause quite a jerk when they open for resistance. Some type of shock cord at the attachment point reduces the shock.

# CHAPTER NINE

# Choosing a Boat

I recently attended a presentation at the Cruising Club of America by a couple who sailed a 36-foot sailboat around the world via the Cape of Good Hope over an eight-year period. They had a wonderful experience and were still enthusiastic several years after the trip's conclusion. What I found really interesting was they had no refrigeration whatsoever, no watermaker, no air conditioning, no microwave, no washer or dryer, no TV, no outboard for the dingy—in other words, nothing that we modern cruisers think is essential. Thus, one of the things to consider when choosing a boat, its machinery, its accessories, and its electronics is how each contributes to your voyage's enjoyment. The sailing couple said they became used to a lack of refrigeration. They learned how to store things without cooling, they made choices based on shelf life, and they canned meat when it was available for future use. Maybe this austere approach is too much for most of us, but it does mean a simpler life with more time to enjoy the voyage rather than worrying about fixing this or that equipment.

We have met hundreds of voyagers under sail over the years. Very few had all the conveniences we power voyagers consider essential. And yet they all seemed to be enjoying themselves.

On *Teka III* we had many of the "necessities," including an effective refrigerator and freezer. However, we did not have central air conditioning. We used fans to move the air around and found only two or three nights when sleeping was uncomfortable because of the heat. We did install a small room air conditioner in the pilothouse that came in handy a number of times when we were heading west in

the tropics. We run it off the inverter due to its low power drain. If you decide to centrally air condition your boat, it will affect many of the systems. You need constant power. For many boats, that means running the generator 24/7, consuming considerable fuel and adding to maintenance. Often, it means the boat is designed to keep the air out; thus, with the AC off, it is miserable. Will the AC fail? Of course. It is certainly possible that you will want a backup generator to make sure you always have a spare if your main generator goes out of service. You must be willing to endure noise during the nights in quiet anchorages. Fellow cruisers may become angry at the noise

**Figure 9–1.** *Seascape*, an Albin 36, was shipped from Los Angeles to Rotterdam, cruised the French canals, and then crossed the Mediterranean from Spain to Turkey. The owners, John and Joan Brair, lived aboard full-time for eight years.

**Figure 9–2.** Washing day in paradise. Many cruisers do not have washing machines; a bucket works. (cruisingunderpower. fastmail.net)

pollution. Your fuel capacity will have to be increased to handle the generator's fuel—on a 15-day passage, that means somewhere around 300 additional gallons just for electricity. You need a bit of reserve fuel

because refills are not always located where you are, so you may want at least 500 gallons extra to make sure you don't run out of AC fuel. Of course, you may say that cool air is one of your top priorities. If so, you just have to consider the design changes that may be needed to support this need.

## The Spiral Model of Boat Choice

Some yacht designers use a system called the Design Spiral to optimize the process of designing a boat. The model evolved from a software development tool proposed by Boehm that was then adapted to boat design by Stephen Hollister (see endnotes). I have modified the model as shown in Figure 9–3 so that we can use it for boat choice as well as design. The idea is to decide what you want in your boat: What is its function? Which attributes are important? How important is each attribute? Which designs are feasible? What trade-offs

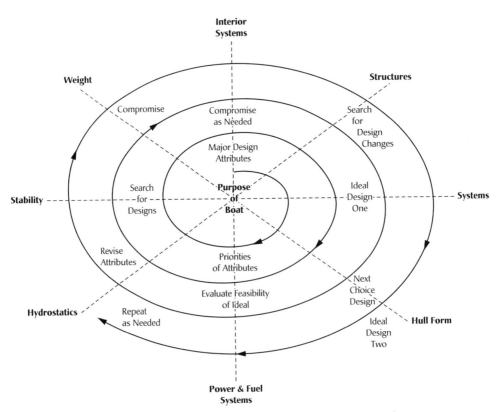

**Figure 9–3.** The Design Spiral of Boat Choice helps determine which boat fits your needs.

or compromises are needed? Revise attributes as necessary and repeat.

**The purpose of the boat.** This begins the whole process. Consider these examples of purpose:

1. A voyaging powerboat capable of crossing any major ocean passage of the world, for use by a full-time cruising couple who are retired or have large blocks of cruising time.

2. A coastal cruising powerboat capable of making limited ocean passages to such areas as the Bahamas or Caribbean, to be used during the winter months by a retired couple.

3. A voyaging powerboat capable of minimal ocean crossings of 2,500 miles, to be operated by a retired couple of limited means who also plan to live aboard.

4. A powerboat for limited coastal cruising to destinations like southeast Alaska for a full-time, live-aboard couple who have limited cruising time.

**Major design attributes.** The second step is to develop a set of design attributes, ranked in order of priority. These attributes will be related to the purpose determined at the beginning of the spiral. Here are some examples, rating in a hypothetical priority order for Purpose 1, shown previously:

- Range: minimum 6,000 nautical miles at 8 knots
- Easily handled by a two-person crew
- Extremely seaworthy; able to survive severe storm conditions
- Stabilized with reliable antiroll system
- Large owner's stateroom with private head
- Large separate pilothouse
- Flying bridge
- Air conditioning
- All-electric galley
- Beautiful finish inside and out

A different set of attributes is seen for Purpose 3, shown previously:

- Cost of purchase less than $200,000
- Low cost of operation, maintenance, and moorage
- Easy to handle for older retired couple
- Reliable stabilization against roll

- Stand-up engine room with easy access
- Side decks for ease of docking
- Washer/dryer
- Center queen bed with private head in owner's cabin
- Minimum steps to climb
- Easy on/off the boat

**Weighing the importance of attributes.** After you define your purpose and develop a priority list of attributes, it is time to evaluate each more carefully. One way is to assign a weight for the importance of each, such as a 1–10 scale or 1–100 scale. Quantifying the importance of each attribute is a help in determining which ones you can give up, if needed. For example, if your absolute limit in purchase price is $200,000 because that is all your savings and you have limited cash flow, then it will probably be rated 10. On the other hand, the earlier set of attributes did not even consider costs—these boaters are probably pretty well off and consider cost down the list in terms of importance. However, these people want to be able to travel anywhere in comfort, so they would rate range very important, say 9.

While yacht designers may use computer programs to quantify these and additional factors affecting your boat choice, you can do your own analysis using this simplified technique. The Design Spiral of Boat Choice can be used whether you are building a new boat or buying an existing one. It should also be completed by both parties if a couple is buying the boat. It can help resolve conflicts about desirable attributes that may vary by person or gender.

## Choosing What Is Important

Everyone wants something a little different in their boat. In the next few sections, we will briefly discuss some attributes that may be important to some and irrelevant for others. Thinking through some of these issues may help you make a better decision. It will also show that compromises and trade-offs are integral parts of choosing a boat. There is probably no ideal boat; they all have their pluses and minuses.

**What are your cruising plans?** Do you plan to circumnavigate? If so, you will need a quite different

# Designing the *Boojum* 25: A Matter of Choices

## Michael Kasten

When I met them, the owners of *Boojum* were already quite accomplished ocean voyagers. Prior to commissioning the design of *Boojum*, both of them had sailed *solo* but more or less in *tandem*, i.e., each in their own boats, across the Pacific from Seattle to Auckland. TC Vollum made this trip in her 20' Flicka sailboat, and Charles Vollum sailed in his own 24' Pacific Seacraft. They arranged several rendezvous at each port along the way, but for the most part did not sail together, therefore accomplishing their voyages entirely solo.

Having already done this kind of thing under sail, TC decided that she wanted to be the first woman to circumnavigate under power, to do it *solo*, and to do so in the smallest boat that could make the trip in safety. If anyone could do it, certainly TC would be the one.

With this in mind, Charles and TC came to me with their request, and we got started. Besides the usual seaworthiness and seakindliness requirements, there was TC's mandate, "It's got to be cute!"

We started quite small at 20 feet; then, in order to gain accommodation space, we went to 22 feet. Finally, in order to achieve a private head compartment the design was increased to a whopping 25 feet, at which size TC put on the brakes and said, "No bigger." Her experience sailing the 20-foot *Tikaroa* across the Pacific had taught her that bigger is not necessarily better.

Since *Boojum* would be a true all-ocean passagemaker, sufficient fuel was required for at least a 3,000 NM leg before refueling. Another requirement introduced early was that the vessel be trailer able, and therefore limited to a maximum of 8 feet of beam, fewer than 15,000 pounds, and not over 12.5 feet from keel bottom to pilothouse top for the sake of the usual 14-foot highway bridge clearance while on a trailer. Further, Charles required standing headroom in the pilothouse. Because he stood a full 6'6" tall, accommodating Charles' height was no small feat.

Hmmm . . . you say? Conflicting requirements . . . you ask? Well, yes—but those were not to be the last of such disparate requests. Also required was that the vessel sit on the hard at low tide upright. Thus we introduced twin keels—actually becoming a tri-keel arrangement if you include the skeg/rudder combination aft. Roll attenuation was given a high priority; therefore, a paravane rig was added. A "get-home" strategy was needed, so sails were added. And finally, since Charles is a wizard with technology, the equipment and systems eventually became rather elaborate for such a small vessel.

The upshot of all this is that as we added features and equipment, we also added displacement; and with added displacement came added fuel, and so on. We did squeak under the maximum desired trailering weight, but just by a nose.

As it has turned out, *Boojum* is really quite a remarkable little yacht. I use the word *yacht* intentionally because this is a vessel that lacks nothing, despite her diminutive size. It is amazing what we fit into that boat—including a queen size double berth aft, plus a full size settee for dining that can sleep another two adults forward.

We did many other things, including:

- Provision of fuel for 3,000 NM
- A positive stability range of 180 degrees (in other words, fully self-righting)
- Twin keels so *Boojum* could sit upright while ashore or aground or on a trailer
- Foil-shaped paravanes for low drag
- A fold-down ladder on each side that is hinged coaxially with the paravane poles so the ladder can be deployed separately when *Boojum* is on the hard or for swimming while afloat
- A sliding water-tight pilothouse door that can be pulled tight into the house side via an eccentric to achieve a true WT seal
- A foldup anchor davit so that the forward tug fender can be used for pushing a barge or another boat
- A fold-down mast for which I designed stainless quick-release turnbuckles
- A reclining pilot's chair complete with extendable footrest
- Forced air heat throughout

Figure 9–4. *Boojum* underway with paravanes deployed. (Steve Vollum)

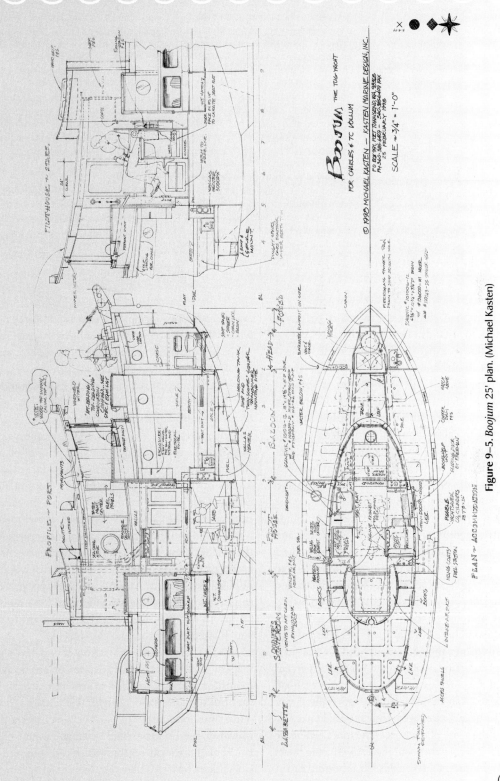

**Figure 9–5.** *Boojum 25' plan.* (Michael Kasten)

*(continued)*

- A watermaker
- Hot and cold running water
- A fuel-polishing system and an oil change system
- A controllable pitch propeller system
- Side scan and forward-looking phased array sonar
- Autopilot and VHF
- Fish-finder, radar, SSB, and iPod-integrated stereo
- Windshield wiper—and the list goes on

Basically all the equipment a gadget freak could ever wish for was put aboard, with a few extras thrown in for good measure. It might be simpler to describe what we left out.

Needless to say, *Boojum* is a heavy little beast for her length. Underway, Charles reports that her motion is very easy without the paravanes. With the paravanes deployed, roll amplitude is negligible. Heavy displacement is a big advantage here, in particular for such a small vessel. Steering and tracking are also reported to be excellent with NACA 0012 series foil shapes used for the rudder, bilge keels, and centerline keel. The accommodation space is perfect for two and quite spacious for one–very much as intended. As for being cute, you judge.

About the planned circumnavigation—not long after construction was started, Charles and TC invited me out to dinner one night where they announced that they would need a much bigger boat. The reason was that their family size would soon increase. Now they have two extraordinary kids, JJ and Tommy. Raising and home-schooling their children has become their entire focus, and all notions of solo sailing on the briny deep have faded well into the background.

Since then, *Boojum* has traveled around New Zealand, where she was built, and then extensively throughout the Pacific Northwest, including the coast of Canada. There is always the inevitable chatter about plunking her on the deck of a cargo vessel where she would then be off to Scandinavia, Ireland, or the canals of France.

Meanwhile, I have designed several larger boats for Charles, up to and including one 60 feet in size. TC, however, has remained true to her original notion: "Bigger is not always better."

kind of boat than someone who wants to cruise the Caribbean islands. For long-distance voyaging, seakindliness, range, fixable and simple systems are most desirable. For coastal or Caribbean cruising, seakindliness may still be important to you, but range and easy maintenance may be less important. There are also people who want a sturdy boat, but are voyaging in calm waters like the inside passage to Southeast Alaska or the great loop via the Intracoastal Waterway and canals. Almost any comfortable size and design boat can fit the bill for inland work. If your primary cruising grounds include the Bahamas, a shallower draft boat is desirable. Some spend extravagantly for a passagemaking yacht and seldom leave the dock. Their dream is vast; their actions are constrained. It is critically important to get some voyaging experience before purchasing a boat. Your priorities could change with experience.

**What are the financial considerations?** First, there is the purchase price of the boat. Then add all the improvements and equipment needed to fit your cruising plans. This latter amount can run 25 percent or more of the purchase price for a new or used boat. Insurance fees can be considerable, especially if you are world cruising. They are normally based on a percentage of the value of the boat—the more expensive the boat, the higher the insurance. All cruising boats will need periodic maintenance, such as bottom cleaning and painting, engine oil changes, and mechanical adjustments. When we were younger, we used to do all the bottom painting ourselves. Now we hire someone. I still change the oil and service the engines, thus cutting the costs considerably—and I know it is done right! Taxes can add quite a bit to the cost. Many states have sales tax on boats amounting to around 10%.

Surprisingly, fuel has been a less significant portion of total costs, although with the price of oil continuing to rise, it will become more of a factor in the future. If you are on a budget, fuel can become more critical. Let's say you are doing a 3,000 nautical mile passage from the Canaries to Antigua. If fuel costs $5 a gallon and your boat gets 3 nautical miles per gallon, the cost of this passage is $5,000. If your fuel economy is only 1.5 miles per gallon, however, the cost would be double—$10,000. In Appendix C I have put together some data on actual fuel consumption for a number of various boats. If these costs are important to you, you might examine the data closely.

Many costs are tied to location. If you have a permanent slip, you pay monthly fees of $10.00 foot/month or more. If you like to stay in marinas, fees vary, but some are $2 foot/night. If you like to anchor out, as we do in *Teka III*, you can save a great deal. However, there will be times when you want to store your boat for the off-season, which can come at considerable expense. Other fees include check-in and

-out fees for various countries, health care, food, and alcohol. Overall, we found that food costs remained pretty similar to the USA wherever we went, although there were many variations in individual item prices, such as wine (which we love).

Resale value of your boat may be an important consideration, especially if you are planning on relatively short ownership. You may be able to minimize the depreciation by buying a used boat of a desirable make. You will probably recover more of your investment, but don't expect miracles. Few break even on the exchange.

**What size boat?** Many of the cost factors mentioned are related to size, so this could be an important factor to some. From a practical standpoint a boat between 40 and 55 feet may be ideal for balancing size/cost relationships. As boats get larger, it is more difficult to find marinas where they will fit—much advance planning is needed. Our boat at 52 feet can barely fit into a 50-foot slip, the largest common slip in North American marinas. Anchorages may also be tight for a bigger boat, thus restricting where you can seek refuge. When you start getting into megayacht marinas, fees go up exponentially. For this book, I generally use a maximum of 65 feet (20 meters). Above this size, most boats get heavier and harder to handle for a cruising couple. Maintenance is more complex and demanding, not to mention cleaning and detailing the boat. You are getting to the size where a full-time captain or crew may be needed. In addition, some ports will require a pilot. You may also be forced to follow the shipping lanes, unlike smaller vessels.

Size is also related to seakindliness (see Chapter 7). The longer length usually means less pitching and slower accelerations from motion, thus less seasickness. Rolling can be gentler as well. Longer waterline length means somewhat more speed, although the increase is not substantial. Since it may take more power to drive the heavier hull, however, fuel consumption can increase.

**Stock or custom boat?** For resale, it is hard to beat a stock boat, even if it has been partially customized. However, if you plan to keep the boat for a long time, say 10 years, a custom boat offers more choices for design. For example, Beebe often designed what he called "canal runners," or boats that could cross

oceans and then cruise the canals of Europe. These boats, as far as I know, were all custom designed and built because of their specialized draft and height requirements.

Building a custom boat takes a lot of time and energy, but it is a way to get what you want. Any trade-off decisions or compromises are made by you, not the builder or previous owner. You are more likely to be satisfied *if* you know what you want. For example, a couple building a custom boat decided that a covered aft deck was absolutely essential. They had one on their previous boat and found the layout immensely enjoyable. In addition, they wanted air conditioning in the owner's cabin at night without a generator running, so they designed an oversize battery bank (1,700 amp hours) to provide power through an inverter. These are attributes that would be difficult to satisfy with a stock boat.

## New versus Used Boat?

**New boats.** One of the biggest advantages is that you get to choose equipment, layout, engines, accessories, anchors, etc. This is also a disadvantage because it takes time, money, and energy to make the selections and ensure that all the installations are correct. The owners of Nordhavn 52, *Dirona*, found that they needed to add 25% of the base price for factory options and another 30% for postdelivery items, so the final price was more like 150% of the base price.

**Figure 9–6.** *Dirona*, Nordhavn 52, owned by Jennifer and James Hamilton, anchored in Nisqually Flats, South Puget Sound, with Olympic Mountains in the background. (James and Jennifer Hamilton)

# The Commissioning Process: A Survival Guide

## John Torelli

When our Nordhavn trawler sales representative Jeff Merrill told my wife Maria and me that the commissioning process for our new boat would take approximately four to six weeks after the boat arrived from the yard in China, I was already stressed from the eight-month build cycle. It had taken us four years of research and some creative financing to reach the point of ordering our dream boat, and we were not excited about this news. I kept asking myself what could possibly take four to six weeks to complete on a brand-new boat that was checked out prior to leaving the yard? The simple answer is, a lot.

After now surviving two new Nordhavn trawler commissionings, I can honestly say that with a little preplanning, establishing realistic expectations, and implementing a few other secrets we discovered along the way, the process doesn't have to be a long, drawn-out nightmare! As we start planning for our third trawler purchase and its required commissioning process, we thought it would be wise to dust off our "precommissioning checklist" that has served so well in the past to help us set realistic expectations. While not foolproof by any means, these simple steps have allowed us to save time, save money, and keep our stress levels as low as possible.

**1. Establish Realistic Schedule Expectations.** If the dealer or builder estimates your commissioning process to take six or eight weeks, realize that this is just an estimate. Today's boats, with their complex systems, take time to check out and troubleshoot problems. Remember, the whole intent behind the commissioning process is to run all systems through their paces and look for potential trouble before you head off on your own. If there are issues with the boat, this is the time you want them discovered and addressed. Whether it is a fluid leak that requires a simple bolt tightening or a partial system removal and replacement that may take days, now's the time to fix it. The crew is working to an estimate, so try not to make serious or costly schedule commitments around the completion date. Most builders will provide you with a grace period after commissioning where there is no charge for leaving the boat docked at their facility. Use this window to firm up plans to fly in family or crew to join you on board. If you are hiring a captain to help with training or delivery, negotiate a schedule window for his services. I remember one couple who hired a captain to provide them with training and delivery of their new boat, but they were stuck paying his daily rate while the boat sat tied to the dock waiting to finish the commissioning process. No one aboard was happy, and the couple ended up spending thousands of dollars for a captain they could not use.

**2. Don't Add.** This may sound funny, but there is a lot of merit to this statement. Adding items during commissioning is costly and timely. Most builders will charge you an hourly rate for anything added during the process and, believe me, it is not inexpensive. I honestly think they inflate the rate to discourage people from making changes or adding items. Understand everything you want when you order the boat and have as much of it installed at the factory as possible. If you are going to add items, possibly with a subcontractor, you may want to schedule that after you have taken delivery of the boat and during that small window when the builder allows free dockage. We found that having all our interior work performed after the commissioning process worked well. The designer had access to make measurements during commissioning and then went off to make the carpets and window covers, requiring only a day for installation. When he was done, no one else came aboard to dirty things up.

**3. Understand the Process.** Obtain a copy of the commissioning checklist and proposed schedule (if you can) and then conduct weekly follow-ups with the supervisor. If you stay out of their way and let them do their job, things will go smoothly. We found that making an initial visit when the boat arrives to meet with our sales representative and commissioning supervisor allows us the chance to perform a walkthrough and discuss the commissioning plan. We then limit visits to once a week, usually on a weekend when the crew is not working on the boat. We take notes and e-mail them to our sales representative to forward to the commissioning crew.

**4. Training.** As with any new boat, there will be a shakedown cruise and time training on board. Again, this needs to be planned after commissioning so you know everything on the boat has been formally checked out. We had a scary experience on our first boat when our sales representative cleared the way for us to conduct an afternoon of training during the last week of commissioning. After a few hours of close-quarters maneuvering, the gear shifter was losing its responsiveness and we headed back to the slip. Just as we entered the busy harbor, the transmission became stuck in neutral. While we did finally make it safely to the slip with some help from vessel assist, it was an experience we could have done without. Only after we were securely tied to the dock did we realize that the commissioning crew had failed to tighten all the screws to the Morse controls; the shifter lever came loose after a few hours of use.

**5. Paperwork.** Make sure to have all your paperwork (final payment, insurance, offshore delivery, LLC, etc.) in order. There is a lot of paperwork associated with taking delivery of a new boat and most of it is tied together one way or another. Offshore deliveries can take a full day by themselves and involve attorneys, delivery captains, sales representatives, and documentation companies. If everyone is not on board with their paperwork at the right time, you can end up wasting an entire day.

So there you have it—five simple-but-important steps to surviving a new-boat commissioning. While these steps have proven effective for us in the past, we recognize that with each purchase new opportunities will arise that will require our attention and patience. The key word is patience!

# Consider a Power Catamaran

### Bill Parlatore

**M**any of us in the passagemaking community have watched the progressive evolution of the power catamaran. In the last decade, we've seen truly impressive power cats voyaging around the world in safety and comfort. These designs often combine lightweight composite construction with sound engineering to create strong structural integrity that offers many advantages over traditional displacement hull forms. While sailing cats have been around a long time, the catamaran concept is much better suited, in my opinion, to a power boat.

Too many people confuse heavy with strength, and the ability to make faster passages in a lighter boat is not to be dismissed. Being able to outrun weather at speed is just as important as the economy of needing less fuel for voyaging long distance. The power cat offers both. And many power cats have shallow draft, something to be appreciated in paradise.

With engines set far apart, maneuverability is outstanding, eliminating the need for thrusters of any kind. It also has a very stable ride, not needing complex machinery such as active fin stabilizers to reduce roll. As a result, even a large power cat can be outfitted simply, while still providing outstanding performance characteristics underway and at anchor. The "less is more" mantra describes the power cat genre well.

A cat's narrow hulls make for exceptional efficiency and fuel economy, which is an important consideration when planning long-distance cruising with today's fuel costs.

It is true that ultimate load-carrying ability of a power cat is somewhat less than that of a displacement powerboat, but that is not the issue it might seem. The late Malcolm Tennant, a well-known New Zealand designer, preached fighting the urge to bring everything aboard, something that is easy to do with so much space. (He also crusaded against granite countertops and heavy hardwood interiors.) Cruising boats tend to get loaded down with all kinds of real or imagined "must have" essentials. But I believe it is a matter of perspective and approaching the situation with a certain attitude. Instead of carrying 800 gallons of water, install a watermaker and lose the weight. Instead of loading the boat with one's library of books, download them onto a Kindle or iPad. Ditto one's CD and DVD movies and music onto an MP3 player or iPod. It has become the way of the world for many people anyway. Instead of a massive davit crane to bring the dinghy atop the boat deck, a simple pair of davits will hold a large dinghy up close and personal between the two hulls at the stern. Again, think simple.

There is much that can be argued for choosing a power cat as one's voyaging boat, but the four key features that support the choice are comfort, efficiency, speed, and stability.

Robert Beebe didn't know about power cats, as they have only recently come of age, but they are perhaps the passagemakers of the future for many reasons. It's all about attitude.

Figure 9–7. *Chrysalis*, a 65', Malcolm Tennant–designed catamaran, described in "Building Your Own Boat" later in this chapter. (Mike Petersen)

Delivery time can also take years, not months. New passagemaking boats are not built and sold at the dealership; they are all presold. All are special orders.

**Used boats.** The advantage here is "what you see is what you get." You can determine whether you like the boat before making a financial commitment. You get to do sea trials where the boat is run through its performance afloat. You hire a certified and experienced surveyor to identify any weaknesses or faults.

If problems are found, you may be able to get the seller to pay for repairs or replacements. Often, you can find bargain boats that have taken a substantial drop from their real value. The market for ocean-crossing yachts is slim. Buyers have a significant advantage if the seller is motivated.

On the other hand, a used boat may contain a lot of obsolete equipment. When we bought *Teka III* she was 15 years old and had much of the original

Figure 9–8. *Lifeline*, a 49' conversion from a Bass Straits (Australia) crayfishing boat. Owners Sue and Phil Goodrick converted her themselves and then voyaged from Australia to Thailand, Malaysia, Indonesia, and the Philippines. (Cruisingunderpower.fastmail.net)

electronics. We spent at least 30% of the purchase price fixing things and updating electronics. We still bought a very proven, capable boat for perhaps one-fourth the cost of a new boat. We have gone through at least one major electronics upgrade about every five years—it seems there is always a newer, better product available or that the old one is causing difficulties.

Buying a used boat can be a real financial advantage if you are on a budget or you do not want to wait for delivery and commissioning. After buying our boat, we spent about a month in the boatyard fixing and improving systems. Then we were off on our adventure! If you are on a seriously restricted budget, you might consider buying a coastal trawler and shipping it to far-away cruising grounds, such as the Mediterranean. Note the photo of *Seascape* at the beginning of this chapter. They had a wonderful voyage at minimum cost.

## Hints for Purchasing a Used Boat

1. Before hiring a surveyor, do a thorough analysis yourself by going over the boat with a fine-toothed comb. Crawl through every space. Lift every floorboard. Examine under the engine. Look at the shaft seal. Check the rudder post and seals. Let out the anchor chain and check for rust. Check life preservers and fire extinguishers. Check design and condition of seacocks. Check age and condition of batteries and wiring. Look for leaks that might have caused damage or rot. Turn on every electrical item and see whether it works. Check fuel and water tanks for rust or corrosion. Take notes and photos of anything you find wrong. If you still like the boat after this thorough inspection, you can provide your list to the surveyor to make sure the items are included in the survey report.

2. Ask for a full copy of the seller's maintenance log and ship's log. Look carefully through these logs to find previous problems. Were they fixed? What about maintenance—was the oil changed at specified intervals? Be suspicious if no logs were kept. You might ask for copies of all receipts for repairs for the boat as a weak substitute.

3. Get oil samples from main and auxiliary engines and have them analyzed for unusual wear elements. For example, high copper levels might mean that main bearings are failing. These samples can also tell you whether there is antifreeze in the oil—usually a symptom of a failed heat exchanger or a leaking head gasket.

4. Arrange a sea trial when the seakeeping capability of the boat can be checked—unless it is a well-known model with much published data. Check out the antiroll system. Make sure the autopilot works under both compass control and GPS control. Checking the boat on a calm day will tell you little about these important qualities. Make sure the rudder is responsive and turns the boat well at low and high speed. Rudder overhauls and redesigns can get expensive.

If you are buying a boat with a comparable fleet of existing boats, search the Internet for logs and blogs for these boats. Owners often note problems with a particular boat, engine, or system. If you are aware of these potential problems, you can pay close attention during the purchase negotiation. You may also find fixes to the problems that will eliminate them in the future.

## Building Your Own Boat

If you have skill and time, you could consider building your own boat. However, it takes considerable perseverance and many years of time. For example, Dan Walsh and Sally Hass decided to build their own boat, *Spirit of Balto*. The keel was laid in May 2001 and the final boat launched in April 2006—five years later. Except for the basic steel hull and the painting, Dan did almost all the work himself. His mechanical work and woodwork are excellent and appear to be just as good as any modern production boat. However, he did have welding, woodworking, and mechanical skills before starting the boat project. If you did not have such abilities, the learning curve could be steep and expensive. Sally says Dan lived and breathed "Balto" for those five years—the task was all consuming, but the end product is great.

Another do-it-yourself project started when Mike and Kim Petersen found a fiberglass catamaran hull designed by Malcolm Tennant in a farmer's field in New Zealand. It was just a shell, with nothing inside. In 2003 the Petersens bought the hull, shipped it to Florida in 2004, and began the finishing process as a family project that included their two children. They had no previous experience that would help on this major project. It took them eight months to complete the entire interior, including woodworking, engines, plumbing, electrical, and all the other things necessary to complete the boat. They then moved aboard and crossed the Atlantic to the Mediterranean and back. (Kim has described the experience in a book—see endnotes.)

Aside from the issues of developing the skills needed to build a boat and the considerable time for building, there may be a resale issue. Many people are

**Figure 9–9.** *Spirit of Balto*, a 52' long, 18' beam, 6' draft steel boat built by Dan Walsh and Sally Hass over a five-year period. With 2,200 gallons of fuel, they have the range to cross oceans. Sally says their dream is to voyage to the Mediterranean. (Bob Lane/Dan Walsh)

**Figure 9–10.** Mike and Kim Petersen finishing *Chrysalis*, their 65-foot Malcolm Tennant catamaran before embarking on their voyage to the Mediterranean. (Mike Petersen)

reluctant to buy a used boat that was home-built; thus, you may be unable to recoup your investment when it is time to sell. However, with careful attention to costs and bargain-hunting, you may be able to go cruising on a much more limited budget.

### Which Material to Use?

At present, there are four main choices: fiberglass, steel, aluminum, and wood.* There are advantages and disadvantages to each. We will highlight only some of the important issues here. Choosing a boat material can be directly related to your cruising objectives.

**Fiberglass (composites).** The most common building material for passagemakers is fiberglass, which lends itself to easy mass production of hulls after the initial mold is constructed. Custom fiberglass hulls are usually pretty expensive because you cannot build a mold for a single hull at a reasonable cost. Thus, more labor-intensive procedures are required, such as building cored hulls. Many choices of fabrics and resins are available. It is difficult to know the quality of the layup of the hull except by the reputation of the builder. In the past, many builders experienced blisters in the hull due to the wrong choice of resins. Fiberglass hulls can offer savings in maintenance, but as they get older they may require painting, just like a steel or wooden boat. Fiberglass is relatively easy to fix almost anywhere in the world. Small damaged areas can be repaired with epoxy putty; however, larger areas of damage may require hauling and weeks of work. Fiberglass requires insulation to reduce sweating caused by cold water condensing the warm air inside the boat. Resale on high-quality fiberglass boats is excellent.

**Steel.** For full displacement boats, such as our passagemakers, steel is high on the list of preferred materials. Steel is relatively inexpensive for material and labor. It is very strong and can absorb impacts quite well—it will dent or deflect, but does not usually break without tremendous force. Steel is the heaviest building material, which adds to the vessel's displacement, but that, in fact, may contribute to a more sea-kindly and comfortable ride. Steel is great for custom boats because they can be designed using computers that provide patterns for computer-controlled cutting making the panels ready for welding. Steel can be repaired relatively easily throughout the world. Steel is superior to any other material for abrasive resistance. It also resists metal fatigue; it is more ductile. Steel does rust and needs constant attention to seal any breaks. There are alloys of steel that are more resistant to rust than others. Cor-Ten steel adds copper, nickel, and chromium to create a stronger steel that is corrosion resistant. Steel also needs painting and insulation within the hull to protect against condensation. It may be noisy and can soak up heat on hot sunny days. Resale value is usually good.

**Aluminum.** This material offers some great advantages for boats. Aluminum costs almost twice as much as steel, but is easier to cut and faster to weld, thus realizing labor savings that offset higher initial costs. Aluminum requires less maintenance, especially if you leave it unpainted. Like steel, aluminum can be lofted and cut under computer control, thus speeding up the

**Figure 9–11.** *BaaBoo*, a 52' steel trawler built in the Netherlands, shown here visiting Cannes, France.

---

*Ferrocement is almost dead as a boatbuilding material due to poor construction techniques and rusted steel. Used hulls are very cheap, but may be flawed. The material is almost impossible to survey. See George Buehler, *The Troller Yacht Book* (Booklocker, 2011) for a more complete discussion on materials choice.

# Why Choose a Motorsailer?

### Don McIntyre

What is a motorsailer? After all, (sailing) yachts have motors. To me a real "motorsailer" allows you to motor efficiently, with or without sail, while keeping a watch from inside the boat, not outside in the cockpit, unless you decide to go out. The percentage of motor to sail is up to the individual—(mine is 50/50 percentage for motor/sail). They all offer another way to enjoy boating: standing watch in your slippers, sitting in a comfortable helm chair watching the spray hit the windows instead of you. As to going to windward, a good motorsailer can plod along all day into nearly anything, with a large, slow-turning, four-blade prop, and a John Deere engine, like trawlers have been doing forever. Did I mention the flopperstopper stabilizers underway? They are even better at anchor.

It took three years and 50,000 Chinese man-hours to build my new boat, *Ice*. It is a 40-ton, 50-foot, self-righting, ice-strengthened, steel, go-anywhere 50/50 motorsailer. It has a 4,500-mile range at 7 knots under John Deere power; a huge stand-up watertight engine room; five-star fit-out; and carries all my toys, including a Polaris flying inflatable boat. I sit watch in a comfortable Stidd helm chair, looking out through 20mm of thick, heated, armor plate pilothouse windows—that is, unless the moon is out, when I may head up onto the flybridge. Margie and I can go anywhere in comfort, anytime, any weather, any wind direction or strength, even zero. Sails are optional if we feel lazy and we don't want to get wet.

**Figure 9–12.** The motorsailer *Ice* owned by Don McIntyre is a 50' George Buehler design built by Seahorse Marine: beam 15.6', draft 6.1', 1,981 gallons for fuel, 264 gallons for water, engine is a John Deere 4045TFM. (Don McIntyre)

process and saving money. Aluminum has to be thicker than steel by about 50% to offset steel's advantages in strength and flexing, but it still winds up 35–45% lighter than steel. This thicker aluminum is more difficult to dent and has a 12.5% higher resistance to ultimate failure. The biggest problem with aluminum is that it is subject to electrolysis if stray current exists in the water (a common problem in marinas) or if there is an electrical fault in the boat. Extra care must be taken in design and installation of electrical components *and* sacrificial zincs are needed throughout the underwater parts of the hull. (Note that all boats require zincs underwater to protect their metal parts; however, aluminum is the most subject to damage from missing or worn-out zincs.) Resale value is excellent.

**Wood.** It is a great building material for the do-it-yourself person. Wood requires skill with tools, but it is a relatively easy, clean material to work with. Many people find working with wood is rewarding and relaxing. Newer techniques of wood boat building often involve using epoxy layers over the wood, resulting in hulls that look just like a fiberglass hull. These newer methods can also result in lower maintenance, always the major drawback of wooden boats. Building wooden boats is a big industry in Turkey—there are numerous yards with generations of boat-building experience. Several George Buehler–designed yachts have recently been built in Turkey. In addition, Michael Kasten has related the process of building the Indonesian *Phinisi*—a seagoing yacht built of rot-resistant woods—at a reasonable price. The drawback of wood is primarily keeping it dry and away from fresh water, such as deck leaks. Rot can quickly cause major problems unless expensive and exotic woods like teak are used that resist rot. Resale value of wood yachts is generally lower. Many people fail to recognize their full value and feel the high maintenance will be unacceptable. However, this may be an opportunity for a budget-constrained voyager to get a really capable yacht at a bargain price. (See the sidebar in Chapter 13 about buying and restoring *Passagemaker*, p-248.)

# Overall Boat Design and Appearance

## Beebe's Comments on Accommodation
## Design Choices

In recent years, responding to the requests of clients, I have found myself concentrating on Passagemaker types that will provide a real home afloat for the owner and spouse. This makes sense to me—for the truth is, such vessels are becoming so expensive they don't make much sense unless they are used practically full time. Ideally, they should be used as homes afloat; then their cost can be viewed as the cost of any comparable home. Granted this premise, we can see a design will not fill the need unless it provides nearly all the amenities of shoreside quarters.

We are thus faced with a demand for superior accommodations. How to supply this need? One way is by using double-decking. This can be seen at its practical limits in *Mona Mona*. She is a real home afloat for living in the Mediterranean and, with her 1,200 gallons of fuel, can cross the Atlantic and return. But she does have a high A/B ratio of 3.0, with lots of glass.

| | |
|---|---|
| LOA | 50'0" |
| LWL | 47'6" |
| Beam | 16'0" |
| Draft | 5'0" |
| Displacement | 33.0 tons |
| D/L | 308 |
| Fuel | 1,200 gal |

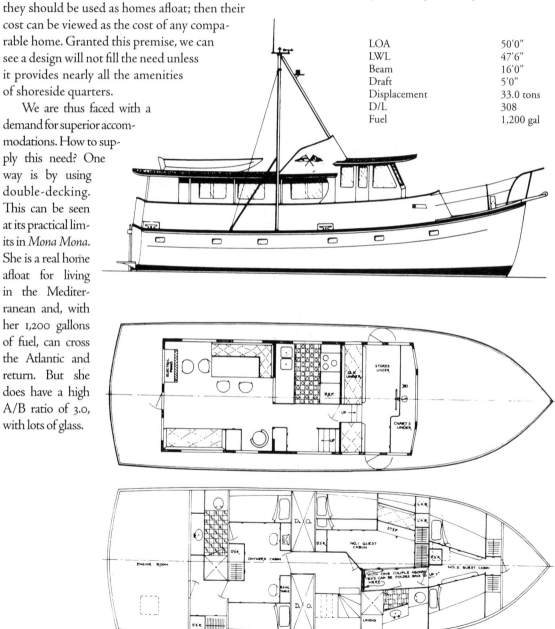

**Figure 9–13.** *Mona Mona*, an early Beebe design, circa 1972.

## Accommodation Decisions and Design

The problems of the motorboat are different from those of the sailing cruiser. Not only does the motorboat have larger engines but their maintenance also demands more elbow room, workbenches, and the like. Then, too, fuel tanks become a major problem. If flopperstoppers are a part of the stabilizing gear, their positioning is of vital importance.

A sheltered steering station is essential, with an open-air station also desired by many owners. These must be capable of being completely blacked out to protect the watchstander's night vision. The galley and dining area will generally be larger than in the sailing cruiser. The comfort of the cook is a cardinal principle. Large saloons with no convenient handholds must be viewed as dangerous at sea. With the motorboat's ability to drive hard into a head sea, an arrangement must be available for the crew berthed forward to come aft to sleep. As I learned aboard *Passagemaker*, while standing at the forward end of her fore cabin, such a vessel is quite capable of throwing you up against the overhead.

The possibilities offered by motorboat layouts for increased glass areas, compared to sailing vessels, must be approached cautiously, with consideration for location and suitability of storm shutters.

The designer must balance all of these factors, and more besides. Complicating his task immensely is one bane of his work—that human bodies do not change in size along with a change in boat length. Hence, a layout that might work well at, say, 50 to 55 feet LOA, may not be practical or desirable in a smaller version.

Looking at what has been done in this field, several distinct patterns emerge. It is possible to classify many yachts by type of accommodations. Figure 9–14 shows my own classifications.

**Type A.** This is the most common arrangement [in 1975], found in many sizes, from 50 feet down, among what are called trawler yachts. The first boats of this type appeared in the Pacific Northwest and were sometimes called "tri-cabins." [See Figure 9–1, *Seascape*; *Teka III* also illustrates this type.] The Type A sketch shows how the boats are divided into three distinct sections: the bow with guest cabins and head; the amidships area comprising a central cabin at or a bit below the sheer line, with the engine room beneath; and the owner's cabin aft with its own head and shower. There is usually a lazarette aft of this, but as it is by no means necessary it must be charged as part of the aft cabin in figuring space. The proportions of each section can be varied somewhat to suit individual owners. In the well-known Grand Banks 42, for instance, the breakdown from forward to aft is 13 feet, 14 feet, and 15 feet.

The advantages of this layout are these: it is simple and economical to construct, it concentrates the saloon and galley amidships, it provides a large engine room—though with rather restricted headroom—and it has a reasonable A/B ratio.

The main disadvantage of this layout, and one that in my opinion inhibits its use for really long-range passagemaking, is the inability to black out the piloting area unless all other activities in the living area cease. This is hard to manage when someone has to wash the supper dishes or work up the evening stars, or if the off-watch crew wants to play cribbage. Banishing the watchstander to the topside steering station during this period is unsatisfactory. The lights from the cabin may bother him anyway, the weather may be inclement, or a radar watch may be desirable at the set, which is normally located below.

This layout has no double-decking and is about as simple as possible. Whether it is satisfactory is up to the individual skipper and his crew.

**Type B.** Probably the next most popular configuration is shown as *Type B*. This arrangement was brought to perfection by William Garden. His *Kaprice* and *Blue Heron* are great beauties. Unfortunately, this usually does not work out to best advantage unless the boat is 60 feet or so. Some attempts to use it in shorter models do not work out so well.

What has been done is to sink the saloon-galley down into the hull, aft as much as possible, and still put the engine under it. In smaller craft, this results in the engine being what I call "sole buried." That is, the only access to the engine is through large hatches in the sole. While there are thousands of motorboats

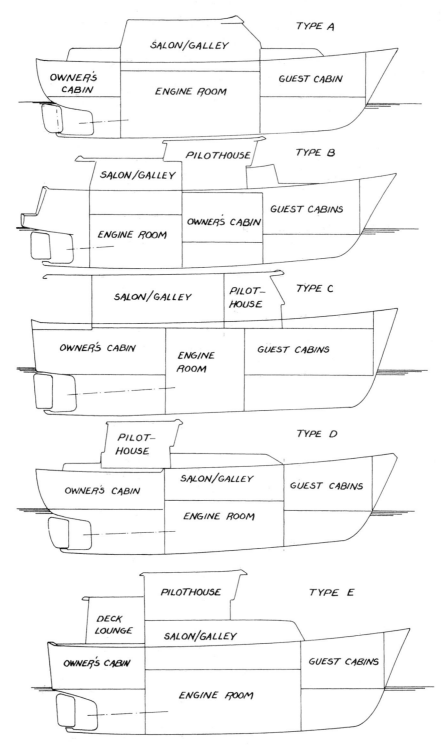

**Figure 9–14.** Beebe's classification of various motorboat layouts.

**Figure 9–15.** Nordhavn 55, *Global Adventure*, in Hong Kong Harbour—a good example of Beebe's Type D. (Nordhavn)

built this way, tucking the engine away inaccessibly in a seagoing vessel does not seem to me a sensible thing to do, inhibiting the regular inspection of machinery while underway.

The pilothouse is forward of the saloon and raised to give double-decking in its area, with a stateroom under it and other cabins forward. The result is all the cabins are jammed into the bow, certainly not the best place in a blow.

This model nevertheless provides a superb saloon-galley area and usually an excellent pilothouse with enough room to be a social center—it is as large as the stateroom under it. In fact, for in-port living and entertaining it is hard to beat.

**Type C.** Clearly, for the greatest amount of interior room in a given length, double-decking must be used as much as possible. We call this arrangement *Type C.* The sketch shows how much room there is. The Grand Banks 50 shows this design feature taken about as far as it can go. And it should certainly be arranged to take advantage of the superb expanse of top deck, with regular stairways instead of vertical ladders.

Type C, however, is expensive, difficult to make handsome in sizes less than 50 feet, has a poor A/B ratio, and has other drawbacks. Nevertheless, it has a lot of appeal as a real home afloat. However, one of them, *Mona Mona*, worked out for cross-ocean voyaging.

**Type D.** To take care of the objections to the common Type A layout, the configuration shown as *Type D* evolved. The revisions are these: make the aft cabin full width without walkways and then place the pilothouse over it and aft of the center living cabin. The living cabin may be full width or with only one side deck [a common design strategy of many modern passagemakers]. Because this configuration is double-decked in the pilothouse, it has a clear interior room the length of the pilothouse over a similar boat that is not double-decked. For instance, a 42-foot boat in Type D would have the equivalent room of a 48-footer in Type A. This is an appreciable increase with no added length.

As for the size of the pilothouse, you have a deck area as long as the aft cabin to be divided between inside and outside spaces. The proportion to be allotted to each is an individual choice. One might say that a yacht expected to spend the majority of its time in warm waters could well have the outside space larger. *Passagemaker's* pilothouse was 5 feet from aft bulkhead to the steering wheel bulkhead. It was about perfect for the watchstander's convenience, but when the rest of the crew showed up for happy hour, it got a bit crowded. Six feet would have been better; seven luxurious. For outside eating on deck around a table, 7 feet is about the minimum.

**Type E.** Would it be possible to design a configuration with as much room as a Type C, yet with a more seaworthy shape and a lower A/B ratio? Some preliminary work for a client, who eventually turned to another designer for a Type C, convinced me that the answer could be yes. The sketch shown as *Type E* shows this. It consists of the essentials of Type D as a base: an amidships full-width saloon/galley, and the cabin on the aft deck over the owner's cabin. But instead of this cabin being the pilothouse, it is an on-deck saloon connected with the outside area. It could be a bar, library, or TV room. The pilothouse is placed forward of it, on top of the midships cabin.

It may not look it, but Type E has as much room inside as the double-decked full-length Type C. In addition, it has several other features that recommend it: the A/B ratio is smaller; the pilot-house is aft of amidships—much the best place, in my opinion—and there is enough area aft so she probably will not sail around her anchor, as Type C does mightily. If there were full headroom in the engine room, she would have a bit of triple-decking, so we must be concerned about her inertial rolling, as discussed in Chapter 8. But the aft and high position of

the pilothouse allows it to be made with lighter, thinner glass than would be safe when the pilothouse is far forward. Visibility for all types of maneuvering would be superb, and the seating forward of the pilothouse is a highly desirable outside lounging area in good weather.

Unfortunately, we run into trouble with our incompressible people again. It appears that the layout must be at least 55 feet long unless the draft is much increased over the usual 10 percent of the length. But Type E has a lot of appeal.

## Other Important Choices

After studying Beebe's five types of interior layout, we can see there is a wide number of choices that will work depending on the objectives of the owners. Since all boats are compromises, here are a few things to consider:

**Flying bridge or not?** A large flying bridge is a great place to socialize. It has a sweeping view for observing what is happening in the marina or anchorage. It is great for seeing obstacles in the water and for docking. It provides sensory input from wind

**Figure 9–16.** *Pamacea,* a 65' Moonen, built of steel in 1990 in Holland and owned by Neil Gloier and Pam Odle. Neil spends almost all his time at sea on the flying bridge, even during ocean crossings. *Pamacea* is powered by twin Volvo 292 diesels, cruises at 9 knots, and can carry 3,200 gallons of fuel. (Neil Gloier)

and waves that is not possible from within the pilothouse. At night, if you have a folding bimini top, you can really enjoy the stars. It enhances safety when navigating in coral or shoal waters. Many people say they would not have a boat without a flying bridge. Personally, we love flying bridges, although we have only a very small one on *Teka III*. We have learned to live without it because ours cannot serve as a social center and it is too exposed to use in bad weather. We have found that we like to be where the electronics reside: in the pilothouse. There are a few downsides for flying bridges. First, you need duplicate electronics readouts, controls, steering, autopilot, radios, and gauges. The second is increased windage. This can be more of a problem if your bridge is forward of amidships, as so many are. It increases sailing at anchor and makes control during docking or during gales more difficult. Finally, it may affect the vessel's stability, although the designer should have figured it when developing the stability characteristics of the boat.

**Pilothouse location.** Just to reemphasize the point made in Chapter 8, a pilothouse aft of center and as low as practical presents the most comfortable ride in rough seas. If the pilothouse is relatively low, it might be great to add a flying bridge when better visibility is needed.

**Outside lounging.** Again, a large flying bridge, if protected from the wind while underway, may be great for this purpose. Our boat has a very large, comfortable, covered area behind the pilothouse, which is a favorite hangout during passages or at anchor. It is also a fine place for entertaining and dining. Access to the galley is much easier than with a flying bridge. The area can be enclosed during inclement weather so it is still usable.

**Ventilation.** The boat should have sufficient hatches, dorade vents, opening windows, and fans to provide cooling and fresh air, especially in the pilothouse, galley, and sleeping quarters. It is surprising how many modern cruisers absolutely depend on air conditioning to keep comfortable on their boats. Dorades are designed to provide ventilation in the cabin or pilothouse, even during heavy rain or spray conditions when hatches must be closed; they trap the water, but allow air to enter the boat. Dorades are a must if you want to travel without air conditioning, especially in the tropics.

Figure 9–17. Aft lounging deck on *Teka III* with the author shucking oysters while Hugo and Marjie Carver look on. The area can be completely enclosed for inclement weather.

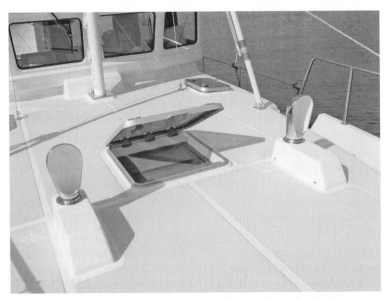

**Figure 9–18.** Dorade vents and hatches in a Nordhavn 35 forward cabin. Great ventilation here.

**Watertight compartments.** Some boats, usually 50 feet or longer, have one or more watertight compartments. This is especially important in the bow, where damage from a collision would be more probable. It is also good if the engine compartment is contained in watertight bulkheads. On our boat we have four compartments. Some designers feel this is overkill. If a major leak happens in one of the larger compartments, the free-surface instability would probably sink the boat anyway. However, water in only one compartment seems easier to deal with than throughout the boat. Other than the extra costs, there are at least two major downsides. Each compartment needs its own set of bilge pumps—we have four in the engine room, including an engine-driven pump. In addition, wiring and plumbing connects must be made at deck level or carefully sealed as if they were underwater connections.

**Fuel tanks.** If you plan to do extensive cruising in the Pacific, where distances are greater than in the Atlantic, you need plenty of fuel capacity. Look at the range of the boat at reasonable cruising speed to determine what you need in the way of tankage. It is surprising how many passagemakers have to add fuel bladders or extra tanks for such passages. (Some even need extra help for Atlantic crossings.) Adding temporary tanks may be a possible solution, but they can affect the boat's stability. On *Teka III* we have 2,000 gallons of capacity—making a range of over 5,000 nautical miles at 7 knots. This capacity gives us a lot of freedom to select refueling based on price, such as duty-free fuel. It also gives a great feeling that no matter what the weather or route diversion, we will always have the fuel with "no worries," as the Aussies say.

**Mechanical line handling aids.** A desirable feature on larger boats, say 45 feet and up, are winches at strategic locations, preferably manual, except for maybe 1 or 2 powerful electric winches. These winches are especially useful for docking, hauling in heavy items, Med mooring, and retrieving anchor gear. With a winch on each side of the boat and a pair on the stern, you can pull the boat in almost any direction without bow thrusters, stern thrusters, or engine power—once you have affixed the lines to shore or other boats. An electric winch with cable on the boom is also essential. It can not only haul up your dinghy but can also haul up and down suitcases, life rafts, or other heavy items. Electric seems better than hydraulic unless you are lifting really heavy items because no engine needs to be started to use the electric winch.

**Portuguese bridge.** This structure protects the forward pilothouse and its side doors from cross seas that might decide to come aboard. Watchstanders can go outside to look at approaching boats or look at the stars without the fear of being swept overboard. It deflects the seas from this vulnerable area and is a desirable asset for an ocean-crossing motorboat. There is little downside other than taking up space. Be sure the bridge drains overboard very rapidly because a freak breaking wave could create free-surface instability if it does not immediately drain.

**Bow thruster.** For single screw boats, this is an important feature; however, it can usually be added if the boat is missing a thruster. For Mediterranean mooring (see Chapter 19), when you have to set your anchor and back up in a straight line between two parked boats, it is almost essential. When transiting the locks in the Panama Canal, the bow thruster allows you to control the position of the boat in its mid-lock position. Backing out of a marina or getting away from a dock with the wind blowing you onshore is much easier with a thruster.

## Choosing a Tender

You see all kinds of tenders on passagemakers and coastal cruisers. Selection will depend on a number of factors, including your cruising area, the size of your boat, the weight of the tender, the speed you want to travel, and the attractiveness of the tender to thieves.

**The voyaging tender.** For the objective of cruising throughout many places in the world, you cannot beat a lightweight inflatable RIB (rigid inflatable boat) of 10–12 feet. Why so small? Why not a 14- or 16-foot model if there's room? Many places where you land your dinghy will be beaches, sometimes with great tidal ranges. A heavy dinghy will be almost impossible to move once it is on the beach. If the tide is rising, you have to figure out a way to keep it from getting caught sideways to surf or wakes. If the tide is falling, you may have to await the next incoming tide to dislodge it. A smaller dingy with a reasonable size motor of perhaps 15 hp can be dragged up or down the beach by several strong people; or, if you use two or three fenders, it can be rolled by a couple of "old codgers." You can always find a place at the dinghy dock for a small RIB.

**What about hard-sided fiberglass or aluminum tenders?** Full fiberglass tenders, such as the Boston Whaler designs, are great on the water, but rather heavy on the beach. In addition, they need fenders to protect them from docks and the side of

Figure 9–19. Dinghy dock at Georgetown, Bahamas. In popular anchorages it can be difficult to find docking space for tenders.

the boat. Inflatables need no fenders. Aluminum tenders are lighter, but they are extremely noisy with waves slapping against them while tied to the boat. Many dinghy docks are not spacious enough to tie up larger tenders. When launching and lifting hard-side tenders, one has to be especially careful that they do not hit the mother vessel and cause damage to one or both boats. Keep overall tender weight in mind; a heavy tender with a big motor may affect the boat's stability because it is a heavy addition, way up from the center of gravity.

**Security for tenders.** In many parts of the world dinghies are routinely stolen while moored next to the mother ship or while tied to some dock or hauled out on a beach. It helps to lock your dinghy at docks or when attached to the boat. However, in many locations the only safe place for overnight storage is back on top of your boat. In the Caribbean, there was a saying: "Raise it or lose it!" Even dinghy davits on the stern are no guarantee that the boat won't be quietly stolen during the night. The more expensive and newer your dinghy looks, the more likely it will disappear. You will often see cruising people, especially salty world sailors, painting their motors some ugly color and making their dinghies appear old and unattractive.

**Tender speed and seaworthiness.** We like a planing dinghy that will zip along on top of the chop. It is always nice to be able to go 20 knots after

spending days at a time at 7-1/2. For most inflatable RIBs, this can be done with 15–20 hp—a relatively small lightweight motor. Choosing an inflatable that is relatively dry in a chop is important. Ask other owners. We owned an Aquapro for a number of years that was much wetter than our Avon. Most inflatables are quite seaworthy, although they can flip in a serious blow, especially if under tow or on a long tender away from your anchored boat. If a big wind comes up, it is best to get the tender back on board or at least alongside before the wind hits.

There is no perfect boat. All boats are compromises. Your boat choices can be rationalized using the Spiral Model of Boat Choice, but in the end buyers have to integrate all the pluses and minuses *from their own point of view, given their objectives.* For people who want to go world voyaging, there are many options, even if their budget is constrained. Older used boats abound. If you are good at building things and you have the time and energy, you might want to build your own boat. Keep in mind that many people who put off their voyaging plans until they are financially secure and able to buy the boat of their dreams either do not live long enough to begin the voyage or their health deteriorates so that further voyaging is not possible. Many dreams have been dashed by waiting.

CHAPTER TEN

# Interior Layout

*One of the joys of personal boats is that the range-of-design approaches and suit-
ability-to-task varies far more than anything that runs on rubber tires on land.*

*Boats are one of the last areas of design where there can be HUGE differences
of opinion, and everyone can be right, depending on their personal cruising plans
and needs. While so much of the rest of the world runs in the "I'm right and you're
wrong" mode, cruising boat selection is refreshingly and maddeningly diverse, with
good humor shared among those with very different views and opinions.*

*We all are humbled by the fact that in the boating world, 2+2 very rarely
equals exactly 4.*

*John Marshall*

Interior layout and choices have fundamental
impacts on boat size and systems. As noted in
Chapter 9, boat choice depends greatly on the interior systems and structures that fit your purpose and
design attributes. If you follow the web posts of people seeking passagemaking yachts, there is a great
deal of diversity in what appeals to people. However,
it is clear that the market is leaning toward more
luxurious boats, with lots of space and amenities. If
such a boat fits your needs and budget, that is great,
but you pay a price for too much size and complexity.
If your budget is constrained or you want simple and
reliable cruising, you may have to forego some of the
desirable items that make the cruising experience as
comfortable as staying at home.

Most of us cannot imagine heading from Singapore
to the United States with the meager equipment
used on *Passagemaker*'s maiden voyage. Of course, in
those days there were not nearly as many systems
and equipment choices. Manufacturing "goodies" and
essentials for voyaging have proliferated over the

years as more of us are cruising. While we are lucky
to have many relatively affordable priced items for
outfitting our boats, Beebe and many other voyagers continue to recommend simplicity for maximum
enjoyment of the experience.

## General Layout Considerations
### Living Above Versus Below Deck

We often hear from ex-sailors who have moved to
trawlers that they are "tired of living in a cave" and
enjoy being able to see the world around them. Having a galley where the cook can see out and a saloon
where everyone can enjoy the surroundings is a real
plus. However, not all boats are designed this way.
One can build a Diesel Duck so that only the pilothouse has a view. Other living accommodations are
below deck, just like in a sailboat. This arrangement
has its pluses. First, you avoid the large expanse of
windows that may be subject to breakage during a
storm. Second, you have full access to both sides of

# The Economical Passagemaker

## Robert Beebe, 1975

In all the discussion of passagemakers in the previous chapters, the emphasis has been on taking our fund of experience and evolving the perfect next boat, if such a thing is possible! We must face the fact that a vessel with all the desirable design features plus comfort and convenience equipment to make her a true home afloat becomes quite expensive—well beyond the reach of all but a fortunate few. Can we lick this? Can we develop an economy model that will lengthen the list of owners?

Throwing all this into the pot and sticking to my preference for a minimum LWL of 40 feet, an economical passagemaker might look like Figure 10-1. Design 105 shows certain basics I would like in any boat. No overhang aft and very little forward seems indicated by conditions previously mentioned—economy, slip rentals, etc. The vertical stern offers two advantages: it is best for a stern platform, an item I would not do without, and it makes possible an outboard-mounted rudder so there is no hole in the hull and easy access for repairs. An anchor-handling bowsprit is also required. The heavy guardrail is needed not only for rough overseas docking but also to protect the stabilizing-gear hinge.

She is 42 feet overall. The enclosed pilothouse is from amidships forward. It is long enough to permit a high bunk in line with the ports, recommended for single handing. When not used for this, it could be lowered and used as a set-tee, though there is also a permanent seat for the watchstander. The engine will be under the pilothouse with nearly full headroom. Aft, right on the center of gravity is the galley and dinette for four, and abaft that, the owner's quarters with head and shower. The mast, primarily for the stabilizing gear, rests on the bulkhead between cabin and galley. It is located forward of the ideal position, but not excessively so. The mast can carry some sails to play with, but if sails are the emergency power, it would be good to have more area. We must remember that a motorboat's sailing rig is a touchy question. If large, ballast must approach sailboat amounts to prevent the vessel taking a knockdown from rig windage alone.

| LOA | 40'6" |
| LWL | 40'0" |
| Beam | 14'0" |
| Draft | 5'0" |
| Displacement | 20.5 tons |
| D/L | 320 |
| Fuel | 650 gal |

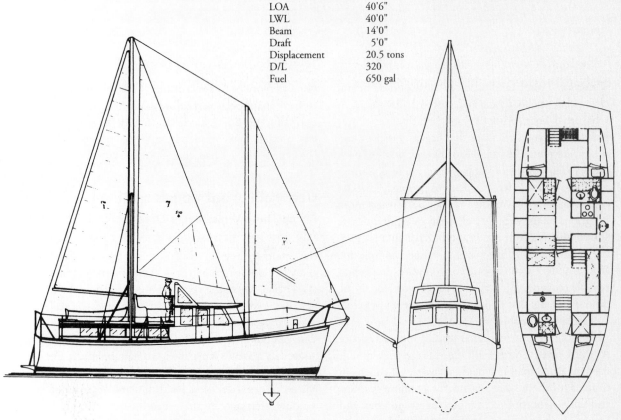

**Figure 10–1.** Profile and accommodation on Beebe's 42' economical passagemaker (Design 105).

I prefer this layout to one having the pilothouse farther aft and the galley forward. We found it easier to put up with motion away from the center of gravity in the pilothouse, where everyone is or can be seated most of the time, than in the galley, where the cook has a stand-up job. It is also easier to provide a truly dark pilothouse for the watchstander with this arrangement. The engine room is under the pilothouse with headroom of 5 feet 6 inches. With a displacement of 20.5 tons, she would have a D/L of 320 and need 650 gallons of fuel to go 2,400 miles at an S/L of 1.1. She could easily be made "French-canal capable." She is well suited for world cruising and broadens the field of husband-and-wife long-range cruising for those without the experience, strength, or inclination to consider a purely sailing voyage.

The basic contract cost for *Passagemaker*, a 50-foot vessel weighing 27 tons, was $40,000 in 1962. We could have left the yard for this. But about $3,000 worth of extra work was done for improvements, such as the aft head and furniture generally. A 3 kW diesel generator was purchased at a very favorable price in the United Kingdom and was installed by us two years later. Our plan was to upgrade the interior over the years as budget permitted. During this period she continued her cruising. (When she was sold, the new owner accelerated this program, installing a deep freeze, refrigerator, larger generator, diesel heat, radio transmitter, and other assorted goodies. None of these impressed me on a cruise I made with him. As a result, 10 years later, the cost has almost doubled.) [Note: The $43,000 Beebe paid for *Passagemaker*

in 1962 was worth $326,740 in 2012, figuring a 4.14% inflation rate.]

I think our approach to improvements makes sense. We started cruising sooner than if I had waited till my funds could purchase a fully found vessel. We were just as comfortable in our bunks in the beginning as at the end, but the cook was happier when *PM* eventually acquired a bigger stove, refrigerator, and deep freeze. Our meals may have had more variety then, but I don't think they were any better. Still, a happy cook is—or should be—a principal objective of any designer. We certainly did less maintenance in the early days. Our navigation put us where we wanted to go, with only a couple of days using the radio direction finder (RDF) and no need for radar or Loran. These days, my wife and I are working up a new boat, and when we start cruising, she will be even more austere than *Passagemaker*.

your deck without any structures to impede you— you can easily walk around your boat in seconds. Third, the lower location of living area near the center of gravity means less motion in seaways. Fourth, it is less expensive than building elaborate above-deck structures. Fifth, you have a lower profile, with less windage, less exposure to breaking seas, and possibly a lower center of gravity. Finally, you have a great deal more space when the entire beam of the boat is available for living space.

Yacht designer Michael Kasten says a critical factor for a below-deck saloon is the amount of light below. This is the result of the number and sizes of openings, such as hatches, port lights, and deadlights. The color scheme and type of wood used are also important. He states, "We ordinarily specify medium or light toned

woods such as cherry, fir, or pine, mainly to preserve the sense of lightness. Combined with white or other light tones painted on flat surfaces of the overhead and on bulkheads above the wainscot level

**Figure 10–2.** The use of light colors and art change the look and feel of under-deck spaces on the FPB 64. It also expands the visual space perception. (Steve Dashew)

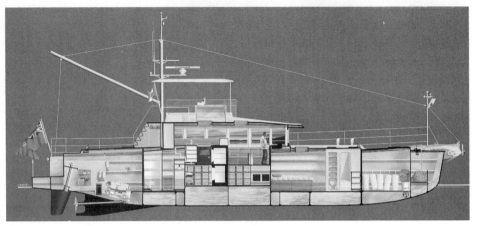

**Figure 10–3.** Profile view of the open arrangement on Dashew FPB 64. (Steve Dashew)

(lower part of the bulkhead or wall), the interior is kept light." Kasten summarizes his design strategy: "Even though I'm not at all claustrophobic, I still have an aversion to cave-like spaces. Since boats are by nature smallish compared to houses, it is one of our primary goals to make the interior of a boat as un-crowded and as livable as possible, whether the galley and saloon are up, or down."

**Figure 10–4.** Looking forward at the open interior on Dashew's FPB 64: to port is the galley, with the pilot chair forward; note the fantastic all-around views and overhead hatches for ventilation. (Steve Dashew)

## Open Versus Compartmentalized Layout

An open layout is one in which there is relatively continuous galley/saloon/pilothouse layout without stairs, doors, or other impediments between areas— sort of like a combination kitchen/great room in a home. Many trawlers have used this general arrangement over the years, but today we are seeing more double-deck boats with numerous stairways between parts of the boat. This is sometimes confusing for a new person on board, when it is difficult to tell where each passage leads. The compartmental approach allows much more design flexibility and more space in a given length of boat. Open layouts may be aesthetically pleasing, but they do suffer some problems compared to the compartmental approach. At night, everyone is forced to go to a stateroom to read or watch videos because you don't want to spoil the night vision at the helm. Cooking meals after dark becomes problematic for the same reason. On the other hand, flow-through ventilation is encouraged with the open layout—there are no obstacles to

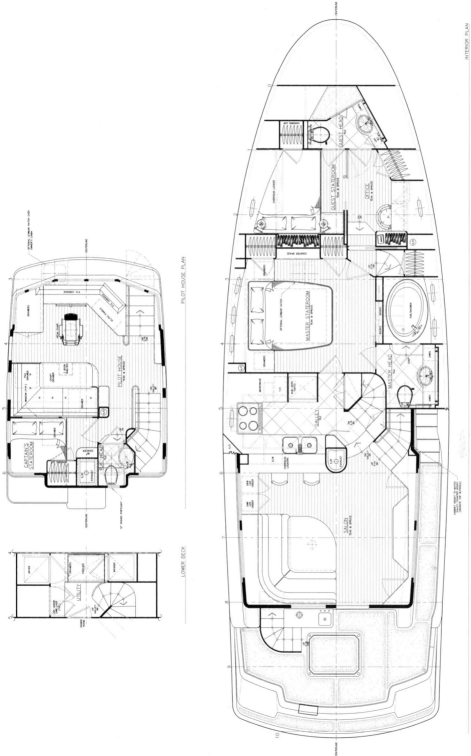

**Figure 10–5.** Compartmentalized layout of Nordhavn 55 (engine room not shown). This boat has a starboard-only side deck to maximize saloon room. This arrangement makes maximum use of space. (Nordhavn/PAE)

**Figure 10–6.** View looking forward on the interior of a Nordhavn 64 saloon and galley. Can crewmembers reach the overhead handholds? How will the chairs and table be secured at sea? (David J. Shuler)

prevent air movement throughout the boat. The open arrangement allows all crew members to socialize more easily—it does not isolate those in the pilothouse from the rest of the boat.

### Hybrids or Combinations

Some designs combine both these approaches by separating the pilothouse, which is often located above the engine room, and the galley/saloon, located somewhat lower but with views from the cabin interior. This approach, illustrated by the design of *Teka III*, was a favorite layout for Beebe's boats of 47' or more. He often designed them with aft owner's cabin, including head and shower facilities. The engine room sits below the pilothouse and has full standing headroom. Steps lead down to the galley, located near amidships and the saloon and table just forward of the galley. A guest stateroom is provided forward, and there is another head and shower. A large line and anchor locker, with a crash bulkhead, is in the extreme bow.

In this case, there needs to be a way to isolate the pilothouse from the forward area. One way is a pocket door to cover the area above the stair access, perhaps with a curtain to block off any light. This system works well, except people may forget the sliding door has been closed and knock their heads. Access to the aft owner's cabin can be problematic. It is

possible to provide a passageway alongside the engine room to go from front to rear; however, this takes fuel tank space and makes for a smaller engine room. Another strategy is to have a separate entrance to the aft cabin at deck level. This later approach is used on *Teka III*. We thought it would be inconvenient, but after some experience, we found we liked it, especially when guests were aboard. Owners and guests were completely separated by the engine room, so maximum privacy results.

## Roaming Around the Boat

In this section, I am going to take a stroll around the boat, much as you would at a boat show—try to point out some special considerations to consider as a voyager, rather than for living aboard at the dock. There are no right or wrong decisions for most design choices; they depend on the owner's purpose and preferences.

### Saloon

Often your first impression upon entry is the saloon and galley. The saloon usually contains a table with enough space to seat the owners, their family, and guests—for most boats this will be four to six people. Beebe recommended at least 22 inches for each person. This space allocation is a bit tight—think of a coach airline seat. We found it handy to have a telescoping table that can be lowered to seat level for another berth or for lounging while watching movies. For sitting comfort, it is great to have a couple of lounge chairs, but the trade-off is loss of storage space and the need to secure this furniture at sea. Fixed seating contains storage underneath and in back for large items, such as life preservers, survival suits, large spare parts, spare bedding, and other bulky items.

The type of windows and window coverings are also important in the saloon. Some boats have installed darkly tinted windows to reduce heat from the sun and improve air conditioning efficiency. However, some people find this darkens the view of the ocean and makes the sea appear more ominous, as if a storm were coming. Blinds for the windows should be able to be fully retracted so there is unimpeded visibility. Curtains should be used only if they can be fully retracted. At sea, it is more comfortable to be able to gaze at the horizon—the chance of motion sickness is lessened. At anchor, you normally want to be able to see all the boats around you clearly—one of our friends calls this "watching harbor TV."

## Galley

Design of this area is mostly up to whoever is doing the cooking, although there are a few considerations. Counter space is important. Ask yourself whether there is enough room for cutting, mixing, and preparing meals. The U-shaped kitchen is probably best for preparing meals at sea because the cook does not need to hold on as much when there is little distance to move in each direction. However, like every area of a true seagoing boat, there should be adequate handholds to prevent falls.

Choice of cooking method is important here. Many cruising boats like propane gas cooking, while others prefer all electric. Electric is safe and requires no filling or storage of explosive gas bottles. However, it does mean you will probably be running the generator a lot and your cruising costs will be higher. If the generator is not already running, you have to start it and possibly have a short warm-up time before you can cook. With gas, all you need to do is turn on the remote solenoid to allow gas to flow to the stove; then light it. There are three major downsides to gas cooking. First, an outside storage locker is needed with overflow vents to the outside air. Second, you must be careful to avoid leaks when connecting gas since explosions are possible. And third, you have to refill the tanks—not always an easy task when world cruising. In the Mediterranean, propane gas is seldom available, and butane must be used. It works OK, but doesn't burn quite as hot or as cleanly on propane cooking stoves. Sometimes you cannot find anyone to fill the tank since pressurized tanks may be filled at remote locations. We had to adapt some European Camping Gaz bottles for use on our stove in several countries. However, we saved a great deal on generator time and diesel use by using gas.

Most cruisers consider a microwave essential. We recommend using a combination microwave/convection oven. This allows you to avoid using the gas oven, which creates a lot of combustion by-products that can be offensive in tight spaces, especially in winter. And speaking

**Figure 10–7.** Looking forward at the galley on FPB64 (see also Figure 10-4). Note the refrigerator and freezer under counter, storage along the countertop, handholds above, and the lips on counters. (Steve Dashew)

**Figure 10–8.** The galley of Nordhavn 64 showing wall refrigerator/ freezer. (David J. Shuler)

of winter, since most of our boats have single-pane, solid-glass windows, condensation can be a byproduct of cooking. We like to use our rice cooker and plug it in on the aft deck so that no moisture enters the boat while cooking. We try to avoid cooking pasta when the boat is closed up in cold weather. We recently added a two-burner propane camping stove that can be used on the aft deck for pasta, crabs, and other moisture-creating cooking needs. This gives us more menu options.

We rarely see dishwashers on cruising boats. Manual dishwashing in a double sink seems to suffice. If you elect to have a dishwasher, you will need to power it. Plumbing is also more complicated. Trash compacters have been a popular addition to cruising boats, but we actually removed ours and replaced it with pull-out pantry shelves. We found we did not use it. When at sea, we disposed of biodegradable waste overboard. Plastic, glass bottles, engine room waste, and similar items were rinsed and stored in garbage bags on the upper deck until we arrived in port for proper disposal.

Look at storage drawers, shelves, and pantries. Are there enough of them? Will you be able to secure them for rough seas? How easy is the access? Do you have a place for a spice rack? Where will you put your larger electric appliances, such as a bread maker, rice-cooker, crock-pot, and blender? On a boat these items cannot be stored on the countertop because they can become flying missiles in rough water.

Refrigeration choices depend on your electric strategy. If you run AC generator 24/7 or you have a large, strong battery bank with large inverters, you could use a normal household refrigerator. If you elect this choice, you need to be sure there is a secure way to close the door. Otherwise, the door and the refrigerator's contents could come flying out. If this is not your strategy, some other choice, such as cold plates that store the cold for 12 to 24 hours are more practical. We have used a Technicold cold plate system that operates both the freezer and refrigerator using the same compressor. It has worked flawlessly for 12 years and requires an hour or two every day to keep the temperatures at the desired level. A plus for this system is that it ran just as well on European power of 50 cycles as it did on our American 60 cycles sources. Steve Dashew has found good success with evaporative cooling, using Frigoboat with Danfoss compressors. One of the things he likes about this system, in addition to its excellent efficiency, is that you can convert a unit easily from refrigerator to freezer and vice versa. He uses three separate units, so he has a choice of the amount of refrigeration versus freezer space—a nice option for cruisers.

## Pilothouse

We discussed the issue of pilothouse isolation. Here are a few more observations. A good helm chair is a must for the watchstander. It should have arms to help brace you in rough seas and a comfortable place to put your feet. Some have found seat belts are needed to hold you in when motion is really severe—we have never experienced conditions this rough. We like the chair to be adjustable so we can get a nice high vantage point. Location of computer

**Figure 10–9.** Pilothouse on a Nordhavn 64 showing an extensive array of electronics. (David J. Shuler)

**Figure 10–10.** Selene 54 pilothouse shown without pilot chair, which I would want to add. The great visibility of the pilothouse seating is a plus. Note the simpler single electronics display and the chart area on the left. (Selene)

screens and readouts can be problematic if they are too bright or distracting. Some people like them low and straight ahead; others may prefer readout to the left or right of forward so there is less distraction. We prefer the off-center position.

An unobstructed view of all directions is desirable; however, some boats do not allow a rear view. This is a real disadvantage, especially in large following seas when you want to observe wave heights and patterns. In addition, it makes fishing more difficult if you cannot see the stern. When Mediterranean mooring, you need a good view of the stern; a remote steering and control station may be needed.

If you have a boat with the owner's stateroom below the pilothouse ("in the cave"), you may want to consider a berth in the pilothouse so that when an anchor watch is needed, you will be able to instantly see your surroundings before returning to sleep. Also, when a couple is the only crew, it is often useful for the off-duty person to be close by in case of problems. A comfortable bench seat can serve a dual purpose for sitting and sleeping, eliminating the berth.

Another big plus for a pilothouse is a good-sized chart table so that at least half of a chart can be displayed at one time. Even if you have great electronic charts and chart plotters, you still should have backup paper charts. It is desirable to have chart storage in the pilothouse as well, but the extra space is often just not there.

## Master Stateroom

Several considerations are important. First is its location in the boat: forward, amidships, or aft. A forward stateroom is great for ventilation while at anchor because a hatch over the bed can be opened to let in a fresh breeze. On the other hand, this is the noisiest place in the boat because waves or even wavelets slap against the bow, sometimes keeping would-be sleepers awake. At sea this is perhaps the liveliest place in the boat since pitching and waves near the bow have their strongest impact on both motion and noise. Unless you can put your head out of the bow hatch, this location has poor visibility while at anchor. Note how Steve Dashew eliminates some of these problems by putting his forward master stateroom much nearer to the center of the boat with the sleepers' heads at almost the boat's center of gravity (see Figure 10–2).

An amidships stateroom offers the best ride since it is low in the boat close to the center of gravity—motion will be at a minimum, and noise should be low if the engine room is well insulated against noise. Like the bow, night visibility at anchor or underway is poor. Another drawback is that access to the engine room is often through this stateroom, causing sleep disruptions during regular engine room checks. In addition, maintenance using this entrance means the potential of dirty, oily trails on the carpet. The aft stateroom can offer fine visibility, if bed layout allows views through aft portholes. However, this is a noisy location while underway with the prop right below the bed. Motion is also a problem, although not quite as severe as in the bow. If you were to select double beds in the aft cabin with heads facing forward, large ports or hatches at the foot of the bed would offer a continuous view while at anchor or underway.

The direction of your sleeping head in relation to the boat's motion and center of gravity is also important. If your head is athwartship (across the

**Figure 10–11.** Selene 54 amidships stateroom that is typical of this location. Its fore-aft bed orientation may be a plus for minimizing motion at sea, but where are the handholds to make sure you stay in the bed? (Selene)

boat from side to side), your inner ear will experience more motion than if your head is on a fore and aft axis of the boat. However, if your boat rolls too vigorously, you may need something like a leeboard or belt to keep you from rolling out of bed. Generally, it is better to get your head as close to the center of gravity as practical to minimize acceleration and rolling motions.

Regardless of where the master stateroom is located, I recommend a chart plotter/GPS be installed at bedside for anchor watch. By marking your location when you go to bed you can see exactly how far you have moved. When you wake at night, you can tell at an instant if there is a potential problem. If not, it is easy to fall back asleep. I also set the GPS anchor watch alarm. If the unit is right beside your bed, you are less likely to sleep through an alarm. I find that a small compass mounted near the GPS can be handy to tell how your position is changing at night due to wind or current shifts.

## Guest Staterooms

Here there are significant choices depending on your guests and family expectations. If you have children,

you may want multiple smaller staterooms to house them so they have their own private area. If you want to impress your guests with luxury, you may want a beautiful forward stateroom with a queen-sized center bed. Our personal preference is to provide somewhat minimal accommodations for guests so that the limited space is used for other purposes.

## Office

Some think that a boat needs an office, much like a home needs a study. Others who have been sailing most of their lives feel that a "nav station" is a must. Most cruisers probably do not need an office or nav station, but some who are engaged in serious writing or business activities may require one. Sometimes it is possible to convert a seldom-used guest cabin to an office. On a serious ocean-crossing vessel, the pilothouse is the navigation station because that is where all the communication and electronic aids reside.

## Heads

Most passagemakers (except the smallest) have two heads. This is desirable because heads have a habit of breaking down at inopportune times. It certainly makes the crew happier if they do not have to use a bucket. In 50' and bigger passagemakers, it is desirable to have two full heads with sinks and showers.

## Storage Space

Seems like we never have enough storage space—spare parts, provisions, and other important stuff just expands to fill the available space. A large bow locker for lines, chains, anchor accessories, spare paravanes, sea anchors, and other assorted important items is useful. If this compartment has a strong bulkhead, it can also be used as a crash compartment in case of an unexpected and potentially destructive encounter with a rock, floating object, or another boat. A lazarette aft is also desirable, even if it is just a deck box that is securely fastened. Something passagemakers need to consider is storage for new and used oil and hydraulic fluid. A large, built-in tank in the engine room is great for new oil. Sometimes, during world travels the appropriate oil may not be available at the time you need an oil change. It is better to carry plenty of spare supply—we carry up to 40 gallons. Likewise, you need at least enough hydraulic fluid to completely fill your system in the event of a catastrophic leak. On *Teka III*, that is another 40 gallons. We carry only an empty 5-gallon oil pail for used oil. We have never found it difficult to recycle it between oil changes.

### Shop Space

I have seen a number of passagemakers with an entire large cabin used as a shop, including drill press, saws, sander, grinder, welders, and other assorted gear. We have a small worktable in the engine room with a drill press. We have a bench grinder and a vice mounted on a separate shelves. I use this engine room shop quite often. We also have a portable workbench (made of 1/2-inch plywood with reinforced edges) for use on the aft deck. It is outfitted so a vice can be

**Figure 10–12.** Lyle Petke, owner of *Puffin,* is a Puget Sound Marine Pilot. He built a shop table over the Cummins engine on his 46' William Garden trawler (note the exhaust pipe). The bench slides back and forth and is removable. Other tools are shown in the background.

installed for holding parts. This has come in handy for repairs while underway, such as for toilet overhaul or pump rebuilding. I have observed some boats that have fabricated a fairly large workbench over the main engine, with a drill press and vice mounted on it. It must be removable, and it is sometimes moveable fore and aft—an interesting and creative use of space.

## Comfort Systems

Here we look at ventilation and air conditioning, heating, entertainment, and handholds. Some comfort considerations have been covered in earlier sections, such as the importance of a good watch chair and sleeping and eating near the center of gravity.

### Ventilation and Air Conditioning

Fresh, cool air is certainly a major comfort item for most of us. Is it practical to forego air conditioning? Again, it depends on your cruising plans. In the Northwest, air conditioning is almost never needed, but the opposite is true in the Southeast, where summer heat and humidity can be stifling. It is certainly an advantage for any voyaging vessel to have air conditioning available. Some like to run their air conditioning 24/7, making extensive use of the generator or shore power. If you do run your generator continuously, try to avoid anchoring near others since they may be offended by noise interrupting a tranquil anchorage.

Another strategy, used by Steve Dashew, is to run the air conditioning for an hour or two before retiring, cooling off and drying out the boat for better sleep. If you have a well-insulated boat, this strategy may work. Others, including your author, do without by making effective use of fans and ventilation. Most voyaging sailboats have no air conditioning—they do without.

**Figure 10–13.** Fantastic Vent used in *Teka III*'s aft-cabin hatch to exhaust hot air. It works on 12 volts and takes little power. It really cools the cabin.

Happiness without air conditioning is dependent on great ventilation in terms of hatches, dorades, opening ports, and fans. It is also better to anchor out rather than go into a marina where little breeze may exist, or it may be from the wrong direction. At anchor, any breeze is forced into the boat, and the air is freshened automatically. We found a 12-volt exhaust fan, such as the Fantastic Vent used in RVs, works great to pull in large amounts of cool outside air even when there is little breeze. We have to use a sheet or light blanket even in the tropics with this fan pulling in air right above our beds. This exhaust fan is particularly useful for center and aft staterooms that do not allow forced ventilation from hatches or dorades. The exhaust fan can be mounted in any hatch, and then all the doors and windows are closed except the ones you want to provide cool air, usually ports in the staterooms. Since these fans work by lowering the pressure inside the boat, most hatches not being used must be closed. If there are too many opened, no air will move.

Small oscillating fans are also a great help. We have one or two in every stateroom, the galley, the pilothouse, and the saloon. It is amazing how much more comfortable it is with a little moving air. In the pilothouse I often use a larger 110-volt fan, run through the inverter, to provide extra air to the watchstander. We do have a small 6,000 BTU room air conditioner in the pilothouse for extreme conditions, such as crossing the Atlantic from east to west, where you get a large dose of afternoon sun in the pilothouse windows and you are frequently running downwind, so forced ventilation is nil. This small unit cools the pilothouse and even the galley and saloon while running on the inverter.

Having an opening window right in front of the helm position is a must for comfort and safety. When we first bought our boat, none of the forward-facing windows opened. Temperatures inside the pilothouse could get uncomfortable, even though it was pleasantly cool outside. A center-opening window that tilts up from 1/3 at the bottom has made life much more pleasant.

### Heating Systems

If you have central air conditioning in the boat, you may have a reversible unit that can change into a heating system in winter. However, you still have the noise and electricity draw of air conditioning, meaning that you have to have the generator or shore power. The most popular heating for voyaging boats is diesel-fired hot water heaters. This system works like a home heating system in which a boiler heats the water and a pump circulates it around the boat, often through radiators with fans to circulate the air throughout the cabin. These heaters take relatively little power to run, and diesel consumption is also pretty miserly. On some boats, it is possible to use engine hot water to heat the boat, much like your car. An engine-generated hot water heater is great for heating while underway and takes no additional energy to run; however, it cannot provide heat when the engine is stopped. While cruising in Europe, we relied heavily on small electric space heaters, purchased locally. In the colder months while we were at marinas, these little heaters did a good job at low cost.

However, we had to wire a separate circuit to use these 220-volt heaters.

If you have space and it fits your ambience, a diesel bulkhead heater is a good way to go in the saloon area. They are quite effective, sip little fuel, and are relatively inexpensive. They do require running a chimney through some part of the boat to the outside, a potential source of leaks. You also have to make sure that there is enough air entering the boat for combustion. I have often seen these little heaters installed, even though the boat has a central, diesel-fired hot water system. Sometimes the larger system is overkill for the warming needed, or you may want to minimize energy consumption—or you may be tied up too close to another boat to operate your main diesel system.

### Entertainment System

TV and audio systems for a boat are comparable to home systems—the choices are many and diverse and depend on the desires of the owner. Flat-screen TVs have made it much easier to install larger TVs; you can use any size you can find space for. We have installed several Bose sound systems with great success. One of their strongest advantages is the use of small speakers. They can be mounted almost anywhere on brackets that are combined with a woofer for bass and can be located almost anywhere that is out of the way.

**Figure 10–14.** A 42", pop-up flat-screen TV. (Steve Dashew)

The other major issue with world voyaging is the differences in systems. There are a number of TV systems in the world and all are incompatible with each other. It is great to find a system converter to view PAL system TV programs on an NTSC system TV. DVDs are also different for each region of the world. It is possible to buy DVD players that will play any system. This is handy for world cruising and for exchanging DVDs with other cruisers.

A pilothouse radio/CD unit, perhaps an automobile unit, comes in handy for entertainment during night watches. If it can connect with earphones, that is even better since there will be less chance of disturbing others at night.

World cruisers will find satellite radio is available in many locations, including the United States, Caribbean, Asia, and Europe. We found that some United States programming was available because NPR was often available in addition to BBC. When out of satellite range, the only inexpensive way to get news is via short-wave radio, with its sporadic reception problems. If you have onboard Internet, programs can be streamed through your computer (at some expense).

### Handholds

Recently, I was touring a 50-year-old 65' Romsdal. The passages were pretty tight for a tall fellow like me. When I asked the experts, they noted that it was designed that way—it is great in a rolling sea since you always have something to hold you in place. My preference is for a more open environment, but the price is the threat of being thrown across the boat when hit by an unexpected wave. The answer is lots of handholds so there is always someplace to grab when moving around in rough conditions. Even in the head, handholds are essential. Pay attention to handhold heights (see Figures 10–4 and 10–7 for a look at the handholds on Dashew's FPB 64). If all the handholds are ceiling mounted, shorter people may not be able to reach them.

# Interior Layout: One Woman's Perspective

## Mary Umstot

Climbing aboard a boat, I look for places to sit, eat, entertain, sleep, and work. Is the space user-friendly? Too much? Too little? Too tight? Although checking out the interior calls to me, there also needs to be an intermediate phase, going from the outside to the inside of the boat. I like a large aft deck, open to salt air and fresh breezes, yet covered from the weather. You spend a lot of time here soaking in the ambience of the marine environment whether at the dock, at anchor, or underway.

Stepping inside, my eyes take in the entry to the living space and the "flow" from one end of the boat to the other. Does the space flow uninterrupted with harmony; or do walls, stairs, separating counters, and abrupt corners affect the feeling of freedom? I like an unencumbered walkway with windows on both sides to bring the light in.

How full is each room? In the social area, chairs, coffee tables, lamps, sofas, television, stereo, and family photos individualize the owner's need to feel at home. At sea, all these items have to stay put as well as look pretty when not travelling. Do people eat at a bar counter or a real table?

One of the most important considerations is the position of the galley in relation to its function of meal preparation. Being able to stand in one position to reach everything necessary to prepare a meal is a plus. Also, its openness to the eating area offers flow between cook and helpers, cook and eaters, and cleanup crew. And, most important, it must have a window or two! Bringing the outside in lets the cook see the horizon, catch a glimpse of the action others see and report, and feel the effects of light.

Storage in the galley should offer places for the usual pots, pans, dishes, and glasses. Other appliances that make you feel like you are in your own kitchen also need storage places to keep them handy. One recommendation from women who cruise extensively is to bring along a set of six special china dishes and crystal wine glasses. They add a new dimension to entertaining on special occasions.

And then there's an important area in any vessel: the pilothouse. I like a pilothouse that is amidships or a bit farther aft away from the big waves that you meet at sea. Ours is the first place one steps when entering. It is roomy with sofa

**Figure 10–15.** A favorite spot on *Teka III*—the aft-deck lounging area.

**Figure 10–16.** The galley on *Teka III*, showing the large window at the end of the counter. Note the spice rack and the bungees holding the canisters on the counter. The cabinet at the lower left houses pull-out drawers that serve as a large pantry.

seats arranged around a table to allow several people to gather, so the person in the helm chair can have company while on watch. Windows allow a 360-degree view, adding an extra dimension to information displayed by the screens of electronic equipment. A chart table is essential to display paper charts or guidebooks when navigating. With a walk-around deck outside the pilothouse, people outside and inside aren't too far apart while doing tasks such as docking.

Staterooms should entice people to just flop down to rest or snuggle in for a good night's sleep. I like to have a view of the outside through large ports or at least overhead hatches. Many boats give me a feeling of claustrophobia because they are dark and enclosed. I consider a head and shower adjacent to the master stateroom essential. I also like lots of storage for books, clothes, medical supplies, and other assorted items in the staterooms and head. If the bed has easy access to underneath storage, that is a real plus.

I keep an eye out for storage areas on board, too—places for supplies, tools, and the extra parts needed to fix anything that may go wrong on the journey. A place for charts and nautical reference books must not be overlooked on a voyaging boat—we carried hundreds of them on our cruise to the Mediterranean. Our boat had so much storage space it was both a blessing and a curse: a blessing in that we had lots of nooks, crannies, compartments, and drawers; the curse was knowing where everything was located. It's particularly helpful to have a small safe to store valuables, extra money, credit cards, passports, airline tickets, and jewelry. Someone needs to be responsible for the safe's combination or for hiding it in a retrievable place, so that you don't wind up without access to your valuables.

We conclude this chapter with a section on interiors by the founder and long-time editor of *PassageMaker Magazine*, Bill Parlatore. He has more experience in a variety of voyaging boats than anyone I know.

## Voyaging Interiors: Observations from Experience

*Bill Parlatore*

I have been fortunate during my years of building *PassageMaker Magazine* to be aboard most every type and style of trawler and ocean-capable passagemaker. I have spent considerably more time aboard than a brief walkabout during a show. In fact I have lived and traveled for many thousands of sea miles on almost all the traditional and nontraditional choices currently available.

The following comments are taken from my notes of these trips, observations made after spending countless days on these boats offshore. Little issues that come to light during a brief sea trial take on new meaning after weeks at sea.

My aim here is to point out certain design and construction elements to be considered when sorting through the many details

**Figure 10–17.** Bill Parlatore, founder of *PassageMaker Magazine*.

that make up a modern passagemaker. Beyond the sheer romance of owning a true passagemaker, understanding the elements of its interior provides some focus to those seriously considering such vessels. And that is important, whether the plan is to circle the globe or simply be comfortable during extended island hopping.

Any yacht going to sea will have some form of stabilization. And yet, even with the most modern roll-reducing equipment, all boats will rock and roll when conditions get to a certain point: as good as modern systems are, the illusion of a flat ride in all conditions is quickly dissipated offshore.

Many modern trawler yachts have large, open interiors—wonderful spaces when in port and at anchor. Whether one cruises locally, entertains family, or simply lives aboard full time, open spaces make for comfortable and luxurious living. But, when I look around such saloons, I always wonder where the handholds are. It can be exceedingly difficult to move around large interiors without something to hold onto. On many of today's yachts, much of the furniture is freestanding, which can be pretty useless—and dangerous—when the boat is rocking and rolling. I don't care how big or how much the yacht costs, I have been there more than I care to remember, moving around on hands and knees because there simply was nothing stable to hold onto.

Another important consideration is the length and style of saloon seating. In upswell conditions, where the forward accommodations of the boat are usually rendered unlivable by the motion, having saloon settees long enough for off-watch crew to sleep on is essential. Despite the best of intentions, what usually begins as an orderly assignment of bunks in staterooms for the crew during an upcoming passage, conditions can reduce such planning to primitive and minimalist living in whatever space is most tolerable.

And on the subject of sleeping on settees, I find almost all U-shaped saloon settees hard to sleep on. I'm over 6 feet tall, and on some boats U-shaped seating is all there is, save the saloon sole. The current trend is to offer the master berth, whether queen or king, in a centerline configuration. Crew with bunk-making duties like this feature because it is easier to make up a bed when one can walk around it. No problem with that, but do you have any idea how hard it is to move around a cabin like this when the boat is rolling? Forget that the ship is stabilized; it can be a nightmare.

I was once aboard a quintessential passagemaker, where I was privileged to get the master stateroom, a midship cabin more or less in the center of the boat. The entry was off the starboard companionway. As we made our way north along the edge of a waning gale, I had to time my entry from the doorway to the centerline berth because there was not a handhold in between, and this trawler was moving about rather friskily in the quartering seas, despite being fully stabilized.

The head, located on the opposite side—to port—could only be reached by moving across the entire cabin. I had to time my entry carefully, waiting for the roll to reach its maximum on one end of the roll period; then I lunged across the cabin to reach the centerline berth, grabbing onto the comforter for support. Then I waited for the end of the next roll to dash across to the master head. There was not a handhold in between. (Had I owned the boat, I would have installed all sorts of solid towel bars, handholds, even sturdy artwork to grasp as I hurled alongside the beautifully finished, but utterly bare, bulkheads.)

I recall another trip across the Gulf of Maine where I was spread-eagled across the master berth in the aft cabin. Every few moments, the seas launched me up into the air off the mattress because I could not hold on to anything. I soon gave up and slept on the saloon cabin sole because the boat only had barrel chairs that had to be tied to a railing. Imagine that when you step aboard your next boat.

Not to make sweeping generalities, but I find most guest accommodations are usually designed as an afterthought within available space. I've been on fairly large boats where I could not close the stateroom door unless I was seated out of the way on the berth. And who would find it acceptable to buy a boat with stacked guest bunks so small that the unfortunate crew member assigned to the top bunk can't even read a small paperback, the overhead being so close to his nose that vision is impossible?

Inspect all usable storage, which is often lacking in many guest staterooms. Can you really hang a blazer or two in that hanging locker, or is it not deep enough? Is that lower locker long and wide enough for shoes? I've spent time on a lovely trawler with two seemingly nice guest cabins. We could sleep just fine in one stateroom, but we were forced to use the second stateroom for our clothes and as a dressing area. I doubt many people would have picked up on that from a casual glance at the accommodations plan on this popular and expensive yacht. It just didn't work, at least from my view, because the cabin could have been done much better. And that is my point.

The proximity of accommodations is also worthy of a good look. Over the years, I have been on passages on boats with inadequately thought-out accommodations plans. One trip comes to mind as the perfect illustration: when I crossed an ocean on a large, expensive trawler. While it never would have come to light before we left, I soon found that the berth in the guest stateroom was situated so that my pillow was only inches away from the master stateroom's toilet. I heard every bodily function.

The illusion of separated space disappears underway when that separation is only 1/2-inch plywood with teak veneer. Every tap of the toothbrush, everything, was heard clearly, and it was impossible to tune it out.

Steps and stairways need to be ergonomically designed. They were meticulously done on Northern Marine's *Spirit of Zopilote*. Too often, the depth of the steps do not allow room for the ball of one's foot, making for an easily slipped condition or forcing crew to turn around to take the steps backward. I find steps are rarely done well: too many people slip and fall because builders squeeze steps into spaces that are too short.

Can the heads be safely used at sea? Can you easily close the door as the boat moves about? Are there handholds around the head and shower compartment beyond fixture plumbing, which can become too hot to touch? Is there a way to brace while using the head or in the shower? Or are you willing to forego such luxury until conditions moderate? Think about it . . . this is pleasure boating, after all.

The pilothouse is often the social center when underway, where off-watch crew hangs out with the on-watch crew, have meals, nap, tell sea stories, and generally enjoy each other's company as the miles go by, the steady beat of progress as the engine rumbles on, the ever-present heartbeat of the passagemaker. On some boats, it is no simple task to get up and down to the pilothouse without holding firmly onto handrails, especially in any kind of swell or weather. Sometimes it is quite a feat to get meals, drinks, and appetizers up to the pilothouse. There is always the risk of dropping a bottle of wine or glasses, or having a food tray slip out of one's grasp as the boat lurches to one side. Somehow this got missed during the design of the boat, an important part of the overall flow and ergonomics of the boat.

While on the subject of ergonomics, some boats don't cater to tall or short crew, and handholds and storage lockers and cabinets are located beyond their comfortable reach. We seriously looked at an extremely lovely custom trawler that had come on the market. It was, and is, a beautiful boat, but my wife could not reach roughly half of the galley cabinets, some over the full-sized refrigerator. What was the builder thinking?

And no discussion of interior spaces can avoid the subject of ventilation. Midship staterooms have much to recommend them, but they generally lack good natural ventilation, most often because there is a pilothouse or other structure above it. That means air conditioning or heating most of the time, which complicates the energy requirements of the boat, making generator(s) vital.

Walking the docks at a recent Trawler Fest, I couldn't help but notice that in the wonderful 70-degree weather of coming fall, some boats had hatches open and a wonderful breeze blowing through the interiors. Other trawlers at the same docks, however, notably the multilevel dreadnoughts, all had air conditioning on, water pumping out the sides of the hulls, and every living space closed up without the prospect of natural ventilation of any kind.

I toured an exquisite trawler with Steve Seaton some years ago. As we walked along its foredeck, he commented that the foredeck's hatches above the various cabins would greatly benefit if one were able to rig an awning across the entire foredeck. He said this would cool the cabins below, easily 15 degrees, perhaps enough for all aboard to be comfortable in their cabins without need for a running generator and air conditioning. Wouldn't that be delightful! Yes, it would. And being able to take a shower under an open overhead hatch, or relaxing on a berth with the smells of paradise coming in to ignite the imagination, is an elixir second to none.

Now let's integrate interior spaces with systems and access. Engine room access via staterooms will disrupt crew trying to sleep. But it also means that dirty, oily work will have owners and engine guys walking through carpeted staterooms with parts, lubricants, buckets, tools, rags, and so on. Having the only access through a master stateroom (or through the master head's shower) is a feature to avoid.

I enjoyed time on a gorgeous steel passagemaker after it had crossed from Europe to the United States. The superb, commercial-grade engine room had access from a massive dogged door on the starboard side deck. While this seemed exceedingly shipshape and maybe even ideal sitting at the dock (out of living spaces), I imagined what it would be like to conduct an 0300 engine room check while traveling through a rain squall. Adding to this was the fact that once inside the engine room hatch landing, one had to turn around to descend a vertical ladder that consisted of gnarly round rungs, somewhat painful in boat shoes with no arch support. Forget flip-flops or bare feet; this ladder required steel-reinforced work boots. As elegant and well-built as this yacht was, truly a beacon of European craftsmanship, the engine room access on this trawler was about as inviting as rappelling out of a Blackhawk helicopter at night.

Another issue that is largely unnoticed is the occasional disconnect between designing living space accommodations and equipment installations. There are boats out there where certain equipment that is used underway, such as stabilizer fin actuators, gets located literally next to the headboard and pillows of the midship master berth. The whine of this equipment is maddening, even for a short time. No one could possibly be tired enough, or drunk enough, to sleep on such a berth underway.

It is no secret that all boats are a compromise, and while designers work hard to fit it all together, some designs succeed better than others, at least when it comes to providing a comfortable and safe home for passagemaking owners. The most successful voyagers tend to make do with less and try not to worry so much about the perfect boat as they do about visiting new destinations and meeting the rest of the world, up close and personal.

# CHAPTER ELEVEN

# Passagemakers' Systems

Passagemaking vessels are generally more complex than coastal vessels. It would take an entire book to cover each system in depth (see Appendix E, Recommended Ship's Library). This chapter concentrates on those systems that are essential for voyaging across oceans and in remote places. If your goal is coastal cruising in the Northwest or the Mediterranean, you may not be concerned with all these systems because parts and skilled technicians are widely available. However, if you are in the wilds of Patagonia or on a major Atlantic crossing 1,000 miles from nowhere, you will have some additional systems needs than those of the normal cruiser.

Your choices for these systems are governed by the type of boat you select and your desire for luxury versus simplicity. For the most part, the objectives are reliability, repairability, serviceability, and simplicity—four valuable criteria for an oceangoing boat. The chapter begins with engine room issues, including the engine itself, fuel management, backup power, shafts and props, wet versus dry exhaust, and hydraulic options. We then consider electrical, both DC and AC, control systems, electronics, and bilge pumps.

## Engines

### The Engine Room

A spacious engine room with enough area to reach every system is a must. Stand up space is a real plus. Single engines have a real advantage in this area for obvious reasons because you can normally walk all the way around the engine and inspect all areas easily while underway. Access must be easy. If you can only

enter through the master stateroom, crew will be reluctant to check the engine space while the room is occupied. Small entries where you have to essentially crawl into the engine room should also be avoided. On *Teka III*, we do checks every two hours day and night. Others, including Beebe, recommend hourly checks—the important thing is that you do regular engine room checks.

A key factor throughout the boat is serviceability, defined by Bob Senter, an expert on John Deere and Lugger engines, as "installation layout and access to potential service and maintenance point—something sadly lacking in some boats. A boat with a big engine room can still have ill-conceived installations with poor serviceability." For example, in my boat, the auxiliary engine, a Westerbeke 58, is mounted so close to the fuel tank on the side of the engine room that it must be loosened from the engine mounts to service or replace the exhaust manifold. While removal is an infrequent event, it still makes maintenance difficult. Another engine room example on our boat was the location of the hydraulic heat exchangers on a firewall aft of the fuel tank with difficult, convoluted access. Routine cleaning was almost impossible. I relocated them to a much better place soon after the purchase. Some items, like the heat exchangers, can be moved. Others, like the auxiliary engine, are practically impossible to relocate. You should carefully examine every important part of the boat to make sure you have access and serviceability.

But what if you have a wonderful closed-circuit TV that shows a constant engine room view? I think this little luxury is really nice, but we never had it

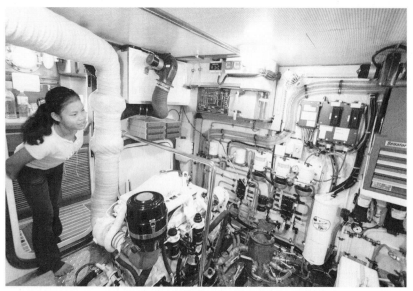

**Figure 11–1.** Engine room on Diesel Duck 48, *Ice*. Note the raw-water manifold to the right of the engine and the easy access to fuel filters and valves mounted on the forward firewall. (Don McIntyre)

onboard—and I wouldn't trust it. You can tell more by sight, sound, and smell when you actually enter the room. Also, there are small areas that need attention such as: Is there any water or contamination in the bottom of your fuel filter bowl? Are there unusual oil drippings under the engine? Are fluids accumulating in the bilge? Do all the gauges read correctly? Are batteries cool? Do you smell any diesel fuel? If so, track down the source. Does it smell hot? Use a laser temperature gauge to track down the source of the smell. It could be many things, such as a belt going bad, an alternator bearing failing, or an electrical connection with high resistance. It helps to have a clean, brightly painted engine room as well because problems are more easily identified if they can be easily seen.

### Selecting an Engine

If you are buying a new boat, building a boat, or repowering an existing boat, you usually have the option of choosing from a variety of engine manufacturers and engine size. It is difficult to compare engines; they are mostly excellent but vary quite a bit in fuel consumption, expected longevity, engine power and torque rpm, robustness of electronic

systems, and so on. It is important to select an engine that is properly loaded during ocean crossing, usually done at lower horsepower and rpms. Bob Senter says a properly loaded engine will be running around 50% at cruising speed. He points out a number of bad outcomes from underloading, including:

+ Abnormally high crankcase vapor blowby (and much faster fouling of the oil-vapor coalescing filters), causing oil leaks and seal failures.
+ Faster oil deterioration and more sooting.
+ Coolant and lube oil flows may be marginal at low rpms in some engines.
+ Turbocharger boost may be too low for the load conditions, creating undesirable byproducts.
+ Piston rings may not seat properly, resulting in buildup of carbon and possibly piston and liner scoring.
+ Injectors, valve ports, and manifold may carbon up, as well as the turbocharger.
+ Sustained low rpm in a hot engine room also promotes alternator overheating at high DC loads for inverters and house batteries.

Bob Senter and Steve D'Antonio note that some of these problems can be lessened if you run the engine to full rpm (wide open throttle) for 10 minutes once a day, preferably at the end of the cruising day. Other experts have told me that it should be even more often—every 4 hours for 10 minutes or so.

Other than fuel consumption, one of the more important qualities is an engine that runs at reasonably low rpm—the higher the cruising rpm, the more noise. The low-revving engine reaches its torque peak at a slower speed as well. A lower-turning engine will also probably have less wear and last longer. An additional consideration is ease of repair. Some modern engines can experience major problems from fuel system malfunctions or using the wrong type of antifreeze. Before choosing an engine, you may wish to get advice from engineers or mechanics on the reliability and repairability of a given engine.

Captain Beebe worked out a table to compute the horsepower required based on displacement and the speed to length (S/L) ratio. His recommendations are included in Appendix A. I tried comparing Beebe's method with other horsepower computation formulas and found quite a bit of variance. In addition, when comparing actual fuel consumption with predicted consumption for a Nordhavn 46, actual range on an ocean crossing was only 74 percent of the predicted range (at S/L 1.0, predicted range was 4,290; actual range was 3,168). There are several ways of predicting range: the Beebe method, the manufacturer's engine tables, the designer or builder's predictions, and observing the performance of surrogates (other similar boats on actual ocean crossings). Appendix C provides a table of real-world fuel burn data based on actual passage reports from voyagers. I suggest that you find a comparison boat for the one you have or are considering and carefully examine the reported fuel consumption of owners. Determine the cruising speed, wind conditions (did they encounter significant head winds?), and generator usage. Boats that run their generators 24/7 show higher consumption.

## Single or Twin?

Most ocean-crossing boats have single engines, as do most commercial fishing boats. The arguments for single screw are:

- lower initial cost,
- economical fuel consumption,
- greater range,
- more engine room space,
- less maintenance,
- better shaft and prop protection,
- reduced drag with only a single shaft and rudder,
- lower engine position for more space in the engine room, and
- lighter boat weight.

Single engines have proven reliable, but many voyagers want get-home options like a wing engine, sails, or hydraulic drive.

Twin engines offer built-in, get-home capability should one engine fail or the propeller become entangled in a rope or net. They also provide greatly improved slow speed maneuvering. They are mounted higher in the boat and can result in decreased draft. Having two identical engines also allows switching parts from one engine to another in the event of multiple system failures. On the minus side, additional fuel tanks are needed or range is decreased. The cost of operating and maintaining two main engines is considerably higher than with a single. There is increased noise and vibration from twins. There is more drag due to the addition of skegs or minikeels to protect the propellers and rudders. With propellers and rudders away from the boat's center and its protective keel, there may be increased likelihood of damage in spite of the separate skegs. There is less space and more heat in the engine room. To gain reliability with twins, there must be separate fuel systems, including tanks and filters; otherwise, contaminated fuel causes both engines to die at the same time. It may also be advisable to have separate electrical systems because failures of electrical and electronic components may be more probable with modern engines.

## Get-Home Options

There are three major options for get-home capability if you do not have twin engines. The first is a small wing engine with separate shaft and prop; second, a hydraulically driven motor, run off an auxiliary engine, hooked up to your main shaft; and third, sails.

**Wing engines.** A popular get-home option is a wing engine that operates completely independently from the main; with a separate fuel source, filters, starting system, transmission, cooling, shaft, and propeller. It will not commonly have its own rudder—it depends on the main rudder for steering. Wing engines are generally about 25 percent of the main engine's power. For example, on a Nordhavn 43, a 27 hp is used; on a Nordhavn 47, 40 hp; on a Nordhavn 57, 70 hp; and on a Nordhavn 62, 85 hp. The wing engine on the N57 is said to run the boat around 5 knots in flat sea conditions. Some smaller Nordhavns have

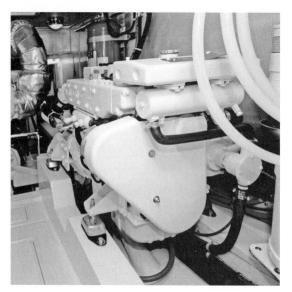

Figure 11–2. A wing engine on a Nordhavn 64—they can provide about 25% of the power of the main engine and can function as a get-home option because they are independent from the main engine. (Nordhavn/PAE)

complained about poor speed performance with their much smaller engines; however, they do result in getting home when needed, just a little slower.

A substantial advantage of this type of wing engine is the reduced chance of fouling the prop with nets, lines, or other debris because it has a folding prop that is less likely to catch floating objects. The downside of having a wing engine is that it is one more engine to maintain and it is almost always separate from the generator engine. In addition, unless you like to troll, it may be difficult to keep the engine properly exercised. An engine that sits around a lot usually does not fare as well as one that gets used regularly. Soot and carbon buildup is common. These engines need to be loaded and preferably run at max rpm for 10 minutes and 80% rpm for one hour at least once a week during regular use periods. Another possible problem is poor rudder control. Some owners report the tendency to yaw, problems with autopilot control, and non-existent slow speed rudder control. When using the wing engine, you have to maintain enough water flow past the rudder to control the boat. This problem could be significant

if the wing engine was required during a storm when headway is slow.

**Hydraulic get-home drives.** The advantage of a hydraulic drive is the saving of an entire engine and its ancillary equipment. The hydraulic drive is run off the main ship generator, usually with a power takeoff. This pump supplies power to a hydraulic motor that drives a large chain that is manually hooked up to the main shaft. The hydraulic motor speed can be controlled from the pilothouse in both forward and reverse. Newer designs for hydraulic auxiliary drives, such as the Wesmar model illustrated in Figure 11–3, use a gear that is directly attached to the shaft with a coupling clutch. The clutch is activated directly from the helm with no need to engage it manually in the engine room. All units are designed for variable speed forward, reverse, and neutral. Wesmar offers two models: a 25 hp and a 100 hp. The larger unit requires a significantly larger auxiliary engine, hydraulic pump, tank, and cooling.

There are several disadvantages to the system. If the main propeller is fouled or damaged, the get-home is useless. In addition, a fairly major hydraulic installation is needed with supply tanks, hoses, cooling, filters, and so on. If no other hydraulic systems are used on the boat, this is certainly another system to install and maintain. If the hookup is manual, it takes perhaps 5 or 10 minutes to accomplish. In tight channels or near the rocks, this time could be critical. The newer designs can be activated as fast as a wing engine, so this problem is eliminated.

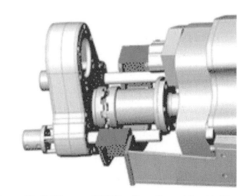

Figure 11–3. Wesmar APU (Auxiliary Propulsion Unit) hydraulic come-home unit shown in standby position. When engaged, the cogs mesh together to drive the main shaft. (Western Marine Electronics)

**Figure 11–4.** Hydraulic get-home with manual chain drive. Lower sprocket is on the driveshaft; upper sprocket is the hydraulic drive mounted on an adjustable steel plate. The chain at the left is not connected, but is ready for connecting; then the plate is moved upward for tension.

On the plus side, the large prop moves the boat more effectively than the small folding prop of the wing engine, and the force is in front of the rudder, giving good control in most sea conditions and speeds. A 58-hp engine drives *Teka III*'s hydraulic get-home at an easy 5–6 knots. You also avoid the idle engine problem because the engine is routinely used for generating AC power. Finally, you have more space in the engine room.

**Sails for get-home and more.** Several prominent designers are in favor of the sail option, including Steve Dashew on his FPB 64, George Buehler on his Diesel Duck designs, and Michael Kasten on many of his designs. Beebe used sails quite often as his get-home design strategy. Sails are best included in the initial design, when stability can be determined for the boat's sailing rig. You may have to

include more ballast with a sailing plan, but after your initial investment, costs are low because there is no mechanical system to maintain. There is no need to worry about a fouled prop because no prop is needed; however, a rudder is still necessary. An added plus is that you can motorsail in certain conditions and improve your fuel economy. We have already discussed the possibility of sails as an anti-roll strategy (see Chapter 8).

However, there is a significant downside. If your engine fails with inadequate wind, you may be at the mercy of the currents, which could result in loss of the vessel, just like in the olden days of sailing when vessels often drifted onto reefs. Another serious drawback is getting into a port. Sailing large motorboats is not as easy as a boat designed for sail—the boat cannot be maneuvered in tight channels. You may have to summon a tow, if one is available.

**Figure 11–5.** Get-home sail on Dashew's FPB 64. (Steve Dashew)

**Figure 11–6.** This tangled mess of nets and lines being held by owner Bill Smith was caught on the prop of Nordhavn 62, *Autumn Wind*, on the way to Horta in the Azores. A hydraulic drive would not have helped. You either have to remove the tangle or use a wing engine or sails to get home. (Nordhavn/PAE)

### Dry or Wet Exhaust?

**Dry exhaust.** Long favored by commercial fisherman and many long-distance designers, dry exhausts eliminate the problem of failing raw water pumps—the bane of wet exhaust installations. It also means less seawater needs to be processed in the engine room, decreasing the possibility of leaking hoses. There is no problem with corroded heat exchangers, and sacrificial zincs will not be needed in the engine cooling system. In addition, the exhaust gases are released high up above the boat and are usually dispersed by the wind or boat movement. On the other hand, boats have to be designed so that the hot muffler and exhaust can be routed through the pilothouse or other living spaces. Exhaust gases and soot don't always get blown away, especially when the boat is running at slow passagemaking speeds. Dry exhaust boats sometimes emit a large amount of soot on startup. One foreign marina required an offending boat be towed away from other boats prior to start up. Dry exhaust requires a keel cooler

to cool the engine. These require regular cleanout, and they often accumulate growth more rapidly because they cannot be covered with antifouling bottom paint.

**Wet exhaust.** Long favored by coastal cruisers and some passagemakers, exhaust noise is rapidly cooled and quieted. Wet exhaust is cheaper to install because it does not require the elaborate through-the-boat passage of hot gasses. Exhaust gases are cooled rapidly with seawater and routed using inexpensive hoses to the outlet somewhere astern. These gases can cause problems due to the "station-wagon effect" that causes smelly diesel gases to enter the rear of the boat, often forcing cruisers to close their aft doors. This problem is easily eliminated by having exhaust gases exit elsewhere. On *Teka III*, we modified the boat so that most gases exit underwater, with a relatively small 2-inch outlet, above-water pressure relief on the side of the boat. This smaller relief hose also serves as a siphon break to prevent water from being sucked back into the engine. We have not experienced any diesel or exhaust fumes since this modification.

Wet exhausts on auxiliary engines can also cause severe problems if water backs up into the engine and drowns it by letting seawater enter the exhaust manifold and engine cylinders. All engines should have a siphon break between the raw water pump and the engine's heat exchanger. It should be a minimum of 1 foot above the loaded waterline and preferably more. This siphon break can be plumbed using a small nipple in place of the usual duck valve that is routed out of the boat's side through a small seacock. This keeps any salt spray out of the engine room and provides another check on cooling water.

As mentioned earlier, one major drawback of wet exhausts is failure of the rubber impellers in the raw water pump. Cruisers must carry numerous spare impellers and pumps to ensure against this failure. Changing impellers annually may head off potential problems. However, there are other solutions to this problem. The Gilkes raw water pump, installed on our Gardner engine, has lasted 30 years and an estimated 130,000 nautical miles without a failure or overhaul. It has a bronze impeller and effective bearings and seals that require a bit of grease every

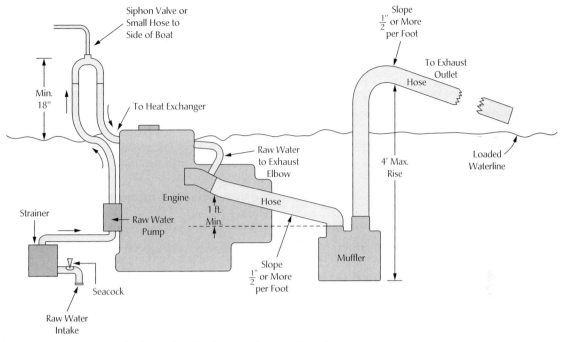

**Figure 11–7.** Raw water and exhaust plumbing for wet-exhaust main engines and generators.

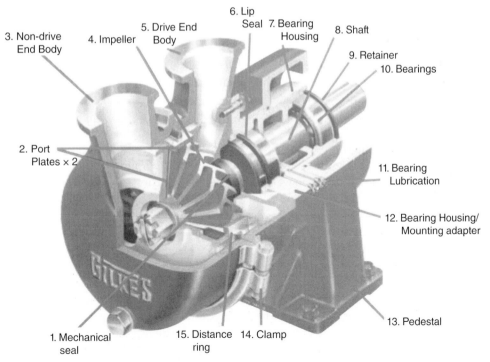

**Figure 11–8.** The Gilkes Series M raw-water pump is long-lasting with high-quality components at a high price. It can be belt- or gear-driven. (Gilkes)

500 hours. It is expensive, but it works. Yes, heat exchangers need servicing, but this is not an expensive or difficult job. Also, most auxiliary engines are water-cooled wet exhaust systems, so you still have to deal with the same maintenance issues. Like everything else, there are tradeoffs and compromises with the exhaust system.

## Fuel System Management

Ocean-crossing boats—often running 3,000 nautical miles or more without refueling—need a lot more fuel and fuel management than coastal cruisers. Our first concern is tank numbers, design, and location. Ideally, fuel is stored amidships, down as low as possible and even below the waterline. This is built-in ballast to increase stability. However, as fuel is used, the tanks empty and weight decreases significantly, meaning that stability declines as we near our destination—not a good thing. Some designers place large tanks on the sides of the boat—wing tanks—so that when they are emptied, they do not pose such a threat to stability. On *Teka III*, we have four regular tanks and one large day tank—five tanks total. The outside tanks carry 500 gallons on each side; we empty these tanks first. This leaves us with three tanks low in the bilge, just forward of the engine room. We empty the two side bilge tanks into the day tank—which holds 250 gallons—meaning we can run at least four days on the day tank alone.

All fuel going into the day tank is pumped and cleaned with a Racor filter, so we can identify any fuel problems before they happen because fuel is prefiltered before it enters the day tank. We also use a De-Bug fuel conditioner to help remove any remaining microbial growth. Does it work? We don't know for sure, but in the past 13 years we have never had an algae problem and we have never used a fuel treatment. Fuel from the day tank is sucked through a set of Racor filters that are switchable and changeable underway. Most passagemakers use this system.

While there is controversy about which micron filters to use, we always opt for the finest mesh available, usually 2 micron, for all our filters. We figure the more we can remove with each filtering process, the better. Except during the first year of cruising when we were

just getting our systems designed and modified, we have never had a fuel system failure or even a forced switch between our dual Racor filters while underway. However, many diesel engine experts recommend using 10 micron primary filters and depending on the engine filter, which is usually 2 to 7 microns, to remove the finer particles. Experts predict premature failure of the primary filter if too many particles clog this filter. (Steve D'Antonio recommends a fuel pressure gauge after the lift pump, but before the injection pump, to monitor this potential problem.) Fuel starvation to the injection pump can result in pump failure, especially on newer engines; you may want to follow your engine maker's recommendations. We have never experienced this problem, perhaps because our fuel is prefiltered as it enters the day tank. Our Racor filters are changed annually—they do not clog regardless of running hours.

**Fuel usage measurement.** When making passages, accurate fuel usage information is mandatory. The simplest and most reliable method is a sight tube, which is simply a tube made of plastic, which runs from the bottom to the top of the tank with a valve or valves to turn it off when not being used. Behind or in front of the tube is a scale showing the number of gallons in the tank. If you have a day tank with an accurate sight tube, you can tell your exact fuel usage on a daily or more frequent basis simply by reading the tube. If your day tank is located low in the boat, it probably experiences minimal fluctuation due to boat motion. I can measure the fuel consumption during the past 24 hours accurately to within 1 gallon. After measuring my 24-hour fuel consumption, I fill the tank to its full position of 250 gallons. When I transfer fuel to the day tank, I use an inclinometer in the engine room to adjust the trim of the boat as needed.

If you don't have a day tank, you must carefully measure the larger tanks to determine fuel used. This is often more difficult because the tanks may be angled with the shape of the hull and they may be so large that it is difficult to get accurate measurements. In these situations, flow sensors on the engine or using Flo-Scan equipment can help. However, these devices need to be checked and calibrated before making passages to ensure their accuracy. Many modern

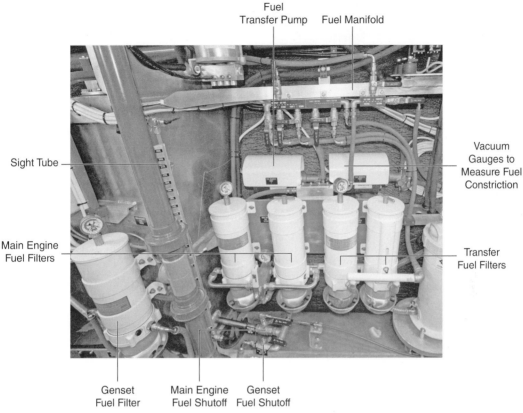

**Figure 11–9.** Fuel system on Dashew's FPB 64 showing dual Racor filters, vacuum gauges, and sight tube to the left of the filter bank. (Steve Dashew)

electronic engines have accurate fuel consumption data available via the engine's computer. Before relying on this data for an ocean passage, cross check its accuracy with other methods, such as a sight tube.

Another consideration is the location of the fuel pickup tube and the shape of the tank. You need to know if 100% of your fuel is available. It could be that the pickup tube is high enough to leave a lot of fuel in the tank, but you cannot get it to the engine. In addition, some tanks are designed so that they taper at the bottom so when you think you have fuel, it may be getting really low. When the boat is in rough seas, these problems can be worse as fuel sloshes around in the tank. If your tank has an inspection port, open it and determine the location of the fuel pickup and the nature of the tank's shape, especially at the bottom. Of course, you have to pump most of the fuel out of the tank to see these areas.

### Engine Gauges

Most engines come with a set of electronic or electric gauges to monitor engine performance and conditions. While these gauges, when linked with alarm systems, are certainly essential, another set of manual gauges should be installed for backup readings on all critical engine components. A favorite brand is the Murphy line of gauges, although they are not the only ones available. I recommend direct-reading temperature gauges for engine coolant, engine oil, hydraulic oil, and raw-water outlet water. You need pressure gauges for engine oil, transmission oil, and hydraulic oil. Another essential engine room gauge should include fuel vacuum or pressure to warn you when filters are beginning to clog. Additional gauges are handy for coolant level and oil level.

When doing periodic engine room checks, I look at all these gauges as a matter of habit, just to make

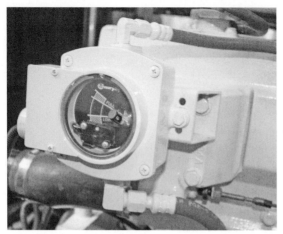

**Figure 11–10.** Coolant level Murphy gauge on FPB 64. (Steve Dashew)

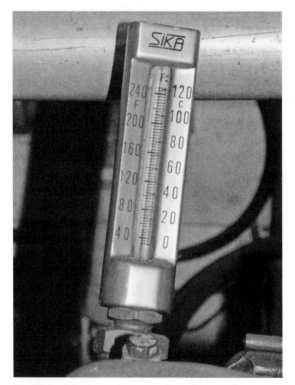

**Figure 11–11.** Engine coolant temperature direct-reading gauge.

sure everything agrees with my electric instruments. A pilothouse exhaust temperature gauge for all your engines, main and auxiliary, is essential. These gauges, also called pyrometers, let you know the loading on the engine—too high or too low. They

can also forewarn of possible prop fouling. If my exhaust temperature is running higher than normal, I usually have a small line wrapped around the shaft, causing just a little bit of drag. At the first opportunity, I check it out.

### Engine Room Ventilation

**Engine room temperature.** When your engine room is too hot, problems can result, including premature component failure, excessive operating temperature, and inefficient combustion due to hot air. In addition, have you ever had to do engine checks, fuel transfers, or fuel filter changes at 125-plus degrees Fahrenheit? If you like saunas, this temperature may be OK, but if you want to do it in comfort, you need a cooler engine room, no more than 30 degrees above ambient temperature (with a maximum of 130 degrees Fahrenheit). Higher temperatures mean premature failure of many temperature-sensitive components. High temperatures can be dangerous because it is possible to get heat stroke from excessive temperatures. Two factors seem most important here: the size of the intake and exhaust vents and the size and capacity of the exhaust fan used.

Milt Baker relates his experience with excessive engine room heat as his new Nordhavn 47 closed in on Puerto Rico in hot sunny weather and very warm seawater:

> *Happily, our boat speed is up. Unhappily, so is the engine room (ER) temperature. We measured after this morning, using two sensors, and it was 150 degrees F at the overhead near the main engine. Dean and I just changed another main engine Racor filter; after about five minutes in the ER, we both emerged closer to 150 than 98.6.*
>
> *ER temperature has become a key determinant of the quality of life on board (or lack thereof). To cool it down we have turned off the generator, re-opened the main saloon hatch into the ER, and opened the door from the ER into the master stateroom. We've set up a new path for cool air in and hot air out, at some discomfort to those of us onboard. But it seems to be working. After two hours like this, engine room temperature has dropped to a relatively cool 130. The bad news is*

that the heat is dispersed through our living spaces: the staterooms, pilothouse, and main saloon—it had to go somewhere! [The problem was resolved by installing a high-capacity Delta "T" Systems axial fan to get cooler outside air into the engine room and force the hot air out. Axial fans are much more efficient than less expensive squirrel cage blowers at moving air into engine rooms.]

**Engine vent location.** Another special consideration for passagemakers is the location of the engine vents and their susceptibility to downflooding, or seawater entering during severe conditions or during extreme heeling. If seawater gets in the vents, even in small amounts, electrical connections can short and cause severe problems. John Spencer relates his problem with this on *Uno Mas* during the Nordhavn Atlantic Rally:

*We [had] some water access the engine air vents located in the cockpit when we rolled to port when the larger wave came from a different direction and hit us on the beam. The water accessed the lazarette through a PVC pipe carrying wire and cable to that area. As she rolled back, the water sloshed UP into the vents on both sides of the inverter, shorting it immediately. The smell was the strongest electrical burning smell I have encountered. This caused the lack of AC power in the stabilizer pump, which resulted in shutting down the Niaids [stabilizers]. [The problem was resolved when an expert swam over from another boat and rewired the stabilizer pump.]*

You cannot simply plug the vent holes. Engines need air. Turbochargers are especially sensitive to lack of air pressure. The only time you want to plug your engine room vents is in the event of fire. In that case, you want to starve the fire of oxygen and let your automatic fire extinguisher do its job. The engines should be shut down immediately if there is fire. For vessel stability, the engine room vents should be as high as possible and baffled to prevent seawater from entering. On coastal cruisers and some passagemakers, I see vents at the deck level or even below. This installation is inexpensive, but is quite threatening to the boat's stability because water can easily enter

Figure 11–12. An easy-to-read engine room temperature gauge is useful. Note the sight tube gauge below and fuel control valves on the right. (Steve Dashew)

in the event of a large wave or extreme heeling. If enough water enters, the vessel instability increases because of water sloshing around in the bilge, exacerbating motion and heeling.

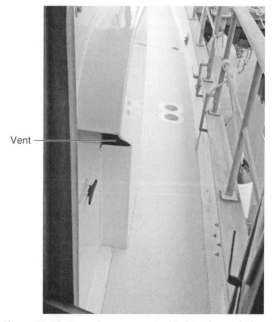

Figure 11–13. An engine room vent added to a lower deck, inboard, improves stability and minimizes seawater incursion.

## Transmission, Stuffing Box, and Propeller

**Transmission considerations.** A passagemaker needs a high-quality, reliable transmission. The two most popular seem to be Twin Disc (long a favorite of commercial fishing boats) and ZF (also used on many newer commercial boats). The key here is finding a transmission that will not fail in the first place; and if the worst happens, it should have some come-home capability. Anyone who has participated in the cruising community can attest to the large number of transmission failures on sailing vessels. It seems they fail much more often than the engines themselves. Our more-robust transmissions do not seem as failure prone. However, you need to become familiar with troubleshooting transmission problems *before* you go voyaging. For example, some transmissions, such as the Twin Disc 509 on my boat, have come-home capability by locking up the transmission in gear if the oil pressure were to fail. I have never had to use it, but I know it is there and how to find the screws that engage the come-home. You also need to know what to do if you have engine failure and must use your wing engine, hydraulic drive, or sails to get home. Most transmissions allow the shaft to freewheel during these situations, but they may also have limits and precautions.

Another consideration for voyaging boats is the reduction gear. Slow-moving displacement vessels move more efficiently with a large reduction gear in the transmission, such as 4:1, and a large propeller that moves water in big volumes at slow rpms. It is possible that efficiency can be doubled with the proper gearing and propeller combination.

**Stuffing box or Aquadrive.** Some marine engineers prefer the old-fashioned stuffing boxes to the newer, dripless connectors. Dave Gerr says that dripless connectors are OK, unless used with an Aquadrive thrust bearing (see sidebar). The nature of this system is to allow the shaft to pull aft 3/8 to 1/2 inch in forward and the same when put in reverse. This can cause the pressure to come off the seal and spray a little salt water in the engine room. Gerr favors using Teflon-impregnated stuffing material in a traditional stuffing box.

Regardless of which stuffing box system is used, it needs constant monitoring. Hugo Carver, marine engineer and boat builder at Knight & Carver, says poor shaft lubrication caused by an overtightened stuffing box or clogged water lines can cause the packing gland to get very hot, create steam, and result in catastrophic failure of the propeller shaft. It seizes up and twists the shaft until it breaks and water enters the boat, sometimes disastrously. It has even been known to tear the stern out of a boat. To guard against this uncommon but potentially fatal problem, check the stuffing box regularly to see if it is getting warmer than usual. We use a traditional box and allow dripping of a drop every minute or so. This means the packing gland and shaft seal are always cool to the touch. When I overtighten the gland a bit, it will get warmer, but never hot. If your

## What Is an Aquadrive?

In an Aquadrive system the propeller shaft is hooked up to the engine by a thrust bearing that absorbs propeller thrust, eliminating the usual stiff hard coupling, with its need for exact alignment. The system uses CV-joint shafts to transmit engine power to the propeller shaft, while allowing the engine to move in any direction. It isolates vibration from the hull and makes for a smoother, quieter boat. However, experts say one should always carry a spacer, just in case the Aquadrive unit should fail.

**Figure 11–14.** Looking astern at an Aquadrive unit installed to reduce vibration in the propeller system. This boat appears to be using a dripless stuffing box connector. (Aquadrive)

packing is hard to reach, put a remote temperature sensor on it to make sure it is running cool.

**Propeller.** Although a complete discussion of propellers is beyond the aim of this book, a few important considerations are highlighted here. First is prop strength. Voyagers hit logs, run aground, wrap nets around props, catch kelp, and so on. A really strong propeller is an asset when far away from home. When we bought *Teka III*, she had a five-bladed prop that was so worn by use and electrolysis that the blades were like knife edges—they would literally cut you. In addition, the five-bladed prop didn't back as well as I expected, in spite of a large rudder. We replaced it with a four-bladed, *nibral*, heavy-duty prop called a "workhorse." (Nibral is a mixture of copper and nickel and is stronger and more resistant to electrolysis than normal bronze props.) After 50,000 nautical miles of use, it still looks new. It chews up logs and stumps in the passage to Alaska like so much seaweed. The four-bladed prop backs well, and we have not noticed any change in vibration levels. Actually, a three-bladed prop is more efficient, but has a greater chance of vibration due to its lower frequency of vibration (higher is better).

# Control Systems

There are three basic sources of control energy: electric, hydraulic, and mechanical/manual. The first two are most important to us because our boats are too heavy for mechanical, hand-powered control methods. We need power for our bow thruster, active fins, anchor windlass, winches, autopilot, rudder control, and engine controls. Manual or mechanical controls are getting rarer. In Chapter 8 we discussed manual methods for retrieving paravanes. Manual engine throttle, shift, and shutdown controls are still commonly used, although they are becoming rarer.

### Electric Control

The most popular control energy in smaller passagemakers is electricity—usually 12 or 24 volts DC, but sometimes 115 volts or higher AC. (The sources of electric power are discussed later in the chapter under electrical systems.) In this section, we assume we have power from batteries or power-generating

sources. Electric power is clean and relatively easy to install. It is fine for light-demand and intermittent control systems, especially in dry places. However, most control motors in wet locations, such as an anchor windlass or bow thruster, have more chance of corrosion and failure, hence require more maintenance. Electrical control systems are more likely to create a fire on board.

### Hydraulic Control

Larger passagemakers often use hydraulic controls, generated by hydraulic pumps on the engine. These hydraulic systems are often load-sensing, in that the hydraulic pressure varies according to the draw on the motor. If no system is being used, the pump just idles along, waiting on a call. Sensing lines are connected to each component to call the pump into action. Each hydraulic motor has two more lines besides the sensing line: one for high pressure coming from the pump, and one for return of the oil to the reservoir. These systems typically work at up to 3,000 pounds per square inch (psi), which is a lot of pressure when you consider that household water lines run at around 60 psi. All this pressure releases a lot of force to move things fast. It can also run for long periods without overheating, unlike an electric motor that gets hot in a hurry if stressed or run continuously.

There are some downsides to hydraulics. They cost more to design and install; they involve many hoses that take more space; they sometimes leak, dripping oil in unwanted places; they require a large oil storage tank; the oil must be cooled, usually with raw water heat exchangers; valves and controls are required to change system flows; additional filters require changing; and more spare oil needs storing. Hydraulic motors can be noisy, although we have not found that to be a problem. For many, hydraulic systems means learning another new system. I remember when I first looked at all the valves and hoses in my engine room, it was intimidating—would I ever learn what everything did? Yes, I did. The systems are not as complicated as they first appear. Figure 11–5 shows all the systems that may be controlled by hydraulics.

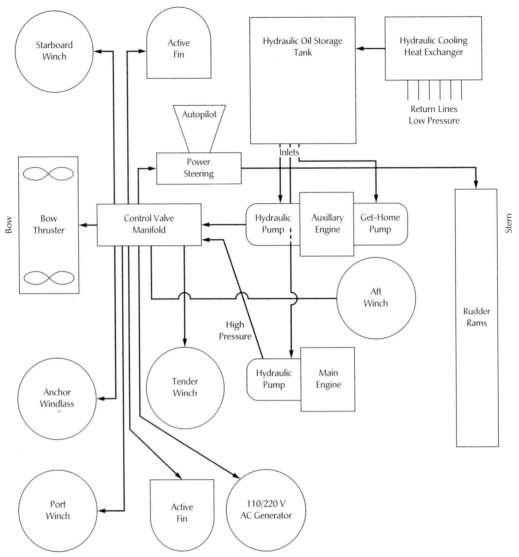

**Figure 11–15.** A simplified view of a passagemaker's hydraulic system. Not all boats have these same systems. (In reality, each of the hydraulic components would have three lines: high pressure, return, and sensing—these are not all shown in this schematic illustration.)

## Bow and Stern Thrusters

Bow thrusters are becoming almost standard on all passagemakers. Cruisers find bow thrusters handy for docking, Mediterranean mooring (bow anchored away from the dock and stern tied to the dock; see Chapter 19), backing down long fairways, as well as leaving docks in heavy current or wind—basically any time we need to move the boat around in close quarters. Some boats now have stern thrusters as

well as bow thrusters, so the boat can move sideways. Stern thrusters can be handy for backing into a tight slip, especially when the wind or current are adverse to your tie-up. On the other hand, thrusters add cost and complexity.

For the first two years we owned *Teka III*, she had no thruster. We made out OK, but docking was tough. Once in Fort Lauderdale it was impossible to get off the dock, even with spring lines. We had to get someone in a dinghy to pull us off by acting like a tugboat. Transiting the Panama Canal was challenging, even when we were tied to a tug. The turbulent currents of the locks resulted in some damage to our teak when we were forced into a tugboat. On our second trip through the canal, we were center tied. It would have been extremely difficult to maintain position without the bow thruster. Keeping the boat in the center of the lock as the water pours in is a tough task requiring really strong line handlers to pull in the lines and keep the boat centered.

Hydraulic bow thrusters are ideal because they have lots of power and can be run continuously. Without hydraulics, you are limited to electric thrusters. This usually means a separate battery bank in the bow to carry the heavy loads. Electric thrusters are often less powerful and can only be run for relatively short periods of time.

What is the downside to installing thrusters? Aside from the costs of the powering system, there are few disadvantages. If you have hydraulic thrusters, you may have to run the auxiliary engine to get full thruster power for docking. While some engines idle at high rpm and have power even at idle, our engine idles too slowly to provide thruster power, so the auxiliary must be started. This can cause premature engine wear due to inadequate loading while the engine is idling, awaiting a thruster action. Another problem is that thruster blades grow barnacles easily and must be cleaned more often than the main propeller. In warmer waters, this means swimming to the bow with a snorkel and a mask and scrapping off the growth. During haulouts, the blades need to be removed and thoroughly cleaned. The space between the two blades is inaccessible while the blades are in place and impossible to clean. Running the thruster frequently helps delay marine growth.

## Rudder System

Most boats use some type of hydraulic rudder control, but many are not part of a central hydraulic system and use small electric pumps to energize the systems. While these systems work, they are more prone to problems. Electrical connections fail; air gets into the system and requires extensive bleeding to remove it. Hoses are generally clamped and can work their way loose. We once experienced a failure with our 37-foot trawler, when a hose worked off, dumping all the hydraulic fluid in the bilge, with complete loss of steering. Luckily, we had just arrived in an anchorage and could make a temporary repair with motor oil to get to a place where we could buy hydraulic oil.

Passagemakers need a reliable steering system and the ability to use an emergency tiller in case of catastrophic failure. A number of boats have removable plugs in their aft decks so a pipe and tiller can be connected to steer manually. Beebe's favorite method is an outboard rudder behind the transom, with the rudder arm entering through the hull and protected by a cover to prevent water intrusion. This method moves the rudder aft and allows more keel and a

Access to the Rudder Shaft and Emergency Steering

Figure 11–16. Beebe rudder design as implemented on *Teka III*: Note the cylindrical fiberglass cover to the right of the spare anchor that allows access to the rudder shaft for an emergency tiller. Also note that the rudder is aft of the transom, protected by the swim bridge.

flatter mounting of the engine drive train; however, it requires a substantial swim bridge to protect the rudder from damage when backing. To use the emergency tiller, you need two block and tackles or boom vangs, with locking devices to hold the tension—one for each side of the tiller. If the boat steers straight, it should be relatively easy to control the course. If not, it is probably a constant two-person job. If you do not have outside access to emergency manual rudder control, better do some planning for this possible emergency. Without a rudder, you are at the mercy of the sea.

## Anchoring Systems

Details about anchoring are covered in Chapter 19. Here we look at some of the mechanical, electrical, and hydraulic control issues. A good strong windlass is absolutely essential for the voyager because you spend many nights at anchor away from the dock. Some boats have pilothouse-operated windlasses where you just press a button to hoist. I am not very impressed with this system because of its distance from the anchor itself. If you haul your anchor at the bow, you can see how much tension is on the rode. You can see when the mud starts arriving, indicating washdown is needed. You can vary the speed to make sure the chain is clean, or even reverse it if needed. When the anchor heads toward the chocks, you can make sure it is cleaned of mud and weeds and that it settles in its place.

A powerful washdown pump near the anchor is mandatory. We have an AC pump that works well. Some boats use hydraulic pumps. It might be hard to get a 12- or 24-volt pump that could create enough pressure and flow.

Planning for windlass failure is much like planning for rudder failure, although you are generally in minimum danger should you experience this unfortunate event. We use a hydraulic windlass that has never failed, but I have an extra long block and tackle made up so I can retrieve the anchor and chain by hand if need be. One end fastens to the mast; the other is attached to a chain grabber for catching and pulling in the chain. On previous boats with electric windlasses, I have found that spare connectors, fuses, circuit breakers, and other assorted electri-

cal fittings can usually resolve a problem within an hour or two—unless, of course, the windings on the motor have burned out. Then, it's time for the block and tackle.

## Autopilot System

It is difficult, but not impossible, to hand steer across oceans, but I wouldn't want to. Hand steering in daylight and good weather is OK, but try it in 12-foot following seas on the blackest of nights—challenging and scary. An autopilot should work in all sea conditions, not just calm seas. When it gets rough, the autopilot steers better than you can, and it is much more relaxing. Autopilots are so important that many builders and owners are installing fully redundant systems—if one fails, they simply turn on the other.

We did not have the space for this option, so we simply carried backups for every component in the system. The only failure we had was on our way from Rota, Spain, to the Canary Islands. All of a sudden, the boat made a hard turn to starboard, and the rudder seemed to jam in that position. I turned off the autopilot and began troubleshooting. At first, I thought the rudder arm was jammed; it was not. I found that we could manually steer, so there was something haywire with the autopilot. A systematic check found the heavy-duty stainless steel multistrand cable for the rudder arm position indicator had fatigued and broken. I rigged some monofilament fishing leaders for a temporary replacement and we continued on our way. Later I replaced the cable with 1/8-inch Amsteel Spectra line, figuring it would not fatigue or break—no problems since.

Search reports from cruisers to find the most reliable and trouble-free autopilot. Word of mouth is the best source.

If you have jog steering, which works when the autopilot is out, this is a much easier steering method than using a big wheel. In fact, Steve Dashew's FPB 64 boats have no traditional steering wheel installed. Unfortunately, because most jog systems work using autopilot systems, if the pilot is lost, manual steering with the wheel may be your only option.

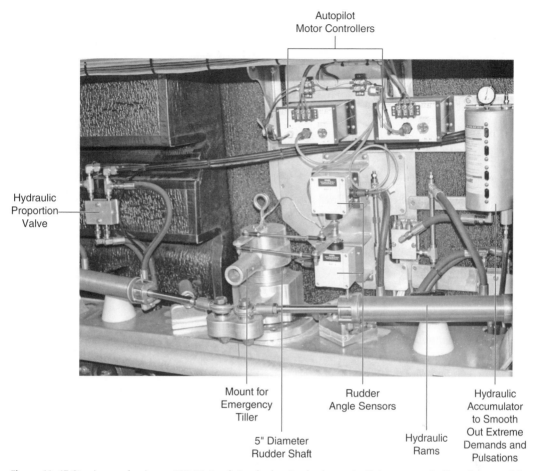

Autopilot
Motor Controllers

Hydraulic
Proportion
Valve

Mount for
Emergency
Tiller

5" Diameter
Rudder Shaft

Rudder
Angle Sensors

Hydraulic
Rams

Hydraulic
Accumulator
to Smooth
Out Extreme
Demands and
Pulsations

**Figure 11–17.** Steering mechanics on FPB 64, *Sarah Sarah*, showing backup autopilot components. There is a complete duplication of all systems.

**Figure 11–18.** Steering knob on Dashew FPB 64, *Sarah Sarah*. You hand steer with the black knob on the right; bow thruster is on the left. A manual steering wheel backup can be connected if needed.

## Engine Controls

Electric and electronic engine throttle and shift controls are the norm nowadays. These systems make it smooth and easy to shift and control engine speed. They also offer remote control from the flying bridge, or even wireless to allow docking while standing by the gunwales. What's wrong with this system? Nothing, as long as it works. We have this convenient system, using MicroCommander, on *Teka III*. It worked flawlessly for about six years, and then we were shocked when we headed into anchor in a cove on Antigua when the boat would not slow down or go out of gear. I immediately headed for the engine room, disconnected the cables, and manually slowed us down. We managed to get the shift to work and then full operation of the system returned. Luckily, we had plenty of room to recover, and no harm was done. What if it had happened in a crowded marina? Several times, ferry boats in the Seattle area have had such failures and crashed into the docks, sometimes with significant damage. We never found out why our system was intermittently failing. The manufacturer gave us a special deal on a new control unit, and we bought it. The lesson here is to be prepared. Know how to manually operate your throttle and shift controls in the event of failure. Be careful of speed in tight quarters and test your controls before you are committed.

Bill Parlatore relates another similar experience:

*I was on a boat where the MicroCommander electronic unit [quit working] . . . backing down a packed fairway in Ft. Lauderdale. We could not slow down or get out of gear, and we kept going astern at a couple of knots. Before anyone could do anything to get below from the fly bridge, the stern of this Sparkman & Stephens yacht squarely hit a floating house held off the shore by two steel poles, which bent in half. The owner and his dog were thrown onto the floor of the floating house, only shaken up but otherwise unhurt. The stern of the boat was damaged. It turned out a ground wire for the engine room control box had come off.*

This is a reminder to go around your boat and tighten connections on a regular basis. Also double-check new installations to make sure all electrical connections are tight.

Bob Senter notes that premature transmission failure is almost always caused by the gear shift not being fully engaged, which allows the gears to slip, creating heat, and often failure. He says to disconnect the shift at the engine and make sure the lever goes all the way into gear.

## Bilge Pumps

We have eight bilge pumps installed on *Teka III*: three normal size electric, three large electric, one engine driven, and one manual, hand-operated pump. The small pumps handle routine water intrusion, mostly in the stern compartment from the shaft drips. There

**Figure 11–19.** Hydraulically driven central bilge pump on Diesel Duck 48, *10&2*. The gray intake valves are below, with the labeled red handles.

is one large DC pump in each compartment, with automatic switches mounted about 6 inches higher than the bilge floor. These pumps are alarmed so that when one starts pumping a horn goes off in the pilothouse. The larger pumps have 1-1/2-inch hoses, so they can move a lot of water. In the past 14 years of cruising, none of the backup pumps has automatically started. Boats with hydraulic systems can install a central hydraulic pump with hoses to various compartments. These pumps can move a lot of water fast. Some voyagers with extra space bring gasoline–powered portable bilge pumps like the ones used by the Coast Guard. One hopes all these pumps are not needed, but if a major inflow of water occurs from either fresh or salt sources, vessel stability is seriously degraded, as we saw in Chapter 7 on stability.

## The Electrical System

Electrical system design depends on the demand. If you have 24/7 air conditioning, you probably need 24/7 generator power. If you decide on an all-electric galley with electric cooking and baking, you need to plan for generator usage during the times you run these appliances. Other than air conditioning, some refrigeration systems, and cooking demands, you can usually run with minimal generator use—thus lowering cost, noise, and reducing maintenance.

### Generator Options

For 24/7 AC power, multiple generators are often needed just in case one has trouble—you don't want to be without power. Some cruisers elect one larger and one smaller generator, but often the smaller generator is not powerful enough. Having two generators of the same size is another option—this also has the advantage of complete parts interchangeability. Of course, two generators take up more engine room space; this approach may be more appropriate in boats of 60 feet or more. Smaller passagemakers should consider other options for staying cool and cooking. Most generators consume 1 gallon per hour per 10 kilowatts, adding to tank requirements and costs and decreasing range.

**Hydraulic generators.** This option is not widely used, but it has potential. A variable displacement pump is combined with a specially controlled hydraulic motor to achieve significant AC power, such as 10 to 15 kilowatts (kW). Most generators run at a fixed speed, say 1,800 or 3,600 rpm. A hydraulically driven generator can be operated at almost any engine speed when significant hydraulic power is developed (usually 1,000 rpm and up). The motor then automatically maintains 3,600 rpm to generate 3-phase AC power (230 volt, 3-phase power). Kar-Tech and High Country Tech are two companies that make electronic generator controllers to ensure cycles remain constant regardless of engine speed.

This approach allows you to use AC from power generated by your main engine without starting the auxiliary generator. Think of the savings on a 15-day ocean voyage with the generator *and* the main engine running 24/7. Sure, there is some power drain on the main engine, but not much. It also has the advantage of loading the engine a bit more when operating at low speeds for long periods of time. When at anchor, you can use the same hydraulic generator, this time run from a pump on the auxiliary engine. Again the powering engine's speed is not critical so long as it creates enough rpm to energize the hydraulic system and does not *lug* (strain itself).

What is the downside? Aside from the expense of installing a major hydraulic system, the hydraulic circuit requires a sensitive flow gauge to adjust the cycles to the proper speed. Once set, the cycles are pretty stable, but it is possible that something may plug the system and cause a decline in cycles. Most electrical appliances are not too sensitive to cycles as long as you keep them to within about 5 percent variance. Many, but not all, 60-cycle appliances will even run on European power, which uses 50 cycles.

Generator              Constant-Speed
Hydraulic Motor

**Figure 11–20.** A 10KW 220-volt, 3-phase generator, with the hydraulic motor to the right of the generator.

## Inverters

Most modern cruisers use one or more inverters to change 12- or 24-volt battery power to 115-volt AC power for electrical appliances such as refrigerators, microwaves, entertainment systems, and other small home appliances. Some boats run computers or other electronic systems on AC power. If so, it is wise to have an additional dedicated inverter that is not connected in any way to shore or generator power to prevent surge or dropouts when the inverter is switching from battery power to shore or generator power. Computers lose data and reboot. Fuses sometimes blow.

If you have large alternators on your engine, say 150 amps or more, you can often use only the inverter for AC power unless you are air conditioning or cooking. This may save a lot of generator usage. We use the generator for heating hot water and for the watermaker. While we can run our refrigerator and freezer on the inverter, we usually turn them on while making hot water, thus easing the load on the alternator and inverter. The size of your inverter depends on your alternator, battery bank, and demand appliances. There are many sources that help you do the calculations. However, keep in mind that you may spend a lot of time at anchor with your generator operating. This needs to be factored into your calculations—batteries only support so much draw.

You can replace some generator needs by using a large battery bank (as discussed in the following section) and several heavy-duty inverters wired in parallel. Steve Dashew employs three 3,000-watt, 70-amp DC, Victron Energy Converters to create the massive conversion capability of 9,000 watts at 200 amps of DC charging. That is really a lot of power.

## Battery Choice

There are many options for batteries. Each type has its proponents and critics. For ship power (the batteries that power the inverter and other DC systems at anchor or underway), you need deep-cycle batteries that are designed to be discharged at anchor, recover, and then do it again the next day. There are three basic types of deep-cycle batteries and many variations in power and size.

**Wet-cell batteries.** We started out with four high-quality, expensive 8D deep-cycle batteries, weighing about 165 pounds each. Now that's pretty heavy. We had a couple of failures. The first was covered by warranty, but the next happened in Barcelona, Spain, a long way from a distributor. We decided to replace them with Trojan T-105 Plus 6-volt batteries. Even though it takes twice as many batteries (8 batteries), they weigh only 62 pounds each so they are easier to replace. Because these batteries typically run golf carts and forklifts, they are easily available worldwide and they are probably the lowest-cost option. We replaced our bank after 7 years and thousands of discharges, even though they were still working, because we were headed for a remote area in

NAIAD Active Fin Control    3 × 3000 Watt Inverters

Autopilot Controls    Ground Connections (Yellow)    Fuse

Figure 11–21. FPB 64 electrical room, showing the three Victron Energy Converters. Electronics control boxes are arranged on the bulkhead at the left. (Steve Dashew)

Alaska in which any type of service is difficult and expensive. Wet-cell batteries require good ventilation because they give off hydrogen fumes when charging, which can explode. They also require regular checks of battery water levels. If you expect to cruise the roaring forties in a self-righting boat that rolls 360 degrees, these batteries are not for you. They could coat the engine room with acid if the tops came loose.

**Gel-cell batteries.** These batteries use a thickening agent to keep the electrolyte from moving around. They are sealed and require no maintenance. Their downside is that they cost more and are more sensitive to overcharging. It is possible to charge them to too high a voltage and ruin all the batteries. The amount of power stored is similar to wet-cell batteries, and the weight is similar to slightly higher.

**Absorbed glass mat (AGM) batteries.** A glass mat is used to separate the lead cells and hold the electrolyte in place. They are spill-proof and vibration resistant. They use the same voltage set points for charging and can replace wet cells without major changes. AGM batteries are also sealed like the gel-cell, so they have the same advantages, including no gassing during charging.

A major advantage of both gel and AGM batteries is that they can discharge higher loads faster than wet cells—3:1 ratio for gel or AGM between battery bank size and largest load versus 4:1 for wet cells. This is a significant plus if you are powering a bow thruster that requires large amounts of power instantaneously. You may be able to use a smaller battery bank to achieve the same results. Gel and AGM are subject to overcharging, so charging circuits need to be carefully monitored. The other downside is higher cost.

**Battery sizes.** It is becoming more popular to use a large bank of 2.2 volt batteries to give power for running large inverters during anchorages or at the dock when adequate shore power is not available. Trojan makes two sizes of 2.2-volt wet cells: 24-plus inches high and 208 pounds or 31-plus inches high at 285 pounds. You would need 6 for a 12-volt system and 12 for a 24-volt system. If you selected the large size and 24 volts, your battery bank would weigh 3,420 pounds—probably

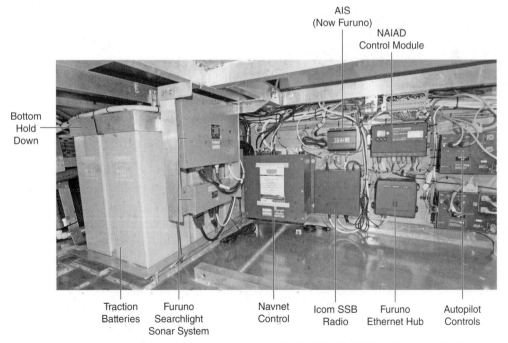

Figure 11–22. Note the size of the traction batteries on the left in this FPB 64–28" high. The battery hold-down brackets are also robust. The electronics black boxes are easy to access; some are redundant backups. This area is called "the basement." (Steve Dashew)

more than your main engine. Steve Dashew has chosen a bank of 2.2-volt traction batteries weighing 194 pounds each and 28 inches high. These batteries allow freedom from generator noise, fumes, and maintenance for most of the time. Needless to say, such large batteries may affect the trim of the vessel and should be included in determining stability.

## Shore Power

**Transformers are simple and cheap.** Finding the right shore power to match the boat's system is almost impossible without some type of converter or transformer. Most of the world uses 220 volts and 50 cycles. The least-costly solution is a transformer that is wired to convert 220 volts to 110 volts. Many budget-wise sailors simply buy a transformer and do the conversion right on the deck. A 2,000 to 3,000 watt

Figure 11–23. Marvin Day sorting out electric connections during the Black Sea Rally. There is a lot of voltage loss in this number of connections. Note the lighter wire used for 220-volt shore power connections. Shore power is necessary for battery charging and refrigeration if you intend to leave the boat for a few days.

transformer is heavy, but still portable. We bought one when we arrived in Portugal and wired it into the boat's system with a series of switches. We had two 220-volt European female plugs—one for the transformer and one for our hot water heater. We had wired one of the 30-gallon electric hot water heater's elements for 220-volt shore power. We also had outlets fore and aft for connecting 220-volt appliances and space heaters. However, the transformer did not change 50 cycles to 60 cycles, so a few of our appliances would not work, including our small air conditioner and the microwave. Although our Technicold refrigerator/freezer was listed at 60 cycles, it worked just fine on 50 cycles. Our electronics for TV and sound also were good on 50 cycles. Most European shore power uses 30 amp circuits with specialized plugs. Polarity was sometimes reversed, so one needs to check voltage and polarity every time. Hookups can be incredibly complex (see Figure 11–23 from the Black Sea Rally).

**Use inverters.** Another strategy, used by Dashew on the FPB 64, is to use massive batteries and three inverters in parallel to provide all the boat's AC needs. The boat can use whatever shore power is available, even if weak, and make up the difference from the massive battery bank or by running the generator. They do not need to be concerned about the amount or quality of shore power—the inverters provide the appropriate cycles.

**Use isolators and power conditioners.** Electrical isolation devices are used to convert voltage in a number of ways. Atlas has a unit that inputs 190 volts to 250 volts and outputs 110/220 and other combinations. It allows using two shore power cords and circuits to squeeze more power for air conditioning and other high-draw uses. Of course, this assumes that two separate power outlets are available—a rarity in our experience. Atlas power also provides frequency converters so that 60 cycle motors and appliances can be run on 50 cycle shore power. These systems work, but they are costly, bulky, and generate a lot of heat.

**Specify multivoltage/multicycle appliances.** Another option is to specify systems and appliances that work on either 50 or 60 cycles. This may not be easy, but because most of the world uses

50 cycles, most products have some compatibility built in or they can be ordered with more flexible electrical requirements. Some boats that intend worldwide cruising specify 220-volt, 50 cycle wiring and appliances so they match most countries' electrical systems. An added advantage is that lighter wire can be used for these higher-voltage systems.

## Night Lighting for Voyagers

Night passages are inevitable for the voyager. There are three major considerations: inside lighting to maintain night vision, outside lighting for underway navigation, and running lights.

**Interior lighting.** Modern pilothouses bristle with electronics, many with night vision settings that dim the light to a much lower setting. However, it may be difficult to get the light level low enough. If you need your chart program running, its night setting may be good, but often computer icons at the bottom of the screen do not dim, creating night-vision killing glare. Other than turning the lighting or equipment off, you can devise various covers with red plastic covers. We did this on our computer screen and it worked reasonably well. You can also find marine monitors that are specifically designed to reduce lighting to almost nothing, but they generally cost more. Also important is isolating the pilothouse from the saloon or other areas that might use white lights at night. Various curtains can be devised to inexpensively fill this need. We run red lights in the galley and engine room at night so crew can get a snack or check the engine without impairing their vision. Check out your night lighting at the dock before departure to make sure it is dim enough.

**Lighting the way while underway.** This is one of the most difficult problems we have encountered. Often, due to heavy seas or because of debris or fishing floats in the water, you want to look ahead at night. We have a large halogen light mounted near the top of the mast. Unfortunately, when it is on, the reflection from our white and light colored foredecks overpower our eyes and we can see very little on the sea ahead. I have been checking fishing boats at Fisherman's Terminal here in Seattle to see what they do about this vision issue. It seems they all mount their large lights well forward on a forward mast. Frequently, the forward decks are painted black as well so that no light is reflected. Many have pilothouses near the bow. While most of these strategies would not apply to our boats, the placement of a strong light near the bow may provide such a night vision aid (see Figure 11–24).

**Running lights.** Large, reliable, bright running lights are a plus—we want to be seen by other ships at night. However, the forward steaming light can cause some of the same problems discussed in the floodlight discussion. It wasn't until we had spent perhaps 100 nights at sea that Hugo Carver, the builder of our boat who was along for a passage along the coast of South America, solved the problem with a simple light deflector. It allows

Figure 11–24. Bow light on FPB 64 shows minimum reflection from the deck and allows good vision of the sea ahead. (Steve Dashew)

our light to be seen by other boats, but shields the foredeck from its bright white light. This simple fix made a major improvement in night vision. An important part of this design is the nails that prevent birds from perching or nesting at that location. Even underway in strong winds and seas, we have birds land on our paravane retrieval lines and balance there all night long. Obviously, we want to prevent this when it might obscure our running lights.

**Night vision aids.** There are night vision scopes, infared TV cameras, and other high-tech ways of seeing better at night. We have used the night vision scope mainly for observing shore when at anchor on a dark night. However, we find the radar is a more effective way of determining our boat's position in the dark. We have not found these aids useful at sea. If you want to try these aids, check with other cruisers who have used them for first-hand feedback about their effectiveness. High-powered, handheld searchlights are fine if you want to spot other boats in an anchorage or if you are searching for a buoy number, but these lights destroy your night vision for a while. Also, remember not

to shine a spotlight on a boat entering an anchorage at night—it blinds them just when they need their night vision the most. To allow them to see your boat, shine the light on your mast or turn on your deck lights.

## Electronics Systems

Electronics have become increasing complex and are changing so rapidly that it would be impossible to cover all the issues in this book. We highlight a few considerations that might influence your choices. We discuss reliability, repairability, and redundancy issues, followed by a brief discussion on key electronics systems needed for ocean voyaging. It is easy to become attracted to the many systems now available, but some are merely fun to have and do not significantly contribute to the safety or enjoyment of the voyage.

### Reliability, Repairability, and Redundancy

Electronic systems are becoming more reliable, but Murphy's Law implies that they will break, usually when you need them the most. We believe in redundancy for every major essential electronic system. Independent components that run without the central computer system are desirable from both reliability and repairability standpoints. If you can yank out a GPS unit and replace it with another, it is cheaper and easier than having to replace some multitask unit. To analyze this issue, list each system you consider to be essential. Second, determine if you are capable of repairing or replacing it. Third, how time-critical is replacement? (If your chart program fails, do you have backup paper charts?) Fourth, is there another system that can provide the information? (At sea, you may be able to use Automatic Identification System [AIS] to identify ships in your path if your radar fails.)

### Critical Electronics Systems

While it is difficult to put systems in a priority order, I have attempted to list the more important ones first. However, mariners must determine their own priority based on their competence and personal needs. In this section, I have not included the EPIRB; it is covered in Chapter 19 on safety issues.

Figure 11–25. Mast steaming light reflector devised by Hugo Carver. The stainless nails are to prevent birds from landing or sitting on this area. The porcupine is for lightning dissipation (see Chapter 19).

**GPS.** I put this high on the list because we have to know our position. I grew up before GPS and its predecessor, LORAN, in the days when dead reckoning and chart plotting were critical skills. Ocean voyagers also needed a sextant to determine position. It is sometimes amazingly difficult to navigate by dead reckoning—land features are often confusing and rocks are hard to spot. Today, it is really simple with GPS. We have two GPS units installed in the pilothouse: one in the aft cabin where we sleep, and one handheld for emergencies or when traveling in the dinghy. In the event of severe lightning storms, we store one or two GPS units in the oven to minimize the effects of a nearby strike.

**VHF radio.** In the event of an emergency, VHF sends signals to all vessels within its reception area—it is indispensable for emergencies. When entering ports, you must be able to contact officials and marinas. At sea, contact with ships is via VHF. Like the GPS, we have two VHF radios in the pilothouse plus a handheld for dinghy and emergency use. In addition, without a VHF radio you might miss a call for sundowners with other cruising boats.

**Depth sounder.** Obviously, you need to know the depth when approaching shoals, harbors, anchorages, and channels. The sounder often gives advance warning when you are entering shoaling water, preventing a grounding, or worse. We use a Furuno color depth recorder with a high-powered dual frequency transducer that allows readings in deep water. We find this helps us confirm our position by comparing with the chart. It also highlights bottom conditions that may cause severe waves or breakers. We have two additional depth sounders, a forward-looking unit that is useful when creeping slowly through coral or rocks, and a small unit in the aft cabin for observing depth while at anchor.

**Autopilot.** We discussed autopilots earlier in this chapter. This is one of the top aids in voyaging. Hand steering at sea, especially in rough conditions, can be challenging and tiring. Some boats with weak rudder design may be difficult to hand steer. Linking the autopilot with the GPS gives an excellent course tool that allows for currents and other factors that can result in course corrections if using compass alone.

On ocean voyages, we always use GPS control of the autopilot. We have a complete duplicate set of components, but they are not installed and ready to use. I feel confident that I could replace any of the components while someone hand steers.

**Radar.** Radar allows us to see in the dark, the fog, and in rainstorms. A good open array radar can pick up small fishing boats anchored without lights on the blackest of nights. It also helps avoid ships, rocks, buoys, islands, and other objects that may not be clearly seen with the naked eye. It allows you to accurately mark your anchoring position by noting distances to various shore points. It shows what other boats are doing in the anchorage during a blow. We find radar is constantly in use. In fact when we are at sea during the night, we turn on both our radars. One looks for fast-moving distant ships; the other for small boats or floating debris within a 1-mile radius. Your main radar should have Automatic Radar Plotting Aid (ARPA) capability. This allows you to see the speed and course of approaching vessels, the closest point of approach, and the time to the closest approach.

**Chartplotter/computer.** Electronic charts surely make navigation easier, but it is also important to keep old-fashioned paper charts aboard. These charts are needed for backup in the event of computer failure and for route planning to view the overall route. On ocean crossings, electronic charts are pretty useless until you approach land. Computers with AIS capability can identify the name, course, speed, and type of ship through their AIS transmissions. These are a useful adjunct to radar and aid in contact with ships because they can be called by name. The computer also allows downloading weather faxes, grib weather files, and e-mails. (These uses are discussed in Chapter 18.) Most boats carry redundant laptop computers with software installed so they can be substituted whenever needed.

**Single Side Band (SSB) radio.** Many voyagers are ready to use their SSB radios as anchors because this is the most difficult piece of equipment to install and operate successfully. Why would you want it? The first reason is emergencies. Like the VHF, you can contact stations in the part of the world where you are cruising. These stations are normally anxious to help out in any kind of emergency, often arranging to contact the appropriate Coast Guard. In addition, most cruising sailboats, which far outnumber motor cruisers, monitor SSB or HAM channels at certain times of the day. There are usually cruising nets that offer local insights into weather, port happenings, boat locations, and other items of interest. You may use the SSB for low-cost e-mail and weather with Sailmail or Airmail. It took us a while to get our SSB running, but now we use it constantly while voyaging.

**Satellite phones.** While prices are coming down, sat phones are still fairly expensive, especially with Internet services. Not all services offer worldwide coverage, so investigate before you sign up. Owning a handheld unit may be the least expensive way to go. A fixed dome costs more. Carefully study the fees—it is possible to get a six-figure phone bill if surfing the Internet. If you depend solely on a sat phone for emergencies, you need an extensive phone book. If you are adrift in the South China Sea, who will you call? If you need maintenance or repair advice, who will you call? What about time and date differences? Will anyone be at the other end? An extensive e-mail list of important contacts should also be available whether you use SSB or sat phone. What do you do about redundancy? Seems logical to have both SSB and satellite phone. Both can help in an emergency.

## CHAPTER TWELVE

# Selected Passagemaker Designs

There is a wide variety of sizes and designs of passagemaking yachts available, and I can include only a limited selection in this chapter. I asked each builder or designer to submit up to two displacement-hull designs, 65' or less. Additionally, I encouraged a variety of lengths, from boats in the 40'-plus range up to the 60'-plus range. Some of the boats are available for do-it-yourself construction or for custom building in the yard of your choice. Others, especially the fiberglass hulls, come from builders who own the hull molds. Even production boats are built based on firm orders from customers and may be considered as semicustom boats. This chapter provides both an overview of the many available designs and my brief impressions of each.

Captain Beebe's comments in the first edition still apply here:

> We owe a debt of gratitude to all the designers who contributed their knowledge and experience to make up this chapter. The remarkable diversity of solutions to the problem of the seagoing motorboat shows how much scope there is for different approaches to achieving what essentially is a single specification—that the product be a seaworthy motorboat with the [ability to cross oceans].

The previous three chapters—Chapter 9, Choosing a Boat; Chapter 10, Interior Layout; and Chapter 11, The Passagemakers' Systems—are essential prerequisites to this chapter. Keep your own spiral of design in mind as you peruse these designs. The chapter is divided into two sections. The first section features boats from boatbuilders, including Dashew, Kadey-Krogen, Nordhavn, and Seahorse Marine. The second section includes boats from eight designers: Pat Bray, George Buehler, Dave Gerr, Michael Kasten, Charles Neville, Bruce Roberts, Stephen Seaton, and Malcolm Tennant. Both sections are presented in alphabetical order.

## Boatbuilders' Designs

### Dashew FPB 64

Steve Dashew, a renowned sailor, was the developer of the Sundeer and Deerfoot line of sailboats. His sailboats are long, narrow, and fast; and he continually won major sailing races in his boat, *Beowulf*. A few years ago he moved into the powerboat world. He spent a lot of time developing his concept that built on his knowledge of sailboats—long, thin, relatively shallow draft and light displacement boats that could go fast and cover vast distances. The result was *Windhorse*, an 83-foot vessel that has covered much of the world (50,000-plus nautical miles) since her launch in May 2005. From his experience in developing and equipping *Windhorse*, Dashew decided to build a line of boats he calls the Functional Pilot Boat (FPB). So far, he has seven FPB 64s completed or under construction. He shared much of the development process and his decisions on design and equipment on his website and in magazine articles. No other designer has been as open about all aspects of design and voyaging.

Steve and his wife Linda state their boat design objective: "Our design goal has always been to

## Dashew FPB 64

| | | | |
|---|---|---|---|
| Length overall | 64.95' | Stabilization and estimated efficiency loss | Active fins |
| Length waterline | 63.6' | PC | N/A |
| Beam | 17.04 | L/B | 2.56 |
| Draft | 4.5' | D/L | 244 |
| Displacement | 90,000 lbs. | Heel angle at max righting moment | 60 degrees |
| Standard engine | John Deere 6068 TFM 263 hp | Max value of righting lever | 2.25 (varies with tankage) |
| Fuel capacity | 3,400 gallons | ISO Design Category | N/A |
| Number fuel tanks | 4 plus day tank | Minimum range positive stability* | 130 degrees |
| Water capacity | 1,800 gallons | | |
| Holding tank capacity | 80 gallons with Vacuflush | | |
| Speed/range at S/L 1.19 without stabilization | 9.5 knots/5,500 nautical miles | | |

*See the stability curve on page 65.

**Figure 12–1A.** *Windhorse,* Dashew's "unsailboat," powers through the chop at high speed. (Steve Dashew)

**Figure 12–1B.** The FPB 64 profile. (Steve Dashew)

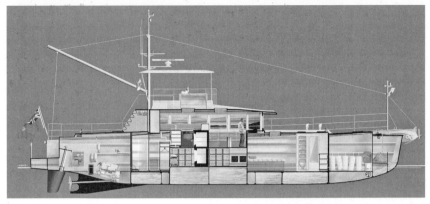

**Figure 12–1C.** Accommodations and machinery layout, profile view. (Steve Dashew)

**Figure 12–1D.** Accommodations and machinery below deck. (Steve Dashew)

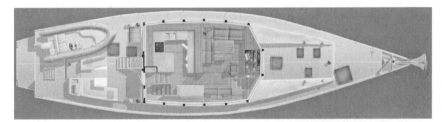

**Figure 12–1E.** Accommodations and layout of upper deck. (Steve Dashew)

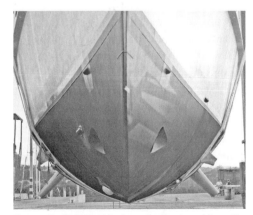

**Figure 12–1F.** FPB 64 bottom details viewed from the bow. (Steve Dashew)

**Figure 12–1G.** FPB 64 bottom details, viewed from the stern. (Steve Dashew)

cross oceans in maximum comfort and safety, while minimizing passage times. Now we're taking a new approach to this process." Here is what they want to accomplish:

+ Maintain high average open-ocean speeds to be able to avoid dangerous weather and make the most of favorable conditions.
+ Maintain steering control downwind in big seas.
+ Make progress uphill in breaking head seas while maintaining excellent maneuverability.
+ Possess a fallback mode if boat is disabled in dangerous weather.
+ Ability to recover from a knockdown.

The key requirements in the design are these:

+ Comfort on long offshore passages
+ Ability to deal with extremes of wind and sea
+ An ocean crossing range at a 10- to 11-knot cruising speed
+ Self-righting capability (full recovery from a wave-induced capsize)
+ Smooth ride in trade wind head seas
+ Systems that allow sitting at anchor for days without using the generator
+ Low maintenance
+ Easy way to leave the boat in storage for extended periods

Dashew's design uses length and fine entry to provide a smoother ride in head seas. Most passagemakers have a wider, fatter bow—often with a lot of flare, which exacerbates the problem in big head seas. The bow hits the big wave like a breakwater and either stops or pounds so violently that you must slow down. The long, skinny boat with modest beam and a sharp entry can power right through head seas with little loss of speed or crew discomfort. The underwater lines curve in and flatten out at the stern. There is little target for a large following sea. The flatter portions aft create lift, much like a semidisplacement hull design, but they are much narrower, so the lift effect is limited. It also appears to be distributed along the entire hull length.

The boat is built of aluminum, with all standards exceeding Lloyds' standards. The windows are 3/4-inch safety glass in front and sides—they are strong

enough to survive a rollover. However, you may recall from Chapter 8, Stabilizing Against Rolling, that this vessel has an excellent stability curve and would recover rapidly if it were ever knocked down or rolled. There is even a flap in the engine-room ventilation that automatically closes in the event of inversion, making downflooding unlikely.

The FPB 64 layout is outstanding for comfort at sea. All living, sleeping, and working areas are close to the center of gravity, resulting in minimum motion for the crew. The pilothouse is connected with the main saloon and galley and is quite low, again a plus for comfort. The engine room is aft, so noise and heat is removed from living spaces. I mentioned earlier when discussing interior design that the combination galley, pilothouse, and saloon can be great for socializing, but makes running at night more challenging. The pilot area cannot be easily segregated from the other livings areas, so subdued colored light must be used. Some will find the rather minimal space for a 64-foot boat is a drawback here—you will certainly get a lot more space in a more conventional trawler. If you plan to spend most of your time at the dock, the extra space may be one of your requirements.

Outside appearance may also be a concern. The Dashews do not paint their aluminum hulls, thus they tend to look like workboats, or even military boats. This may turn off the owner who wants a shiny boat to polish and show off at the dock. One of Dashew's design objectives is minimum maintenance. Anyone who has spent time cleaning, buffing, polishing, and retouching a 64-foot boat knows it takes a lot of time and effort.

Steve has also been a leader in systems engineering. Several of his installation designs have been illustrated in earlier chapters. The large water tank capacity is designed so that as fuel is used during a passage, it can be replaced by making water, thus maintaining a steady displacement weight. One starts with a relatively low amount of water and adding more as needed while making the passage. He is also an innovator in electricity management—heavy-duty traction batteries weighing more than 2,000 pounds (see Figure 11–22) provide electricity while at anchor. Large inverters and alternators provide whatever power is needed without reliance on a constantly running generator. Almost all electronic systems have built-in backups, and Steve favors independent units that can be repaired and replaced without troubleshooting the entire system. Access to and troubleshooting of systems is outstanding with large areas underneath the upper deck allocated to batteries and electrical equipment.

## Kadey-Krogen

There are currently seven Krogen models available from 39 to 64 feet—most have ocean-crossing range. Here we highlight two passagemakers: the 52 and the 64. In Chapter 13, Proven Passagemakers of the Past, several Krogens are also discussed.

Kadey-Krogen is one of the oldest surviving builders of passagemakers—it has been in business since 1976.

Krogens are lighter weight than many passagemakers because they use a closed-cell PVC sandwich core above the waterline. Below the waterline, they employ solid fiberglass with an aramid (think Kevlar) fiber reinforcement that adds a bulletproof-strong layer to the hull. Krogen advertises that it uses hull integrity—never simply lengthening a hull to add space. Each hull is completely designed and integrated as a separate unit.

**Krogen 52.** The Krogen 52 has the familiar look of most of the Kadey-Krogen line with a high bow,

| Krogen 52 | | | |
|---|---|---|---|
| Length overall | 52'8" | Speed/range at S/L 1.0 without stabilization | 6.89 knots/3,537 nautical miles |
| Length with bow platform and swim platform | 57'8½" | Stabilization and estimated efficiency loss | TRAC active fin, 9 square feet |
| Length waterline | 47'6" | PC | 0.61 |
| Beam | 17'3" | L/B | 3.05 (deck/molded beam) 3.06 (LWL/BWL) |
| Draft (max load) | 5'7½" | D/L | 292 (50% load) |
| Displacement (max load) | 76,700 lbs. | Heel angle at max righting moment | Max load 43 degrees Light load 59 degrees |
| Standard engine | John Deere 6068AFM75, 231 hp | Max value of righting lever | Max load 1.48 Light load 1.45 |
| Fuel capacity | 1,400 gallons | | |
| Number fuel tanks | 4 | Max degrees positive stability | Max load 88 degrees Light load 87 degrees |
| Water capacity | 400 gallons | | |
| Holding tank capacity | 140 gal grey and 140 gal black | ISO Design Category | A |
| Speed/range at S/L 1.2 without stabilization | 8.27 knots/2,378 nautical miles | | |

**Figure 12–2A.** Krogen 52. (John Beatty/Kadey-Krogen)

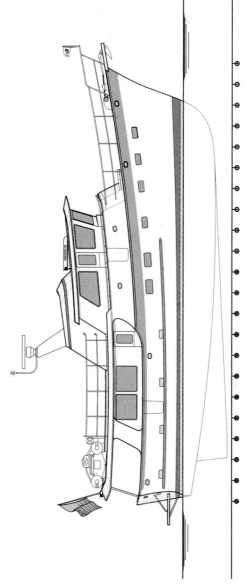

Figure 12–2B. Krogen 52 profile. (Kadey-Krogen)

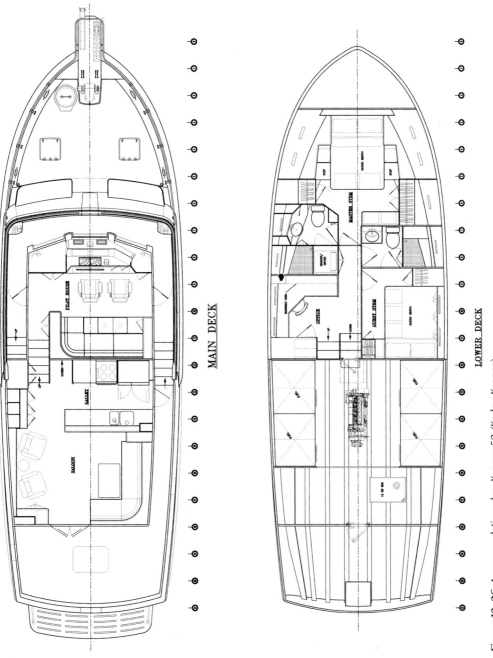

MAIN DECK

LOWER DECK

**Figure 12–2C.** Accommodation plan, Krogen 52. (Kadey-Krogen)

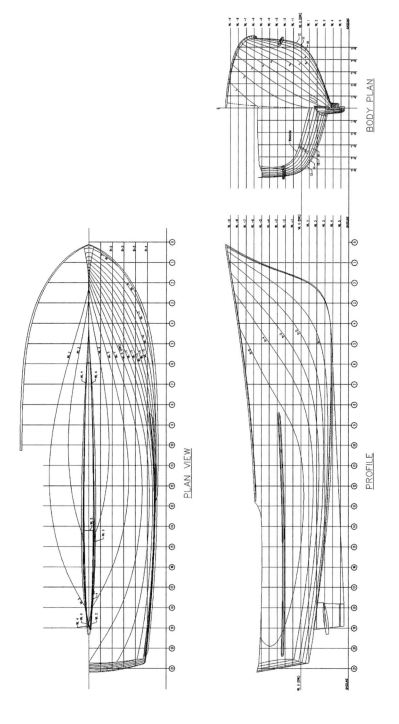

**Figure 12–2D.** Lines for Krogen 52. (Kadey-Krogen)

forward pilothouse, and master cabin farther forward. Its typical Krogen hull form shows fine entry and exit, moderate D/L, and Krogen's trademark hourglass stern; the hull should be efficient with excellent fuel consumption. The interior layout has proven popular over the years, but will probably be less comfortable on ocean passages than the Krogen 64 (discussed next). A forward pilothouse gives great visibility, but results in more motion at sea and more windage up front, making for more difficult maneuvering in high winds and more sailing at anchor.

**Krogen 64.** The Krogen 64 has a pilothouse located more amidships, so the motion at sea is easier. It is still high, providing excellent visibility, but is somewhat far away from the boat's center of gravity, where the motion would be easiest. The plan shown here has the master stateroom amidships rather

| Krogen 64 | | | |
|---|---|---|---|
| Length overall | 64'0" | Speed/range at S/L 1.0 without stabilization | 7.9 knots/4,463 nautical miles |
| LOA with bow platform and swim platform | 70'4" | Stabilization and estimated efficiency loss | TRAC active fin/12 square feet |
| Length waterline | 62'9" | PC | 0.63 |
| Beam | 20'6" | L/B | 3.12 (deck/molded beam) 3.19 (LWL/BWL) |
| Draft (max load) | 6'1" | | |
| Displacement (max load) | 173,000 lbs. | D/L | 289 (half load) |
| Standard engine | John Deere 6068AFM75, 231 hp | Heel angle at max righting moment | N/A |
| Fuel capacity | 3,000 gallons | | |
| Number fuel tanks | 4 | Max value of righting lever | N/A |
| Water capacity | 600 gallons | Max degrees positive stability | N/A |
| Holding tank capacity | 250 gal grey and 250 gal black | | |
| Speed/range at S/L 1.2 without stabilization | 9.5 knots/2,467 nautical miles | ISO Design Category | A |

**Figure 12–2E.** Krogen 64 profile. (Kadey-Krogen)

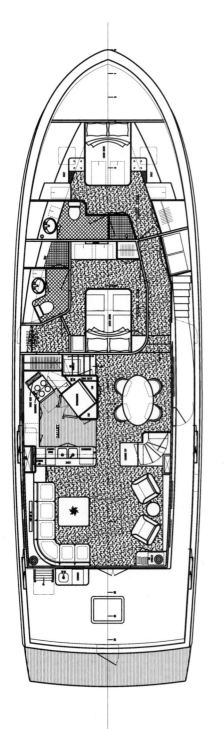

**MAIN DECK**

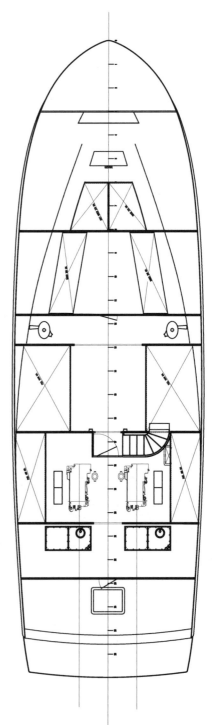

**LOWER DECK**

**Figure 12–2F.** Krogen 64 accommodation plan, showing guest stateroom forward; an alternate plan with forward owner's stateroom is also available. (Kadey-Krogen)

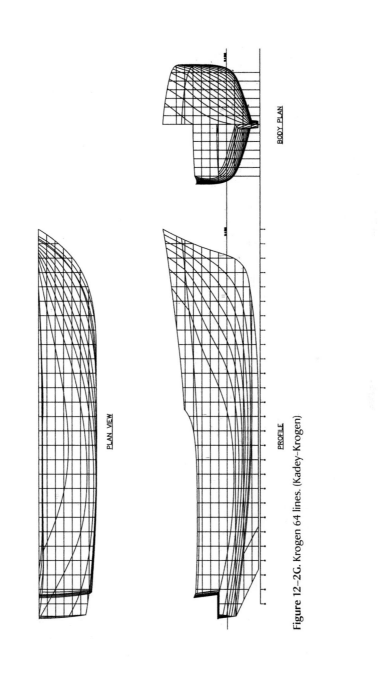

BODY PLAN

PLAN VIEW

PROFILE

**Figure 12–2G. Krogen 64 lines. (Kadey–Krogen)**

than in the bow—again, for comfort and quietness. I was glad to see a separate entrance from the saloon to the engine room, so periodic checks do not bother people in the master stateroom. It looks like there may be another engine room entrance on the aft deck. This would be great for maintenance activities, but might present opportunities for downflooding unless there is a strong waterproof door that is kept closed. I like the built-in swim step. A swim platform like this should not make noise when waves or swells arrive from the stern while in an exposed anchorage.

## Nordhavn

Nordhavn's history is related in Chapter 13. They currently offer 16 models, from 40 to 120 feet. The two models explored here are the N43 and the N63. Jeff Leishman is the designer for all models, with input from Jim Leishman, Nordhavn customers, and other staff. The N56, 62, 64, 68, and 76 are built by Ta Shing Yacht Building Company in Tainan, Taiwan, a long-time builder of Nordhavns. Its entire yard is now devoted to Nordhavn construction. The N40, 43, 47, 55, 60, 63, 75, 86, and 120 are built by South Coast Marine in Xiamen, China.

**Nordhavn 43.** The Nordhavn 43 replaced the N46 (the first Nordhavn discussed in Chapter 13, page 253) in 2004. The N43 improved on the N46 design by flattening out the underwater lines to provide more heft for fuel, machinery, and provisions. The waterline remains exactly the same, but the overall length

| Nordhavn 43 | | | |
|---|---|---|---|
| Length overall | 43'0" | Speed/range at S/L 1.0 without stabilization | 6.2/4,734 nautical miles |
| Length waterline | 38'4" | | |
| Beam | 14'10" | Stabilization and estimated efficiency loss | Paravanes or active fins |
| Draft | 5'6" | | |
| Displacement | 65,000/52,480 lbs. | PC | .60 |
| Standard engine | Lugger 1066T 165 hp | L/B | 2.7 |
| Fuel capacity | 1,200 gallons | D/L | 418.7 light |
| Number fuel tanks | 2 | Heel angle at max righting moment | N/A |
| Water capacity | 300 gallons | | |
| Holding tank capacity | 50 gallons | Max value of righting lever | N/A |
| Speed/range at S/L 1.2 without stabilization | 7.4/2,958 nautical miles | ISO Design Category | A |

**Figure 12–3A.** A pair of Nordhavn 43s–*Special Blend* (foreground) and *Kosmos* (background) in Nuka Hiva, French Polynesia. This model Nordhavn is available with or without the flying bridge. (Christi and Eric Grab)

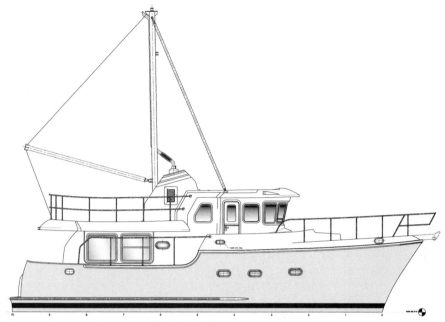

**Figure 12–3B.** Nordhavn 43 profile. (PAE/Nordhavn)

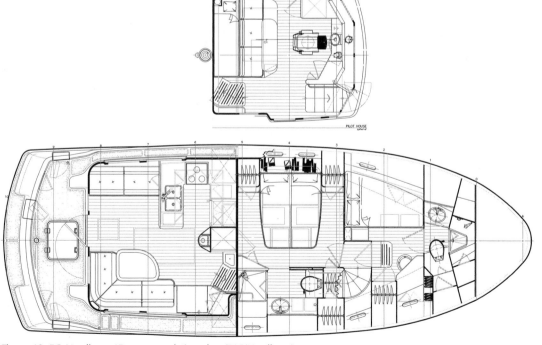

**Figure 12–3C.** Nordhavn 43 accommodation plan. (PAE/Nordhavn)

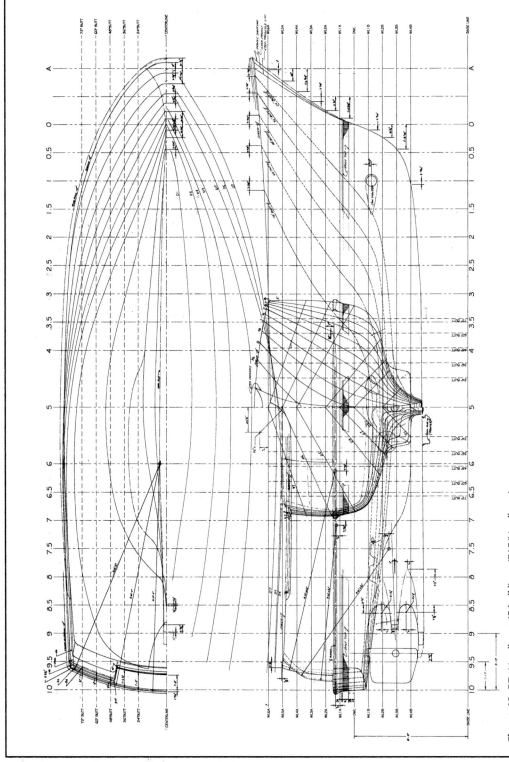

**Figure 12–3D.** Nordhavn 43 hull lines. (PAE/Nordhavn)

decreased by 2'9"—from 45'9" to 43'. The beam was reduced by 7" to 14'10" by reducing the stern overhang and aft deck. Fuel capacity was increased from 1,075 to 1,200 gallons. N43 owners have made numerous voyages, as shown in the data in Appendix C, Real-World Fuel Burn, and other examples cited elsewhere in the book.

The Nordhavn 43 hull is a little fuller going forward when compared with the N46. The pilothouse is farther forward and higher off the water—a disadvantage for motion. Engine access is through the master stateroom, a disadvantage noted earlier. The master stateroom bed is athwartships, allowing more motion when at sea because the sleeper's head is away from the center of the boat. The forward bunk and head are probably unusable under rough-sea conditions. The N43, being a shorter- and taller-looking version of the N46, is seen as "boxy" by some, but fitting all those amenities into such a small space requires such a boat. The N43 may not be as beautiful as the N46, but it is functional.

If you compare the lines of the N43 and N46 (see Chapter 13), you can clearly see the flattening of the aft sections for more load carrying. The stern shows a small, built-in platform that may aid entry from the dinghy. The step design toward the stern along the keel is to provide better access to the engine and drivetrain. The N43 is heavier than the N46 with a light load D/L of 419.

The starboard side deck appears a bit narrower on the N43, but should be adequate for docking. The port side has a small "toehold" deck that provides limited emergency access as long as one holds on tightly. Overall, the N43 is one of the best choices in small passagemaking boats, although costs have risen rapidly, making this model more expensive. There are compromises required by its length that make it a less comfortable sea boat than some of the larger Nordhavns.

**Nordhavn 63.** This model was new in 2011 and promises to develop a good following. In my opinion, it is one of the most attractive of all the Nordhavns.

| Nordhavn 63 | | | |
|---|---|---|---|
| Length overall | 62'6" excluding bow pulpit | Speed/range at S/L 1.2 without stabilization | 9.1 knots/1,820 nautical miles |
| Length waterline | 57'5" | Speed/range at S/L 1.0 without stabilization | 7.58 knots/3,550 nautical miles |
| Beam | 18' | Stabilization and estimated efficiency loss | TRAC active fins |
| Draft | 6'8" | | |
| Displacement | 178,500 lbs. maximum 147,800 lbs. minimum | PC | 53 (1/2 load) |
| | | L/B | 3.46 |
| Standard engine | John Deere 6081 AFM 330 hp @ 2,300 rpm ZF 3.958 reduction transmission | D/L | 317 (1/2 load) |
| | | Heel angle at max righting moment | N/A |
| Fuel capacity | 2,500 gallons | | |
| Number fuel tanks | 4 plus a supply tank | Max value of righting lever | N/A |
| Water capacity | 600 gallons | ISO Design Category | A |
| Holding tank capacity | 120 gallons black, 110 gallons gray | | |

Figure 12–3E. Nordhavn 63, *Silver Spray*, in the Bahamas. (Nigel Macleod)

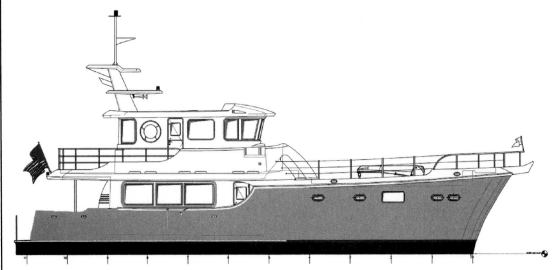

**Figure 12–3F.** Nordhavn 63 profile view. (PAE/Nordhavn)

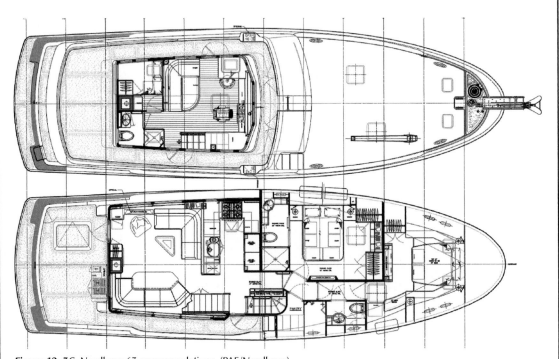

**Figure 12–3G.** Nordhavn 63 accommodations. (PAE/Nordhavn)

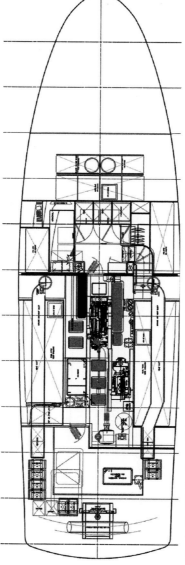

**Figure 12–3H.** Nordhavn 63 lower level machinery and tank space. (PAE/Nordhavn)

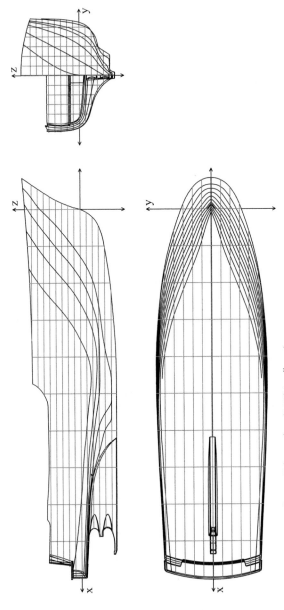

Figure 12–31. Nordhavn 63 lines plan. (PAE/Nordhavn)

The Nordhavn 63 has a high pilothouse, which has great views, but is subject to more motion. The pilothouse is spacious and includes a pilot berth and head, which can be convenient for watchstanders. The saloon is large with plenty of space for sitting or sleeping. Its aft position means it will be more comfortable at sea. The galley appears spacious. Stairways from the pilothouse to the main deck and lower deck join, making it convenient to move from one level to another.

A large, amidships owner's stateroom contains an athwartships bed, not the ideal position in rough seas. The master head separates the stateroom from the engine room, making it quieter. There is actually one lower level in the boat with a crew bunk and engine room access. It is unclear to me how this level is accessed. The forward stateroom will be uncomfortable when at sea.

There is a good-sized aft deck at main deck level and pilothouse level. The boat's design with its more aft pilothouse makes it less likely to sail at anchor and improves the motion at sea. As far as shortcomings, its minimal fuel capacity of 2,500 gallons makes long passages more challenging. Also, many Nordhavn owners run their generators 24/7, decreasing range and speed. Like many boats this size, there is a lot of complexity with plenty of opportunities for things to go wrong. Overall, the N63 looks like a fine addition to the Nordhavn line.

### Seahorse Marine

**Diesel Duck 462.** Bill and Stella Kimley founded Seahorse Marine in 1985, then based in Richmond, California. The early boats were built in Taiwan. In 1989, they moved to Zuhai, China (about 60 miles from Hong Kong) and developed two yards, one

| Seahorse Diesel Duck 462 | |
|---|---|
| Length overall | 48.45 |
| Length waterline | 46.82 |
| Beam | 14.87 |
| Draft | 5.67 |
| Displacement | 67,514 lbs. |
| Standard engine | IVECO NEF 150/123 hp |
| Fuel capacity | 1,600 gallons |
| Number fuel tanks | N/A |
| Water capacity | 250 gallons |
| Holding tank capacity | 60 gallons |
| Speed/range at S/L 1.17 without stabilization | 8 knots/2,560 nautical miles with 10% generator plus 10% reserve |
| Speed/range at S/L 1.0 without stabilization | 6 knots/5,200 nautical miles with 10% generator plus 10% reserve |
| Stabilization and estimated efficiency loss | Sail and/or paravanes |
| PC | .66 |
| L/B | 3.28 |
| D/L | 294 |
| Heel angle at max righting moment | N/A |
| Max range of positive stability | N/A |
| ISO Design Category | N/A |

**Figure 12–4A.** Seahorse Diesel Duck 462, *Seaducktress,* owned by Peter Geerlof, near Hoonah, Alaska.

**Figure 12–4B.** Seahorse Diesel Duck 382, *Traveller*, owned by Brian Sanders. This is a very functional 40-foot passagemaker. Note paravane rig and foresail used for motor sailing.

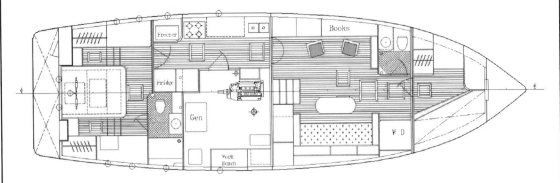

**Figure 12–4C.** Seahorse Diesel Duck 462 accommodations. (Seahorse)

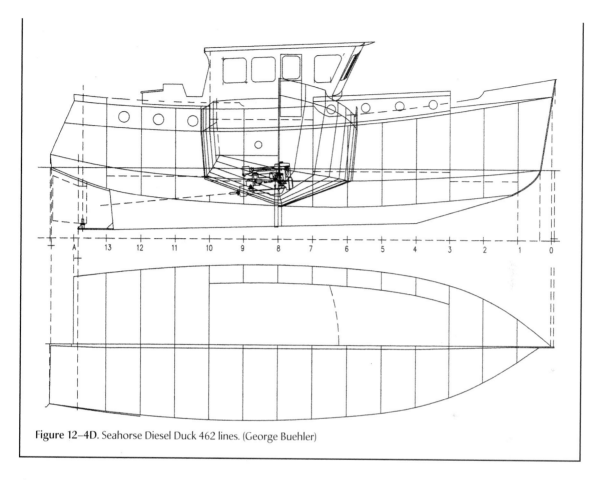

**Figure 12–4D.** Seahorse Diesel Duck 462 lines. (George Buehler)

for FRP boats and one for steel boats like the Duck. Their first steel Diesel Duck was completed in 2003. Since then, they have built 12 Diesel Duck 462s and currently have 3 more under construction. Seahorse also built two custom Diesel Ducks, a 55' and a 48', plus a Neville 44. They also build a Diesel Duck 382 that is about 10 feet shorter than the 462 at 41' LOA. Five of these smaller boats have been delivered or are under construction. The Diesel Duck is a capable sea boat that has accomplished some significant voyages. Seahorse has also built or has under construction six sedan versions of the 462, but the company and George Buehler, the designer of the 462, do not recommend this version for ocean passagemaking.

The Diesel Duck 382s and 462s have been the most affordable new passagemakers available, although prices continue to rise. The boats are proven passagemakers, with numerous ocean-crossing voyages, including two passages from Japan to the West Coast of North America via Alaska. They have voyaged to the South Pacific and throughout Southeast Asia. One Duck has voyaged from China to the Mediterranean.

The Seahorse Diesel Duck has been a popular alternative to the more expensive Nordhavn designs in this size. These boats are nicely finished with many features, such as a stand-up engine room, that make for good passagemakers. The living areas are below deck with limited views, a disadvantage to some, but also more comfortable in rough seas. Many of these boats are fitted with paravane stabilizers in addition to sails. The walkthrough design on the port side of the engine room makes good use of space. This area also serves as the galley. The aft master stateroom will probably be noisy and somewhat uncomfortable in heavy seas, but the saloon area offers a more central, comfortable sleeping area while underway.

The bow compartment berth is fine for anchor, but will have too much motion at sea. The pilothouse is reached by a fairly long ladder. It is rather small and may be crowded for a crew of four while at sea. There is an aft seating area in most boats to expand the deck space.

## Designers

### Patrick J. Bray

Based in White Rock, British Columbia, Patrick Bray has been designing and researching hull designs for 30 years. He does a lot of tank testing of new designs. He was a first prize winner in a conceptual design competition in Barcelona, Spain, in 2007 for his 75-foot trawler, Trekker 75. He also received special mention for his work on fuel-efficient hulls.

For this chapter, Patrick submitted his Latitude 49—a high-speed trawler that runs efficiently at 11 knots, with an S/L of 1.7. This is the smallest hull with a bulbous bow within our selected designs. Patrick states the bow is effective from 8–13 knots. The 49 grew out of an earlier design for a 47-foot version, Karvi 47, and the Cape Scott 85. Two fiberglass versions of the Karvi 47 were built; unfortunately, the builder went out of business before more could be completed. The 49-foot version shown here is built of aluminum.

**Latitude 49.** The Latitude 49 is interesting. It has good accommodations with an aft center master

| Bray Latitude 49 | | | |
|---|---|---|---|
| Length overall | 48'7" | Speed/range at S/L 1.0 with stabilization | 7 knots/5,000 |
| Length waterline | 42'4" | Stabilization and estimated efficiency loss | Fixed twin keels |
| Beam | 16' | | |
| Draft | 5'0" | PC | 0.62 |
| Displacement | 55,000 lbs. half load | L/B | 3.26 |
| Standard engine | John Deere 300 hp | D/L | 324 |
| Fuel capacity | 1,200 gallons | Heel angle at max righting moment | 70–90 degrees |
| Number fuel tanks | 4 | | |
| Water capacity | 300 gallons | Max value of righting lever | 2.213 feet |
| Holding tank capacity | 150 gallons black 150 gallons grey | Maximum positive stability | 180 degrees |
| | | ISO Design Category | N/A |
| Speed/range at S/L 1.2 with stabilization | 8 knots/3,500 miles Maximum speed 11 knots | | |

**Figure 12–5A.** Patrick Bray's Karvi 47, almost identical to the Latitude 49. (Patrick Bray)

**Figure 12–5B.** Latitude 49 profile. (Patrick Bray)

**Figure 12–5C.** Twin bilge keels used for stabilization on the Latitude 49. (Patrick Bray)

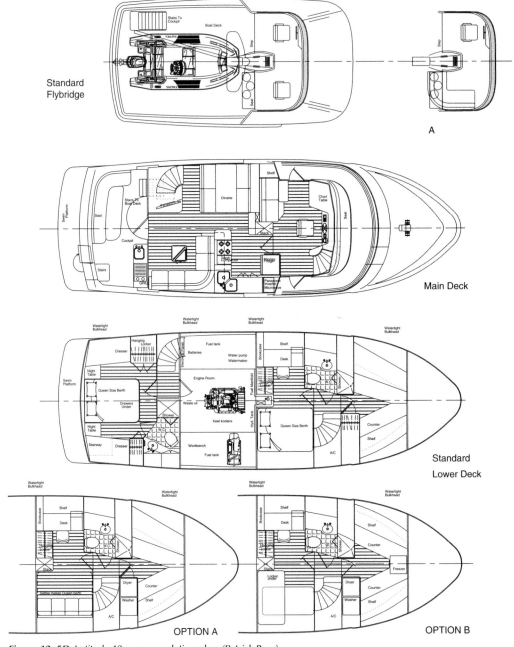

**Figure 12–5D.** Latitude 49 accommodation plan. (Patrick Bray)

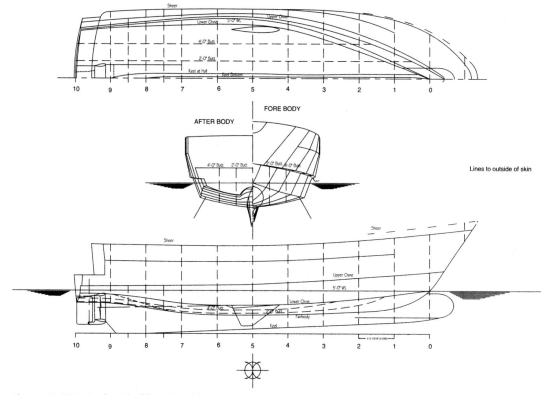

**Figure 12–5E.** Latitude 49 hull lines. (Patrick Bray)

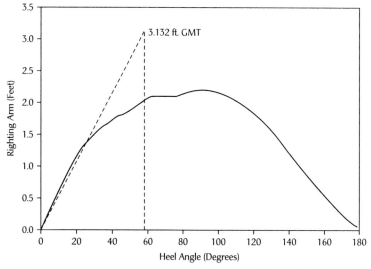

**Figure 12–5F.** Latitude 49 intact stability curve. (Note: No allowance has been made for free surface in the tanks or water on deck; weather-tight superstructure is included in calculation. The only downflooding point is through the stack.) (Patrick Bray)

stateroom. Engine room access is good, although anyone sleeping aft may be disturbed by the hourly engine-room checks. It has two baths—essential in a boat this size. I like the standard double bed amidships fore and aft. This should be a fine place to sleep at sea. The boat relies solely on bilge keels for stabilization. I would want to know these will work in rough conditions. The hull lines appear flatter than most, possibly to achieve the higher speeds of the hull design—the S/L ratio is 1.7 at 11 knots. Patrick says they designed the hull to be efficient at these higher displacement speeds. Will this flatter design be seakindly in head seas? The stability curve is excellent, although doors are weatherproof, not waterproof, and the glass is 1/4" except for 3/8" for pilothouse windows.

## George Buehler

Growing up in Oregon, George has always loved boats. When he graduated from high school, he went to Maine to work in the wooden boatbuilding yards. Around 1978 he began designing boats, first by carving models and later by using computers. His design expertise was developed by self-help; he learned by studying and doing. His design philosophy is that boats should, above all, be FUN! He criticizes the typical "trawler" yacht: "Many are wonderful vacation homes, but most aren't suitable for open-water cruising. They're so high and fat that they'll beat you to death in a seaway, be difficult to dock in any wind, and have systems aboard that require skilled technicians to keep operational." His objectives for design are simplicity, reliability, and affordability. George is now based on Whidbey Island, north of Seattle.

George prefers longer, narrower hulls with the major living spaces below deck. His Diesel Ducks, built by Seahorse Marine, are well known and covered earlier in this chapter. In this section, we present yet another Duck design, called the 41—one George says would be relatively easy to build as a do-it-yourself project in either steel, aluminum, or wood. The other is a longer boat, the 71-foot Ellemaid. (This is six feet longer than my standard maximum of 65 feet, but it is easily handled by a couple and has some real advantages in speed and economy.)

**Diesel Duck 41.** The Diesel Duck 41 provides an economical alternative to most of the boats in this chapter. The fuel consumption reports, while limited, indicate the hulls are easily driven with excellent economy. If you do not mind living below deck as you would in a sailboat, the design offers plenty of advantages and is less expensive to build. The hard chine design is simple to construct. The use of steel allows a great deal of interior layout flexibility as well.

| Buehler Steel Diesel Duck 41 | | | |
|---|---|---|---|
| Length overall | 40' | Speed/range at S/L 1.1 without stabilization | 7 knots/3,500 miles |
| Length waterline | 39.14 | Stabilization and estimated efficiency loss | Sail or paravanes |
| Beam | 13'6" | | |
| Draft | 4'6" maximum | PC | .609 |
| Displacement | 39,666/61,612 lbs. | L/B | 3.09 |
| Standard engine | 40–80 hp | D/L | 280 |
| Fuel capacity | 800 gallons | Heel angle at max righting moment | N/A |
| Number fuel tanks | N/A | | |
| Water capacity | N/A | Max value of righting lever | N/A |
| Holding tank capacity | N/A | ISO Design Category | N/A |
| Speed/range at S/L 1.2 without stabilization | N/A | | |

**Figure 12–6A.** Diesel Duck 41, also named *Diesel Duck*, owned by Marlene and Benno Klopfer. They had a yard build the hull in aluminum and finished the boat themselves. They have circumnavigated South America. (Marlene and Benno Klopfer)

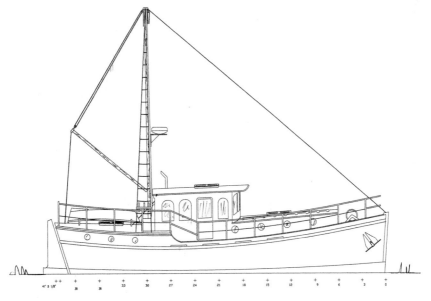

**Figure 12–6B.** Diesel Duck 41 profile. Pilothouse windows can be rounded or rectangular (George Buehler)

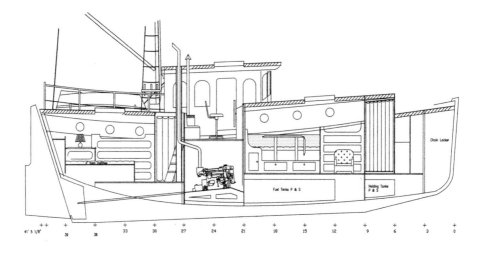

41' 5 1/8"    39    36    33    30    27    24    21    18    15    12    9    6    3    0

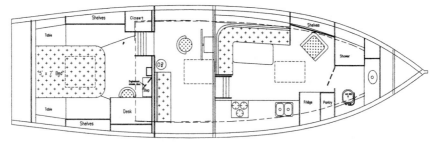

**Figure 12–6C.** Diesel Duck 41 accommodation plan showing pilothouse over engine room. (George Buehler)

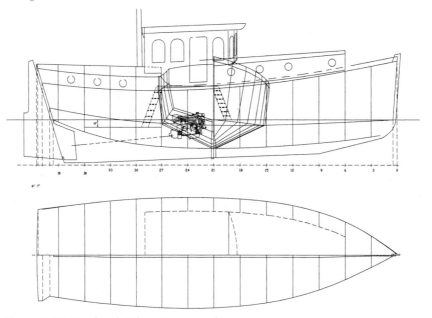

41' 7"    39    36    33    30    27    24    21    18    15    12    9    6    3    0

**Figure 12–6D.** Diesel Duck 41 lines. (George Buehler)

**Ellemaid 71.** This design is the narrowest of all models with a length-to-beam ratio (L/B) of 5.0 and a beam of just 14'1" for a waterline length of 66'11". It is a double-ended design that can be built in steel or wood. With a speed length ratio (S/L) of 1.0, the boat should cruise at 8.18 knots, without stabilization, in calm water. If you combine this with a moderate size engine, say 180 hp, the boat should be able to travel long distances at relatively high speed.

This boat shows the same general style of most Buehler designs, except it is narrower and double ended. One problem with such a long boat is marina costs and availability. Once you exceed 50 feet, costs rise and available marinas decline. If beam were taken into account, then the boat would be narrower than most any passagemaking boat, but realistically, marinas continue to charge on a per foot basis rather than total size. This boat should be comfortable at sea with most living areas and the pilothouse close to the center of gravity. The sleeping quarters in the stern and bow would not be as comfortable at sea. One might want to design more slumber opportunities in the saloon and pilothouse. I would choose the galley in the passageway where motion would be kinder than nearer the bow.

If I were building this boat, I would add another 1,000 gallons of fuel to improve range and allow faster speeds, if needed, for weather avoidance. This boat should be capable of making 10 knots for long distances with proper fuel capacity and power.

I would also prefer some type of stabilization in addition to sails. George does not like any stabilization other than sail, but he has not taken one of his designs across an ocean—I suspect he would change his mind if he did. The boat might be a good candidate for an antiroll tank because there is plenty of deck space to mount the tank. Paravanes could also be added easily to this steel boat. On the other hand, the current owner of *Hooligan* is happy with sail stabilization. He states: "The sails are great as noted in the commissioning blog; we did an equator run in February—15 to 20 knots and 3 meter seas—and she is solid as a rock with a double reef mizzen and the jib up. I see no reason to even think about vanes, plus all the gear and complexity; sails seem to be a pretty good option!"

## Dave Gerr

Dave is a well-known expert in yacht and small-craft architecture. He is Director of the Westlawn Institute of Marine Technology and president of Gerr Marine. He has written four books and authored more than 400 articles. He believes that longer, lighter designs make better passagemakers than the more common broad, heavy boats in use today since the former can travel faster with better overall efficiency. The boat submitted for this section is his Imagine, built as the *Imagine*, also known as the Kanter 57.

| Buehler Ellemaid 71 | | | |
|---|---|---|---|
| Length overall | 70'10" | Speed/range at S/L 1.0 without stabilization | (speed would be 8.18 at S/L 1.0) |
| Length waterline | 66'11" | Stabilization and estimated efficiency loss | Sails N/A |
| Beam | 14'1" | PC | N/A |
| Draft | 6' | L/B | 5.04 |
| Displacement | 156,000 lbs. | D/L | 211.5 |
| Standard engine | INVECO NF150 150 hp | Heel angle at max righting moment | N/A |
| Fuel capacity | 1,600 gallons | Max value of righting lever | N/A |
| Number fuel tanks | 2 main/50 gallon daytank | ISO Design Category | N/A |
| Water capacity | N/A | | |
| Holding tank capacity | N/A | | |
| Speed/range at S/L .86 without stabilization | 7.0/4,887 nautical miles 10% reserve, no gen time | | |

**Figure 12–6E.** *Hooligan*, a steel Ellemaid 71, owned by Drew Gardener, who is based in Singapore. This steel boat was built in Izmir, Turkey, by Kaya Cakar at Ashboat Yachts. (Drew Gardener)

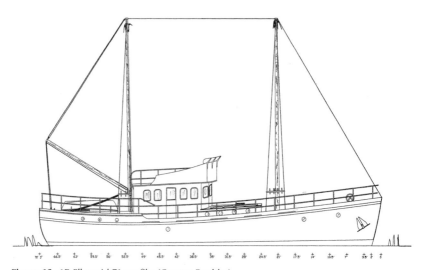

**Figure 12–6F.** Ellemaid 71 profile. (George Buehler)

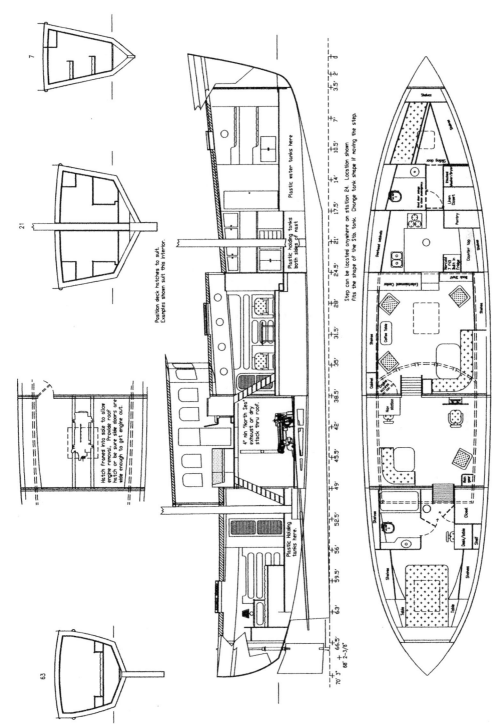

Figure 12–6G. Ellemaid 71 interior without passage. (George Buehler)

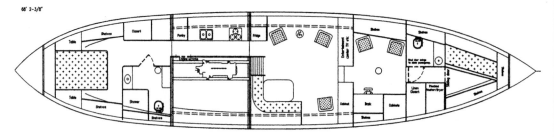

**Figure 12–6H.** Ellemaid 71 accommodations, showing plans with passageway. (George Buehler)

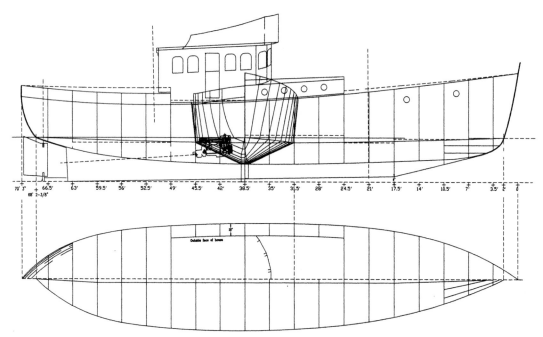

**Figure 12–6I.** Ellemaid 71 lines. (George Buehler)

**Kanter 57.** This boat would be excellent if you wanted to go shorter distances in a hurry, such as from Fort Lauderdale to the Bahamas. It offers excellent speed, with good economy, on an ocean passage at 8.3 knots, faster than most existing passagemakers. Without any generator time, the fuel consumption would be about 2.3 nmpg, an excellent figure for this size boat. As far as the layout and boat accommodations, I like its sleek, low appearance; however, there is a price—engine room space and access is extremely limited. This is a significant drawback for an ocean-crossing boat. Also, engine access is gained by raising the steps to the forward area, an awkward method, especially if people were going in and out of the engine room. The aft master stateroom at deck level seems inconvenient for access, although it would provide excellent views when anchored. On the plus side, it should be fairly comfortable at sea and a good distance from propeller noise and vibration. The pilothouse is high and forward of amidships—it offers great visibility, but it creates more motion for the crew. This boat might benefit from antiroll tank stabilization rather than the more trouble-prone active fins.

## Michael Kasten

With a degree in philosophy, but an interest in boats, Michael became involved in boat design by working in boatyards, doing small design jobs, and building his own boat. He eventually founded his own firm, which has been designing sail and powerboats for a number of years. We present two designs here: the 43' Roberta Jean and the 50' Vagabond. Kasten's boats have a low, classic style with aft pilothouses.

| Gerr *Imagine* 57 (Kanter 57) | | | |
|---|---|---|---|
| Length overall | 56'6" | Speed/range at S/L 1.17 without stabilization | 8.3 knots/4,597 nautical miles with 8% reserve; economical mode |
| Length waterline | 50'5" | | |
| Beam | 14'6" | | |
| Draft | 5'9" | Stabilization and estimated efficiency loss | Active fins |
| Displacement | 69,800 lbs. maximum | | |
| Standard engine | Cat 3306B 215 hp@ 2,000 rpm | PC | 0.66 |
| Fuel capacity | 2,180 gallons | L/B | 3.89 |
| Number fuel tanks | 3, including one 400-gallon day tank | D/L | 205 |
| Water capacity | 400 gallons | Heel angle at max righting moment | 48 degrees |
| Holding tank capacity | 90 gallons | | |
| Speed/range at S/L 1.7 without stabilization | 10 knots/2,227 nautical miles with 8% reserve; normal cruise | Maximum positive stability | 115 degrees |
| | | ISO Design Category | N/A |

**Figure 12–7A.** Kanter 57, *Imagine.* (Dave Gerr)

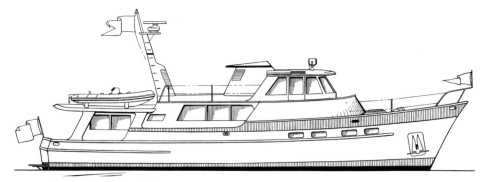

**Figure 12–7B.** Imagine 57 profile. (Dave Gerr)

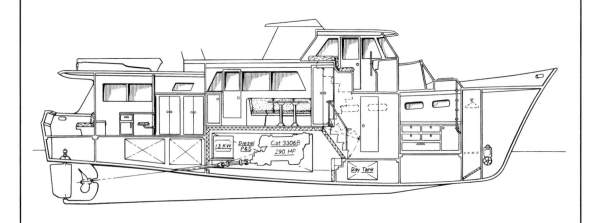

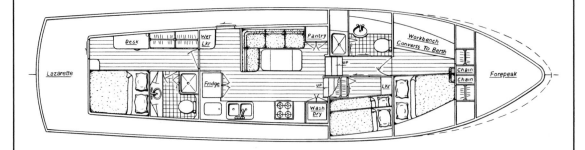

**Figure 12–7C.** Imagine 57 accommodation plan. (Dave Gerr)

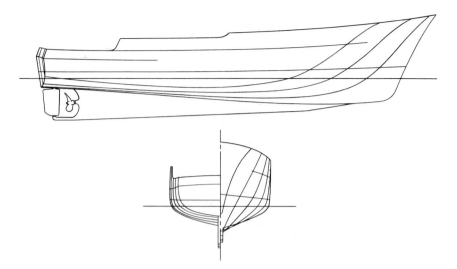

**Figure 12–7D.** Imagine 57 lines. (Dave Gerr)

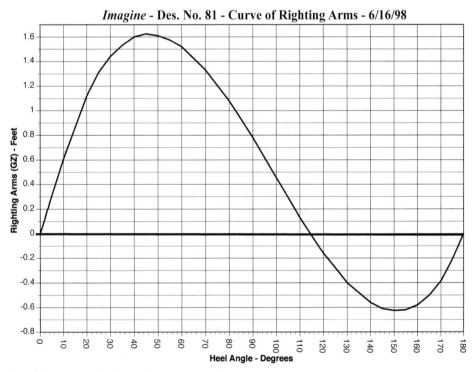

**Figure 12–7E.** Imagine 57 stability curve. (Dave Gerr)

**Roberta Jean 43**. Michael calls this series of yachts, from 43 to 60 feet, his "Dream Yacht" style. They have a long raised foredeck and an aft pilothouse, with a fantail stern. This yacht was designed with a deeper body to provide more room and seagoing comfort. The height of the 43 is low enough so the boat can cruise the European Canals if desired.

The Roberta Jean has much of its living space on the lower deck, like the Diesel Duck design. It leaves plenty of space for the engine room. The galley is located in the center, the best place for making meals at sea. The stateroom is forward and would probably not be usable at sea; however, there is space in the saloon and in the pilothouse for slumbering crew. There is only one head.

This boat offers a lot in a small space. The beam is only 12'6", so there is less room than some other 43-footers. It is also quite light due to its aluminum hull. However, it is a seaworthy design that is easily driven. It should be an economical passagemaker.

| Kasten Roberta Jean 43' Aluminum | | | |
|---|---|---|---|
| Length overall | 43'0" | Speed/range at S/L 1.0 without stabilization | 6.4 knots/4,740 nautical miles includes 15% reserve |
| Length waterline | 39'7" | Stabilization and estimated efficiency loss | Paravanes, 2–5% |
| Beam | 12'6" | | |
| Draft | 5'1" | PC | 0.64 |
| Displacement | 46,120 lbs. heavy | L/B | 3.5 |
| Standard engine | John Deere 4043 TFM 125 hp @ 2,400 rpm | D/L | 305 full load |
| Fuel capacity | 817 gallons | Heel angle at max righting moment | 86.1 degrees |
| Number fuel tanks | 3 | | |
| Water capacity | 200 gallons | Max value of righting lever | 1.32 feet loaded |
| Holding tank capacity | 60 | Max degrees positive stability | 180 degrees |
| Speed/range at S/L 1.2 without stabilization | 7.7 knots/2,600 nautical miles includes 15% reserve | Downflooding angle | 81.3 loaded |
| | | ISO Design Category | A |

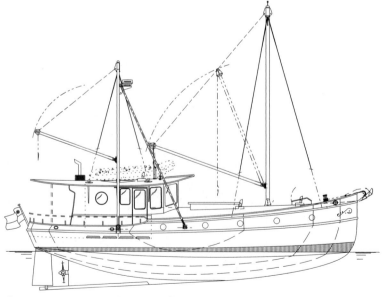

**Figure 12–8A.** Kasten's Roberta Jean 43' profile. (Michael Kasten)

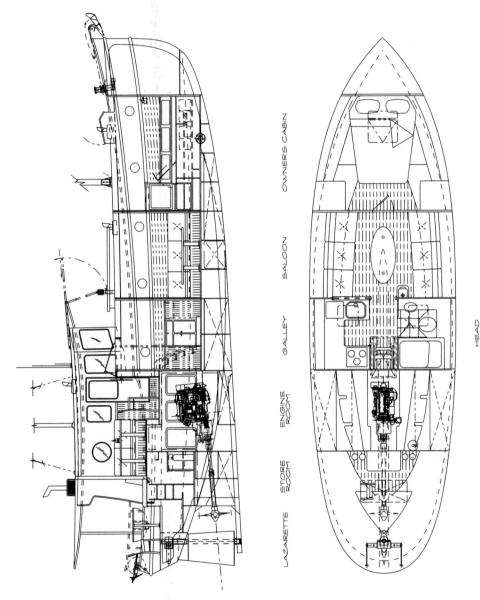

LAZARETTE  STORE  ENGINE  GALLEY  SALOON  OWNERS CABIN
                ROOM    ROOM

HEAD

**Figure 12–8B.** Kasten's Roberta Jean 43' accommodations. (Michael Kasten)

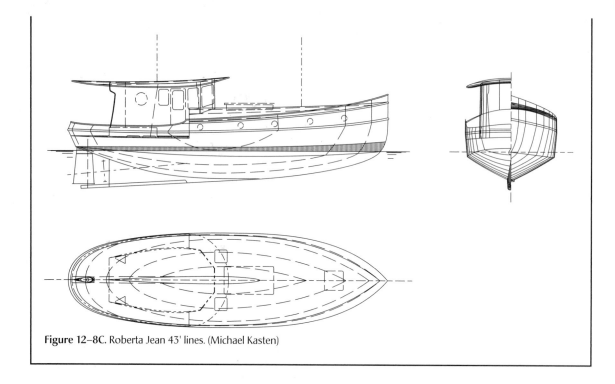

**Figure 12–8C.** Roberta Jean 43' lines. (Michael Kasten)

**Kasten Vagabond 50'.** The Vagabond series contains several designs from 49 to 53 feet. All are European-canal-capable. This line was based on West Coast fishing trawlers. They are relatively narrow beamed and easily driven. They may use bilge keels and paravanes for stabilization.

This boat is one of my favorites in this size. I like the saloon/galley layout with a large seating area aft and a table for eating and working. Kasten also makes room for two easy chairs without sacrificing too much space. The galley is particularly large and is convenient to the saloon and pilothouse. I also like the covered aft deck with seating. This part of the boat is popular on *Teka III* and gives a place to enjoy the sea while underway or at anchor.

The lower-deck layout is good, although I would prefer an amidships owner's cabin that is quiet at anchor and more comfortable underway. It appears the guest and owner's cabins could be switched fairly easily. One possible drawback is the steep ladder or steps needed to reach the lower accommodations.

As long as there are good handholds and a backward posture is used, this is probably OK, and it certainly saves space. A plus for this hull is the openness to natural ventilation, requiring much less generator time and expense.

Kasten keeps this steel hull fairly light with a D/L of 247; it can be driven economically. Placement of engine room vents on top of the deckhouse makes for a down-flooding angle of 85.5 degrees—a real safety advantage. The hull also tests out with a 180-degree range of positive stability. While I certainly would not want to test this, it appears the design is particularly seaworthy.

## Charles Neville

In the third edition of *Voyaging Under Power*, two Chuck Neville designs were shown: Neville 39 and Neville 48. Here we show his Werner Bay 50 and Neville 56. Neville and Steve Seaton were partners in a Florida design firm for about 11 years, starting in the mid-1970s and ending when Seaton moved to the Northwest in 1988.

### Kasten Vagabond 50' Steel

| | | | |
|---|---|---|---|
| Length overall | 50' | Speed/range at S/L 1.0 without stabilization | 6.9 knots/4,500 nautical miles, includes 15% reserve |
| Length waterline | 47'4" | Stabilization and estimated efficiency loss | Paravanes, 2–5% |
| Beam | 13'7" | PC | 0.64 |
| Draft | 5'4" | L/B | 3.7 |
| Displacement | 59,900 lbs. heavy | D/L | 247 heavy |
| Standard engine | John Deere 6068 TFM 175 hp @ 2,300 rpm | Heel angle at max righting moment | 101 heavy |
| Fuel capacity | 940 gallons | Max value of righting lever | 1.738 feet heavy |
| Number fuel tanks | 2 | Range of positive stability | 180 degrees |
| Water capacity | 300 gallons | Heel angle at downflooding | 85.5 heavy |
| Holding tank capacity | 40 gallons | ISO Design Category | A |
| Speed/range at S/L 1.2 without stabilization | 8.3 knots/2,400 nautical miles, includes 15% reserve | | |

**Figure 12–8D.** Kasten 53' *Passage of Time*, owned by Alan Wagner. Note engine vents on top of the pilothouse. (Alan Wagner)

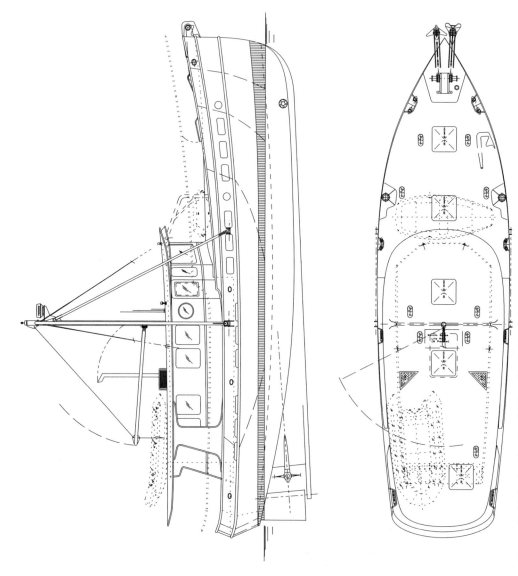

Figure 12–8E. Kasten Vagabond 50' profile. (Michael Kasten)

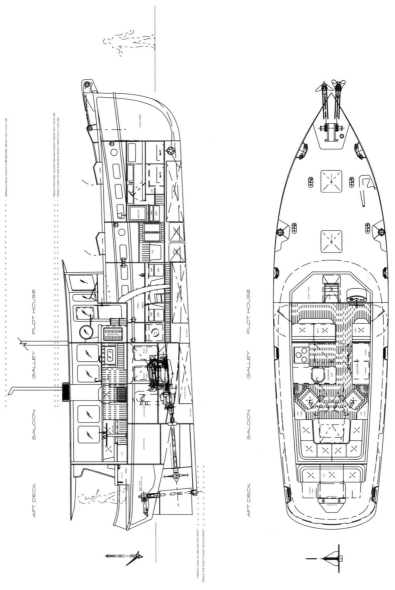

**Figure 12–8F.** Vagabond 50' main deck accommodation plan. (Michael Kasten)

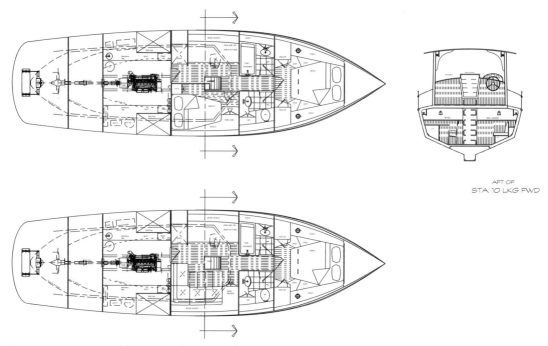

**Figure 12–8G.** Vagabond 50' lower deck accommodation plan. (Michael Kasten)

AFT OF
STA. 10 LKG FWD

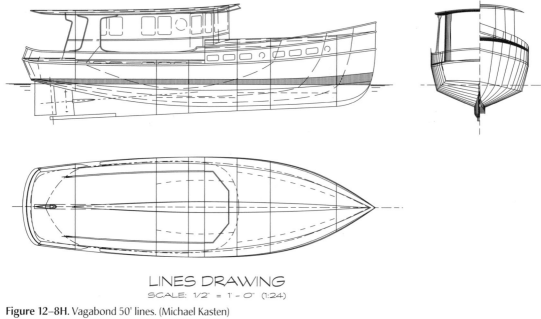

LINES DRAWING
SCALE: 1/2" = 1' - 0" (1:24)

**Figure 12–8H.** Vagabond 50' lines. (Michael Kasten)

**Werner Bay 50.** This boat started out as a 53-footer, but as the design process moved along, the owners decided that the size and heft of the boat were just too big for the remote areas they planned to cruise, so they downsized to 50 feet. They were used to cruising in smaller sailboats and did not feel they needed the extra room. Chuck says this is the only time this has happened to him—most owners let the size creep up to get more space. Designed for steel with an aluminum deckhouse, the version illustrated here shows a conventional pilothouse with side decks to allow easy access fore and aft on both sides of the boat. It could be modified for a wide body or asymmetric shape with limited side decks, for more interior space.

A hefty boat indeed with a D/L, fully loaded, of 495. In spite of its weight and 16'5" beam, it still is a bit cramped in places, especially the saloon. It is not clear where the crew eat their meals since the table in the saloon is tiny—if I were building

| Neville Werner Bay 50 Steel (with aluminum deckhouse) | | | |
|---|---|---|---|
| Length overall | 50'8" | Speed/range at S/L 1.0 without stabilization | 7.4 knots/3,600 nautical miles; includes generator and 10% reserve |
| Length waterline | 45'6" | | |
| Beam | 16'5" | | |
| Draft | 5'6" | Stabilization | Active fins 7.5 square feet |
| Displacement | 104,400 lbs. full load | PC | 0.628 |
| Standard engine | Cummins 6CTA 8.3 250 hp @ 1,800 rpm | L/B | N/A |
| | | D/L | 495 (full load) |
| Fuel capacity | 2,436 gallons | Heel angle at max righting moment | 55 degrees full load 62 degrees light ship |
| Number fuel tanks | | | |
| Water capacity | 222 gallons | Max value of righting lever | 2.06 full/1.71 light |
| Holding tank capacity | 52 gallons gray 110 gallons black | Maximum stability | 106 degrees full/100 degrees light |
| Speed/range at S/L 1.2 without stabilization | 8.1 knots /2,670 nautical miles; includes generator and 10% reserve | ISO Design Category | N/A |

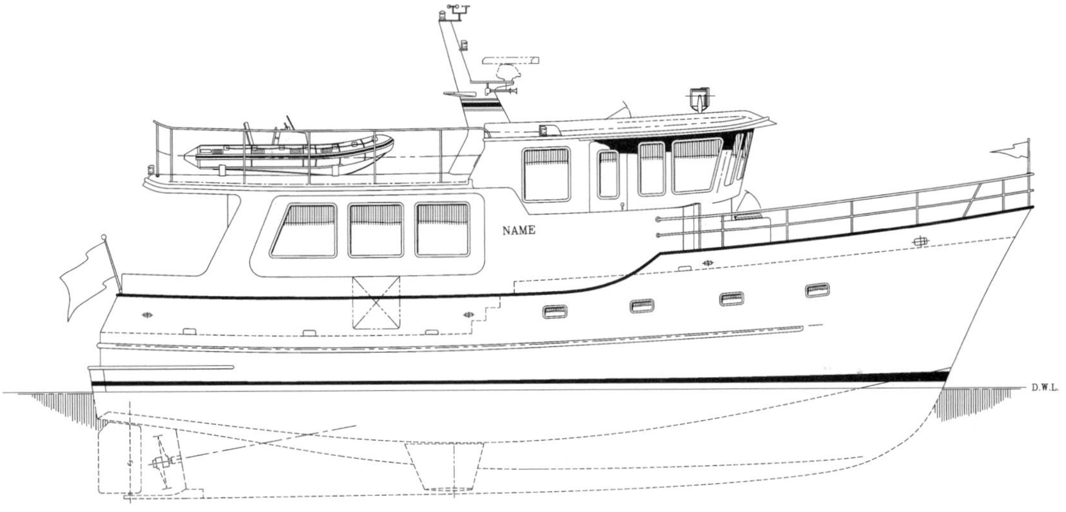

Figure 12–9A. Werner Bay 50' profile. (Charles Neville)

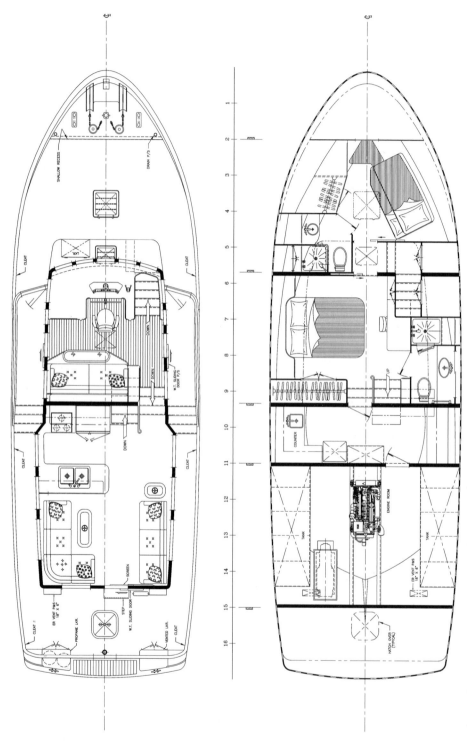

**Figure 12–9B.** Werner Bay 50' accommodations. (Charles Neville)

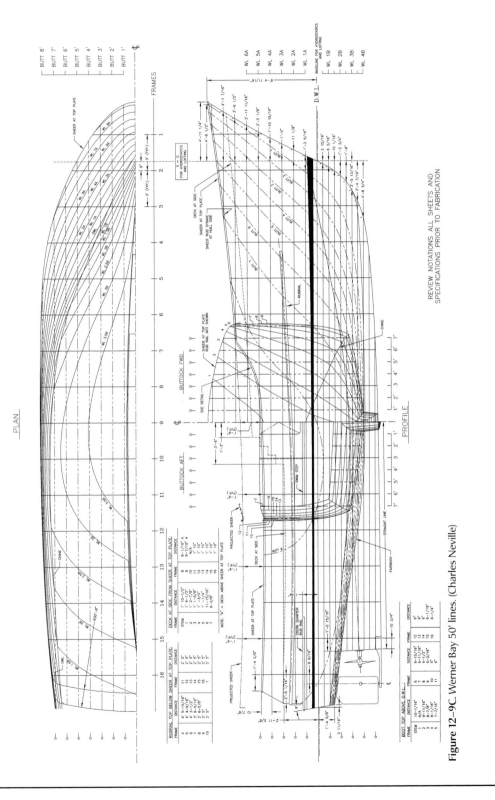

**Figure 12–9C.** Werner Bay 50' lines. (Charles Neville)

this boat, the table would be greatly enlarged. It seems a bit of wasted space to have two stairwells leading to the below deck area, although it would offer more privacy if boisterous grandchildren were aboard. The forward bunk beds would be unusable at sea, so the saloon would probably serve for sleeping while underway. Sleep in an athwartships bed is not quite as good as a fore-and-aft mounting, but its amidships location is good. A large space is devoted to a laundry, freezer, and perhaps a shop area. As an avid do-it-myselfer, I like this unusual plus. Unfortunately, the only engine room entry is through the master stateroom, making engine room checks at sea more invasive. Areas for entertaining are limited, although with the dinghy in the water, the cabin top could probably serve in lieu of a flying bridge.

**Neville 56.** This boat is an evolution of the Neville 47 into a roomier boat with a separate utility room. The larger size allows a single chine with a deep forefoot and a fine waterline entrance angle so that it may be more easily driven and more comfortable in head seas. This boat, like the 50', is designed for steel with an aluminum deckhouse. The boat aims to provide spacious, open areas and plenty of head space in the stand-up engine room.

The upper accommodations of the 56' are quite similar to the 50'. With a hefty 19'6" beam, there is more space in the pilothouse with room for two chairs, plus the "berth seating" at the rear. Saloon space is also greatly increased, but more eating and working area is needed, plus enough sofa space for crew to sleep on passages.

The major advantages of the extended length are the lower accommodations. Only one stairway leads down to a long hallway. A small utility room off the hallway provides access to the engine room and lazarette, allowing easy engine room checks without disturbing sleepers. The fore and aft placement of the master stateroom's bed is also a major plus for slumber at sea, putting the sleeper's head about as close to the boat's center as possible. The forward stateroom provides luxurious space while at anchor or a marina, but will be uncomfortable at sea.

The displacement of the 56' (164,700 pounds) is 60,000 pounds heavier than the 50', giving this boat a tremendous heft to punch through head seas. The price, however, is more fuel consumption. Range is still adequate with 2,700 miles at S/L 1.0 of 7.4 knots. And this includes allowance for generator use and a 10% reserve.

| Neville 56' Steel (with aluminum deckhouse) | | | |
|---|---|---|---|
| Length overall | 56'8" | Speed/range at S/L 1.0 without stabilization | 7.4 knots/2,700 nautical miles; includes generator and 10% reserve |
| Length waterline | 54'2" | | |
| Beam | 19'6" | | |
| Draft | 6'0" | Stabilization and estimated efficiency loss | Active fins, 12 square feet |
| Displacement | 164,700 lbs. full load | | |
| Standard engine | John Deere 6125 AFM 341 hp @ 1,800 rpm | PC | 0.637 |
| | | L/B | N/A |
| Fuel capacity | 2,746 gallons | D/L | 458 full load |
| Number fuel tanks | N/A | Heel angle at max righting moment | 47 degrees full load |
| Water capacity | 411 gallons | | |
| Holding tank capacity | 117 gallons gray/158 gallons black | Max value of righting lever | 2.092 feet at full load |
| Speed/range at S/L 1.2 without stabilization | 8.8 knots/2,100 nautical miles; includes generator and 10% reserve | Maximum stability range | 97 degrees full load 91 degrees light load |
| | | ISO Design Category | N/A |

**Figure 12–9D.** Neville 56' profile. (Charles Neville)

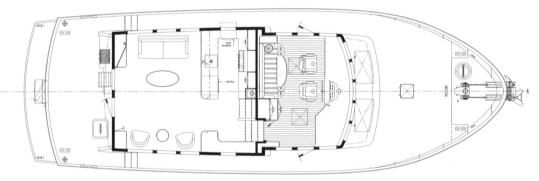

**Figure 12–9E.** Neville 56' upper deck accommodations. (Charles Neville)

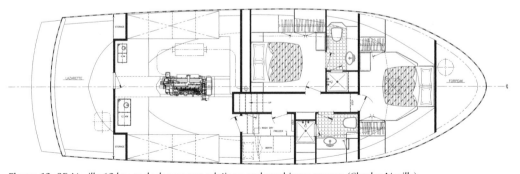

**Figure 12–9F.** Neville 62 lower deck accommodations and machinery spaces. (Charles Neville)

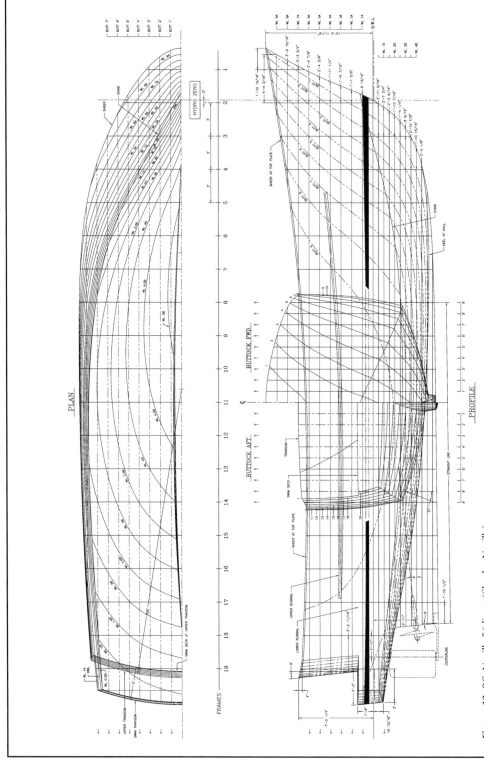

**Figure 12–9G.** Neville 56 lines. (Charles Neville)

As with all steel/aluminum designs, it is relatively easy to redesign the interior spaces to suit the owner—many of the comments relating to both Neville boats could be easily rectified during the design phase.

## Bruce Roberts-Goodson

Like many designers mentioned in this book, Australian-born Bruce Roberts-Goodson spent time in a boatyard developing his skills. He expanded his technical knowledge through the Westlawn Institute of Marine Technology. In 1966 he and his partner,

Andrew Slorach, founded Bruce Roberts Yacht Design. In 1972, he moved his operations to the United States. Later, he opened additional offices in Holland and Ireland. Bruce's approach is not only to sell plans but also materials needed for construction, either by do-it-yourselfers or at boatyards. He also publishes a number of books about techniques and methods. He has many designs, but most are aimed at coastal cruising, not passagemaking. An exception is his steel Trawler Yacht Voyager 485 shown here.

This is a hard-chine steel boat with lots of space for a 49-footer. It has a nice saloon and galley with

| Bruce Roberts TY485 Steel | | | |
|---|---|---|---|
| Length overall | 52'2" including swim step 49'2" length over deck | Speed/range at S/L 1.0 without stabilization | 6.9 kn, 2,894 nm |
| Length waterline | 47'4" | Stabilization and estimated efficiency loss | Active fins |
| Beam | 17'3" | | |
| Draft | 5'8" (3/4 load) | PC | 0.68 |
| Displacement | 84,610 lbs. to CWL | L/B | 2.85 |
| Standard engine | 225–350 hp | D/L | 435 (3/4 load) |
| Fuel capacity | 1,440 gallons | Heel angle at max righting moment | 25 deg |
| Number fuel tanks | 2 | | |
| Water capacity | 300 gallons or more | Max value of righting lever | 0.73' |
| Holding tank capacity | 100 gallons | | |
| Speed/range at S/L 1.2 without stabilization | 8.3 kn, 1,686 nm | ISO Design Category | A |

**Figure 12–10A.** Roberts TY 485, *Nikola Tesla*, in Greenland on her way from Europe to North America. (Brank Kresojevic)

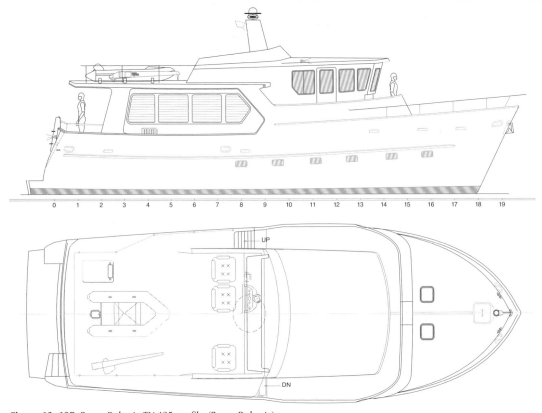

**Figure 12–10B.** Bruce Roberts TY 485 profile. (Bruce Roberts)

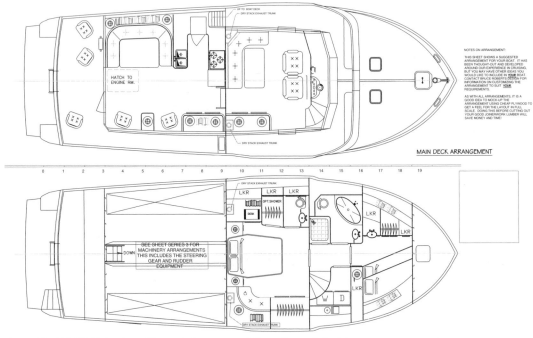

**Figure 12–10C.** TY 485 main and lower deck accommodations. (Bruce Roberts)

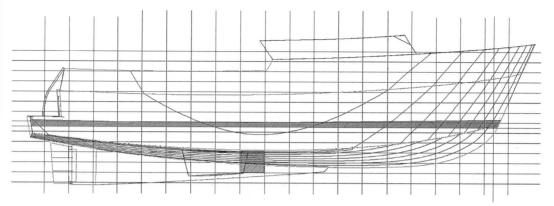

**Figure 12–10D.** TY 485 lines, profile view. (Bruce Roberts)

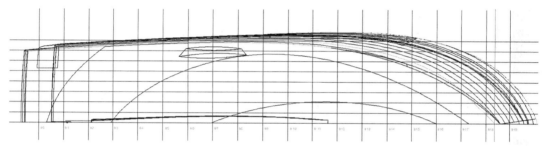

**Figure 12–10E.** TY 485 lines, plan view. (Bruce Roberts)

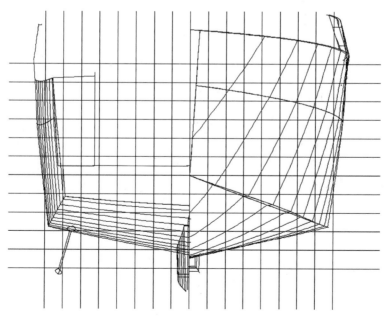

**Figure 12–10F.** TY 485 hull lines, sectional view. (Bruce Roberts)

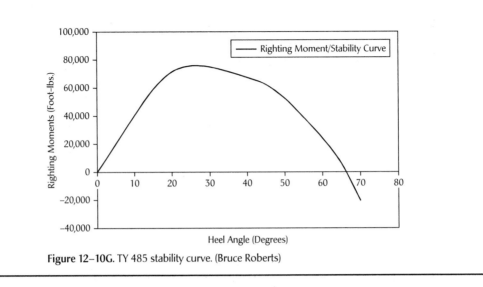

**Figure 12–10G.** TY 485 stability curve. (Bruce Roberts)

plenty of seating space. The pilothouse is large with two helm chairs, an unusual plan in this size boat; however, it is located pretty far forward. The sleeping area is below the pilothouse and forward deck. The owner's stateroom is located amidships with its bed fore and aft, probably the best layout for comfort at sea. There appear to be two toilets, but only one shared shower. The forward guest stateroom consists of bunk beds and will be untenable in rough seas. The boat has a good-sized flying bridge for getting outdoors and entertaining. There is also a large aft deck for lounging. Engine room access is through a hatch in midsaloon. This may be better than an entrance in the master stateroom, although I would want to make sure it was easy to open for engine room inspections. Overall, she is a nice passagemaker that may be built by the owner or a small shipyard. This could be a way to save money, especially if the materials were provided precut from the designer.

## Stephen R. Seaton

The only repeat designer from the first edition, Seaton has been designing passagemakers for his entire career, beginning in 1969. His design history is discussed in more detail in Chapter 13. Seaton has designed a large number of boats for various celebrities and for Northern Marine, a builder of expedition yachts. He began his career working for the famous yacht designer Bill Garden, in Seattle, Washington. He then went to work for Morgan Yachts in St. Petersburg, Florida. Later he ran his own boatyard, Hidden Harbor, in Sarasota, Florida. He has experience in both design and building.

We selected two designs, the Cape Scott 54 and Seaton 64. Both are heavy displacement, go-anywhere boats.

**Cape Scott 54.** This design was for owners who want to live aboard. Accommodations are plentiful and spacious. The boat is designed for steel.

The Cape Scott 54 packs a lot into 54 feet. The large forward owner's stateroom looks like it would be great in port, but subject to a lot of motion at sea. The amidships TV/guest cabin would probably be popular during passages. The large aft saloon also offers opportunities for sleep at sea and offers space to "get away" when the boat feels too small. The boat is unusual for one with beam-to-beam living quarters—it has a small side access area amidships on each side that should be handy for boarding and docking. However, the tradeoff of this design is that the crewmember who is handling dock lines may have to run fore and aft through living quarters, an awkward arrangement. The high pilothouse allows great views, but suffers from a forward position that means more motion in seaway. The pilothouse

## Seaton #494/Cape Scott 54 Steel

| | | | |
|---|---|---|---|
| Length overall | 54'3" | Speed/range at S/L 1.0 without stabilization | 7.1 knots/3,894 nm |
| Length waterline | 50'6" | | |
| Beam | 18'3" | Stabilization and estimated efficiency loss | Active fins, 0.3 knots loss |
| Draft | 6'10" full load | | |
| Displacement | 125,300 lbs. light load | | |
| Standard engine | John Deere 6081 AFM 330 hp @2300 rpm | PC | 60.9 |
| | | L/B | 3.01 |
| Fuel capacity | 2,475 gallons | D/L | 481 (max displacement) |
| Number fuel tanks | 3 main; 2 day tanks | Heel angle at max righting moment | N/A |
| Water capacity | 650 gallons | | |
| Holding tank capacity | 230 gallons gray/360 gallons black | Max degrees positive stability | 142 degrees (max displacement) |
| Speed/range at S/L 1.2 without stabilization | 8.5 knots/2,740 nm | ISO Design Category | N/A |

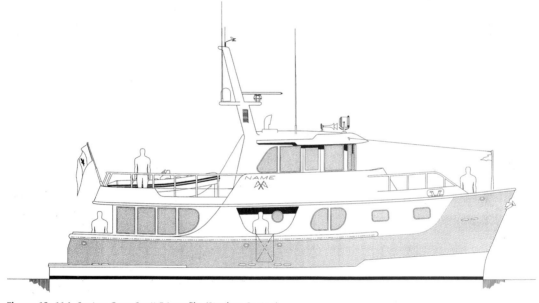

**Figure 12–11A.** Seaton Cape Scott 54 profile. (Stephen Seaton)

**Figure 12–11B.** Cape Scott 54 main deck accommodations. (Stephen Seaton)

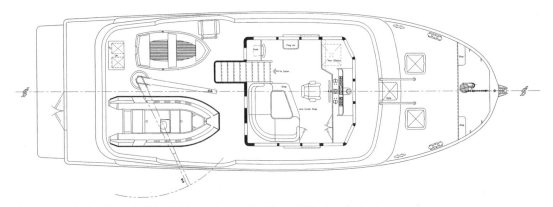

**Figure 12–11C.** Cape Scott 54 flying bridge and upper deck layout. (Stephen Seaton)

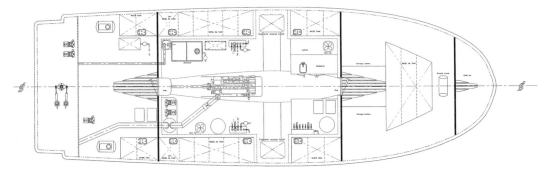

**Figure 12–11D.** Cape Scott 54 engine and machinery layout. (Stephen Seaton)

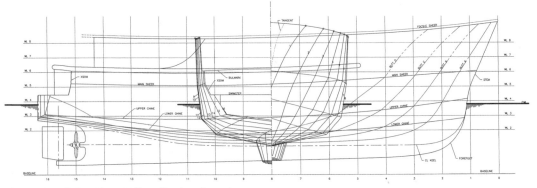

**Figure 12–11E.** Cape Scott 54 lines. (Stephen Seaton)

accommodates three people plus the watchstander with ease, and there is a lot of room for charts and navigation equipment. Engine room access appears difficult, with access through an aft door on the outside of the boat—a significant safety hazard for periodic engine room checks at sea. There are also two waterproof hatches on each side—again, not convenient or safe for engine room checks.

**Seaton 64.** This boat is a revival and modernization of a design done 20 years ago, but never built.

The 64 is a tall boat, even without a flying bridge. Unless you have a special need for a flying bridge for fishing or because you want to be out in the weather, it might be better left off. There is little room for entertaining at that level, which is one of the main advantages of a flying bridge. It is also quite a climb to reach that area. There is a reasonable amount of space on the aft deck and the pilothouse level for entertaining small groups, but it would not be suitable for large gatherings. The aft-of-center pilothouse

| **Seaton Design 472/64** | | | |
|---|---|---|---|
| Length overall | 64'2" | Speed/range at S/L 1.0 without stabilization | 7.7 knots/4,010 nautical miles |
| Length waterline | 58'11" | | |
| Beam | 20'4" | Stabilization and estimated efficiency loss | Active fins, 0.3 knots loss |
| Draft | 6'10" full load | | |
| Displacement | 153,310 lbs. light | PC | 60.3 |
| Standard engine | John Deere 6125 AFM 400 hp @ 1,900 rpm | L/B | 3.22 |
| | | D/L | 367 max displacement |
| Fuel capacity | 3,310 gallons | Heel angle at max righting moment | N/A |
| Number fuel tanks | 6 main, plus 2 day tanks | | |
| Water capacity | 550 gallons | Max value degrees pos stability | 138 degrees at max load |
| Holding tank capacity | 250 gallons gray/420 gallons black | | |
| Speed/range at S/L 1.2 without stabilization | 9.2 knots/2,240 nautical miles | ISO Design Category | N/A |

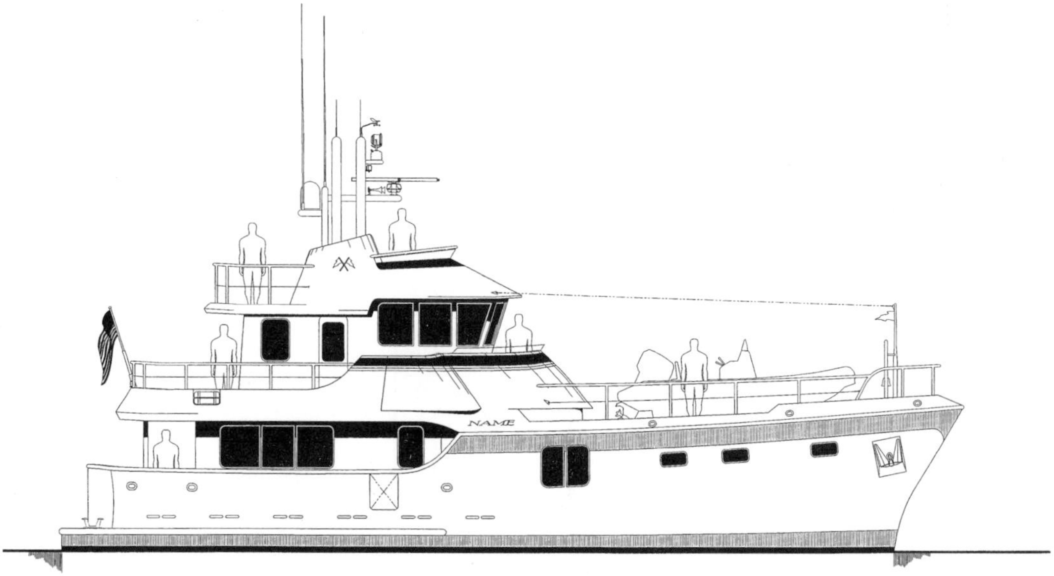

Figure 12–11F. Seaton 64 flying bridge version. (Stephen Seaton)

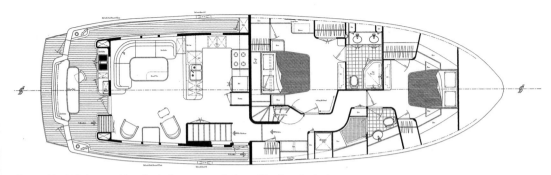

**Figure 12–11G.** Seaton 64 main deck accommodations. (Stephen Seaton)

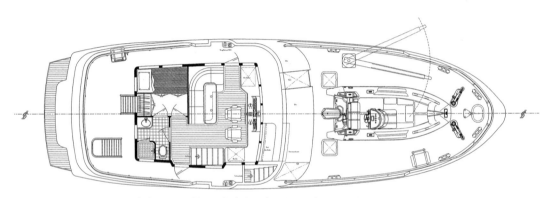

**Figure 12–11H.** Seaton 64 pilothouse and boat deck. (Stephen Seaton)

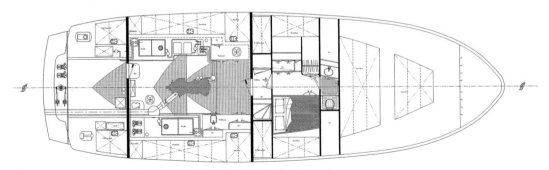

**Figure 12–11I.** Seaton 64 engine room, tanks, and cabin. (Stephen Seaton)

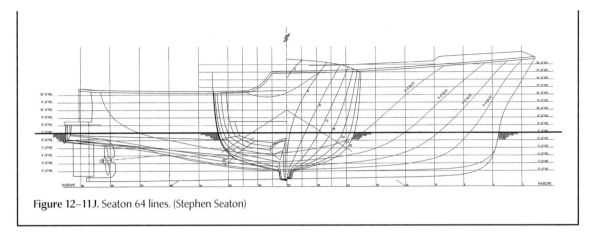

**Figure 12–11J.** Seaton 64 lines. (Stephen Seaton)

should provide a better ride at sea than the more forward one in the Cape Scott 54; however, it is a long way off the water, so you will feel the roll more than a lower design.

The amidships owner's stateroom should be quiet and comfortable in its central location. The forward stateroom may not be usable at sea unless conditions are pretty calm. There is a small sleeping cabin on the engine-room level that should be comfortable, if claustrophobic, at sea. Perhaps this is designed for a crewed boat. The pilothouse has a great pilot berth complete with a head and shower. With four heads and showers to maintain, the boat offers lots of opportunities for boatyard mechanics.

Engine room access for periodic checks is excellent, but it is unclear how you access the area for maintenance or battery replacement without tracking through the living areas. Stand-up headroom is a plus, as is the large built-in workbench. The boat uses a wet exhaust system.

The saloon combines with the dining area with a wraparound sofa and table. Two lounge chairs are used for additional seating. The galley looks large, with almost too much floor space for rough-sea cooking. It is unclear whether there is enough food storage space. It looks like the only TV viewing areas are in the staterooms. Overall, this looks like a fine passagemaker offering many luxuries and a great deal of complexity.

## Malcolm Tennant Catamarans

After Malcolm Tennant died in an unfortunate accident in 2008, Tony Stanton continued the Malcolm Tennant Multihull Design company in New Zealand. The Tennant design team is responsible for all the catamarans illustrated in this book. I found no other ocean-crossing catamarans of 65' or under. Even a 65' catamaran has almost a 23' beam—a very wide boat with attendant problems with marina space and haulout facilities. However, they offer a lot of space, need no stabilization, cross oceans faster and more economically than most monohulls, and are capable of high speeds once they arrive at their cruising grounds.

**Domino 20.** In spite of the length and breadth, the Domino 20 has some shortcomings on space. There is only one stateroom. The second stateroom is a narrow bunk-bed arrangement in the port hull. There is also only one head and shower, an inconvenience if more than a couple is onboard. Engine room access appears to be through hatches on the rear deck, outside the main cabin. This could make it difficult, if not dangerous, in extreme sea conditions, to do engine room checks. On the plus side, the starboard hull contains a small workshop and spare storage area. The combined saloon, galley, and pilothouse offer great visibility and plenty of opportunities for socialization. I would prefer a captain's chair rather than a bench for the helmsperson.

The large rectangular space offers plenty of opportunity to modify the interior design, although the need to keep the weight near the hull's center limits these options. I would definitely design access to the engine rooms from inside the boat. The large flying bridge provides room for social gatherings and a getaway for crew members.

## Tennant Domino 20 Catamaran

| | | | |
|---|---|---|---|
| Length overall | 65.5' | Speed/range @ 10 knots | 4,000 nautical miles, with 10% reserve |
| Length waterline | 61' | Speed/range @ 20 knots | 2,000 nautical miles, with 10% reserve |
| Beam | 22' 11" | | |
| Draft | 4'9" | Stabilization | No stabilization required |
| Displacement | 88,185 lbs. max | PC | N/A |
| Standard engine | Twin John Deere 6081 AFM; 300 hp M2 rating | L/B of hulls only | 15.6 |
| | | D/L | N/A |
| Fuel capacity | 2,900 gallons | Heel angle at max righting moment | N/A |
| Number fuel tanks | 6 | | |
| Water capacity | 507 gallons | Max value of righting lever | N/A |
| Holding tank capacity | 262 gallons | | |
| Speed/range @ 11 knots | 2,900 nautical miles, with 10% reserve | ISO Design Category | A |

**Figure 12–12A.** *Domino*, Tennant catamaran owned by Marie and J. P. Dufour. (Bill Parlatore)

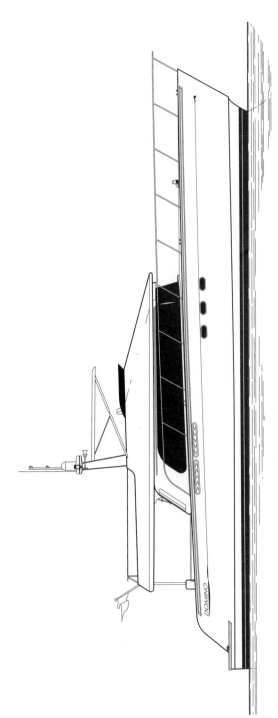

**Figure 12–12B.** Tennant Domino 20 passagemaker profile. (Malcolm Tennant)

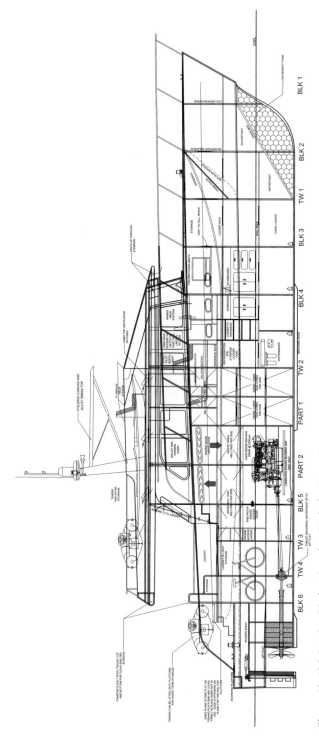

**Figure 12-12C.** Domino 20 elevation plan. (Malcolm Tennant)

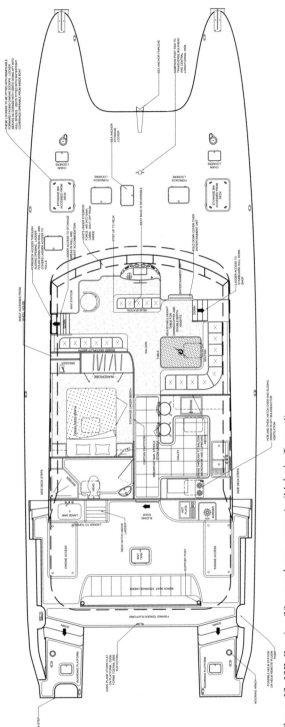

Figure 12–12D. Domino 20 general arrangements. (Malcolm Tennant)

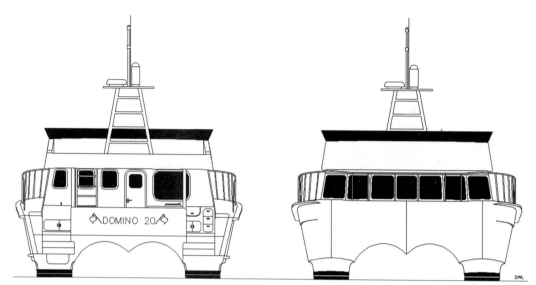

**Figure 12–12E.** Domino 20 front and rear views. (Malcolm Tennant)

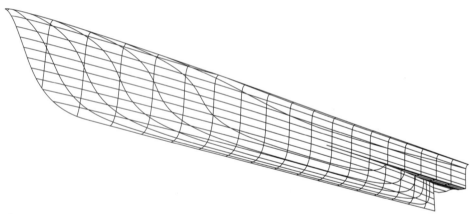

**Figure 12–12F.** Domino 20 hull lines, showing the displacement hull of these catamarans. (Malcolm Tennant)

## CHAPTER THIRTEEN

# Proven Passagemakers of the Past

The idea of including older proven passagemakers is new to this edition. When the earlier editions were written, most boats were relatively new because power voyaging and passagemaking were in their infancy. It's been more than 35 years since the first edition was published, and there is now a rich history of proven passagemakers. This section can also serve to whet the appetite and provide leads for purchasing a used boat. Prices of new boats are out of reach for many, but opportunities for good used boats abound.

There are a number of ocean-capable boats that are not included here simply because I could not verify ocean-crossing voyages for them or I was unable to get complete information. For example, the Hatteras LRC boats are displacement designs with ocean-crossing capability, but I found no evidence of any significant passages completed by these boats, so have not included them. They have been widely used on both coasts of North America and throughout the Caribbean. Many Defever models are also ocean capable—Pelagic, a 40-foot model, actually rounded Cape Horn.

The chapter is organized into sections for each builder or designer, roughly in chronological order from oldest to newest. We begin with the granddaddies of all passagemaking yachts, the Romsdals and Malahides. Then we turn to boats from Willard, Skookum, Cheoy Lee, and Stephen Seaton, followed by the current status of a couple of Beebe designs from the 1970s. Next comes Knight & Carver, an early builder of

long-range passagemakers. Kadey-Krogen has done much to encourage coastal passagemaking with some notable offshore voyages as well. Then we turn to Nordhavn, a company that revolutionized passagemaking by producing large numbers of passagemaking boats, beginning with their 46- and 62-foot models. Finally, Cape Horn Trawlers built a number of strong steel passagemakers.

## Romsdal North Sea Trawlers

*According to Norway's Bergen Maritime Museum, in Bergen, Norway, the history of the Romsdal-style boat goes all the way back to the 1870s, and a boat builder named Lars Jensen Hameraas. He built the first of these incredibly seaworthy fishing cutters (sailboats) to a design closely related to the Scottish trawlers of the time. The success of Hameraas' boats was so universal that soon all of the other Romsdal builders took inspiration from him, and the tradition of the Romsdal-style became rooted in maritime history.*

—Bill Parlatore, *PassageMaker Magazine,*
Spring 1998

In ancient times, the Vikings invaded Scotland and Ireland, bringing with them their beautiful curved-bottom, seaworthy boats. Originally, the boats were all sailing vessels. Around the turn of the century, the boats were converted to power,

Figure 13–1A. The *Rekord,* a Romsdal built in 1914, showing the working boat heritage of Romsdal yachts. The boat was originally 42 feet long, but was eventually extended to 61 feet. She is still powered by a 90 hp, 2-cylinder Brunvoll engine that was installed in 1934. Built as a motor freight vessel serving the Fjords of Norway, she eventually voyaged to the Caribbean where she continued as a commercial boat. She now serves as a yacht based in Maine and part of the World Ship Trust. (Captain Jim Sharp)

The wood boats were built strongly with 2-inch thick fir planking and 5-inch square laminated frames. The keel and keelson were 8 × 9 inches and the deck planking was 2-1/2 inches thick. The space between the outer and inner planking was filled with many tons of concrete ballast—required to provide stability for the high pilothouse. These boats had no stability against roll; although their long roll period was slow, it was still more than most of us would prefer. Some boats have been retrofitted with paravanes or active fins.

The power for this 70-ton boat was provided by a single Swedish Penta 6-cylinder diesel, rated at 128 continuous hp at 1,800 rpm. She drove her 47-inch, 3-blade variable-pitch propeller with a 4.55:1 reduction gear. She had a 4 kw generator and a single battery bank, rated at 200 amp hours (not much electrical power was needed in those days). She had 2,500 gallons of fuel capacity (range 4,000 miles) and 1,000 gallons of water. She had five small staterooms and three toilets and showers. She could sleep 13.

Romsdals have a strong following among trawler aficionados. People have spent years and millions of dollars restoring these grand old boats.

first gasoline and then diesel. The 100-year-old fishing boat, *Tordnskjold* (see Figure 2–1), is an example of this type of fishing boat. Even though it was built in Washington State, the fishermen and boatbuilders of the Northwest were mostly Norwegians—the hull shape spread throughout the world.

In the 1950s Peter Varney, owner of Lido Yacht Sales, in Newport Beach, California, decided to develop and market yacht versions of the Romsdal fishing boats. The 65-foot, 70-ton *Edvard Grieg* was the first of 7 boats Varney imported beginning in 1960. The boat, along with most future boats, was delivered on her own bottom after a 10,000 mile voyage from Norway to California. A total of 22 Romsdals were built from 1959 to the mid-1960s in Norway before yards discovered they could build more lucrative oil-tending vessels for the local market.

The first Romsdals were built of wood, although in later years several steel versions were completed.

## Malahide North Sea Trawlers

Another source of North Sea trawlers was born in the early 1960s at Southern Marine Shipyard in Malahide, County Dublin, Ireland. The yard began converting British Admiralty surplus boats into robust, no-frills, knockabout private yachts in the late 1950s. In 1962, it bought a large yard and built huge new sheds and many other improvements. By the end of the 1960s, however, it was increasingly difficult to find Admiralty or surplus fishing boats to

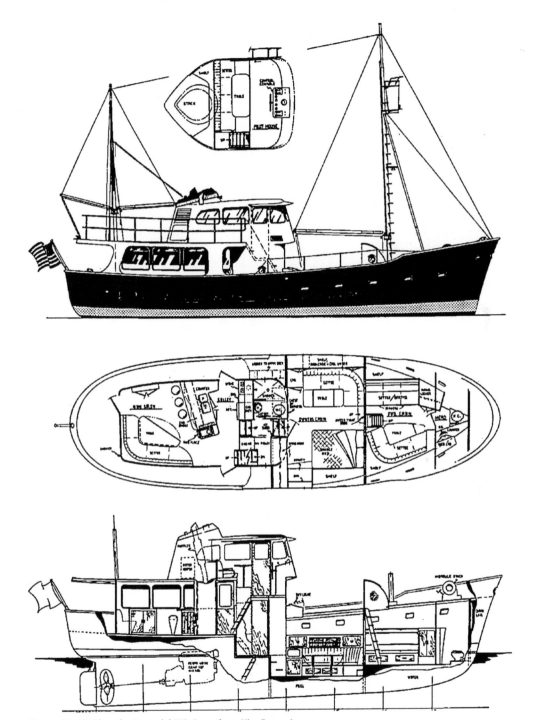

**Figure 13–1B.** Plans for Romsdal 52', Orca class. (Jim Rogers)

**Figure 13–1C.** Restoring the 1960 Romsdal, *Viking Fjord*, is expensive and time-consuming, especially when new frames are required. Look closely between the frames on the left to see the concrete ballast.

**Figure 13–1D.** The 55' Romsdal, *Delfin*, restored and owned by Carl Loeb. She was built in 1965 of steel with an aluminum pilothouse by Romsdal Boatbuilders, Alesund, Norway. Beam 15'6"; draft 7'6"; displacement 125,000 lbs.; fuel 2,450 gallons (5,000-mile range); water 600 gallons; power Cat 3306 270 hp@2200rpm; generator 20kw Northern Lights. (Jim Rogers)

## Sea Quest and Bill Wood

Like many Romsdals, the 65-foot *Sea Quest* has had a varied and interesting life since she was built in 1961 by the Hagen Shipbuilding yard in Hjelset, Norway. She began cruising with an Atlantic crossing and a trip through the Canal to California on her own bottom. She participated in marine surveying and science projects, with various teams of scientists from Scripps and the California Marine Institute on board, during her annual trips to Mexico. She went through several West Coast owners and made numerous trips to Mexico and one to Alaska.

A Japanese owner bought *Sea Quest* in 1998 and began a million-dollar-plus refit and repair job. When he ran into some financial difficulties, he sold the boat to Bill Wood, who continued the refit in Port Townsend and San Diego. In 2005, Bill and his wife Betsy Ann cast off

and headed to Mexico, stopping in all the popular cruising ports in Mexico. They had such a great time that they decided to keep going south. They stopped in El Salvador, Costa Rica, went through the Canal, the San Blas Islands, Columbia, Venezuela, Trinidad, the Windward and the Leeward Islands, and eventually up to Massachusetts.

Departing Cartagena, Colombia, for Aruba, the Woods thought they had a good weather window to make the passage north along Colombia. The passage is known for extremely rough seas in the winter when the "Christmas Winds" arrive from the reinforced trades that push up against the Andes Mountains as they terminate on the Colombian coast. Because this was April, they expected favorable conditions. When they departed it was glassy calm. By nightfall, the wind and waves had risen until it was blowing a

continuous 55 knots with higher gusts. Seas were 26 to 27 feet with the top 5 to 6 feet breaking. Quartering the waves, *Sea Quest* was making slow progress off the Rio Magdalena until around midnight, when they were hit by what was probably a rogue wave. With a loud bang and a shudder, it slammed into the boat and rolled over the high bow, stopping the boat as if it had hit a sandbar. The breaking wave swept over the port bow, bringing tons of water with it, hitting their lashed launch with such force that the bow chain ripped its chain plate out of the deck. The force of the water washed the stern cushions off the boat, her lashed deck cargo was strewn about the deck, and her life ring, including mounting hardware, was ripped off the front of the saloon house. The Woods fought this weather for 34 hours until they were finally able to duck behind a cape at Santa Marta. They spent four days resting, cleaning up the mess, doing repairs to the chain plate, and remounting the life ring before they could get going again.

Weather on the trip up the Colombia coast was the worst the Woods encountered on the entire trip. And it was not the only "adventure." Returning to the boat in El Salvador, they found a swarm of bees filling the pilothouse with thousands more trying to get in. The pilothouse smelled of honey for months after. When the boat was working its way north through the Caribbean Islands to Florida, its main anchor was lost and recovered three times. The trip back to Massachusetts ultimately took a year and eight months.

Figure 13–1E. *Sea Quest* in Port Townsend, Washington, prior to her voyage to the east coast of the United States via the Panama Canal. Note paravane poles and bow thruster—nice additions. (Bill Wood)

modernize. It was also increasingly difficult and expensive to make the conversion, which required a complete gutting of the old hulls. With the decline of Romsdal production due to the North Sea oil boom, demand for North Sea trawlers was growing. So Malahide turned to producing new boats and supplying the American market.

The Malahide yard could not keep up with hull construction, so it turned to other yards to supply the hulls, then finished them in Ireland. Hulls came from Norway (5), Portugal (11), Ghana (2), and Irish government shipyards. The basic hulls were sailed from their place of construction (1,500 miles from Portugal) to Ireland. Out of 17 new hulls constructed, 6 went to the United States, 6 to the UK, and the rest spread between Belgium, Holland, Germany, and Spain. The hulls ranged from 52 feet to 68 feet.

Figure 13–2A. Malahide 65' *Ursa Major*, in Baja, Mexico. (Joyce Gauthier)

Worldwide Marine marketed the boats with 5-foot scale models at the New York and Miami boat shows. Americans were even more passionate about these trawlers than their builders. The builders felt they had really cracked the U.S. market.

Figure 13–2B. Romsdal and Malahide parade in Ballard Locks, Seattle, Washington, 2003. (Ken Wagner)

An article in *The New York Times* on January 25, 1970, announced the arrival of "Five luxury craft due from Dublin" in May—"Safety and Comfort noted." The importer, Lynn Akers of Worldwide Marine Ltd., described the purpose of these boats: "[Yachtsmen] desire a rugged vessel that a man and his family can live in, go anywhere in, in any weather, at any time and stay there, and do it with a minimum of crew."

According to Myles J. Stapleton, who joined Malahide in 1963 as its chief designer: "1970–1975 were boom times for the yard. We were over 70 personnel, including 10 Portuguese shipwrights, who came with their families to Dublin to share our success."

Unfortunately, success was short-lived. With the oil crisis in late 1973, inflation caused major increases in labor and material costs. Interest rates soared. In addition, Taiwanese boat builders were making major inroads with low-cost trawlers. U.S. orders began to dry up. Near the end of the 1970s, the two founders of the boatyard, Alf Tyaranson and Jack Fielding, died suddenly within a few months of each other. This was the final blow to the yard. A new owner tried to revive the business, but the gates closed in 1983.

There is a strong kinship between Romsdals and Malahides. They look pretty much alike. Their hull designs are similar. The size is generally the same, although there were a number of larger Romsdals made. Owners of both boats are very loyal to the boat and would not think of trading for other types. As with Romsdals, Malahide owners spend extravagantly on restoring and updating their vessels. It is rare to see a derelict North Sea trawler.

## Willard Marine

Vega Marine launched its first production fiberglass boat, the Vega 36, in 1961. For a year, until Skookum introduced its 42-footer in 1962, it was building the largest fiberglass hull in the world. Boat construction started on the Southern California waterfront in the 1950s as individual projects under the direction of owner Bill Tighe. Sometime after 1974, the name was changed to Willard Marine, Inc.

During the period from 1961 to 2002, Willard Marine built 39 Vega 36s, 176 Willard 30s, and 32 Willard 40s in various pilothouse, sedan, and motorsailer configurations. By 2002, Willard was deeply involved in building military boats to meet post-9/11 needs. A Willard executive said that from 1961 to 2001, Willard built thousands of military craft and 235 pleasure boats. The last Willard production trawler was produced in March 2002—it simply did not have the space and resources to continue producing pleasure craft.

All production Willards are full displacement hulls with canoe sterns and single engines. Most models have a mast that can be fitted with steadying sails. Because Willards are round-bottomed with considerable ballast (7,000 lbs. on the 40), they tend to roll vigorously. A few of the larger ones are fitted with active fins. Some have installed paravanes. Others have found success with "bilge chocks" or bilge keels as described in Chapter 8. Many owners, including those doing ocean passages, have not installed stabilizers. Their hulls are slippery and can be easily powered, gaining considerable fuel economy. They cruise between 6 and 7.5 knots and burn between .75 and 1.5 gph, depending on the model.

While a number of Vegas and Willard 30s have made significant voyages, including one related by Bill Parlatore in *Passage-Maker Magazine* about a trip to Bermuda, this boat is probably more suitable for coastal cruising than open-ocean passages. The Willard 40s are often seen in the Caribbean and Pacific coast of Mexico. In 2007, the Willard 40, *Aloha*, participated in the Baha Ha-Ha—mainly a sailing event—from San Diego to Cabo San Lucas, Mexico. The Vega 36 trawler, *Hornblower*, completed a voyage from California to Hawaii in 1987. The 2,300 nm trip took approximately 16 days at 6 knots and used 330 gallons of fuel—less than one gallon per hour. The boat had Naiad stabilizers. Another Willard 36 cruised from Oregon to the Galapagos Islands in the 1970s and remained there for a year performing research. When we were cruising in the San Blas Islands of Panama, we encountered a family of four cruising in a Willard 40, including two full-grown teenage boys. They were spending the year cruising around the Caribbean and diving at every opportunity.

Figure 13–3. Willard 40, *Candor*, built in 1981, at La Conner, Washington, 2012.

## Skookum Marine

The first manufacturer of fiberglass passagemakers was Skookum Marine, founded in 1962 in Seattle by Ben, Bernie, and Julian Arthur. Tom Fay and Bill Peterson later joined the firm. Soon they moved to Port Townsend, Washington, to get away from the crowds of "onlookers" who were disrupting production. In 1962, they built what was then the largest solid fiberglass motorboat, a 42' fisherman designed for Pacific offshore salmon charter fishing. In 1969, Skookum Marine started building the 53-foot fiberglass Skookum, the largest fiberglass hull at the time. They used the same hull mold to build motor yachts, fishing boats, and sailing vessels. The interiors of the boats were custom designed for each owner's needs. The basic hull and all the modifications were designed by Edwin Monk & Sons. Eventually 55 of these hulls were built. By the 1980s, the market for yachts and fishing boats was declining, foreign competition was underpricing U.S. manufacturers, and government rules and requirements were proliferating; thus, they decided to end production in 1990—after more than 400 boats from 28' to 70' had been built.

The 53-foot Skookums are go-anywhere boats that have voyaged throughout the world. Some of them were outfitted as motorsailers for tuna fishing off Midway in the Pacific islands. Others ventured to Australia and other parts of the world. My own enthusiasm for long-range ocean voyaging was sparked by the Skookum 53, *Sea Raven*, which had voyaged from Friday Harbor, Washington, through the Panama Canal to the Caribbean coast of Mexico in the early 1990s. We wanted to buy a seaworthy and seakindly boat when we discovered this one—it certainly fit the bill. Unfortunately, we did not like the interior layout, so we kept looking until we found *Teka III* in 1996.

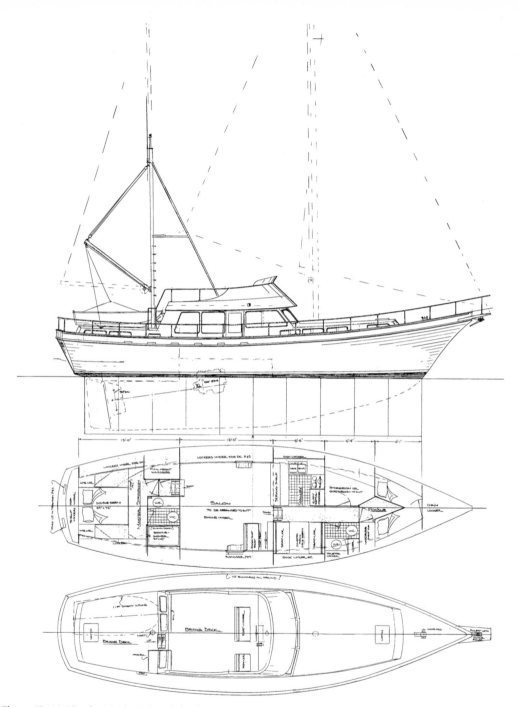

**Figure 13–4A.** Plan for Monk-designed Skookum 53, 1977. (Bernie Arthur)

**Figure 13-4B.** Skookum 53 *10&2* in Greenland. Her 135 hp Lugger burns 2.5–3.0 gph including a pony motor for charging and a hurricane heater, cruising at 7 to 8 knots. (Ross Anderson)

Ross Anderson describes his experience of 10 years cruising aboard *10&2* between 1994 and 2004 as "wonderful." He cruised to Newfoundland and Labrador three times, Greenland once, then through the Caribbean, the Panama Canal, and on to Alaska as far as Glacier Bay. On his return in 2003 and 2004, he brought her back to New England via Cape Horn, the Falklands, Fernando de Noronha, and most points in between. He says she was the best sea boat he ever travelled on, and he's had lots of experience because he grew up with schooners. Before his trip around the horn, he replaced the original Detroit Diesel 4-71 engine with a 135 hp Lugger. The Skookum carries 1,600 gallons of fuel and 600 of water. The paravane stabilizers worked well.

## Cheoy Lee Trawlers

Cheoy Lee is one of the oldest boatyards that is still producing yachts. It began in Shanghai in 1870, moved to Hong Kong in 1936, and is currently moving to a new site on the Pearl River, 60 miles west of Hong Kong. After World War II, Cheoy Lee began producing yachts in teak and during the early 1960s pioneered the use of GRP (glass-reinforced plastic)/foam sandwich (fiberglass) on yachts. More than 4,500 yachts were produced over the years.

It currently specializes in larger yachts—over 50 feet and up to 144 feet. It also continues building commercial vessels, ferries, and tugs in its 400-person yard.

In Chapter 2, which discusses the history of power voyaging, I highlighted the voyages of Larry Briggs, who accomplished three circumnavigations on Cheoy Lee–built boats, the 53-foot *Champion* and the 55-foot Cheoy Lee LRC, *Chartwell*. These feats alone put Cheoy Lee in a leadership position for early passagemakers.

Another fascinating story is Sheppard Root's 1977–78 voyage from Hong Kong to Fort Lauderdale in a stock 40-foot Cheoy Lee trawler. Shep, as he likes to be called, was on a banking assignment in Hong Kong when he read the first edition of *Voyaging Under Power* and began corresponding with Bob Beebe. He did not want to spend the time and money on a custom-built ocean voyaging boat, so he explored the existing options in Hong Kong. He found that a stock 40-foot Cheoy Lee trawler fit his needs perfectly.

The displacement hull already had considerable fuel capacity: 830 gallons. To this he converted one of his 3 water tanks into an additional 270 gallons of fuel, making a total of 1,100 gallons. Even though the boat had twin Ford diesels, they were small at 72 hp each. Shep found little difference between running with a single versus twin engines, although he designed a shaft coupling so that the shaft could be locked or even disconnected to run on a single engine, if needed. He installed a Cheoy Lee option, Lexan storm windows, for protection in extreme conditions. He had no time to fit paravanes and went without any stabilization for the entire trip. He says that the roll was mostly tolerable, but at times the boat rolled horribly. There were only seven or eight days like this when he really wished he had stabilizers.

The only major equipment failure was the autopilot, which failed soon after leaving Singapore. He and his one crew member, Jeff, hand steered for the next 5,000 miles until it was repaired in Israel.

Shep designed the voyage to take advantage of the various weather windows so that the entire voyage could be completed in one year. His planning worked well. One storm in the northern end of the Red Sea, however, was pretty bad with winds approaching hurricane force and steep nasty waves. Excerpts from some of the log entries from *China Blue* reflect the reality of this night to remember:

**2100 May 11**: *It must be blowing Force 10 out there. Ship after ship coming down on us. Got to stay out here in the middle to keep away from the shore reefs and oil rigs. I'm staying head to the seas. Have reduced rpms. Couldn't run off I don't think. The seas are so nearly vertical that I don't think we could run even if we could turn around and I'm afraid it's too late for that . . . It's like going the wrong way on a one-way street. Ship after ship. Can't see anything through the spray except the lights of the nearest ships. The big ships are starting to wander. It must be getting rough for them too. Can't maneuver well. Occasionally falling off the wind is throwing us off into crazy, dangerous roll.*

**2200 May 11**: *Must be blowing 60-plus knots. Can't hear the engines over the wind. Big damn ships coming down on us. Nothing I can do. Gear is flying and water is starting to squirt in. Getting cramps in my arms and my mouth is dry. Jeff trying to bring glasses of water but it's too rough. All spilled. Feels like we're doing aerobatics. Must be falling off 50 degrees to a side. When we fall off a wave, I'm lifted off the pilot seat. If an engine goes, this boat is going to sink. I know it.*

**2300 May 11**: *The scene outside is chaos. It looks like a deathscape. The weather is so bad now that it's more interesting than frightening . . . The radio. I talk with a guy sitting on an oil rig over the VHF. He says his instruments read Force 12—70 knots continuously with 90-knot gusts. I say "Jeff, it's blowing a hurricane plus. Don't you see, . . . if it's blowing that hard it can't last for long. It must be almost finished!"*

**0330 May 12**: *It can't be worse than a strong gale out there now. Compared to what we had this is*

nothing. I can steer with one hand and stay behind the wheel just by wedging an elbow against the column that supports the overhead. Not necessary to use the death grip any more.*

**0430 May 12**: *Jeff and I both feel like we're going to pass out. Inside the boat is a wreck, but everything still seems to be working. The bilges have been pumped. The engines are still ticking smoothly. All we need to do is stay awake and away from the reefs until the sun comes up. Now we're just waiting for daylight and Suez.*

The route of *China Blue* was from Hong Kong to Singapore; then to Sri Lanka and across the Indian Ocean to Aden. From Aden, it braved the Red Sea; transited the Suez Canal; and wound up in the Mediterranean, including Haifa, Malta, and Gibraltar. Crossing the Atlantic took Shep and Jeff to the Canaries, Cape Verdes, and then a 2,160 mile run to Barbados. Finally, they worked their way north through the Caribbean Islands to Fort Lauderdale, where the voyage officially ended 13 months and 20,000 miles later.

Speed for the voyage ranged from 6.74 to 7.40 depending on winds and currents. Nautical miles per gallon ranged from 1.93 to 3.24, with 3 nmpg being rather typical. Cost per mile ranged from 13 to 25 cents depending on fuel prices.

**Figure 13–5.** *China Blue* anchored off the Pitons on St. Lucia in the Caribbean. (Sheppard Root)

## Stephen Seaton's Boats

When I asked Stephen Seaton for a couple of photos of his "passage-makers of the past," he sent me 15! They were all different and all interesting. I decided on *Zopilote* and *Spirit of Zopilote*. Both of these boats were built in Seattle or Anacortes, Washington, by either Delta Marine or Northern Marine, and both boats have crossed oceans. Their history also intertwines with that of Bruce Kessler, one of the most renowned power voyagers, who has contributed a great deal to the field, including founding the FUBAR, discussed in Chapter 20. Bruce's circumnavigation in the early 1990s did much to create interest in power voyaging.

**Figure 13–6A.** Seaton's first passagemaker, the steel *Nahama*, built in 1969 by George Sutton. Shown here when owned by Philip Emmerson and called *Katahdin*—cruising in the ice near Frobisher Bay, Baffin Island. The boat is now called *Combahee* and is owned by Roderick Arnold. (John Emmerson)

Stephen started designing ocean-crossing trawlers in 1969, beginning with *Nahama*, shown in Figure 13–6A. He has been featured in all previous editions of this book, starting with the first edition. Because Seaton is a designer and not a builder, his boats are all pretty much custom, although many are partial replicas of earlier designs, combined with the desires of his new client. He is happy designing for any building material, including fiberglass, steel, aluminum, and even wood (yes, some clients still want wooden boats).

## Beebe's Passagemakers

Over the years, Captain Robert Beebe designed many boats specifically as passagemakers, ranging from 40 to 55 feet. Many of his earlier designs were built in wood and have since disappeared. Some were built abroad and have been lost to history. Because every boat was a custom design, there is no "brand," such as the Nordhavn 46, to track. However, his legacy lives on in many more modern designs. His influence was great on the design of my boat, *Teka III*, which has been used in many of this book's illustrations; her final design was a cooperative effort between

Captain Beebe, Paul Kotzenbue, and the Knight & Carver boatyard.

If the market dynamics had been different in the early 1980s, we might have seen a production line of boats called the "Passagemaker 54." Beebe and Knight & Carver were using *Teka III* as a prototype for this new line of boats. Beebe trademarked the term "Passagemaker" for the sale of this line and would have received commissions. Unfortunately, the rise of inexpensive Taiwanese-made trawlers and increased U.S. costs doomed this endeavor, much as it did the Malahide North Sea trawlers described earlier in this chapter. When the trademark expired it was not renewed.

In this section, we explore the history of two other Beebe passagemakers, *Steel Magnolia* and *Passagemaker* herself.

### Steel Magnolia

Beebe Design 96, built in steel, was launched in 1980 as *Bold Endeavour*. She was built for an owner in Texas; however, he died before his dream of ocean voyaging was fulfilled and little is known of her

# Bruce and Joan Kessler, *Zopilote*, and *Spirit of Zopilote*

Bruce Kessler had always been interested in boats. He grew up in Washington State in a family with commercial fishing roots and connections; he was always visiting on boats and hitching voyages at every opportunity. Instead of becoming a commercial fisherman, though, he went to Hollywood and became a successful director of movies and TV. His successful career allowed some time off for voyaging, and he says his main interest began when he was searching for the perfect long-range fishing boat. He had a "go fast" sport fisher that he took to Cabo to pursue the great fishing available there, but its range was limited. His whole life and approach to boating changed one day when he tied up to a large, beautiful tuna boat down in Cabo. He decided a full displacement boat, like that one, would allow him to go wherever he wished to find the big ones.

Bruce began looking around for a boat that would fit his needs. He did not want a commercial boat because the engine is usually forward to make room for fish holds. He wanted a standard, amidships engine location. He also had a preference for fiberglass, rather than steel or aluminum. While he was searching, he discovered a fiberglass bare hull at Delta Marine, which at that time was a strictly commercial boatbuilder. He told them he wanted to make a yacht out of the hull. They were reluctant because they had never built a yacht since their founding in 1975, but things were slow for new commercial boats and the 70-foot hull was too small for the Bering Sea crabbing industry. They finally agreed. Bruce hired Steve Seaton and his partner, Charles Neville, to convert the hull into a long-range yacht, and the boat was launched in 1985.

Bruce and Joan took *Zopilote* to Alaska and then through the Panama Canal to Maine and back through the Caribbean to Los Angeles. They left California in 1990 headed to Hawaii, searching for the world's best fishing grounds. Then they decided that Australia called, so they made their way south via the islands of Palmira, Christmas, Tahiti, Cooks, Tonga, Fiji, New Caledonia, and

**Figure 13–6B.** Bruce and Joan Kessler's *Zopilote*, a 70-foot Seaton design using a commercial fishing hull. (Bruce Kessler)

**Figure 13–6C.** *Spirit of Zopilote* is 62'6" LOA, 18' beam, 6'6" draft, displacing 165,000 pounds. She has a range of about 3,000 miles with 3,300 gallons of fuel. She is powered by a 300 hp Cummins engine. (Photo by Arthur Grace, courtesy Bruce Kessler)

finally to Sidney. They fished in Australian and New Zealand waters for a couple of years, and then decided to head home via the Mediterranean. In doing so, they headed to Bali, Singapore, Sri Lanka, Maldives, and the Red Sea into the Med. They covered most European countries and eventually headed back via the Azores and Bermuda to Florida, returning to California in May 1993. *Zopilote* was sunk by a rock pinnacle off Dall Island,

Alaska. A sad and unexpected loss after almost 100,000 miles under her keel. Luckily no one was hurt.

Bruce and Joan wanted a replacement that was similar to *Zopilote*, but smaller. They decided that 70 feet was just too much boat. Two or three extra people were needed to operate her—they wanted a boat the two of them could handle, so they commissioned Stephen Seaton to design the *Spirit of Zopilote* for

them. They contracted with a new yard, Northern Marine in Anacortes, to build it. Bruce and Joan spent 18 months living on-site, supervising the construction. Bruce focused on systems and engineering, while Joan covered layout and finish. There was, of course, a lot of collaboration to get the boat right. The boat was completed in 1997 and they have been actively cruising ever since, but have not repeated their circumnavigation feat.

history after his death. Sometime in this period she was renamed *Steel Magnolia*. Around 2002 she came on the market and was purchased by a true voyager—Roy McNett. Roy had read *Voyaging Under Power* and knew this was the boat of his dreams. He bought her without looking at another boat. In an article for *PassageMaker Magazine*, Roy described some of his feelings about the boat:

> *Although she's certainly everything I could want in a boat, I realize she's not the perfect boat for many readers. To me, she's beautiful, graceful, and a delight to live with (just like Jane, my wife!). She's calm, strong, and steady in a storm. She's gorgeous in the sunset as we return in the dinghy from an evening ashore for shopping and dinner. But to others with differing views of boating interests, she might seem too large, a bit ungainly, a tad rough around the edges, or, as one lady politely described her, "too functional . . . too utilitarian" for her tastes. Steel Magnolia is functional; she was designed by Beebe to cross oceans, comfortably and safely. She has a respectable A/B (above-water area to below-water area) ratio of 2.6 and a D/L (displacement/length) ratio of 291.*
>
> *Readers who enjoy dockside entertaining at marinas might be appalled at Steel Magnolia's lack of a spacious saloon with extremely large windows, plush couches, oriental carpets, and a big-screen television. Beebe designed her as an offshore passagemaker, not a marina princess. I wouldn't want to be standing near one of those large saloon windows if caught broadside by a rogue wave in the Gulf loop current. While the wheelhouse, with its wonderful 360-degree view,*

> *is the center for most of our activities and entertaining, the galley and dining saloon can seat nine people reasonably comfortably for a sit-down dinner. With no previous offshore experience, Jane quickly learned all the wheelhouse nav systems, radios, radar, and alarms. She can confidently stand a solo six-hour watch at night, waking me only if necessary.*
>
> *Steel Magnolia has taken me many thousands of miles safely and comfortably from New Bern to the Rio Dulce with only a few white-knuckled moments, all of which can be attributed to the captain, not the vessel. I've lived aboard Steel Magnolia for almost five years and have logged over 6,000 nautical miles at her helm. And I'm confident she'll take us many more miles to other countries and other wonderful anchorages. Thanks, Capt. Beebe.*

**Figure 13–7A.** *Steel Magnolia* is 50'LOL, 47'6"LWL, 15'beam, 5'6" draft, 55 tons displacement, 3306 Cat 175 hp, 20kw Kohler generator; she also has paravane stabilizers. (Roy McNett)

# Beebe's *Passagemaker*: Saving this Classic Boat

## Peter Quentrall-Thomas

How many times have you looked at the beautiful lines of a lovely old yacht but wondered about the work involved in bringing her back? How much will it cost? How long will it take?

I had the good fortune to become the current guardian of the original *Passagemaker* motor yacht, designed and built with loving care by the author of the first edition of this book, Captain Robert Beebe. Unfortunately she had spent six years on the hard in Trinidad & Tobago at Powerboats' excellent facilities. The harsh tropical sun had not been kind to her. But beneath the peeling paint and rotting deck was a solid hull and frame and she possessed interior fittings along with an engine, generator, water maker, radar and other electronics, all in good condition.

But let me back up and describe the steps leading to her purchase. I had retired and decided to go sailing. So the first step was using the Internet to see what yachts were available and what sort of prices were being asked. Prices are directly related to age and condition. The older the boat and/or the worse her condition, the lower the price is. And when it comes to wooden hulls, it is truly a buyer's market. But before you even consider buying any old boat, especially a wooden-hulled one, you must be either well off or handy with lots of time because there will be plenty of work to do—not just to get her in the water but also on an ongoing basis. If you are looking for a "sail it and forget it" boat, look elsewhere. But if you want a fulfilling project, a liveaboard lifestyle with plenty of room and comfort, look at an older boat.

In terms of price, many an owner has taken as little as one dollar rather than see their pride and joy go under the chainsaw, even when the scrap value might have been several thousand dollars. Realistically, expect to pay between $20,000 and $100,000 depending on the boat's size and condition. And budget at least $10,000 to place her back in the water, even in a basic condition. [Peter spent approximately $13,000 in 2008 to bring her back to life. His largest costs were $3,180 for paint and $1,200 for

**Figure 13–7B.** A restored *Passagemaker* trying out her sails in 2010 in Rio Dulce, Guatemala. (Peter Quentrall-Thomas)

new batteries. He also had to buy some used sails, buy a new outboard, service his life raft, and service the engines.] To this you must add your own "sweat equity." I invested two months (working 7 days a week) before *Passagemaker* was launched, overhauling seized equipment like the 110-volt Lorfrans anchor winch. That was a lesson well learned. The local agent came and said the winch was beyond repair and I should buy a new one. With nothing to lose I stripped it down, freed the armature, cleaned the contactors, and two years later it's still giving great service.

Having decided you can afford it, how do you determine whether a boat is structurally sound? In the case of a wooden boat you must do a haulout to allow a thorough examination of the hull. Today's marine surveyors are reluctant to examine wooden boats because so many problems can be lurking just below the surface. But if you go over the whole hull, trying to force an ice pick into each and every timber, you will find any suspicious soft spots that need to be opened up on the inside to see whether just the plank has to be replaced or whether the rot has spread to the interior frame. Don't worry

about the holes the ice pick will make because you are going to apply antifouling before she goes back in the water, anyway.

Another potential source of major problems is the through-hull fittings. Carefully go round the exterior, noting how many there are and their approximate locations, and then find the matching fittings inside. If they are showing any signs of corrosion they must be replaced. While you are crawling around in the bilges, check out the condition of the various frames and other timbers. They must be rock solid.

Moving up the hull to the topsides, it's a good idea to go round the interior first looking for any signs of water penetration and then matching that spot with the deck above it. Again the ice pick will soon reveal any rotting deck covering. In the case of *Passagemaker*, I pressure washed the deck to remove old blistered paint, and the jet of water went right through in several places as the plywood was only being held together by the paint!

The main engine must be run and the gearbox and prop checked for nasty noises, vibration, oil leaks and the like. Ask for the service record to gain some idea of the boat's history. Well-maintained diesel engines will run for years and years. Generators and electronics should all be tested. If you don't know how, get someone who does. These are not cheap items and replacing them can easily exceed the initial cost of the boat.

And last, but not least, check the wiring. Old boats tend to have accumulated many bits of equipment as each owner added his own touches, such as deck wash down pumps, mast lighting, electronics, and electrical outlets of various voltages. Many of them have become obsolete or unwanted with the passage of years and have been removed, but the cabling is nearly always left in place, "just in case." *Passagemaker* was no exception and I am still, three years later, removing unwanted cables. The older the cable the greater the fire risk as the insulation becomes brittle with age. Plus, they make it devilishly hard to trace a fault.

Would I buy *Passagemaker* now, knowing all the work that had to be done? Like a flash. There is really something wonderful about restoring a boat with a long history. I often pause in the middle of a job to imagine the men who built her nearly 50 years ago in the John Thorneycroft shipyard in Singapore. Their pride still shows in the workmanship that is so evident throughout her spacious interior.

[Peter circumnavigated the Caribbean in *Passagemaker*, covering some 7,000 nautical miles. He intends to circumnavigate South America and explore some of the major rivers there. He says, "there's plenty of life in the old girl yet."]

## Knight & Carver

John Knight and Hugo Carver were friends at the California Maritime Academy, where they both studied Marine Engineering. After graduation, they spent a few years in the Merchant Marine, but left the sea to pursue an interest in smaller craft. Hugo learned about small boat construction while working for Willard Marine Company. John worked for Hawthorne boats in San Diego building custom sport fishing boats. In the mid-1970s they joined forces to create Knight & Carver Marine Construction, which was later renamed Knight & Carver Custom Yachts (K&C), located in San Diego. They are placed a little earlier in order because of their links with Beebe boats.

About 1975, they began building Airex foam core custom fiberglass yachts, many of them passagemakers. This system allowed them to build hulls without an expensive mold—a major improvement for custom boats, such as those designed by Beebe. Over time, they experimented with different resins and reinforcements. These Airex hulls are still in use today and have been durable and strong over the years.

In 1978, Knight & Carver built *Rowan*, a 52' Beebe design aimed at crossing the Atlantic and becoming what was then termed a "canal runner," meaning it had the capability in water and air draft to fit the tunnels of European canals. The boat had a removable

**Figure 13–8A.** *Teka III*'s construction with Airex foam core in 1981. A jig of the boat is built, panels are attached and faired, and then fiberglass layers on the outside are completed. The hull is then rolled over and the inside supports are attached and fiberglass laid in, making a high-strength core. (Hugo Carver)

pilothouse top as well as twin engines, one mounted on top of the other, with a belt-drive to a single shaft and propeller. This allows running on each motor separately or using both at once if maximum power is needed. Unfortunately, the couple that built her died soon after she was completed. The second owners used her for diving and photographic voyages on the Pacific Coast of Mexico. *Rowan* was renamed *Endeavor* a number of years ago and then sold in 2008 (see Figure 13–8B). Knight & Carver also built *Mirage*, a Beebe-designed 54-foot diving boat.

**Figure 13–8B.** *Endeavor* (formerly *Rowan*), designed by Robert Beebe and built by Knight & Carver in 1978, is a 52' Airex core fiberglass boat. She is now owned by Bob and Gail Toombs of Orcas Island, Washington.

In the early 1980s Knight & Carver built both *Teka III* and *Neptune's Chariot. Teka III*, owned by the author, made two round-trips from the west coast of the United States to Europe under her original owner, Rod Swanson, and one round-trip with Mary and me. *Teka III* started as a Beebe design and was improved and finalized by Knight & Carver, Rod Swanson, and yacht designer, Paul Kotzebue. Several other hulls with different structures were modeled after the *Teka III* design. *Neptune's Chariot*, designed by Paul Kotzebue and K&C, was built for Larry Briggs (see Chapter 2). She is exceptional because her gigantic fuel tanks hold 10,000 gallons. With this range, fuel planning for circumnavigation was easy.

Another canoe stern design from Paul Kotzebue and K&C was *Andaleena*, a 62' twin-screw long-range fisherman. The boat fished around Hawaii and was later moved against the trade winds to Cabo San Lucas. They say *Andaleena* recorded 3,000 miles to windward on the voyage, but it was actually farther because of climbing all those waves.

Knight & Carver also built two Malcolm Tennant 78-foot catamarans in 1999–2000. These big cats were designed to cross oceans at 20 knots with a 3,000 mile range and are currently in commercial charter service. One of the more recent projects was building

an 82-foot by 42-foot all carbon fiber, wakeless vessel. This boat can cruise at 55 knots using its four engines without a significant wake. Over the years, Knight & Carver built more than 100 custom boats, ranging from 31 to 100 feet.

High building costs in the United States when compared with China have led to a decline in new boat construction. Knight & Carver is now focused on being one of the foremost yacht repair and refit facilities on the West Coast, with service capabilities up to 4,000 tons.

## Kadey-Krogen

James S. Krogen and Art Kadey created one of the most prolific models of ocean-going trawlers ever built: the Krogen 42. Two hundred and six hulls were built from 1977 to 1997, when it was replaced by the Krogen 44. Art seems to have been the driving force behind the 42-footer. In the mid-1970s, he presented Jim with some rough drawings of a full-displacement cruising boat that he wanted Jim to design. In 1976, they decided to become partners in a venture to produce the new design. Jim did the design work, and Art was in charge of getting the boat built in Taiwan. Their first boats were described as "rough," with primitive molds and integral plywood fuel tanks. The first boats cost only $68,000.

Most of these boats are used for coastal cruising, although a number have made significant ocean voyages, including the *Searcher*, which followed an unusual and interesting route. The boat was shipped to England in 1987 and proceeded to cruise Denmark and Sweden, then down the coast of France across the infamous Bay of Biscay, to Gibraltar and into the Mediterranean. They travelled throughout the Med as far as Turkey. Departing the Med in March 1992, they cruised down the coast of East Africa to Mauritania, Dakar, Senegal, Gambia, and Guinea-Bissau and then on to the Cape Verde Islands. They departed for Trinidad in June 1993, covering 2,250 nm in 15 days, stopping only for an oil change in mid-Atlantic. After spending 9 months in Trinidad, they ran up the Caribbean Island chain, including a non-stop passage of 583 nm from Puerto Rico to Long

Island in the Bahamas. *Searcher* finally arrived back in its home port of Stuart, Florida, in June 1994 after a seven-year voyage.

Beebe and Leishman analyzed this model in the third edition of this book. For an ocean crossing, the motion would be much more comfortable with either paravanes or active fins for stabilization (although it seems that *Searcher* had no stabilization). My limited personal experience on these boats is that they have a healthy roll in beam seas and need stabilization for comfort. The forward pilothouse windows and doors are also vulnerable to green water. They need to be covered with storm covers in the event of a serious storm. The Krogen 42 was built with a foam core to reduce weight. That strategy resulted in some hull-deformation problems and was changed to solid glass in the mid-1980s for below the waterline construction. Its hull is more efficient than the Nordhavn 46, which is built of heavier solid fiberglass. Fuel consumption of the Krogen is about 1.6 gph at 7 knots, while the Nordhavn 46 is about 2.10 gph. The A/B ratio of 2.2 (discussed in Chapter 12) shows that the 42 is not as top-heavy as it looks. The high forward pilothouse makes for excellent visibility, but may exacerbate motion when at sea.

## Krogen 54' Passagemaker

Between 1988 and 1990, Kadley-Krogen built eight of the Krogen 54s. It was replaced by the Krogen 58, which is still in production. I found two significant ocean voyages by Krogen 54s, both crossing the Atlantic.

**Krogen 54' Patty.** In 1989, delivery captain Philip W. Campagna piloted a new Krogen 54 (Number 7), *Patty*, from Miami to the Mediterranean. His 4,800 mile voyage was uneventful, except that, when leaving Gibraltar, they had an unusual experience that is no longer possible. Here is how he describes it:

*On July 19, we called Gibraltar control and cleared the bay in a light mist and fair winds. Nearing Europa Point, the VHF came in slightly broken up, but I could still detect the familiar Midwestern accent. "Gibraltar . . . Harbor Control . . . this is . . . American warship . . . entering . . . bay."*

*I thought, "Must be one of our destroyers or a cruiser coming in for a few days." Then she appeared out of a light haze off our port bow, with one of those long, sleek, sheer lines that are rarely seen these days. Destroyer? Cruiser? Not with those guns! That's history! A battleship! A helicopter buzzed around in circles, warning ships to keep a safe distance. We made a 30-degree turn to starboard to clear the radius of the helicopter. As the gigantic vessel passed, we made out the name on the stern: IOWA . . . a great sight to behold! This still modern warship was carrying her age proudly over the seas, thrilling all who beheld her wherever she sailed.*

**Krogen 54' Horizons.** We first met Maude and Frank Ruffin in April 1999 as we left the San Blas Islands of Panama. We travelled together on what turned out to be a rough, 250-nautical-mile, overnight passage. The forecast was for 3–5 foot seas and 15 knots of wind, but the actual seas wound up with steep 9–10 feet seas and 25 knots—on the beam! *Horizons* had to refuel in San Andres with a Mediterranean mooring layout in strong winds—it was a challenge. Actually, this was the first time we had seen a Krogen 54.' We were impressed by its high bow and great visibility, but were glad we did not have the windage that made docking more challenging. We lost track of them for a while and then met up again in 2001 when wintering in Barcelona, Spain. We enjoyed each other's company and camaraderie during that time. Frank had complained of problems with his Ford Lehman engine. It seems the first owners of the boat had used it only a few times and had not properly maintained the engine. By the time they arrived in the Mediterranean, they decided to replace the troublesome Ford with a Lugger. The replacement worked out well and they really enjoyed their new trouble-free engine.

## Krogen 48' Whaleback

The Whaleback, introduced in 1993, was designed as a long-range cruiser with 1,000 gallons of fuel, giving her good range powered by a 210 hp Cat engine. She has a Portuguese bridge for good protection and the pilothouse has excellent all-around views. Thirty Whalebacks were produced before being replaced with the 48' North Sea in 2003. One of the more interesting adventures of a Whaleback owner is related here by Maurice and Louise-Ann Nunas.

# Our Australasian Seas Adventure

### Maurice and Louise-Ann Nunas

Maurice Nunas was director of National Spectrum Management Operations in the Canadian Department of Communications (like the FCC in the USA). Louise-Ann Nunas worked in accounting and as an office manager. They migrated to Asia, where Maurice worked as government relations director for private industries, and Louise-Ann was a counselor at the Canadian Education Centre and volunteer for the Canadian Association. In Singapore, they bought *Akama*, a 1993 Krogen 48' Whaleback, and cruised the waters from Thailand to Indonesia, eventually becoming full-time liveaboards. Upon retirement in 2002, they slipped the lines and set out on the voyage of their dreams.

*Thinking back over the past six years, we have so many memories. They run the gamut of emotion from pure terror to elation. Our planned three-year trip in Australasia took over five years. We went to many wonderful and exotic places in Singapore, Malaysia, Sabah, Borneo, Helen Reef (Palau), Papua New Guinea, the Solomon Islands, Vanuatu, New Caledonia, New Zealand, Australia, and Indonesia.*

*We started out on 15 September 2002, full of anticipation and some trepidation about what we were about to do: explore Australasia on our own by sea. Our friends and relatives thought we were nuts. "Aren't you afraid of pirates and storms?" was their collective mantra. Frankly we were a bit scared, but our fear was more than outweighed by the anticipation of the fun and adventure to come.*

*Cruising down the Santi River in Malaysia, heading to sea, we felt a bit like Columbus. We were heading into the unknown, armed only with our ship, our wits, and our charts. We did not even know exactly where we would go, other than it would be "wilderness cruising" around the South China Sea. In some cases the charts merely said, "UNSURVEYED," with only a row of soundings between major islands and vague indications of depth and obstructions everywhere else. Cruising guides were few and scant.*

Maurice and Louise-Ann continued their voyage throughout Australasia, including Borneo, Papua New Guinea, the Solomon Islands, Vanuatu, New Caledonia, New Zealand, and Australia. One exciting weather event happened on their voyage to the top of Australia:

*Heading across Australia's Bay of Carpenteria, en route to Darwin; for the first time in five years we were in the company of many boats, mostly sailing yachts heading for the Darwin to Indonesia rally. In good weather, the crossing takes about two days. The bay is known for violent storms that whip up big square waves in the shallow water, and we got caught in one of the worst storms we'd endured. The waves were higher than the boat and the winds gale force and more. More than once we had to bear off our course, then claw back the lost miles whenever the sea eased. We were never afraid for our lives. We'd already had too much sea time in bad weather for that. We knew Akama could take it. But we were severely punished, and things that had never moved about slid back and forth noisily.*

*When we got to a safe anchorage we surveyed the damage. To our astonishment, there was nearly none. Despite the shifting of nearly everything that was not screwed down, and despite having fallen off several big waves, only a few dishes broke and one battery fell over, spilling acid into the bilge. We were relaxed and sipping coffee less than an hour after anchoring, and for the first time were truly in awe of Akama's ability to transport us safely.*

*Then the sailboats began to arrive. They had blown-out sails, broken rigging, and salt water everywhere. All their crews were clad head to foot in foul weather gear and many were pouring water out of their boots. For days afterwards, the VHF was buzzing with harrowing tales of the storm and ever-inflating estimates of the winds and the waves. Until then, we had assumed that when the going truly got rough we'd be better off in a good sailboat.*

After departing Australia, their route took them to Bali, Singapore, Thailand, and back to Malaysia. They had to sell *Akama* due to ill health, but they had a grand adventure.

**Figure 13–9.** Krogen 48' Whaleback, *Akama*, anchored off Koh Pethra on the West Coast of Thailand. The arm is for an anchor stabilizer. The boat is 48'2" LOA, 16'8" beam, 4'9" draft, displaces 56,000 lbs @ half load, and is powered by a single 210-hp Cat 3208. (Maurice and Louise-Ann Nunas)

## Nordhavn

Since Nordhavn launched its first N46 in 1988, the company has been the leader in ocean-going motor boats. The company was founded in 1978 as Pacific Asian Enterprises, in Dana Point, California, by Dan Streech, Jim Leishman, and Joe Meglen. At first, it built sailing vessels in Taiwan for the relatively crowded U.S. sailboat market. It was not long, however, until they came under the spell of Captain Beebe's vision of ocean-crossing passage-makers and saw a future market for long-range powerboats. Dan Streech likes to describe the genesis of the N46 model:

**Figure 13–10A.** This informal gathering of Nordhavns at Hawkesbury River in 2010 at Castle Lagoon, Australia, shows how ubiquitous Nordhavns are in world voyaging. The boats include N55 *Moana Kuewa*, N47 *Elfreda Beetle*, N46 *Suprr*, N43 *Barquita*, and N43 *Opal Lady*. (Christine Boaman)

*The N46 was conceived by Jim and Jeff (Leishman) in the bar of a restaurant about 25 years ago (1986). Fortified by some beers and a fresh bar napkin, the course of history was changed.*

Jeff finalized the design of the N46 in 1987 as part of his final graduation requirements from the Yacht Design Institute, later merged with the Westlawn Institute of Marine Technology.

Over the next 15 years, Nordhavn built 82 hulls. These boats have been some of the most prolific power voyagers ever created. A number of 46s have circumnavigated, including Jim and Susy Sink on *Salvation II* in 1990–1995 (see sidebar), Heidi and Wolfgang Hass on *Kanaloa* (circumnavigated twice; see more information in Chapter 16, World Cruising Destinations), and Scott and Mary Flanders on *Egret* (see Chapter 2 for information on their voyage). Ghanim al-Othman, a Kuwaiti, also completed a circumnavigation on *Othmani* (see sidebar in Chapter 18). The N46 model leads all other Nordhavn boats in miles travelled and circumnavigations—it has been the workhorse for world voyagers.

Some of the other major voyagers with N46s include *Suprr*, owned by Bob and Margaret Edwards, travelling from the Mediterranean to Australia via the Panama Canal and Hawaii. John Keen's *Not Yet II* voyaged from Southeast Asia to the Mediterranean and Black Seas. *Envoy*, owned by Wayne and Patricia Davis, cruised with the NAR (Nordhavn Atlantic Rally, see page 375) and continued in the Mediterranean. *World Odd@Sea*, with John and Dulcie Harris, cruised the NAR, the Mediterranean, and on to England. Andy Lund's *Resolution* voyaged up and down the Pacific Coast; then through the Panama Canal to the Eastern United States; then from Rhode Island to Falmouth, England; and continued to Scandinavia and the Mediterranean.

There are many photos of N46s throughout the book. However, it is interesting to examine the original lines shown in the illustration. Note the smooth flow of the underwater lines with the almost canoe stern aft. This shape provided seakindly qualities to the hull that have made it popular with voyagers. The pilothouse was relatively low and amidships to minimize accelerations in rough water. The hull is relatively low with an A/B ratio of 2.3, giving it minimum windage and a low center of gravity. Many of the N46s used paravanes for stabilization, although a number of purchasers elected active fins.

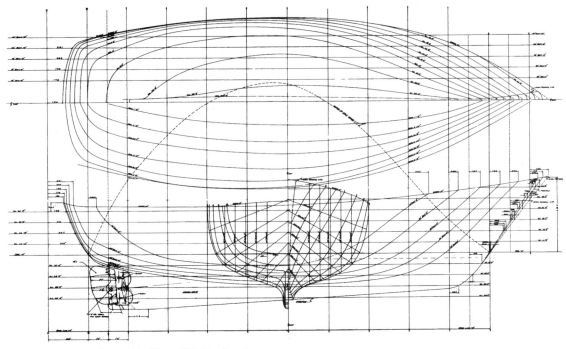

**Figure 13–10B.** Nordhavn 46 hull lines. (PAE/Nordhavn)

# *Salvation II*'s Voyages and Circumnavigation

In 1990, Jim and Susy Sink bought Nordhavn 46, Hull #10. As newcomers to ocean voyaging and passagemaking, they learned the ropes taking their new boat up the coast to the San Juan Islands of Washington, and then on to Southeast Alaska and Glacier Bay. Not wasting any time, they cruised down the Pacific Coast (in December), through the Panama Canal, and onward to their home in Houston, Texas. From there, they began a great circle route up the East Coast, through the Great Lakes, and down the Mississippi River to the Gulf of Mexico—a 6,000 mile trip. After completing this voyage, they decided to try for a world circumnavigation.

Their trip across the Atlantic in the spring of 1992 took the established route through Bermuda and the Azores. They endured a couple of gales on the way to

**Figure 13–10C.** *Salvation II* arriving at Dana Point after completing its circumnavigation. (PAE/Nordhavn)

Falmouth, England, but the N46 handled them with ease. From England, they journeyed through canals and up the Rhine River to Austria, through the canal, and down the Danube to the Black Sea. From there, they headed into the Mediterranean. In a letter dated Jan 1, 1993, they summarized their experience:

> It's New Year's Day here on the Turquoise Coast of the Aegean Sea, near the ancient city of Ephesus, not far from three great cradle-lands of civilization.
>
> Salvation II logged 10,000 miles, Texas to Turkey, in 1992. Crossing the mighty Atlantic; cruising the south coast of England; up the Thames to London—two glorious weeks at St. Katherine's Dock. Parading Parliament on the fourth of July, Captain of the Queen's Barge on board as our guest. Across the English Channel, the North Sea, the Ijsselmeer, Frisian Islands, Keil Canal, Baltic Sea to wonderful Copenhagen. Then south on the Mittelland and other lovely canals through the spectacular heartland of Germany. Up the fabled Rhine and the meandering Main to the summit of the new Main–Danube Canal (1,332 feet above sea level). At the front of the line for first locking on opening day. Finally, carefully down the troubled Danube through central and Eastern Europe; laying claim to be the first ship in history to transit the inland waters (2,223 miles and 93 locks) Baltic Sea to Black Sea!
>
> Onward through the Bosporus to fascinating Istanbul, Sea of Marmara, the Dardanelles, into Kusadasi for a Thanksgiving feast, and Christmas holidays with newfound friends in this most congenial country.

After spending two years cruising the Eastern Mediterranean, they departed via the Suez Canal and Red Sea to Thailand, Malaysia, and Singapore. They completed their circumnavigation via Hawaii to Dana Point in October 1995. Theirs was the first of the Nordhavns to circle the world, logging 50,000 nautical miles.

## Nordhavn 62

The second model introduced by Nordhavn in 1992 was the N62. PAE built 38 of these boats. The N62 adapted the lines of the classic Northsea trawlers like Romsdal and Malahide with an aft pilothouse and large foredeck. Many feel that of all the Nordhavns, this is one of the most aesthetically pleasing boats.

In spite of its 18-year production run, these boats seem to have done fewer major voyages than the N46s. As of 2011, two circumnavigations are known: *Rover* and *Karma*. Jimmy Buffett has done more than 50,000 miles on Hull #2, *Continental Drifter*, including a round-trip voyage across the Atlantic. David Crannell on *Adventure* travelled to the South Pacific and Australia before shipping the boat back on *Dockwise*. *Autumn Wind*, owned by Bill and Arlene Smith, also travelled to the Marquesas and later on the NAR crossing the Atlantic. Braun and Tina Jones' *Grey Pearl* completed the NAR and the Great Siberian Sushi Run (GSSR) to Japan via the Aleutians and is currently in Indonesia. *Seabird*, owned by Steven and Carol Argosy, set off from Florida and joined the GSSR voyage to Japan. They are travelling with *Grey Pearl* in Southeast Asia. Ken and Roberta Williams toured the Mediterranean on *Sans Souci* and crossed the Atlantic on the NAR. They sold the boat and traded up to a larger 68-foot Nordhavn with the same name—also a GSSR voyager.

Two other Nordhavn models have been retired: the N50 and the N57. Philip Eslinger, owner of

**Figure 13–10D.** Nordhavn 62, *Grey Pearl*, on the Nordhavn Atlantic Rally. Note the bulbous bow installed on the hull. Specifications are 62'6" LOA, 19'4" beam, 6'draft, 325 hp Lugger, and 2,450 gallons of fuel. (PAE/Nordhavn)

*Flat Earth*, an N50, has travelled from Alaska to the South Pacific in his boat. His misadventure with a net on the way back from Hawaii is related in Chapter 15. Two N50s, *Sundog* and *Four Across*, crossed the Atlantic on the NAR, while another N50, *Downtime*, went on the Med Bound Rally, organized by Milt Baker. Twenty-nine N50s were built between 1996 and 2005.

The most famous N57 is *Bagan*, owned by Sprague Theobald, who completed a circumnavigation of the North American Continent, including the Northwest Passage. *Ice Dancer II*, owned by Dick and Gail Barnes, has covered more than 70,000 nautical miles through the South Pacific, including Peru, Australia, Tasmania, both islands of New Zealand, and most of the tropical island groups. Three other N57s crossed the Atlantic in the NAR: *Atlantic Escort*, *Emeritus*, and *Goleen*. *Shaka* is reported to be in the South Pacific. Forty N57s were built between 1996 and 2007.

**Figure 13–10E.** Nordhavn 50, *Flat Earth*, anchored just north of Sandy Cove, Glacier Bay, Alaska. The N50 is 51'2" LOA, 16' beam, 5'8" draft, 80,000 lbs. displacement, with a 300-hp Lugger engine and 1,320 gallons of fuel. (Philip Eslinger)

**Figure 13–10F.** Nordhavn 57, *Ice Dancer II*, anchored in the South Pacific. The N57 is 60'7" LOA, 17'7" beam, 6'2" draft, 122,000 pounds displacement, powered by a 325-hp Lugger with 2,000 gallons of fuel. (Dick and Gail Barnes)

## Cape Horn Trawlers

Peter J. Sever, founder of Cape Horn Trawlers, did not intend to become a boat builder—he sold his computer business, intending to buy a good boat and go cruising. His primary criterion was safety, but he had many other desires as well. His favorite boat at that time (1990s) was a steel Romsdal, but it was priced higher than he wanted to pay for a boat that was already 30 years old. He insisted on steel as the ultimate strong boatbuilding material. Here were the criteria Peter used for his boat:

• First and foremost, the vessel had to be extremely safe and reliable. We did not want to spend much of our sabbatical living in fear—or any time at all being in legitimate danger at sea. As captain, I wanted that secure feeling, deep in my gut, of total, absolute, complete trust in my vessel's strength and integrity, under any circumstance in which nature's whims or my own mistakes could place us. I had created a list of misfortunes—"What Ifs"—and wanted a positive escape plan for each scenario. This trip was meant to be fun, not terminal.

• Second, it had to be a very seakindly, comfortable and quiet vessel underway.

- *Third, it had to be a very comfortable home! At this stage of life we like to live reasonably well.*
- *Fourth, I admit that we wanted a pretty yacht too. We did not want to appear ostentatious in third world countries, but also didn't want to be embarrassed pulling into good yacht clubs.*

When he could not find any boats to suit him, he decided to build his own. He describes his epiphany as follows:

*So, one evening in a Ft. Lauderdale hotel, exhausted from boat-hunting, I decided: I was going to build a truly great boat at a reasonable price. My boat was going to be tough, safe and traditional like that Romsdal—except double bottomed, with heavier-duty windows/doors and with more modern layout and equipment. Plus my study of existing naval research showed that hard chines were a preferable hull form than round bilges and no one else was making hard chined trawler yachts. I would include the best features of boats we had seen, workboat construction, with none of the drawbacks.*

Peter worked on the design for his new custom 56-foot trawler with Bob Johnson to create his "ideal boat." (Later Cape Horns were modified by Lengkeek Vessel Engineering, Charles Neville, and Sparkman & Stephens.) He built his new design in Canada, launching the finished boat, *Eden Bound*, in March 1994. His boat had many features not found in other trawlers of the time, such as a double-bottom hull, self-righting stability, Z-drive propulsion, and backups for all critical systems. He was pleased with the results of his efforts, and the boat performed well in heavy seas and even survived with only scratches from a major collision with a runaway tug. His only criticism of the new boat was that it was too small. He wanted more space for all the equipment needed for redundant systems and living space—65 feet was a better size for his needs.

Peter found that people were asking him, "Where can I buy one of these boats?" He had

**Figure 13–11A.** Cape Horn 65, *Anjumal* (now named *Windermere*), showing the benefit of bilge keels for drying out and the hard-chine hull shape, reminiscent of modern commercial fishing boats. (Wray West)

so many inquiries, he decided in 1998 to found a corporation, called Cape Horn Trawlers, to build more of these yachts. Over the next 9 years, there were 15 Cape Horns built, ranging from 52' to 82'. While specifications varied a bit, the Cape Horn 65 was 65' LOA, 20' beam, 5'9" draft, displaced, at full load, 210,000 pounds, carried 5,500 gallons of fuel, giving a range of over 4,000 miles, and was powered by a 440 hp Cummins diesel. An unusual feature was the use of keel cooling *and* wet exhaust to eliminate the soot and heat of a dry exhaust. Another unique

**Figure 13–11B.** Z-Drive, Kort-nozzel, and rudder on Cape Horn 65, *Windermere*. Note the extreme protection for the rudder, rare in a trawler. (John Richards Jr.)

design option was the use of Thrustmaster Z-drives to provide propeller thrust in any direction, much like a modern tugboat. Most Cape Horns have active fins and bilge keels (see Figure 13–11A). This unusual combination is discussed in Chapter 8. They were all built in Ontario, Nova Scotia, or New Brunswick, Canada.

Cape Horns have crossed the Atlantic and Pacific, with numerous trips through the Panama Canal from coast to coast. One of the most interesting was the experience of *Eden Bound* during the tsunami at Phuket when she experienced a near knockdown.

**Figure 13–11C.** Cape Horn 63, *Two by Sea*, purchased by Jim Long in 2002, has cruised extensively in the Caribbean. (Jim Long)

The owner reported that he was aboard and tied to the dock at the time the tsunami arrived. The first indication of the tsunami was when the boat heeled over, submerging the portlights. Because she was tied to a floating dock, maneuvering was out of the question. He cranked up the engine and positioned the Z-drive 90 degrees against the force of the current using full throttle. To this he added the full power of his hydraulic bow thruster. He fought the wave sideways, while other boats went crashing by, landing ashore. Some of his docklines snapped, but he maintained control. The boat sustained only some cosmetic paint damage. This event seems to support Peter's objective of building a boat that can survive almost any catastrophe at sea.

This chapter shows not only the variety of boats that have accomplished major voyages but also the tremendous variations in itineraries—the old saying the "world is your oyster" holds true when you own a passagemaking vessel. These passagemakers were built strong to cross oceans so a few or even many years and miles of cruising do not seem to create that much wear and tear. Some express fear of buying a used boat, perhaps because they liken it to a used car. But many of these older passagemakers are still going strong 40 or 50 years later. The worst thing for boats is sitting around in marinas in the sun and salt, where they deteriorate much faster than when underway on voyages.

## CHAPTER FOURTEEN

# Voyage Preparation and Planning

Your cruising objectives are the guiding principles for the planning needed for your cruise. If you are undertaking an inshore passage, such as voyaging to Alaska or the Great Circle route, you can find help nearby and assistance almost everywhere. If you are taking slightly longer, intermediate voyages, such as a Caribbean trip to the Bahamas or farther south to Trinidad, you need more preparation, but help is still relatively easily obtainable. If you are crossing oceans and headed to far-off locations, a maximum amount of preparation is needed. In this chapter, I concentrate on the latter—the big voyage.

## Voyage Planning for *Akama*

### Maurice and Louise-Ann Nunas

Our first step is a written long-term plan highlighting countries we plan to visit or avoid. We always have a plan for about five years ahead, the detail being little more than where we would like to be year by year. We research routes and destinations at leisure; we don't dwell on the detail. Without a plan, one might stay in one place forever! We are setting out to explore as many areas as possible, eventually ending up back in Canada before we grow too old or infirm to carry on this lifestyle.

Next we make a medium term plan. Each year, we consider where we are and where we want to go during the next year. Making this plan entails knowing on a month-by-month basis where we will be moving. Generally, the most important aspect is climate. We try to stay where it is warm, but not hot, and move during favorable climactic seasons. This plan is also not very detailed, the time frame being monthly or bi-monthly. On this plan we list little more than the distances for the passages, major ports, the best and worst times to go, and the time we plan to go (usually stating just the month).

Once we settle on a good intermediate plan, which is fun and informative work, we make a detailed plan for the coming season (usually the next six months). Now our research turns to the specific sites that we want to see in each country. We generally know within a few weeks specifically where we will be, sometimes reserving a marina berth and scheduling specific maintenance. Although we have dates and times, our overall cardinal rule is DON'T BE DRIVEN BY SCHEDULE. So, if we are not ready to go, or if the weather is not cooperating, we stay put, keeping an eye out to be sure that we don't box ourselves in for the next few major moves.

One of the things we ensure when making our more detailed plans is setting aside time for sightseeing. We've met several "yachties" who were going around the world in two years. Invariably they are a haggard bunch, and if you ask them about it they all opine that they

**Figure 14–1.** *Akama*, a Kadey-Krogen 48 Whaleback, owned by Maurice and Louise-Ann Nunas, anchored in Thailand. (Maurice Nunas)

should have set aside much more time. Even Jim and Susy Sink told us that four and a half years to circumnavigate was way too fast.

The chapter explores several aspects of voyage planning: getting experience, information sources, routing, gathering crew, provisioning, mechanical preparation, fuel consumption, communication, and emergency planning. Each topic could become a chapter in itself, but here I provide only an overview of these subjects as a start for your voyage preparation.

## Get Experience

Some cruisers have the advantage of having cruised or owned several previous sailing or motor boats. Before beginning our entry into ocean voyaging, we had owned fishing boats and coastal cruising boats for many years. If you don't have that experience, you can offer to crew on others' boats, hire an experienced captain to go along on your initial cruises, or learn slowly by cruising close to home until you gain experience. We brought our boat up the coast from San Diego to Washington on her initial voyage. We then circumnavigated Vancouver Island and made a trip to Alaska. After that, we felt ready to try a longer voyage, so we headed down the U.S. and Mexican coast, through the Panama Canal to Central America, and onward to Florida. We got used to overnight passages and voyage planning. We encountered a lot of different weather and sea conditions to test us. All in all, the experience made us feel comfortable about beginning an ocean-crossing voyage. It also gave us a chance to see what needed improvement on the boat before we left.

One unusual way to prepare for an ocean voyage is the experience of Leonard Stern on *Indifference*. He and his spouse tested the boat on a 14-day, nonstop voyage back and forth across Long Island Sound. They were able to fine-tune the boat, practice launching and retrieving their paravanes, get used to a watch schedule, and even change oil while underway. They practiced using the SSB radio and receiving weather faxes, and checked out their radar skills. This practice run simulated a 14-day passage between Bermuda and the Azores.

## Mine Information Sources

This is where you get to do your own research. You might begin by joining the SSCA (Seven Seas Cruising Association) and scouring all the back issues about cruising where you might want to go. *PassageMaker Magazine* has been an excellent source of power cruising for many years. Back issues have a wealth of information. There are many wonderful books that help with planning. Imray publishes a large number of useful cruising guides to all areas of the world. Nautical bookstores often feature limited distribution cruising guides to unusual areas (see the sidebar by Scott Flanders, next page). Internet searches of owners' websites can net many useful gems, as can e-books.

An important resource for your voyaging experience will be the ship's library. We try to include reference books on every topic we may encounter while voyaging. We search out good books on weather, route planning, anchoring, electrical systems, diesel engines, medical emergencies, navigation, electronics, seamanship and heavy weather handling, docking, knots and rigging, cooking and provisioning, and any other topic we feel might be relevant. Try to include some foreign language–conversation books and, if possible, a book of nautical terms in the language of places you will be visiting.

## Evaluate Health Risks

This is a personal issue that all voyagers face, especially as we age. Ocean cruising takes you away from your doctor and from medical facilities you may need. In fact, if you experience a heart attack or stroke, it may mean death; whereas, if you were at home, you might have been saved. Health risks are particularly scary when a husband and wife team is voyaging on their own. What would happen if your spouse died while aboard? A close friend of ours had that experience while cruising off the islands in Greece. Luckily, the wife was fully competent to pilot the boat until authorities could be notified. This is the only case we have heard of someone on a yacht dying at sea, so the risk is pretty low. If you are at risk for significant health events, you need to determine in advance how emergencies can be met. What medicines will be needed? Is there an emergency number to reach your doctor in far-away places? Are you trained in first aid? Are the right reference books on board? Is there any special equipment needed, such as a defibrillator?

# Read All About It

**Scott Flanders, Voyage of *Egret* website**

In 1994, we subscribed to *Cruising World* magazine, soon followed by *Ocean Navigator* magazine. This was not because we were or wanted to be sailors, but they had great tales of far off places. The articles were written by regular folks who actually WENT somewhere. A few years later along came *Passage-Maker Magazine*. After reading two issues we picked up at a newsstand, we subscribed and later bought every back issue. The wheels were now turning and those thoughts of long-distance cruising turned into reality. I say this as I drive *Egret* currently 411 nm due west of Guinea-Bissau (Africa) and 1,767 nm from our landfall of Bahia de Salvador, Brazil.

We have every one of those articles from each of the three magazines from 1994 on, aboard *Egret*. They are cut out and arranged in files geographically, then by subject: weather, medicine, technical, and "interesting." The file Mary and I read and reread time and time again (now Steve is reading) is labeled "Chile." This file contains every article from Gibraltar through Chile. Over time we've noticed a consensus amongst the different authors. Of particular interest are Beth Leonard's aboard *Hawk* [author of *Blue Horizons* and *Voyager's Handbook*] and John Harries aboard *Morgan's Cloud*. In doing research I am not interested in "how I cheated death" tales but the nuts and bolts of the voyage south along the Argentine coast and the intricate details of the Chilean canals. These two pieces—particularly Beth's—are priceless. Today, we only subscribe to *Cruising World*, which we pick up once a year when we visit family and friends in Fort Lauderdale. We enjoyed the other two magazines. They performed their duty of inspiration and knowledge. I recommend, at a minimum, that you buy the past six years' issues of *Cruising World* and do exactly what we did in creating your own files.

These articles provided the spark for the fire. At first the fire smoldered; then little flames appeared with more high latitude information coming faster and faster. The idea of taking *Egret* to Chile was beginning to take shape but needed a catalyst. The catalyst came in the form of the most incredible cruising guide we ever read. What is even more incredible is the minuscule audience it serves. Authors Mariolina Rolfo and Giorgio Ardrizzi devoted eight years of their lives living in Patagonia aboard their Amel sailboat, researching and writing the *Patagonia & Tierra del Fuego Nautical Guide*. This is a large hardbound book complete with every possible bit of information a cruiser could need. In addition, there are pictures and an extensive history of the area. In December 2004 we sent them an e-mail looking for information. What we got back was three pages of information complete with answers—specific to our questions—that gushed with enthusiasm. As we weave through the intricate Chilean canals, we will refer to this guide extensively. We encourage every one of you to buy this book if for no other reason than to support their tremendous effort. Best value for a hundred bucks you'll ever get.

Health insurance may also be in order. Many United States policies, including Medicare, do not cover foreign doctors or hospitalization. When I fell off a quay in Horta, Azores, and broke some ribs, Mary had to pay the fees before they would treat me. On the other hand, in Porto de Roma, I cut my foot and had to go to the emergency room. There was no charge there. It appears that medical treatment will often be available, but be prepared to pay cash in advance. It is also advisable to bring along x-rays if you have some skeletal condition that may worsen while cruising, such as spine compression. In some developing countries, it is a good idea to carry empty syringes in case you need an injection. In some countries, used syringes are the norm.

## Routing: Where to Go and When

We will cover this topic in more detail in later chapters on ocean crossing and weather. As a general rule for planning, you need pilot charts of the area you would like to travel. These charts summarize mariner's experiences throughout the earth in terms of wind direction and strength, sea states, tropical storms, and fog; and they do it by month.

When we were cruising in the Eastern Mediterranean, we seriously contemplated completing a circumnavigation from west to east via the Indian Ocean and north through Japan to Alaska. We bought charts and cruising guides, but when we studied the pilot charts more closely, we came to the conclusion that the best time to go across the Indian Ocean was during the transition season between monsoon winds. This is also the beginning of the cyclone or hurricane season. Thus, we would have been taking a risk of being caught in a tropical storm or worse—a risk we were not willing to take. Even if we had made it to Southeast Asia, we had a similar monsoon problem with travel from Singapore to Japan. To top it off, the time with the fewest gales in the North Pacific is also the time with the highest

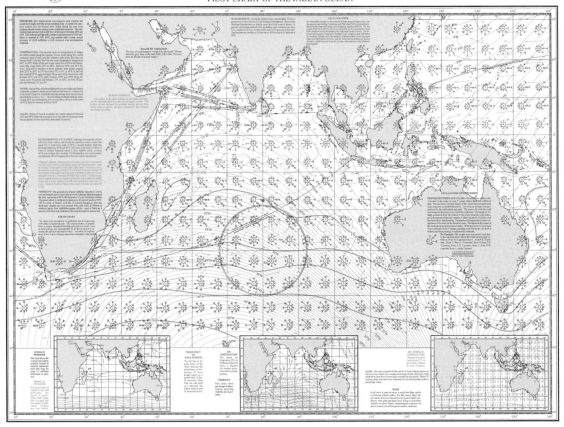

**Figure 14–2.** Example of Indian Ocean pilot chart for May. Winds are favorable, but almost every year a tropical cyclone happens in May. (National Geospace-Intelligence Agency)

number of days of fog. These factors accumulated into an analysis that the trip would be a risky and difficult adventure without much fun. Since one of our primary cruising objectives is to enjoy ourselves, we opted not to pursue this route.

If you choose the right timing and route, your voyage will be more pleasant and safe. Study the pilot charts for wind direction and force by month. Look at the possibilities of gales. Look at the strength and consistency of the winds. If the chart predicts a larger percentage of days with an average wind of 25 knots, you can expect some pretty big waves and a lot of motion. If the wind averages 15 knots, the voyage will be more pleasant and comfortable. In addition, you want to avoid tropical storms, hurricanes, and cyclones, so choosing the season is important. Also

search Internet weather sources for wave heights *and direction*. For example, a trip from San Diego to the Marquesas may result in large quartering seas on the stern, meaning perhaps 1,000 miles or more of corkscrew motion—a very uncomfortable prospect. On the other hand, a departure from Southern Mexico or Panama to the Galapagos and then on to the Marquesas will most likely afford much smoother, more comfortable wave trains.

At one time weather was the only major constraint on where to go. Today, piracy also restricts our decisions. Check the Internet before transiting potentially dangerous areas. In addition, check your insurance to make sure they will cover the area you plan to visit. Sometimes insurance companies put conditions on cruising area, number of crew

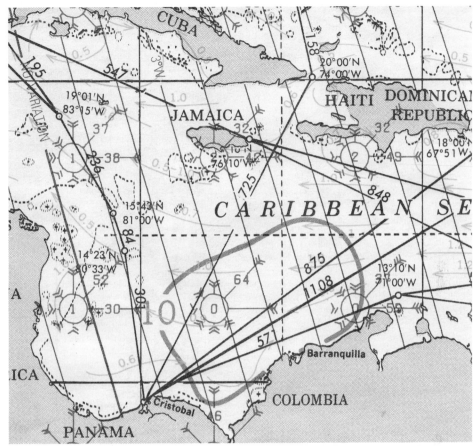

**Figure 14–3.** Pilot chart for January. The large area marked with a "10" off the coast of Colombia is average wave height. The small circles are "Wind Roses," showing the wind direction and force for the area around the center. The circle right above Colombia shows a 0 in the middle indicating no calms. The longest arrow shows average wind as Beaufort Force 5 (17–21 knots) for 64% of the time. Northeast to east winds are expected almost continuously. You would not want to be headed east toward Trinidad at this time of year.

required, experience levels, seasons, and other factors. Check early in the decision making process to avoid disappointment. Be sure to carry proof of insurance. Some countries and many marinas require such proof.

Fuel capacity and consumption are a major consideration when route planning. You need to figure out how far you can go, plus reserve, to determine your maximum range. If you exceed this range, you either don't go that route or you take on fuel bladders to extend your range. This latter option has been used by a number of cruisers on longer passages, including *Egret* and *Starr*, discussed in other parts

of this book. If you pursue this option, you should also evaluate stability with the increased load. See the "Resource Planning" section later in this chapter.

## Who Will Go?

Early in the planning process, you need to decide whether you will use additional crew for all or part of your voyage. If so, who will you invite or hire? What qualifications will you look for? What are the logistics of pick-up and drop-off? How flexible is their schedule? Having friends or crew along on long ocean passages allows easier watch schedules and reserve help if one person is injured or gets sick.

# Insurance for Ocean Voyaging

## Milt Baker

Getting insurance coverage to cross an ocean can be hard, especially for a first-timer with little or no offshore experience. Determining what kind of experience is needed can often be like chasing a moving target; every underwriter seems to use a different yardstick.

According to Al Golden, principal of International Marine Insurance Services (IMIS), whose company insures many ocean-crossing motor yachts and sailing yachts, attitude is perhaps the single most important determinant of whether a skipper will get offshore insurance to cross an ocean. "The right attitude makes all the difference," said Golden. "With that, everything else falls right into place." And, as far as underwriters are concerned, it takes an experienced insurance professional like Golden (who has crossed the Atlantic in his own yacht) to be a good judge of what constitutes the right attitude.

What else are underwriters looking for? Serious cruising experience—a record of increasingly challenging coastal cruises, preferably rounded out with at least some bluewater experience—a round-trip to Bermuda, for example. "The underwriter wants to know that this guy is not going to start hollering Mayday and abandon his yacht if a little weather comes up," says Golden.

One underwriter prefers three years of ownership of the vessel making the crossing or a yacht within 10 feet of its size. The owner of an ocean-capable motor yacht who has no personal offshore experience but who has a bluewater-experienced crew onboard for the crossing will usually get an OK from an insurer.

A U.S. Coast Guard master's license carries some credibility with insurers because it shows commitment. A British "yachtmaster" certificate, however, carries more because it requires demonstration of the practical skills needed to manage a yacht at sea. Hands-on onboard training with offshore-experienced skippers counts for a lot, especially when certified in writing.

In negotiating coverage with one of his company's underwriters, Golden made the point that there are many reasons a skipper may not have a record of offshore cruising, including the fact that the skipper has to work for a living. "Then he retires and wants to go cross an ocean," Golden chuckles. Even a skipper with only coastal cruising experience may get an "up check" from an insurer if he can show that he has done his homework, has prepared his yacht well, and is approaching the ocean-crossing with the all-important right attitude.

Although sometimes mentioned in books and by experienced cruisers, Golden says the companies he deals with rarely require a "voyage survey." When one is requested, it's often because the yacht in question is not a brand known to be built for serious offshore work. Nevertheless, a voyage survey voluntarily obtained by an owner can be an important benchmark in establishing that the owner has the right attitude.

However, living in close quarters at sea sometimes creates friction that spoils the experience for both parties. Although most sailors elect a two-person crew, many power boats have at least three-person crews on ocean voyages. A study reported by Beth Leonard of 55 circumnavigating sailing vessels found that more than half were crewed by couples and over 70% were family crews. Only four of the circumnavigators regularly took on additional crew, and three of these were single-handers.

An important question to ask yourself when selecting outside-the-family crew is are you willing to support them as if he or she were family? You are responsible for anyone entering a foreign country as crew, even if they leave your boat. If they get into legal trouble, commit crimes, get sick, or become derelict, you are responsible. You could have to pay a crew member's airfare for returning home. If you pick up crew in a foreign port, it is possible that you will not be able to remove them from your boat without paying dearly.

To ensure that crew skills are well documented, bring along any certifications of boating competence, such as U.S. Coast Guard Auxiliary course, U.S. Power Squadron course, or Coast Guard license. We found that many countries wanted such proof upon entry and that any one of these certifications seemed OK. (While we are on the topic of paperwork, be sure your vessel documentation paperwork is current and will remain current during the voyage. We found the Coast Guard would issue a documentation certificate early if we requested it. Also make sure any radio licenses are current.)

An important planning consideration is how to handle last-minute crew cancellations. Do you have backup people? Are you willing to go with only a double-handed crew? Are you willing to take the risk of an unknown person at the last minute? We have not experienced such a late cancellation, although we have done a number of passages when we would have preferred an additional crew member or two. Our

# On Crew Selection

### Ken Williams

Adam said, ". . . For safety reasons, we have decided not to leave until we can find a crew person (or potentially a couple) . . . ." Roberta and I were talking at lunch today, and have one more thought for you regarding crew for your upcoming passage. We read through your website, and noted the focus on making sure that the chemistry is right with whoever joins you on the trip. There are PLENTY of Nordhavn owners with stories to tell about the "trip from hell" when they brought someone on board who was not a good fit. But, that said . . . if you get enough of a response to have your pick, I'd try to give significant weighting to finding someone who plugs any skillset-holes that you might have. Ocean crossing is serious business. I don't have any sense of how skilled you are technically, but I'd bias towards bringing someone onboard who brings some skillset to the voyage that you need.

When our GSSR [Great Siberian Sushi Run] group was headed to the Bering Sea, we wanted someone who had been there before, and decided we wanted a commercial fisherman. We didn't worry about chemistry. Our #1 priority is: "safety." Anything that helps achieve that goal is what we want. As it turned out, Bill Harrington was a delight to have onboard, but I don't think we ever agonized about it, one way or the other. Had he been a total jerk, we still would have brought him onboard, because he had skills and knowledge that would help get us to the other end of the Pacific safely. And, we knew that on arrival, whether he was a good guy, or a bad guy, on reaching the other side of the puddle, we'd be continuing our trip without him.

The bottom line is that, if you get the luxury of having multiple applicants, I'd encourage you to do a serious assessment of what skills could be required should things go wrong, and where your weaknesses are. If you find someone who plugs the gaps, grab them. Safety trumps fun every time. Besides, if they are truly annoying, it'll give you some good stories to tell.

personal feeling is that we are perfectly capable of a double-handed passage and have done many of them. However, on long ocean voyages, Mary feels much more comfortable if there are three of us onboard. With only two people, if one becomes incapacitated, it puts a heavy burden on the remaining person.

## How Will You Find Your Way?

Nowadays, almost everyone uses electronic charts. They certainly help with navigation chores and route planning. However, computers and chartplotters do fail; or the data on the chart program may be missing, inaccurate, or incomplete. When we were cruising in the Black Sea, we found one of our vector charts was quite inadequate for ports. Luckily, we had another complete program and dataset that did have better information. We were constantly changing back and forth between programs and chart data. During this same period, our main computer crashed and we had to use the laptop as our only backup.

We always carry paper charts for the places we visit, which we keep displayed on the chart table. It is great to have the "big picture" as you cruise along. We plot our courses and mark our position at various times during the day or night, especially during passages. Paper charts are expensive, but you can get excellent copies in the United States through various chart-printing companies because U.S. government charts are not copyrighted. These charts are black and white and come in various sizes. We use colored pencils to highlight shoals and deep water lines. It also helps to color in the shore lines in brown.

Various pilots and cruising guides are indispensable for entering ports. They usually provide better detail than charts, but also may indicate where marinas are located and services can be found. Some even show stores and marine suppliers on shore. They normally provide VHF frequencies for key authorities and may provide anchor location information.

You will be very dependent on your GPS for all navigation activities. We have four separate units on our boat, so there is always redundancy. It is great if you have two GPS units hooked up to your autopilot. If one GPS fails, you can quickly change to the backup. That said, we have not had a GPS failure during the past 12 years. During our early cruising days we had a unit that would lose signal at the most inopportune times, causing us lots of anxiety and stress. We changed brands and have had no failures since then. We do keep one of our backup units in the oven where it may be less subject to lightning damage.

## What Will You Eat and Drink?

Food is not much of a problem on modern boats with refrigerators and freezers. Some cruisers prepare meals in advance and put them in the freezer for passages. If the cook is subject to motion sickness, this is a great idea. It also frees up a lot of time for watchstanding when you have limited crew on board. We only generally plan our meals for passages. We make sure we have plenty of food, including some luxuries. For example, we celebrated a birthday in mid-Atlantic with a turkey dinner with all the trimmings.

Food does not stay fresh on long voyages, so after a week or so you will be dependent on a freezer for frozen vegetables and other similar items. Bread keeps in the freezer, but it is even better if you have a breadmaker along. We really enjoyed a fresh loaf of bread in the afternoon, although it was always gone by the end of the day. Milk is available on UHT boxes that keep well for several months; fresh milk is seldom available.

One voyaging consideration is backup food should you have a refrigeration or freezer failure. We always have enough staples and canned foods along to survive until we reach port. Luckily, our refrigeration and freezer system has worked great. There are a number of cruiser's cookbooks that specialize in food preparation without refrigeration.

Some items that you take for granted at home may be hard to come by in foreign lands. We are coffee aficionados and had a great deal of trouble finding coffees that we considered up to Starbuck's standards. Some spices are missing from foreign shelves. Limes are almost nonexistent in the Mediterranean, although lemons abound. If you like tiny peas, like we find frozen in the stores here, they are impossible to find in Southern Europe. They generally like their peas and corn mature and hard. On the other hand, throughout the Med they had great peaches all summer long at reasonable prices. Spinach is often available by the kilo—and that's a lot of spinach. Tomatoes and colorful peppers were available everywhere.

## Resource Planning

Fuel is the most important consideration. Before you make an ocean voyage, you need to do several longer passages so you know your fuel consumption. Do not depend on the boatbuilder's consumption figures until you have verified them yourself. Be sure some of the test runs are in open sea with relatively significant waves using your stabilizers. Also

consider your anticipated generator use and fuel consumption (about 1 gallon per hour per 10 kw). You can then estimate the amount of fuel needed for the passage. Add a reserve—I like at least 20%—and you will know how much fuel you need. If you are doing shorter passages, it is prudent to look at fuel availability and prices. For example, in the Caribbean, fuel is much cheaper in Trinidad and Venezuela. If you can bunker here, you can save lots of money. Some countries offer opportunities for duty-free fuel when leaving their shores.

If you are travelling to distant shores, you need to consider lubricating oil. It is sometimes hard to find oil that meets the manufacturer's specifications, especially in smaller, less-developed countries. We were lucky to have a 40-gallon oil tank so we could stock up when we found high-quality oil. If you don't have an oil storage tank, you need to find a place to secure at least a couple of oil changes. Be sure to tie the cans down well. A loose, 5-gallon oil can is dangerous rolling around in the lazarette. You should also carry at least one complete change of hydraulic fluid. Luckily, it is usually pretty easy to buy this lubricant almost everywhere.

Water planning is also needed. If you have large tanks, you may be in good shape for an ocean crossing even without a watermaker. However, some parts of the world, such as the Caribbean Islands, have very limited water. If you do not make your own, you may have to pay a pretty steep price to refill your tanks. A good watermaker is a strong plus for any voyage. Check it out at sea before you depart.

## Prepare Engines and Transmission

In Chapter 17 we cover maintaining your engine during voyages. Here I emphasize a few things to do before your voyage. The first is what is called a WOT (Wide Open Throttle) test. Run your boat for 15 minutes at WOT and check engine temperature, exhaust temperature, raw-water flow, rpm (does the boat attain its full rpm at WOT?), boat speed, and engine room temperature.

Clean your bottom and propeller just before leaving and make sure all your zincs are renewed. It is surprising how much efficiency is lost when the propeller has even a few barnacles. Remove and clean all strainers. Check and free up all seacocks. Memorize their location—try to find them at night with the lights off. Replace all the impellers on your raw water pumps. Get a spare alternator and check it out. I recommend getting a duplicate of your main alternator and switching new for old before embarking. That way, you are certain both alternators work. You definitely don't want to have an alternator failure at sea without a replacement. Modern trawlers need DC power and plenty of it. Carefully check all your hoses and clamps and replace any with the slightest problem.

Change oil and filters in both your engine and transmission. Some transmissions, such as Twin Disc, have a grease nipple at the aft end where the shaft connects—grease it well. You may also have intermediate shaft bearings that need greasing before and during the voyage. Check your shaft-log connection. Make sure the water lubrication system is working. After changing fuel filters, make sure you have plenty of spares. Run every bilge pump and make sure the automatic switches operate.

## Check Rudder, Autopilot, and Stabilizers

While at the dock, have someone move the rudder from side to side while you examine its operation in the stern. Look for any looseness in the system. Are moving parts well lubricated? Many rudders have grease fittings. Check the autopilot rudder position sensor to ensure there is no wear. If it uses cables to connect it to the sensor, you might consider replacing them before a long voyage because metal fatigue can cause failure at an inopportune or dangerous time.

Test your autopilot in rough seas with the boat in different positions relative to the waves—head sea, beam sea, following sea, quartering on the stern, quartering on the bow. Make sure it works well in all these positions. If not, adjust it as needed until it works flawlessly. Hand steering on a dark night with large following seas is no fun!

Check out your stabilizer system under similar conditions as for the autopilot. Make sure the system works at cruising speed. You might also add or subtract a knot of speed to see how the system reacts. Make any adjustments before leaving. If you use paravanes, be sure all your shackles and lines are as good as new. I always install new nylon snubbers before making a long ocean passage.

## Deck and Interior Preparation

For deck preparation, the word is secure, secure, secure. Make sure everything is firmly tied down. Pay particular attention to anchor tie-downs. We use ultra-strong amsteel spectra line to secure the anchors. A loose anchor during a storm can do significant damage, and you don't want to go forward to fix it when in the midst of large waves. Tenders are also threatened by sea and wind. Extra tie-downs and a very secure cover are musts. We move all our fenders to the upper deck and secure them firmly to the mast.

Before departure put on storm covers and ensure that all hatches are fully secured or able to be secured. Deck plates over the anchor locker need to be firmly tied down.

We install lifelines to the bow and along the upper deck for possible use in these locations if we should have to go there. We also carry clip-on harnesses, used by sailors, to prevent being washed overboard.

We use Rain-X on all our windows to shed salt water fast. In fact, we do not even have windshield wipers; we removed them. We find the treatment gives us excellent visibility in almost all situations, and there is no salt buildup on the windows. We do take advantage of calmer periods to clean the windows with fresh water and a squeegee.

Inside the boat, we use towels to prevent shifting of glassware and dishes. We put nonskid plastic on all the tables and galley counters. We use bungee cords to hold down items on the counters. We have no movable furniture to secure; if we did, we would have to figure a way to secure it. Be sure all drawers have catches that hold them firmly in place. In rough seas, drawers have a way of coming open. Any electronics need to be firmly attached. We use tie-down straps or even bolt the items to the shelf.

## Electronics and Communication

A thorough shakedown on all electronic and communication systems is needed. Run all your electronics for at least 24 hours, nonstop, before departure.

You want to identify any problems early. Test the EPIRB to make sure its battery is current and that it lights up properly in the test mode. Make sure the proper person is listed on the EPIRB emergency contact list. Ideally, that person should be kept appraised of your position and situation on a daily basis, usually via e-mail. Our daughter posted our daily position on Google Earth to update our friends on progress on our last Atlantic crossing.

Check out your radios, especially the SSB. Many power boats have trouble with their SSB installation. Find an expert to troubleshoot and fix these problems, which are usually related to the antenna, ground system, or interference from other electrical and electronic systems. You may be able to make successful passages using only a satellite communication system and an Internet hookup. An ideal situation would be both, which gives you lots of flexibility and redundancy.

## Develop Emergency Plans

Make sure all your emergency equipment is serviceable, available, and useful. Inspect life preservers, making sure they each have a light and whistle attached. Make sure each crew has his or her own prefitted preserver kept in their bunk for immediate use, if needed. If you have survival suits, try them on. Make sure you have plastic bags to go over feet for easy entry into the suits. Check your life raft to make sure its inspection is up to date and that it is properly secured.

Develop plans for emergencies (see Chapter 19) such as fire, flooding, crew overboard, or abandon ship. Make up an abandon-ship bag. We use a waterproof bag, such as those used by kayakers and canoers. We place items like a handheld GPS, a small watermaker, fishing gear, stocking caps, flashlights and batteries, extra flares, and a laser signal device. Additional items, such as handheld VHF, extra food, water, passports, money, ships log, and other valuables, are listed on the outside of the bag so they can be filled at the last minute.

Preparation and planning may seem like big tasks, and they are, but that is part of the adventure. I have always enjoyed the planning—reading and dreaming of faraway places to cruise to. This is why we buy these oceangoing boats. Preparation can be tedious, but your objective is a pleasant and uneventful voyage during which you are safe and have no problems. Thoughtful and thorough preparation doesn't guarantee this result, but it helps.

## CHAPTER FIFTEEN

# Crossing Oceans

*At long last the weeks and months of planning have come to an end. Everything is done that has to be done to make the ship "fully found and ready for sea." It is time to go, time to leave the shores for the vast reaches of the open ocean. It is also time to think about the duties and responsibilities that lie ahead, the routines to be followed, the preparations for any emergency.*

*Abandoning the land to sail thousands of miles on the open sea has always been a significant occasion. No matter how many times I have done it myself, it has never lost its sense of mystery, of anticipation; there's even a little dread.*

—Robert Beebe, 1976

The opening quote from Captain Beebe certainly mirrors my feelings at the beginning of an ocean-crossing voyage. The mystery, anticipation, and anxiety are very real. I end this chapter with a section on the anxieties experienced by us just before the departure on our first ocean voyage. Once at sea, the anxieties are greatly reduced, and feelings of comfort and routine seem to dominate. There is always something to do and see. There are fish to be caught, machinery to check, weather to monitor, e-mails to be sent, shortwave nets to contact, sunsets to be photographed, naps to be taken, and books to be read. The steady rumble of the engine is comforting. The motion of the boat in seaway becomes less noticeable as the body adjusts to the give and take with the waves.

In this section, we build on the previous ones about planning and preparation—we will now be doing it! We discuss the effects of route choice on passage comfort, finding buddy boats, training crews, watchstanding, running at night, en-route machinery checks, fuel management, arrival issues, emergencies at sea, and finally warding off seasickness. Even though I highlight some potential problems, all of our passages have been relatively free of drama—we have arrived safely, comfortably, and on time.

## Choose a Comfortable Route and Season

The old sailing axiom, "fair winds and following seas," can also apply to powerboats, although many of us are content to motor through calms with little or no wind—that is certainly one of the major advantages of power boating. Avoid routes with lots of headwinds and head seas. Winds from ahead not only slow you down but also create much more pitching, which is one of the more uncomfortable boat motions. Christi and Eric Grab, on *Kosmos*, assert in their text box that the "wind is not your friend" as it is with sailboats. While no voyager wants to be thrashed around by big and confused seas driven by the wind, we find that a 15–20 knot wind on our stern is very comfortable and does not create motion uneasiness for us or our crew. Because we do not use air conditioning, the wind keeps the boat cool and comfortable as well. The difference in comfort aboard *Teka III* versus *Kosmos* may be partially due to our longer waterline length; 10 feet really makes a difference in pitching motions. Anyhow, we find it useful to generally follow the sailing routes that normally have winds behind you and favorable currents. One of the best sources for route planning is Jimmy Cornell's *World Cruising Routes*,

# Comfort

## Hugo Carver II

After some time pondering what it is that I enjoy, or more correctly, derive from cruising, I have decided that the correct feeling is "comfort." My suspicion is that many (perhaps most) people experience some degree of apprehension, nervousness, or downright fear while aboard a boat no matter how large or small.

While bringing a 57-foot yacht back from the Hawaiian Islands as captain of this small vessel, I got a feeling that I subsequently have thought of from time to time—comfort. Being a couple thousand miles from land in any direction you would think might cause some concern; but I noticed an overriding feeling of comfort. I don't know all of the reasons why, but being on a good boat, having a good crew, and being confident in your abilities must be important factors.

Between Hawaii and the mainland is a large calm spot called the Pacific High. The wind in the North Pacific circles around this high and like the eye of a hurricane there is no wind in the center. We crossed this calm area under power with our wake being the only disturbance leading off to the horizon. I noticed that in spite of being far from civilization we felt comfortable. We thought that a swim call would be welcomed so we shut the engine off and our speed slowly bled off as we coasted to a stop. No wake, not even those little ripples in the bathtub or in a wine glass. There was no threat of any change in wind or waves, no sign of waterborne problem with sharks or jellyfish, and no concern with dissension within the crew.

We stripped down and dove into the water. It was that perfect temperature: a bit refreshing yet not at all chilling. We could have stayed in for hours floating and gliding in this pure expanse of salt water, which must be as pure and comfortable as embryonic fluid. Some of us swam a long distance away from the yacht so the small craft looked really small in this huge salt millpond. It seemed that swimming took no effort and that one could soar through the water without bothering to surface for a breath of air. It felt as though I could dive a long way down, close my eyes and enjoy a peaceful nap; however, eventually my automatic mechanisms kicked in to catch some air. It was as it must be to be a marine mammal, and a reminder we are not that remote from them in our development. The water is very deep in the mid-Pacific at 2 miles or more. Searching with eyes wide open yielded nothing but deep blue sea of the most beautiful hue. After a long time we reluctantly returned to our yacht, the only dot of humanity and sign of civilization in this vast expanse. After a welcome meal and a toast to the perfect place, we started the engine and continued our voyage for another eight days. For me, returning to the mainland was a letdown after some time in this perfect place.

Each time I cruise I look forward to the feeling of comfort that a voyage on a small craft provides me. For others it may be the middle of a desert or isolation of a mountain that might bring some of that special feeling as my "middle of the ocean" brings to me. But the ocean is so much larger and deeper, plus the environment is the same salinity as our body fluids so we have an affinity for the ocean. I can understand a bit why some feel apprehension where I felt comfort. Some feel apprehension with most places and activities so I feel sympathy for them because that comfortable "returning to the womb" feeling may be important for our well being.

If you have concerns and apprehensions, my advice is to occasionally travel in a capable small craft to a place as far as possible from civilization and just float .... Just disconnect from all earthly material and social commitments for awhile. I think a long time is good. Most of us would be surprised at how rarely we really get far away from the rush, the hubbub, and general sensory overload of today's world.

Figure 15–1. Mid-Atlantic calm at sunset.

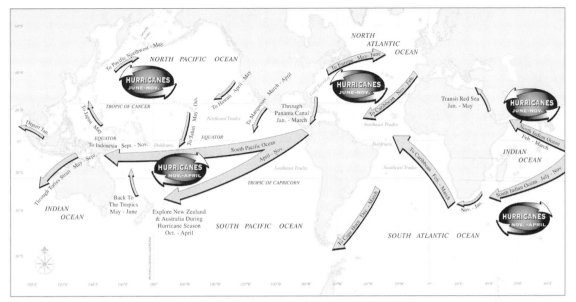

**Figure 15–2.** *The Voyager's Handbook* provides this excellent summary of world cruising routes that are discussed in detail in *World Cruising Routes*. (Beth A. Leonard and Paul Mirto)

now in its sixth edition. Beth Leonard's *The Voyager's Handbook*, Second Edition, also has many useful insights into voyage planning.

## Finding Buddy Boats

While it is not always possible, it is great to travel with others, at least loosely, on long ocean voyages. On some occasions, you may find an organized voyaging group, often called a rally, such as the Atlantic crossing rally sponsored by Nordhavn or the Black Sea Rally sponsored by the Atakoy Yacht Club in Istanbul. These rallies can be fun and increase safety by going in the company of others who might be able to help in the event of an emergency. On the other hand, rallies usually have schedules, meaning the voyage will go on even if the weather is not great. The Nordhavn rally encountered some really nasty weather while heading toward Gibraltar from the Azores. If you had been travelling alone or in a small group, you might have diverted to Lisbon and waited for a calmer time to head to Gibraltar. One of our most unpleasant passages was in the Black Sea heading from Romania to Bulgaria during a night passage in a gale. If we had been on our own, we would have

waited at the mouth of the Danube for the gale to pass. (See Chapter 20 for more on rallies.)

We find that belonging to cruising networks usually provides insights into who is going where and when. In many major ports or wintering places, VHF networks calls are a daily event. In many parts of the world, there are regional daily SSB nets, where people check in and share information. Many ocean crossings happen around the same time due to seasonal storms and cruising at the destination. For example, when we left the Canaries for Antigua, there were about 50 boats all headed in the same direction. There was an SSB net twice a day to share weather, fishing results, shark sightings, equipment problems, and other items of note. Only two other boats were power voyagers. We kept in close touch with *Suprr*, a Nordhavn 46 we had befriended in the Balearic Islands. Partway across the Atlantic one of its paravanes hit the prop. They were about two or three days ahead of us, but we thought we might have to go to their aid. It would have been a long tow, but they were able to continue with their main engine at low rpms in spite of the vibration from the bent propeller. The important thing here is that we would have gone to their location and either

# Kosmos' Circumnavigation: Crossing Three Oceans

### Christi Grab

When we were preparing for our circumnavigation, time and again we read that in the cruising life the highs are higher and the lows are lower than in land life. We didn't quite "get it" then; now we fully understand what that means.

Our first passage [from San Diego to the Marquesas], which took twenty-one days, was hard on us. The seas were rough for every single day of that trip: 6- to 10-feet swells at ten-second intervals topped by wind waves of 4 to 6 feet, all coming from the port aft corner, making for a horrible corkscrew motion. We both had mild seasickness problems and were perpetually physically uncomfortable. I was dismayed to find out that I suffer from lethargy at sea, and I would get so lethargic that I wouldn't even eat. Along with the lethargy came depression. By the end of the passage, I was so depressed that I was crying daily, pulling my hair out in handfuls, and had suicidal thoughts. I never had suicidal thoughts before in my whole life. Eric also struggled with lethargy, though not as severely as me. He constantly worried that something would go wrong, making him stressed out and unhappy. Now we understand why the conventional wisdom is to build up to long passages. It was truly trial by fire.

After that passage, we believed we could take anything and that sea time would be easier from there on out. Wrong! The first passage was definitely the hardest—but only because it was the longest. As we continued across the Pacific, the waves continued to get bigger and bigger. By the end, 10- to 12-feet swells from the port beam were the norm, regularly rolling *Kosmos* over 30 degrees. Traveling became physically more challenging. We both struggled with seasickness, Eric more so than me. We both struggled with lethargy (which we just found out is a form of seasickness), me more so than him. I would get lonely, homesick, and depressed. Eric would get stressed out about the myriad of "what-if's" that could potentially go wrong. When the seas were rough, we'd often take our misery out on one another

and have big fights. It took us six months to cross the Pacific from end to end, with fifty-eight days at sea and one hundred and eighteen on land. Those fifty-eight days were some of the hardest of our lives.

What kept us going was the fact that we absolutely loved the land destinations. We stopped in 18 places between San Diego, California, and Cairns, Australia. Two of the islands were physically impossible to get to without a private boat, and they were almost magical. Most of the rest were incredibly difficult to get to without a private boat, and they were unspoiled paradises. Obviously, the islands that didn't see many tourists had limited (if any) hotel accommodations. The few places that were easy to get to and had plenty of hotels, such as Tahiti, simply didn't wow us. We knew that in the South Pacific, boat was by far the best way to travel and we were willing to put up with any kind of sea conditions to get to those exotic paradises.

Once we made it to Australia, we had to make a choice: continue traveling by boat or switch to more conventional

modes of transportation. From Australia on, we could easily travel via planes or trains, and hotels were readily available. We simply didn't need a boat anymore. But after weighing the pros and cons, we decided to press on with the boat.

Over the next month, we worked our way up the Great Barrier Reef. The super-protected waters were so flat and calm; it was like a paradise for us. Our next major passage was from Australia to Indonesia, eight days across the Arafura Sea. The wind was dead and the seas were flat as a pancake—it was like being on dry land! We felt like we were somehow "cheating" by not having to "rough it." With the water so calm, we were making exceptional speeds. While we were in heaven, our sailor friends were in hell. With no wind, they were stuck, moving just a handful of miles per day.

Right after our best passage of all time came our worst—the Java Sea. Sadly, we had missed our weather window and the monsoon winds had changed for the season. The passage from Bali, Indonesia, to Singapore should have only taken eight days but actually took twelve,

**Figure 15–3.** *Kosmos* in the magical South Pacific. (Christi Grab)

thanks to unfavorable sea conditions (10- to 15-foot head seas at rapid intervals with particularly sharp waves) forcing us to go painfully slow. Our poor boat was beat up, but sustained no major damage, which was amazing considering just how bad the conditions were.

We broke the Indian Ocean up into three legs. Legs one and two were fabulous, with conditions much the same as the Arafura Sea. Leg three was fairly rough with 3- to 4-foot sharp swells at rapid intervals that were always either on our nose or confused. But compared to the South Pacific, it was a piece of cake. Because of the adverse sailing conditions, our engine hours across the Indian were roughly the same as most of the sailors'.

Next was the Red Sea, which was another miserable passage. Conditions were constantly changing. In our ten days at sea, we experienced virtually every kind of condition imaginable—head seas, beam seas, following seas, confused seas. The wind seemed to change direction every couple hours and would vary wildly in both direction and velocity, sometimes going from 20 knots to zero and back again in a matter of hours. For most of the time, conditions were unsuitable for sailing, forcing the sailors to stop in some less than ideal ports to fuel up. We were thankful that we had a large-capacity tank that could make it all the way from Oman to Egypt without ever having to stop.

We transited the Suez Canal into the Mediterranean, where we did short hops to the Canary Islands off the coast of Africa. Our Atlantic crossing took twenty days. We never had extreme conditions on either end of the spectrum; most days were mildly rough at 3 to 10 feet from the aft. Had it been our first long passage, we would have probably complained that it was difficult, but after having experienced far more uncomfortable conditions, we didn't think it was too bad. Perspective is everything! The rest of our time in the Caribbean was much the same, mildly rough.

We transited the Panama Canal and started on the dreaded journey up the West Coast of North America. We were braced for hellacious conditions: ugly head seas the entire way; but somehow, we lucked out. [The year] 2009 happened to have an unusual weather pattern and conditions were exceptionally mild (though still not fun), usually with head seas of about a foot coming at rapid intervals. We hadn't realized how much of a tolerance to the seas we had developed until a crew member joined us for a leg. The two of us thought the passage conditions were pretty darn good, but our poor crew member was sick as a dog the whole time!

performed a tow or cruised along with them while they ran with their wing engine. Remember, there is no one to rescue your boat when you are a thousand miles offshore. It is comforting to have help nearby.

## Crew Decisions

Crew choice was discussed briefly in Chapter 14. Once you have made the decision about whether to have a couple or family crew, hire crew members, or ask friends for their assistance, you will need to develop a training and orientation program. If the new crew member is experienced, you may be able to provide a detailed tour highlighting all the important mechanical, electronic, and emergency equipment on board. If you have found someone inexperienced to accompany you, then training will be in order. The Nordhavn 46, *Jenny*, developed a 38-page manual for crew that is more like an owner's manual with great detail about all aspects of the boat. Even with experienced people, I have found detailed instructions on Post-Its are useful for providing instantaneous feedback on operation of unusual or complicated equipment such as the autopilot or the DSR emergency radio broadcasts on VHF and SSB.

Because most crew members will be expected to do engine room checks on their watches, careful training, including actually observing and critiquing the member, is important. There are all too frequent stories of crew-members that have inadvertently turned some valve, resulting in the fuel being cut off or other adverse outcomes.

When taking non-family crew, make sure the passport is current for at least six months from the time the person is expected to leave the boat. If a visa is required, make sure it is entered in the passport. Make financial agreements with the crew about who is going to pay for airfare home, visas, food, entertainment, and other incidental costs. Make clear when and how the crew is expected to depart. When someone leaves your boat, you need to clear the departure with immigration on your passage document (zarpe), which includes the crew list. Otherwise, when you get ready to leave, you may not be allowed to exit without proving your crew's departure.

### Watchstanding

Standing watch on a motor vessel is easier than on a sailing vessel, where attention to weather, winds, and sail trimming is critical. A sudden squall with too much sail can cause a knockdown if it is strong enough. Many sailing vessels reef down their sails

# Nordhavn 46, *Jenny*, Crew Manual

## Table of Contents

at night to prevent such surprises. When cruising under power, this problem is not as acute because the boat will be less sensitive to extreme changes in wind—a 60-knot gust on the beam will cause the boat to heel, but it is unlikely to significantly affect the motor boat's stability. Night watches on ocean passages can be very pleasant but also very trying because you are defying your body's signals to sleep. The pilothouse is a wonderful control center with dimly glowing red lights and gauges, and the constant picture of the radar as it rotates, searching for anything that might be out there.

With a dual-handed crew, a pilot berth is a nice luxury. The off-duty person can be close by to lend assistance if needed. We don't have such a berth on our boat, but if conditions warrant, I may sleep in the pilothouse on our bench seat. If we have additional crew, I almost always sleep in my cabin because pilothouse sleeping means constant awakening as calls come in on the VHF or cabinets are closed, or when another crew member decides to join for a while.

## Watch Schedules

Developing scheduled watches at night seems to be an almost universal practice when the crew is three or more. However, double-handed crews often use more informal systems, even though they always keep someone on duty.

Most cruisers seem to settle on three-hour watches at night. The night is often divided as follows: 9 p.m. to midnight, midnight until 3 a.m., 3 a.m. to 6 a.m., and 6 a.m. to 9 a.m. Some continue watches throughout the day and early evening, sometimes on 4-hour shifts instead of 3. However, others use

Figure 15–4. Mary on watch in the Atlantic off Portugal. We had lots of ship traffic in the shipping lanes here. We found that ships may prefer talking to a woman—Mary always got more responses to VHF calls than the male crew did.

# Training Watchstanders
## James F. Leishman

Introducing a friend to passagemaking ranks as one of the greatest pleasures of voyaging. It's an opportunity to introduce them to an activity they can enjoy throughout their lives, and it can add considerable satisfaction to your own cruise. Of course, there are specific qualifications that any person standing watch alone must meet, including the ability to stop the ship, to disengage the autopilot, and to use its dodger. VHF radio operation, recognition of ship lights and the ability to determine the direction they are travelling at night, and the [use of the radar's computer or] hand-bearing compass for collision avoidance are also important. The watchstander must be familiar with the engine instruments and must be able to enter hourly positions into the logbook. Additionally, each new crewmember should be shown the location of each fire extinguisher and how it

is used, know the location of life jackets, and understand the procedure for abandoning ship—including the release of the life raft and the activation of EPIRBs aboard.

These are all simple tasks that can be taught to a receptive student within a few hours. School can start at the beginning of a voyage, but ideally these basics should be taught prior to departure because there's no guarantee that weather and sea conditions will be conducive to teaching. If the new crewmember knows what's expected of him before the voyage and if the skipper can recommend reference material, the basics can be learned ashore. With a couple of orientation sessions aboard the vessel prior to departure, a responsible yet inexperienced person will be fine crew.

The captain must remember that he is *always* responsible for the safety of

the ship, and he will need to treat crew of varying capabilities differently. A new crewmember should thoroughly understand that he *must* request assistance in even the most basic situations. If the captain is the only one aboard with experience, then he should be called. With more experience aboard, another crewmember may be on call as the first to be summoned when specific routine situations arise—ship sightings, rain squalls, changing conditions, etc. If the watchstander feels uncomfortable with *anything*—if he hears an unusual sound, smells something odd, notes a change in any engine instrument—he *must* report immediately to a designated person. It's far better to err on the side of caution in these situations as the ship will be more safely operated, and other crew can rest without concern.

informal watches during the day, with watches being assumed by whoever is available and willing.

The "dogwatch" from midnight to 3 in the morning is most difficult for the majority of people unless the person has traditionally worked the night shift. As captain, I usually assign myself to this watch because it is the most challenging watch of all and breaks up your night's sleep into two segments.

We never use rotating watches because it seems to be relatively easy to adjust to a new sleeping schedule after two or three days. If a watch time is changed, you have to adjust all over again to the new schedule. It is always good to take advantage of the crew's natural sleep patterns. For instance, we had one crew member, Bob Hermann, who was a "night owl." The 9 p.m. to midnight shift was easy for him because he was usually up during that time period anyhow. On the other hand, Mary is always ready to sleep between 9 and 10, and would find the first night watch more difficult. However, she feels pretty chipper when aroused at 3 in the morning and likes to watch the sun rise. When we have four people for watchstanding, Mary does not take a night watch, although she often checks on the watchstander when she awakens during the night. She can easily do the 6 to 9 watch in the morning as well.

Double-handed watchstanding is another matter. Beth Leonard (author of *The Voyager's Handbook*; see the suggested reading list in Appendix E) did a study of thirteen couples who had completed shorthanded offshore voyages on sailing vessels. Eight were experienced couples that had sailed at least 5,000 nautical miles, and the other five had completed one or two offshore passages of five days or more. She found that all cruisers were likely to have a night watch schedule in place, but it was more flexible for experienced cruisers. As cruisers gain experience, they adjust the watch to fit individual sleep patterns. They also tended to evolve toward longer watches, sometimes 6 hours or more. Informal daytime watches were the norm for both groups.

On *Teka III*, Mary and I keep flexible watches as well. Normally, I will begin my watch around 9 p.m. and stay up as long as I feel comfortably awake, usually around 2 a.m. I listen to books on tape or CD, I listen to satellite radio programs—anything to keep me awake and alert. When I finally feel like sleep might be catching up, I wake Mary and she takes over until she feels too sleepy; then we exchange again. In the daytime, watches are informally shared depending on who was napping and what is happening at the time. After the first day and night, we find this arrangement works well and is easy to execute.

Peter Pisciotta, a delivery captain who moves boats up and down the Pacific Coast with one crew person, normally uses a formal schedule of 3 hours on and 3 off at night, and 4 on and off during the day. He notes that 4-hour night shifts are preferred, but most crewmembers find this amount of time on duty too difficult.

## Watchkeeping Lessons Learned

- Avoid stimulants like coffee or NoDoz to help keep you awake. It may prevent you from going to sleep when off watch.
- Use your usual bedtime routines before retiring, such as brushing your teeth or taking a hot shower. Change out of your watch clothes and into your bed clothes. The routine helps your body know it is time to sleep.
- Keep busy on watch. Move around. Don't lie down. Listen to books or radio. Do frequent gauge and radar checks.
- Make it easy for the on-watch person to connect with the captain. When double-handed crewing, I always sleep within easy walking distance, but preferably not in the pilothouse.
- Get a sugar injection upon waking for a wee-hours watch. A little fruit juice or tea with honey may suffice to get you through the middle-of-the-night slow energy period.
- If you cannot sleep, go to the pilothouse and offer to take over the watch. If you are at the end of your watch, but still wide awake, let the other person sleep. This recommendation applies primarily to double-handed crewing.
- In the event of adverse conditions, it may be necessary to shorten watches or for two people to be on watch.
- Sleep whenever you can in short-handed situations.

## Duties of the Watchstander

The primary purpose of the watchstander is to make sure the boat and its crew remain safe. This means avoiding collisions at sea with ship, other boats, nets, rocks, and anything else that might endanger the vessel. When voyaging under power, we have the advantage of being able to run the radar 24/7 so we can almost always see major objects, like ships, well off in the distance. When you get a radar return, it is time to evaluate the course of the ship and determine its closest point of approach. In the daytime this is easier than at night. You can simply look at the approaching vessel's location in relation to a fixed point on your boat, such as a stanchion or the bow. If the approaching vessel is constantly changing position, you should not be in danger of collision. However, if it remains in the same relative position, it is time to change course or slow down. Never speed up and try to go in front of a ship to avoid a collision, for it puts you right on the bow of the approaching vessel—a very dangerous place indeed.

There are two major aids for the watch person: radar with ARPA (Automatic Radar Plotting Aid) and AIS (Automatic Identification System). Between these two systems, it is relatively easy to track oncoming ships to see if there will be a problem. Radar, with ARPA, is my first choice. You simply select the target you want to track on the radar and click the cursor. The computer uses your course, speed, and the oncoming ship's course and speed to determine how close it will come to you. If it misses by a mile or more, we continue watching and tracking it to make sure there are no course changes or calculation changes. If it is less than a mile, we take some type of evasive action, even if we theoretically have the right of way. The second aid is AIS, which broadcasts a ship's position, course, speed, name, and cargo over an automated VHF transmitter. If you have fitted an AIS receiver on your boat, you will be able to see the information on your computer. Most programs also calculate the closest point of approach as well, so it is a good cross-check with the radar. Obviously, all watch people need to know how to operate these two systems.

It is also critical for the watchstander to be able to identify ships by their lights. We use an aid on the pilot station that shows all common ship lights. This helps prevent confusion and helps make more accurate identifications. Be sure to highlight the urgency of seeing both a green and red light with a white one in between signaling an imminent collision. (See Chapter 19 for more on collision avoidance.) In addition, it is good to emphasize identifying tugs with barges. There have been many serious accidents where a boat went behind a tug, but ran into the towline and sank.

Recording information in the passage log is also an important duty. There is no official book you can buy for this purpose. Some use a regular logbook. We designed our own that fits our instruments and situation. Before leaving shore, we reproduced the form and had it spirally bound in books of about 100 pages each (see Figure 15–5). We fill it out every two hours. Some voyagers do it every hour. The log contains your position, data from engine and electrical instrument readings, boat speed according to the GPS, nautical miles travelled, barometer, sea conditions, wind direction and speed, sightings of ships or boats, and any other events that seem worthy of note. The log allows the next person on watch to see what has been happening and how conditions are changing. We also use the miles travelled divided by the time to compute our actual speed for the 2-hour time period. The captain can also view the log at any time and look for any anomalies that may affect the boat.

## Running at Night

Inexperienced owners and crews who have not run the boat at night may find the experience disconcerting. It is analogous to flying an airplane in a cloud except that everything is black. When the full moon is shining, running at night is pure magic, with the water shimmering in the moonlight. On a clear, moonless night the stars light up the sky enough to make out the horizon and make for a delightful watch. When it is cloudy and stormy with heavy seas and strong wind the night is intimidating. The boat motion, combined with the lack of a horizon or reference point makes one feel uneasy. All you can see is the white crests of the nearby waves as they arrive and pass you by, illuminated by your running lights. This is the time you hope your

**TEKA III:**
**Bi-hourly Trip LOG**
Date: 12-12
Route: @ 1015

| | 1000 @1015 | 1200 | 1400 | 1600 | 1800 | 2000 | 2200 | 2400 |
|---|---|---|---|---|---|---|---|---|
| | T | I | M | E | | | | |
| Distance to waypoint | 1450 | 1438 | 1417 | 1402 | 1588 | 1374 | 1360 | 1346 |
| Position: | 19 47.6 | 19.47.3 | 19.46.3 | 1945.6 | 19 44.9 | 19.44.2 | 1943.5 | 19 42.7 |
| | 36 28.9 | 36.41.3 | 37.03.3 | 37 19.9 | 37 34.2 | 37.49 | 38 03.5 | 38 13.6 |
| Course: | 283 | 283 | 283 | 283 | 283 | 283 | 283 | 283 |
| Barometer: | 1016 | 1016 | 1014 | 1017 | 1014 | 1015 | 1017 | 105 |
| Sea state: | NW 3/5m | same | NW 3m | NW 3m | NNW 2m | Same | NW 2 m | NW 2. |
| Wind speed/direction | NN 15 | | NN 10 | NW 10 | NW 12 | N 10 | N 10 | N 8/10 |
| GPS speed | 6.7 | 7.0 | 7.5 | 7.0 | 6.9 | 7.2 | 7.0 | 7.1 |
| Knotlog: | 7.0 | 6.7 | 6.8 | 7.0 | 6.9 | 6.9 | 6.9 | 6.9 |
| Actual average speed | | | 7.0 | 7.5 | 7.0 | 7.0 | 7.0 | 7.0 |
| RPM: | 1150 | 1150 | 1150 | 1150 | 1150 | 1150 | 1150 | 1150 |
| Oil pressure: | 40 | 40 | 40 | 40 | 40 | 40 | 40 | 40 |
| Coolant (engine) temp: | 155 | 155 | 155 | 155 | 155 | 155 | 155 | 150 |
| Exhaust temp: | 625 | 625 | 660 | 650 | 625 | 600 | 625 | 625 |
| Oil temp: | 145 | 140 | 140 | 140 | 140 | 140 | 140 | 145 |
| ~~Gear~~ (transmission) temp: | 150 | 145 | 150 | 150 | 150 | 150 | 150 | 150 |
| Fuel filter gage | 0 | 0 | 0 | 0 | 0 | 0 | 0 | 0 |
| Gear Pressure | 200 | 200 | 200 | 200 | 200 | 200 | 200 | 200 |
| Engine room temp | 109.6 | 109.6 | 112.3 | 110.1 | 110.3 | 109.2 | 104.4 | 105.3 |
| @ outside temp | 88.0 | 93.0 | 80 | 80 | 75.6 | 73.6 | 72.5 | 72.0 |
| Voltage--12V | 13.70 | 13.7 | 1365 | 13.70 | 13.70 | 13.7 | 13.70 | 13.76 |
| Bilge pump cycles: | 0 | 0 | 0 | 0 | 0 | 0 | 0 | 0 |
| hyd oil tank | 105 | 105 | 105 | 1.5 | 105 | 105 | 105 | 105 |
| Engine room inspect: | OK | | | | OK | small air leak injector | ok | OK |
| Paravane inspect: | OK | | ok | ok | ok | OK | ok | ok |

Trans

12 DEC
Sightings:
1200 UTC  (1100 Local)

19 47.6 N
36 33.8 W

Changed clocks GMT−2

Sunsets 0555 ½ way

B-day cake too!

@ 1900 local
2100 UTC
||
Turkey, Dressing, Gravey & Pot + Cranbenn —Yum

Figure 15–5. *Teka III*'s bi-hourly informal trip log is kept in a spiral binder. The log allows the captain and each crew member to observe the events as the day develops: weather, engine performance, fishing, sightings, sea conditions, etc. Each day I enter a summary of important information, fuel consumption, distance made, and distance to go, which I then transfer into the formal ship's log, our legal document.

autopilot is working, for steering in rough seas in the dark with only the compass for reference is difficult.

A major problem encountered at night on power voyaging boats is pilothouse light. All the wonderful electronic gadgets give off light that tends to partially blind night vision. On *Teka III* we found even the masthead steaming light reflected off our extensive light foredeck interfered with night vision. Boats with multiple screens right in front of the pilot chair may have the most problem unless the screens allow dimming until they are just visible. Most normal computer screens are a particular problem due to their icon panels at the bottom or top of the screen. Even though the chart program may dim OK, the bright spots on the screen are a particular problem. When considering the purchase of any pilothouse item, make sure it can be dimmed to very faint levels. It is possible to improvise covers for overly bright displays with red plastic sheets and a bit of tape.

Fishing fleets are a particularly difficult problem when you encounter them at night. It is often impossible to determine where the nets are laid. Often, they will be speaking a different language or not monitoring the radio at all. We have travelled at night between Sicily and Sardinia among a large fleet of fishing boats that peppered the radar in all directions like it had the measles. To make matters worse, there were numerous strobe lights showing net positions; however, we had no idea if the net began or ended at a given strobe. Calling the boats in our poor Italian resulted in silence. We decided to slow down to about 4 knots and creep through the fleet, hoping we did not encounter a floating net. It worked, and we wiped the sweat off our brows. It was a very difficult evening.

Around daybreak, off Cape Arena in Northern California, we picked up a long line with our paravane. We were able to release it without entangling the propeller, but it was a challenge. We also picked up a crab trap off Oregon, but were able to release it without much difficulty by stopping and backing up.

If you have the luxury of two radars, like we have on *Teka III*, you can run both at night, one on long range, say 12 miles, looking for ships so you have plenty of time to take evasive action if needed. The other radar we keep on 1 to 2 miles looking for small blips of fishing boats, sailing vessels, or other things that may not show

up at the longer range. It is not uncommon for a motor yacht to collide with an unlit wooden fishing vessel that is anchored for the night well offshore. You may be able to pick up these boats on radar at short range.

The most difficult situation is running at night in the rain with big seas. In this case, you may not be able to see other boats with radar. Ships may be visible, but rain and sea clutter filters prevent having the most accurate view. This is the time to have an extra pair of eyes on watch, preferably on the Portuguese bridge or flying bridge, if you have one, or in another safe position outside the pilothouse.

When travelling with other boats in relatively close formation, careful attention to visual contact and the radar are needed. A few years ago on the Eastern Mediterranean Rally, a large steel powerboat ran into the stern of a slower sailboat, causing considerable damage. When radar range gets too close, it is difficult to pick out another boat's position and speed.

## Machinery Monitoring at Sea

Our total dependence on engines means we have to pay special attention to anything that affects the engine's operation. The most important thing is monitoring the gauges for any change in engine or transmission temperature, rpms, exhaust temperature, oil, or transmission temperature. Some gauges allow ranges of normal operation to be set, with alarms if the range is exceeded. This is useful, but even slight changes may become apparent and should be checked out by visually inspecting the engine room periodically (usually hourly or every two hours). This must be done immediately if a gauge indicates a potential problem. We also monitor and record engine room temperatures to make sure it stays within acceptable levels of cooling. At night we keep a red light on in the engine room and use a flashlight for most engine checks; otherwise, you lose your night vision in the bright light of the engine room.

The engine room check must be tailored to your particular situation; however, most engine rooms have common things to check. Here is a list of items I feel are important:

1. When entering, look around for any visible exhaust gas or any steam or water that would indicate a leak.

## *Egret* Night Encounter: Freemantle to Mauritius

**From the log of Scott and Mary Flanders**

Last night was memorable. The most important item to keep an eye on when running at night is the radar. We have a saying, radar never lies. Last night it wasn't up to its usual tell-tale performance. However, we had high seas (not rough; just high); *Egret* was surrounded by rain squalls showing up everywhere on 12 nm radar. I was preparing OMNI Bob's [weather] report for 1200Z when I looked up and saw CLOSE what appeared to be a city after being at sea for more than a week. There was a ship moving very slowly down sea off to starboard on a course that paralleled *Egret*'s and would pass well less than a mile away. I dropped Bob's report and started fine-turning the radar trying to figure out its course. The front and rear white lights were visible and it had very bright deck lights but no visible running lights. In the heavy swell there were only moments when both boats were on top of waves at the same time. In the meantime I could barely get a return on radar even after dropping down to 6 nm and to 3 nm. This was very strange for such a large target. I called Mary and Dick up to keep watch as well. I changed course drastically to port. THEN it turned toward Egret. So we ran the engine up to 2,000 rpm and kept turning inside its turn radius. At this point we were probably less than 3/4 nm away. Mary said she thought she saw TWO ships close together. Then she said they appeared to be Asian fishing boats like we have seen in the past. These boats are about 100' long, wood, and have stern storage projections out over the usual flat transom. After the boat turned to port (south) it/they maintained its course and came no closer. Obviously I called on the radio and there was no [radio response or] AIS. That was the end of it, but all our legs were literally shaking for a while after.

It appears they were two Asian fishing boats waiting for *Egret* to pass before resuming or starting fishing. I assume there wasn't an English speaker aboard like on all commercial ships these days, because if there was they would have communicated. At least I would hope so. And now it is something after 0400 on Thursday since relieving Dick. After Dick went below I turned up the radar from 12 nm to 24 nm and turned up the gain to full (because it is calm and there is no "snow" on the screen. Oh no, not again, there was a single target just outside 12 nm radar range. I put the EBL (electronic bearing line) on the target and started to watch. It appeared at first to be holding position but in the end it went away. It was probably a small pocket of rain.

Smell can also be a guide. If you smell something unusual or hot, track it down. If you smell diesel fuel, track down the leak. Listen to the engine. Are there any unusual noises? If so, use a mechanic's stethoscope to identify the source of the noise. Check the exhaust hose for wet-exhaust systems and make sure it is not too hot. Check the entry and exit raw water temperatures.

2. Look under the engine for any fluids that may be leaking. Check the bilge for water or oil.

3. Use a flashlight to backlight the bowl of your primary fuel filter to see if there is any sediment or water. If so, drain off the contamination. Check the vacuum pressure gauge on the filter to make sure it is not becoming clogged.

4. Examine your alternator belts. Are they running free and true, and not flapping as they go around? Do you see a lot of carbon building up on the outside of the alternator, indicating a misaligned belt?

5. If you have backup gauges mounted directly on your engine, check them. Are they normal and do they agree with your instrument panel?

6. Feel the shaft packing area to make sure it is no more than warm to the touch. It should not be hot.

7. Examine all hydraulic fittings for leaks and overheating.

8. You may find that a laser remote temperature sensor is very handy during your engine room checks, especially if you have established normal operating temperatures on key components. One hint here is to mark each location for temperature with a bright dot of paint or fingernail polish so you take the temperature at the same place each time.

9. If you are running your generator, inspect it for unusual temperatures or sounds. Be especially attentive to the raw water output temperature and the exhaust hose temperature.

## Underway Fluid Management

**Fuel management.** We have three major concerns: fuel, oil, and hydraulic fluid (if used). Monitoring fuel while underway is critical. Beebe recommends a "How-Goes-It Curve" to summarize fuel consumption management during passages (see Figure 15–6). We have plotted the curve on every passage over

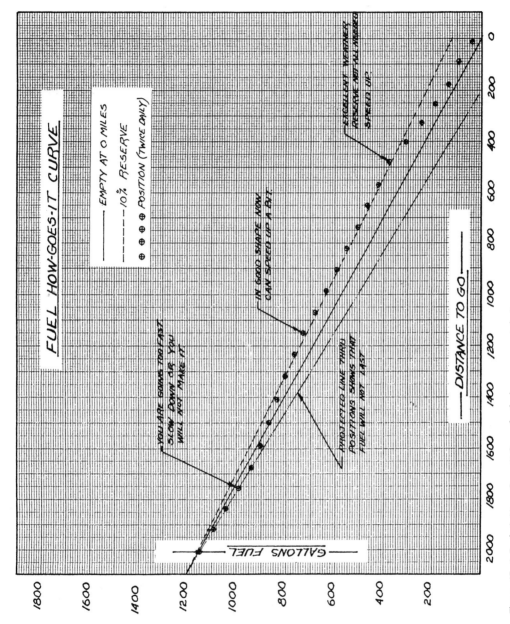

Figure 15–6. Beebe's How-Goes-It Curve for fuel management during passages.

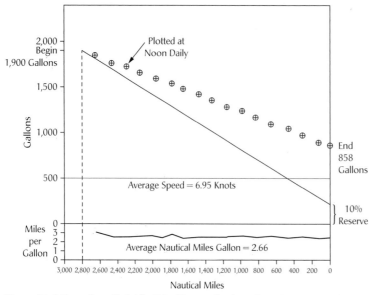

**Figure 15–7.** How-Goes-It plot for *Teka III*'s crossing from Gran Canary to Antigua.

On some boats, such as ours, the oil dipstick is protected by a surrounding tube that allows oil level to be checked while the engine is running. I know exactly where the full level is on the dipstick when the crankcase is full and the engine is running, so it is a simple matter to check oil consumption and add the appropriate amount. The second major issue is changing oil during passages. In this case, you need to talk to the technical department of the engine manufacturer. Oil change schedules are based on an intermittently run engine that allows contaminants to build up more rapidly, and oil deteriorates as a result. If you are running your engine at operating temperature for 24/7, then fewer oil problems are created, and oil change intervals can probably be extended. You might look at the oil change recommendations for your engine when it is used as a generator to get an insight here. Our Gardner

1,000 nautical miles. We have loads of excess fuel capacity so plotting the curve is not really needed, but it makes me feel good to see the plot.

**Oil management.** There are two major issues here. First, an oil level check should be done daily.

---

# Log of *Egret*: Fuel Management
## Scott Flanders, October 4, 2006

Position report: N18 43.02 W21 10.77, course 209 degrees, distance traveled 140.7nm, average speed (*see note below) 5.9 knots, fuel burned 43.67 gal, fuel burn 1.81 GPH, MPG 3.22, 3–4' N swells, apparent wind 4.6 knots N, 2610 nm to go, 1,410.77 nm from Gibraltar.

Yesterday afternoon we transferred the 89.5 gallons of fuel in the cockpit bladder into the port tank. Later the wind picks up, clocking more to the port

side (ENE). The stabilizers were taking a beating from the low rpm so at 2030 we added 100 rpm (from 1,350 to 1,450), and that settled things down. At 0030 this morning Mary reduced rpms to 1,400 with declining seas and at 0500 Steve went back to 1,350 rpms. We have had a many hour head current plus the inefficiency of somewhat rough water giving us the decline in distance traveled and GPM average for the past 24 hours.

Let me take the time here to make an important point. You see I am stressing MPG. This is assuming you know the distance to travel and have pre-planned sufficient fuel with a strong reserve. This also assumes you have

a way to accurately measure your fuel remaining at all times. I personally don't believe in electric gauges. In the boats we used to build, electric gauges were a fairytale but were all we could install. I believe in sight gauges, shrouded sight gauges. They never lie. GPH/speed is figured at no wind/no current with a modest load. In real life cruising there is a bottom line for efficiency and performance, MPG. These figures are only good for the past 24 hours and perhaps a little ahead in similar stable weather. MPG is infinitely variable because of rpm, gph, wind, wave direction and height, current, boat weight, just to mention a few. The balance is curiosity and math.

*Speed is up a bit now at 6.4 knots with little wind or waves (both are favorable so if this current will reverse or go away we'll be rockin'.) We'll see. In the big picture it doesn't really matter. We'll get there when we get there.

engine has a 400-hour change interval under normal circumstances, so we always begin a passage with new oil and make no changes until we arrive at the destination, regardless of the number of hours.

**Other fluids.** Check hydraulic fluid levels and coolant levels to be sure they are topped up. If either of these fluids disappears, try to determine the source of the leak—they do not burn up like fuel or oil.

**Daily check.** At noon each day, I check the fuel consumption and oil consumption. I also transfer fuel into the day tank at this time, recording the amount used and plotting it on the How-Goes-It graph. Coolant and hydraulic oil are also checked. I record all the fluid consumption in the ship's log.

## Handling Emergencies at Sea

While there is always a chance of your boat catching fire or capsizing during an ocean passage, these outcomes are pretty remote. You need to be prepared with firefighting equipment and knowledge. You also need a way to survive if you must leave your sinking boat. Life rafts are the most common method for emergency exit. Most cruising boats use this method. A few rely on dinghies for survival; however, this is more problematic due to seaworthiness concerns, emergency equipment, and sun screening. EPIRBs are also essential to fast rescue if you are stranded. There are a couple of emergencies I will emphasize here. If you are prepared, you may be able to save your boat and avoid a sea rescue. (See more on emergencies in Chapter 19.)

### Nets or Ropes around the Propeller

My greatest anxiety related to our first Atlantic crossing was the possibility of getting a major mess of nets and lines entangled in the propeller. Without a wing engine, we would have been at the mercy of the sea—adrift. Because we were nearly a thousand miles away from the nearest land, the possibility of a tow was minuscule. Rescue ships cannot tow yachts, and there are few "buddy boats" large and strong enough to tow another boat a thousand miles. Read about this in the following "Every Boater's Nightmare" sidebar.

So what are your options if you encounter a net ball 800 miles offshore in rough conditions? Once you evaluate the extent of the problem, it is time for a little planning and options review. If you have antiroll tanks or paravanes, that will help dampen the roll while you are dead in the water. If you have a parachute anchor, this might be a good time to deploy it. Perhaps you could drift for several days until the seas calm down a bit. If you have a wing engine, and the nets are well away from becoming entangled in its propeller, then you may proceed using the wing until the seas calm down or perhaps all the way to safe harbor. If you have auxiliary sails, you might use the sail until it calms or you get close enough to land for a tow. If you are near North American or Central American waters, you may want to contact the Coast Guard on SSB or satellite phone. It is possible they may have a ship that can tow you. Unless you are a very experienced and well-equipped diver, it is pretty dangerous to go under the stern of the boat while it is pitching and rolling. Try it in a choppy anchorage sometime to see how difficult it really is. The safest bet is to take other options, at least until it is calmer.

There are also some equipment needs for solving this type of problem. Good dive gear with wet suits is mandatory. This is probably the time to have a portable compressor aboard. The Hooka—an air compressor plus hose—makes diving to clear fouled propellers or to clean the bottom a more manageable chore. This unit keeps the air generation on board. The diver has a long hose and a regulator, plus the usual mask. Using this rig, you can move much more easily than with a large tank on your back. This can be critical at sea when the rolling and surging can make any underwater task more difficult.

Good serrated knives are a must (see Figure 15–9). Have plenty of them on board and be sure you can tether them to your hand. If you are on a larger boat, you might want to have a compressor on board capable of powering air tools with cutting blades. These will cut through any rope and most cables and they can be used underwater. Handles with suction cups also come in handy for working under the boat.

# Every Boater's Nightmare

**Phil Eslinger,** *Flat Earth*, **June 15, 2009**

I have been diving for over forty years and am very comfortable in the water. This was one of the three most dangerous days I have ever had while diving. I long for the boring calm days when absolutely nothing happens.

This morning, a little after 5 a.m., I woke up very badly. The door to the engine room is right next to my bed. When the engine bogged down, loaded up, and changed pitch, I was on my feet in an instant. Five seconds later, I had a pair of shorts on and was wearing hearing protectors. I was in the engine room looking at the shaft and the stuffing box to confirm what I already knew: the prop was fouled and bogging the engine down. Chris was on watch and became aware of the problem while I was getting dressed. He pulled power on the engine, but didn't know what else to do. I ran up to the pilothouse and put the engine in neutral. Because the seas were rough and cold, I went below and got into one of my wet suits. Then I ran up to the boat deck, grabbed my fins, mask and the other Spare Air that was still full. By this time, Rick was waking up and wondering what was wrong. Because we were still in the twilight of dawn, I took a dive light down with me.

As soon as I jumped in the water, my worst fears were confirmed: A huge clump of net and rope was wrapped around the prop and shaft, so much so that you could barely see the prop from the front side. I immediately swam back to the swim platform and exited the water. I told Rick and Chris that the Spare Air would not do it. I had to have complete dive gear. Chris and I ran around gathering up all of my gear and assembling it in the saloon. This took about half an hour. Carrying the tank down from the fly bridge in stiff seas with no way on was very dangerous. I knew things were not going well when the first tank I brought down had lost its O ring, which keeps air from leaking out of the seal between the regulator and the tank. Rick mostly watched and helped where he could. Chris and I discussed details to make this as safe as possible. I chose to go with very heavy weights, 25 pounds worth of weights—10 pounds more than

normal. This proved to be both a good thing and a bad thing. With 6- to 8-foot seas, I was worried about the boat slamming down on top of me as it pitched and rolled. More weight would allow me to sink with the boat instead of getting hit over the head with it. I got a special line-cutting knife I had recently bought with a serrated edge for cutting line. We set up the man overboard tackle at the side door to help me get in the boat. With 6-foot pitching seas, the swim platform becomes a death trap that could kill if it came down on top of you.

An hour after we stopped the boat, I went back into the water with full dive gear on. Getting under the stern of the boat, I grabbed tightly to the fouled netting and began sawing away at the lines. I quickly realized that the knife I was using was golden. No other knife would be able to penetrate the massive tangle of lines that was wound around the prop. I worked for about 20 minutes sawing away at the mass of net and rope, which had stopped us dead in the water. Suddenly, my mouth filled with water. To get a little water in your mouth while diving is not unusual, and there are procedures to deal with it. I pushed out away from the boat and did the first of these procedures: I blew out through the regulator to clear the water out. Immediately, my mouth filled with water again. So I did the next procedure: I reached up to push the purge valve on my secondary stage to use tank air to clear out the regulator. There was only one problem with pushing the purge valve; there was no regulator. All I was left with was the mouthpiece still between my lips. About this time, my brain and my body began having a conversation:

Brain: "Well this is another fine pickle you've gotten me into! This is the same situation Sandi got into when she drowned and almost died. Is it time for panic yet?"
Body: "No don't worry. I've still got breath. I'll just swim up to the boat."
Brain: "You mean THAT boat way up there? While you were talking, all of that weight you have on made you SINK. The surface must be more

than 10 feet away now. Are you ready for the adrenaline, yet?"
Body: "No, I can still make it; I'll just kick with my fins."
Brain: "Well, you're not doing anything. With all that weight, you're barely maintaining 10 feet, not going up. Here comes the adrenaline."
Body: "Listen Brain, I don't have the energy for adrenaline. All I have to do is press the inflator valve on my buoyancy vest. Here we go!"

Needless to say, after all that I was exhausted when I got back to the boat. Rick and Chris literally had to haul me back to the boat by the safety line while I tried to keep from inhaling water from the waves breaking over my head. Getting into and out of the boat in all that gear was eating up my energy as much as anything else. I collapsed in the saloon, soaking the rug, the chair, and everything else. I sat there for 20 minutes trying to get my energy back and my courage up to get in the water again.

I repaired the regulator and made up a line to tie the knife to my wrist, one I could get out of in case it got tangled. I feared the thought of going under the boat again, but we were disabled 800 miles from land. I jumped back in the water and started sawing on the net. In about 5 minutes, the line tied to the knife slipped off my hand. I pulled back from the mess and reattached in over my wrist, only to find that there was nothing on the other end! Looking down, I could see the "special knife" spiraling down to Davy Jones's Locker. For a brief second, I thought about going after it. But I really wanted to say what Bill Paxton's character, Hudson, in the movie "Aliens" said, "GREAT, JUST GREAT! NOW WHAT ARE WE GONNA DO?"

I climbed back into the boat and collapsed in the saloon again while Rick scoured the boat looking for some other cutting tool that would work. He found a Leatherman jackknife that had a serrated blade on it. Rick asked me if I thought putting the boat into gear would help. I said that would be the worst thing that could happen. It would undo all of my work and wrap the loose netting even tighter.

Finally, I worked my courage and energy up again to go back in the water. I sawed away at the mass for another 20 minutes while riding a roller coaster under the boat. I began making some progress. I managed to free most of the loose mass (about half of the total) from around the prop and pushed it away in a large cloud of rope and net. The other half was wound tight around the shaft in a 3-inch thick bulk. I sawed all the way through the mass at one point, but it wouldn't budge. I realized that I was going to have to take it apart in sections, but I had no more energy. I surfaced and Rick and Chris pulled me in and helped me into the boat. Again, I collapsed into the chair in the saloon. I had to balance what I had left inside me with safety. I told the crew that I didn't think I could get all of the line off the prop. I could get a large portion of it, but some of it was just too tightly wound around the shaft.

I also told Rick to try putting the boat in gear. Most of the loose stuff was off, and the tight stuff couldn't get wound any more tightly. Rick ran it in forward and reverse a few times while I rested. He said that he thought we could limp in at a lower power setting. He said, "That stuff is all around us out here. There is a huge patch of it just off the starboard side of the boat. "Yah," was all I could manage as I got up and steeled myself for another trip into the water, my FIFTH. As soon as I got below the surface, I realized that the large patch of net Rick had seen was the stuff from around our prop! If I could yell under water, I would have! I took a few minutes clearing the last remnant of net from around the shaft and then surfaced. Apparently, putting the engine in gear had broken the tangle where I had sawed through it but could not remove it. I was beat up and exhausted. I had half a dozen cuts and abrasions on my hands and only enough energy to shower and collapse in bed. The boat had been disabled for 3 hours and I had been in the water for 5 dangerous dives. The boat fared little better. The interior was trashed from rough seas and a wet diver. At least one of the crew had gotten seasick as the boat flopped around. But we were SAFE and on our way unencumbered again.

**Figure 15–8.** Nordhavn 50, *Flat Earth*, in Palmyra, south of Hawaii. (Phil Eslinger)

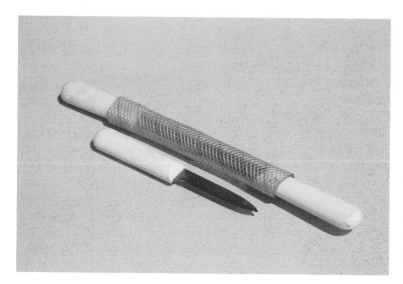

Figure 15–9. Serrated knives for clearing nets. A diver who removed several lobster pot lines each day in Maine gave me the hint to buy them by the dozen and store in a section of waterhose.

## Mechanical Failures at Sea

Running 24 hours a day for weeks at a time allows plenty of time for things to go wrong. Making sure you keep clean fuel going to the engine is the best way to prevent main engine problems, but other things besides fuel issues can cause difficulties. The only problem we had on all our ocean passages was a broken autopilot rudder sensor cable. It failed due to metal fatigue over a 6-year period of constant use. The fix was easy. As soon as I replaced it with fishing leader, we were off again. We did find that our watermaker's raw water input would collect air in the strainer until it would stop working. We lived with this problem for many years by not using the watermaker while underway (we have 600 gallons in our full water tanks). We finally fixed the problem on the advice of Hugo Carver: Simply run a small hose from the top of the strainer to well above the waterline. This lets any air that collected to be expelled. The simpler and more reliable your systems, the fewer problems you are likely to have at sea.

## Arrivals: Time to Take Care

Most yachting disasters happen upon arrival at the end of the voyage. The captain and crew are anxious to get into a nice quiet anchorage and relax for a full night's sleep. Visions of beer, wine, or martinis arise. However, this is the time to be especially careful. The following sections discuss some considerations in various situations.

### Avoid Night Arrivals in Strange Harbors

Things get confusing when closing on a harbor at night. Charts may be inaccurate, waypoints can be wrong, lights on shore can be confused with navigation lights, unexpected shipwrecks may provide obstacles—in other words there are plenty of opportunities for disaster. I have almost always tried to follow this rule. When we approached Flores in the Azores, we slowed way down during the night so we could make a daytime arrival. The one time we broke this rule was almost a disaster. We arrived at English Harbour, Antigua, just after dark after a long passage from the Canaries. Our pilot showed a range marker and a distinct channel after entering. We were also in contact with our friends on *Suprr*, a Nordhavn 46, anchored there. They agreed to shine a searchlight on the channel's central entrance using their dinghy to guide us in. This strategy worked fine; however, after entering the bay we found the anchorage and channel full of anchored boats with little space in between. To make matters worse, we still had our poles out and could not stop in the dense anchorage to raise them for fear the wind would carry us into an anchored

boat (we had planned to raise them in the channel). Our situation became even worse as anchored boats started shining their powerful spotlights directly at us rather than on their masts, blinding our night vision. Somehow we crept through the anchorage and found a spot, but it was a wonder we did not hit someone. With hindsight, I would have anchored outside the harbor until daylight permitted a safe entry.

### Do Not Bet Your Life on Charts (or Guidebooks)

Few areas of the world have really accurate electronic charts. Paper charts may also be off by quite a bit. This can result in disaster when entering through a coral reef under poor visibility, an all-too-often possibility in tropical waters. For example, on March 18, 2011, at 5 p.m., the 48' Defever, *All Points North*, struck the barrier reef at Xcalak, Mexico, resulting in the loss of the vessel. Luckily, the crew survived unscathed, at least physically. They were heading south, toward Belize, after a hard day's run, hoping for a quiet anchorage. Everyone was tired and ready to stop. There was a range marker, but only one tower was visible because the sun was in their eyes. The break in the reef is small, shallow, and not buoyed. This is where the fatal error occurred—they decided to use their electronic chart's guidance to find the entrance. They had a guidebook with the coordinates of the entrance, but believed the chartplotter rather than the guidebook. The captain decided to navigate in the pilothouse, which was covered with crusted salt. His mate was on the flying bridge keeping a lookout. Due to the seas, they ran at a full 8 knots toward what they thought to be the entrance. Here is what happened:

> We hit the reef going 8 knots with strong following seas. It was over immediately. In a matter of perhaps 30 seconds we grounded in a few feet of water. The waves turned us broadside, facing generally south and the boat tipped precipitously to starboard. What we didn't know at this point was that the starboard stabilizer fin structure was

*forced upward into the hull, and it is likely that at that point the hull suffered a breach. All we knew was that we were in trouble and had to get off the boat before it rolled over (it never did). As I got on deck, I hoped that perhaps the waves would push us over the reef into the deeper water beyond, but this was not to be. We were stuck fast. I looked for Susie, and turned to see her falling violently from the upper deck to the lower. She picked herself up, we got on our life jackets, and I managed to get the dinghy down from the top deck. We got on board and traveled over the reef to the relative safety of the inner harbor. Susie was bruised but otherwise OK.*

## Watch Out for Bars

Many harbor entrances have bars to cross to gain the safe channel. Often, but not always, there are jetties at the bar entrance. Usually there is a river or estuary that empties into the ocean through this entrance. When the river flow and tide are running against the incoming swell, breakers and rough seas are formed. Crossing a bar in these circumstances is quite dangerous. On the Pacific coast of the United States, numerous boats have been lost crossing bars. The rule for entering such a channel is to wait for slack tide, preferably high slack tide, which also gives you extra depth. Never enter on an ebb tide when surf will be at its worst.

## Crossing the Bar
### Scott Bulger

Some say that cruising, like flying an airplane, is long periods of boredom punctuated by moments of sheer terror. Well I guess it was inevitable. We finally had one of those terrifying experiences that no one wants to have. We were attempting to enter the channel to Puesta del Sol in Nicaragua. We had left Barillas marina in El Salvador and traveled 11 hours to arrive 1 hour before sunset. We'd had a good crossing, a bit more bouncy than most of the trip as the seas were mostly on our bow, but not bad by any measurement. I'd read the Rains guide over and over about entering the channel and felt fully prepared for arrival. I had the marina provide waypoints entered on both chartplotters. The boat, having recently been prepared to cross the Tehuantepec, was as sea shape as she had ever been.

I began to get concerned when I noticed on my radar that I was actually seeing breaking waves along the entire shoreline, something I'd previously not been able to tune my radar to show so crisply. I wondered if I had gotten better at tuning or if these waves were showing up because they were so large. At sea we weren't feeling any significant rollers, really nothing more than a few feet. However, as we closed on the sea buoy and began our approach (about 2 miles out) I became increasingly aware and concerned about a series of rollers that would pass under us every 4 or 5 minutes. They were in sets of three or four and were SUBSTANTIALLY larger than the surrounding seas. I'd been hailing the marina for at least 30 minutes but only getting sporadic response. They were sending a panga to meet us and I was trying to keep an eye out for him. I made certain we were on the approach as described in the guide, and by the marina manager. As I observed the large rollers passing under the boat I started to become really concerned when it appeared to me that they were breaking across the entire shoreline, including in the channel entrance, which we believed we were approaching.

I asked my wife to join me on the bridge so she could spot the waves behind us. We reached a point where if the channel didn't become obvious I was going to turn back out to sea. Then a set of rollers arrived. As I looked back and saw the wave standing up and beginning to steepen I realized it was time to abort. Each second the wave was getting steeper and steeper, and I realized we were going to have a problem. I didn't know if the boat would accelerate and start surfing, but I knew this was going to be an experience unlike anything we had ever had. I guess a 40,000-pound trawler doesn't surf well because as the wave arrived, the nose buried, and the stern started moving to the port; it was then I knew we were going to broach. The boat began to heel with the face of the wave and the stern swung parallel to the wave. We ended up about 45 degrees to the horizon as the wave peaked and we started down the backside. As the boat heeled, the noise inside was dramatic as the contents of every locker and container shifted. Fortunately only a pair of binoculars and a

*(continued)*

compass were tossed loose as everything else in the cabin was secure. The righting moment of the boat was fantastic; it snapped right back into shape and I spun the wheel to continue the momentum of the broach to head back out to sea. Thanks to the Edson speed knob, the turn was rapid as I added full power. We moved quickly ahead to face the oncoming waves and climbed up and over them, returning to safe water within seconds. I knew [we] were through the worst of it when we completed the turn, but my wife continued to whimper as we climbed up and over the remaining rollers until we were back in water deep enough that the swells were gentle.

After calming down I got back on the radio and hailed the marina manager, asking about conditions. I had asked him several times if conditions were good and he said "Yes, it is very calm." I asked him if he could see the channel entrance, and he said he wasn't in a place he could see it, but that he had called a person in the beach facility and they advised the conditions were fine. He then added that the panga was leaving the marina and would be there in just a few minutes. We circled for 15 minutes and then we saw the panga coming. I asked the marina manager if the panga driver spoke English and he told me no, but that he would translate for us. Then he came back on the radio and said "The panga driver says to go

NOW." I pulled in behind him and we started into the entrance channel, but we were about a mile farther south than the location where I had attempted to enter. This approach was much better as we observed breaking waves on each side of us, but the channel remained clear. Then another set of the rollers arrived. I'll never forget the look on the panga driver's face as we looked down on him from about 25 feet above his head and less than 100 feet behind him. I think because we were in the channel and the waves weren't steepening up as they did before we had a much more sedate ride in.

We arrived at the marina and tied the boat up. I didn't even care if we had the fenders out; I just wanted that boat tied to the dock. In conversation with the marina manager and the panga driver I was to learn that these conditions had only started a day or so ago, and I was the first boat to come in and experience this problem. The panga driver even broke the VHF antenna off his boat in the rough conditions. They think the recent swell must have shifted the entrance channel and moved it about a mile south and made it much narrower. They assured me these were not the normal conditions.

Figure 15–10. Nordhavn 40, *Alanui*, in the Panama Canal. (Scott Bulger)

## Seasickness: The Spoiler on Ocean Passages

Seasickness results from motions and accelerations that are natural for a boat at sea. Experts in this area say the most important prevention is to recognize the onset of seasickness. While symptoms vary, they most commonly begin with yawning and drowsiness, then abnormal fatigue and lethargy. After these initial symptoms, stomach discomfort and nausea appear. Concentration on tasks becomes more difficult, and vomiting almost always results. Subsequent attacks of vomiting, typically with less warning happen time after time. With the first signs of symptoms, you need to react immediately—don't put it off until you are sick at your stomach. Here are some recommended actions:

+ Take seasickness medication.
+ Go on deck where motion is less, amidships or aft.
+ Use "horizon viewing." Look at waves, clouds, distant sails. Manually steering the boat by visual, not compass reference, may help.
+ Ride the waves. Stand up and let your legs adjust to the motion of the boat. Or sit upright and let your trunk and neck muscles keep your head and upper body balanced. Get in rhythm with the sea; don't fight it.
+ Let the skipper know. Perhaps a course change can ease the motion.
+ Stay on deck. Avoid going below. After sleeping, go on deck at once. When you go off watch, lie

down in bed quickly—it is easier to adapt when lying down.

+ Pace yourself if you have duties below. Alternate below time with deck time. Be alert to symptoms onset.
+ Plan ahead if you are the cook or navigator to minimize time spent looking down.
+ Avoid alcohol.
+ Eat whatever you want, but do not overeat.
+ Don't starve yourself to avoid seasickness—you can become weak, confused, and even totally incapacitated by lack of nutrients. Take broth, saltines, and candy to replace fluids.

+ Watch others. Seasick crew members are more prone to accidents and falling overboard.
+ Have a plan to manage seasickness. Stock up on medications and patches.
+ Stock up on bags, buckets, paper towels, juices, etc. for someone who is seasick.

We have travelled over 50,000 nautical miles on the ocean and have had very few incidents of seasickness among our guests. Mary and I have never experienced seasickness in any ocean conditions. None of our Atlantic crossing crews was ever seasick in spite of a couple of significant gales.

# Ocean Fishing

One of the joys of crossing oceans is the opportunity to catch fish. This is especially true in warmer waters inhabited by tuna, wahoo, and mahi mahi (dorado). We have been successful in catching these species and hooking some even larger billfish, which escaped. After leaving the Canaries, bound for the Caribbean, we caught so many dorado that we had to quit fishing for a few days because of oversupply. When we started fishing again in mid-ocean, we started hooking really large, strong fish. We had no chance of landing them on our 60# test line and medium weight rods and reels, but we had some very exciting moments. If you go voyaging into Alaskan waters, salmon and halibut abound, creating a culinary delight. If you enjoy fishing, be sure to get Scott and Wendy Bannerot's book, *The Cruiser's Handbook of Fishing.* It offers complete information on fishing anywhere in the world you may travel. Here are some hints from the book and a diagram of trolling lure types.

**Figure 15–11.** David Umstot displays a mahi-mahi caught in the Atlantic on our way to Antigua.

- Troll the lure between 1.5 and 3 boat lengths astern. A single line might be let out around 100 feet. Multiple lines can be run at varied lengths–it makes the fish think a school is running away and they charge the bait. (Note: We never slow down for trolling in warmer waters; 6–9 knots seems just fine.)
- If using surface baits (this simulates flying fish), the bait should "pop" or break the surface at least once every 5 seconds, without coming completely out of the water.
- Larger baits can be run closer to the boat, while smaller ones need more distance behind.
- Increasing the trolling line's angle increases the lure's surface action.
- Always run the lure on the face of waves, not on the crest or back of the wave. If it is breaking a little that is even better. Lures run best going downsea rather than upsea.

*(continued)*

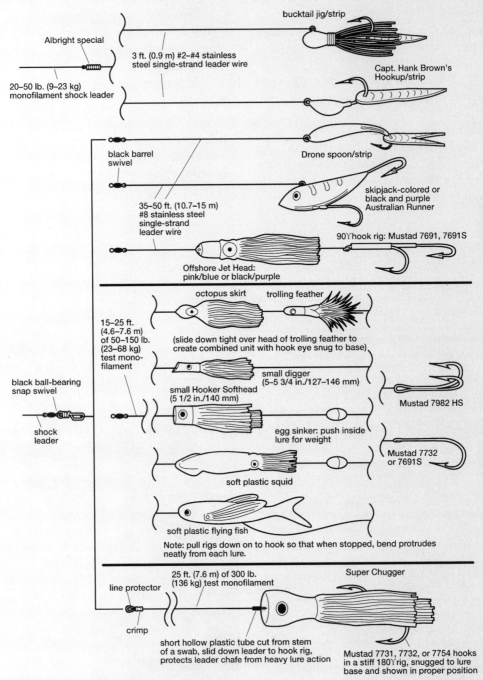

Bucktail jig/strip

Albright special

3 ft. (0.9 m) #2–#4 stainless
steel single-strand leader wire

Capt. Hank Brown's
Hookup/strip

20–50 lb. (9–23 kg)
monofilament shock leader

black barrel
swivel

Drone spoon/strip

35–50 ft. (10.7–15 m)
#8 stainless steel
single-strand
leader wire

skipjack-colored or
black and purple
Australian Runner

90Ỵhook rig: Mustad 7691, 7691S

Offshore Jet Head:
pink/blue or black/purple

octopus skirt       trolling feather

15–25 ft.
(4.6–7.6 m)
of 50–150 lb.
(23–68 kg)
test mono-
filament

(slide down tight over head of trolling feather to
create combined unit with hook eye snug to base)

small digger
(5–5 3/4 in./127–146 mm)

small Hooker Softhead
(5 1/2 in./140 mm)

Mustad 7982 HS

black ball-bearing
snap swivel

egg sinker: push inside
lure for weight

shock
leader

Mustad 7732
or 7691S

soft plastic squid

soft plastic flying fish

Note: pull rigs down on to hook so that when stopped, bend protrudes
neatly from each lure.

25 ft. (7.6 m) of 300 lb.
(136 kg) test monofilament

Super Chugger

line protector

crimp

short hollow plastic tube cut from stem
of a swab, slid down leader to hook rig,
protects leader chafe from heavy lure action

Mustad 7731, 7732, or 7754 hooks
in a stiff 180Ỵrig, snugged to lure
base and shown in proper position

**Figure 15–12.** Sample trolling lures as illustrated in *The Cruiser's Handbook of Fishing.* (Scott and Wendy
Bannerot)

# Anxieties and Realities about Ocean Passages

The anxieties and apprehension preceding an ocean crossing are many, especially for first-time voyagers. In 2002, Mary and I wrote an article for *PassageMaker Magazine* entitled "Atlantic Anxiety: How One Couple Felt Just before Their First Ocean Crossing." A summary of the article, which highlighted our concerns about the voyage, follows.

## "His" Anxieties and Realities

**Will we encounter a bad storm?** Would we encounter a perfect storm? There have been such storms in May when we planned to go. We decided to hire a weather router from Ocean Marine Nav to help provide weather windows and avoid the possible storms. We had a smooth passage through the Gulf Stream, encountered a cold front that gave us some wind and seas, but nothing too uncomfortable. The long run from Bermuda to the Azores was uneventful, but cool and moderately windy as our course was just south of the jet stream's storm track. We had strong, near gale force winds off Portugal, but again it created no problem for us or our boat.

**Will we have a major mechanical failure?** I had a great deal of confidence in our Gardner engine, but what if the raw water pump failed? Or the alternator? What if a net was caught around the prop or the rudder came off? We had no problems with anything in the engine room during the voyage, but I was prepared with spares for almost everything. The biggest potential problem was nets on the propeller. I had scuba gear with one tank, but I knew if the tangle was bad, it would be impossible to remove. As I mentioned before, I installed sails to get home in case of such an event when we re-crossed the Atlantic.

**Will we run into something?** We heard stories of boats ramming containers and sinking, although I was never able to confirm those stories. We worried a bit about collision with ships or other boats, although we sighted very few of either on the voyage. We did have a "ghost ship" that appeared to be a medium-sized fishing boat pass in front of us only a few hundred feet ahead. This happened on our way to Bermuda in the heart of the Bermuda Triangle. It was spooky because they had no running lights and did not respond to radio calls. We suspected the crew was asleep. We did pass a barely floating 55-gallon drum that would have made a dent had we hit it at full speed. Another cruiser observed a runabout of maybe 18 feet long floating bow-up in the middle of the ocean. It had Florida numbers on its bow. They reported it, but never found out who owned the boat.

**Would the crew get along with us?** Living in close quarters with others is stressful. For the most part, we all got along well, but there were times when tempers flared. One problem I found was giving crewmembers enough responsibilities on the voyage to keep them interested and challenged. I wanted to do most of the mechanical checks myself rather than delegate to the crew. I also did the navigation, weather, and route planning. When we decided to take a somewhat different path to the Azores, due to the jet stream's position, one crewmember thought the change unnecessary and recommended against it. As the captain, I made the decision for the course change. Interestingly enough, the two sailboats who were buddy boating with us both parted with their crews in the Azores, even though they had planned to go the entire crossing.

## "Her" Anxieties and Realities

**Can I stand being alone out there on the big ocean?** Early on in owning our boat, I announced, "I don't do nights and I don't do oceans!" That has changed over the years of cruising on board *Teka III*. But our longest passage to date had been between Puerto Madero, Mexico, and Bahia de Cocos, Costa Rica—a trip of 60 hours. We traveled quite a distance offshore on that trip. In fact, it was so far that I couldn't find land on the radar. Yet I knew if we made a turn to port, land lay over there somewhere. The prospect of crossing the Atlantic Ocean, even in segments, posed one big coping situation for me. Completing such a trip would be the ultimate step up. We figured 6 days to Bermuda, 11 to the Azores, and 6 more to Lisbon (exploring land at each place). I had said, "I'll wait to see how I handle the first leg. If I choose not to go the 11 days, I will fly."

A merchant mariner had put a seed in my mind in 1997 about life on the ocean. He said, "The sea has a rhythm. Go with it." I repeat this to myself quietly every time we embark on a journey, small or large. I also remind myself to "trust *Teka*." This has a tendency to calm me.

I am happy to report I didn't fly to Portugal. Why? By the time we arrived in Bermuda, I had gotten caught up in the adventure. The next leg would take twice the time, but I found we had a routine on board and seemed to stay busy all the time. Unless I chose to worry, I didn't. And I teased the guys. If I deserted them, they'd miss my "galley magic." Each boat out there works out its own system for meals, but that role felt very comfortable to me.

**Weather: will the seas get too scary?** Although I trusted my ship and Denis completely, I worried about things I could not control. The weather bothered me. Reading *The Perfect Storm* and seeing the movie last year made dramas at sea real. We weren't going swordfishing in the far North Atlantic in the wrong month. However, storms do occur anywhere in the open ocean. We purposefully planned the crossing to avoid hurricane season, but there's more to weather than hurricanes. Fronts take different tracks at times, like marching soldiers, glaring at you from the printed weatherfax. Could we be so lucky that none occurred in our path? Can the budget afford the services of a weather "guru" to guide us? There's no place to run and nowhere to hide out there should things go haywire in a hurry.

As much as I worried about the potential weather, we were spared any major storms. In fact, the United States West Coast showed us much larger waves than those in the Atlantic. Early in my cruising days, if it was really rough, my coping strategy was to retreat to the center of the boat and play solitaire, not looking at the waves. Now I can watch.

To confess, I have not mastered the "one-pot meal." I felt the need to create, more than just feed, the hungry crew and captain. It became very rough every night about 6 p.m. I am positive the largest waves rolled against us as I worked in the galley. When a big one would toss things about, I'd yell, "Keep the wheels out of the ditch!" Up in the pilothouse someone would shout back, "We can't tell which ones are the big ones!"

**Sister ships: Is someone out there who cares?** The prospect of being alone, outside of USCG range, and needing help made me think hard about going with other vessels. This seemed extremely important on the Bermuda to Azores leg. Who would be interested and available? We met two sailing cruising boats during the summer of 2000 on the East Coast, and they agreed to join us in Bermuda for the 900-mile trip to the Azores. We kept in touch via e-mail to establish rendezvous timing there. Although we did not travel exactly together to the Azores, we knew they were back there for "backup," coming to our aid should that be needed. It means a lot to hear a friendly voice over the SSB, even if you have to shout to be heard, or keep changing channels to find a better one. We joined up again in the Azores and celebrated in a grand fashion.

**Will everyone stay healthy?** What if someone got sick or injured along the way? Did we have the right knowledge and medical supplies to deal with it on a temporary basis? Perhaps we should make a "Doctor at Sea" e-mail arrangement. If no crew joined us, how would I run the boat if something happened to Denis? That really bothered me. I cannot fix mechanical problems, first off. And I would probably be too stressed to think straight, too. Fortunately, no one came down with anything or had an accident while at sea. Denis did have quite an accident, resulting in three broken ribs and an injured leg and ankle. But the injury happened at the dock in the Azores, where plenty of help materialized almost immediately.

**Mary's final thoughts.** My days at sea were full with keeping the crew happy and fed; pulling up and studying weather reports; planning, preparing, and cleaning up after meals; studying books about places coming up; and standing watches. On land, laundry, groceries, sightseeing, and socializing with sister ships kept us busy. Even though I stayed subconsciously fearful, manifested by fitful sleeping and frequent checking of things, I am glad I did not fly. Now I can proudly say I have joined an elite group of cruisers who have crossed the Atlantic on their own boat!

## CHAPTER SIXTEEN

# World Cruising Destinations

The previous two chapters on planning and ocean crossing prepare us for arrival, for "being there" at our destination of choice. There are thousands of rewarding and exciting destinations. Beginning passagemakers would be wise to gain experience in destinations that are relatively close to home, such as the Bahamas, Caribbean, Alaska, or the Sea of Cortez. There are numerous books and articles on these destinations, so they are not be covered here—instead I emphasize more distant spots traveled by ourselves and other cruisers.

When Captain Beebe wrote the first edition of this book the focus was on cruising in Europe, with considerable emphasis on enjoying the French canals. The idea was to design a boat with the ability to cross oceans, then comfortably cruise in the canals after arrival. This generally meant a very low profile so the boat could fit in the tunnels of the canals. Currently, minimum depth in the Canal du Midi is 5'2"; height is 9'9" at the tunnel or bridges' center. (Sides may be as low as 6'5".) Beebe designed a number of what he called "canal runners" to fit within this space. However, the depth of the canals has been decreasing from 5'6' to 5'2", so many boats designed in the 1970s may churn up a lot of mud or run hard aground. The low height makes it difficult, if not impossible, for any modern passagemakers to fit—you would need a custom design.

In this chapter I explore world cruising with input from those who have been there. The chapter begins with a voyaging opportunity close to home: Cuba. We then move farther afield to the Mediterranean, South America, the South Pacific, Australia, Southeast Asia, and Africa. Some areas of the Indian Ocean

have closed due to the high risk of piracy. The beautiful and interesting coasts of Venezuela and Colombia are also high-risk areas and are generally to be avoided.

**Figure 16–1.** Papua, New Guinea, is but one of the destinations at your feet. This shot was taken on a walk to Doini Island Plantation Resort from N55, *Moana Kuewa*. (Christine Bauman)

# Cruising the North Coast of Cuba

*Marie Dufour*

*Domino* [a 65-foot power catamaran, owned by Marie and J. P. Dufour and designed by Malcolm Tennant, was built in Paraguay, and launched in 2009 (see page 230)], just clocked her first 10,000 nautical miles, which in 15 months' time is pretty good for a brand-new ship. She performed like a champ, keeping us safe and averaging 11 knots through her travels, burning on average 8.5 gallons/hour. We've discovered 22 countries, caught half a ton of fish and 30 lobsters, met dozens of cruisers from around the world, and made many friends along the way. Each anchorage has been a discovery, and we've been amazed at the boat's performance at every change of sea conditions.

You must enter Cuba at one of the international marinas (on the north coast, this means Puerto Vita, Cayo Guillermo, Varadero, or Marina Hemingway). If your boat is too large for the marina or if the marina is full, you can't enter the country. Our intention had been to do our entry at the Marina Cayo Guillermo and to cruise the reefs around that area, reputed to be the nicest on the north coast. We elected not to enter at Puerto Vita, the easternmost

entry point, but opted for Cayo Guillermo. However, when we reached Cayo Guillermo and informed the Guardia of our intention, a long discussion took place between the Guardacosta cruiser that met us and the headquarters at Cayo Guillermo.

Bottom line: we could not enter at Cayo Guillermo. Why not? No particular reason was given. Perhaps the marina was full, perhaps the boat was too big, perhaps there was not sufficient staff that week; with many apologies, the Guardia allowed us to anchor overnight at Cayo Guillermo, with orders to proceed to Marina Varadero 140 miles to the west in the morning. We were allowed reasonable overnight stops as long as we did not land anywhere. The point is that, in Cuba, you cannot anchor your boat out and dinghy over to the marina to do your entry.

In the morning, we headed for Cayo Diablito, 38 miles to the west. According to our friend Jeff on *Kejfam*, this was the best snorkeling spot in the world. Jeff was right.

The diving at the western end of the Cay is spectacular. A forest of multicolored sea fans leads to a vast collection of giant elkhorn corals opening their branches to the sun in the shallows. Long and deep trenches between the corals are home to peaceful nurse sharks. Thousands of fish dart in and out of the coral collection. Without any doubt, this is one of the most spectacular snorkeling places yet. Cayo Diablito, however, lies at the westernmost limit of the northern reef and is the last of such anchorages. The more western anchorages lie between mangroves, except for the outer side of Cayo Cruz del Padre, where the reef is spectacular and diverse.

[Clearing in at Marina Varadero] took seven teams of officials, a "sniff" dog, and less than two hours: physician, veterinarian, agricultural inspection, customs, immigration, port captain, and the dock master relayed each other until all our papers were in order. We had prepared a document in Spanish and made several copies to ease the process. (Nigel Calder's *Cuba: A Cruising Guide* is the authority on the subject.)

Figure 16–2. *Domino* in the Varadero Marina, Cuba. (Marie Dufour)

The marina is undergoing improvements—someday it may be up to par with international standards. But it is well protected from the elements, and security is excellent. We withstood a storm with 40 knots of wind without problem and left the boat overnight for side trips. You can walk to the market at Santa Marta or ride your bike to the international hotel strip at Varadero itself. A taxi ride in one of the ubiquitous '50s American cars will cost you $5, although your driver will ask for $10. Changing money is easy at the Cadeca (Casa de Cambio) in Santa Marta, but it is better to change your Euros or Canadian dollars rather than your US dollars (USD). There is a 10% penalty on the USD (down from 20% previously), plus a couple of taxes, so that by the time you're done changing you've paid 15% tax. No such thing with other currencies. The CUC (Convertible Universal Currency) is the currency used by the tourists, while the citizens use the national peso. Do carry some pesos to buy your fruits and vegetables at the local market.

Confusing? What is not confusing in Cuba? There are stores for the locals, where the meager merchandise on the shelves is sold in pesos. And there are stores for the tourists, where everything is sold in CUCs, at international prices, gouging the tourist. The Cuban worker is paid in pesos, only has access to the "pesos stores" to shop, and will do anything to earn CUCs. That is why many of them turn to the tourism industry: doctors, university professors, dentists would rather be hotel waiters or taxi drivers, just to earn some CUCs and have access to higher quality goods.

Some cruisers complained that it was impossible to cruise Cuba if you didn't stay at a marina. This was not our experience. We filed a float plan with the harbormaster who gave us a cruising permit for the coast between Varadero and Cayo Falcones: 60 miles of coastal cruising.

### Cayo Cruz del Padre

Looking at the chart and reading the cruising guide, I was not sure I wanted to attempt shooting the reef at Cruz del Padre. The channel is a narrow, winding trail with shallow depths. But the day was spectacular, the visibility excellent, and the morning breeze barely a ripple on the water. JP studied the charts some more, marked all the waypoints on the Navnet, and we carefully made our entrance through the extended and treacherous reef. Once more, I can vouch for Nigel Calder's excellent drawings and instructions in his 15-year-old *Cuba: A Cruising Guide*. Once into the groove behind the reef, safe with 12' of water under our hulls, we went as far east as we could to seek as much of the little protection afforded by the tip of Cruz del Padre, within short distance of the lighthouse. We dropped anchor with 10' of water below us, over sand and grass, and set it carefully. The winds had a tendency to strengthen in the afternoon, but always from the same direction. We were the only boat around, and we spent three spectacular days, filled with swimming and snorkeling and underwater hunting.

Every day, an hour before slack water, we loaded the dinghy with water bottles, a handheld VHF, and a GPS and crossed over to the reef, each time venturing a bit further, between 1 and 2.3 miles away from the mother ship. We snorkeled for hours, caught a number of lobsters, but mostly were astounded by the variety of corals.

Would we go back to Cuba? We'd like to snorkel more of the northern reef. But next time, we would enter at Porto Vita, only spend one night at the marina, and then cruise for two weeks, diving on the reef, and exiting at Varadero.

## Cruising the Mediterranean Sea
*Mary and Denis Umstot*

Spending time in the Mediterranean is a top goal of many cruisers. We spent five years there and thoroughly enjoyed it. The area is a large and varied cruising area with many alluring ports and anchorages. The countries are alive with history and culture. Wonderful and unique foods are a highlight. I have taken short excerpts from Mary's book, *Voyaging to the Mediterranean Under Power*, to provide insights into cruising this area.

### Spain: Pickpockets and Festivals

"No! No! No!" I shouted at the nicely dressed twenty-something-year-old Spanish man in the Metro Subway station. He backed up, holding his hands so I could see he held nothing, and appearing as innocent as he could. But innocent he was not. He and his pal had just performed one of the many

**Figure 16–3.** In the Mediterranean you can enjoy anchoring right in the midst of history as shown here in Tropea, Southern Italy.

pickpocket schemes cruisers had been warned about while traveling around Barcelona.

A handout to newcomers alerted us to many schemes. A popular one went like this: A person in front of you hesitated, bumped into you, or stumbled in getting his footing and at the same time accidentally dropped a bunch of change on the ground in front of you. If you bent over to assist in retrieving it, your hip pockets became visible and available—

voila! But there is also the tried-and-true method of just sticking a hand in your pocket to search for wallets or money.

### St. Tropez, France

We anchored in a nice spot on the south side of the bay. During the night, the fun started. The weather changed and gale-force winds (35–40 knots) were predicted by midnight. Midnight came, and we bolted out of bed. The rigging started singing, and the boat began bouncing up and down with OTN (on the nose) waves from the north. The wind at that time registered only 20 knots. We had to pull anchor and relocate before the wind got up to 40. A quick check of the chart showed that if we went about 2.5 miles across the big bay, we could possibly be out of harm's way—protected from the north wind. We bounced along listening to the wind creep up to 40 knots during that 1-hour trip to go 2-1/2 miles. We safely re-anchored by 2 a.m., resettled our psyches, and finally went back to sleep.

Next morning arrived bright and clear. We moved back across the bay and took the dinghy to St. Tropez, where we gawked at the megayachts in the harbor and the fashionably dressed folks strolling through town.

### Italian Harbors and Islands

**Beautiful harbors.** Our Italian waiter touched Denis gently on the shoulder; then verbally and nonverbally as only the Italians can do, exclaimed, "Bellisimo!" On our first stop along the Italian Riviera in June 2002, we celebrated our anniversary at Santa Margherita Ligure, anchoring just below a restaurant perched above the bay. After the waiter presented us with the menu, he walked over to the large picture windows and stared out at our boat.

Portofino, with its busy harbor of fishing boats, pleasure craft, and megayachts all lined up tightly together, had a Mediterranean feel about it. The homes surrounding the harbor were painted pastel colors, had balconies for openness, and shutters for privacy. Cobblestone streets ran through the village. Tourists mingled

**Figure 16–4.** Portofino is one of the most picturesque harbors in Italy.

with the locals, creating a melodic sound of languages to match the already colorful scene.

**Elba.** At first the port authorities in Elba would not allow us off the boat to tour the town. Someone had to be on board at all times, something we never quite figured out. At one point they did give permission to leave for a limited time, but only if we called the port office on the radio and discussed it with them first.

## Mediterranean Mooring at Porto de Roma

Mary describes one of our early experiences with Med mooring:

> Coming into the port through the breakwater, we met men in a marina dinghy to help us to our assigned spot and assist us in Med mooring. Med mooring is done throughout the Mediterranean and is supposed to be a simple job. Instead of tying sideways, as we do in the States, the boat is tied with stern lines to the dock and secured at the bow by an underwater line pulled on board. Rather than using 52 feet of space by side-tying, we used only 16 feet. Many more boats can be accommodated using the Med moor method. What is supposed to be simple can become complicated, which we found out over our time in the Med. Wind can affect positioning. Currents get involved. Boats need to be squeezed open to make adequate space. And then there's the prop wrap, which happened to us.
>
> The men in the dinghy pulled up to the dock and jumped out to wait while we reversed into position. No other boats had to be dealt with, so it looked as if we would have an easy job. But while our prop was still reversing toward the dock, one of the men got ahead of the game and pulled the underwater line up that went to the bow. It got wrapped around the prop. Nothing could be done until we hired a diver to cut it away. He took quite a while to do that job too, coming up with small pieces of rope at a time. The marina men did not appear upset about our situation, shrugging shoulders and looking bored while we got untangled.

During the next four years we had lots of practice with Med mooring and became quite competent. There are two Med mooring situations: marinas with slime lines and using your own anchor. (We cover procedures for using an anchor and more on Med mooring in Chapter 19.)

At marinas, there are usually light lines that lead from the dock to a heavy line anchored offshore, sometimes to a giant chain running mid-channel in the marina or harbor. The idea is to back up close enough to the dock to pick up the small line (called the slime line because of marine growth accumulation) with a boat hook. Often, the stern lines from the boat can be secured to the dock here. While the boat sits there out of gear, someone on board walks forward with the light line to the bow and then pulls up the large, slimy mooring line from the bottom, pulls it through a hawse hole on the bow, and wraps it around the windlass capstan. The line is then pulled in, with the help of the windlass, until the stern is away from the dock, but still close enough for your *passerelle* (gangway attached to the boats used for walking ashore from the stern) to reach.

**Figure 16–5.** Passerelles come in many shapes and sizes from this simple one on *SeaScape* to expensive built-in remote-controlled units. In the Mediterranean, this equipment is a must—the photo shows the port at Bizerte, Tunisia. Surge often prevents mooring, close to the dock. You may need to be 6 or 7 feet away.

All this creates quite a mess. Gloves are essential, and the washdown pump gets a workout. There is always a balancing act between bow and stern lines to keep the proper distance from what is often a concrete wall.

**Italian Islands.** There are many interesting islands off the central Italian coast, including Isola d'Ischia, with its famous formidable island castle. If you arrive on the weekend, you may have to jockey for a place to anchor. Lots of marina-based boats come for the day, but the anchorage is almost deserted at night. In medieval times, local citizenry fled to safety across the cobblestone causeway and moat bridge during a siege. Several thousand people would hunker down inside the castle.

Another island of note is Procida, which is only 4 miles away from Isola d'Ischia. It looks untouched with fishing boats anchored everywhere, but not many pleasure boats. The houses along the harbor and up the hillside near the castle sparkle in their pastel colors of blue, pink, and yellow. It was one of our favorite towns to visit.

### Surprising Tunisia

Our background knowledge of northern Africa turned out to be wrong. We thought all of it was desert, based on the *Lawrence of Arabia* movie and

**Figure 16–6.** Procida, "the pastel island" off the coast from Naples.

the WWII movies about the battle with General Rommel, aka "the Desert Fox." True, there is a lot of desert in Tunisia, but in Tabarka, the nearest city to Algeria in the northwest corner, it is very green; it was once the "bread basket of Rome." It was also where the animals came from for the gladiator events in the Coliseum. One day, we took time to explore the area nearby—visiting ruins of ancient slave markets, temples of worship, and homes, their frescoed floors still visible.

We had several problems at our next port, Bizerte. Wind caused havoc with Med mooring. Another was the official asking for whiskey, more than once. They knew we had liquor on board because we had to list it on the boat inventory papers. He became quite a pest until he finally was told in Arabic by John, our traveling partner, we would not do it. A bottle of whiskey in Tunisia was worth approximately $100 U.S. No wonder he wanted one.

### Croatian Imprints

Weather kept us totally involved during our two months in Croatia. In Croatia, the nasty weather revolves around boras. *Boras* are the winds that come down off the high mountains so intensely that they scour all vegetation away. Looking up as we traveled on the Velitski Canal, we were reminded of a moon landscape. These winds are well-respected, and travel is limited when boras are occurring.

We dropped the hook at about a dozen different islands, with names like Korcula, Pag, Rab, Cres, Hvar, Vis, and Mljet, and one bay called Rogoznica. The cruisers all called it "Rosie's knickers." There are no sandy beaches in Croatia, and people seem to arrive at the seaside early to spread their blankets or mats on the "softest" rock. However, each of the islands has a castle, cobblestone streets, interesting buildings, and lots of shops.

Dubrovnik's walled city sat on a cliff dominating the scenery all around. During their recent war in then-Yugoslavia, much of Croatia escaped damage, yet some remnants (shell holes in the walls) were visible. Some houses are still not rebuilt; all we could see were piles of rubble.

In Starigrad, an unusual storm came through. We could hear the thunder and see the lightning just before dawn. The skies opened up, and the rains really came down, hard. Everyone got up to watch the drama, not quite knowing what to expect. While we watched, water in the whole bay seemed to be sucked out of its opening, only to rush back in like a tsunami, three times. After losing about six feet of water under the boat, as measured by the eye on the seawall, enough water remained so that boats Med moored to the wall were not damaged. However, the passerelles were damaged. The quick up-and-down jolt bent the gangway attached to the boat, requiring extensive repair after the

Figure 16–7. Cruising along the coast of Rab, Croatia.

storm. Some dinghy davits close to the seawall also were affected. Everything settled back down after a few minutes, and luckily no one got hurt, but the town got flooded. Later, in discussing this phenomenon with townspeople, they told us that a similar storm ten years ago had pulled all the water out of the bay, stranding the fish on the bottom, where they flopped around like crazy.

## Looking for Zorba!

The Greek Islands have enticed thousands of people over time who come, see, play, stay a while, and take home stories and memories. Greece, with its many islands, is strategically located in the Mediterranean. To go from west to east—Italy to Turkey, or south to north—Red Sea to Black Sea—you have your choice of places to explore. Most people focus on islands in the Aegean Sea, yet the Ionians offer interesting places, too.

There are two ways to reach Athens from Corfu: one is the Corinth Canal, which costs money to transit, and the other is longer and more scenic around the Peloponnese peninsula, with its three fingered fjords. We chose that one. Land trips included Olympia, where the first torch was lit; Sparta, where the fierce warriors lived and learned to fight (according to guidebooks only healthy children survived infancy, as sickly ones were thrown into the mountain ravines); and Mystras, an ancient place atop a mountain near Sparta. We anchored near castles

a lot—Corfu, Methoni, Monemvasia, and Navplio, the first capital.

From Athens, we stopped at nine islands while working our way to Turkey. Beautiful anchorages

Figure 16–8. Exploring an old fort next to Ormos Navarinou, Greece. Nice beach, but this cove is too exposed for us to anchor overnight.

awaited us at each, but getting to them sometimes involved going through some rough water. In Greece, the wild winds are called meltimis. They can come on strong and last quite a while. They can put you into port or keep you there and they are nothing to mess with since each island is not too close to another. Altogether we visited 22 islands, 17 in the Aegean and 5 in the Ionian. While the Aegean is famous for its meltimis; the Ionian has to cope with earthquakes. We narrowly missed one in Lefkas. Our friends who where anchored there described it as feeling like they were aground, but still moving and shaking around.

## A Taste of Turkey

Turkey is a wonderful cruising destination with fine marinas, protected harbors and anchorages, fantastic food markets, friendly people, and some spectacular historical sites. They also have excellent and reasonable marine repair facilities. They can do practically anything you might wish to accomplish at a fraction of the price elsewhere. We could write a whole book about our time in Turkey, which included two winters, along with lots of summer cruising. In this section, a few tidbits may whet your appetite.

Exotic Istanbul, a blend of modern and traditional, sits atop a bluff overlooking the Bosphorus Strait, an extremely busy waterway for shipping

**Figure 16–9.** Typical Black Sea port on the Northern Turkish coast. *Teka III* on the far left, anchored.

between the Black Sea and the Mediterranean. The Bosphorus also separates the European and Asian sides of the famous city. A tourist's five senses can be overwhelmed quite easily.

First, the ears. Beginning at dawn, the first call to prayer from a minaret, which floats across the air over the city, is followed by four more calls before the day is finished, after sunset. When the calls are sung by a man on the scene through a microphone, it has more impact than when a recorded version is played, but the result is the same—people stop for prayer. Men pray in the mosques or their shops; women pray at home. Then there is the Turkish language, melodic to listen to, but hard to speak. We tried to learn some words, as we did with all the other languages we encountered, but never took official lessons. Fortunately for us, the signs were often in English as well.

Eyes worked overtime to take in the beauty of such buildings as the Blue Mosque and Aya Sofya, monuments to the rich history of a Christian and Muslim country. Istanbul was originally called Constantinople. It is one of the most beautiful and historic cities in the world.

## Black Sea

With equal amounts of excitement and anxiety, we awaited the signal from Commodore Teoman Arsay's 63' ketch, *MAT*. At 10 a.m., July 3, 2004, Teo fired the cannon on board, announcing to us and to the world that our KAYRA journey around the Black Sea had begun.

KAYRA, known in Turkish as the Karadenzi Yat Rallisi, made a 2,042 nautical mile counterclockwise circumnavigation of the Black Sea. We were scheduled to stop at 34 ports along the coastlines of northern Turkey, Georgia, Russia, Ukraine, Romania, and Bulgaria during the next two months. The vessels flew flags representing the USA, Canada, Turkey, England, France, Germany, the Netherlands, Sweden, Israel, Antigua, and St. Vincent.

We lined up according to our number and headed around the corner and into the Bosphorus Strait. It's a 25-nautical-mile stretch of water that divides Istanbul's European side from its Asian side and drains the Black Sea into the Med via the

Sea of Marmara and the Dardanelles. It was packed with activity. There were large and small ferries crossing and re-crossing, privately owned vessels out for a Saturday spin, fishing boats, northbound or southbound commercial vessels, and the constant outgoing current from the Black Sea to deal with that day. A large number of sailboats, tacking back and forth between the two main bridges, narrowly missed each other and sometimes us.

The Black Sea was a wonderful experience, but would have been much more challenging calling on our own. Officials in some of the ports would have been particularly onerous without the help of a local representative to smooth out the process. Unless you speak Russian, communication is challenging since few people speak English. If I were going without a rally, I would visit Ukraine, Romania, and Bulgaria, skipping Russia and Georgia. The north coast of Turkey is friendly and easy to visit, but marinas are few. You may have to tie up to a commercial pier or anchor out.

**The Middle East**

We visited Cyprus, both North and South; Syria; Lebanon; and Israel on our own, with one other buddy boat. However, thinking back, we felt going by airplane rather than boat would be more comfortable and much easier. Most of the interesting places required travelling inland, so the boat had to be left at the port. Clearance procedures and navigation requirements in that unstable area meant long delays in clearing the boat and out-of-the-way routes between countries. You had to pay moorage in marinas or harbors and pay hotel bills while ashore. There was always a little uneasiness about leaving the boat in strange harbors. The following incident shows how unnerving travel in this area can be:

It took 25 hours to go by sea from Herzliya, Israel, to Larnaca, South Cyprus. All during the trip we heard the Israeli Navy calling vessels at this or that location. Our buddy boat, S/V Conestoga, headed to a different port than we did. We kept our two-hour report-in schedule until we thought we couldn't hear each other. Just before midnight, Bob's voice came loud and clear over the VHF radio with this message, "This is the *sailing* vessel Conestoga calling the vessel off my bow. What is your intention?" He did it more

**Figure 16–10.** Balaclava, Ukraine, once home to Soviet submarines.

than once. We waited and then contacted him ourselves. His report: A boat had shadowed him, speeding up when he did, slowing when he did, but never speaking to him. Finally, the other boat shone a spotlight on him and then left. Was it an Israeli gunboat? A fisherman? A pirate? Who knows? Bob's position was 80 nautical miles off the Lebanon/Israel border, so go figure.

# Patagonia, Cape Horn, and the Chilean Canals

Just the mention of Cape Horn sends shivers down the back of most voyagers. This area has the reputation of being one of the worst pieces of ocean to cruise. Why then do so many decide to cruise there? The area has pristine anchorages, huge glaciers, and snow-covered mountains. It has many of the same features of British Columbia and Alaska, but it is much more remote—you may not see another boat for weeks at a time. This is a place for the truly adventuresome cruisers who do not mind cold, windy weather and big seas. In this section, I provide some excerpts of firsthand accounts of motor boats that have recently passed that way: *Pelagic*, a 40′ DeFever Passagemaker; *Egret*, a 46′ Nordhavn; *Ice Dancer II*, a 57′ Nordhavn; and *Diesel Duck*, a 41′ Duck. The 75′ *Radiant Star*, a converted North Sea fishing vessel, had come this way in January 1995 on her way from Scotland to Seattle.

Figure 16–11. Cape Horn from the pilothouse of *Diesel Duck*. (Benno Klopfer)

Figure 16–12. Brazo Noroeste as seen from *Diesel Duck*. (Benno Klopfer)

**Weather.** Ken Murray on *Pelagic* describes the weather in the southern summer this way:

*At that time of year in the Southern Hemisphere, summer was just getting started. The mountains that rise on both hands still were covered with snow down to about 200 feet above sea level and the air was a brisk 50–60 degrees most of the time. When the sun was out, which wasn't often, it had an intensity seldom experienced in other parts of the world. It was easy to believe there was a hole in the ozone when the sun hit you. I could spend weeks trying to describe the weather in any 24-hour period. That particular summer was a nasty one. As Hal Roth shared in* Two Against the Horn, *the water was flying through the air much of the time. The description of Dick and Gail Barnes on* Ice Dancer II *adds another perspective: South polar fronts pass here every two to three days. High winds, clouds, and rain are the norm, not the exception. There are no swells to contend with, except when near ocean entrances and long fetches.*

**So why would you go there?** When the skies clear, the area is spectacularly beautiful with high mountains, glaciers, and other delights. *Ice Dancer's* owners describe the area like this:

*Monday's anchorage was another small basin, maybe 200 feet in diameter, with a narrow and shallow entrance. Without the cruising guides and scanning sonar, we would not attempt entry. Both of these, and last night's Caleta Burgoyne showed us landscapes that looked like professional gardeners had planted and trimmed. Among the mix were Bonsai-shaped trees, colorful, wild fuchsias, holly-like bushes, plants with trumpet-shaped orange flowers, and beautiful covering plants. What a nice surprise. On Tuesday afternoon, we experienced sunshine with blue skies, rain, hail, and gale-force winds. The highest peaks have fresh snow, along with last winter's accumulation and glaciers. Many hillsides are barren with only glacial-polished rock showing. It is all very interesting.*

**Shore-tie anchoring is required.** Finding anchorages with shallow enough water and swinging room is a real problem. Marlane Klopfer on *Diesel Duck* describes it like this:

*Some of the caletas where we stopped for the night offered excellent shelter from the prevailing winds. But in some places violent gusts were coming down the mountains and if there was little swinging room and rocks close by, we needed to bring out the two stern lines. First, we would set the anchor, and then launch the dinghy. I would get into the dinghy with oars. [There were so] many rocks close to shore and all the kelp which could easily foul the motor; only rowing was possible. Then I would attach one end of the floating line to which we had a carabiner hook fastened onto the dinghy and row ashore. Tied up the dinghy so it wouldn't drift off and climbed (usually over slippery rocks) onto shore and found a tree where I could fasten the line. Benno would then winch the line tight and tie it up on either the port or the starboard stern cleat and I rowed back to the boat to get the other line. Did the same thing again so that we now had one line to starboard and one to port in addition to the anchor. I know it sounds easy, but it's a lot of work and not so much fun when it rains or drizzles.*

Dick Barnes on *Ice Dancer II* describes the anchoring places like this: *We anchored last night in a small cove, dropped anchor and tied two stern lines ashore. It was just as well, there is a nasty front passing today, and we have sustained winds of 30 knots and gusts of 40. With this system, you don't swing at all, but it takes about a half hour to rig it up and take it down.*

**Problems with charts.** Like many other places, the electronic charts for this area are poor. *Ice Dancer's* owner puts it this way:

*My electronic Nobeltec charts for this region are off by 1.5 nm to the south and .6 nm to the east. All of the land masses are screwed up, but further north they are mixed, with some right on and others terrible. So, here I am running back and forth looking at small scale (poor detail) paper charts, drawings*

**Figure 16–13.** The 41' *Diesel Duck* stern tied in Patagonia. (Benno Klopfer)

*in guide books, the electronic version, and what the radar shows is really going on. In big canals it doesn't matter, but some areas are choked with pinnacles and ridges. I have the scanning sonar set at 400 feet out and 10 degrees down or about 60 feet. I just leave it on. It has saved our bacon more than once.*

**Figure 16–14.** Nordhavn 57, *Ice Dancer II*, anchored in Chile—this is certainly one good reason to go there! (Dick and Gail Barnes)

The Chilean Canals. Scott and Mary Flanders on *Egret* took particular delight in the vast network of canals. Here is Mary's description: *I can't see anyone not enjoying cruising the Chilean Canals! The scenery is spectacular and it is for the most part protected waters. It can be* *windy, but wave action is rarely over 3' at its worst because there is little fetch. I'm speaking about the main channel, the Beagle. There are plenty of fjords and anchorages to tuck into to get out of the wind if you find yourself in that position. Along the Beagle we are in communication by radio*

# Hanga Roa Bay, Easter Island, Chile
## Scott Flanders, the Voyage of *Egret*'s Log

Did we roll [at anchor] or what? Yup, buried the master head port light from time to time–[like being in a] glass-sided boat. Friday afternoon and night we were boat-bound in a rocking machine. Saturday morning was beautiful with a relatively slight swell. Fuel day. The catamaran is working hard to keep her place on the boat deck instead of being discarded after nearly sweeping us off the boat deck in rolly conditions while we were trying to launch her. We made five rental car trips to and from the gas station with eight jerry jugs, 56 gallons–more than 400 lbs of fuel per load. It took from 11:00 a.m. until nearly dark with a quick stop for a sandwich our only break . . . We had our fastest turnaround time on the second load when Frank and I got the pumping routine down to production levels; but gray hair kicked in on the third load and we slowed down a bit each time. So that was Saturday.

Sunday was different. With Advil working its magic, off we went in the rental car to explore the island. We took a clockwise route trying to catch the sun at its best angles for picture taking at the various places of interest. Easter Island is the REAL DEAL, *Egret*'s highest compliment. Everything you have read about since childhood and later is here and accessible. Moais (Easter Island head carvings) are everywhere. There are over 650 of these stone guys around the island taken from a single quarry. How they transported them is still a mystery. One of the most impressive sites was the quarry where there are still figures lying unfinished cut into the hillside as if it were a weekend break. No one knows for sure the early history of the island

but it is thought Polynesians arrived in two waves. The Moai have two distinct different types of configurations. The earliest were the "short ears" with a more rounded head and the latter group are the "long ears" and long faces. The latter group is by far the most prolific. On some of the figures there are similar designs on the back. Starting from the waist there are three horizontal curving lines representing a rainbow, a circle above–the sun, two large abstract birds facing each other–man and woman, a smaller bird above the birds–child, and two different images on either side of the child again representing male and female.

Returning from the day's outing in the catamaran dink [was an experience]. There were four of us, Ken the Single

hander, who was with us for the day and a full fuel tank in the little fat dink. There was a HUGE surf running into the harbor breaking ALL the way across instead of leaving us the 75' "hole" we normally scoot through. Grande surf; mucho scary surf–you get the picture. We waited until it went calm, then made our way out. After the point of no return the first wave popped up–flying catamaran; Ken taking his own ride. There were four more [waves]. The last was breaking (not good) and we blasted through in a ball of spray–wild! Scary! An inflatable would never have made it through. Perhaps a largish, 12-plus footer with just two people [could have, but] certainly not a heavy rib with seating. So perhaps we should rethink the main dink scenario.

**Figure 16–15.** Scott and Mary Flanders with Easter Island Moai. (Scott and Mary Flanders)

with the various coast guard stations, and sometimes while at anchor in a cove. However often the mountains block radio communication; in that case we e-mail the Chilean station at Puerto Williams our location each day. I feel good about this, as if Heaven forbid, an emergency should arise, the word would get out. We also have a satellite phone to use if necessary. When we cruised the "glacier loop" this winter, Scott and I did not see another boat. Of course, there are many more cruisers in the summer here, but we have gotten to know others who winter here and along with the locals it can be a social whirl if you are inclined.

## South Pacific Highlights

*From the Log of Selene 48, Furthur, and Brian Calvert*

### Hanamenu Bay, Hiva Oa, Marquesas

The bay is on the northwest side of the island out of the trade wind's swell. The bay looks like Yakima River Canyon, stark rock walls with ragged tops. At the end of the bay past the black sandy beach is a palm tree forest. We notice some signs of life as we ride the surf to the beach. A local man and two small boys come to welcome us and show us where the pools are. We are ecstatic to find a tropical pool of cool water surrounded by flowers and large ferns. The water is crystal clear spring water. We relish the cool soak, admiring the surroundings. On our way out, our new friend, Louie, gave us a large bag of fresh limes grown right there in the valley. We agree Louie has it made; he even has a couple of horses. Back on the boat we enjoy the evening with bright stars above and no other lights but ours. We will stay here another day or try one more anchorage on Hiva Oa before heading to Nuka Hiva.

We had an early morning visitor; our new friend, Louis, dropped by in his boat to give us a bunch of fresh fish. Again his generosity was amazing. We ventured through the surf to pay back the visit with goodies for his small boys. I went to his home where his family was merrily preparing fish for drying. Louis and I went for a walk through his "estate" where he told me—remember he speaks almost no English and I less French—that his whole family lived there and they live off his hunting and what he

grows. I do count Louis as one of the most fortunate men I have ever met.

We did the 8-mile trek across the top of the island to the next anchorage, Haiapa Bay. The cruising books describe this as the best anchorage on the north side of the island. Again the scenery is spellbinding and it appears there is more of a village ashore. I did a quick scuba dive under the boat to find white sand where we dropped the hook, with a beautiful coral reef not too far away. The joy of diving 40 feet in just swim trunks (86-degree water) is enough but the schools of tropical fish and the many coral types made this a wonderful dive.

We went ashore and walked into the village, where kids were jumping from a bridge into a stream. I took some mid-air pictures and showed them the results on my camera. What unfolded was far from expected. The village is a Garden of Eden with well-kept gardens, flowers, and fruit orchards. The paved road goes past the church and brought us to the "Yacht Club," a small shack occupied by an island character named William. He has been keeping record of all the cruising boats that stop by since 2004. I note that there were only two boats so far this year and about six last year—not exactly Roche Harbor! William bounced around his shack bringing us all kinds of treasures of fruit, bananas, grapefruit, some weird spiny thing, and coconuts. His generosity was amazing. We made arrangements to see him in the morning to return some gifts. The Copra boat comes here tomorrow and it will be interesting to watch the occasion.

### Ofalonga Island, Ha'apai, Tonga

Ending our stay in Ha'apai we checked out with the local officials, and headed to the northernmost island in the group, Ofalonga. En route we stopped three times to watch whales frolic under clear tropical skies.

This uninhabited island is guarded by a large coral reef forming an ideal lagoon all the way around the island. I dropped the hook in the southern end where the reef jets out providing good protection. After a bit we launched the dinghy and made our way through the easy to see pass to the whitest sand I have ever seen. I had noticed that the water temperature on boat depth sounder was up over 80, 5 degrees warmer than in Vavau—not what I expected. Then when

**Figure 16–16.** Selene 48, *Furthur,* in Tonga. (Brian Calvert)

I put my pinky in the water inside the lagoon, a large smile came over me. This was water more like the Tuamotos, warm, warm, warm. We snorkeled about the reef, seeing many fish and live coral, enjoying the freedom that isolation and warm water enable.

After a stint in the water we took a stroll around the beach. There was not a trace of human life; we made the only human footprints in the sand. We had this little piece of paradise to ourselves; this is what I had come for, the treat of a lifetime. As we made our way back to *Furthur* in the dink, I spotted a spout just past the boat. We zoomed out to find three humpback whales breaching and playing about. At one time they came right for the dink—yes, three 40-foot whales heading for us in a 11-foot boat, yikes! They dove under the boat and I popped on a mask and fins, and that was all—so I am the only one I know to "snorkel" with the whales. Wow something that had not even made the "bucket list," and had been checked off.

To top off the perfect day, the full moon rose in the east just as the huge sun set in the west. We dined under the full moon, which illuminated the white sand on the beach and sparkled on the water.

### Fiji: Adventures in the Yasawa Islands

Leaving the protections of the inner reef and the lee of the main island, the Yasawas are much windier and rugged. The west side has a perpetual westerly swell, and the east side [has] the perpetual howling wind—we go up the west side. Impending lack of light forces us to a small, albeit rolly, anchorage with 25 knots of wind cascading off the adjacent hill. There is a small resort in the bay, but we do not go ashore. We head north and take protection in the large bay on the north side of Naviti Island.

This is the home of the Sosomo Village, a primitive home to 250 villagers and a beautiful bay full of reefs. As per custom, we go ashore to pay our respects to the chief. This is a unique case as the chief is a woman so when we land the dinghy we are taken to the "Lady Chief" by her entourage. The elderly lady comes out and sits as we present her with our cava gift and a perfume sample provided by my good friends in Mexico. She accepts the gifts and welcomes us to her village. This ritual is essential to the culture in the Fiji villages; they own the surrounding water, land, reefs, and everything in them. The chief rules with absolute power and must be honored if you are to visit any of the villages. I think it is a great custom and [I] fully participate. Once accepted you are thoroughly welcome by these wonderful people. We are given a tour and meet the "mayor" who is the brother of the "Lady Chief"; we also meet Pastor Kali of the local Assembly of God Church. He is a well-educated fellow. He invites us to a Fijian feast the next night.

We spend the day kayaking, snorkeling, and exploring the shoreline. As darkness falls we take the dinghy ashore armed with ukulele and balloon kit to attend the feast. The balloon tying again is a huge hit and kids come out from every direction, bright dark eyes full of excitement. I must have made 50 dogs, rabbits, and horses for them and they all loved them. As we have seen before, the kids eagerly share and make sure the smallest ones get the balloons first. Their behavior is amazing and I am moved by the experience. The feast is a marvel, the food has been cooking underground all day, and the ladies bring the many dishes to the grass mats that have been prepared for us to eat on. There is no electricity here and the village is mostly dark, but they fire up a small generator and they proudly produce one small electric light. The food is incredible, much better than other local foods we have eaten in the South Pacific. We have tuna wrapped in leaves with coconut milk, a meat-stuffed pumpkin, marinated clams, boiled fish, and many other great dishes.

After dinner the cava is brought out and so is the guitar. The major and I play music as the cava is passed around. Even young Jess gets his first cava. I coached him before that if he takes it—and it will taste bad—that under no circumstances can he spit it out or show signs of how yucky it is. He slugs the cup back, smiles, and asks for more!

## Suwarrow, Cook Islands

*Christi Grab on Nordhavn 43, Kosmos*

One of the most special places we visited in the world was the island of Suwarrow, an atoll in Cook Islands that has been designated a wildlife preserve. Suwarrow is probably the most isolated place we visited on our journey, 150 nautical miles away from its nearest neighbor and 300 miles from a population center.

What makes Suwarrow special is that no ferries or planes go there; it can only be accessed by private boat. About 120 boats a year visit the atoll. The only inhabitants are the park ranger and his family [it is a national park].

The pass into the atoll can be tricky as it has a couple coral heads in it, but the water is clear so the hazards are visible in the daylight. Boats are only allowed to anchor near the ranger station and dinghy to shore near the ranger station. The anchorage is protected from the prevailing winds and calm. Because the environment is so fragile, cruisers are forbidden to go to any other part of the island unescorted. While we were there, the ranger took the boaters out daily to one part of the island or another.

The island is a breeding ground for several species of sea birds, including frigates, brown noddys, sooty sterns, tropicbirds, boobies, and petrels. Each time we visited another part

of the island, literally thousands of birds would be flying around us. Many wildlife species that are rapidly becoming endangered on other South Pacific islands, such as coconut crabs, thrive in Suwarrow, so there is more diversity of creatures than in most other places. The underwater life is even more enthralling. The water is warm and clear, with more than 100 feet of visibility. The fish are abundant and huge, the coral is brilliantly colored, and the variety of species is amazing.

Above all, we loved the sense of camaraderie amongst the cruisers. Because we were limited in where we could go and when, all the cruisers were usually in the same general vicinity, making interaction especially easy. We bonded on our trips around the island. When back at the anchorage, the area on shore we were allowed to roam freely had a lovely white sand beach covered with coconut trees that provided shade from the hot tropical sun. The constant wind kept us cool and bug free. It was a location that lent itself to socializing and the ranger encouraged it. We had potlucks every other night. The ranger's wife would bring traditional local foods for us to try and the ranger would crack open green coconuts for everyone to drink. We'd stay up late into the night.

Figure 16–17. Suwarrow, Cook Islands. (Christi and Eric Grab)

# Indonesia: A Delightful Surprise

*Christi Grab on* Kosmos

When we planned our route, Indonesia was an unavoidable part of it. Many people expressed concern about us going there; didn't we know it was filled with pirates and American-hating Muslim extremists who would blow us up? Indonesia turned out to be one of our favorite countries, bearing little resemblance to the Western world's perception of it. Indonesians in general are kind, welcoming, and quick to flash a smile. With over 17,000 islands, the diversity is incredible, with both landscape and cultures. We only stopped at five islands and wished we could have visited more.

On Timor, we explored the city of Kupang, where every child we saw came up and talked to us. We also took a tour up to the mountains, where we went to several villages that still live in traditional grass hut houses, without running water and electricity, just as their forefathers had.

On Flores, we visited the Crater Lakes at the Kelimutu volcano, a natural wonder that is a sacred site to the locals. The three lakes are each a different color; what is amazing is the lakes each change color over time as the mineral content changes. In the city of Ende, the locals were so fawning that we felt like rock stars. At least a dozen teens approached us to practice their English.

On Rincha, part of the Komodo National Park, we saw Komodo Dragons in the wild and went scuba diving at what turned out to be our favorite spot in the entire world.

On Karimata, the locals greeted us with gifts of fresh fish and calamari and were eager to talk to us. We found that in areas that don't see many tourists, the locals were thrilled to have us. They went out of their way to make us feel welcome and safe. To be honest, we probably would not have enjoyed these four destinations as much if were we not on our own boat. Getting from island to island would have been problematic. Several tourists told us horror stories about the local ferry system, with rickety boats and unsanitary conditions. All four areas were relatively poor; the hotels and bathrooms were not up to our standards. Finally, because we had our own kitchen, we never had to eat food that was questionable, and when we craved western "comfort" foods, we could make it for ourselves.

# Papua New Guinea: Going Back in Time

*Maurice and Louise-Ann Nunas on* Akama

Experiencing other cultures was fascinating. The remote Hermit and Ninigo Islands off the northeast cost of Papua New Guinea were prime examples. The people there intentionally live a primitive existence without any infrastructure. Simple gardens and fishing provide nourishment. Their only source of currency is from collecting sea cucumbers that they dry in the sun. There is no running water, sewage, electricity, or shops. They move about the atoll between the small islands in dugout canoes with sails made from bits of bed sheets, bags, and old poly tarps. Cruisers don't go there; they should. The people were truly interested in us, as we were in them. Our experience here was to be repeated over and over. Perhaps our favorite memory was when we went inland in

**Figure 16–18.** *Kosmos* anchored in Rincha, Indonesia. (Christi and Eric Grab)

Figure 16–19. Krogen 48', *Akama,* in Papua New Guinea. (Maurice and Louise-Ann Nunas)

Borneo to the village of the Ikan people. There we were treated as honored guests, with numerous toasts of their local home brew. At one point a newborn baby was passed around and each of us was asked to bless her. Only a few generations ago these people were the famous "headhunters of Borneo."

## Madagascar and Mozambique: High-Risk Destinations

*Heidi and Wolfgang Hass on Nordhavn 46, Kanaloa*

*Heidi and Wolfgang Hass have completed two circumnavigations on Kanaloa. They have many favorite places, including Fiji, New Caledonia, and Vanuatu. However, for them nothing beats Africa, so in spite of the piracy warning, I am including their comments about these destinations. Perhaps in the future, it will be safe to return.*

Madagascar is one of the best kept cruising secrets. Here you find cruising the way it was 30 years ago in the Caribbean and the South Pacific. Unfortunately with the Seychelles off limits due to piracy activity at the moment, it is a bit hard to reach. Cruising near Mayotte and Tanzania became a huge problem lately, since criminals copy the pirates from Somalia.

They have not kidnapped cruising folks yet, but have boarded boats and demanded money. The border between Mozambique and Tanzania has been a hotspot for years. However, the risk to visit Madagascar is well worth it, [although] a slightly different route has to be considered.

Figure 16–20. Simple local fishing boat in Madagascar. (Heidi and Wolfgang Hass)

# *Idlewild's* Unusual Circumnavigation 2005–2006

Canadian Ben Gray constructed *Idlewild*, a George Buehler–designed 57' long, slim (11'), shallow draft (3'6"), trawler powered by only 55 hp. He built the boat out of aluminum and proceeded from his ranch in Alberta, 2,000 miles down the river systems of Canada that involved portages, groundings, and other difficulties. On reaching the Arctic Ocean, he turned west past Alaska to 15 miles south of the Bering Strait, and then turned back toward the East through the Northwest Passage and then headed south in the Atlantic toward South Africa. From East London, South Africa, to Freemantle, Australia, he made one of the longest passages by any yacht of this size, under power: 4,499 miles in 29-1/2 days. He used 977 U.S. gallons (3,700 liters) for this passage. Total mileage for the circumnavigation was 26,827 nm in 329 days, of which 202 were at sea. (See endnotes.)

**Figure 16–21.** *Idlewild* in Russian waters, 2006. This is one of the most unusual circumnavigations under power. It began with a 2,000 mile trip up the rivers of Canada to the Arctic. Paravanes were installed in Australia. The first half of the trip was done without stabilization. (Ben Gray)

When we first visited Madagascar and Mozambique both countries [had severe economic problems]. It was a disaster and we have never seen people so poor and in [such] desperate need for some clothes and food. This [has] all changed for the better, and it is a delight to cruise the calm waters along the western side of the island. Supplies are more plentiful, Visa credit cards are accepted, and people couldn't be happier to make some money showing you the beauty of this country; and beautiful it is. Some locals [warn of potential trouble for] yachts that are left near Nosy Be, but so far no one has reported any trouble.

The people of Mozambique have always been kind to us and we can only report the best. The last time we visited the beautiful diving island of Bazarutto, people had just gone through their first cyclone ever. It destroyed every dive resort, not to mention the small huts of the local people. When we left for South Africa, we had only two pair of shorts each and two dull knives, left from the items we

donated to help out. It cost us a bundle to replace all the towels, parts, cutlery, and so on, but these people are worth it a hundred times.

Only a small number of cruising areas have been covered here. Many more great areas are available to the long-range voyager. The whole Caribbean offers numerous, relatively close-to-home opportunities, as do the Canadian Maritime provinces. Northern Europe, including Scandinavia, has been rewarding to those who have gone there for the limited cruising season. The Philippine Islands are rated highly by many who have cruised there. In short, a study of nautical magazines, books, and cruising guides will give you even more options. Round the world voyaging has become much more difficult due to piracy in the Indian Ocean. Voyagers who want to circumnavigate must go around the Cape of Good Hope. For those with enough resources, Dockwise and other marine shipping services offer another option for bypassing the more dangerous areas.

# CHAPTER SEVENTEEN

# Maintenance, Repairs, and Haulouts In Far-Away Places

Passagemakers consist of many complex and interacting systems: some mechanical, some electrical, and others electronic. With such a plethora of failure possibilities, we can be sure that something will happen over time. Ideally, we would ensure that all our systems are 100 percent reliable before leaving port, but this is an impossible dream. Systems will fail and things will burst, break, or leak.

**Figure 17–1.** The author changes a steaming light midocean.

Our objective is to foresee as much as possible and learn how to deal with the inevitable problems.

As an example of how things can go wrong in spite of extensive preparation, I am including Braun Jones' story about what went wrong during his passage from Seattle to Tokyo, while participating in the Great Siberian Sushi Run (GSSR).

What do we observe from the accompanying *Grey Pearl* account? First, there is a wide variety of things that can go wrong. In this case, few related to the main engine; however, malfunctioning heads can be almost as bad as a malfunctioning engine. They had a fine array of spares, and most of the problems were fixed by replacing the defective parts or units. However, they apparently overlooked the hot water heater thermostats, resulting in an unhappy crew in that far-north, frigid area. The preventive care taken before the trip was a source of some of their problems. Improperly installed gaskets, seals, and other items resulted in some premature failures. This is why I like the do-it-yourself approach. It does not mean you will do a perfect job, but at least you will take great care to get it right . . . and you are not under the time crunch that yard personnel face. Finally, the right tools are essential to make repairs and work around problems.

We have made two Atlantic crossings with almost no maintenance issues. Our first crossing from Florida to Lisbon had only one problem—a paravane system that I had recently installed using blocks to route the lines from the deck to the

# The Rest of the Story

**Braun Jones, *Grey Pearl,* Nordhavn 62**

As can be expected on a long voyage, there will be equipment failures. The weather, saltwater environment, motion of the boat, and constant use of systems combine to produce significant stress resulting in malfunctions. The GSSR voyage from Seattle to Japan was no different. Each of the participating boats experienced its share of failures. Here is a list of some failures and resulting repairs on the boats that are representative of the variety of things that can go wrong. Should a similar failure occur on your boat, this list may help you with the diagnosis and repair.

**Preventive Care.** To minimize problems underway and considering the length and remoteness of the voyage, a comprehensive pre-departure inspection plan was developed. This included inspecting, maintaining, or replacing every system, engine, hose, connection, control, etc., on the boat. Thus, extensive work was performed by the owner and specialized contractors. The work was checked upon completion and then tested during sea trials, which resulted in the typical discovery of installation and parts problems. These were then resolved. Regardless of this careful checking and problem resolution, some failures choose not to appear until the voyage was well underway, in some of the remotest of areas—"Murphy's Law."

The underway failures were of two types: (1) "worked on" systems; those worked on before departure and believed to be correctly installed or repaired; and (2) other; those that occurred just because *it's a boat getting heavy use.* The following list describes both types of failures and elaborates on what went wrong with the "worked on" systems to provide a "how not to do it." The list is organized by symptom, problem, and problem resolution.

1. While at sea, with the stabilizers activated, there was a loud banging and pulsating noise in the port Naiad actuator. Sleep was interrupted in the captain's state room—a big problem. Diagnosed and replaced failed port Naiad potentiometer [part of the active fin stabilization system]. According to

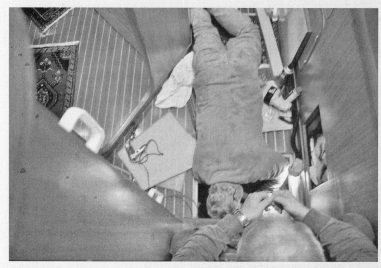

**Figure 17–2.** Repairing the stabilizer actuator. Things always seem to break in inaccessible places. (Braun Jones)

Naiad, these are wearable parts in the Naiad system. Both port and starboard potentiometers were replaced two years ago.

2. No hot water in remote Alaska for 7 days. Dinghying to other GSSR boats for occasional showers. Met by them with clothespins on their noses. Recently installed a new hot water heater and the thermostat failed due to water intrusion. Leaking overhead water hose allowed fresh water to run down a power wire to thermostat junction box because of *no drip loop* in power wire. Replaced burned up thermostat after eventually arriving in port and receiving an air shipped part. Correctly installed drip loop in wiring, and added a spare thermostat to parts locker.

3. Hot water level lower than usage would indicate. Repair leak from a hot water tank fitting that was improperly installed. This is a Whale hose plastic to brass adapter fitting that has an O-ring in it and is to be *hand tightened only.* It was on very tightly and may have been improperly wrench tightened, which split the O-ring causing a leak. Replaced O-ring and hand tightened fitting.

4. Shower water collecting to bather's ankles. Shower pan won't empty. Rebuild and replace failed shower sump pump.

5. Band-aids and medicines wet; medicine chest cabinet soaked with salt water after a particularly rough 3-day run. Repair leak around deck inlet for fresh water by removing the fitting, bedding it, and reinstalling.

6. The 20 kw generator leaking salt water. Found a torn rubber cap connected to one end of the heat exchanger. Replaced the caps *at both ends.* Before departure, the heat exchanger had been removed for cleaning and it appeared the installer may have used a sharp tool to refit the rubber end cap over the engine block receiving flange. This improper technique could have caused the rip in the rubber cap, which eventually leaked at a remote Aleutian island. If one end was done improperly and leaked, could the other end be far behind? Replaced them both.

7. Various small plastic mystery pieces on engine room floor. Repaired broken main air filter [Walker] Airsep gauge. No apparent reason for failure.

8. More fog in two showers than outside in the constantly foggy Aleutians. Replaced two failed head exhaust fans. Seawater had intruded into fans via deck exhaust clam covers due to heavy seas constantly washing over deck and sloshing up into the clam covers, through a mesh grate and into fan ducts. New predeparture procedure is to plug up vents with Nerf [foam] balls to seal out heavy seas.

9. Black water tank full and won't empty. Heads unusable. Although chilly, the men are using stern bustle for overboard platform, but the women are upset—they demanded action and boycotted the galley. Diagnosed, located, and repaired a fine crack in the Sealand waste discharge hose, which admitted air into the line, but was not big enough for waste to leak out of crack to reveal it, making it difficult to locate the leak. This proved "Techamediae's law" that air is finer than waste. Part of the diagnosis involved a novel approach fashioned by the crew to back flush a suspected clogged hose with pressure water. When pressure water was applied, a fitting blew off, dousing the captain with waste water. After intense questioning by the captain, the crew "discovered" a check valve installed backward, causing the back flush. Crew claimed no prior knowledge. Captain suspicious. All ended well since the heads were working again, the women were happy, and chow resumes.

10. Starboard Naiad fin locked up at sea. Couldn't move it with a crowbar. Diagnosed and repaired waterlogged Naiad actuator junction box wiring. The water ran into the box due to excessive condensation caused by external cold seawater on the warmer interior of the hull. The resulting short locked the actuator in a fully extended position. Relocated and sealed the box to prevent recurrence. Vowed to get out of cold Aleutian water ASAP.

11. Early one departure morning when raising the anchor off the remote Aleutian island of Kiska, the hydraulic windlass quit. Investigation revealed a ruptured hydraulic hose that drained all fluid. Decided to repair the hose at the next anchorage. Retrieving the anchor requires the use of a bar to manually raise the 300 lb. plough anchor and 200 feet of chain (approximately 3 lb./ft.). The weenie bar furnished by Maxwell Windlass Company is wholly inadequate in these circumstances. On the *Pearl* we have a 6-foot long, 2-inch thick "cheater bar" specifically made for this purpose. After the unscheduled exercise and with the anchor raised, we sail on to Adak Island. On arrival we were instructed by a native Aleut Indian to raft to an old WW II Navy tug in 25 knots of crosswind. Windlass and bow thruster shared a hydraulic system. With no hydraulics, there was no bow thruster to maneuver alongside the tug. Expected a hard docking, and rigged extra fenders. On final approach, well-trained crew did an excellent job getting crash fenders dynamically positioned, all of which were squished flat on impact (the fenders).

Repair began on a split high pressure hydraulic hose, caused by 10 years of chaffing on a sharp piece of original factory molded fiberglass. The rupture and high pressure quickly sprayed and dumped 7 gallons of fluid throughout the inverter bilge. Hydraulic hose repair in remote locations is particularly difficult because the fittings are properly pressed on in a machine shop, using appropriate presses and the right equipment. The *Pearl* carried hose in the diameters of all installed hose, in assorted lengths, and with attached fittings. However, in this instance it was not possible to run a length of spare hose. A splice had to be made, which requires a connector fitting to be installed into the hose. A helpful mechanic at Adak airport volunteered to use a surplus Navy press to help us out by attaching the fitting. Using questionable technique, he pressed on the fitting to a new piece of hose. When this splice hose was attached on the boat and the hydraulic system powered up, the fitting promptly blew out, with the same nasty results (dumping 7 more gallons of oil) as the original failure. Not trusting the airport volunteer a second time, we "field fit" a high pressure connector from the Pearl's spares. This is a two-man job with big wrenches and lots of muscle. This worked, restoring the use of the windlass and bow thruster. Side note—decided to get this hose repair redone at the first shipyard that the *Pearl* visited that had the proper equipment to do an "as new" job. This turned out to be at the Nordhavn factory in Taiwan. After a thorough inspection by the Nordhavn hydraulic experts they pronounced the field fitting as good as new and advised letting it be.

12. Forward bilge taking on water. Diagnosed that Whale manual emergency diaphragm discharge pump is siphoning seawater due to heavy seas and filling the bilge. Shut seacock.

13. Forward bilge filling with more water when bilge pump is running. Bilge pump leaking at its diaphragm. Installed new bilge pump. Rebuilt old one for spare.

14. Crank case vapor breather filter hose on main engine split, oozing oil. Replaced.

15. Excessive water in forward engine room bilge. Visible flow down the bilge bulkhead. Water was hot and tasted fresh. Traced leak to a Whale hot water hose that blew out at a "T." Replaced junction. Lowered thermostat temperature of hot water tank. The maximum that the Whale fittings can withstand is 150 degrees. Any greater temperature causes tubing and fitting failure.

16. Naiad hydraulic fluid reservoir tank temperature 15 degrees too warm, as noted by shooting with a temperature gun. The tank is one of the temperature spots regularly shot during routine underway inspections. The auxiliary cooling of the Naiad fluid is by a "continuous duty" Jabsco Water Puppy pump that is prone to failure (i.e., not continuous duty). The pump ingests seawater, and in Alaskan waters pump heads should be cool to touch and sweating from condensation. Pump head was warm and dry. Replaced pump. Tank temperature returned to normal. Old pump is swimming with the fishes.

17. Furuno NavNet radar fails to show targets (ships or land). But array is

*(continued)*

revolving, sweep is apparent on monitor, and AIS targets appear. Disconnected all leads at both NavNet black box and monitor and at antenna array. Inspected for loose wires, poor connections, etc. carefully and tightly reconnected. Nothing obvious found, but the Furuno manual "troubleshooting" in several sections directs this procedure, so believe this fault has happened before. Radar works after reconnections.

**The People.** Diagnosis and fixing these problems was made possible by the extraordinary efforts of captains Wayne Davis and Kell Achenbach, both highly experienced yachtsmen, who crewed on the *Pearl* during the GSSR—spending over 9 weeks voyaging through the Aleutians, to Russia and Japan. Wayne and Kell have years of experience on their own boats and crossing oceans. They have seen it all and when these issues occurred, many at the wrong time of night and in remote places, it was business as usual. They are real pros.

And when the three guys were consumed with the problem du jour, who ran the boat? That would be Pat Davis and Tina Jones. Both of these women are highly experienced, having also crossed oceans in their own boats. They both performed more than their share of the boat's chores, watchstanding, and general deck work. Together with Wayne and Kell, what an outstanding team to have on board when something goes wrong!

So there is the rest of the story, all in all not so bad. There were other failures but this is a reasonable sampling of what can be expected on an extended voyage. The key as in most things in this life is the right people to deal with the situations. Hopefully, in a small way, this review of problems proves helpful with similar issues you may have.

**Figure 17–3.** *Grey Pearl* in Pybus Bay, Alaska, on the Great Siberian Sushi Run. (Braun Jones)

paravanes broke. It turns out I had underestimated the forces on the system in rough seas. We recovered the broken system and ran on one paravane for the rest of the way to Bermuda. Since then, we use fixed paravane lines on ocean crossings so as not to stress the blocks and winches. Crossing from Spain to Antigua, we had only two minor problems. The autopilot rudder position sensor cable broke and I had to replace it with heavy-duty leader wire. It had failed due to metal fatigue. The fix was easy and caused only a minor inconvenience. The other item is displayed in the opening photo—replacing the mast steaming light. It was no problem with our built-in mast steps. We try to fix things in port, and our strategy has worked well; our passages have been almost trouble free. We have aimed to install relatively simple, reliable, well-maintained systems and components. In this chapter, we examine what spares to take and how to manage them; which tools you need; what manuals and technical information are required; troubleshooting; getting help; plus hauling out and storage issues. Appendix D provides Milt Baker's list of recommended spares for Atlantic-crossing boats.

## What Spares Should I Take?

### How Would a Failure Affect the Safety of the Voyage?

Perhaps the number one criterion for spares choice is this: how will it affect the voyage in terms of its safety and success? Comfort is secondary. If your main engine fails, you are in for big trouble, even if you have a come-home system. If your watermaker fails, you can ration water until you can either get more water or repair it. If your anchor windlass fails, you may be unable to anchor or to free your anchor and leave. In many places there are no marinas for refuge; thus, you would have to be lucky to find someone to raft up to—a situation that could become dangerous. If your air conditioning fails in the tropics, open the windows and break out the fans—it is merely uncomfortable. Alternators are absolutely essential to power the numerous electrical and electronic devices on our boats. Who would go to sea without a spare?

You have to develop your own spares approach based on type of voyaging, the remoteness of locations, your vessel's complexity and condition, your budget, availability of fly-in replacements, the required tools, and your ability to make repairs. Phil Eslinger writes about his experiences with spares in the South Pacific and how his philosophy changed as a result:

*Polynesia was a true eye opener for the crew of* Flat Earth *[Nordhavn N50]. We had put some miles on her, but never had much go wrong. On the way down to Tahiti, a passage of about 2,400 nm, we had a whole series of pumps fail; some we had spare parts for and some we didn't. We ended up cruising the last 1,200 nm without stabilizers or air conditioning and only limited use of the generator. Why did these parts fail? Heat? It was just their time? Getting replacements was a nightmare . . . Once you leave the confines of civilization, you have to learn to be self sufficient. And boy, did we learn. "Overnighted" parts from the US took three weeks to get there. Then they would be the wrong part (three more weeks) or we'd need another one to complete the repair (three more weeks).*

*In the middle of all this, Scott and Mary Flanders pulled into our anchorage aboard* Egret *[Nordhavn 46].* Egret *had crossed the Atlantic with the NAR, spent a couple of years in the Med, crossed the Atlantic again, down the east coast of South America, around Cape Horn, up the west coast of South*

*America, across to the Galapagos, and then to French Polynesia. Scott had the same generator we did and helped us fix the freshwater pump. We helped him mount his spare inverter. I learned from Scott how ignorant I had really been. Scott had spare parts for EVERYTHING. He had a spare pump and a rebuild kit for EVERY single pump he had on board. There wasn't an inch of wiggle room down in his engine room because of spare parts. Scott even had a spare anchor chain snaked around below his engine in the oil drip pan. I can't imagine how much over gross* Egret *must be. It is the essence of self sufficiency.* Egret *was a huge epiphany for me about how woefully ill-prepared I was. It will take a couple of years to get* Flat Earth *to the level of preparation that Scott had* Egret *right now.*

### What is the Probability of Failure?

A second issue is the probability of failure. To my knowledge, no passagemaker carries extra valves and pistons because of the low probability of needing them. Failure of these items is rare. However, raw water pumps are failure prone, and spares must be carried. So how do you figure out rates of failure? Manufacturers often make lists of parts they recommend for various voyages, such as inshore and offshore. Studying the

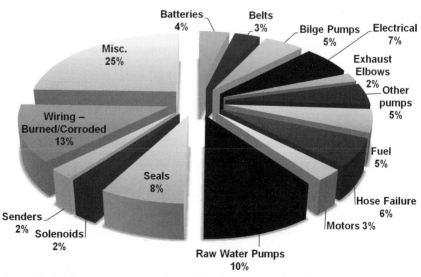

Figure 17–4. Failure rates on marine items. (Wheelhouse Technologies)

experience of other cruisers with similar boats can give excellent insights. What failed on their boat is likely to fail on yours. You can also work with companies, such as Wheelhouse Technologies (often seen at Trawler Fest), to build specific spares packages for your boat. They work through the manufacturers to determine failure rates, inventories, troubleshooting, and documentation. They even pack and label the spares and provide computerized listings of the contents.

## Types of Spares

Generally spares can be divided into those required for service or routine maintenance—they are expected to be replaced during the voyage. Next come parts assemblies or parts kits for items that could require repair. Finally, the generic items needed to improvise and complete repairs. Spares can also be installed as redundant items or systems, such as dual GPS units or autopilots.

**Service spares.** These include fuel filters, oil filters, oil, hydraulic fluid, coolant, belts, impellers, engine hoses, water filters, and zincs. Always carry plenty of these spares. Fuel filters are especially important because you never know when you will get some bad fuel. I carry at least 12 Racor filters and 6 secondary filters. While we have never received a really bad fuel load, you never know when disaster will hit. For example, when our boat was new, the previous owners took on a full fuel load in Puerto Rico and headed for the Azores. Before long, they discovered filters clogging very rapidly. They only had 3 or 4 spare filters on board, so they resorted to cleaning the dirty filters in kerosene (used for heating) and reinstalling them. They made it to the Azores, but it was a stressful voyage with lots of dirty work cleaning filters.

Another key item is a full supply of belts with at least two backups for each one. Loss of drive belts for alternators or other key components can have disastrous results. In addition, if a belt breaks, it is often due to misalignment rather than wear and tear. When installing a new one, carefully check the alignment pulleys and adjust them as needed. A spare engine oil tank is really handy on a passagemaker. Finding oil is easy, but getting the correct grade and specifications is more challenging. Some parts of the world carry only basic engine oils in single grades. If you use hydraulics, be sure to have enough extra oil to refill the system in the event of a major leak or burst hose.

**Parts and parts kits.** Here is where you rely on experience, common sense, and manufacturer's recommendations. Essential spares include a full alternator, starter, fuel lift pump, coolant pump, heat exchanger, and raw water pump. An exhaust elbow is also essential for all wet exhaust designs. Other items to include are any solenoids, such as one for fuel. What about just using parts kits? I carry both an assembly and a repair parts kit. If a failure happens in port, for say an alternator, you can take the spare parts to the repair facility to make sure they install the correct ones. At sea, I have had little success with using repair kits for water pumps. It seems there is always something wrong with the pump that prevents its proper operation. I now carry several water pumps for my Westerbeke auxiliary engine. When one fails, I install a new one.

Of course, many systems can fail during a long voyage as we saw in the opening story. You will need spares for bilge pumps, toilets, fresh water pumps, watermakers, refrigerators, and shower sumps. The more complex your boat and systems, the more spares you need. I recommend carrying as many complete assemblies as you can afford. It is always easier to pull out the old unit and drop in a new one than to try to complete complex repairs at sea. Don't forget the rigging cables, which can develop fatigue and fail. Some spare cables and clamps can solve this failure if it happens.

**Generic spares and repair products.** As far as I am concerned, you can never have too many generic spares, such as sealants, glues, special oils, greases, hoses, threaded steel rods, stainless steel bolts, nuts and screws, aluminum and bronze plates, WD-40, dielectric grease, lacquer thinner, alcohol, paint thinner, acetone, duct tape, electrical tape, masking tape, gasket materials, fiberglass repair kit, antiseize compound, Teflon tape and paste, electrical wire, fuses, switches, various PVC pipes, fittings, valves, and cement. The list goes on and on. The idea here is not only to facilitate installation of parts kits, but to provide the raw materials to construct work-around solutions when no part is available or a failure has happened without the correct spare.

Two products used to repair metal, including tanks, deserve special mention. If you need to repair stainless steel, Devcon/Permatex makes stainless steel putty that bonds ferrous and nonferrous metals and does not rust. J-B Weld is a metal-mending product used for filling small cracks. It has little structural strength and must cure for about 72 hours. Experts recommend mixing it warm, since it does not mix well at cooler temperatures.

**Installed spares.** When feasible, spares can be installed so that in the event of failure, you just switch to the other identical and redundant system. This adds a lot to the boat's complexity and cost, but makes dealing with failure much easier. We have redundant GPS units—two in the pilothouse (both hooked up to the autopilot) and one in our aft-cabin stateroom for anchor watch. We also have two radars, which not only provide redundancy, but allow us to view near and far targets at the same time. Likewise, we have two VHF units in the pilothouse. We also have backups for every bilge pump—a much larger pump is mounted about 6 inches above the normal pump to provide backup and to provide more capacity in the event of water intrusion. Our water system has a backup 12-volt pump built into the system—either pump will work when needed. Many passagemakers elect dual autopilots since this equipment is so important for long-range voyages.

**Managing your spares.** There is a continuum of effort in spares management. On the one hand, you can pay Wheelhouse Technologies, or similar companies, to build the list of spares, buy them, provide documentation and manuals, and pack them in sealed plastic and waterproof boxes. On the other hand, you can do all the research yourself, order the parts, check them when they arrive (some would recommend that you actually install the spares and put the old units aside as backups—that way you know how to install them and you know both units will fit and work), package them, inventory them, and store them. In other words, the latter method offers more insight into what you have and how to use them, but it involves tremendous time and effort.

## What Tools Do I Need?

Selecting tools depends on how skilled you are at using them, how much space you have to store them, and the specialized requirements of your boat. Even if you are not particularly skilled with tools, you may find that tools will be needed by a mechanic to complete repairs—having the right ones on board can save time and money. Many tools are generic and can be used for all onboard repairs, such as socket sets and wrenches, Vise-Grip pliers, pipe wrenches, C-clamps, and assorted Crescent wrenches. Be sure your tools include wrenches that are large enough to fit the needs of your boat, often larger than one inch. In addition, you may have to carry both metric and SAE tools. Include various-sized pry bars and steel pipes.

### Don't Leave Without These Tools

In addition to the normal tools indicated previously, there are some you will find invaluable during your voyage. A Dremel set is handy for cutting off screws, finishing metal repairs, getting in tight places, and numerous other uses. I would be sure to have a portable electric drill and two sizes of electric-powered drills, including a 1/2-inch chuck drill for heavy jobs. (Include a couple of complete drill-bit sets.) A Sawzall comes in handy for many jobs, including cutting metal parts. A circular saw can be used for cutting plywood for repairs, or it can be fitted with a metal-cutting blade for sawing through chain. A heat gun is absolutely essential for installing or removing hoses on tight-fitting barbs. A gear puller may be needed to remove some reluctant assembly. A come-along is a cable winch with a ratchet handle used to move heavy things, like batteries, when needed.

A set of various-sized wooden or plastic plugs is a must for temporarily closing leaks in hoses. Every seacock should have a plug of the appropriate size attached to the seacock for emergency repairs. Also be sure to have numerous and varied steel and brass caps and plugs to fill any hose end or opening in the engine or hydraulic system.

Install a vise somewhere on the boat. There are innumerable times when a vise is needed to free some marine part. Captain Beebe recommended a portable workbench for the aft deck, complete with a vise. We built such a workstation with vise on *Teka III* and have found it helpful on a number of occasions.

Diving gear and tanks are essential in case of propeller or anchor fouling. Hooka diving gear, discussed earlier, is great for dealing with problems with the boat's running gear. This system uses an onboard air supply and an umbilical hose to supply the regulator of the diver. Of course, either type of diving approach requires training and certification for safety.

A digital camera, capable of close-ups, is great for photographing parts before and during disassembly. It is much easier to get things back together if you have pictures.

### Take These Instruments Along

**Voltmeter.** Perhaps the most essential diagnostic instrument is a voltmeter. I carry both a digital voltmeter and an analog one. I find the analog one is easier to read when doing quick voltage checks and resistance checks. The digital provides precise results when accuracy is important.

**Temperature sensors.** Infrared thermometers with laser dot sighting are useful for finding developing problems before they become critical (see the sidebar, "Taking Your Boat's Temperature"). These sensors determine accurate temperatures from several inches away by using infrared sensors. They are usually combined with a laser sighting to show where the center of the sensor is pointed. The idea is to take routine measurements of the boat's mechanical systems to determine if there is a pending problem, as indicated by overheating. Many voyagers make dots on their engines to indicate the proper sighting place so that readings will be consistent over time. If you have a worksheet, the data can be entered and reviewed for changes. I take these temperatures daily when on passage.

Here is how Wayne Beardsley on *Long Legged Lady*, a Grand Banks 49, describes using his temperature sensor:

*One of the things that I've done for increased peace of mind is to acquire an infrared digital heat sensor. The IR sensor allows me to measure the*

## Taking Your Boat's Temperature

When taking readings of your boat's temperatures, here are some parameters that may help identify problems (temperatures should be taken on metal, not rubber; take temperatures at full load rated speed or maximum throttle):

- *Intake water at strainer to output from heat exchanger:* 10–20°F difference.
- *Stuffing box:* No more than 30°F higher than seawater temperature.
- *Exhaust elbow at hose:* Maximum of 150°F.
- *Heat exchanger or keel cooler inlet and outlet:* Small temperature change (10°F), not exchanging heat well (insulated); large temperature change (25°F), slow flow—exchanger becoming clogged.
- *Engine room temperature:* 30°F over ambient temperature; 130°F maximum.

*temperature of anything that you point at, from up to several feet away. This is enormously useful for measuring the temperature of different engine components that normally are not equipped with instrumentation: alternators, stuffing boxes, heat exchanger inlet and outlet temperatures, oil coolers, etc. They can also be used to measure exhaust manifold temperature cylinder-by-cylinder for those boats not equipped with exhaust pyrometers. I've taken baseline readings of all these components under normal operating conditions, logged the readings, and in some instances have written the baseline temperature on the component with a marking pen. I bring the IR sensor with me during my normal engine room checks and take a quick reading of all the key systems.*

**Voltage detector.** Another useful instrument is an AC voltage detector, such as the one shown in Figure 17-5. With this simple sensor, the hot AC wire is identified by merely touching the wire or outlet. Let's say you plug into shore power, but get no voltage in your boat. With the AC sensor, you start at the dockside: is there power coming out of the shore power? If not, perhaps there is a circuit breaker in the off position. If it is on, you proceed to your cord: is there power in the cord?

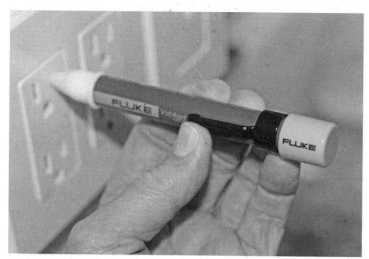

**Figure 17–5.** The Fluke VoltAlert voltage detector glows when AC voltage is sensed, even through insulation.

*cut away ropes or cables, or whatever might be fouling the prop or running gear. I am also bringing an underwater camera so I can photograph a problem under the boat, if I might need some time to find a solution.*

## What Technical References Are Required?

Complete shop manuals and parts lists on all onboard equipment are essential. These are best obtained before you leave, although it may be possible to download them from the Internet or manufacturer if you have that capability. If you study these manuals before departure you may find special tools or parts kits are needed. Get them before you go! I also recommend that any digital manuals be printed prior to departure. There is nothing worse than having to run back and forth between the engine room and the computer to read the manual.

In addition to shop manuals, I like to have a complete library of how-to books covering such topics as diesel engine repair, marine electrical systems and repair, fiberglass repair, refrigeration, hydraulics, and plumbing. Good general marine mechanical books, such as Dave Gerr's *Boat Mechanical Systems Handbook* and Linda and Steve Dashew's *Offshore Cruising Encyclopedia* are great sources of general information (see Appendix E).

## Troubleshooting Strategies

Whole books have been written about troubleshooting diesel engines. Steve D'Antonio suggests some strategies summarized here:

+ *Know your engine:* Spend enough time in your engine room while underway to know how it looks, feels, sounds, and even smells. You will be able to detect subtle differences if you have this knowledge.
+ *Run your engine at wide-open throttle (WOT) rating:* This is the rpm the engine should turn when fully loaded. Run it regularly at WOT for

If yes, you continue until it reaches the boat plug: is there still power? If so, check the boat: is there power before and after the main circuit breaker? The beauty of the AC detector is that it detects the power through the sheathing cord. You do not have to go directly to the bare wire or fitting.

**Mechanic's stethoscope.** This simple device makes it easy to listen to your engine. A steel probe provides the sound and vibration sensing that is then transferred to your ears. You can actually hear the movement inside your alternator. You can listen to your engine in various positions to determine whether there are any unusual noises or to identify the source of a noise. You can even listen to your propeller noise.

### Possible Tool Additions

We have a drill press and a grinder in the engine room. I use both quite often. The drill press allows precision drilling and fitting when making repairs. It makes drilling through 1/4-inch stainless steel a breeze. The grinder and wire brush help fabricate anything we need out of steel or aluminum.

If you have the room for a compressor, air tools can come in mighty handy. Here is what Don Stabbert on *Starr* takes along:

*A 4" pneumatic air angle grinder with plenty of hose, and ten 4" cut-off wheels to be used underwater to*

10 minutes and observe any problems, such as under-revving, overheating, unusual smoke, or propeller mismatches. During passages, often made at low rpms to save fuel, a short period of WOT daily is good for the engine. During WOT runs, check the vacuum on your Racor filter gauge—it should be changed at or before 6 Hg and should not go above 8 Hg.

+ *Engine does not crank:* If the engine doesn't crank at all or cranks slowly, the problem is likely electrical in the starter slave relay, cables, connections, or battery condition.

+ *Engine cranks, but will not start:* If it cranks, lack of fuel or air in the system is the most likely cause. The first item to check is the fuel supply solenoid. Is it working? If you can hear a click or thunk, it is probably working. If not, check the wiring to make sure it has power to activate it. If power, but no click, the solenoid probably needs replacing.

+ *Bleeding the fuel system:* Bob Senter, the Lugger/Deere expert, says do not bleed or crack the injector lines on the pressure side where the pump provides fuel to the injectors—it is very dangerous in high-pressure common rail injector systems. Begin bleeding to find out if there is fuel and/or air at the engine's fuel filter. If there is a mixture of fuel and air, keep pumping fuel until all the air is expelled. If no fuel, check further—are all the fuel valves on? Is the Racor turned on and unclogged? Steve D'Antonio uses a small outboard fuel tank, loaded with clean diesel, with a bulb for pumping and an in-line filter (should be 2 micron) for further troubleshooting. He removes the fuel line going from the fuel lift pump to the filters, then pumps fuel by hand. If it flows nicely, he knows there is a restriction earlier, perhaps in the primary filters, lines, or the lift pump. He repeats this process until he identifies where the fuel is being restricted. Then he knows what to replace or fix.

+ *It starts, but it smokes:* White smoke is usually an indicator of incomplete combustion or perhaps failing glow plugs. It can also be an indication of bad injectors or low compression. At start-up, white smoke is normal for the first minute. Blue smoke on start-up or when throttling up after prolonged idling usually indicates leaking valve seals. More persistent blue, gray, or white smoke, accompanied by high oil consumption, may indicate more serious problems with injectors, pump, or piston rings. Black smoke indicates overfueling, which can have a number of causes, such as a fouled propeller, restricted air filter, mismatched propeller pitch and size, or a faulty injection pump.

+ *It starts, but doesn't run well:* These problems are usually fuel-related. Surges may mean air in the fuel, clogged filters, contaminated fuel, or low centane ratings. A bad injector can be identified by disabling injectors, one at a time. When a good injector is disabled, it will result in even rougher engine performance. When you get to the bad injector, there will be no change, so it can be replaced. On newer engines, you may have to have a laptop with the proper software to evaluate injectors. On older engines (unless they use a common rail injection pump), an injector line can be cracked to eliminate its operation. Poor running may also be due to carbon buildup in the cylinders or even on the injectors. Running the engine at WOT periodically during the day will rid the engine of these harmful by-products.

Many more things can go wrong, requiring much more thorough troubleshooting. Often, the repair manuals will provide specific troubleshooting guidance. With the newer electronic engines run by computer, it is important to follow the manufacturer's troubleshooting guide and computer readouts.

Troubleshooting electronic problems is even more complicated and difficult, especially for the new integrated, interrelated systems. My bias is to keep electronic systems relatively independent, so that if one fails, you can just remove it or plug in a new one. This is obviously the simplest strategy for world cruisers. Finding technical assistance for modern electronics is almost impossible throughout much of the cruising world.

## Getting Help

**Make contacts.** Before starting an extended voyage, it is important to develop contacts for technical assistance, parts support, and shipping services.

# How a Simple Repair Turns into a Nightmare!

**Benno Klopfer,** *Diesel Duck* **41, 06/10/2009, Angra dos Reis, Brazil**

Coming from Paraty [near Rio de Janerio] on the way to Angra dos Reis, I noticed a charging problem. Somehow the voltage of the house-bank batteries was dropping and not rising while the engine was running. The house-bank's alternator is mounted piggyback on top of the Perkins diesel engine. It is a 100-amp Balmar alternator, controlled by a fancy Balmar regulator, and already had over 3,000 hours on it. I suspected that the alternator's brushes were worn down after all the hours of good service. But there were no spare brushes or parts for this alternator on board *Diesel Duck*.

We had met Klaus, who runs the cruising station for the Transocean Cruising Club here in Angra dos Reis, and he said he knew of a starter and alternator repair shop in town. With his Range Rover we were soon there and Pedro, the honcho at the shop said, "No problem." These were the only English words he knew, and my Portuguese knowledge was even less. In no time the alternator was clamped into the vise and Pedro, the expert, attacked the beast with a metric Allen key trying to open up a U.S.-made alternator. The key didn't fit. Meanwhile, I was trying to tell him there is a difference between metric and standard. In a short time, four customers plus myself and Pedro were involved in a heated discussion about metric, standard, and George Bush.

Suddenly, Pedro found in the depths of his toolbox a 3/16 Allen key. Voila! The alternator came apart and I was feeling a lot better. Pedro reached for a 6 mm socket driver to remove the 1/4-inch hex head screws, which were holding the brush holder. I started the discussion again about 6 mm and 1/4 inch and that it was not going to fit. Pedro smartly grabbed a 7 mm socket driver, which is bigger, but of course it was too big. The discussion heated up as there were now seven customers and me, plus Pedro. Pedro remembered the U.S.-made vise-grip pliers, his secret weapon. In a flash, both brush holder screws were removed and Pedro was holding up the culprit, the brush holder. The whole group was happy and clapping their hands. The brushes had worn flat right down to the wire.

Did Pedro have new brushes? He smiled and went down the road. Five minutes later, he was back, presenting me and the whole discussion group with a new brush holder complete with brushes. Pedro was the boss and Tavio, his right hand man, got the job to assemble the alternator. Tavio went to a wall cabinet where he pulled out a tiny drawer and plucked two new hex head machine screws out. One of the old screw heads had been damaged by the vise grips. Surprisingly, the socket driver fit this time. It was going well. Now Tavio was bending over and I could see he was putting some muscle into the turning of the screw. A little cracking sound was heard. Something no good had happened. Did he try to fit a metric machine screw into a standard thread? Yes, he did! He then broke or snapped the screw while forcing it into the hole. Pedro, the boss, must have heard the breaking sound too when the screw snapped. He waved to me with a sour smile and said, "No problem," pointed to the wall clock, made an eating sign with his hand, indicating to me to buzz off, have lunch, and come back at 2 o'clock.

I was back at 2. Pedro was holding my alternator like a Christmas present and smiling. Tavio was smiling too. "Completo" and the bill was "completo" too: 75 bucks. I hoofed back to the boat, fitted the alternator, and started the engine—a crackling sound, a little smoke out of the $310 Balmar smart regulator. Nothing worked. Maybe the regulator had already been defective prior to fitting the alternator, I thought. Out comes the spare Balmar smart regulator, it gets fitted, and I have another try with the engine. More smoke. Now this regulator is fried too.

That's it. I removed the alternator and opened it up. What a mess! The brush holder was not aligned, the mounting holes were not drilled in a 90-degree angle, and the negative brush lead was not wired to the negative stud. Instead, it was wired to the case. The isolation Teflon sleeve was destroyed. Should I take the alternator back to Pedro? was my first thought. Nope, these guys here are not up to snuff in fixing isolated ground Balmar alternators! To get us going, I wired the house bank's batteries to the engine's own alternator, which is only 75 amps and normally feeds just the engine starting batteries.

Months later, in St. Thomas USVI, I had the Balmar alternator professionally repaired and bought a new smart regulator.

---

Talk to suppliers to find out who is most knowledgeable and willing to help. Get e-mail addresses and, if possible, cell phone numbers. Sometimes there will be numerous time zone changes making phone contact difficult. Locate branch offices in areas you plan to cruise for nearby assistance.

**Use local shops.** Local repair services can be useful for many systems. For example, alternators and motors are usually repaired locally; however, as noted in the above sidebar, there are sometimes shortages in skills. Hydraulic hoses can be repaired or replaced almost anywhere. It may be helpful to take the illustrated parts list to the shop as well as any specialized tools, such as SAE hex wrenches or sockets. If you have a repair kit, use it. Substitutes of local materials may be unsatisfactory.

**Contact other cruisers.** An excellent source of expertise and help is other cruisers. If there is a VHF net, there is normally a call for anyone needing assistance. It is surprising how many cruisers have worked as mechanics, electricians, boatyard repair people, or computer programmers. When I made a net request in Aruba for help with a malfunctioning watermaker, another cruiser completely rebuilt it, bypassing the complex valves that had broken and making a much simplified, more reliable system. When our friends on S/V *Zelda* found their alternator had failed, we supplied a rebuild kit from our spares—there was no kit available in Horta.

**Fly in experts.** For most of us this is a last resort due to costs and availability of technicians. If you can find someone willing to fly in to fix your problematic system, they must make travel reservations. In some more remote areas, getting there may take days, not hours. Many of the most highly skilled people have full schedules and cannot afford the time for fly-in help. The technician must also bring all the parts and tools to do the job. If an unexpected problem develops, parts need to be ordered, delivered, and cleared through customs. This can sometimes take weeks. What will the technician do? Lie around on the beach for a paid vacation?

## Haulouts and Going on the Hard

In most cases, boats must be hauled at least once a year for bottom cleaning, propeller cleaning, antifouling, and zinc replacement. If you have a large boat, your first task is to find someone with a Travelift or ways that can handle the boat. Most boats under 65 feet can be lifted out of the water and blocked on land. However, the bigger the boat, the more careful you need to be in selecting boatyards with enough lifting capability. Once you find a yard that says they can lift your boat, check the condition of the Travelift and especially the slings. Do they look worn or frayed? Does the lift have double

slings at both ends to spread the load and provide backup? For an example of what can happen, see the sidebar, "A Haulout Gone Bad," excerpted from *PassageMaker Magazine.*

**On the hard.** This term describes the time your boat spends on land, blocked, and supported so that maintenance and painting can be completed. It is also common to leave the boat on the hard when departing for extended home visits. Many cruisers leave their boats during the off-season (hurricane season in the southern United States and the Caribbean, and winter season in the Mediterranean), either in the water, with opportunities for leaks and bottom growth, or on the hard. There are some special considerations for going on the hard:

*Jack stands:* These stands resemble the jack stands used for car repair, only they are a lot bigger. They normally have a three-leg base and a screw adjustment for height. It is possible that these jacks can settle and actually result in the boat falling. In addition, in earthquake zones, failure of the stands is common. One way to minimize these problems is to use ratchet tie-down straps used by truckers to tie down their loads. These straps can be run to opposing jack stands to prevent them from falling over. If you find a yard that uses only logs for jack stands, beware—they are even less stable.

*Level the boat:* Yard workers often put blocks under the keel to support the boat; however, most trawlers have more draft in the stern than in the bow. Thus, you will normally need more blocking under the bow. This is important to make sure the water runs off the boat properly and to make it easier to work inside with level floors.

*Bring a ladder:* Many yards scrimp on ladders. They may be rickety wood ladders or rebar welded to pipes. Both types are dangerous and should not be used. (While we were in Marmaris, Turkey, a cruiser fell off a ladder and had extensive head injuries as a result.) We carried a 12-foot aluminum ladder in our 14-foot dinghy for such purposes. It is high enough to reach the swim step and can be easily climbed and secured by tying a line to the boat. If you have no room for a ladder, you may be able to buy one locally; then sell or give it away when you leave.

# A Haulout Gone Bad

## Don Perrine

My wife, JoAnne, and I had researched our options regarding where to spend the 2006 hurricane season, and we had selected Chaguaramas, Trinidad, as our destination. We had decided to have our 14-month-old, semicustom Nordhavn 47 trawler hauled out before we flew back to the United States to visit family and friends for a few months. The cost would be about the same as that of leaving the boat in a slip. The most suitable boatyard for the haulout appeared to be Peake Yacht Services in Chaguaramas. The yard had a 150-ton Marine Travelift, which seemed more than adequate to move our 47-foot, 50-ton-displacement Nordhavn.

Shortly after arriving in Trinidad, we signed a contract with Peake Yacht Services for the haulout. The contract required us to provide certain information about our vessel, including her displacement weight, which we specified as 50 tons. After nearly one week of preparing our boat to spend time on the hard, we were ready. We stood off until we were requested by radio to enter the boatyard's mobile lift bay. Upon entering the bay, we began securing lines. The boatyard staff was trying to pull the boat to center her in the bay, but I told them she displaced 50 tons and showed them how I can maneuver the vessel easily using the bow and stern thrusters.

I noticed that the slings were covered with plastic sleeves, which alleviated my concerns about possible scuffing of the topsides. I also saw that the yard had a diver who would ensure that the slings were correctly positioned under the hull. These had been my two main concerns and both had been addressed, even though I had not requested any special measures, so I felt confident. Plus, I saw that the yard hauled out boats all day long at this time of year. I proceeded to shut down the main engine and generator, and we secured the stabilizers and everything else that needed to be fastened down for the haulout. JoAnne and I then disembarked in preparation for the haulout itself, as instructed.

The Travelift hoisted our boat from the water and wheeled her over the concrete apron. With the keel about 2-1/2 feet above the concrete, the crew began scraping marine growth off the bottom, and I stepped under the hull to take some photos. Within several minutes, while both the crew and I were under the boat, the aft sling gave way.

The loud crack of the sling breaking and the deafening crash of our beautiful boat hitting the unforgiving concrete blended into one powerful note. Instinct and adrenaline fired my immediate reaction as the boat went into free fall. I dove out from under the hull, across the concrete, landing with a headfirst "home plate" slide. I was sure the boat was going to fall on me, and I remember clearly thinking, "If I can get far enough away, it might just crush my legs, not kill me."

When I looked back, the boat was being held steady only by the front sling. I had survived, although I was scraped, bloody, and reeling in disbelief. I must have shouted, "I can't believe it" half a dozen times. Even now, I can hardly believe what happened. JoAnne had watched the whole episode from the other side of the boat, horrified by all that had occurred in the blink of an eye. She had watched as the hull struck one worker's back and injured another worker's arm. Because she couldn't see me on the other side of the boat, she assumed the worst.

The good news was that we had all been spared serious injuries. However, it would be some days before JoAnne and I would fully realize how profoundly a split-second event would affect our lives.

Our boat had struck the concrete with a force calculated at 480,000 lb. The rudder shoe had hit first, driving the rudder itself up into the hull approximately 8 inches. Then, the aft section of the keel had made contact with the ground and had been forced up, breaking open a section of the hull above the aft keel to the hull joint.

From the outside, the damage didn't appear to be catastrophic. However, the view from the inside, as well as "open and inspect" work and surveys, showed that the damage was extensive.

[After extensive negotiations between the owners, Peake Yacht Services, and their insurance company, the boat was classed as a total loss. The full article is recommended reading for all boat owners.]

**Figure 17–6.** The Nordhavn 47, *Jade Explorer*, just minutes before it fell when the sling strap broke. Note the single straps on both bow and stern. (Don Perrine)

**Figure 17–7.** Preparing *Teka III* for a summer of storage in Guyamas, Mexico. Note six jack stands on each side. Straps are not yet attached to the stands. Note higher blocks on the bow to level the boat. The sun cover was to reduce exposure during the hot months; however, a tropical storm demolished it.

## A Case Study of Injector Pump Failure and Repair in the Remote South Pacific Aboard Diesel Duck *Ice*

*Abridged from Don McIntyre's Blog*

I debated whether to even include this case because we do not have the final problem identified and there are many complexities. However, it does illustrate the difficulties in diagnosing and solving problems when away from sources of expert help. It shows that mistakes are easy to make and help is hard to come by. Think of this case as you might have done in a graduate seminar—the problems are identified, but solutions are up to you. What would you have done if you were stuck in Tarawa?

*Ice* has experienced fuel problems several times over her short life. It all started with a replacement injector pump during sea trials. Then they encountered a microbial bloom in their day tank, which resulted in sludge that had to be cleaned. Next, another apparent injector-pump failure, replaced at sea. Finally, the series of events, unfolding over

a three-month period, involving the removal and replacement of additional pumps. The logistics and communication problems in this far-away location of Tarawa presented special problems. Here is a rough chronology of the problems encountered.

- *Ice*, a custom version of the Diesel Duck 462, built in China by Seahorse Marine. The yard fills day tank with 158 gallons using drums of diesel from a local service station. Gulf Coast Filter installed as main fuel–polishing and transfer filter.
- *Ice* sits for nine months while Seahorse finishes the boat.
- *April 2008*: Diesel injector pump shutoff solenoid fails during sea trials, and injector pump is replaced. Electrical fault is suspected because pump was rated 12 volts, but boat's system is 24 volts. (He later finds that a 24-volt system specifies a 12-volt solenoid—strange indeed.)
- Don McIntyre begins his voyage. Discovers slime in the Racor on passage from Hong Kong to Philippines, indicating microbial bloom in the day tank and deteriorating diesel fuel. Adds biocide and has tank cleaned. Only the day tank seems infected.
- *July 2008–April 2011*: Boat in Philippines for use as a demo; little use.
- *April 2011*: Departure for Palau and Tonga (beginning with 156 engine hours)
  - Changed four Racor filters en route at 8–9 Hg vacuum.
- Departed Palau for 2,500-mile passage to Kiribati. Experienced a number of problems:
  - Rev-hunting with a 300 rpm revving up and down—only in rough water. Changed Racor and on-engine filters. Problem continued.
  - Engine would not reach maximum rpm. Fuel starvation? Slowly dying.
  - Strange up-and-down Racor gauge readings. Occasional air bubbles in the Racor.
  - Twice engine stopped—fuel starvation. Fuel blockage cleared with compressed air.
  - Complete fuel blockage from day tank. Drew fuel from another tank and through the Gulf Coast Filter.

- Even with satellite phones, communication from far-away places is difficult.
- Communicating with non-English-speaking distributors may result in errors.
- If there is a possibility of two parts, such as gaskets, applying to your engine and you do not know for sure which is correct, order both.
- Infrequent flights complicated logistics.
- Shipping and transportation of spares was often delayed.
- Internet access was very limited, making research more difficult.
- Special tools may not be readily available. Flying in an expert might eliminate this problem.
- It is especially useful to have a technical helper, such as the builder or mechanic, with contacts and knowledge that you can depend on.
- Using sails as get-home has some drawbacks because of limited mobility once anchored and the possibility of grounding on windless days.

## CHAPTER EIGHTEEN

# Weather, Waves, and Storm Strategies

The three topics in this chapter—weather, waves, and storms—are related and also link back to voyage preparation and planning. Each of these three topics can fill entire an entire book. Thus, I will only highlight a few things that need emphasis for ocean voyaging. Earlier in the book, when we discussed the philosophy of power passagemaking, I highlighted the importance of good weather as a major factor in enjoying the lifestyle—hence your ability to understand the weather and plan to avoid storms is critical to the success of your passage. I am not a meteorologist nor an oceanographer, so my knowledge is limited to experience and study of the topics. To get a thorough understanding, I recommend studying technical sources that cover the topics more completely. (See Appendix E for recommended resources.)

## Weather

### Study Historical Data before You Depart

In Chapter 14 I mentioned that pilot charts are an excellent planning source for voyaging. Other sources can also be used. For example, the National Weather Service publishes a record of hurricanes and tropical storms for every year, showing their tracks and development over time. If you study the patterns over the past ten years or so, you get a feel for where storms originate and what tracks they may take.

Sometimes this allows more detailed examination of paths than the pilot chart, which only shows predominant paths. There is a lot of variation that can significantly affect your voyage.

I chose to show the hurricane track chart from 2005 in Figure 18–2 because that is the year we crossed the Atlantic on the way back from the Mediterranean. Two storms, Vince and Epsilon, affected our voyage. We were tied up to the dock in Rota, Spain, waiting for a weather window when Vince made an unexpected appearance. You don't expect a tropical storm in this part of the world, but we had one. Luckily, all we had was wind and surge. We tended lines and fenders, and made sure everything was secured. It would not have been pretty if we had been at sea when it struck.

The threat was not over with Vince. When we were on our way from the Canary Islands to Antigua, tropical storm Epsilon developed right on our great-circle route. We had several anxious days watching it spin in

Figure 18–1. Hurricane Adrian in June 2011 off the coast of Mexico. (NOAA)

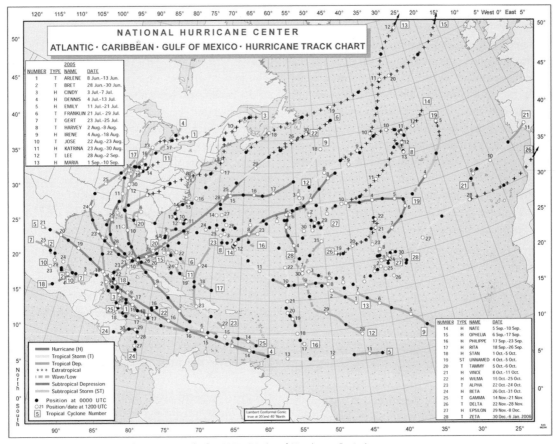

Figure 18–2. Atlantic Ocean hurricane tracks for 2005. (National Hurricane Center)

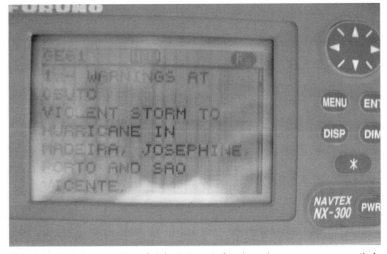

Figure 18–3. Navtex warning of violent storm to hurricane in our area—we were tied to the dock in Rota, Spain, but it was still disconcerting.

first this direction, then in another—it could not make up its mind. We changed our course to a more southerly waypoint to avoid any potential meet up, although one weather router was predicting a turn toward the African coast, which would have put us right in its path. Luckily, it followed the NOAA predictions and missed us entirely, although we did get some residual swell. These late-season named storms formed at unlikely times in unlikely places. Study of historical records might not have helped much. But much of the time, the historical paths provide indicators of when and where a safe passage can be made.

### Don't Forget Pacific Storms

Sometimes we forget that the ocean off the western coast of Mexico is a fertile spawning ground for Pacific hurricanes and tropical storms. For boats voyaging along the Mexican coast or on passage to the South Pacific, these storms are extremely important. In addition, these storms sometimes form offshore and head inland, so even an anchorage or port may be vulnerable. The results of taking a chance on a late-season departure to the South Pacific can be fatal. *Peregrine*, a 66-foot steel Romsdal, reportedly left Acapulco in June 1974 and was presumed lost during Hurricane Dolores with her crew of six (see Figure 18–4). Figure 18–1 taken during a June storm

off the coast of Mexico, shows how vast hurricanes can grow—they can cover a lot of territory.

### Watch Out for Known Trouble Spots

The lower latitudes, especially the Roaring Forties of the Southern Hemisphere, are places where gales blow often and waves get very big. Few voyagers go there on purpose. Many experts rate the Drake Passage, south of the tip of South America, as the roughest water of the world. What follows are a number of topographic situations that can create rough conditions for passagemakers.

**Winds are compressed and accelerated by two mountain ranges.** There are many places in the world where winds rush from high to low pressure through a set of mountain ranges, causing a venturi effect with accelerating winds. For example, the Gulf of Tehuantepec, off the coast of Southern Mexico, is gale-prone, storm-prone, and spawns many of the Pacific hurricanes. The heavy weather is caused by a gap between two mountain ranges that allows the high pressure air in the Gulf of Mexico to flow into the Pacific, making a venturi in the process. Many larger boats have been lost in this area. One merchant mariner told me the roughest water he ever experienced was in this location— the seas literally blew right over the ship. Small boats, such as passagemakers, can make safe passage by staying close to shore, even though the wind may be ferocious. We encountered a "Tehuantepecer" when going south from California toward the Panama Canal. All the forecasts were favorable, but the nasty winds came in spite of the good predictions. We hugged the shore (they say you are close enough if you can hear the dogs barking), while the wind blew over 60 knots at times. We were heeled like a sailboat due to wind forces. When the trip was over after 39 hours and we reached Puerto Madero, we found that the windward half of our boat

**Figure 18–4.** *Peregrine,* before leaving on her ill-fated voyage to the South Pacific. (Jim Rogers)

was covered by dirt, mixed with salt. We had quite a cleaning job.

Another example of this weather phenomenon is the Gulfe du Lion in the Mediterranean, off the Southern Coast of France between Spain and Italy. High pressure in Northern France spills into the Mediterranean, and moves toward the low pressure in Northern Africa. Strong gales and storms occur in this region, even threatening large ships.

**Where mountains meet the ocean.** Off the coast of Columbia, on the line between Aruba and Cartagena, the Sierra Nevada Mountains meet the Caribbean Sea. At certain times of the year, when the trade winds are strongest, there is a constant gale in that area with monstrous steep waves. This is primarily a wintertime phenomenon and is called the "Christmas Winds." (Read the experiences of Romsdal 65, *Sea Quest*, in Chapter 13. They tried this route when the winds were screaming and found out how bad it can get.) When we travelled this route, we took great care to arrive in early December, before the winds—an easy passage.

Another troublesome location where the winds are compressed against mountains is in Northern California off Cape Mendocino and Cape Arena. The winds accelerate and create frequent gales, especially within 20 to 100 miles of shore. These winds are strongest in midsummer when the Pacific High is at its strongest, pumping strong north-northwest winds along the coast.

**Where strong currents meet opposing seas.** One of the most famous areas is the Gulf Stream, which flows from the Gulf of Mexico past Florida and into the North Atlantic. Current runs between 3.5 and 5 knots going north—it is the swiftest major current in the world. If a northerly wind opposes the stream, very steep breaking seas are created. When crossing the Gulf Stream from Fort Lauderdale, Florida, to the Bahamas, you can observe the stream from shore if you find a lookout on a third- or fourth-story building. With strong northerlies, which often follow a cold front in the winter, you will see the breaking seas—we say "the elephants are marching!" Even large resupply ships hunker down in such situations. Of course, southerlies have the reverse effect—seas are quite calm, even with significant winds.

Off the southern coast of South Africa, the warm Agulhas current from the Indian Ocean meets the cold Benguela current of the South Atlantic. The Agulhas current is actually turned back by the more powerful Benguela current. These conflicting strong currents cause some extreme seas and need to be traversed with caution. In addition, the Agulhas is considered the world's most dangerous current because it flows between two land masses—Africa and Mozambique. The cautions about sailing against the current apply equally here as in the Gulf Stream.

## Avoiding Difficult Passages

Scott Flanders, aboard *Egret*, notes that capable powerboats have a significant advantage over sail boats because they can wait for calms in challenging passages; sailing vessels must have wind. He uses the example of cruising around the infamous Cape of Good Hope area on their five-capes circumnavigation:

> In *Egret's* case, [the passage] was not dangerous whereas under sail it can be. A perfect example was rounding the last cape [of our voyage], Cape of Good Hope. Three of four small sailboats we met in Mauritius suffered major damage with ripped-off dodgers, skewed solar panel towers, and one knockdown. *Egret* did not [even] have spray on her pilothouse glass for the most part until nearing Cape Town. Sailors need wind and wind from the right direction to sail. The South African coast can be truly dangerous. *Egret* waited for a big 5-day high from the SW and drove through [with] no wind. Leaving Cape Town for Namibia [we had a similar advantage over sailors]. This can be a tough trip for sailors and it was super calm for *Egret*, to the point we could drive right along the beach of the Skeleton Coast and see the sea lion colonies and wrecks along the shore. The simple key is waiting for calms in potentially dangerous areas versus pushing the wind windows under sail.

Tidal effects can cause similar amplification, albeit temporary, effects on waves. Between mainland British Columbia and Vancouver Island, a narrow body of water called the Johnstone Strait can cause considerable havoc for smaller craft. The current in this channel runs quite strong due to strong tides of around 12 feet. Westerly winds, often gale force, are funneled down this channel against the tidal current of up to 5 knots, creating short steep, breaking seas, and tide rips of 7 to 8 feet. These conditions are dangerous for smaller vessels. We experienced these seas on our first voyage to Northern Vancouver Island—many years ago. We were zooming down the channel in our 37-foot trawler (with 5 knots of current) when up ahead we saw whitecaps. I thought: "it's only a tide rip; we'll be through it in a few minutes." Once we entered the boiling froth, the bow was constantly burying itself in the steep waves and we were scared. We picked a slight lull, turned around, and headed for a small anchorage on the opposite shore where we spent the night. Early the next morning there was no wind and the seas were placid.

# Weather Tools for Voyaging

## Use the 500-Millibar Charts

Safe and comfortable voyaging in temperate waters is enhanced by consulting the 500-mb charts issued by NOAA and other weather agencies. The chart does not show pressure like the normal surface analysis chart, but the heights of the 500 mb surface, expressed in meters above the surface. It is a way of depicting the three-dimensional surface on a flat chart. However, these height lines do behave roughly the same as isobars on surface maps. Winds aloft flow along the lines and closer spacing of bars indicate stronger winds. In Figure 18–5, winds aloft range from 40 to 65 knots according to their wind arrows. The surface winds also relate to the 500 mb speeds, being roughly one half to one third of the speeds shown on the chart. The lines on the chart are called "streamlines"—the bold 564 line indicates the southern boundary of strong surface winds.

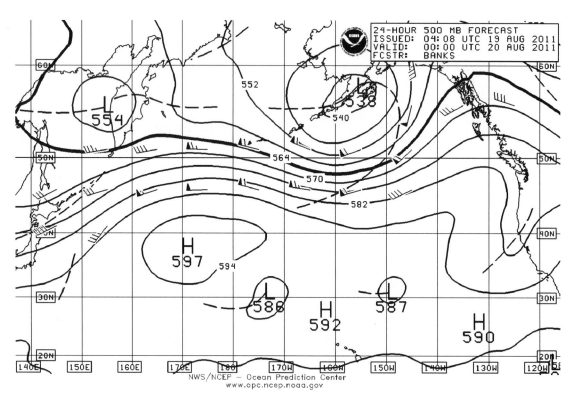

**Figure 18–5.** 500-mb chart for the Pacific Ocean, August 19, 2011. The heavy black line at 564 mb indicates the southern edge of strong winds. (NOAA)

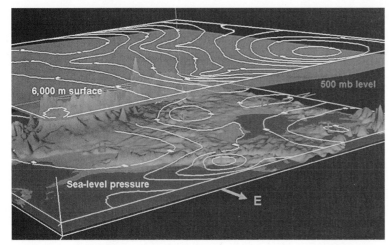

**Figure 18–6.** Three-dimensional depiction from 0000 UTC 10 Dec 2005 showing: sea-level pressure in yellow contours; the height of the 6,000 meter constant altitude surface depicted in pressure values (mb, white); and the 500 mb constant pressure surface in transparent green shading. (Joe Sienkiewicz and Lee Chesneau)

of the constant pressure in meters. For convenience, they leave off the last zero of the elevation; thus 5,640 meters (18,504 feet) is noted as 564 on the chart.

**Route classification using the 500-mb chart.** Captain Mike Ma-Li Chen and Lee Chesneau, in their book *Heavy Weather Avoidance and Route Design*, discuss using the zone between 540 and 570 on the 500-mb chart to devise safer and faster routes for both ships and cruising boats. They classify zones as A, B, C, and D. As far as trawlers are concerned, the only safe and comfortable route is south of the 570 line, the "Available Zone." If you are routing a ship, there are more options called the "Be Careful Zone" and "Cautious Zone." The "Difficult Zone" is to be avoided by all due to high winds and rough seas. Figure 18–7

Figure 18–6 illustrates the three-dimensional nature of weather. Because the 500-mb chart measures constant pressure, the altitude of that pressure will vary. Meteorologists measure this in the height

**Figure 18–7.** A 500-mb analysis for the North Atlantic Ocean valid for 10 Mar 2008. The 564 mb height contour is shown in bold red. The colored arrows show the surface wind speed and wind direction as estimated from the NASA QuikSCAT satellite. The color bar in the upper right shows the color coding of wind speeds. Yellow and orange arrows are GALE force, the brown arrows STORM force, and red (southwest of Ireland) are HURRICANE FORCE as you would see reflected on OPC's surface pressure charts. In this area of hurricane-force winds, the upper winds are blowing 115 knots. (Joe Sienkiewicz and Lee Chesneau)

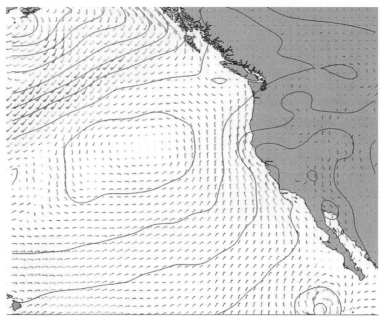

Figure 18–8. GRIB forecast 21 August 2011. Note the higher westerly winds on the northern portion of the forecast, indicating its closeness to the 700 line on the 500 mb chart. Also note the 30-knot winds off the coast of Northern California, showing the effect of compression against the mountains. At the bottom right, a tropical depression with 30-knot winds may form into a hurricane.

shows the comparison of surface winds and winds at 500 mb. As you can see, staying well south of the 570 line results in less wind and fewer waves. The difficult area near Ireland is experiencing hurricane-force winds.

## GRIB Forecasts

GRIB (gridded binary file) forecasts are computer-generated with no input from meteorologists. They are generated four times per day based on Wwave3, a program that generates sea level wind and wave forecasts; and GFS (Global Forecasting System), which forecasts surface winds, pressures, and precipitation. We have used GRIB forecasts since 2002 and have found them reliable. In some parts of the world, like the Black Sea, local forecasts were unavailable or in foreign languages that were not interpretable. The GRIB filled the gap. Forecasts can be downloaded from the Internet or through a number of services. The free GRIB.

US software is available for download to read the files. When obtaining a GRIB file you select the geographic area you would like and the degree of details desired. Figure 18–8 shows a GRIB file downloaded for illustration.

## Weather Routers

Many passagemakers make use of commercial weather routers—professional meteorologists specializing in marine weather, often with a cruising background themselves so they can relate to the voyager. Their main advantages include expertise well beyond most cruisers, access to specialized computer models, like the NASA QuikSCAT satellite image shown in Figure 18–7, and reports from other cruisers or ships providing actual on-site weather conditions. What follows is an example of advice provided by weather routers (Ocean Marine Navigation [OMNI]) to *Teka III* as we re-crossed the Atlantic from east to west:

To: Captain Umstot—M/Y TEKA III
Fm: O.M.N.I./USA

1140Z 06 DEC 2005

Hurricane Epsilon at 0900Z was located near 32.9N 33.9W moving south (185/deg) at 04kts. Max winds are estimated 65kts near the center. Gales extend outward an estimated 75nm from the center, except up to 100nm SW of the center. No basic change to the forecast track/intensity. Epsilon should take on a more SW, then West course the next few days and gradually weaken to a tropical storm/depression than a remnant low.

Forecast at 07/0600Z 30.5N 35.0W Max 50kts—Gales outward 75nm from center.

Forecast at 08/0600Z 28.0N 37.5W Max 30kts

Forecast at 09/0600Z 25.0N 40.0W Max 25kts—Remnant Low.

Outlook at 10/0600Z 23.0N 41.4W Max 25kts—Remnant Low.

Along the rhumbline route toward w/p 20N 30W thence rhumbline Antigua, expect:

Tue/06: ENE-NE 08—15kt, NE 1.0—1.5mtrs through pm.

Wed/07: NE-ENE 15-20kt, NE-ENE 1.5-2.0mtrs.

Thu/08: NE-ENE, 15-21kt, ENE 2.0-2.5mtrs.

Fri/09: Ease NE-ENE 12-18kts, ENE 2.0mtrs through aftn. Veer ESE-SSE 12-18kts, become confused 1.5-2.0mtrs toward eve-night.

Sat/10: veer early SSE-SW 12-20kts, confused 1.5-2.0mtrs am. Veer SW-NNW 15-21kts, confused-NNW 1.5-2.0mtrs during pm.

We were quite concerned about the tropical storm and were diverting to 20N 30W to stay out of its path. This prediction shows successful avoidance and moderate seas of about 6 feet. We avoided the tropical storm. Actual conditions taken from our log for the 6th were NE 10–12 knots, low seas. For the 7th, still NE 10–12, but seas building to 2-plus meters (8 feet). The following was the forecast for 10 December:

1100Z 10 DEC 2005

Captain, since the front is nearing your location, sending this update to update its location/forecast.

A developing 1006mb low center near 32N 30W will gradually deepen to 999 mb while moving to 30N 30W through Sun/11th, then should track north toward 35N 30W through Mon—midday. The trailing cold front extending SW across 20N 39W will move eastward, but should also weaken during Sun/pm-Monday. The front will bring veering SE-SW winds and some gusty winds with some mixed sea conditions as the front nears/moves through. Conditions should steadily improve west of the front by Sun/pm into Mon/am.

Outlooks indicate the low will continue to move NW'ward and become absorbed into a cold front moving east across the western Atlantic through Tue/13th. The front will continue to move eastward while the prevailing ridge pattern begins to weaken late Wed/night and Thursday.

The rhumbline route toward w/p 20N 30W thence rhumbline Antigua remains valid, expect:

Sat/10: Veer SSE-SW 12-20kts, confused-NNW 1.5-2.0mtrs. SW-WSW 17-22kts, gusty 25-28kts, NW-N

1.5-2.5mtrs, nearing the front during late Sat/pm.

Sun/11: Shift early am/hours. WSW-NNW 17-25kts, gusty, NW-N 2.0-2.5mtrs. Mostly NW-NNW 15-21kts, NW-N 2.0-2.5mtrs by sunrise. Tend to ease NNW 14-18kts, NNW-N 2.0-2.5mtrs late.

Mon/12: NW-N 15-18kts, NNW-N 2.0-2.5mtrs, tend to subside closer to 2.0mtrs during pm/hrs.

Tue/13: NW-NNE 10-16kts, NNW-N 1.5-2.0mtrs, become NNW & NE 1.0-1.5mtrs pm/hrs.

Wed/14: NNE-ENE 10-15kts, NE-ENE 1.0-1.5mtrs.

We expected gusty headwinds for a while and some significant seas. Our log for the 10th shows SW to W winds at 15–25 knots, with 3–4 meter seas (9–14 feet). Front passed at 1845. Altered course and slowed to 1,000 rpm for better night ride. On the 11th, winds moderated to NW 10–15, but swells still big. Not too uncomfortable.

No question—our next ocean voyage will again use a weather router. For those crossing the Atlantic on a budget, you might consider Herb Hilgenberg, an esteemed Canadian weather router who does it as a hobby—he does not charge. The catch is that you must make daily contact on HF (short-wave) SSB radio, which can be tiresome and sometimes difficult. His services are used widely by sailing vessels and some power boats. Even if you don't sign up with Herb (Southbound II), you might tune him in on SSB frequency 12359 in the evening. When we crossed the Atlantic eastbound, our sailing buddies used Herb, while we used OMNI. We compared recommendations, finding both sources useful.

## Weather Communication

If you have onboard Internet access, then it is just a matter of figuring out which websites have the best, least-costly reports. At a minimum, you should be downloading the NOAA weather fax data, which includes lots of valuable and essential information. GRIB files are also valuable and quite easy and economical to download.

**Using the SSB radio.** Before satellite phones, the short-wave (HF) radio was the only source of long-range communication at sea. It is still quite useful and economical, but as many power passagemakers have discovered, it is difficult to get tuned so that interference is eliminated or minimized. Antenna problems, grounding, and interference are issues for experts. Do not expect the normal electronics technician to do a correct installation—go to an expert. Most of the information available on the Internet is also available using the SSB radio, usually for low or no cost. Over the past 10 years, HF e-mail programs have become widespread, with Airmail (for HAMs) and SailMail being the most common. You can send and receive e-mails that may include specialized weather products, like NOAA high seas forecasts and GRIB forecasts. Weather faxes are available for download off the air from NOAA broadcasts in Boston, New Orleans, Pt. Reyes, or Honolulu. The disadvantage of weather faxes received by SSB is that you have to receive them at the proper time and this is not always convenient. Also, the quality varies. Sometimes, you may not even be able to get them via radio. If you have the satellite capability and can afford the cost, Internet download is the best way to go.

**Contacting others with the SSB.** There is usually an active net for ocean voyagers because we all desire weather information that allows us to know what is happening so we can depart during safe weather windows. These nets typically run twice a day and pass along weather information from their locations. Other useful information about ports, fishing, pirates, etc., is provided by participants in the net. Often amateur, but capable, weather forecasters provide radio updates and information in real time for cruisers. We have found these nets quite useful. It is an advantage to have a HAM general license so you can participate in HAM marine nets.

## Waves: The Real Danger

Much of the previous weather discussion was about wind. Wind does not usually cause heavy trawlers much problem, but the waves created by high winds do. Wind exerts between 10–12 pounds of force per square foot while a breaking wave can create over 2,000 pounds per square foot! Total wave energy increases exponentially to the fourth power of the wind speed. In other words wave energy at 60 knots will be 1,300 times greater than 10 knots.

Wave formation is rather complex, involving the fetch over which the waves will move, the duration of wind, and its strength. For example, a steady 30-knot wind blowing for 20 hours over a 340-mile fetch produces the following waves:

- Most frequent wave height                                8.5 feet
- Average height of all waves                             11.0 feet
- Significant wave height
  (average of the highest 1/3 of all waves)   17.0 feet
- Average height of highest 10% of all waves   22.0 feet

Sea state grows most rapidly when the wind first begins, then slows down as the seas get bigger with longer periods. This makes the relative wind speed lower than when the winds first started.

When do big waves become threatening? If non-breaking waves exceed the boat's beam, they are a threat when taken on the beam. Head seas become dangerous if they exceed the boat's overall length. Thus, for a 50-foot boat with a 16-foot beam, it is dangerous to take the waves on the beam if they exceed 16 feet. On the nose, the danger point is 50 feet. Of course, this applies only if the seas are not breaking. Breaking seas are discussed next. Also, recall the preceding example in which the average wave height of 11 feet may have maximum waves of 22 feet. There may be little danger from average waves, but a really big one may present an entirely different situation.

## Breaking Waves

The greatest danger is from breaking waves. These waves can damage even large steel ships. Almost any well-constructed passagemaker can survive big waves if they are not breaking, but a breaking wave can disable or sink almost any boat. Most vulnerable are hatches, windows, and ports. At 60 knots, almost all larger waves are breaking. At lesser wind speeds over 10 knots, there are varying numbers of breaking waves—most will not be dangerous until wind speeds increase to gale force or higher, unless a countercurrent is present, such as the Gulf Stream.

A plunging breaker has tremendous side force that can roll a boat on its side and possibly capsize it (Figure 18-9). Contrary to popular belief, research indicates a wide-beam boat is more susceptible to capsize from a breaker than a narrower-beamed craft. A broad-beamed boat rides up the face of the breaker and heels to a much larger extent than a narrow beam boat. Then when it is stuck by the plunging breaker, it tends to bury its leeward deck, which acts as a tripping force to ensure capsize. The narrow-beamed boat tends to slip sideways away from the breaker's force. Steve Dashew has argued that his FPB 64 is designed to slide sideways rather than roll. The research seems to support this approach.

If a plunging breaker hits from the bow, it is unlikely the boat will roll, but it is possible to pitchpole (flipping end for end) if the wave is big enough and very steep. A more likely scenario is that tons of water will come crashing down on the boat, severely testing its windows, hatches, and other openings. Even large ocean liners and cargo ships have been damaged by such waves. The sidebar "Othman's Circumnavigation and a Huge Wave" (page 339) conveys what can happen when hitting a big wave head-on, although this wave was apparently not breaking. Othman did not report any damage to his Nordhavn 46 from the encounter.

If you are running with the waves, the results can be similar to meeting a breaker head-on; however, some of the force may be lessened by the forward motion of the boat. If a plunging breaker comes aboard, it may poop (i.e., break over the top of) the boat, especially if there is cockpit aft, threatening stability and causing damage.

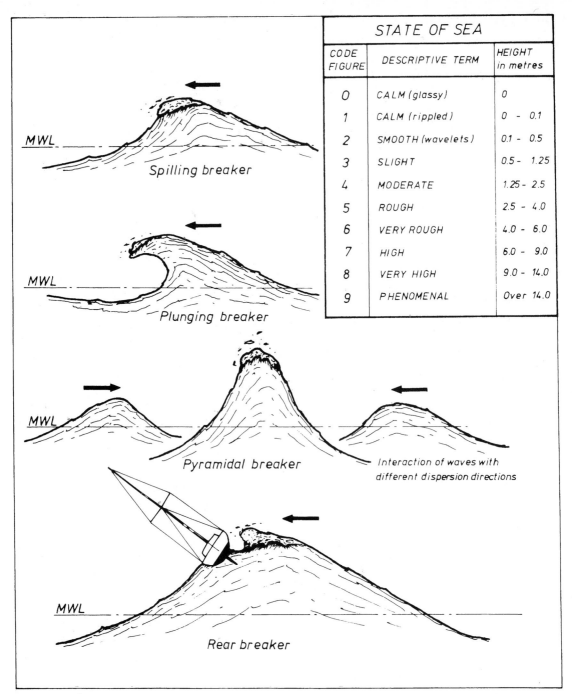

The following table appears within the figure:

| CODE FIGURE | DESCRIPTIVE TERM | HEIGHT in metres |
|---|---|---|
| 0 | CALM (glassy) | 0 |
| 1 | CALM (rippled) | 0 – 0.1 |
| 2 | SMOOTH (wavelets) | 0.1 – 0.5 |
| 3 | SLIGHT | 0.5 – 1.25 |
| 4 | MODERATE | 1.25 – 2.5 |
| 5 | ROUGH | 2.5 – 4.0 |
| 6 | VERY ROUGH | 4.0 – 6.0 |
| 7 | HIGH | 6.0 – 9.0 |
| 8 | VERY HIGH | 9.0 – 14.0 |
| 9 | PHENOMENAL | Over 14.0 |

**Figure 18-9.** Deep-water breaking wave types. The plunging breaker is most dangerous because of its tremendous side force. (C.A. Marchaj)

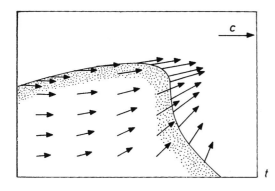

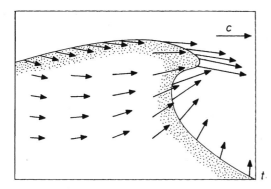

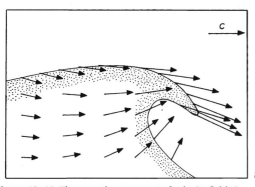

Figure 18–10. The growth movement of velocity fields in a plunging breaker in deep water. Note the vertical face (in the middle illustration) that may cause extreme heel of the boat; then in the bottom illustration, the forces toward rolling. (C.A. Marchaj)

# Othman's Circumnavigation and a Huge Wave

Ghanim al-Othman, a Kuwaiti, had a dream of being the first Arab to circumnavigate in a small power boat. While he was always interested in the sea, his boating experience was limited to a 39-foot powerboat, in which he travelled to some local ports. He decided to buy a Nordhavn 46 in Singapore and bring it back to Kuwait for his first ocean voyaging experience, taking 39 days.

He began his circumnavigation in January 1998, stopping in Dubai, Oman, Maldives, and India on his way to Southeast Asia. From there, he made his way via Indonesia to Hawaii and then California—almost 16,000 miles. Othman thought that by sticking close to the equator, seas would be calm, but there were strong headwinds, sometimes up to 50 knots, and adverse currents. Off the island of Kosrae, in Micronesia, he encountered a rogue wave estimated at 40 feet high: "The seas were like 12 feet," he said, "All of a sudden, I saw this huge, giant wave. I couldn't believe my eyes. My crew and I opened our mouths in silence. Once we hit it, the boat dived. All of a sudden, we could only see water. We kept on seeing water, and I was praying to see the sky again. After that, I decided to return to Kosrae and wait."

Othman learned navigation and weather as he progressed, gaining knowledge from other yachts and from a U.S. navigation firm. His charts were inaccurate and out of date. He had to dodge storms and low-pressure areas all across the Pacific. When he arrived in Hawaii after a tough three-month slog, people were shocked that he had travelled during the hurricane season, arriving in July.

He had some other adventures along the way. In Singapore, he ran aground on some rocks and the boat heeled over on its side at low tide. He spent a very fretful night trying to right the boat—he was afraid of downflooding when the tide rose. However, the boat just popped up and everything was fine. In Palau, he got blood poisoning from a minor coral cut, his leg swelled up, and he experienced a lot of pain. In spite of the doctor's recommendations to stay around for observation, he took a bunch of antibiotics and continued the journey.

Othman completed his circumnavigation, travelling approximately 29,000 miles. His progress was closely followed by Kuwaiti press and television. He survived groundings, blood poisoning, scurvy, and storms; unfortunately, he died after the voyage in an aircraft accident.

A 55-foot steel lobster boat, caught in a storm 150 miles off Chatham, Massachusetts, was lying stern to the seas when she was overtaken by a steep breaking wave and pitchpoled. The boat did not right itself; it later sank.

## Forecasting Wave Heights

Avoiding breakers is your first priority. This means avoiding areas of high winds and waves that may cause these events. There are several wind/wave forecasts that can be useful for these predictions.

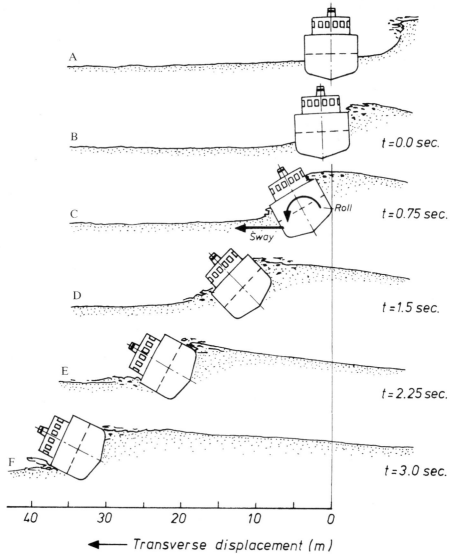

**Figure 18–11.** A re-creation of the capsize sequence of 114–foot fishing vessel *Helland-Hansen*. A 16-foot breaking wave approached abeam (A and B). The captain reduced speed to 6 knots, but the wave rolled the boat to a list of about 60 degrees (C, D, and E). Subsequent waves caused her to heel to 80 degrees, the point of vanishing stability. She sank sideways after 20 minutes. (C.A. Marchaj)

Figure 18–12 shows sea heights in meters and is available through weather faxes from NOAA. At the time of the chart's publication, it is evident that we wouldn't want to cross the Atlantic using the northern route to Ireland—the seas would be horrendous and very dangerous.

## Storm Strategies

If you pay close attention to weather planning, the chances of getting caught out in a storm are quite low. In more than 55,000 nautical miles of cruising, including two Atlantic crossings, we have never experienced anything worse than a gale with winds

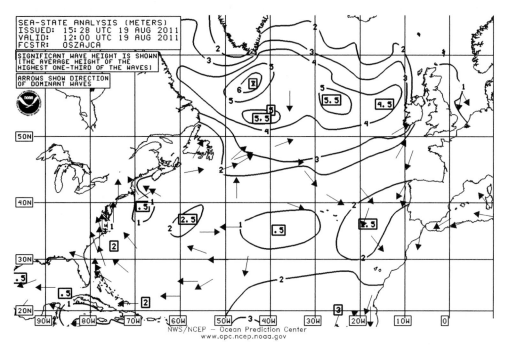

**Figure 18-12.** Sea-state analysis from NOAA for August 19, 2011, showing high seas between Newfoundland and Ireland. Note the significant wave heights of 6 meters or 20 feet. We might expect some waves double that height . . . and this is August! (NOAA)

of about 35–50 knots. We have been both careful and lucky. That does not mean we haven't seen some significant seas that caused concern or discomfort.

We begin this section with a sidebar story about *Resolution*, a Nordhavn 46 on passage from New England to the Azores. Andy Lund and his crew, Mike McFadden, encountered horrendous conditions—their experience illustrates storm tactics and hopefully motivates us to avoid these potential weather conditions.

## How Do You Ride Out a Storm?

The first question is: How bad are the seas? Are they breaking? Are they steep, with short periods? If conditions are really severe, most experts recommend powering slowly into the seas, with an eye open for any especially large, steep, or breaking seas. If an especially nasty wave comes your way, try to sidestep it. If that isn't possible, apply enough power to prevent broaching. If a big freak wave comes your way, you may have no option but to hit it head-on and let it roll over the boat. If everything is tied down well and if all the windows and hatches remain intact,

you may escape with merely a fright or minor damage. However, you will probably never see such a wave unless you venture into the areas of rough seas in the northern or southern oceans.

If the seas are large, but not steep or breaking, you may be able to run downwind with them. This tactic is more comfortable because it effectively slows down the sea's impact and effective wind speed. This is a time to know your boat: How well does it handle in following seas? Does it have a tendency to broach (be thrown sideways) due to bottom contours, rudder, or keel design? If so, you may have to turn into the waves at an earlier point. *Teka III* normally rides well in seas of 12–14 feet on the stern, or even aft quarter. I attribute this to Beebe's design strategy of extending the keel and moving the rudder farther aft. We also have a very large rudder that helps keep the boat straight and prevents broaching. An effective rudder also helps with the slow-speed control needed to ride out the storm.

When deciding on a bow-on or stern-to course, keep in mind that "force intensity increases roughly as the square of wind speed and average wave height,"

# *Resolution* in a Storm

## Michael McFadden

*T*his is Mike McFadden's description *of the storm we just went through [on our passage from Newport, Rhode Island, to Horta, Azores]. He's been aboard [my Nordhavn 46, Resolution] from Bellingham, Washington, through the Panama Canal to Florida, then from New York across the Atlantic. For those of you who haven't met him, he's one of the brightest, nicest, most conscientious and finest people I know. Andy Lund.*

**Subject:** Kickin' the storm's ass
**Date:** 6/14/2005 20:08:29
Well, boys, we made it through the worst of the storm. It came on us quick this morning; then at about two in the afternoon all hell broke loose, and it was time for some evasive tactics—Dirk Pitt style.

So, we were running on the paravanes because both port and starboard stabilizers are now officially out—the starboard stabilizer has a stainless steel bar that snapped—gone. Port side is leaking hydraulic fluid so bad [that] we went through the supply in about five hours. System warnings came on, telling us that it would seize up completely if not shut down immediately! So bam—off with the breaker. With the paravanes deployed, we cruised last night feeling the storm . . . But, the best part was today.

**Figure 18–13.** The Atlantic during the Nordhavn Atlantic Rally showing normal conditions at sea—this is not a storm. (PAE/Nordhavn)

We've been having problems with the boom staying in place as the "clincher cleats" (the ones on most sailboats that [are supposed to hold] the boom straight), were not working causing massive slack on the paravanes. So last night at 2 a.m. we had to go out there and juryrig a knot to keep the boom in place. Problem is that it still had 4 feet of give, two on each side (we couldn't get it tight enough as the boat was rocking so hard, and the boom was swinging with massive strain).

This was ok for a while, until the worst of the storm hit us today mid afternoon. Everything is all over the floor. The doors are duct taped so no water gets in. No way you're eating anything but crackers and more crackers. The chairs that are not latched to the floor are racing across the saloon—aft chair in the lead; no it's the forward chair. Wait, the forward chair just slammed back into the wall; aft chair wins with a victorious crash into the table.

Anyhow, that damn boom kept getting jacked back and forth, letting the port paravane snag under the swim step on the dinghy "dowap." Now that 35-pound weight is right behind the prop tearing up the swim platform. Immediately, I thought we were screwed—there goes everything; no more paravanes. Next, a huge wave hits and the whole boat rocks to starboard, losing what's not already lost to the floor. I'm on my ass in my underwear because it's so damn hot in the boat. Water's crashing everywhere and we're listing heavily side to side—good thing we put on the storm windows the day before.

I put on a mustang jacket, a life jacket, some long underwear, and my soaking wet shoes from the night before; grabbed a harness; and strapped myself up to the back deck as I went out to solve the problem. Immediately I was getting tossed around [something awful]. I was soaked in three minutes,

as waves were crashing through the scuppers, and pounding over the deck. The other guy on the boat (Zach) came out there in the same attire, it was bad ass—I'd never seen a sea so rough! At this point, 40 knot winds, 15–20 ft. seas, and an occasional 30 footer—it's like a fish story: they always seem bigger looking at them than they really are.

We manage to unhook the paravane chain from the swim platform, losing the fish gaff in the process, as it was torn out of my hands when weight yanked free. Within five minutes it was stuck again; same process, this time lost the boat hook. So I had to go on the top deck and free up the extra lines from the boom so we could cleat them off on the aft deck, thus creating a snug fit and solving the slack problem of the paravanes. Up on the top deck I was behind the dinghy lying on my ass, harnessed to the boat, and undoing the knots I had tied the night before in the dark. I looked out, and saw the biggest wave I'd ever seen. It crashed down on me, I got the f*#k out of there, went back around to the back deck and tied that boom down to the cleats, raised the paravanes with the boom winch, and we were set.

The whole time, those deck chairs had rocked loose, and were crashing into our ankles with every movement of the boat. Almost threw 'em over, but, well, found a new place for them—hope they are there in the morning. I came inside, soaking wet, ate some more peanut butter crackers, and made fajitas for dinner.

As of 9:30 our time, we are seeing 10 foot seas and about 15–20 knots of wind. Should be all done with this in about 24 hours, and then we'll do a full damage report. The lines on the boom are chaffing and need to be replaced. The wire on the port side of the boom winch also needs replacing. I told Andy I would not get back on the boat until these items are taken care of and the paravanes are amply restored. Problem is the little string of islands [Azores] in the middle of nowhere that we're going to. However, over a thousand yachts come through there every year, so hopefully we can get the repairs done in time.

Four more days to go.

# Maneuvering in High Seas

The boat's behavior in rough, high-seas conditions will be influenced more by the waves and wind and less by the rudder and propulsion. This means that more time and power is needed in severe conditions. William Van Dorn (author of *Oceanography and Seamanship*—see suggested reading in Appendix E) points out that orbital forces contained in high waves can result in some unusual reactions—even the opposite of what is expected.

In large following seas, as the crest reaches the stern, the wave particles may be rotating so that the current reaching the propeller and rudder are actually opposite from normal—it is like the boat is in reverse even though you are powering ahead. The propeller loses much of its thrust, and much of the remaining thrust is diverted sideways away from the boat, causing the stern to swing to starboard for a right-hand screw. Applying normal rudder correction makes things worse. It is possible the boat could yaw to port and may even slide down the crest and broach. So what can you do? Van Dorn recommends reversing the normal rudder direction and even putting the boat temporarily in reverse—a counterintuitive move that I would be unlikely to attempt. One might also apply even more power to try to get normal rudder control. Even better, if you feel like you are losing control, change course slightly to starboard to offset this effect. This latter recommendation seems most realistic to me. If you are still experiencing control problems, change course more radically or completely change direction to power into the waves rather than running with them.

The following tactics recommended by Van Dorn and others may be considered for dealing with high seas:

1. There is an underlying rhythm to seas and waves. If you need to reverse course, do it during a group of lower waves.
2. Allow speed to build up before putting the rudder hard over.
3. Turning off the wind is easier than turning upwind.
4. Boats with right-handed propellers will turn easier to port.
5. If going to windward, steer as close to the wind as possible. Maximum forces against you are at 30 degrees off the wind.
6. Running before high seas is precarious: if too slow, risk of pooping; if too fast, risk of surfing, yawing, or broaching. Most vessels will be better quartering the seas.
7. Avoid running in troughs in heavy seas. When a large crest reaches you while running in a beam sea, stability is radically decreased due to the effects of weightlessness similar to that experienced when going over a bump when skiing. The forces of gravity are much lower in this case.
8. Freak waves of three to four times average height can occur; keep a sharp lookout and meet them end-on or head-on.
9. A straight course is seldom the best course—view the sea as an obstacle course, through which you thread your way. Use your boat's power and maneuverability to avoid any breaking waves. Power slowly into head seas unless you need a radical change in direction. The faster you go, the more impact from the arriving wave trains.
10. Avoid surfing large seas unless you have a faster boat and skill in riding the waves.

and it varies with relative heading. Shifting course from end-on to 30 degrees off the bow or stern nearly triples the forces. Of course, during a storm waves and wind come from many directions and gusts at various speeds—the sense of direction can become so confusing that it is impossible to determine where you are in relation to the wind and waves.

**Paravanes and storms.** Paravanes also help to prevent broaching because they react to a broach by increasing the force to keep the boat on course. Paravanes also work at the slow speeds you might need during the storm. Active fins are not of much use unless you are moving at a pretty good clip. If you have both fins and paravanes, this is the time to launch the paravanes to augment or even replace fin action.

**Drogues and sea anchors.** Drogues are towed behind the boat to slow it and help give better directional control. Sea anchors are much larger and are used to keep the bow to the waves and slow down drift. We have both on our boat, but have never used either system. Drogues have been proven to work to maintain control when going with large seas. Sea anchors, on the other hand, are not seen as being very effective in extreme conditions. They do seem to work well in more moderate conditions, such as keeping the boat under control while removing a net or rope from the propeller. Commercial tuna fishermen use them at night to drift so they can resume fishing the next day without moving too far from the fish.

U.S. Coast Guard reports found the Jordan series drogue effective for preventing broaches and loss of control in large following seas. However, the largest boat used in the test was a USCG 44-foot motor lifeboat. No tests were done with larger or heavy-displacement trawlers; in fact, the whole project was aimed primarily at sailing vessels. The report indicated that loss of boats over 60 feet to breaking seas is rare, and drogues for larger trawlers may not be needed.

## Preparing for a Storm

When it looks like a storm is unavoidable, it is time to get ready. Some items, such as installing storm windows, may be impossible once the storm has begun. Here are some actions to take beforehand:

+ Install storm windows.
+ Prepare covers for any forward windows that could break. This may mean having plastic or plywood covers available and ready to install. Have installation equipment and fittings readily available.
+ Clean and Rain-X all windows in the pilothouse.
+ Close any through hulls/seacocks not required for running.
+ Be prepared to close dorade vents. These sometimes have inside screw-down covers, or the dorade scoop must be removed and replaced with a plug.
+ Close any ports and secure tightly.
+ Check contents of "ditch bag."
+ Test EPIRB.
+ Get out and check life jackets.
+ Check life raft tie-downs.
+ Secure hatches. Install storm covers, if available.
+ Install lifelines around the deck and flying bridge just in case you have to go out during the storm.
+ Tie down dinghies and other loose items, such as gasoline containers.
+ Prepare extra lines for possible emergency use.
+ Tie the anchor securely so that it cannot possibly be loosened during the storm.
+ Remove any canvas that might blow away, such as a Bimini top.
+ Securely fasten covers for anchor hawseholes.
+ Deploy paravanes if installed.
+ Fill water tanks as full as possible if you have a watermaker.
+ Transfer fuel so that tanks are full, filling the lowest tanks first. Be sure the day tank is full.
+ Check coolant and oil for the main engine.
+ Start and warm up the auxiliary engines.

+ Secure inside of the boat, including dishes and glassware (towels and socks as stuffers work well for this purpose).
+ Bring pillows, sheets, and sleeping gear into the saloon area or near the center of the boat where motion is least powerful.
+ Prepare emergency dry food, such as jerky and granola bars. Fill water bottles for use during the storm. You might want to make sandwiches in advance. Fill thermoses with hot drinks if weather is cool.
+ Pump out contents of holding tanks.
+ Prepare drogue if you have one.
+ Take precautions for seasickness, including barf bags for sick crew.

It is interesting that after all our cruising, the worst gale we encountered was in the same place that Captain Beebe described, off the coast of Northern California near Cape Mendocino. We were going south just like *Passagemaker* and it was a dark night. We could only see the white crests of the waves as they passed around the boat, illuminated by our running lights. The autopilot was under full control and worked without a hitch. I tried for awhile to hand steer, but in utter darkness and 12-foot seas it was almost impossible. After going off course a number of times, I re-engaged the autopilot. When daylight finally arrived, we saw large (perhaps 15-foot) pyramidal waves—the only large waves of this type we ever saw. When we passed one, we would simply slide down its side; they were not breaking.

As long as you watch the weather and stay away from the gales associated with 500 mb parameters and tropical storms, you should experience none of the problems described in this chapter. In our ten years and 50,000 plus miles of world cruising on *Teka III*, I can count only ten days that were particularly rough with gales or near gales and big seas—none of these were more than merely uncomfortable. Scott Flanders on *Egret* reports similar experiences. In seven years and 41,000 miles of cruising, they encountered only nine days of bad weather, often for just part of the day. He also notes that only eighty-six days were spent at sea far from ports of refuge. Only five days of bad weather happened while on such passages—about 6% of the total open-ocean time. Of those five days, none were even approaching survival status.

# Heavy Weather Handling

## Robert Beebe

The literature of sail cruising is loaded with advice and examples about handling vessels in heavy weather. For power voyaging, there is not nearly as much advice available, and what there is seems largely concerned with coastal motorboats and "recreational" boats—such as fishing launches. Some of this advice is applicable particularly about running inlets and handling in thunder squalls. But for a small motor craft 1,000 miles at sea, not much has been written—the experience is just not there.

*Passagemaker*'s experience may be of some use, though her gales were not too severe. The first hit us at the south end of the Red Sea with winds of just about gale force, around 30 knots from astern. The problem was that we had to head about 20 degrees across the wind to avoid going ashore somewhere near Mocha. And we were uncertain about how far off downwind we could safely go without tending to broach. It soon became clear that we could head as far off as we needed, except before the very biggest waves. As a matter of prudence, we took these from dead aft. It was not until this wind died out after sunset that I realized it had never occurred to me to slow down: We ran at 7.5 knots the whole time.

Our hurricane off Bermuda was a strange experience. The sky became overcast and it started to rain, the barograph went down like a rock, and the wind increased. The trouble was that, to us, the wind appeared to be from the wrong direction for a tropical storm. It turned out later the storm had formed over Bermuda and headed northeast so it was already north of us. At the time we had sailed up and ran off with the wind on the port quarter, which of course is the wrong tack for a tropical storm. The rain was so heavy it flattened the waves, but as closely as we could determine, the wind reached 55 knots. It had been 85 knots at Bermuda, but was dying rapidly. We eventually entered what must have been the remnants of the storm's center because the barograph started back up as rapidly as it had gone down. We were able to go to power only and head directly for Bermuda in a dying sea.

A day ahead of us, a yacht (a 77-foot motorsailer) had a very hard time of it, but she came through undamaged.

Our second hurricane was encountered on the passage from Sandy Hook, New York, to Delaware Bay; this storm was coming up the New Jersey coast. The weather bureau said we could beat it if we started *right now*; but what they didn't tell us was that conditions were building up for a typical nor'easter, in addition. The result was plenty of northeast wind all night as we ran down the coast. At about 0200, when I took over, we took down the sail and continued to run with the wind and sea on the quarter, our only choice. She rode the big swells easily, and we had no real problems in wind velocities as high as 50 knots.

Our worst gale, which I noted earlier, was encountered off Cape Mendocino, California. After a summer in British Columbia, we were going down the Pacific Coast toward San Francisco, where we had an onboard party planned for the next day. The night before, the wind started to increase from astern. By 0300 it was bad enough for me to be called. I was on the bridge for the next 27 hours. Conditions were not bad until dawn. After that, the winds gradually increased in strength until they reached full gale. This was not a storm but a gradient wind powered by the hot interior valleys of the West making a "thermal low" while the cold ocean air rushed in to fill the vacuum. It soon became so strong I felt it advisable to take the wheel and head off directly before the waves at low speed. Around sunset, the waves began to "roll," giving them a most frightening aspect. I was concerned about being able to stay dead before the waves after dark on a moonless night. Much to my relief, I found this was no problem: the waves could be seen well enough to manage that.

We kept on southward. The trouble was San Francisco is southeast, getting more easterly the farther we went. I had visions of the gale sweeping us right past the Golden Gate and putting us back in Monterey again. But after midnight the wind gradually started to slacken, and we could steer across it

a bit more each hour, until the course was attained for San Francisco. Shortly after dawn we were steaming through a windless sea. The party was a great success. We were on schedule despite a difficult night.

Now, in all these incidents we ran off before the weather; in the last, dead before it, in the others, across the wind to varying degrees, at all times using flopperstoppers. Would it be possible to do this in winds of higher velocities, say in the 65-to-75-knot range? The answer is, I don't know. I rather suspect that in those conditions, the recommendations for sailing vessels under such "survival conditions," found in books on the subject, would be applicable to power vessels as well. But the essence of the argument—and there is an argument—about the best methods of meeting heavy weather is that running off raises the danger of "broaching," while lying "ahull" (that is, with engines stopped and the drifting vessel allowed to take what attitude she will to the seas), raises grave danger of heavy damage from breaking seas because in this situation almost every vessel will lie broadside to the seas.

Broaching means the boat turns uncontrollably beam to the wind and sea. It is caused by going too fast down the face of a wave that is coming up from astern. The bow buries deeply with enormous increase of resistance forward. The rudder is unable to provide the force necessary to stop the turning motion that results. The turn is so quickly made that large centrifugal forces are generated that, when combined with a breaking wave pushing against the side, can capsize the vessel. The same forces in extreme conditions have also caused some vessels to "pitchpole," or turn end-over-end.

It is these end results of broaching that have caused some experts to urge lying ahull. They point out that the forces acting on a hull lying broadside to the seas are much less if the vessel is stopped than they are with the addition of centrifugal forces from the sudden broaching turn. This should make the vessel less liable

*(continued)*

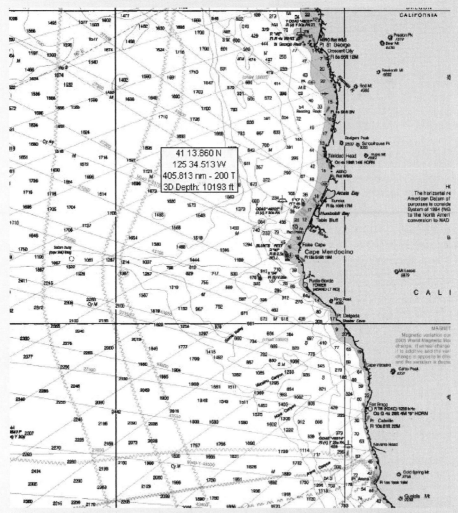

**Figure 18–14.** The gale-prone Cape Mendocino, California. In addition to strong winds, currents meet here, and the seabed has many deep underwater canyons and ridges that distort waves.

to capsize. If it does, it would be better to be rolled over from the broadside position, with inertial forces helping to bring the vessel upright through a full roll, than it would be to chance the damage from pitchpoling. Actual incidents are cited to show the difference in danger and damage.

All of this sounds quite grim, and of course it is. Although many professional seamen have gone to sea all their lives without meeting such conditions, nevertheless one must realize that it can happen. What is really needed in this case is something like a submarine. Vessels going far to sea should have extensive

preparation for preserving their watertight integrity under any condition.

The roster of sailing vessels that have pitchpoled or been capsized, yet righted themselves and returned safely to port, is quite lengthy. So we can see such an incident need not mean certain death—no matter how traumatic the experience. The key, of course, is keeping the sea out of the boat. It is this concern that inspired my earlier remarks on glass areas.

Returning to broaching, our experiences with *Passagemaker* showed she had less tendency to broach than I had hitherto experienced. The "rooting"

tendency was there—you could feel it as she put her bow down and accelerated before a wave. But her big rudder proved to have enough "command" to keep her from actually running off course. The drill was to watch the waves astern, and when a particularly vicious one appeared, to put the stern dead before it. As the bow went down, the helmsman's line of sight was shifted to dead ahead. If the bow showed the slightest tendency to turn to either side, the rudder was immediately slapped hard in the opposite direction. This always worked, yet I hesitate to imply that it always would, the sea being so full of surprises.

## CHAPTER NINETEEN

# Safety and Anchoring

This chapter is divided into several related sections, all about keeping the boat and its crew safe. We cover collision avoidance, staying afloat, lightning, life rafts and survival suits, piracy and theft, medical emergencies, and anchoring (including more on Med mooring). We do not have the space to go in depth on these topics, but when you finish the chapter you will have an idea about which topics need more coverage for your voyaging needs.

## Offshore Safety

Offshore means far away from shore, where you will not encounter crab pots, fishing nets, or rocks. When at sea, there are actually fewer dangers, except for weather, to threaten your boat. However, any accident can be made more severe by the distance from help—there is no Vessel Assist, or similar services, on the high seas. You might be able to call a tug, but this may involve salvage claims or very high towing fees.

### Avoiding Ships and Other Boats

At sea, this task is relatively easy, thanks to radar with Automatic Radar Plotting Aid (ARPA) and Automatic Identification System (AIS). Powerboats have a significant advantage over sailing vessels—a continuous supply of power. We can run our radar constantly and even set alarms to let us know when a target comes into range. There are a couple of potential problems with radar. In heavy rain and seas, it is often difficult to see the ships that would be easily spotted in calm, clear weather. Additional attention is required under these circumstances.

Another problem is not using enough range to pick up a ship in time. Ships can be moving at 20 knots or more and can close a 5-mile separation in 15 minutes or less—not much time to take evasive action. We like the radar on at least the 12-mile range so we have enough time to avoid close calls. One of the problems with using a 12-mile or more range is that the radar might not pick up a small sailboat with a weak radar reflection. If you have two radars, one can scan on a 2-mile range looking for small targets while the other can scan for more distant ships.

**Radar ARPA.** Most radars can be fitted with an automatic radar plotting aid, which is a computer board that is hooked up to a high-speed compass and a GPS. When a ship is seen on the radar screen, you select it with the cursor. Then you have to wait a bit while it tracks both boats until it has reliable information on course and speed. It will then show the following data on the radar screen:

+ Target's course
+ Target's speed
+ Target's range and bearing
+ Target's closest point of approach (CPA), in feet or meters, or miles
+ Time to target's closest point of approach (TCPA)

Multiple targets can be selected, but most radars track only one at a time. If you find the first target is OK, you can select the next target to track. In rough conditions, the data can vary from minute to minute because it is dependent on your course stability and the radar's stability. Thus, you must continually

Figure 19–1. This radar display image was taken at night during the Black Sea Rally—most boats are on the same course. We have seen the radar filled with this many targets in the Mediterranean between Italy and Greece when multiple ferries meet at the same general location. Our ARPA gets a real workout in that case.

monitor the track to make sure you are not coming too close.

**AIS.** This system differs quite a bit from ARPA because the data comes from the target vessel directly, rather than as a radar reflection from the vessel. If the vessel has its AIS "on," then the system should provide much of the following information via VHF transmission every 2 to 10 seconds:

+ MMSI number
+ Navigation status: "at anchor," "underway with engine," "not under command," or "fishing"
+ Rate of turn to right or left, in degrees per minute.
+ Speed over ground in knots.
+ Course over ground relative to true north
+ True heading from 0 to 359 degrees
+ Latitude and longitude.
+ UTC seconds (only) since these data were generated

The following data will be transmitted at a less frequent interval (6 minutes):

+ IMO ship identification number (assigned by the International Maritime Organization to commercial ships)
+ Radio call sign
+ Boat's name
+ Type of ship and cargo if applicable
+ Dimensions of the ship in meters
+ Location of the GPS unit on board the vessel
+ Type of positioning, such as GPS
+ Draft of ship in meters
+ Destination
+ ETA UTC time of arrival month/date/hour

AIS decoders take the data and display it on some type of screen, such as a chartplotter or navigation program. The software's computer calculates a CPA, TCPA, and posts it on the screen. Alarms may be set to warn of potential collisions. Multiple targets may appear simultaneously. AIS can give a more consistent prediction than ARPA, provided it receives the signal. However, be aware that if a tug is pulling a barge, only the tug will show on the AIS radar, not the barge. In this situation, radar is the more accurate. Using both systems is ideal. One problem I have noted at night, when the tracking is most useful, is that it's difficult to get my computer screen

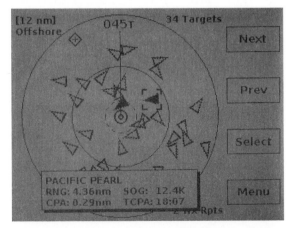

Figure 19–2. Screen shot of a Watchmate AIS receiver, working as a separate dedicated component from the radar, showing all the traffic in a 12-mile area (this can be filtered) with tracking on the *Pacific Pearl*, which has a 0.29 CPA. (Vesper Marine)

**Figure 19–3.** The navigation display on Nordhavn 52, *Dirona*, off the west coast of Vancouver Island combines ARPA and AIS on one screen. Blue triangles are AIS, the white circle is an active ARPA target, and the white diamonds are lost ARPA targets that are no longer applicable. (James Hamilton)

dim enough to read the AIS information without being blinded. I don't experience this problem with the ARPA display on my Furuno radar, which can be dimmed to a satisfactory level that doesn't spoil night vision.

### Communicating with Ships at Sea

When dealing with ships, it is good practice to call on the VHF if there is any clarification needed for which course to take. For example, if your CPA is too close for comfort, you would call the oncoming ship; give your boat name, type, size and position; and state that you are altering course to go astern of the ship. AIS is a great aid here because you can call the ship by name, rather than ship at X and Y latitude and longitude. You are much more likely to get a response with the vessel name. If there is a female watchstander on duty, have her make the call. We find that ships' crew are more likely to respond to a woman's voice than to a man's. Also consider that some ship watchstanders will have limited English skills, so speak slowly and clearly. Learning and using the approved phrases by IMO for standard marine communication phrases (SMCPs) makes communication clearer and more consistent.

### Can Other Boats See Us?

We find that a lot of cruising boats have weak running lights. This is nice for night vision, but it means you are much harder to see at night. Use the largest, strongest running lights that are practical. Locate them where they will not reflect on the forward deck and affect your night vision. Light deflectors may be used to reduce reflections, but still allow you to be clearly seen by other vessels.

## Near-Shore Safety

Problems multiply as you get closer to shore. Chances of collision increase. Rocks and shoals are everywhere. Logs, nets, and kelp are more likely. Small fishing boats, almost invisible on radar, are a problem. Narrow channels with traffic make passages more challenging. Fog is a frequent problem. Charts may be inaccurate. In other words, there are many additional things that can go wrong when you are close to shore.

### Chart Inaccuracies

Coastline and depth surveys are often more than a hundred years old. The original surveys were done with lead lines (lead weights on the end of a marked line with knots every fathom, or 6 feet). As recently as 2001, NOAA noted that about half of the depths in U.S. waters were from lead line soundings. In fact, until 1940 that was the only way to record depths. It wasn't until the 1980s when modern side-scan radars came into use that truly accurate bottom-depth contours were possible. Data is most accurate in areas frequented by ships or commercial traffic. Areas frequented by pleasure boats are not as current. This is the conclusion we reached in our article for *Passage-Maker Magazine*:

> *Hazards "reported" on charts are sometimes deceiving. Their positions are usually recorded during an emergency (such as a fire or sinking) or by eyeballing a location—often positioned to the nearest latitude and longitude on the chart.*
>
> *There are several thousand unsurveyed wrecks and obstructions marked on charts and many more*

that are still uncharted. When you are in the area of a reported hazard, keep up your vigilance for a considerable distance away from the mark on the chart.

Also, since so many soundings are from lead line or single-beam data, there still may be potential dangers lurking below the surface. If you are cruising in an area with older sounding data that shows an irregular bottom, it would be prudent to stay in the deepest, most commonly used channel rather than taking a shortcut.

The bottom line is to be careful out there. We are still a long way from fully accurate bottom charting of all U.S. waters.

## Arriving at Christmas Island

### Dick and Gale Barnes, *Ice Dancer*, Nordhavn 50

We arrived at two in the morning, in very heavy rain. The rain obscured radar images. Our electronic charting of this area was poor. The worst was the non-detailed, world vector chart by Nobeltec. It had Christmas Island misplaced by 25 miles. We note that Fanning and Washington Islands, which are on our current route, are similarly mischarted on the vector charts by about 15 miles. Our older, raster electronic charts of this area are imperfect, but at least within one-quarter mile of actual position. Our new paper chart of the island was drawn in the 1950s, with unknown horizontal datum, meaning that you cannot rely on your GPS for precise navigation. Our strategy is to find and confirm all islands and reefs near our course by radar. On Wednesday morning, we motored offshore waiting for daybreak before finding an anchorage. (June 2, 2005)

Figure 19–4. Lead line sounding photo circa 1928. The photo caption is "Wind that sucker up and let her fly!" The lead is thrown ahead as the boat moves so that it will be straight up and down when the ship reaches the thrower's position. (NOAA Historical Library)

The situation is even worse in other places. We found ancient surveys for the Sea of Cortez while cruising in Mexico. *Ice Dancer* reported similar conditions at Christmas Island (see the sidebar "Arriving at Christmas Island").

### Running Aground

Experienced cruisers say "it is not *if* you run aground but *when*" you will run aground. If you cruise the shallow waters of the Intracoastal Waterway, there is a good chance you have already found the bottom. We did. In central Georgia we were confused by changing channel markers and missed a key marker in spite of our chartplotter. However, it was a mud bottom and the tide was rising, so no problem. We also found the bottom in some skinny water in the Bahamas and had to wait on the tide again—no problem. Running aground in the Pacific Northwest can have more severe outcomes. The tremendous tides of 20 feet or more mean your boat can be completely dried out, even if it is not holed by some sharp rock. If it heels over too far on its side, the possibility of damage or sinking is great due to downflooding through ventilators or other openings in the boat.

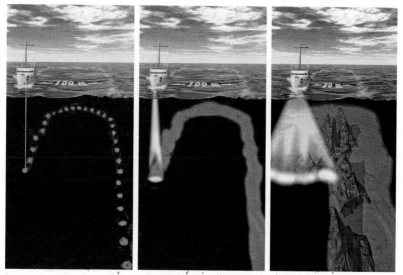

**Figure 19–5.** The evolution of depth sounding for nautical charts from lead line (left), to single-beam depth sounders (middle), to modern multi-beam sonars (right), showing how pinnacles were hidden by the older methods, but show clearly with the new techniques. (NOAA Office of Coast Survey)

# Going Aground on a Falling Tide

If you go aground on a falling tide where the amount of tide is equal to the draft of the boat, you have trouble, especially if it is on a sloping bottom. Here are some steps you may be able to take:

- Work to free the hull by reversing and using the bow thruster to wiggle the boat a bit. If it does not come free, try to use the engine and rudder to get the boat to heel upslope with the keel toward the deep water.
- If you have a really heavy dinghy, and the boom is long, you can put it in the water, load it with people, and lift it just above the water at right angles to the boat. Be sure to put the weight on the upward side of bottom so the boat will dry out upslope. It is possible this will reduce your freeboard, so you can try reversing with the engine again.
- If the previous suggestions do not work, prepare to be heeled over and dried out. If you are not facing the

mast upslope, fasten a rope to the top of the mast and run it to shore. Use a block and tackle to pull the boat so the keel runs toward deep water. If the shore is too far away, a long line to an anchor might work. Keep this pressure in place even when the water starts to return.
- If the boat is leaning the wrong way, get some timbers (carried in the bilge for this purpose) under the spray rail or gunnel to keep the boat from settling all the way on its side. It is also helpful to have some plywood pads to support the bottom of the timbers. It may be possible to wedge shorter timbers under the hull to support it nearer the turn of the bilge.
- Next, cover any potential down-flooding openings on the water side of the heeling boat. Use duct tape and heavy plastic to cover engine vents. Use wood or plastic plugs to cover wet exhaust outlets. Cover fuel and water tank vents and fuel fills with duct tape. If you are heeling toward the deep water, tape doors and

windows on that side as well. Anything that might let in water should be taped. Even bilge pump outlets may need taping unless you have one-way valves to prevent water's entry.
- If the heel is steep enough, you may need to plug engine dip stick holes and make sure battery acid will not leak. Turn off the propane valve.
- If necessary, you can pump all the water from the tanks to lighten the load a bit.
- It is a good idea to set an anchor in deep water to prevent any further grounding when the tide rises.
- If you have an extra engine–powered bilge pump, test it and place it in ready status.
- When the tide starts back in, carefully monitor the bilges and openings to make sure nothing is leaking. If the side of the boat remains watertight, it should right itself.
- If you seek help from a towing company, be sure to get a contract that protects you from future salvage claims.

**Figure 19–6.** This Nordhavn 57 was lucky—its fin kept it upright as the tide went out. Generally, fins are designed to break away if they hit something like a rock. In this case, the boat probably settled gently on the fin. Think of the damage here if the boat had rolled to 90 degrees or more. (PAE/Nordhavn)

## Hitting Objects in the Water

There are many opportunities to hit things that are floating around. We have seen or hit numerous logs, tree stumps, crab pots, lobster pots, kelp, nets, and even a 55-gallon drum riding low in the water. Others have seen boats floating bow-up, and containers knocked off ships by storms. Some of these items can cause serious damage if hit at cruising speed. The most likely adverse outcome is a bent propeller, snagged paravane or fin, or a tangled mess around your shaft. A rare event might be an actual hole in the hull, caused by hitting something especially big and unmoving at just the right angle, say a floating container. In the Pacific Northwest, a "deadhead" is particularly dangerous. This is a large log that is waterlogged, but still floating vertically in the water. Its end may be only inches above the surface, but if you hit it, you can put a hole in the bottom of the boat. A number of commercial fishing boats have had this unfortunate experience. Deadheads are normally reported to the coast guard and announced on the VHF. If you are travelling by day, you can often see these threats, but at night they

are invisible. That is one reason we don't travel at night in this part of the world.

Of course, hitting an underwater rock is the worst and is almost certain to cause serious damage. A few years ago, a Nordhavn 62 cruised too close to shore along the Baja coast and hit a rock. The boat could not be saved, and one person died during the attempt. Cal and Nancy Massey's Nordhavn 40, *Hale Kai*, had a better outcome when it hit a rock going about 2–3 knots in Kalinin Bay, north of Sitka, Alaska. The starboard fin was broken off about one-third of the way to the tip. Under cruising power, it was discovered that the fin had also bent and was leaking slowly around the seals. The Masseys made it back to Sitka, arranged for an emergency haulout, and fixed the problem. Obviously, fins are a vulnerable part of the boat. A Krogen 42 in the Gulf of Mexico was sunk during a rescue attempt after grounding when the fin broke away from the hull, taking part of the hull with it.

## Fixing Leaks in an Emergency

While we have travelled well over 50,000 nautical miles, we have never had to fix a major leak. However, I have spent a lot of time planning what I would do if I had a bad leak on board. Here are some of the approaches I use; there are many more:

- Make sure to have wooden or plastic tapered plugs for every hole in the boat, including seacocks, exhausts, bilge pump outlets, and sink drains.
- Keep fresh underwater epoxy for fixing holes.
- Have a good selection of plywood, 1/4" to 1/8", along with 2" × 2" and 2"× 4" boards for wedging them into holes from inside the boat. You will need a small sledge hammer for this.

- Have towels, sheets, tarps, or even paper towels handy to plug leaks.
- Have some driller's mud. This is a specialized type of cement that hardens on contact with water or oil and is used in oil or water drilling.
- Have a triangular piece of strong waterproof canvas about 4 feet on each side with a large grommet in each corner and lines attached for pulling it under the boat and stopping water from outside the hull. Launching a diver in the water might help get the cloth installed.
- Know the location of every through-hull, even in the dark. You might have to go underwater to close a seacock.
- Have a good LED strap-on headlight for troubleshooting. This frees both hands to work. Waterproof models, the best choice, can be purchased at dive shops.

## Safety at the Dock

In 2011, a Nordhavn 75 sank at the dock in San Jose del Cabo, Mexico. Apparently sometime during the night, with no one on board, the boat developed a leak in a recently installed faulty bait tank PVC fitting. The leak overwhelmed its electric bilge pumps. Flooding happens rapidly if there is a major leak. One mathematically inclined cruiser calculated that a 1-1/2" leak that is 4' feet below the water line would let in about 88 gallons per minute, or 5,300 gallons per hour. Our 12-volt or 24-volt bilge pumps are not designed to handle this level of flooding.

If someone is on board, a bilge warning horn or alarm may be sufficient to alert people that a problem exists, allowing them to take action to fix it. If no one is on board, the alarm may not get the attention of other boaters, or they may be reluctant to break into a strange boat to find the problem. One solution may be to close all seacocks when leaving the boat. This method is a bit troublesome, but it is practically foolproof. If the boat has waterproof compartments with doors, secure them as well. If you live near the marina, you may want to install remote alarms that can signal problems.

# Through-Hulls and Safety at the Dock

## Steve Dashew

Have you counted your through-hulls? Do you know where they are? Can you get to them? Do you close them when leaving the boat unattended for long periods? And how about fridge and air conditioning plumbing? How secure is it, and what are the unattended risks associated with it?

As boatowners continue to stretch the complexity of systems aboard, the temptation to riddle the hull with underwater through-hulls increases. Owners are often uninformed to the potential problems and risks associated with fittings below the waterline, and many builders and boatyards find it tough to deny the wishes of a paying client.

It does not have to be this way. We are not trying to push our concepts on the back of anyone's disaster, but there are some systems design principles that will mitigate these risks:

- Watertight bulkheads, in particular around the engine room and shaft logs
- Single incoming salt water point with easily accessed valve to turn off when leaving the boat
- Fridge and air conditioning cooling systems that do not rely on pumping salt water through the condensing coils
- Standpipes for below-the-waterline fittings, with shutoff valves above the waterline (fiberglass and metal construction)
- Dual automatic bilge pumps in high-risk (engine room) areas.

# Lightning

The likelihood of your boat being struck by lightning is not great, but the results can be catastrophic. Some parts of the world have a low incidence of lightning; while others, like Florida, have plenty of lightning. BoatU.S. Insurance reports lightning strikes in Florida for trawlers at 2 per every 1,000 boats. For auxiliary sailing vessels, it's 4.5 per 1,000. Higher masts naturally attract more lightning, but it can strike anywhere. A marine insurance surveyor says, "If lightning wants to hit your boat, there's not much you can do about it." We have never been struck by lightning, but have experienced two close calls. One was in an anchorage in Florida when lightning struck a nearby buoy—the flash and crack of

**Figure 19–7.** World cruisers have to worry about lightning strikes, which can have devastating effects on electronics-laden passagemakers. (NOAA Photo Library)

bottom, sometimes up to 3 inches in diameter. Imagine yourself in some remote area of the South Pacific with this type of damage. Not a nice picture. Take every precaution to prevent or minimize lightning damage. If you experience a strike check for leaks around seacocks and look for any holes in the boat's hull. You may want to haul the boat to check for damage. Turn on electronics and electrical items. If they work, you may be OK—lightning tends to immediately kill electronics and electrical items; however, as noted in the sidebar (next page), later failures are possible. Check your engine for smooth, normal operation. Make sure the sensors are working.

What about grounding your equipment? Lightning expert Ewen Thompson says "The NFPA (National Fire Protection Association) recommends interconnecting (bonding) everything to equalize potentials and hence lower the risk of sparks forming between conductors. This is not to say that bonding cures all, since voltages still form along any conductor that the lightning current is flowing in, and there can be induced voltages from magnetic coupling effects into circuits." He continues: "Charges also build up in any conductor that is *not* connected to anything. In this case the total charge is zero but charges accumulate at the extremities and can reach critical densities to initiate sparks. So lightning can complete the circuit by arcing across at *both* ends of the conductor." This means simply disconnecting your antenna wire may not be enough.

Current lightning-protection strategies call for creating a path down the rigging (if you have rigging) to through-hull conductors at or near the waterline and at the sides of the boat, not the centerline. Lightning really likes to dissipate at the surface, not underwater. If your main grounds are below water, they are not as effective. The idea is to provide what is called a zone of protection for people and electronics by routing the lightning around the boat rather than through it. (See Figure 19–8.) When it goes through the boat to the engine or a central underwater ground, there are lots of opportunities for damage or injury.

thunder were simultaneous. The other time was at an anchor in Gaeta, Italy. Several sailboats anchored next to us were damaged by electromagnetic forces from a nearby strike. They lost autopilots, GPSs, and radars.

Lightning tries to equalize the electrical charge built up in the clouds by seeking a ground to dissipate it—water is a good place for it to go—30,000,000 volts of zapping power! Lightning's path is encouraged to go to a "lightning rod," which for cruisers is the boat, usually the top of the mast. Once it strikes the mast, its path will be down to the water, often passing through the mast to the boat's grounding system, through the engine block, and out through the shaft to the propeller or bonded seacocks. However, it will take the easiest path, which may be through electrical wiring, or it can even side flash (or jump) to stoves, refrigerators, or even people as it seeks a path to ground. Lightning also creates electromagnetic fields that can damage nearby boats. Current can jump from one wire to another without any electrical connection.

A lightning strike can ruin pretty much anything electrical on the boat, including engine sensors, autopilot, GPS, computer, alternator, inverter, VHF/SSB radios, battery chargers, and even bilge pumps. If lightning does not have a clear path to the water, it can blow holes in the boat's fiberglass sides or

# Lightning Damage

## Lightning Strike on a 36' Boat

A 2-year-old 36' boat, loaded with modern electronics systems, took a lightning hit at the dock. The voltage surge knocked out the shore power and flowed through the boat to the zincs. Pretty much everything was dead. Engines would not crank; radar, radios, GPS, TV, refrigeration, and chartplotters were all knocked out. The insurance company wanted to repair items rather than replace them. Based on some technical advice, the owners insisted that any repaired items be cycled on and off multiple times a day. After a week of this on-off cycling, things began to fail. The insurance adjuster finally agreed that the components needed replacement. If the cycling procedure had not been used, failures might have happened months later, with denial of any liability by the insurers.

## Lightning Strikes a Nordhavn 72

This boat was struck at the dock with the owner on board. Shore power had been removed and the ship's electrical system minimized. A severe flash and very loud crack signaled the strike, which was later determined to hit the forward whip antenna. The boat appeared to have a total power failure, with a burning odor in the pilothouse, saloon, and engine room. A quick check of bilges and engine room indicated no water intrusion or fire. It turns out that most of the electronics were fried by the high voltage from the strike. The owner went through a check of on-board systems—233 of them—to find out which were operational. Quite a few of the household items, such as refrigeration, were still working. Unfortunately, almost everything with electronic control was not working. Here is a summary of some of the outages:

- Sonar and depth sounders
- Radar
- VHF and SSB
- Satellite phone
- GPS and GPS compass
- Stabilizers
- Autopilot doubtful
- Throttle gear control
- No engine display information. Later, engines were manually started and ran fine, but without any information about rpm, oil pressure, or temperatures.
- Nav PC and associated systems
- 24-volt hydraulic alternators

While the loss was covered by insurance, the owner expected it to take months for repairs. Latent damage is also possible since it make take months or more for a problem to surface.

Add connections to handrails & metal superstructure where possible.
Add surge suppressors to all antenna cables.

**Figure 19–8.** Key elements of lightning protection system on a Nordhavn 62 designed by Ewen Thompson. (Marine Lightning Protection)

Completely disconnected electronics may be spared, but this is hard to do. We put a spare GPS, handheld GPS, and computer in our oven, which is metal and grounded. We hope that these items would survive a strike. Manual backup engine gauges would be helpful in the event engine electronics are knocked out. GPSs, autopilots, chartplotters, and electronically controlled stabilizers may be put out of action. Experts say most modern engines will run without their computer in a manual mode. You might want to check out your engine's specifications for this event.

## Life Rafts and Survival Suits

If your boat were on fire, or sinking due to an uncontrollable leak, you need to be ready. Most passagemakers carry a life raft for these types of emergencies. Much has been written about the difficulties of boarding and using a life raft in rough seas. Remember that the rule is always to stay with the boat as long as it is afloat.

In colder waters, survival suits can make the difference between life and death. Hypothermia is the real enemy—without a survival suit it may be impossible to live more than a few minutes in really cold water. If you own survival suits, practice putting them on; it is not as easy as it looks. Be sure to have two plastic shopping bags with each suit to make putting your feet into the suit easier and faster. Also note that there are different size suits—one size does not fit all.

While we were interviewing the Canadian Coast Guard for an article they told us they greatly preferred looking for a life raft when compared to someone in a

**Figure 19–10.** Steve and Linda Dashew display the recommended position to await rescue if you do not have a life raft. (Steve Dashew)

survival suit. The life raft is much easier to spot, and the chances of prompt rescue and survival are better if you have a raft; however, the combination of both raft and survival suits is best. This allows you to stay warm in the raft.

## Piracy and Theft

As this book goes to press, it is very dangerous to voyage anywhere in the Northwest Indian Ocean through the Red Sea to the Suez Canal. The U.S. Coast Guard and the International Sailing Federation (ISAF) recommend avoiding this area entirely. For those wishing to circumnavigate, going around Cape Horn is the recommended route to avoid pirates. Some voyagers are opting to commercially ship their boats to the Mediterranean to avoid the long sea voyage around Africa. If you choose to make the risky passage through the Gulf of Aden and Northwest Indian Ocean, there are recommended actions and contacts available from many sources, including the ISAF Guidelines concerning piracy in this area. Noonsite also has extensive references and reports about this area.

While other areas of the world also present considerable risk, it is not as severe as in the Gulf of

**Figure 19–9.** Linda and Steve Dashew in their survival suits during a training course in Alaska. This training is highly recommended for cold-water voyagers. (Steve Dashew)

Aden area. The next worst area for piracy is Venezuela, especially the island of Margarita, although problems are also bad throughout much of the Caribbean Windward Islands. The accompanying table shows where piracy has happened in recent years, based on Noonsite reports. If you plan to visit any of these areas, read the appropriate report and take actions to minimize your risk. Many piracy incidents are thefts and burglaries; however, armed robberies and even murders at anchorages or at sea seem to be happening more often, especially off the coast of Venezuela.

## Strategies for Minimizing Risk of Pirate Attacks

Searching through reports and examining our own experience, I have made a list of some of the strategies that may help minimize the chance of a pirate attack. The list is incomplete so I urge you to research this topic more fully.

+ Avoid piracy areas—don't go there! Plan your route and travel to safer areas. For example, in the Caribbean, you might avoid Venezuelan waters entirely and go directly from Martinique to Cartagena, Colombia, or the Panama Canal.
+ Avoid areas where armed violence, ransom, and murder have been associated with piracy. For example, St. Vincent and the Grenadines is one of the more dangerous areas of the Windward Islands; however, theft is more common than armed robbery, so you might want to chance it.
+ Throughout many parts of the world, theft of dinghies and motors is common. In the Caribbean we hear, "lift it or lose it," meaning that any dinghy left in the water may disappear during the night or at the dock, even if locked.
+ Lock up at night and when leaving the boat. Thieves may still gain access, but it will be more difficult. Leave several deck lights on, whether you are on board or not. This might deter pirates.
+ Install alarm systems. We use a motion alarm that gives off a loud signal. We also have a manually activated horn and floodlights that are controlled from our locked sleeping cabin. The combination of noise and light may deter most common thieves.
+ Travel at night. Most pirates do not like to attack ships at sea at night. If you run without lights (this is not legal, so do it at your own risk) and without transmitting on the VHF, that can help—stealth is the strategy here. If you want to remain in contact with a buddy boat, use a SSB channel that cannot be scanned by the pirates.
+ If traveling in pirate waters, you might trail several lines behind the boat with floats to make it

| Country | 2009 | 2010 | 2011 |
|---|---|---|---|
| Aden | | | 1 |
| Antigua | 2 (1) | | |
| Belize | 1 | | |
| Bequia | 2 | 4 | |
| Borneo | | | 1 |
| Brazil | 2 (1) | | |
| Cape Verdes | | 2 | |
| Colombia | 3 | 2 | |
| Costa Rica | | 1 | |
| Dominica | 3 | 1 | |
| Dominican Republic | | 1 | |
| Galapagos | 1 | | |
| Gambia | 1 | | |
| Greece | 2 | | |
| Grenada | 1 | | |
| Honduras | | 2 (1) | |
| Indonesia | 1 | | |
| Italy | 1 | | |
| Malaysia | | 1 | |
| Maldives | 1 | | |
| Marshall Islands | | | 1 |
| Mozambique | | 1 | |
| Nicaragua | 1 | | |
| Oman | | | 1 (4) |
| Panama | | 1 (1) | |
| Papua New Guinea | | 2 | 1 |
| Philippines | 1 | | |
| Red Sea | | 1 | |
| Solomon Islands | 1 | 1 | 1 |
| Seychelles | 3 | | |
| Somalia | 1 (1) | | |
| St. Lucia | | | 1 |
| St. Martin | | 1 | |
| St. Vincent | | | 3 |
| Thailand | 1 (1) | | |
| Trinidad | 2 | | |
| US Virgin Islands | | 1 | |
| Venezuela | 1 | 3 (1) | 2 |
| Yemen | 1 | | |

**Figure 19–11.** Pirate attacks 2009–2011. Deaths in parenthesis. (Compiled by the author from Noonsite reports)

harder to approach your stern; or, if you are lucky, entangle their propeller.

+ Some have recommended towing a dinghy on a long line behind the boat to use for escape if pirated on the high seas. In the worst case, you could jump overboard, cut the line, and swim to the dinghy. The reasoning here is that some pirates find murder on the high seas easy—no witnesses, no hassles. We have never done this.
+ Have copies of all important documents, especially your passports, and store them on a CD placed in a place that is unlikely to be discovered. You might also send scanned copies to your e-mail account if it stores your messages online.
+ Keep money and credit cards stashed in several locations.
+ Keep an old wallet with money and some old credit cards handy for giving away.
+ Guns are controversial, but most experts recommend against them unless you are willing to shoot to kill and are skilled with the gun. If you don't shoot first and kill the pirate, he may kill you. Showing a gun often escalates the threat of violence and may result in deaths.
+ If attacked, try to stay calm and give the pirates what they want. Don't make any quick moves or take any photos.

## Medical Emergencies

Dealing with serious medical emergencies is one of the most stressful events for the voyaging boat. Unless you have medical training, anxiety is often high. Am I doing the right thing? How can we resolve this problem? While power cruisers may have fewer ways to get injured by simply running the boat than do sailing cruisers, there are still ample opportunities for trouble. In our ten years of world cruising we have been relatively lucky to have most problems near land.

We've survived a fall that resulted in broken ribs and an infected leg wound, an ulnar nerve attack to the arm and hand that mimicked a heart attack, a cut foot that needed stitches, and food poisoning in the remote San Blas Islands. Except for the San Blas problem, all incidents occurred in areas close to medical attention.

The best preparation for dealing with medical emergencies is knowledge and access to proper first aid materials. Ideally, at least two crew members will have first aid training for remote medical emergencies. Several organizations specialize in training for marine medical emergencies. In addition, these same companies often provide rather extensive offshore medical kits that include equipment, supplies, and medicines needed to treat almost any accident or sickness. Thorough research before leaving is needed and your boat's reference library should include a number of good books on marine medicine (see Appendix E). The sidebar (next page) provides insights on handling major medical problems at sea.

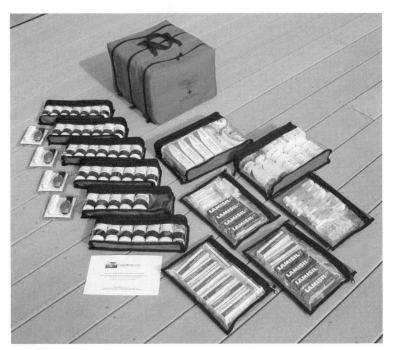

Figure 19–12. The Voyager Prescription Kit by OceanMedix contains the prescription medication component of a vessel's medical kit intended for voyages where professional medical care may be more than 48 hours away. (Denny Emory; OceanMedix.com LLC)

# The Unthinkable: Major Trauma Offshore

Jeffrey E. Isaac, PA-C

For practical purposes we can separate major trauma into three categories: the kind that will kill quickly no matter what; the kind that will kill within an hour or so without medical intervention; or the kind that is not directly fatal but exposes you to risk of death by hypothermia, dehydration, or infection. Regardless of your level of medical training, you can disregard the first category; the cause of death is merely interesting. However, it is the other two that you should prepare for and might be able to do something about.

You don't need to know a lot of medicine to effectively handle the immediate emergency. Bleeding control, spine protection, airway management, and ventilation are all covered in any good first aid course. But, in addition to those basic skills you also need to know how to focus on the problems you can treat and not be distracted by the problems you can't. Your goal is actually pretty simple: give your patient the best chance of survival under the circumstances you're in. Head trauma, one of the most common serious problems aboard small boats, offers a good example. You cannot do anything about brain swelling or intracranial bleeding. But you can protect your patient's airway from blood and vomit and keep him warm, hydrated, fed, and secure from further injury. Let the brain take care of itself while you focus on everything else. Given a chance, most head trauma patients survive.

Severe bleeding is another example. External bleeding from a lacerated blood vessel in an arm or leg can be stopped with a pressure dressing or even a tourniquet if necessary. Internal bleeding from a ruptured spleen is out of your control. Again, focus on the possible. Keep your patient hydrated, fed, protected, and warm; and she, too, will probably survive. Most solid organ injury is not directly fatal, but the combination of blood loss and hypothermia is. A fractured femur or lower leg is rarely fatal. Unless the bones have penetrated the skin, there is only so much space available for bleeding, so shock does not progress. The danger is

in the disability. The patient cannot run or swim to safety, or find food and water without help.

A leg fracture can be splinted to the other leg for quick extrication. Straighten the leg if necessary; then wrap both legs firmly together with padding between them. A femur can actually be splinted this way for a long time. A lower leg will need additional splinting to include the ankle. As long as there is good blood flow all the way to the toes, the patient can endure a days-long evacuation if you pay attention to pain control and the basic body needs. You don't need to worry about putting the bones back exactly where they belong. The orthopedist can do that tomorrow or next week.

Be sure to have your lifesaving tools easily accessible. A comprehensive medical kit, like a life raft, is just expensive ballast if you and your crew can't find it. Consider breaking it up into smaller kits that can be stowed where they're needed. In doing this, remember that a short-handed crew will not just be dealing with a medical emergency; they will be trying to manage a boat underway at the same time.

Keep a basic trauma module just inside the companionway. This should include a pair of protective gloves, a pressure dressing and tourniquet for bleeding, a splint and wrap for injured extremities, and a pocket mask or Numask for rescue breathing. It should also include a couple of extrication straps (long sail ties will do) and a stiff cervical collar to help you move your patient to safety.

Pain medication should also be easily accessible. Pain control is an emergency medical procedure, especially in the shorthanded survival situation. If pain is not controlled, the patient will not be able to protect himself, eat, drink, or effectively communicate. Pain is the most common and treatable cause of respiratory distress in chest and abdominal trauma.

The fear that pain medication will mask symptoms and allow a patient to injure himself further is unfounded. Any patient who is awake and able to

move around will feel pain and modify activity accordingly. A dose of medication sufficient to mask all pain will put the patient to sleep. Unless you have plenty of crew to monitor him, drugging your patient into coma is not a good idea. In a serious situation, we want an injured person awake and talking, but feeling better and breathing easier. Use narcotics if you have to, but medicate with the lowest effective dose. When you call from the [pilothouse] to see how things are going down below, you want an answer. The more the patient can care for himself, the more you will be able to focus on the overall management of the emergency and the vessel.

A near perfect choice for severe pain initially is the narcotic fentanyl for transmucosal administration. This is essentially a lollypop that is placed between the gum and cheek allowing the potent medication to be absorbed through the mucous membranes. It is easy to remove if the patient becomes drowsy. Fentanyl is short acting and the pop does not freeze, break, or melt in storage.

Another useful drug is a broad spectrum antibiotic. While use of antibiotics to prevent infection in high-risk wounds is controversial in the civilized setting, you need all the help you can get when you're far offshore. The sooner antibiotics are administered, the better they will work.

For long-term survival you will need to manage the "ins and outs." This means providing fluid, electrolytes, and calories. If the patient can eat and drink, you're all set. If not, you will need to start an intravenous or subcutaneous fluid drip or try to rehydrate rectally. Managing output may require using a urinary catheter for a disabled patient and managing defecation with an incontinence diaper. This is the part of trauma management that goes beyond first aid and illustrates other skills and materials that you should consider acquiring.

The ultimate goal, of course, is getting a severely injured crewmember safely off the boat and into a hospital, preferably before the diaper becomes necessary.

*(continued)*

But beware of the rush to evacuate—some rescue efforts may not actually improve the casualty's chance of survival. With several crewmembers aboard the typical voyaging boat the risk/benefit of evacuation can be more carefully weighed against the risk/benefit of staying on board. Exercising this judgment is where good seamanship and good medicine really come together.

Instead of an Australian frigate in fair conditions, your rescuer may be a tramp steamer wallowing in 20-foot seas or a helicopter trying to lower a basket in 60-knot gusts. It would be deeply disappointing to have worked so hard to keep your patient alive only to see her drown in the rescue effort, or later for lack of appropriate care. Your patient might have a better chance of survival if you sailed her into port yourself, even if it takes five days. You should gear your training, equipment, supplies, and attitude toward that possibility.

## Anchoring

We prefer anchoring to marinas and have anchored well over a thousand times. We get to observe others as well, which prompted me to put a separate section in the book. It is surprising how many skippers have trouble with anchoring. In this section, we discuss a few strategies we have used for more successful anchoring.

### Anchor and Chain Selection

If you have the correct size anchor and rode, you will solve many potential anchoring problems. The heavier the anchor and chain, the easier it is to set and the better it will hold. Do not believe the manufacturers' recommendations on anchor size. Select the largest, heaviest anchor that you can store and retrieve. Heavy chain also helps hold and set the anchor. All-chain rode is highly recommended. It is almost impossible to anchor in deep water with nylon line unless you have plenty of swinging room—a rare luxury.

On our 52-foot boat, we are restricted by the amount of room required for the bow-mounted anchors. We carry two anchors, a 110-pound Delta with 300 feet of 1/2-inch chain and a 110-pound Bruce with 400-plus feet of 3/8 inch chain. We use the Delta when holding is really critical, such as on grassy bottoms or in hard sand, or in gale conditions. The Bruce works well in the sticky Northwest mud, but is unsatisfactory in grassy or rocky bottoms because its flukes are shaped to pick up larger rocks or clumps of grass. This often results in the anchor dragging rather smoothly across the bottom without biting into the bottom. The lighter chain on the Bruce makes retrieval quite a bit faster than the big chain on the Delta so we often use it when anchoring in deep water (60 plus feet).

There have been many anchor tests showing that some of the newer designs may hold better than older models. One popular new model is the Rocna, shown in Figure 19–14. Many new voyaging boats are using this anchor, including the Dashew designs. On our next long voyage I may trade my Bruce for a Rocna of similar size and weight. The Bruce could cause problems in coral if pieces bunched up in the flukes.

Figure 19–13. A bolt-type shackle cannot work loose like pin shackles.

**Figure 19–14.** Rocna anchor shown on the bow roller of Diesel Duck, *10&2*.

**Figure 19–15.** A Dashew FPB 64, showing its Rocna anchor and the bow line hole for the snubber line. This smooth aluminum donut results in minimum chafe. (Steve Dashew)

## Choosing an Anchoring Spot

In an ideal situation, you will find a nice little bay with plenty of swinging room and protection from wind and waves. Unfortunately, reality doesn't usually work out this way. Some critical variables are covered in the following sections.

**Protection.** In some parts of the world, such as the Pacific Northwest, good protected anchorages are abundant. In other areas, you can only get protection from the prevailing winds and waves. This situation means you may have to depart in the middle of the night if the wind changes. Voyaging up the Pacific Coast from California to Washington state, we anchored in the lee of a peninsula, called Port Orford, due to moderate to strong northerly winds. About midnight, I felt the boat start to roll, even though our paravanes were in the water. A quick check showed a wind change to the southwest, directly into our nitch. We hauled anchor and departed immediately. Luckily for us, the southerly winds continued all the way to Neah Bay, Washington, giving us a nice trip north with the winds behind us rather than bucking them.

**Dangers.** Even an idyllic anchorage can have obstacles lurking on the bottom or underneath the surface. Hidden rocks are the worst danger, but there may be cables, old logs on the bottom, or even engine blocks used for moorings. A careful circle around the area where you intend to anchor equal in radius to your expected scope is a must. I like to look at the chartplotter while making the circle, then make a hard turn back to the center to drop the anchor. When the anchor hits the water, we push the set waypoint button to mark the exact location where we dropped it. If you have extra money and space, you might consider one of the depth sounders that can do a 360-degree scan. These sounders take the guesswork out of

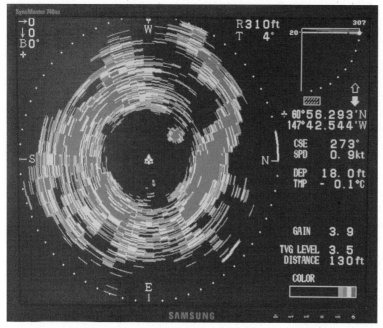

Figure 19-16. Depth sounder display for side-scanning sonar on Dashew's *Windhorse*. This picture gives new meaning to "gunkholing." (Steve Dashew)

Figure 19-17. Transducer for side scanning sonar retracts, but it is really big! (Steve Dashew)

finding obstacles, as can be seen in Figure 19-16.

**Bottom.** Often, the bottom will be unfavorable for anchoring. As you search for a good spot, watch out for grass or kelp—try to find a nice flat bottom with nothing growing there. But not too flat, indicating a smooth rock bottom, which makes setting the anchor impossible. Rocky anchorages are to be avoided whenever possible because holding is more uncertain. If you do anchor on rocks, pay special attention to any position changes due to wind or current.

**Proximity to other boats.** Sometimes you are stuck in crowded anchorages. Finding a place if you are a late arrival may be difficult. Watch the position of other boats to help predict where you will drift to after setting the anchor. Be especially wary of boats with nylon anchor rodes as they may drift erratically during wind or current shifts. Sometimes, a shore tie from the stern can cure the crowded-anchorage problem. If you are tied off, you will not swing. Beware wind changes in the night that may bring the wind abeam. In this case, you may have to let go the stern line.

### Setting the Anchor

We often watch boats enter an anchorage, drop their anchor, drift back a little, and then drop their dinghies and head to shore—without setting their anchor! They apparently expect it to set itself. There are many anchor-setting techniques that work. Here is how we do it:

*After we circle the potential anchoring location and bring the bow to the middle of the circle (upwind), Mary brings the boat to a stop and gently begins to reverse. As soon as we build up a little backward movement, I drop the anchor until it hits the bottom. Then I slowly pay out the chain with some tension on the brake until we have let out the* amount of chain I like for the scope. Mary then cuts the engine, although the reverse momentum of the boat continues. I put my foot on the anchor chain to feel it as it sets. You can actually feel the anchor pull out any looseness and set into the mud, sand, or whatever. The boat stops, and I ask Mary to back down slowly again until the anchor chain comes up tight—it is almost straight out, although angled toward the bottom. We then add power, 100 rpms at a time. I continue to feel the chain with my foot. If the anchor has not set, it feels jerky as if encountering lumps. (If it does not set, I pull it in and try again.) However, it usually sets right away. We add more and more power until reaching maybe 30% power. While

the power is on, I look at trees, flagpoles, rocks, or some other stationary references to make sure we are not moving. If we are well set, we power off and attach the nylon snubber to the chain and pay out enough chain so that all the weight of the boat is on the snubber.

### Anchoring Problems

**The hung-up anchor.** If you cannot hoist your anchor with the windlass and you have tried going ahead in the opposite direction from the anchor set, you may be hung up on something. The first strategy is to let out some scope, say 3 to 1, and drive around in a circle, hoping that a different direction of pull will release the anchor. If this does not work, and you do not have an anchor trip line like the one pictured in Figure 19–19, you may have to dive to free the anchor. When diving, you may be able to attach a trip line to the head of the anchor and pull it out using your windlass. For really difficult problems, I recently heard that a diver's lift bag may do the trick. The bag is attached by the diver to the anchor, filled with air from the diving tank, and can then be lifted with hundreds of pounds of force. I have not tried this method, but it sounds promising.

Imagine that you are anchored in a beautiful tropical location only to find your anchor chain caught in the coral. That's what happened to Eric and Christi Grab on *Kosmos* in Suwarrow:

> Today, we went diving by ourselves, jumping off Kosmos and staying in the anchorage. After our last dive, we were feeling fairly confident. More important, we knew that if we had an emergency, help was nearby.
>
> Our first priority was getting the chain untangled. When the wind is strong, the chain is blown taught, making it difficult and dangerous to maneuver. But right now the wind was calm, and we figured that the chain would have some slack. We got into the water and swam down to the coral head. It looked like when we originally dropped anchor, the slack chain had gotten looped under a large coral formation. Then when the wind picked up and the chain got rigid, it must have wedged itself deep into the coral formation. Now, it was

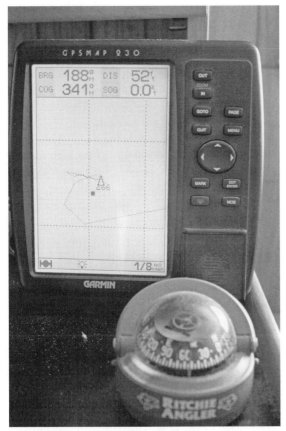

**Figure 19–18.** A GPS chartplotter (with anchor alarm) in our sleeping cabin allows us to view the boat's position during the night without leaving the bed. The compass shows which way we are pointed to detect wind or current changes.

tightly embedded. To make matters worse, the chain had broken off a big chunk of the coral, and the broken piece had collapsed onto the rest of the coral head, creating a ledge that trapped the chain. The broken piece was enormous; too heavy for us to lift. To get the chain free, we would have to figure out how to push the broken piece of coral out of the way and how to pry out the embedded chain. Words do not do justice to how bad the situation was.

We pulled and yanked on the chain to no avail. Then we rearranged the chain in other spots to create more slack and pulled again. The chain wasn't moving at all from under the ledge, so Eric went up and got the boat hook. Using the leverage of the hook, he yanked and yanked from every angle until it finally came out.

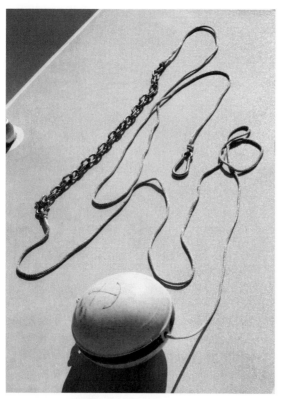

**Figure 19–19.** An anchor trip line runs from the anchor on the bottom to a buoy on the surface. The one shown here uses Amsteel line with chain spliced into the line so that it will sink straight down. A stainless steel ring on top of the buoy allows use of a grappling hook if the trip line is fully submerged.

This is the second time our SCUBA gear has saved us; we never would have freed the chain without going into the water. And our boat hook gets equal credit. It's a good thing we didn't wait any longer to free the chain since it had been rapidly working its way deeper and deeper into the coral. Once it was free, we were able to relax and enjoy the underwater scenery.

In this case, it was almost impossible to clear the chain without scuba gear because it was the chain that was stuck, not the anchor. Anchoring in places where you may find your anchor stuck can be minimized by using an anchor trip line connected from the top of the anchor that leads to a buoy on the surface. If the anchor gets hung up, you pull straight up and it pulls the point out of the rock or obstacle that is holding it.

**Windlass failure.** At the start of Chapter 17, *Grey Pearl* experienced a broken hydraulic line, causing the windlass to fail. It was quite a chore to raise the anchor. It is unusual for hydraulic lines to break, but it is not uncommon for electric windlasses to fail. Electric motors like the windlass that operate close to salt water are prone to failure. Careful annual maintenance may help prevent such failures, but spares should be carried for everything electrical on a voyaging boat.

If you have to manually retrieve anchor chain in 50 feet of water, you will have to lift a lot of weight—185 to 270 pounds of chain on our boat, plus 110 pounds of anchor—and this does not count any mud remaining on the anchor. Luckily, we have never had this unfortunate experience, but we are prepared. I made up a long four-part block and tackle that fastens to the mast on one end and a chain grabber on the other. In theory, we can take in about 20 feet of chain at a time, tie it off, and dump it in the chain locker; then repeat the process until the anchor is in. It might be slow, but I think it will work.

**Sailing at anchor.** This is a common problem with trawlers that have a forward pilothouse combined with a high bow. This structure catches the wind and makes the boat want to sail side to side on the fulcrum of the anchor. Anchoring sails have been the age-old solution to this problem, but that only

**Figure 19–20.** This Malahide 65, *Ursa Major*, uses an anchoring sail to prevent sailing around the anchor, although the sail may not be needed in such calm conditions. Note that the boat already has a lot of superstructure aft. (Joyce Gauthier)

boat in close to the dock and turn at right angles, going slowly outward at 90 degrees. After going perhaps 150 feet, stop the boat and drop your anchor until it touches bottom; then slowly back toward the wall, paying out chain slowly with some tension. When you get near the other boats, or about 50 feet from the pier, set your anchor. Then, slowly back between any boats, pushing them aside with fenders and boathooks. It is great to have a crew of three here, but we have done it numerous times as a couple. If someone is aboard the side boats, they will usually come out to help. When you get close to the dock, secure your stern to the bollards. We found using spectra line with a chain loop on the end worked well to rapidly secure the boat's stern. Finally, balance the pull between bow and stern until you are comfortable and your passerelle reaches the dock.

**Executing the Med mooring.** On *Teka III*, we shared the job of Med mooring. After tying off the fenders on the stern swim platform as well as on the sides if other boats were already moored, and preparing the two stern docking lines, Mary moved quickly to the bow and dropped our anchor on cue while I reversed the boat. That left no one to toss the stern lines to shore until Mary completed setting and locking the anchor in place. All the while, I kept the boat in reverse at idle rpm so we would not drift away from the dock. Mary then scrambled aft, grabbed the stern lines coiled for throwing, and heaved them to someone on the dock. Usually there was help on the dock. If not, Mary would get on the swim bridge while I reversed close enough for her to connect to a ring on the pier. (Fenders tied to the swim steps are essential in case you get too close to the pier, which is often concrete or stone.) Mary then gave those ashore a quick nonverbal demonstration on how to hook the stern line to a ring, bollard, or rusty pipe; otherwise, they might just stand there and hold the attaching line and hook.

works if you have an aft mast for mounting the sail. It is also a lot of trouble.

Another solution to the anchor sailing problem has been developed by Milt Baker for use on his Nordhavn 47, *Bluewater*. He uses a snubber that attaches at water level, providing less movement and leverage for the wind to blow the bow sideways (see Figure 19–21).

### Using Your Anchor for Med Mooring

In Chapter 16 we covered cruising in the Mediterranean and mentioned some techniques and strategies for Med mooring. Here Mary and I discuss the strategy and specifics of using our own anchor rather than lines provided by the marina.

Using your own anchor is common in many older ports or ports without marinas, especially in the Mediterranean. In some ways it is easier, with little chance of fouling your propeller, and it is cleaner. However, you need a boat that can back in a straight line. A bow thruster makes this much easier. You will often be backing into a small space between two other boats. Dropping your anchor in the right spot is essential. Look at other boats to see whether their anchor chains are going straight or whether winds or currents are moving boats out of a straight line. Next bring your

## Arrangement When the Anchor Is on the Roller

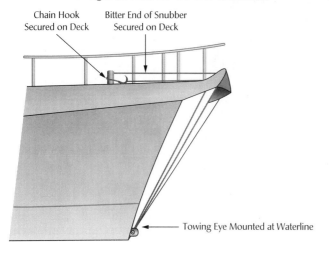

Chain Hook Secured on Deck

Bitter End of Snubber Secured on Deck

Towing Eye Mounted at Waterline

## Arrangement When the Anchor Is on the Bottom

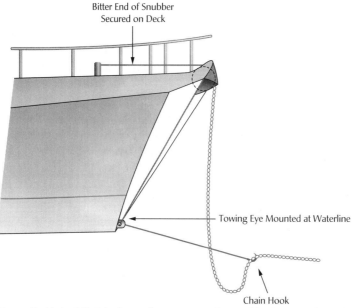

Bitter End of Snubber Secured on Deck

Towing Eye Mounted at Waterline

Chain Hook

**Figure 19–21.** On Milt Baker's Nordhavn 47 an anchor snubber line runs through an eye mounted at the waterline–the direct angle to the anchor chain from lower in the vessel minimizes the boat's sailing around its anchor. The upper image shows the position of the snubber line when not in use. (Milt Baker)

All this time the boat is slowly moving to the quay. If Mary missed getting the line to shore, quick retrieval was a must. Lines like to get tangled in props. Once the lines were ashore and I felt that I could leave the helm, together we finished straightening out the boat and tightening the lines using a pair of winches.

This process usually went smoothly, but there were sometimes unusual problems. Occasionally piers were set up for large fishing boats or commercial vessels with bollards and rings spread far apart, thus making it challenging to find a convenient attachment place. In between were huge ugly black tires for fenders. Not the best arrangement for yachts.

Another consideration is estimating the distance from the pier to drop the anchor. I usually use two to three times our boat length just to make sure there is plenty of scope to keep the anchor set regardless of wind and sea conditions. It is surprising how hard it is to judge this distance. You are normally much farther from the dock than you think. One cruiser friend dropped his anchor so far out that he ran out of chain, and the bitter end was not secured. It took some time in the dinghy and a grappling hook to find the chain and reconnect it.

There are many more safety concerns for voyagers, such as fire- prevention and fighting, life raft survival techniques, retrieving people who fall overboard, running in fog, and taking a dinghy through surf, to name

Holding it won't do. They must secure the lines. We found that our small, light spectra lines with a snap-hook and short length of chain made it easy to throw the line and easy for the person onshore to secure it. just a few. In addition, each topic covered here needs more in-depth treatment, but perhaps I have motivated you to adopt an attitude of safety and to seek out other, more complete sources.

# CHAPTER TWENTY

# Social Dynamics of Voyaging

## Mary Umstot

Voyagers are cruisers with a sense of adventure, coupled with a desire for new experiences, often requiring a change of lifestyle. Being a voyager boils down to being curious about what's out there in the world and having the courage to spring loose and experience it. The fit between this lifestyle and your personal needs will determine your enjoyment and the success or failure of the voyaging adventure.

In *The Voyager's Handbook*, Beth Leonard describes cruisers as "ordinary everyday people who can do the most extraordinary, adventurous things . . . To go cruising requires commitment, determination, time, and money," she points out, "plus having to pull up roots, leaving loved ones behind, and accepting some discomforts and inconveniences." And she's right.

Most long-distance cruisers have been boating for a while—honing boat-handling skills, learning how they react to situations requiring problem-solving tactics, and experiencing different weather events on the water. Knowledge gained by nautical classes, paired with confidence gained through experience, prepares one to try something larger—like blue water voyaging, where passages are counted in days rather than hours and your radar tracks other vessels instead of the outline of land.

## Categories of Voyagers

There are fundamentally two categories of voyagers: couples alone (each boat is a microcommunity) and those with crew (family or friends). Both of these categories fit into the larger web of the cruising community whose role in your boat's and your personal life can be strengthened and deepened by embracing various opportunities.

### Couples Alone

Among voyaging couples, each party should be committed to any plans made. Often at first, one is a reluctant partner. Debra Cantrell, for her book, *Changing Course,* gained valuable insight from the answer to "Who came up with the idea of going cruising?" Of the 110 boaters answering, 80 percent of the women whose partners initially proposed the idea of cruising resisted the thought of living on a boat. Five basic reasons surfaced: not wanting to leave family, friends, career, and life on land; the inability to grasp any notion of long-distance voyaging; "what-if scenarios"; lack of experience; and "what about me and *my* dreams?" Traits of successful couples included a sense of adventure, being open to new experiences and learning, and looking at the world with a "half-full" rather than a "half-empty" viewpoint. They shared mutual respect, open communications, and positive interactions; they also trusted in each others' problem solving and decision making skills. Lin Pardey proposes that to make cruising comfortable and sustainable, the lifestyle could be introduced as "Ten ways to keep your lover." Lin and Larry Pardey have cruised for more than 43 years and accumulated enough sea miles for a circumnavigation five times, so they have the expertise to make this list:

1. *Introduce your partner to boating gently.* Gradually build your partner's boating skills rather than using a sink-or-swim strategy. Start on a calm day.

Build confidence. Create successful experiences. You want the experience to be positively reinforcing, not punishing.

2. *Remember, everyone really IS watching you.* We call this "harbor TV" because everyone in the marina or anchorage is watching you to see if your arrival is entertaining or merely competent. Arrive early in the day before the rush at the anchorage or marina. Create your communication plan before you arrive.

3. *Candidly discuss the fear yelling creates and the power it gives.* Women and men react differently to yelling. Men may see it as a way to make themselves heard—that is, if the yelling is not accompanied by angry nonverbal signals. Women associate yelling with anger and fear. Instead of relying on verbal commands that may be interpreted as yelling, create workable hand signals or wear headsets and talk softly. Apologize if you goof and get out of control.

4. *Give your partner (and yourself) room to make mistakes.* Don't supervise or coach too much—let your partner learn by doing. Mistakes are a part of learning—don't let them ruin your day. Lin says, "Boats are easier to fix than relationships."

5. *Don't make false promises about boating.* Don't lure your partner to sea by promises of peace and comfort. Be realistic about the physical demands of standing night watches or retrieving the paravanes. Because of the need to secure things while underway, things are never as easily accessible as they are in a house. Also learn to give each other mental and physical space in a smaller, more confined environment of the boat.

6. *Make and keep real promises about what boating can offer.* Connect boating with your partner's personal interests; find out what really excites her and try to make it happen. The idea is to make the boat a way for your partner to do new things that are rewarding.

7. *Contingency planning calms fears.* Talk over possible emergencies. Women can take confidence-building classes offered by female instructors so they can feel comfortable about stepping in when

needed. Practice exchanging duties like dropping the anchor to build confidence and experience.

8. *Encourage your partner to talk to other experienced cruisers.* Build opportunities for your partner to share others' experiences. Avoid attending lectures about shipwrecks and storms.

9. *Create an exit strategy.* If a plan sounds or feels wrong, consider an "if … then …" policy. For example, I was concerned about crossing the Atlantic. We agreed that if I still felt uncomfortable in Bermuda, I could fly to the Azores and Portugal. I stayed and enjoyed the voyage, but I had an out.

10. *Be logical about boat maintenance.* Fixing breakdowns and maintenance tend to be what's liked least on the boat. Try to fix everything before you leave port and keep systems as simple as possible.

She sums it all up with this philosophy, "Combine learning how to communicate afloat with some confidence-building boating experiences, and you'll increase your partner's enjoyment and sense of self-sufficiency."

Of course, health, money, and the ability to roll with what obstacles come along while cruising all contribute to the longevity of a cruising lifestyle. Bob Austin relayed some relevant information in his posting entitled: *Fish or cut bait, aka: big decisions.* Bob and his wife left California in 1982 with 19 other boats and three years of cruising plans. They were

**Figure 20–1.** Mary shares *Teka III* responsibilities—here she is analyzing the en route weather downloaded from NOAA weather faxes.

the only ones to achieve the goal. Three boats were lost. Four couples divorced during that time. The rest of the boaters gave up the voyage at some stage and sold or shipped their boats home. In his opinion, the biggest mistakes were people trying to run a business from afar as if they were still there; payments due on boats and houses; a rigid schedule; or not looking realistically at the big picture. Interconnectivity has improved since 1982 with the use of satellite communication for doing business while cruising. Paying bills through automatic payments takes that worry away. But schedules and reality checks are another issue, individually based. Bob also pointed out that both partners have to be "fully committed," and each partner needs to be able to handle the boat in case of an emergency.

## Voyagers Who Take On Nonfamily Crew

Two to four people aboard can easily manage a boat, depending on the cruising time and distance. Besides the couple, a volunteer crew could include family members or friends. How do you select crew members? Prior experience on voyages is probably the best predictor of future success. It is a luxury to get someone who can join for multiple voyages. If you don't have experience with the person or couple, pick people who are fun—those who can laugh about their experiences soften rough spots in a voyage. Selecting people with expertise you lack is also a possible criterion. On the Great Siberian Sushi Run from Seattle to Japan via Alaska, Ken Williams selected a crewmember who had been a commercial fisherman in the Aleutians and could add local knowledge and experience. Ken reports this worked out well.

The ability to stay cool, calm, and collected in tight spaces for lengthy periods of time affects dynamics between couples as well as between couples and crew. Beth points out that couples who do not spend a lot of time with each other on land will find it especially difficult adjusting to a boat length and "being in each other's hip pocket at all times." The same could be said for crew. She says that family members, especially close-knit ones, can handle stress in small spaces much better than friends can. They have a background in interacting together in the same environment.

## Experiences of Women Who Went to Sea

I reported my research in a story for *Latitudes and Attitudes*, "Women Who Answered the Call to the Sea." I interviewed 18 women, ranging in age from 45 to 75 (average age: 58), having a total of more than 150 years of cruising life. At least six of these women were on a circumnavigation.

My interviews focused on only four questions: What lured you to sea? What kept you there? How have you changed? Can you share a story about your life as a "modern day mermaid?"

What lured them to sea included following husbands with dreams, a love of the water and boating in general, wanting to see the world and broaden horizons, meeting new people and experiencing different cultures, and escaping to another realm of possibilities. What kept them there? Camaraderie with others ranked high, as well as being able to store "bad passages" only into short-term memory. How had they changed? Overcoming fears and being less afraid of the unknown came out on top; being mentally flexible, and able to cope with emergencies and new challenges as they arose; learning that all the people in the world are not so different from you; improving language skills; and learning about different customs and traditions.

Their stories were rich and varied, ranging from fear-provoking to awe-inspiring situations. They included weather events, nature at its best, seeing a dream fulfilled, having a religious experience, and taking charge of the boat when the captain became incapacitated.

## Captainship and Leadership

During our years of cruising, we have had some less-than-pleasant crew experiences, especially with people on board for extended lengths of time. Discussions with other knowledgeable voyagers provided new insights on the issues of "captainship" versus "leadership."

Captainship refers to the overall responsibility of the captain for the crew and the boat—the buck stops with the captain, both morally and legally. However, if teamwork is important for a successful voyage, then leadership is also critical. Some self-reflection by Denis resulted in the realization that most of the really important tasks were done by him, the captain, without really using the skills and knowledge of the entire crew.

Another way to approach leadership of a voyage's crew is to use skill or knowledge-based crew leadership. The idea here is to use the abilities of the crew so all on board can feel a sense of accomplishment in the voyage. They can really contribute! To reach this objective, make a list of all the skills and knowledge areas needed for the voyage—we came up with a list of more than 40—some of which are noted in the list that follows. Before the cruise, meet with the crew to discuss matching their individual strengths to the roles needed on the voyage. Then delegate, based on these capabilities, individual areas of responsibility to that person for the voyage. If this is done before leaving the dock, the responsible person can study reference sources and recommend equipment and supplies to carry out their assigned tasks. Certain areas, such as meal preparation and provisioning, might be assigned to more than one person so they could work together as a team and not be overwhelmed.

The tasks still need to be overseen to some extent by the captain, but more in the role of information-receiver than of task-doer. Training may be needed to ensure each crewmember thoroughly understands what is expected; thus, there is some front-end time and investment, but the long-run payoff in success and smoothness of the voyage will be great.

### A Sampling of Skills Needed for an Ocean Passage

- Offshore medicine and first aid
- Diesel engine mechanical
- Navigation and charts
- Electronics operation and troubleshooting
- Weather, including FAX and GRIB analysis
- Cruiser's nets (SSB and HAM radios)
- Cooking and provisioning
- Diving (SCUBA and Hooka)
- Deck security, including lighting
- Water monitor and watermaker operation
- Fuel management and transfer
- Destination research—tourist and formalities
- Destination research—harbors, anchorages, and marinas
- Washing boat and windows
- Wine and beer steward
- Communications manager: computer, e-mail, and satellite phone
- Watchstanding
- Waste and garbage disposal

### Feedback Sessions

Another idea for smoothing relationships, reducing conflict, and solving problems before they become serious is to structure periodic "how-goes-it" sessions. One simple method: each person states two compliments about how the crew is operating and then two suggestions for improvements. The compliments and suggested improvements can be directed to any specific individual or to the crew as a whole. These suggestions are not meant to be criticisms, but ways to improve. Having such meetings may be an effective way to build crew cohesion and satisfaction.

## The Cruising Community: Fellowship of the Voyagers

Cruisers share a sense of adventure, danger, and exploration that is intense and long-lasting. People meet, form friendships, and build ties throughout their voyage. Sometimes people voyage together over vast areas. The community also builds by interconnections between cruisers. Someone will say, "Do you know so-and-so?" Replying that you don't brings out stories of why you should be friends and where you'll likely meet in the future. The community of friends grows constantly as a result of these social interactions. The community is a gathering of like-minded souls from many boats, both power and sail. Cruising community members approach life with an adventurous spirit, evaluating risks and taking them in stride. They enjoy humor, laughing at unusual situations they have survived. They willingly share information, like where to go, what to miss, or where to shop, based on their experiences. They eagerly assist fellow travelers in trouble situations, large or small; and, most importantly, they offer lasting friendships. The beauty of those friendships is the flexibility. Friends made today tend to stay in touch while you make new ones along the way. And it is a special event when pulling into a harbor or marina to find a surprise—someone you originally met half the world away! Traveling south or returning north on the ICW each winter one meets interesting folks, either at anchorages, marinas, or while waiting for bridges to open. If you miss a bridge opening, several boats gather with you, making lazy circles in the water waiting for the next scheduled opening. Often valuable information about places to go and things to see are shared in these moments.

Once when we were tied alongside the outer dock at Palmer-Johnson Marina in Savannah, Georgia, on the ICW a trawler passed with "Port Townsend, Washington" as home port on its stern. They had not seen us, but when we told them we were from Washington, too, we wound up traveling together through three states. In 2003, they crewed for us in Greece. We see each other each summer back home in Washington—they have become an integral part of our cruising community.

While in the Med, we often crossed paths with vessels we met after our Atlantic crossing. With each meeting, we shared information about where we had been and what we had seen—from markets to mosques, bazaars to bakeries, places to buy phone cards to the public transportation available at the different ports.

Imagine dropping the anchor in Cartagena, Colombia, and hearing a hearty "Welcome!" keyed into the mike by people we met six years earlier on *Que Linda*. We hadn't seen them since leaving the Bahamas. And at Zihuatanejo, Mexico, in 2007, a woman on *Sirius*, the sailboat anchored directly behind us, came over in her dinghy for a courtesy call. Ironically, she had just been thinking about *Teka III* when she popped up from her cabin and there we were! We had first shared an anchorage in the small bay at Santa Marguerita Ligure in northern Italy in 2002, and in the five years since at many places in-between Italy and Mexico.

Many long-distance cruisers migrate back to life on land after an average of ten years. They do not necessarily give up boating, but discover that their long voyaging itch has been scratched, leaving them with imprints of people, places, and encounters that cannot be matched. A couple we met on the Black Sea in 2004 purchased shoreline property at Gorge Harbor in British Columbia, Canada. In late summer 2010, they spotted us at anchor, jumped in a small boat to check us out, but found no one to answer their knock, so then waited for us to haul anchor in the morning and gave us a VHF call. We had no time for coffee and a visit, but we made a promise for next time.

## Building Informal Cruising Communities: Encounters in Anchorages and Ports and a Rendezvous

We had no sooner pulled into the anchorage at East Holandes Cays in the San Blas Islands of Panama than someone came around in a dinghy and asked us to join them ashore that evening for drinks around a bonfire. It was a first of many such invitations, and it felt good to be included. Perhaps the most social of all the areas we have travelled is in the Exuma chain of the Bahamas.

Many winter cruisers drift down the Exumas, anchoring and socializing along the way. A usual and memorable way to get involved is to volunteer at the Exuma Cays Land and Sea Park. With only one Ranger for the whole park (112,000 acres), he stays busy monitoring smuggling activities and illegal fishing. Volunteer cruisers help out with cleaning beaches, building things, checking mooring buoys, maintaining trails, and whatever is needed to make the park viable and special for everyone. Pretty much all the day-to-day management and maintenance is left up to volunteers. Of course, this is a great way to build camaraderie and friendships.

And at Staniel Cay, many joined together at the Happy People restaurant to root for their favorite Super Bowl team. Another day, several dinghies were seen roped up together outside a grotto, waiting for people to return after a swimming adventure inside James Bond's Thunderball grotto. Colorful fish swam close to fingers and masks, and the light through the holes in the underwater cave made it seem so familiar. That evening we had a social gathering on *Teka III* where we cooked popcorn and watched the *Thunderball* DVD movie—it was great fun.

Figure 20–2. Cruisers (and one dog) do many tasks at Exuma Park in the Bahamas.

how to sign up, where to show up for picnics, times for softball and volleyball practice or games, where to find mail, who had faxes waiting, and a category called "Boaters' General" in which people could ask for assistance ("where is?" "I need help with"). Local merchants and community news were also included in the morning net. A "Thought for the Day" concluded the program.

## The Croatian Rendezvous in Starigrad

In the Mediterranean, a cruisers' rendezvous was organized in Starigrad, Croatia, two years in a row (2002 and 2003). It took effort to publicize the Starigrad gathering, giving information out through VHF nets and the single sideband radio. With boaters spread out across the Med, it meant some would have to adjust their cruising schedules to attend the get-together. We volunteered to organize the 2003 rendezvous.

Starigrad dates back to 400 BCE, with first Greek and then Roman civilizations. It has friendly

## Rendezvous—The Georgetown Gathering

Our first experience with a organized cruising event came when we joined the Georgetown gathering at the bottom of the Exuma Island chain in the Bahamas. Every year the cruising community sets up a Regatta for the first week in March. Plenty of planning goes into this festival, and boats just keep coming for the event. By the time we arrived on February 17, the boat count had climbed to 389. One week later, the official count totaled 447. This was a lot of boats, but Elizabeth Harbour has room for all in the numerous colorfully name coves, such as Hamburger Beach, Volleyball Beach, and Sand Dollar Beach.

Georgetown, established in August 1792, has much to offer cruisers. It's a place to have mail forwarded, replace supplies, and get repairs made, try the different restaurants, dive or drive to explore local scenery, walk the beaches, and attend all the scheduled or impromptu social events. The dinghy dock at Exuma Markets remains packed all day—sometimes upward of 100 small craft. One often has to climb over several to get to the dock and back with their parcels.

Each morning the cruisers' net offered information on Regatta events:

Figure 20–3. Some of the cruisers who joined the Starigrad Rendezvous. This is where we were when the 6-foot tsunami hit, as described in Chapter 16.

people, many places to eat and provision, plus inexpensive moorage stern-tied to the town wall. Twenty-four boats came in 2003 to tie up or anchor out. Events began with a pot luck dinner that set the mood for other activities. During the week, cruisers enjoyed wine tasting, games, a bus trip to a country restaurant for dinner, picnics, book exchanges, and, of course, the usual exchange of cruising information.

## Formal Cruising Communities for Voyagers

### Rallies

Formal cruising groups—boat rallies—are great for those who are hesitant to set out across an ocean on their own. These rallies not only provide a social network of people with shared interests and goals but they also may provide technical guidance, boat inspections, and set equipment, safety, and communication requirements, and crew minimums. These formalities help ensure that first-time voyagers are reasonably well-prepared for the crossing. There are three regular rallies for oceangoing boats: the FUBAR from San Diego to La Paz, Mexico; the Baha-Ha-Ha, also from San Diego to Cabo San Lucas; and the ARC for crossing the Atlantic. In addition, the Eastern Mediterranean Yacht Rally (EMYR) offers the opportunity for touring the Middle East. Other rallies conducted on a one-time or erratic basis are the KAYRA, or Black Sea Rally, and the one-time Nordhavn Atlantic Rally that occurred in 2004.

**FUBAR.** One event aimed only at powerboats is called the FUBAR (Fleet Underway to Baja Rally), originated by Bruce Kessler. The FUBAR organizes a rally from San Diego to La Paz, Mexico, every other year, and yacht clubs in the Southern California area rotate sponsorship. This has been a great way to build camaraderie and get more timid owners to take the plunge on an ocean passage.

**Baha-Ha-Ha.** *Latitude 38* in Mill Valley, California (near San Francisco), has organized the Baha-Ha-Ha since 1994. This rally leaves San Diego toward the end of October. Over the past 18 years it has averaged about 140 boats a year, almost all sailboats. Going on a rally with mostly sailboats should not

be a deterrent. You will find at least a 10 to 1 ratio of sail to power among cruisers everywhere. However, interests overlap to a great degree. You will be interested in going to the same destinations; you will share many of the same boat systems. You may or may not travel a bit faster, depending on winds and the relative size of the boat. Some sailors like to call power boaters "stinkpots," but it is now more common for sailors to convert to power as they grow older. (Most sailors are interested in your passage-maker and will appreciate a tour.)

**ARC.** Like the Baha-Ha-Ha, the Atlantic Rally for Cruisers (ARC) is focused primarily on sailboats, but in recent years has encouraged powerboats to join. The focus is providing a rally for crossing the Atlantic each way at different seasons. In May, the ARC goes eastbound from Antigua to Europe via Horta in the Azores. In November, they travel westbound, leaving Las Palmas in the Canaries headed for St. Lucia. The rally has run for more than 25 years, beginning in 1985. Approximately 220 boats participate in each rally. It is well organized, with a leader, rules, social events, post-departure seminars, and a fee to pay on signing up. Boats travel independently from one another, although weather guidance is provided, and SSB networks are organized. Many ARC participants make long-term cruising friendships and travel together afterward for months, or even years.

**EMYR.** The Eastern Mediterranean Yacht Rally began in 1990. Yachts from all over the world come to Turkey for this rally, described as "neither a race nor a regatta," but more of a cultural experience. Typically the rally starts in Istanbul; port-hops along the Turkish coast; then on to Cyprus, Syria, Lebanon, Israel, and Egypt; with a final banquet back in Herzliya, Israel. There are opportunities to visit 16 countries over a 59-day period, covering almost 1,500 nautical miles. Rallies are now limited to 80 boats. One year almost 100 boats signed up and this was too much—overnight passages seemed like traffic jams in places. One boat reported the scene as "measles on the radar." Imagine the difficulty of parking this many boats in a marina!

**KAYRA.** The Black Sea Rally, a counterclockwise circumnavigation of the Black Sea, includes six countries: Turkey, Georgia, Russia, Ukraine, Romania, and Bulgaria, totaling more than 2,000 nautical miles

Figure 20–4. Route of the Eastern Mediterranean Yacht Rally. (Hassan Kacmaz, EMYR Committee)

in a 60-day cultural adventure. Atakoy Marina in Istanbul sponsors this rally. Although it was started in 1997, it runs infrequently, so check the schedule. We joined the 2004 Black Sea Rally along with 36 other boats flying flags from eleven countries. The Black Sea cannot easily be visited by an individual boat. There are many language barriers, bureaucracies, and red tape to unravel. This organized rally took care of all formalities, allowing a wonderful experience. Aside from the wide-ranging cultural experiences, the rally group itself provided a unique, multicultural cruising community.

**NAR.** In 2004, Nordhavn sponsored the Nordhavn Atlantic Rally (NAR). Eighteen trawlers participated, ranging in size from a 40-foot Nordhavn to a 90-foot Monk-McQueen. The group departed Fort Lauderdale, stopped at Bermuda and the Azores, and terminated in Gibraltar. All vessels completed the 3,800 nautical mile journey to Gibraltar, a first for everyone. Considerable support was provided by Nordhavn, and the boats travelled in two groups, quite close together. This was the first all-motoryacht, ocean-crossing rally. This

Figure 20–5. The Nordhavn Atlantic Rally arrives at Gibraltar in 2004. (PAE/Nordhavn)

rally has not repeated—although a group of nine Nordhavns, ranging from 40 to 62 feet, banded together with the organizers, Milt and Judy Baker, to form the "2007 Med-Bound" rally. This group followed the same route as the NAR from Fort Lauderdale to Gibraltar.

### Cruising Organizations

**SSCA.** The Seven Seas Cruising Association (SSCA) publishes an informative monthly newsletter with valuable information about cruising spots worldwide. Members fly the SSCA flag while at anchor or in marinas. They also hold Gams (social visits with friendly interchanges) each year in different places so cruisers can meet, learn from each other, and make contacts for future activities. One benefit from our attendance at the 2000 Gam in Maine was meeting two couples who planned an Atlantic crossing the next summer. We decided to buddy-boat (travel together), an arrangement that worked well.

**CCA.** The Cruising Club of America (CCA) is focused on voyagers who have already made significant ocean passages under their own command using either sail or power. While entry is limited to those that have already completed voyages, it is a congenial and interesting group of people with extensive cruising experience. The CCA sponsors domestic and international cruises throughout the world for its members and guests.

## Off-Season Connections: Wintering in the Mediterranean

Cruising around the Mediterranean in winter is not comfortable due to the many gales and storms and cold air temperatures. So throughout the region, cruisers think about their winter plans. Most prefer a reasonably priced marina with a nice town nearby and with other cruisers around— the more the merrier. Some elect just the opposite—wintering in an obscure place with no other cruisers around. This approach may allow deeper contacts with the local community. Selection of a marina is often based on word-of-mouth information from other cruisers. What have they heard? Where are they staying? What are the pluses and minuses of various locations? What will be the expected weather?

What do you do during the winter? Many take advantage of the winter holiday season and book flights home to see family and celebrate holidays, storing boats on the hard or in the water at a protected marina. Returning to the States allows boaters to purchase needed boat items for the next cruising season, enjoy family time, and return with their batteries charged, ready for another year. Others spend their time around the marina with the live-aboard community, engaging in social activities and spending time travelling overland in Europe. In the next three sections, I touch on several of our wintering experiences.

### Barcelona, Spain

Many cruisers wander around the end of Portugal after their Atlantic crossing, continuing through the Gibraltar Straits, along the Costa del Sol of Spain. That path allows them to start long-term friendships with "the Mediterranean cruising community." The consensus of cruisers was that Marina Port Vell in Barcelona would be a great wintering spot.

The year we were in Barcelona at the Marina Port Vell, the live-aboard community entailed 130 members spread out along Docks A through G. Boats flew flags from fifteen countries: England, France, Germany, Australia, New Zealand, Sweden, the United States, Canada, Spain, Latvia, South Africa, Portugal, Uruguay, and Holland. It is there we met the Mediterranean Cruisers' net for the first time. In winter ports, the net uses VHF; during the summer months, when cruisers spread out throughout the Mediterranean, the single sideband radio is used to keep in touch. Each morning at about 0730, a different voice came over the VHF radio, announcing he or she would be the Net Control for that day. Cruisers were then asked to check in so we would all know who was in port, or underway. To keep up with arrivals and departures, those leaving gave boat name and next port; new arrivals announced themselves and their last port. A net priority was to find out if there were any emergencies where people needed help. A daily weather report is included. While the weather report was mostly routine, I remember one exception that still gives me a chuckle:

The reporter announced, "The temperature today will drop drastically to 30 degrees Fahrenheit, and winds will increase to gale force by noon. There may even be some snow." This was enough to catch us totally off guard as we looked out the windows to see the sun shining and blue sky above. It took a moment for everyone to catch on. The date: April First!

The net also communicated other topics: where to find parts; items for trade or give away; and upcoming social events, such as the Sunday morning Barcelona Bicyclists' Club, who met at the gate for an all-morning bike ride. Other than fun and exercise, the goal each week was to find "the best croissant in town." Another social event was the Sunday evening potluck where 70 or more people attended. Cooks tried to outdo one another with gourmet entrees—a truly excellent feast.

With many cruisers together in the marina for a lengthy time, plans for future adventures could be addressed. What about next year? Where are the best ports, marinas, and anchorages? Which attractions should not be missed? How would we avoid difficult passages, such as the infamous Gulf of Lyon between Spain and France? Where should we winter next year? Information sharing was the name of the game.

**Figure 20–6.** Cruiser's potluck in Barcelona, Spain.

## Gaeta, Italy

Porto di Roma offered a new large marina for wintering, but we chose Gaeta. We had heard mixed reports about staying at the new one; yet it remained attractive because of its proximity to Rome and other cities in Tuscany. We spent a month at Porto di Roma in the summer and found that at times surge entered the marina and made it pretty rolly. We suspected the surge might be even more of a problem in winter. Also stores and markets were some distance away from the marina, necessitating a long bike ride or renting a car to get around.

The marina in Gaeta, called Base Nautico Flavio Gioia, had many advantages. Like Barcelona, it is right in the town with a short walk to the markets, stores, and other attractions. On checking in, we were presented a 67-page "Welcome to Gaeta" brochure to all boaters covering marina services, where to find what in the town, how to get around, cultural history, and more. Those who stayed on board for the winter could take advantage of Italian lessons, too. Weekly potlucks on the pier or clubhouse kept everyone entertained and well-fed. Since several of us were going to Turkey for the next season, two of the boating women took it upon themselves to expose us to Middle Eastern music and folk dancing. The wintering community here was much smaller than Barcelona—we were nine American vessels, one Aussie, and four European ones. A goose-bump event happened Easter morning 2003, when the *USS LaSalle*, the Sixth Fleet command ship, came into view flying the largest American flag I have ever seen from the tallest spire on board. While docking, the men and women in uniform lined the deck. Behind them, across the bay, we grabbed the largest American flag we had, and stood waving it proudly to let them know we were also present. Released from attention, these sailors waved first at their side, then turned and waved at us.

## Marmaris, Turkey

Many boaters talk positively about wintering in Turkey. We joined others in trying Marmaris on the southern coast, where there were two major marinas: Yat Marine out by the entrance to the bay, and Netsel, located close to town. Many chose Netsel, especially if they intended to stay on board all winter, which allowed them easy access to supplies for boat jobs, restaurants, shopping, and other cruisers for socializing. Those who opted to stay in Netsel had one common complaint—the size and position of the large cruise ships—which arrived in spring, summer, and fall—blocked the wind from the marina slips, choking fresh air off from the smaller craft moored there.

The other marina, at Yat Marin, across the bay from Netsel, also had dock space, but their main attraction was the huge parking lot for haulouts. The wooden Turkish boats, called gulets, that specialized in taking tourists for day trips along the Turquoise Coast, also used this facility to haul out during the off season. Approximately 700 or more vessels filled the giant lot. They had an unusual system for relaunching everyone in a timely fashion. You were required to give them your launch date, which they wrote on the rudder; they then positioned your boat in the lot based on that date. If you missed your date, and someone behind you needed to get out, they moved you to accommodate the other boat, but charged you for the move. Mini-buses, rental cars, or a small passenger ferry connected the people in Yat Marin with Marmaris town.

## Beyond Fun: Support and Help from Cruisers

Cruisers, by their nature, are inclined to help one another. Support is the glue holding communities together—the following stories accentuate that point. At Porto di Roma Marina, barefooted Denis accidentally cut his heel after stepping on a garbage bag that was sitting on deck waiting to be taken off the boat. His foot connected with a tin can top in the bag and immediately started bleeding profusely. I ran to the stern to look for help. A woman walking a dog approached our boat. I asked, "Do you know if there is a doctor around here?" She answered, "No, but I am a nurse." She boarded, assessed the situation, and quickly went back to the boat she had just left and asked her friend to take us to the emergency room in their rental car. The couple from *Gatti Felice* (Happy Cat) stayed at the hospital with us while Denis was

## We Women Visit a Turkish Bath

What about a Turkish bath? Several women decided to go as a group to see what it was all about. We took a bus to the front door of the hammam. There we met a person who made sure all the men had finished their sessions and then left. Then we changed, put our valuables in a box, keeping the key on a plastic ring over our wrist, and entered the first room, carrying our towels. It was large, with a high ceiling and marble benches along the whole outside circle and center of the room. These were heated. We sat. The heat caused our skin to flake, and our bodies to feel super hot. No problem. Behind the marble seats were channels of cool water and small bowls to scoop up water and pour over the head and body. That motion also washed away dead skin appearing from the sauna-like atmosphere. Then, one at a time, we walked over to a large table where a man dressed only in a red and white sarong placed low on his hips grabbed a very big soapy sponge and started washing first backs and then fronts. We had not spoken a word to the man, yet the washer knew we were Americans. The man soaping me asked where I came from in America. When I said, "Seattle," he threw his soapy sponge in the air and shouted, "Supersonics!" When I stepped back down from the table after my rinse, that man waltzed me around for a minute before pointing me to the showers. Tea in a hot tub was next before the massage, with four to a room for comfort's sake. The unusual part of all this is the Muslim tradition about touching between men and women. It seems that did not apply with foreigners. We all enjoyed our "hands on" treatment. Relaxed and back in street clothes, we returned to the marina. Total time for transportation and treatment: three hours and a reasonable fee. It hit the high mark as a special cultural experience far from home with my cruising sisters!

stitched up and then returned us to the boat. They asked nothing in return except for us to "hide" their son who was coming in secretly for their birthday celebrations. Both husband and wife had birthdays on July 4. She had arranged a flight for their son, and jumped on a chance for us to harbor him until time for the party. We welcomed the chance to help out.

Anchored at Puerto de Andratx on the southwest coast of Mallorca, we sat out a gale one night. Some boats dragged anchor and ended up on the rocks. No one could help them in the morning, but one man on a boat stranded out past the breakwater called over the VHF, "Does anyone know how long this (the storm)

will last?" He explained he was alone on board, had two anchors out that had crossed during all the stormy night, and he could not raise either one of them. Two cruisers, including Denis, immediately launched a dinghy and went to help. The sailboat lurched back and forth with the waves. Through my binoculars, it appeared the rescuers could not even get aboard, but they timed it successfully and were able to board. It took a while, but *Free Union* was finally freed and could then join other boats in the protected fishing harbor the authorities had opened for shelter. The skipper invited us all over for drinks that evening. Later in Barcelona, his three sisters visited from Toronto, Ontario, and came to tell us that he felt compelled to buy and fly a U.S. flag to show his appreciation for the help.

## Cross-Cultural Opportunities

Cruisers have a wonderful opportunity to mingle with local cultures around the world. The idea of touching real people in their real lives exposes them to us, as well as us to them. Try new foods, wrap your tongue around some new phrases, and smile. Interact with the children to open doors for adult interactions. Treat each opportunity as a way to learn about different cultural traditions, and especially the people met along the way. Three examples will illustrate this cruising plus.

**Panama: Bahia Honda.** Domingo Gonzalez paddled his dugout canoe up to *Teka III* in the calm anchorage of Panama's Bahia Honda. The anchorage was deserted, and no village or town could be seen onshore, yet there he was, smiling and offering friendship. We had stopped there to lower our flopperstopper arms for repainting. We needed calm water for that job—one that took several days. Bahia Honda offered us that and more—a chance for a cultural exchange. Domingo looked familiar. We had not met him personally before, but I was struck by recalling a photo in Pat Rains's book on cruising in that area. So I got out the book and showed him the picture. He broke into a big grin. I asked in Spanish, "*Usted?*" (You?) He answered, "*Si, muchos anos pasado.*" (Yes, many years ago.)

Each day he stopped to see us. Sometimes he brought vegetables from his garden. We looked forward to his visits and even dubbed him, "The Mayor." He spoke a little English and we worked hard on our

Spanish. Along with gestures and smiles, we communicated well enough. One day he invited us to come with him to meet his family. While I stayed on the porch trying to communicate with his wife and their two grandchildren, Denis walked over to see several men working on an outboard engine without success. Domingo took us for a walk through his property looking for wild ginger root, with the grandson and granddaughter tagging along, very interested in us as new people in their lives.

On another day, he wanted us to take him in our dinghy so he could show us some sights. So off we went, from the big bay into smaller river channels leading past people and huts on the way to a village. The village had several houses, a small store with a few items on the shelves, a basketball court, and a police station. The lone, and stern-looking, policeman stepped outside his door. He wore all black. His tee shirt had the words, "I am not anti-social. I just don't like you." On the basketball court quite a few young boys kicked a soccer ball around, and I joined them. They all laughed at my efforts. While there, Domingo took us to a house where some women were pounding corn inside a huge stone with a large, heavy paddle. Several children ran around the women, and shyly looked at us. The only man draped himself inside a hammock. Everyone seemed happy and friendly. On the way back to our boat, we saw several youngsters playing with a home-made "Panamanian-stroller," giving the smallest child a ride. After finishing our painting job, we said farewell to "The Mayor," leaving him our 3.5 Tohatsu outboard motor to replace his ailing one—a thank you gift for his friendship.

**Turkey: Sea of Marmar.** Another delightful and unexpected encounter happened on the small island of Paşalimani in the Sea of Marmara. On our way to Istanbul for the Black Sea Rally (KAYRA), we anchored in the small bay along with a few local boats. Few cruising boats come here. Onshore, an off-duty policeman befriended us, taking us to meet a woman we think was a relative. Dressed in white blouse, long dark colored skirt, vest and scarf, she took us into her kitchen and opened up a giant bowl of freshly made yogurt. She spoke no English, but we managed to have a good time indulging in her yogurt, accompanied by fresh cherries and Turkish coffee at her table.

Figure 20–7. Domingo Gonzalez, who we dubbed "The Mayor" of Bahia Honda, Panama.

When we left "the Yogurt Lady," we walked around inside the village and then strolled along the sidewalk next to the shoreline. Several times people stopped us to talk, issuing more invitations for tea. We had to decline them as we had already promised the policeman. At his place we met his wife, a customs officer, and enjoyed tea, cake, and more cherries. That day left us full of good food and excellent memories of sharing time and space with these very friendly people. They gave of themselves freely, and expected nothing in return but our appreciative smiles and waves as we returned to the boats in the harbor.

Figure 20–8. Home-made Panamanian stroller.

**Papua New Guinea.** Maurice and Louise-Ann Nunas, on the Kadey-Krogen 48, *Akama*, tell of the following experiences cruising in Papua New Guinea:

*One of the rewarding things about cruising in areas that are off the beaten path is trading. We traded things such as fishing gear, soap, canned goods, clothing, and balloons and candies for the kids; in return we got fresh fruit, vegetables, and seafood. Supply ships visit some of the remote areas only rarely, so our presence was truly appreciated. We were taken to see villages and schools. Sometimes we spoke before the assembled students and teachers about our culture and lives. Everywhere the children were truly delightful. We often blew up balloons and set them free in the wind. The kids would scramble in their dugout canoes to get them. We had a stock of cheap plastic recorders (flutes). Once we gave one out and that evening floating out to us in the bay came the tune "Mary had a little Lamb."*

*Other cruisers were fun to meet also, and sometimes truly helpful. For example, in Papua New Guinea we lost our Naiad stabilizers and our generator set. With great trepidation we elected to go to the mainland, reputedly a very dangerous place. We found a small bay in which to anchor where, amazingly, we found an expatriate Aussie who was rebuilding a large wooden boat. He'd cruised there and liked it so much that he stayed. He was a great help, and over a five-week period we managed to obtain needed parts and manufacture others. So much for getting boarded or kidnapped by rebels!*

*And, we were also aided by locals. One day while going through some reefs into an anchorage, we discovered to our horror that we had no steering. Using the wing engine as rudimentary steering, we managed to drop the hook in safe water. A hydraulic hose on the steering arm had failed; we had no spare, and there was not even a village anywhere nearby. We flagged down a small, open fishing boat. Unfortunately, the people spoke no English and we had no idea what language they were speaking, probably a local dialect. Since we were in Malaysia we waved the hose and blurted out, "Ini tidak bagus," fractured Malay meaning, "This is no good." They looked at us blankly and without a word went away. We sat*

*there wondering how the heck we could carry on and tried unsuccessfully to mend the hose. To our amazement, the fishermen returned with two hoses, both with exactly the right fittings. They would not take any money, despite our attempts to pay.*

## Activities to Build Social Relationships

Powerboats' configurations can be both a blessing and a curse for building social relationships. If the boat is closed up so the air conditioning can work efficiently, the rest of the world is left outside. In marinas and at anchor, others can get the idea—correct or not—that it's an unfriendly boat. On the other hand, the people may not be unfriendly, but just prefer to be left alone. During our ten years cruising from Seattle to the Med and back we often found this to be true—the closed boat phenomena.

**Sundowners.** Boats without air conditioning leave windows and doors open for answering any call from a fellow cruiser. In addition, open spaces outside, either on the aft deck, large bow area, or big enough flying bridges, render an easier invitation to "Come by and say hello" or "Come aboard." If one has a boat with room, the easiest way to meet people is to invite them over for sundowners. In an anchorage, this could just be as simple as taking a dinghy ride around, introducing yourself, and inviting people over to your boat. For sundowners every boat brings his or her own drink of choice and a plate of snacks to share. Paper plates are acceptable. No setup or take down—more time is therefore spent getting to know each other. These events usually result in plenty of hors d'oeuvres, so it is unlikely there will be any desire for more food—don't plan dinner.

**Potlucks.** Another gathering method is potluck dinners. Again, everyone brings their own drinks and a dish to share for a regular meal. Paper plates are still okay, but attendees can even bring their own plates and silverware and take them home to clean. Potlucks are usually done in the afternoon or early evening.

**Bonfires on the beach.** If you are at a remote anchorage where a bonfire would not bother anyone, you can go around the anchorage and invite people to join you at the beach. This can be combined with sundowners or a potluck as well. It is always great if

# A Newbie's View on the Ocean-Life World

### Lucka Zajec, South Pacific, June 22, 2010

[*We believe this outsider's view—from a Slovenian crewmember on Furthur, a 48' Selene—of the cruising life is a pretty accurate picture of reality as we have experienced it. We hope you enjoy it, too.*]

After just slightly dipping my nose into the world of sailing, the universe decided that I should dip my nose into the world of motorboats as well. The concept of that wasn't difficult for me to accept, but it was pretty funny to watch what a reaction my decision to do this caused in some sailing circles. The opinion on the last sailing boat I was on went as far as me selling my soul to the devil. Well, people would be people and I guess even in the world of boats finding excuses to bring division and a bit of spicy drama is to be expected.

Thankfully those aren't the only aspects of the boating world. Far from it. It seems to me that the people living with the ocean are generally different than the city folks (in a positive way). There is this undeniable shine that sparkles in their eyes and gives away the spirit behind them—it's a spirit of freedom, joy, courage, adventure, traveling, and love for the ocean along with ocean life. Physically people are healthy and fit, covered with different tones of brown skin (except for some English chaps, those go a little more pink), nice lines of muscles, and hair bleached from sea salt and sun. This world is full of interesting people with fascinating stories to tell. Those generally evolve around where they've been, where they are going, the troubles they've had with their boats or other boats in a shared anchorage, information on passes, anchorages, and provisions, funny stories about other boaters' lack of knowledge (those always go with a slightly outraged and marking tone), the mechanical parts of the boat that are working and those that don't, and the joy and drama around the dynamics of the crew (these are fun to listen to and satisfy the need for local gossip and reading tabloids).

Traveling on a certain ocean route also creates a kind of boat community—a mix of bumping into the same boats and meeting new ones. The last but not the least surprising thing that needs to be mentioned is that the world of boats has its own language. After spending half a year learning the names of boat parts, sailing maneuvers, and other names and elements of the disciplines that make the ocean traveling possible, I can now actually listen to a boater's conversation and have a bit of an idea of what they are talking about, but it will take a while longer for me to fully engage myself in a conversation.

What I do like about the language and its topics is that it seems quite equally distributed between men and women. There are women sailing instructors (and I do know one woman captain), women who seem to know just as much as what's going on in the boat as men do, and the majority seems to be willing to learn and do (and not just go for the ride and look pretty, but that is fine as well). Men do seem to be more engaged in mechanical conversations, but I have been listening to those coming from women as well. In that way, the ocean world feels a bit more balanced and definitely interesting. I think everyone would agree that this world is never ever dull.

I absolutely adore this life. For me, it generally reflects what I perceive life to be—a constant change. Nothing is certain, plans change, people come and go, and you never know when or if ever you are going to see them again. Along with that changes the scenery, one beautiful island after another, going from a tiny village to a modern city marina (I prefer the first one, though; don't like the heavy traffic noise), from one culture and language to the next, a rainbow parade of energies, feelings, thoughts, and experiences, excitement that comes with going into the unknown. All of these combined sometimes can be overwhelming and scary. There are moments where I wish I could just hold on to something I know and like for just a little longer—a good friend or a beautiful bay. But then I hold on to the reassuring thought that nothing is ever lost or gone, but lives eternally in the never-ending storage of the heart. So for all of you wonderers out there who are thinking—ocean life, yes or no?—I would definitely recommend it. But a slight warning—it will change you whether you like it or not.

**Figure 20–9.** Selene 48, *Furthur*, in the South Pacific (Brian Calvert, furthur.talkspot.com)

Figure 20–10. A sundowner get-together on the aft deck of *Teka III* in Procida, Italy.

someone has a musical instrument such as a guitar to share.

**Organize a dinner or lunch at a restaurant.** If there is a good or interesting restaurant near the anchorage or marina, you can dinghy around and see who would like to join a party. In many areas, the VHF can be used for this purpose as well. If at anchor, you may even be able to get the restaurant to come pick you up in their skiff—most restaurants are more than willing to bring in customers this way.

**Have a dinghy raft up.** The idea here is for everyone to join dinghies together and enjoy snacks and drinks while drifting slowly through the anchorage. It is fun and requires little or no preparation.

**Organize a shore trip.** Depending on the area, this could be a hike around the island, a rented bicycle trip, or even a rented minibus to travel to distant sites. While in Tunisia, we organized a three-day trip through the countryside to the Sahara Desert. Three cruising couples went with a guide. Another time, we joined with another couple to take a ferry from Roatan to the mainland of Honduras and traveled via rental car to Copan.

**Organize a rendezvous.** This takes lots of work, but has great payoffs. The get-together at Starigrad, mentioned earlier, is an extreme example. Lesser meetings can be arranged so that a group of friendly cruisers

all arrive at a certain anchorage or port at the same time to share activities.

**Have an open house for your boat.** If you have a large motoryacht, people will be curious. You can invite them over to have a tour. We have done this often with *Teka III* and we are only 52' long—not really that big. We had docked at a marina in northern British Columbia when a large boat, formerly owned by John Wayne, came in. The crew docked the boat and then closed the boat up from prying eyes. We were told by others at the dock that when John Wayne was alive and traveled in his boat into those same Canadian waters during the summer, his crew would tie up the boat and then invite everyone at the marina to come on board, have a drink, and "meet the Duke."

Social dynamics contribute a lot to cruising enjoyment. People who run from port to port or anchorage to anchorage miss some of the best and most rewarding cruising experiences. Becoming part of this adventuresome and varied community adds richness to the experience and makes everything much more enjoyable. It also helps cement the bond between couples and relieves some of the tension that comes from living together in close quarters for long periods of time.

Figure 20–11. Nordhavn 43, *Special Blend*, at anchor at Isle of Pines, New Caledonia. This is what it's all about. (Jim and Martha Lyle)

# Successful Long Distance Voyaging Under Power

## Linda and Steve Dashew

When we started cruising 30 plus years ago, we didn't have the experience to differentiate between what looked good at the dock and what worked in the real world of long distance voyaging. By the time we'd crossed the Pacific Ocean from California to New Zealand, we had learned the hard way. Although the four of us, two adults and two young children, loved the cruising lifestyle, we were tired of the motion, constant maintenance, and nagging worry, which we, and most of our fellow cruisers, endured.

Knowing we had to solve the design and systems issues satisfactorily or the family was going to rebel, we set about finding solutions where the bottom line to every decision was first and foremost about comfortable passagemaking. Although we did not start out to be in the yacht design and construction business, others were attracted to this approach. We dealt almost exclusively with experienced and therefore like-minded clients. From our perspective, and theirs, a key ingredient was making sure that both members of the couple had their needs fulfilled. The result has been innumerable circumnavigations and several million sea miles from a relatively small fleet of 50 yachts.

Fast forward to fall 2011, and lunch in Baltimore with old friends and *PassageMaker Magazine* founders, Bill and Laurene Parlatore, and circumnavigator Bruce Kessler. After catching up, the subject turned to why so few trawler owners actually ventured offshore. Bill mentioned that some years ago, while covering the end of a trans-Atlantic rally, almost all the wives among the participants took him aside and told him how unhappy they had been at sea. Linda and I were astonished at this since we look forward to and enjoy our passages together. As the five of us discussed the cause of this unhappy outcome, a common theme emerged: lack of experience, coupled with reliance on advice from lightly seasoned cruisers to those with even less knowledge.

Denis Umstot's update of *Voyaging Under Power* will go a long way toward addressing this deficit in reliable information. In our comments, we'll relate the key lessons we have learned: first, as a couple that loves to voyage together, and second as designers and builders whose clients are similarly inclined. We have also included the comments of several experienced voyagers.

Since the intuition of the (so-called) fairer sex is frequently more in tune with risk factors, comfort, and the unspoken worries that their mates often try to suppress, we'll address this subject from the feminine perspective.

In the context of long-distance voyaging, comfort at sea and security in adverse weather trump all other concerns. Get this right and you will look forward to your passages. On the other hand, if you are physically uncomfortable or have a constant undercurrent of worry about reliability, weather, or crew, there is a tendency to put off going.

Comfort in normal weather and security in storms are handmaidens, based on stability and steering control (discussed in Chapter 8). A yacht that finds its groove quickly and is easily steered is more comfortable at sea, offers a greater array of tactical options with weather, and in the end is safer in dangerous conditions.

The location of the galley, watchstanding position, and offshore sleeping accommodations are also key. The lower you are and the farther aft, the more comfortable you will be underway. Almost all yachts pitch about a point roughly 60% of their length aft. Being on or behind this position is better than being forward of it (the more a vessel pitches into a sea the more important this becomes). In a similar vein, what naval architects call "the slamming zone," where the biggest impact is felt when dropping off a wave crest into the trough, is typically a quarter of the way aft of the bow.

Sue Henry has cruised many thousands of miles with husband Bill in sail and power. When we asked Sue her most important priority in a cruising yacht she responded, "Number one would be seaworthiness, making sure that the boat will stay afloat even in the worst case scenario, a rollover; hull strength, door strength, window strength, coffer dams for the stabilizers, and minimal through-hulls."

Valerie and Stan Creighton started out as neophytes a few years ago and have worked their way down the west coast of the United States to Central America. As they gained more experience their perspective has changed. Valerie says "heavy weather is a major what-if. My general attitude about the what-ifs is all about preparedness and avoidance. Both of those minimize my anxiety and give me some sense of control as we cruise."

"Preparedness involves getting educated, gaining at least a basic understanding of weather (I believe many women skip this step), as well as choice of boat and outfitting that boat."

Debbie and Pete Rossin have owned a series of motor yachts and have cruised for many years along the east coast of the United States and the Bahamas. But long-distance cruising is new to Debbie, and she recently completed her first ocean passage, from New Zealand to Tonga. Debbie was apprehensive at first but now says about her experience, "at the top of the list was that I felt safe on *Iron Lady*. How comfortable the boat is at sea and at anchor and how it stood up to the punishment of a grounding gave me tremendous confidence in the boat. My husband is also much more relaxed about things and that, in turn, makes me comfortable. By the second day out of New Zealand to Tonga on our first really long passage, I was standing watch—something I would never do on our last boat."

John and Sandy Henrichs are another very experienced cruising couple, having been at this for more than 40 years, with definite thoughts on this subject. John comments "... the question is can seaworthiness be combined with a gentle motion ? ... (the) single most important aspect."

Sue Henry feels that "motion is right up here too. You will deal with that 24/7. Seagoing details are going to come into play, too."

Some argue that comfort and security at sea are minor issues. Their theory is that a small amount of time is actually spent on passage and that weather can be avoided with outside routing assistance. This approach fails to address several key points. First, uncomfortable passages tend to reinforce the urge to stay put, to wait for the illusive perfect "weather window," ship the boat, or hire a delivery crew. None of these outcomes is conducive to success in chasing that cruising dream. Second, while modern weather forecasting is quite good—for the first 48 to 72 hours of an offshore voyage—beyond this you need to be prepared to deal with a blow. If you are worried about what might happen and not certain in your gut if the boat or crew is up to those "what-ifs," it is another anchor to keep you in port.

John Henrichs adds, "the ability to maintain speed in poor conditions is a big plus. With greater speed, weather considerations become less of a factor due to reduced exposure."

A key part of the decision-making process is whether or not to carry crew. This affects many interior layout decisions. Our preference is to cruise on our own, which we enjoy much more than with crew aboard. The benefits are total independence, harmony, privacy, and the ability to make decisions based strictly on our own desires. The negative is lack of sleep as our bodies adjust to the watch-on-watch routine the first few days at sea.

Over the years we have seen a few of our clients start out with crew, but in almost all cases they migrate toward cruising on their own.

The Creighton's experience is typical. Valerie says, "the only time we've had participatory crew during multiday passages was for the first few trips we made, along the Baja peninsula on our way south into Mexico between San Diego and La Paz. It was a couple who are sailors themselves and very dear friends, and as green as we were to running overnight. We had a wonderful time; substantively it was a largely unnecessary but fun hand-holding experience for all of us. On all subsequent passages, including a five-day run between southern Pacific Mexico across the Gulf of Tehuantepec to El Salvador, we never even considered enlisting crew and were comfortable with just the two of us."

John Henrichs concurs. "Ease of passagemaking as a couple (is) very high on our list because we don't want a captain on board and will only have help on longer trips. Only after a couple years cruising on longer trips did we realize just how important this is."

The more you gravitate toward being on your own, with occasional guests rather than permanent crew, the more important a layout that facilitates working together as a couple becomes. This means fewer barriers between galley and bridge, with the ability of the off watch to sleep close to the helm in case he or she is needed for a consultation or temporary relief.

Intertwined with this is an interior design that works well in suboptimal weather. Walkways that hold you in place, a galley that braces your body, keeping your hands free to work, fiddle rails to keep things constrained, and handrails placed throughout so that everyone can reach them, are important. In the same vein are a stove and fridge that are easy to use with a big sea running.

A design corollary is that all of this needs to be viewed in the context of a "sneaker" wave, that unusually steep statistical anomaly, which sooner or later will enter your world. That this will happen in ordinary conditions is a given, which is why we always move about the boat with one hand securely attached to something solid. When the sneaker comes, and it will, if your body stays put, and locker doors remained closed, the event will pass unremarked.

Often there is a trade-off between these features and a visually open interior. We find that having constraining furniture kept at counter height, combined with lots of windows, offer the best of both worlds. Avoiding high barriers, whether cabinets or bulkheads, opens the visual space further.

Sue Henry makes an interesting point about open interiors. "Bill and I have spent the majority of our time cruising with just the two of us on board, sharing the responsibilities of operating and navigating our boats. I feel that both from a safety and enjoyment point of view the open and uncomplicated layout works really well in this regard. One of us can be in the galley fixing a meal or getting a snack, sitting at the saloon table or relaxing on the settee and still feel effective as a second lookout underway."

Even head compartment design is important. Cathy Clark, an experienced sailor now converted to power, says "a head located where motion is minimized, with good ventilation, is very important if you are at all prone to seasickness." We would add that handrails that help you on and off the seat are another import sea-going detail. Next, showers should be designed to hold you in place with the boat moving around a bit.

Another topic we hear a lot about is the launching and retrieval of dinghies, and the ease of dinghy operation by all crew members. On larger yachts the primary dinghy tends toward the biggest that can be carried. These can be intimidating to some, and if space is available, a second, easily maneuvered, smaller dinghy will provide independence to anyone unsure of themselves in the larger rendition. In this same context, the launching and retrieval system needs to be evaluated. How easy is it to launch and retrieve on rough versus calm days (at anchor)? If there are just two on board, can this process be carried out safely? Our personal preference is for dinghies to be stored on deck rather than on a roof level. We found that fixed boom systems with external, open winches are more reliable than complicated davits.

Which brings us to the last, but certainly not least, design issue: systems. Even the smallest cruising yacht these days has pressure hot and cold water, heating and air conditioning, fridges, freezers, washer/dryers, a suite of galley appliances, and of course entertainment gear. These can be a source of pleasure, allow freedom from shore power, or keep you tied to the dock in frustration waiting for a service call. Unfortunately, the latter outcome is often the case.

But it doesn't have to be this way. There are a few simple rules, which if followed will go a long way toward keeping the systems end of your cruising on course.

This starts with space and access. Where there is a tension between interior volume and systems, priority should be given to systems. Good access means it is easy to inspect and perform routine maintenance. This tends to catch incipient problems, allowing them to be dealt with while they are easy. Next is the type of gear used. Verify that it has a history of reliability. Some well-known (and costly) brands of kitchen appliances have less-than-stellar reputations. It is worth talking to customer service managers, explaining you will be away from service techs, and asking for recommendations on their most reliable models. We prefer to stay away from anything too new to have a service record. When there is a choice between automated and complex or manual control and simple, our experience is that the latter gives better service over time.

The last piece to the systems puzzle is understanding how things work. For some reason, men seem to gravitate toward the systems and their operation. However, it is equally important for their partners to be up to speed, too. This brings a sense of participation and empowerment, and is also a major safety factor.

There is going to be a learning curve involved, and a formal training period, coupled with good documentation, is essential. This takes time—a commodity that always seems to be in short supply. But the learning curve is so important to making your first year of cruising a success that we would urge this be made a priority, ahead of everything else.

How long does this take? Our norm with a new build is 40 hours of instruction by the electrical and engineering staff at the yard, followed by an additional 40 hours of training on systems and boat handling. These 80 hours cannot be absorbed all at once. Rather, it is best to learn the basics, go away and cruise a bit, and come back for another dose. Having worked with many couples over the years we have found that separate instruction, where couple dynamics are absent, works best.

Finally, a ship's operations manual, with checklists and troubleshooting notes, is a necessity. If this is not detailed enough to see you through when there is no outside help available, consider creating your own, having one put together for you, or even buying a different boat.

We think the most important aspect of the design and systems approach discussed here is that it engenders confidence in a holistic fashion. This encourages the unplugging of the shore power cord, and the pointing of the bow toward distant shores.

We'll see you out there cruising.

# APPENDIX A

# Robert Beebe's Method for Figuring a Boat's Horsepower and Range

This appendix shows how to make up speed-range graphs, how to calculate speed to length (S/L) ratios, and how to make a couple of other applications of mathematics.

In estimating speed and range, we need two graphs to give us two factors: $F_1$ and $F_2$.

For $F_1$, enter Graph No. 1 (Figure A–1) with the vessel's displacement in long tons of 2,240 pounds along the bottom line. Proceed up to the curve and read off $F_1$ on the edge of the graph. In the example shown, the displacement is 46 tons, and $F_1$ is 87.

For $F_2$, enter Graph No. 2 (Figure A–2) with S/L ratios along the bottom line. For any given S/L ratio, there is an $F_2$ on the edge of the graph. The example shows that for S/L 1.25, $F_2$ is 1.65.

The horsepower required at any given S/L ratio is then $F_1 \times F_2$. In the cases of the examples drawn on the graphs, the horsepower required to drive the 46-ton vessel at an S/L ratio of 1.25 would be $87 \times 1.65 = 143.5$ hp.

For S/L calculations, you need a calculator with a square root function. Enter the waterline length of your vessel, converting inches to one-hundredths of a foot (46 feet 9 inches = 46.75 feet), and press the square root function. This will give you your vessel's speed in knots at an S/L of 1.0. To calculate higher S/Ls, multiply the speed at S/L 1.0 by the desired S/L. In other words, the speed corresponding to an S/L of 1.0 for a 46.75-foot waterline is 6.84 knots. To figure the speed at an S/L of 1.3, simply multiply 6.84 by 1.3 to get 8.89 knots. Making a series of such

calculations allows you to make up a table because it is better to have speed in knots keyed to your particular waterline rather than in S/L ratios.

As an example, see the accompanying table (page 391) made up to produce a speed-range curve using these rules. This table is for the Nordhavn 46.

Although horsepower figures in this table are given to two decimal places, it should not be assumed that the results can be depended on to be that accurate. But for plotting purposes, in making a smooth curve, it helps.

Figure A–3 shows the curve made from the accompanying table. The S/Ls are also indicated for reference. At below the S/L ratio of 1.0, the range becomes progressively more inaccurate. The ship could not possibly go more than 7,000 miles at 5 knots, for example. And the range at 6 knots is also overstated. [In fact, it appears that true range may be only 75–80% of the predicated range at around S/L of 1.0, partially due to drag of active fins and/or paravane stabilizers. Active fins or stabilizers can reduce speed by half a knot due to the added drag.]

## How-Goes-It Curve

While actually operating at sea, another useful curve is the "How-Goes-It" Curve illustrated and discussed in Chapter 15. This is a graph with total gallons at the start on the left side and distance to go along the bottom. As an example, take a fuel capacity of 1,200 gallons and a 2,000-mile passage.

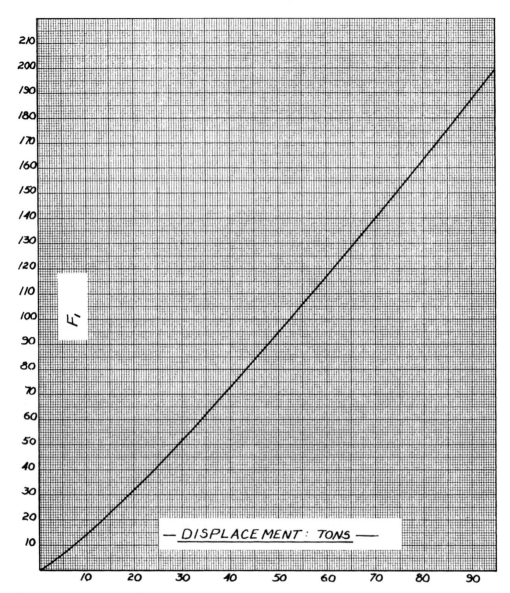

**Figure A–1.** Graph No. 1: $F_1$ Factor.

Draw a line from the full-fuel mark to the zero-distance mark. Then draw a line from the full-fuel mark to the desired reserve-on-arrival figure, say 10 percent.

It is obvious as you plot the fuel remaining each day and the distance to go, the plotted points *must* stay *above* these lines. Ideally, you want to be above the 10 percent reserve line. But if you fall below the solid line, you *know* you are not going to reach your port unless you change what you are doing.

## Wave Length Calculations

Another useful formula is the length of waves. Because waves have a constant S/L of 1.34 (which is why a vessel's hull speed is S/L 1.34), the length of the waves a boat is actually making, measured

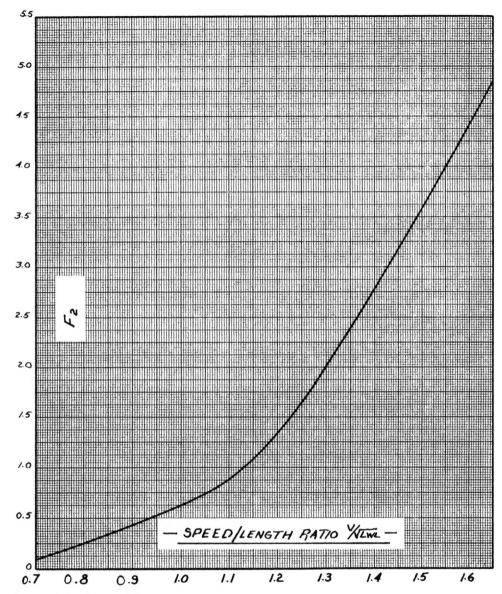

**Figure A–2.** Graph No. 1: $F_2$ Factor.

from the bow to the top of the second crest along the length of the boat, is a measure of the speed the boat is making. The formula is:

$$\text{Length} = \frac{V^2}{1.8}$$

The 1.8 in the denominator is $1.34^2$. The lengths, then, for the speeds we might be interested in are shown in the accompanying table. The lengths shown can be marked on deck to use as a log. Note that the difference between 6 knots and 7 knots is 7.2 feet, for instance.

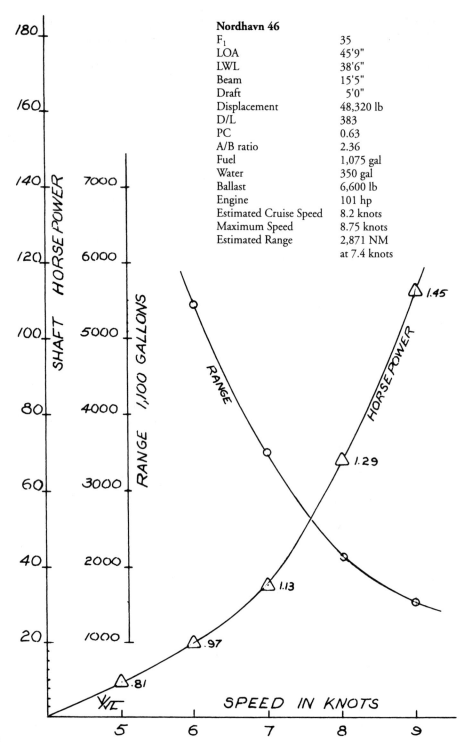

**Nordhavn 46**

| | |
|---|---|
| $F_1$ | 35 |
| LOA | 45'9" |
| LWL | 38'6" |
| Beam | 15'5" |
| Draft | 5'0" |
| Displacement | 48,320 lb |
| D/L | 383 |
| PC | 0.63 |
| A/B ratio | 2.36 |
| Fuel | 1,075 gal |
| Water | 350 gal |
| Ballast | 6,600 lb |
| Engine | 101 hp |
| Estimated Cruise Speed | 8.2 knots |
| Maximum Speed | 8.75 knots |
| Estimated Range | 2,871 NM |
| | at 7.4 knots |

**Figure A–3.** Speed/power/range curve for a Nordhavn 46.

| Speed Knots | S/L | $F_2$ | Hp $F_1 \times F_2$ | Gal/Hr at 0.06 Gal/Hp/Hr | Hours Running | Range |
|---|---|---|---|---|---|---|
| 5 | 0.81 | 0.28 | 12.6 | 0.75 | 1,467 | 7,333 |
| 6 | 0.97 | 0.57 | 25.6 | 1.54 | 715 | 4,290 |
| 7 | 1.13 | 1.02 | 46 | 2.76 | 398 | 2,786 |
| 8 | 1.29 | 2.02 | 91 | 5.46 | 201 | 1,612 |
| 9 | 1.45 | 3.20 | 144 | 8.64 | 127 | 1,146 |

Nordhavn 46 specifications: displacement, 26.8 tons; $F_1$, 45; LWL, 38.5'; fuel, 1,100 gallons.

| V (knots) | Length (feet) | V (knots) | Length (feet) |
|---|---|---|---|
| 3 | 5.0 | 8 | 35.5 |
| 4 | 8.9 | 9 | 45.0 |
| 5 | 13.9 | 10 | 55.5 |
| 6 | 20.0 | 11 | 67.2 |
| 7 | 27.2 | 12 | 80.0 |

# ISO Design Category Definitions

## Michael Kasten

Boats owned and/or operated within the European Union are required to obtain a "CE Mark," which certifies that the boat has been built according to the EU "Recreational Craft Directive." This includes a review of the boat's structure, equipment, and stability according to the standards of the International Organization for Standardization (ISO).

Naturally, not all boats are rated according to this standard because this requirement applies only to boats sold in the European Union. In the United States, for example, few manufacturers or designers bother to apply these ISO standards because they are not a requirement for private yachts bought, sold, built, or operated within the United States.

Even so, it is useful to have a standard against which we can compare boats, even if they are not "required" to comply. It should also be noted that Transport Canada has adopted the ISO rules, and the American Boat & Yacht Council (ABYC) is working closely with ISO as well. In all likelihood, it will not be long before we see a similar set of stability regulations imposed on pleasure craft in the United States.

For power boats, the standard that addresses stability is ISO 12217-1, by which an operational category is assigned to each boat. Each category defines the maximum sea state in which the boat is qualified to operate, whether ocean, coastal, inland, or sheltered inland waters.

## Design Category A

Boats designed for voyages, such as crossing oceans or in unsheltered waters for several hundred miles, are expected to be able to operate in conditions having a "significant wave height" of 23 feet (7 meters) with wind gusts up to 54.4 knots (28 m/s), and are expected to survive in even more severe conditions.

This is equivalent to Beaufort Force 10, which is ordinarily defined as being "Storm" or "Whole Gale" conditions with very high waves; overhanging crests; resulting foam blown in dense white patches with the wind; sea takes on a whiter look; visibility is affected by airborne spray; and wave height is 29 to 41 feet.

The ISO rule defines "significant wave height" as being the mean height of the highest one-third of the waves, or approximately the wave height estimated by an experienced observer. ISO further assumes that some waves will be double this height—in other words to 46 feet (14 m).

## Design Category B

Category B applies to boats designed for a significant wave height of 13 feet (4 meters) and a wind of Beaufort Force 8 or less. Such conditions may be encountered on offshore voyages of sufficient length where shelter may not always be immediately available, or on inland seas of sufficient size for the wave height to be generated. Some waves are assumed to be twice as high, or up to 26 feet (8 meters). Winds are assumed to gust to 41 knots (21 m/s).

Beaufort Force 8 is ordinarily defined as "Gale Conditions" having moderately high waves with greater length; edges of crests breaking into spindrift; foam blowing in well-defined streaks with the wind; considerable airborne spray; and a maximum wave height of 18 to 25 feet. Assuming some waves will be double, we have an ISO maximum wave height of 26 feet.

## Design Categories C and D

A boat given Category C and D ratings is designed for waves of up to 6.5 feet (2m) and 1.6 feet (0.5m); wind speeds of 33 knots (17 m/s) and 25 knots (13 m/s); and Beaufort Forces 6 and 4, respectively. In other words for brief coastal, inland, or sheltered waters in moderate to mild conditions. These categories are probably not of interest except perhaps for the shore boat.

## How Is the ISO Category Determined?

The International Marine Certification Institute provides guidance and worksheets in accordance with ISO 12217-1 for determining which operational design category a boat qualifies for. While the process is somewhat complex, it is interesting to at least know the factors that are considered, so we will summarize them here:

1. **Dimensions:** Length, beam, draft, and other measurements.

2. **Load:** The condition at the minimum operational displacement, and at maximum load.

3. **Offset Load:** A calculation of the amount of heel induced by the maximum number of crew and passengers in the least favorable position, as high in the boat as possible, and all crowded to one side. The vessel must not heel beyond a certain angle and adequate freeboard to downflooding must remain.

4. **Downflooding:** Hatches, doors, and other openings must have proper closing appliances. Downflooding is assumed to occur when any openings that do not have such closures are immersed, for example engine room vent openings. Downflooding heights are determined relative to the waterline for both full and light load conditions. Downflooding heights must be above certain minimums based on the boat's dimensions.

5. **Recesses:** Any recesses "open to the sky" that can contain water on deck are evaluated to make sure stability is sufficient when flooded (e.g., cockpits, fishing wells, decks enclosed by high bulwarks, etc.).

6. **Righting Moment:** The boat must be shown to have an absolute minimum *righting moment* of 18,439 foot-pounds (25 Kn-m) at some point in the range of heel between 30 and 50 degrees. See item #8 for a definition of RM.

7. **Righting Arm:** The boat must be shown to have a righting arm length (GZ) of at least 0.610 feet (0.2 meters) at some point in the range of heel between 30 and 50 degrees, calculated on the basis of the maximum righting moment between 30 and 50 degrees of heel in #6 above. See item #8 for a more complete definition of GZ.

8. **Stability:** At each load condition and at each angle of heel there will be a differing horizontal distance between the center of gravity force vector acting downward, and the Center of Buoyancy (CB) force vector acting upward. This distance is called the *Righting Arm* or simply, "GZ."

*Righting Energy:* Using imperial units, at each angle of heel, if you multiply the length of the righting arm in feet times the displacement of the boat in pounds, you have the righting moment that exists at that angle of heel. *Moment* simply means force times distance, and is expressed in foot-pounds. It is the same as torque.

Once the GZ distance has been calculated over a range of heel angles, the righting arm lengths are plotted on a graph with the GZ distance in feet measured on the vertical axis and heel angle in degrees measured along the horizontal axis. Plotting GZ at different heel angles yields the stability curve, also called the GZ *Curve* (see item 1 in Figure B–1).

Below the GZ Curve an area is contained, extending to the angle of vanishing stability, where the curve again crosses the horizontal axis. The contained area is assumed to represent the total amount of *positive righting energy* available, and is measured in *foot-degrees.*

*Stability Limitation:* ISO considers this positive righting energy area to terminate at the angle of vanishing stability, or at the downflooding angle, or at 50 degrees, whichever is less. At the lesser of those angles of heel, a vertical line is drawn (see item #3 in Figure B–1), truncating the area below the GZ Curve. Beyond that stability limit, any remaining area below the GZ Curve is ignored.

*Heeling Arm:* In order to discover how far the boat will heel with a given wind load directly abeam, the heeling arm must be derived. In order to calculate the force imposed by the wind, first the windage area of the boat's silhouette above the waterline is calculated, expressed in square feet. Then based on a certain assumed wind speed, a force per square foot is applied, which yields a total force expressed in pounds.

In order to discover the heeling moment, the heeling force in pounds is multiplied by the distance in feet from the windage area center to the boat's underwater center of lateral resistance. Thus we find the total heeling moment (force X distance), which is expressed in foot-pounds. This can be thought of as the amount of "torque" attempting to heel the boat.

We then divide the heeling moment by the boat's displacement in pounds, and we have a distance. This is the heeling arm, expressed in feet.

*The Plot:* Since the vertical axis of the GZ Curve is also expressed in terms of feet, we can also plot the heeling arm on the GZ Curve as a distance along the vertical axis at zero heel angle (see $M_w$ in Figure B–1). At that height, a line is drawn parallel to the horizontal axis (see item #2 in Figure B–1).

In the ISO code, at the point where the horizontal heeling arm line first intersects the GZ Curve, that is the angle of heel that is assumed to occur as a result of the wind force that has been applied directly abeam.

We now have an area contained between the GZ Curve and the horizontal heeling arm line, which extends over to the vertical *stability upper limit* line, which is shown in the diagram as Area 2 ($A_2$). The ISO code assumes $A_2$ to represent the boat's *residual righting energy* with the enclosed area measured in "foot-degrees."

9. **Resistance to Wind and Waves:** The International Maritime Organization (IMO), in cooperation

with others worldwide, has been seeking the best way to model the maximum assumed total *heeling energy* using the righting curve as the basis.

In order to plot an area representing the assumed "maximum heeling energy," the concept of a "Roll Back Angle" is used. In this calculation, it is assumed that the boat is already heeled due to a steady wind, for which the amount of heel is found by the method outlined via the intersection of the heeling arm with the GZ Curve.

From that point, the boat is assumed to roll back to windward due to wave action. This is called the *roll back angle.* The amount of roll back (R) is calculated by ISO as follows:

$$R = 25 + (20/D) \quad \phi_R$$

Where: D is the boat's displaced volume, expressed in cubic meters.

R is the amount of roll back, measured in degrees, from the point of steady heel, back *to windward,* (i.e., to the left on the GZ *Curve,* shown as $\phi_R$ in the diagram that follows).

At the calculated roll back angle, a vertical line is struck across the GZ Curve plot. The area enclosed between the GZ Curve and the steady heeling arm line, up to the calculated roll back angle is assumed by the ISO to represent the maximum heeling energy. This is called Area 1 ($A_1$) in Figure B–1, measured in "foot-degrees."

10. **Pass/Fail:** The boat will qualify for its intended category if the residual righting energy exceeds the assumed maximum heeling energy.

In other words, in the GZ Curve in Figure B–1, Area $A_2$ must be larger than Area $A_1$.

## Critique of the ISO Methodology

The calculation of arms, moments, and righting energy (#8); heeling energy (#9); and the comparison of areas (#10) per the diagram all describe the methodology generally used in order to assess a boat's suitability for ocean conditions.

What I have described is a "first-principles" approach similar to that promoted by the IMO

(International Maritime Organization). By first principles I mean that actual physical dimensions, centers, and wind pressures have been employed in the calculations.

While that is the general idea behind the stability analysis used in ISO 12217-1, the ISO method of prescribing heeling arm and wind pressure is in fact calculated quite differently.

Heeling arm is prescribed in ISO 12217-1 as: HA = (Windage Area/WL Length) + Draft Amidships. This ordinarily results in a much larger heeling arm than in fact exists by a first-principles calculation.

Wind pressure is prescribed in ISO 12217-1 as: WP = 0.3 kg / square meter. This yields approximately half the true wind pressures that would exist at the wind speeds given for Categories A and B of 28 m/s and 21 m/s, respectively.

The upshot is that the ISO stability calculations do not yield an accurate picture. All we know for sure is whether the vessel does or does not comply with European law.

What this means from a design standpoint is that the ISO recreational craft data cannot be directly correlated with widely available IMO stability data for commercial craft. This, in my view, is quite an unfortunate outcome.

## What Would Beebe Think?

Item #10 is actually where Captain Beebe's original A/B ratio concept is shown to have validity, since it is extremely difficult to pass this criterion if the vessel has excessive windage combined with insufficient volume below the water. In other words, if there is a larger profile below the water, it is more likely that the boat will have sufficient displacement to "handle" its windage profile above the water.

Beebe probably did not need a crystal ball to know this. He was, after all, a highly seasoned voyager, as well as quite an intuitive designer. It is easy to write off Beebe's A/B ratio as being too simplistic, but it is quite obvious that Beebe was prescient with regard to the ISO and the IMO wind and wave criteria.

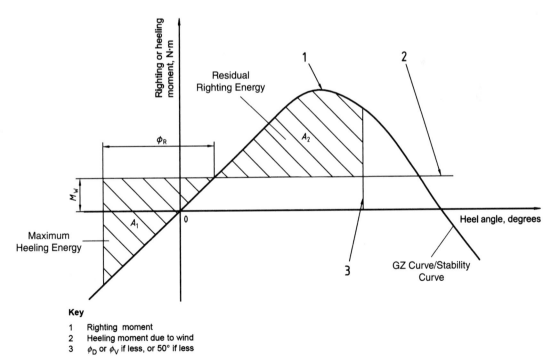

**Key**
1  Righting moment
2  Heeling moment due to wind
3  $\phi_D$ or $\phi_V$ if less, or 50° if less

**Figure B–1.** Roll resistance to waves and wind.

# Real World Fuel Burn for Selected Passagemaking Boats

Based on owner-provided data from answers to a questionnaire from the author, or from owner websites. Conditions and boats vary so figures will not be exactly repeatable, but they do provide some insight and rough comparisons. May or may not include generator time. (Where available, I have noted generator use.)

| Vessel | Make | Size (ft.) | Engine | HP | Single/Twin | RPM | From |
|---|---|---|---|---|---|---|---|
| China Blue | Cheoy Lee | 40 | Ford | 70 | T | | C Verdes |
| Finally | Nordhavn | 40 | Lugger 668 | | S | 1,500 | Hampton VA |
| Nordhavn | Nordhavn | 40 | Lugger 668 | 103 | S | | Worldwide |
| Diesel Duck | Diesel Duck 41 | 40 | Perkins M80T | 78 | S | 2,200 | Colon, Panama |
| Special Blend | Nordhavn | 43 | | | S | 1,500–1,600 | Galapagos |
| Kosmos | Nordhavn | 43 | Lugger 668 | 105 | S | 1,675+ – | Worldwide |
| Kosmos | Nordhavn | 43 | Lugger 668 | 105 | S | 1,500+ – | Ensenada |
| Summer Skis | Nordhavn | 43 | Lugger 668 | 140 | S | | Ft. Laud |
| Le Reve | Krogen | 44 | | | | | New Jersey |
| Emily Grace | Nordhavn | 46 | Lugger 6414D | 143 | S | | Galapagos |
| World Odd@Sea | Nordhavn | 46 | Lugger 668 | 163 | S | 1,550 | Bermuda |
| World Odd@Sea | Nordhavn | 46 | Lugger 668 | 163 | S | 1,550 | Azores |
| World Odd@Sea | Nordhavn | 46 | Lugger 668 | 163 | S | 1,550 | Ft Laud |
| Egret | Nordhavn | 46 | Lugger 668 | 130 | S | 1,350–1,575 | Freemantle |
| Kanaloa | Nordhavn | 46 | Lugger 668 | 143 | S | 1,500 | Mexico |
| Resolution | Nordhavn | 46 | Lugger 668 | | | | Newport |
| Frog Kiss | Nordhavn | 46 | Lugger 668 | 145 | S | | Bermuda |
| Bacchus | Nordhavn | 47 | Lugger 668T | 174 | S | 1,450 | Acupulco |
| Bluewater | Nordhavn | 47 | Lugger 668T | 174 | S | 2,200 | Ft Laud |
| Bluewater | Nordhavn | 47 | Lugger 668T | 174 | S | 1,900 | Bermuda |
| Bluewater | Nordhavn | 47 | Lugger 668T | 174 | S | 1,900 | Beaufort NC |
| Ice | Seahorse/Buehler | 50 | Deere 4045TFM | 150 | S | | Palau |
| Dora Mac | Diesel Duck 462 | 51 | Deere 404ST | 135 | S | | Langkawi, Malaysia |
| Dora Mac | Diesel Duck 462 | 51 | Deere 404ST | 135 | S | 12–1,500 | India |
| Teka III | Knight & Carver | 52 | Gardner 6LXB | 127 | S | 1,200 | Jax |
| Teka III | Knight & Carver | 52 | Gardner 6LXB | 127 | S | 1,100 | Bermuda |
| Teka III | Knight & Carver | 52 | Gardner 6LXB | 127 | S | 1,100 | Canaries |
| Dirona | Nordhavn | 52 | Deere 6068A | 265 | S | | Seattle |
| Seahorse | Skookum | 53 | Lugger | 130 | | | |
| Myah | Nordhavn | 55 | Lugger 1276A | 340 | S | 1,200 | Barra Navidad |
| Salty Dawg | Nordhavn | 55 | Deere 6081 | 330 | S | | Ft Laud |
| Salty Dawg | Nordhavn | 55 | Deere 6081 | 330 | S | | Bermuda |
| Salty Dawg | Nordhavn | 55 | Deere 6081 | 330 | S | | Azores |
| Idlewild | Gray/Buehler | 57 | Kubota | 55 | S | | S. Africa |
| Chrysalis | Tennant | 60 | Cummins | | T | | U.S. |
| Wildwind 4 | Tennant | 60 | Cummins | 330 | T | | Hawaii |
| Oso Blanco | Nordhavn | 64 | Detroit | 400 | S | | PV, Mexico |
| Iron Lady | Dashew FPB | 64 | Deere 6068 TFM | 236 | S | | New Zealand |
| Sarah Sarah | Dashew FPB | 64 | Deere 6068 | 234 | S | 1,700–1,900 | New Zealand |
| Avatar | Dashew FPB | 64 | Deere 6068 | 234 | S | 1,750 | Fiji |
| Pamacea | Moonen | 65 | VovTAM71A | 292 | T | | Canaries |

| To | NM | Speed (knots) | Gals burned | NMPG | Hrs | Stability | Comments |
|---|---|---|---|---|---|---|---|
| Barbados | 2,160 | 7.22 | 840 | 2.57 | 299 | None | Both engines 1978 HK to Fla |
| Bermuda | 1,425 | 6.3 | 625 | 2.3 | | | Round trip |
| | 24,211 | 6.67 | 10,361 | 2.34 | 3,627 | Fins | N40 Circumnavigation; includes gen use |
| Georgetown G. Cayman | 611 | 6.3 | 132 | 4.6 | 96 | Sail | 400 sq ft steady sail |
| Marquesas | 2,995 | 6.2 | 950 | 3.1 | 480 | Fins | Some gen use incl |
| | | 6.1 | | 2.7 | | Fins | For entire circumnavigation |
| Marquesas | 2,835 | 5.67 | 1,002 | 2.83 | 498 | Fins | Blog report |
| Tiverton RI | 1,535 | 6.5 | 590 | 2.6 | 236 | | Via Bermuda; Gulfstream +2–4 kts; 2 hrs gen/day |
| Holland | 3,885 | 6.35 | 1,290 | 3.01 | | | Total for 3 legs |
| Marquesas | 3,000 | 5.95 | 845 | 3.55 | 504 | Fins | 200 amp alternator; sail assist .2 knot ? |
| Azores | 1,844 | 6.4 | 675 | 2.73 | 288 | Para | Incl 12.5 hrs gen use 98% paravane use |
| Gibraltar | 1,185 | 6.77 | 355 | 3.2 | | Para | |
| Bermuda | 1,005 | 7.2 | 444 | 2.26 | 140 | Para | 70% paravane use |
| Mauritius | 3,365 | 6.1 | 1,134 | 2.97 | 558 | Fins | 9.3 hrs gen use |
| Marquesas | 2,872 | 6.9 | 1,110 | 2.59 | 404 | Para | 100% paravanes; no generator |
| Azores | 1,743 | | 605 | 2.88 | | Fins | |
| Newport | 650 | 6.4 | 255 | 2.55 | 102 | Para | 75% paravanes |
| Marquesas | 2,829 | 6.2 | 1,243 | 2.28 | 455 | Fins, Para | Para used after fins failed on Day 4. 3 hrs gen incl |
| Bermuda | 1,035 | 7.4 | 935 | 1.1 | 140 | Fins | Gulfstream push |
| Azores | 1,820 | 6.2 | 1,284 | 1.4 | 295 | Fins, Para | 50% paravanes Fin malfunction drag |
| Portland ME | 2,775 | 6.64 | 2,210 | 1.26 | 418 | Fins, Para | Via PR, Tortola, Bermuda. 10% paravanes Gen: 342 gal excl |
| Tarawa | 2,500 | 6.34 | 712 | 3.51 | 394 | Para | Aux sails used some |
| Sri Lanka | 1,539 | 6.1 | 391 | 3.94 | 252 | Para | Storm forced course reversal for 36 hours |
| Maldives | 392 | 6.1 | 79 | 4.93 | 65 | None | |
| Bermuda | 891 | 6.86 | 375 | 2.38 | 130 | Para | No gen; 100% paravanes |
| Azores | 1,720 | 6.5 | 639 | 2.69 | 262 | Para | No gen; 100% paravanes |
| Antigua | 2,768 | 6.9 | 1,042 | 2.66 | 398 | Para | No gen; 100% paravanes |
| Alaska | 900 | 7.0 | 825 | 1.1 | 118 | Fins | |
| | 1,752 | 7.3 | 757 | 2.31 | | Para | |
| Marquesas | 2,686 | 7.05 | 1,714 | 1.57 | 381 | Fins | Gen: 39 hrs incl |
| Bermuda | 1,025 | 7.29 | 852 | 1.2 | | Fins | |
| Azores | 1,820 | 6.17 | 1,095 | 1.66 | | Fins | |
| Gibraltar | 1,185 | 6.77 | 769 | 1.54 | | Fins | |
| Freemantle | 4,499 | 6.3 | 977 | 4.6 | 708 | None | |
| Gibraltar | 1,805 | 9 | | 2.0 | | None | Catamaran |
| Seattle | | 8–8.5 | | 2.0 | | None | Catamaran; ran partially on single engine |
| NZ | 8,104 | 7.3 | 6,795 | 1.2 | | Fins | Multiple legs; Gen: 2,300 gal excluded |
| Fiji | 1,770+ | 9.6 | 965 | 1.83 | | Fins | Includes Tonga; Gen: 389 gal excluded |
| Neah Bay Washington | 6,572 | 9.39 | 4,414 | 1.49 | 700 | Fins | Refueled in HI. Over 50% headwinds. Excludes 116g gen |
| New Zealand | 1,100 | 8.2 | 687 | 1.60 | 136 | Fins | Gale, head seas adverse current, air cond for 3 days included |
| Antigua | 2,805 | 8.66 | 2,243 | 1.25 | 324 | Fins | Ran both engines |

# Recommended Spare Parts and Supplies for Trans-Ocean Cruising Med Bound 2007 Rally

## Milt Baker

## Pumps

Complete primary bilge pump
Complete high-water bilge pump
Primary bilge pump rebuild kit
Complete waste and gray water discharge pump
Spares for waste and gray water discharge pumps
Fuel transfer pump (boost pump)
Pressure water system pump
Repair kits for all heads onboard
Replacement joker valves

## Filters

Racor filter elements for main engine, wing engine, generators (30- and 10-micron)
Racor filter elements for fuel transfer system (2-micron)

## Bulbs

Anchor light
Port and starboard running lights
Stern running light
Mast steaming light
Extra navigation light sockets
All deck lights
Spotlight/searchlight
Interior lights
Engine room lights

Fluorescent tubes for engine room
Flashlights

## Misc.

Spare hoses for all applications onboard, especially engines and gensets
Grease gun and grease
Fastener kit (nuts, bolts, screws, washers, etc.—various sizes—stainless steel)
Hose clamp kit (various sizes—all stainless steel)
Wiper blades
Strainer baskets for sea-water strainers
Gaskets for sea-water strainers
Whale pressure water hose and fittings as follows:
  equal T
  equal elbow
  equal straight
  stem adaptor
  shut-off valve
Batteries for flashlights
Backup binoculars (7 × 50)
Backup GPS and batteries
Backup handheld VHF radio and batteries
Hydraulic ram for steering system
Seals for steering system
Oil for steering system

## Zincs

- Bottom hull
- Keel cooler
- End propeller main shaft
- Rudder shoe
- Spurs
- Wing engine shaft
- Pencil zincs

## Electrical Parts

- Automotive fuses
- Spare battery switches
- Assorted breakers
  - 5-amp
  - 10-amp
  - 15-amp
  - 20-amp
  - 25-amp
  - 30-amp
  - 40-amp
  - 50-amp
- Double-pull 20-amp
- Double-pull 30-amp
- Alligator clips
- Electrical connector kit
- Class "T" fuses 400-amp
- Class "T" fuses 250-amp
- Other fuses specific to your boat
- Solenoids for engines, generators, windlass

## Fluids

- ATF steering fluid Dextron II/Mercon
- John Deere–approved coolant
- ISO 32 hydraulic oil for boats with hydraulic systems
- 10W40 motor oil for boats with Naiad stabilizer systems (unless otherwise specified by Naiad)
- Lube oil for main, wing, and generator
- BioBor, Stanadyne, and/or other preferred diesel treatment
- 80–90W gear oil for oiler bottles on Trac system and thrusters
- Oil for transmission(s) if different from above

## Main Engine

- Fuel filters (on engine)
- Oil filters
- Air filter
- Air filter cleaning kit
- Thermostat gasket
- Thermostat lower
- Thermostat upper
- Serpentine belt
- Alternator belts
- Workshop manual
- Parts catalog
- Starter
- Starter solenoid
- Alternator
- Alternator pulley and bushing
- Voltage regulator
- Lift pump
- Coolant pump
- Raw water pump (if fitted)
- Impellers (if raw water cooled)
- Cooling system zincs (if fitted)
- Exhaust elbow (if fitted)

## Generator

- Standard spares kit
- Oil filters
- Fuel filters (on engine)
- Raw water pump
- Impellers
- Thermostats
- Belts
- Workshop manual
- Parts catalog
- Starter
- Starter solenoid
- Stop solenoid
- Alternator
- Voltage regulator
- Lift pump
- Exhaust elbow
- Cooling system zinc(s) if fitted
- SPDT relays (check for proper voltage rating)

## Wing Engine

Fuel filters (on engine)
Oil filters
Air filter or air filter cleaning kit
Thermostats
Thermostat gaskets
Belts
Raw water pump
Impellers
Workshop manual
Parts catalog
Starter
Starter solenoid
Stop solenoid
Alternator
Voltage regulator
Exhaust elbow
Cooling system zincs (if fitted)

# APPENDIX E

# Recommended Ship's Library

This is a list of books we have found useful to have aboard during passages. You never know when you will need information to understand and solve problems. These books may provide it.

## Books

Bannerot, Scott and Wendy. *The Cruiser's Handbook of Fishing* (International Marine/McGraw-Hill, 2003). One of the most complete and helpful books on saltwater fishing ever written. A must for cruisers who want to catch fish and shellfish along the way.

Beebe, Robert P. and Umstot, Denis D. *Voyaging Under Power, Fourth Edition* (International Marine/McGraw-Hill, 2013). An essential reference and background book on power passagemaking. I carried both the first and third editions on *Teka III* long before I even dreamed of writing the fourth edition.

Buehler, George. *The Troller Yacht Book, Second Edition* (Booklocker, 2011). If you are choosing a boat, George offers a lot of insight into keeping costs low and still getting a very effective passagemaker. If you are interested in a Diesel Duck or other Buehler designs featured in Chapter 12, this book is a must. The PDF electronic format is in color.

Cornell, Jimmy. *World Cruising Destinations* (International Marine/McGraw-Hill, 2010). A fine reference for planning voyages. The book includes information on most of the major world ports: the people, the climate, formalities, and facilities.

Cornell, Jimmy. *World Cruising Routes* (International Marine/McGraw-Hill, 2008). Contains useful information for planning your voyage: distances, waypoints, cruising guides available, timing, and winds and weather.

D'Antonio, Steve. [forthchoming—title is tentative] *Your Boat Inside and Out: The Photographic Guide to Symptoms, Causes, Cures, and Best Practices for Sail- and Powerboats* (Forthcoming from International Marine/McGraw-Hill, 2014)

Dashew, Linda and Steve. *The Offshore Cruising Encyclopedia, Second Edition* (Beowulf, 2002). Anything you want to know about boat systems is contained in this large reference volume. It is aimed at sailors, but also useful for power boaters.

Dashew, Steve and Linda, *Mariner's Weather Handbook* (Beowulf, 1998). One of the best and most interesting weather books available to voyagers.

Dashew, Steve and Linda. *Surviving the Storm: Coastal and Offshore Tactics* (Beowulf, 1999). An interesting book about storms that includes sections on waves, weather, boat design, and tactics. It is written mainly from a sailing perspective, but has plenty of good information for power voyagers.

Dempsey, Paul. *Troubleshooting and Repair of Diesel Engines* (McGraw-Hill, 2007). An excellent book for understanding how to work with your engines.

Gerr, Dave. *Boat Mechanical Systems Handbook: How to Design, Install, and Recognize Proper Systems in*

*Boats* (International Marine/McGraw-Hill, 2008). This book, by one of the most distinguished yacht architects, aims to show how to design, install, and recognize proper systems in boats.

Gill, Paul G. *The Onboard Medical Guide: First Aid and Emergency Medicine Afloat* (International Marine/McGraw-Hill, 1996). This book is a good source for first aid and emergency medicine at sea. There are several newer books available that we have not had a chance to review.

Hinz, Earl. *The Complete Book of Anchoring and Mooring* (Cornell Maritime Press, 2001). Somewhat dated due to new anchor developments, but still contains many insights into effective anchoring techniques.

Hollander, Neil and Mertes, H. *Yachtsman's Emergency Handbook* (Angus & Robertson, 1989). Full of ideas for handling emergencies at sea.

Leonard, Beth A. *The Voyager's Handbook: The Essential Guide to Bluewater Cruising*, Second Edition (International Marine/McGraw-Hill, 2006). While this book is aimed primarily at sailors, it has many insights applicable to all voyagers, including those under power.

Marchaj, C.A. *Seaworthiness: The Forgotten Factor, Second Edition* (Tiller Publishing, 1996). An excellent technical book on the design of boats for operating in extreme conditions.

Van Dorn, William G. *Oceanography and Seamanship, Second Edition* (Schiffer Publishing, 1993). A classic text on oceanography, waves, and ship dynamics. Brims with useful information.

Wing, Charles. *Boatowner's Illustrated Handbook of Wiring, Second Edition* (International Marine/McGraw-Hill, 2006). A handbook of basic concepts of AC and DC power.

## Most Useful Magazines for Passagemakers

*PassageMaker Magazine*
*Ocean Navigator*
*Latitudes and Attitudes*
*Cruising World*
*Latitude 38* (information about sailors' experiences throughout the world)
*Practical Sailor* (tests many systems for all boats, not just sail)
*Sea* (Pacific Coast to Panama)

# Endnotes

## Chapter 2

7     *Arielle's 1937 Atlantic crossing*    Marin-Marie wrote about the voyage on the *Arielle* in his book, *Wind Aloft, Wind Alow* (Scribners, 1947).

9     *All these details are from*    See Humphrey Barton's book, *Atlantic Adventurers* (Coles, 1962).

10     **Speejacks: The First Power Yacht to Circumnavigate**    The Gowens' story is told by Dale Collins in *Sea Tracks of the* Speejacks: *Round the World* (Doubleday, 1923).

11     *Great seas buffeted her hither and thither*    Description by Jeanne Gowen in Collins, 1923, 21.

11     *Westward: First motor yacht to circumnavigate entirely on its own power*    Don and Ann Gumpertz relate their historic adventures in, "Five Years Around the World" (*International Yachtsman*, premiere issue, date unknown).

14     *June 2007 Crossing the Pacific*    Hugh and Teresa Reilly chronicle their adventures in their blog, "Voyage of the Good Ship *Westward*" (http://classicyacht.org/westward, 2007–2008).

14     *Larry Briggs' Circumnavigations Beginning in 1977*    Based on personal correspondence with the author.

16     *Egret's Circumnavigation: The Southern Capes*    Scott and Mary Flanders discuss their circumnavigation adventures in "*Egret's* Circumnavigation and You," *PassageMaker Magazine* (July/August 2011) and a number of other *PassageMaker Magazine* articles. They also share their stories of the trip on the voyage of *Egret* website sponsored by Nordhavn (www.nordhavn.com/egret).

## Chapter 3

17     *"The chief difference from cruises of the past"*    See Robert Beebe's early thoughts on power cruising in *Rudder* (August/September 1946).

18     *This rugged trip under winter conditions*    Robert Beebe describes the trip in Joe Necomb's *Talaria* in *Rudder* (February 1958).

25     *In fact, what to call long-range motor cruisers*    See Richard Henderson's book, *Sea Sense* (OP, International Marine/McGraw-Hill, 1991) for a discussion of terms.

## Chapter 5

37  *In describing their experience*   See Steve Dashew's discussion at setsail.com.

38  **Keys to Enjoyable Voyaging Under Power**   This section was developed in part through the joint efforts of Denis and Mary Umstot and Christi and Eric Grab, Trawler Fest, San Diego, 2010.

39  *Our minimum stay is about 14 days*   This quote is from Milt Baker's article, "Home Is Where Kanaloa Is" (*Circumnavigator*, 2010), 80. Used with permission of Heidi and Wolfgang Hass.

41  **Transatlantic Aboard Salvation II**   Jim Leishman, co-owner of Nordhavn, relates his experience in crossing the Atlantic. This account is edited and abridged from his original version.

45  **Heading for Antigua, Almost 3,000 Miles Away**   This excerpt is from Mary Umstot's book, *Voyaging to the Mediterranean Under Power* (Booklocker, 2010). Used with permission.

## Chapter 6

53  *It turns out that the S/L ratio was mathematically derived*   See Dave Gerr, "On Standard Hull Speed," *The Masthead* (June 2010), 12–13.

53  *For example, heavy additions*   For a complete discussion see Dave Gerr's article, "Practical Speed and Powering Calculations" in *The Masthead* (June 2008). Also see Dave Gerr's book, *Propeller Handbook* (International Marine/McGraw-Hill, 2001).

55  *The Ideal Passagemaker Design*   This sidebar excerpted from Michael Kasten, *The Ideal Passagemaker* (2000–2009), published on his website. Used with permission.

## Chapter 7

61  *George Buehler, designer of the popular Diesel Duck line of boats*   See his book, *The Troller Yacht Book: How to Cross Oceans Without Getting Wet or Going Broke, Second Edition* (George Buehler Publications/Booklocker.com, 2011).

61  *Of the 300 boats entered, only 85 finished*   William G. Van Dorn wrote about the storm in *Oceanography and Seamanship* (Schiffer Publishing, 1993). Several other books have been published about this event, including John Rousmaniere's *Fastnet: Force 10: The Deadliest Storm in the History of Modern Sailing* (W. W. Norton, 2000); Nick Ward's *Left for Dead: Surviving the Deadliest Storm in Sailing History* (Bloomsbury USA, 2007); and Adam Mayers' *Beyond Endurance: 300 Boats, 600 Miles, and One Deadly Storm* (McClelland & Stewart, 2008).

61  *Hull form and displacement and weight distribution*   See Marchaj (1996), 86.

61  *I relied upon*   Van Dorn (1993) and C. A. Marchaj's *Seaworthiness: The Forgotten Factor, Revised Edition* (Tiller Publishing, 1996).

62  *While all these boats were sailing vessels*   See Marchaj (1996).

62  *However, in one three-year period*   Described in Van Dorn (1993); based on Jan-Olof Traung's *Fishing Boats of the World, Vol. 2* (Fishing News, 1967).

62  *In the mid-1960s*   Romsdals are discussed in Chapter 13.

63    *While the curve in Figure 7–6 shows a 90° point where stability is lost*    See B. Webster and R. Sampson's research project, "Suitability of Stability Criteria Applied to Small Fishing Vessels and Associated Survivability" (University of Newcastle, March 31, 2006), 30.

65    *Boats that are not fully decked over*    See Van Dorn (1993), 249. Also see Roger Long's article, "Critically Damped Vessel Motion" in *Ocean Navigator* (May/June 2011).

66    **International Organization for Standardization (ISO) Design Categories for Recreational Boats**    Thanks to Nordhavn for providing the sources for this summary.

67    *If we could compare stability data on oceangoing motor yachts*    The International Organization for Standardization (ISO) has established stability standards for yachts, although most U.S. yacht companies do not make their ISO computations public. Standards are covered under ISO 12217-1.

67    *According to Ralph Naranjo, the U.S. Coast Guard, in developing its 47-foot motor lifeboat*    Ralph Naranjo discusses these issues in his article, "Power Seafaring Defined" in *Ocean Navigator* (March/April 2011).

68    **Figure 7–10.** *Effects of the sea on boat movement*    Adapted from Van Dorn (1993), 298.

69    *On the other hand, if these 8-foot waves*    See Van Dorn (1993), 300.

69    **Evaluating an Existing Vessel's Stability**    Roger Long's sidebar is reprinted from *Ocean Navigator* (May/June 2011). Used with permission.

70    *Marchaj reports that tank tests of*    See Marchaj (1996), 235.

70    *"Modern, relatively light keelboats, with high freeboard, will skid on their topsides"*    Steve Dashew, "On Stability" (February 2011), setsail.com.

71    **Free Surface and Stability**    This section is based on John Womack and Bruce Johnson's booklet, "A Guide to Fishing Vessel Stability" (Society of Naval Architects and Marine Engineers, 2003).

72    *If the boat has a watermaker, it can be used to keep water tanks full*    For a technical paper on this subject, see P. R. Couser's, "On the Effect of Tank Free Surfaces on Vessel Static Stability" in the *International Journal of Maritime Engineering* (2004), 146.

74    *Good course-keeping in heavy weather*    See Marchaj (1996), 278.

74    *Don Stabbert described his experience with* Starr    See Don Stabbert's article, "When Two Rudders are Better" in *PassageMaker Magazine* (March/April 2004), 118.

74    **Diagnosing Steering Stability**    This sidebar is adapted from R. M. Freeman's paper, "The Rudder: A Hidden Cause of a Common Problem," presented at the National Marine Electronics Association (1978, revised 1997). Available from Wood Freeman, manufacturer of Metal Marine autopilots.

74    *Using this method, the rudder area*    See Van Dorn (1993), 257.

74    *Another rule of thumb*    Attributed to Ed Hagemann in Stabbert (2004).

76    *If you have a rudder made out of a flat plate*    See R. M. Freeman (1978, 1997).

76     *Several brands of passagemaking yachts have installed this rudder and report excellent performance* See Robert M. Lane, "Articulated Rudders," *PassageMaker Magazine* (September 2007). Also see Robert M. Lane, "Devlin Sockeye 45," *PassageMaker Magazine* (March/April 2004).

79     *Patrick Bray, a Canadian yacht designer* See Patrick J. Bray, "Super fuel efficient long range motoryachts," paper presented at the Second Symposium on Yacht Design and Production (Madrid, Spain, 2006).

79     *Another study done as part of the MIT Sea Grant Program* Heliotis, A. D. & Goudey, C. A., "Tow Tank Results of Bulbous Bow Refits on New England Trawler Hulls," MIT Sea Grant Report 9 (September 20, 1985).

79     *Don Bass, Honorary Research Professor of Engineering and Mathematics at Memorial* Don Bass, "Seakeeping for the 90-Foot Multi-species Fishing Vessel with Various Bulbous Bows," report provided to the author (March 2011).

82     *Stability information on sailing vessels is routinely required for participation in races.* The Royal Ocean Sailing Club, in conjunction with ISO 12217-2, has developed numerical factors to rate the stability of sailing vessels (often referred to as IRC—the numeric handicapping system used in sailing races), including the Stability Index or STIX and the Angle of Vanishing Stability or AVS. These numbers are required for a vessel to participate in an IRC race. (In the United States US-IRC oversees these ratings.)

## Chapter 8

84     *"Habitability is more than just available space below deck."* Quote and graphs from C. A. Marchaj in his book *Seaworthiness: The Forgotten Factor* (Tiller Publishing, 1996).

91     *Figure 8–11. Down under in Australia,* Explanation and image from cruisingunderpower .fastmail.net.

95     *One study by* See A. Akinturk, D. Cummings, and D. Bass, "Effects of Paravanes during Sea Trials," paper presented at 28th American Towing Tank Conference (August 2007).

98     *With normal irregular beam seas* See Frank H. Sellars' and John P Martin's article, "Selection and Evaluation of Ship Roll Stabilization Systems" in *Marine Technology* (1992): 84–101.

99     *Steve D'Antonio, an expert on marine mechanical and electrical systems* Steve D'Antonio, "Fin Stabilizers," *PassageMaker Magazine* (November/December 2008).

99     *Others might not give such protection.* Steven and Diane Koch describe their ordeal aboard *Kinship* in their article, "To the Rescue," in *PassageMaker Magazine* (April 2006).

100     *Nancy described their process of solving this challenge* See "Anti-Roll Tanks—A Simple Way to Stabilize," in *All at Sea* (February 2007), reproduced courtesy of Nancy Terrell and *All at Sea*.

102     *Kasten discusses this strategy* See "An Overview of a Few Common Roll Attenuation Strategies for Motor Yachts and Motor Sailors 2002–2010," on Michael Katsen's website: http://www.kastenmarine.com/

102     *Another yacht designer,* See Patrick Bray, "The Advantages of Twin Keels," undated, available through his website.

102    *One study reported in* Marine Technology *found a reduction in roll*    See Martin, John R., "Roll Stabilization in Small Ships," *Marine Technology*, (Oct. 1994).

105    *For a more detailed report*    See Steve D'Antonio's article, "Seakeeper Gyro," in *PassageMaker Magazine* (March 2008).

## Chapter 9

108    *Some yacht designers use a system called the Design Spiral*    See B. Boehm's article, "A Spiral Model of Software Development and Enhancement" in *IEEE Computer* 21, no. 5 (1988): 61–72. Also see Stephen Hollister's book, *The Design Spiral for Computer-Aided Boat Design* (New Wave Systems, 1994).

114    **The Commissioning Process: A Survival Guide**    See John Torelli's article, reprinted from *Passage-Maker Magazine* (May 2011). Used with permission of the author and *PassageMaker Magazine*.

116    *We have gone through at least one major electronics upgrade about every five years*    See Tom Neal's article, "Bringing a Used Cruiser Back to Life," in *PassageMaker Magazine* (March 2008).

117    **Figure 9–9:** *Sally says their dream is to voyage to the Mediterranean*    For details, see Robert M. Lane's article, "Spirit of Balto: Built with These Two Hands," in *PassageMaker Magazine* (November/December 2007).

117    *They then moved aboard and crossed the Atlantic to the Mediterranean and back*    See Kim Peterson's book, *Charting the Unknown: Fear, and One Long Boat Ride* (Behler, 2010) for a description of building *Chrysalis*, a 65-foot catamaran; moving aboard with her husband, Mike, and two children; and voyaging to the Mediterranean.

118    *However, with careful attention to costs and bargain-hunting*    A number of diesel ducks, designed by George Buehler and described in Chapter 12, have been home-built. See Gregory Roscoe's article, "Duck Builders," in *PassageMaker Magazine* (March 2011).

127    **Figure 9–19:** *Dinghy dock at Georgetown, Bahamas.*    Photo by Denis Umstot from Mary Umstot's article, "Lure of the Bahamas," in *PassageMaker Magazine* (October 2000).

## Chapter 10

139    **Ventilation and Air Conditioning**    Dave Gerr's book, *Boat Mechanical Systems Handbook* (International Marine/McGraw-Hill 2009), has an excellent technical discussion of air conditioning and heating systems.

## Chapter 11

148    **Selecting an Engine**    For a more complete discussion of engines, see Dave Gerr's book, *The Nature of Boats* (International Marine/McGraw-Hill, 1992).

148    *He points out a number of bad outcomes from under-loading*    Bob Senter posted these outcomes on the Nordhavn Dreamers website (http://www.nordhavndreamers.com, June 23, 2011).

153    **Figure 11–7.** *Raw water and exhaust plumbing for wet-exhaust main engines and generators*    Based on the Northern Lights technical information paper, "Please Don't Drown Me"; and Dave Gerr's *Boat Mechanical Systems Handbook* (International Marine/McGraw-Hill, 2009), 111.

154     *While there is controversy about which micron filters to use*     Bill Parlatore argues that the Racor primary filters should be 2 micron rather than 10 micron. See his article, "Filtering Fuel: An Offshore Experience" in *PassageMaker Magazine* (March 2007).

158     *Dave Gerr says that dripless connectors are OK*     See Dave Gerr's book, *Boat Mechanical Systems Handbook* (2009).

159     *Actually, a three-bladed prop is more efficient*     See Dave Gerr's book, *Propeller Handbook* (International Marine/McGraw-Hill, 2001).

168     **Figure 11–23.**     Photo by Denis Umstot. Shown in Mary Umstot's book, *Voyaging to the Mediterranean Under Power* (Booklocker.com, 2010) and her article, "Cruising the Black Sea" in *PassageMaker Magazine* (May/June 2005). Used with permission.

## Chapter 12

173     *No other designer has been as open*     For more information on the FPB 64 or the other models Steve Dashew is developing, see his website: Setsail.com.

184     *Nordhavn currently offers 16 models*     The Nordhavn website offers extensive information on all models: www.nordhavn.com.

198     *His objectives for design are simplicity, reliability, and affordability*     George Buehler's design approach and philosophy are described in his book, *The Troller Yacht Book: How to Cross Oceans Without Getting Wet or Going Broke, Second Edition* (George Buehler Publications/Booklocker .com, 2011).

## Chapter 13

235     *Many Defever models are also ocean capable*     Ken Murray writes about rounding Cape Horn in a 40-foot trawler in *PassageMaker Magazine* (March 2003).

235     **Romsdal North-Sea Trawlers**     Much of the information in this section provided by Joyce Gauthier and Jim Rogers.

236     *Some boats have been retrofitted with paravanes or active fins*     Based on an article in *SEA and Pacific Motor Boat* (December 1960). Author unknown.

236     *Another source of North Sea trawlers was born in the early 1960s*     For more Malahide history, see Myles J. Stapleton's article, "The Malahide Shipyard: A Brief History," in the *Classic Trawler Network* (March 2002).

238     **Figure 13–1D.** *The 55' Romsdal,* Delfin, *restored and owned by Carl Loeb*     For *Delfin*'s story, see Robert Lane's article, "Romsdal Reborn," in *PassageMaker Magazine* (July/August 2008).

240     *Willard Marine*     This section is based on Richard Miller's "Recreational Trawlers from Willard Marine: History and Production 1957–2003" (revised version December 26, 2007), which was compiled from material developed by Patrick Gerety from Willard files and personnel, and from other Willard owners. Additional information was provided by Patrick Gerety of Willard Marine. For more on Willards, see Robert M. Lane's article, "Willard Renaissance," in *PassageMaker Magazine* (January/February 2002).

241     *While a number of Vegas and Willard 30s have made significant voyages*     See Bill Parlatore's article, "Little Boat on a Big Ocean," in *PassageMaker Magazine* (November 1, 2002).

241   *Skookum Marine*   The information in this section is based on an interview with Bernie Arthur, 2012.

243   *Another fascinating Cheoy Lee story*   This section is based on two articles by Sheppard Root: "You Only Go Around Once," in *Motor Boating & Sailing* (October 1978); and "Slow Boat from China," in *Motor Boating & Sailing* (December 1978) and on correspondence with Sheppard Root.

245   **Stephen Seaton's Boats**   This section based on information from Stephen Seaton and Bruce Kessler.

245   *Steel Magnolia*   See Roy McNett's article, "Steel Magnolia Returns to the Northwest Caribbean," in *PassageMaker Magazine* (November/December 2006).

247   *Zopilote was sunk by a rock pinnacle off Dall Island, Alaska*   *Zopilote* was salvaged, restored, and renamed *Tatu*. In 2011, she was reportedly a megayacht charter in the Marquesas.

247   *The boat was completed in 1997*   See Bill Parlatore's article, "Northern Marine 64 LRC," in *PassageMaker Magazine* (Summer 2008) for a full description of *Spirit of Zopilote* and photos of the boat (available on the Northern Marine website in addition to the magazine).

248   **Beebe's Passagemaker: Saving this Classic Boat**   For an extended version of this article, see Peter Quentrall-Thomas's article, "Buying an Old Wooden Passagemaker," in *Ocean Navigator* (June 2011). See also his article, "Still Voyaging Under Power After 46 Years," in *PassageMaker Magazine* (October 2011).

249   **Knight & Carver**   Information in this section provided by Hugo Carver.

250   **Kadey-Krogen**   This section is based on information from Larry Polster at Kadey-Krogen and Bill Parlatore's article, "The Legacy of Kadey-Krogen Yachts," in *PassageMaker Magazine* (November/December 2002).

250   *Most of these boats are used for coastal cruising*   Larry Polster, excerpts from the log of *Searcher* 1987–1994. E-mail to author (December 8, 2010).

252   **Our Australasian Seas Adventure**   This is abridged from Maurice and Louise Nunas's article, "Our Australasian Seas Adventure," in *Waypoints* (Summer 2008).

255   *Theirs was the first of the Nordhavns to circle the world*   Jim Sink died in January 2010 at the age of 80.

255   *Braun and Tina Jones' Grey Pearl completed the NAR and the Great Siberian Sushi Run*   Grey Pearl was lost in 2012 due to a fire at her berth in Thailand. No one was on board at the time and the cause is unknown.

256   **Cape Horn Trawlers.**   Based on information from Peter Sever and Cape Horn owners.

256   *Here were the criteria Peter used for his boat*   See Peter J. Sever, *The Cape Horn* (28th edition, March 2003), 4.

257   *I would include the best features of boats we had seen*   See Peter J. Sever, 2003, 4.

## Chapter 14

259   *Voyage Planning for Akama*   This section is adapted and abridged from a posting on Passage-making Under Power (PUP) (January 2, 2006). Used with permission of the authors and PUP.

264     *Only four of the circumnavigators regularly took on crew*     See Beth A. Leonard's *The Voyager's Handbook, Second Edition* (International Marine/McGraw-Hill, 2007), 3.

266     **Prepare Your Engines and Transmission**     For another perspective, see Steve D'Antonio's article, "Prepare Your Vessel for Long-Distance and Offshore Passagemaking," in *PassageMaker Magazine* (November 2002).

## Chapter 15

272     **Kosmos's *Circumnavigation***     Christi Grab is the author of *The Unexpected Circumnavigation: Unusual Boat, Unusual People*, a four-part series about her around-the-world journey.

275     **Figure 15–4.** *Mary on watch in the Atlantic off Portugal*     In Mary and Denis Umstot's article, "Atlantic Anxiety: How One Couple Felt Just Before Their First Ocean Crossing," in *PassageMaker Magazine* (March/April 2002).

276     *Informal daytime watches were the norm for both groups*     See Beth Leonard's *The Voyager's Handbook, Second Edition* (International Marine/McGraw-Hill, 2007).

276     **Watchkeeping Lessons Learned**     This list is based, in part, on Leonard 2007, 440–441.

284     **Every Boater's Nightmare**     This sidebar was adapted from a posting on the Passagemaking Under Power (PUP) list. Used with permission of both the author and PUP.

286     *We hit the reef going 8 knots*     This is from the website of Susan and Mark Lindsey: All Points North.

287     **Crossing the Bar**     For more discussion on bar crossing, see the article by Mark Tilden, "Bar Hopping," in *PassageMaker Magazine* (April 2009).

288     **Seasickness: The Spoiler on Ocean Passages**     Adapted from *Seasickness Prevention and Treatment*, Marine Medical Systems (April 1998).

291     *The anxieties and apprehension preceding an ocean crossing are many*     Abridged and adapted from Mary and Denis Umstot's article, "Atlantic Anxiety," in *PassageMaker Magazine* (March/April 2002). Used with permission.

## Chapter 16

294     **Cruising the North Coast of Cuba**     Marie and Jean-Pierre Dufour hold joint U.S./French passports, so they have no difficulty travelling to Cuba. At the time of writing this book, U.S. citizens have more difficulties cruising in Cuba. Check the latest information.

299     **Looking for Zorba!**     Adapted from Mary Umstot's article, "Allure of the Greek Islands," in *PassageMaker Magazine* (June 2006). Used with permission.

300     **Black Sea**     Parts of this section were adapted from Mary Umstot's article, "Cruising the Black Sea," in *PassageMaker Magazine* (May/June 2005). Used with permission.

301     **Figure 16–10.** *Balaclava, Ukraine, once home to Soviet submarines.*     Photo by Denis Umstot. From Mary Umstot's article, "Cruising the Black Sea," in *PassageMaker Magazine* (May/June 2005). Used with permission.

302     *The 75' Radiant Star,*     See Robert M. Lane's article, "Radiant Star," in *PassageMaker Magazine* (Spring 1999).

302   *As Hal Roth shared in* Two Against the Horn   See Ken Murray's article, "40-Foot Trawler Braves Cape Horn," in *PassageMaker Magazine* (March 2003).

305   **South Pacific Highlights**   See Furthur.talkspot.com.

308   **Papua New Guinea: Going Back in Time**   See Maurice and Louise-Ann Nunas's article, "Our Australasian Seas Adventure," in *Waypoints* (Summer 2008). Used with permission.

310   **Idlewild's *Unusual Circumnavigation 2005–2006***   Based on information from Ben Gray. He has now completed a book of his journey: *An Incredible Journey: The* Idlewild *Expedition*, (Smashwords, 2011).

310   *From East London, South Africa, to Freemantle, Australia,*   Larry Briggs on *Neptune's Chariot* has made several longer nonstop voyages: one from Hong Kong to Long Beach, California (more than 8,000 nm), and one from Singapore to Suez. There could be others, but these voyages are exceptionally long. Note that the 75-foot *Neptune's Chariot* holds 10,000 gallons of diesel!

## Chapter 17

312   **The Rest of the Story**   Braun Jones is owner of *Grey Pearl*, a Nordhavn 62, and a USCG captain. From *Grey Pearl* blog, September 15, 2009. Revised by Braun Jones and used with permission.

315   *Polynesia was a true eye opener*   From a posting by Philip Eslinger, "The Evolution of the Long Range Cruiser," Passagemaking Under Power (PUP) list, August 31, 2009. Used with permission of the author and PUP.

318   **Taking Your Boat's Temperature**   Based on information from Steve D'Antonio and Bob Senter.

319   *Whole books have been written about troubleshooting diesel engines*   See Paul Dempsey, *Troubleshooting and Repair of Diesel Engines, Fourth Edition* (McGraw-Hill, 2007), and Nigel Calder, *Marine Diesel Engines, Third Edition* (International Marine/McGraw-Hill, 2006).

319   *Steve D'Antonio suggests some strategies*   See Steve D'Antonio's article, "Engine Troubleshooting," in *PassageMaker Magazine* (February 2007).

323   **A Haulout Gone Bad**   Excerpts from Don Perrine's article, "A Haulout Gone Bad," in *PassageMaker Magazine* (June 2007). Used with permission.

324   **A Case Study of Injector Pump Failure and Repair in the Remote South Pacific**   This case is adapted from Don McIntyre's e-mails and blog, Blue Treasure.me. Used with permission.

## Chapter 18

328   *(See Appendix E for recommended resources.)*   Recommended reading includes Steve and Linda Dashew, *Mariner's Weather Handbook* (Beowulf, 1998); Steve and Linda Dashew, *Surviving the Storm* (Beowulf, 1999); and other books referenced in this chapter.

332   **Use the 500-Millibar Charts**   See Joe Sienkiewicz and Lee Chesneau, *Mariner's Guide to the 500-Millibar Chart* (NOAA, Revised Edition, December 5, 2008).

333   *Figure 18–6. Three-dimensional depiction*   See Sienkiewicz and Chesneau, 2008.

333    *Route classification using the 500-mb chart.*    See Mike Ma-Li Chen and Lee S. Chesneau's book, *Heavy Weather Avoidance and Route Design: Concepts and Applications of 500-mb Charts* (Paradise Cay Publications, 2008).

337    *For example, a steady 30-knot wind*    See William G. Van Dorn's *Oceanography and Seamanship, Second Edition* (Cornell Maritime Press, 1993), 180.

338    **Figure 18–9.** *Deep-water breaking wave types*    See C. A. Marchaj's *Seaworthiness: The Forgotten Factor* (Tiller Publishing), 226.

339    *Othman's Circumnavigation and a Huge Wave*    This sidebar is adapted from Joseph D'Hippolito's Nordhavn Distance Pennant Program voyage description.

339    *The boat did not right itself; it later sank*    See Carol L. Hervey and Donald J. Jordan, *Investigation of the Use of Drogues to Improve the Safety of Sailing Yachts* (U.S. Coast Guard Report CG-20-87, May 1987).

342    **Resolution** *in a* **Storm**    This sidebar is a message sent by Michael McFadden to his brother, dad, and uncle. (Edited from the original version.) Used with permission.

343    *Of course, during a storm*    See Van Dorn (1993), 361.

343    **Maneuvering in High Seas**    This sidebar is adapted from Van Dorn (1993), 362–363.

343    *They do seem to work well in more moderate conditions*    See Hervey and Jordan (1987).

## Chapter 19

349    *Learning and using the approved phrases by IMO*    IMO Standard Marine Communication Phrases (June 10, 1997).

349    **Chart Inaccuracies**    See Mary and Denis Umstot's article, "How Accurate Are Our Charts?" in *PassageMaker Magazine* (July/August 2001).

352    *Cal and Nancy Massey's Nordhavn 40,* Hale Kai, *had a better outcome*    See Cal and Nancy Massey's description in "Crew Organization and Planning May Prevent an Unexpected Crisis from Becoming an Emergency on Your Vessel" at *Inside Passage News.com* (2009).

353    *One mathematically inclined cruiser*    Thanks to Chris Hallock for this computation, which is based on the following formula: GPM = 5.67 * d^2 * SQRT(H) Where: GPM = gallons per min flooding rate; d = opening diameter in inches or cm; H = depth of opening below the waterline in inches or cm.

353    **Through-Hulls and Safety at the Dock**    See Steve Dashew, SetSail.com (February 11, 2011).

353    *A marine insurance surveyor says,*    See "Lightning! Flash, BANG! Your Boat's Been Hit—Now What?" in *Seaworthy* (BoatU.S. Insurance, date unknown).

355    **Lightning Damage**    Based on Dennis O'Conner's Passagemaker Under Power (PUP) list posting (March 23, 2007); and from the Shearmadness72 website.

356    *While we were interviewing the Canadian Coast Guard for an article*    See Mary Umstot's article, "Standing By: Canadian Coast Guard Search and Rescue Vessels Patrol and Protect British Columbia Waters," in *Nor'westing* (April 2010).

359    *The Unthinkable: Major Trauma Offshore*    Abridged from Jeffrey E. Isaac's article, "The Unthinkable: Major Trauma Offshore," in *Ocean Navigator* (2009). Used with permission.

360    *There have been many anchor tests*    Research back issues of *Practical Sailor* to find anchor tests. Manufacturers' websites will often include tests as well.

363    *That's what happened to Eric and Christi Grab*    From Christi Grab's *The Unexpected Circumnavigation: Unusual Boat, Unusual People Part 1—San Diego to Australia* (2010).

## Chapter 20

367    *"ordinary everyday people who can do the most extraordinary, adventurous things.."*    See Beth A. Leonard's *The Voyager's Handbook, Second Edition* (International Marine/McGraw-Hill, 2007).

367    *Among voyaging couples, each party should be committed*    See Debra Ann Cantrell's *Changing Course: A Woman's Guide to Choosing the Cruising Lifestyle* (International Marine/McGraw-Hill, 2003).

367    *Lin and Larry Pardey have cruised for more than 43 years*    See Lin Pardey's article, "Ten ways to keep your lover," in *Boat U.S. Magazine* (October/November 2010). Adapted from Lin and Larry Pardey's book, *Capable Cruiser, Third Edition* (Paradise Cay, 2010). See also www.landlpardey.com.

368    *Bob Austin relayed some relevant information*    See Bob Austin's "Fish or Cut Bait, aka Big Decisions" in the Passagemaking Under Power (PUP) list (May 7, 2006). Used with permission of the author and PUP.

369    *Experiences of Women Who Went to Sea*    See Mary Umstot's article, "Women Who Answered the Call to the Sea," in *Latitudes and Attitudes* (April 2011).

370    *Another idea for smoothing relationships*    Thanks to Nancy Erley for this idea.

380    *Maurice and Louise-Ann Nunas, on the Kadey-Krogen 48, Akama*    See Maurice and Louise-Ann Nunas's article, "Our Australasian Seas Adventure," in *Waypoints* (Summer 2008).

## Appendix C

396    *Real World Fuel Burn*    Milt Baker was instrumental in developing and gathering data for this table.

# List of Contributors

**Anderson, Ross.** Owner of Diesel Duck, *10&2* and Skookum, *10&2*.

**Arthur, Bernie.** Co-founder of Skookum boats.

**Baker, Milt and Judy.** Owners of Nordhavn 47 *Bluewater*. Organizers of Med-Bound 2007 rally.

**Bannerot, Scott and Wendy.** Authors of the *Cruiser's Handbook of Fishing* (International Marine/McGraw-Hill, 2003). Scott has a Ph.D. in Fisheries from the University of Miami. They cruised on their 41-foot sloop, *Elan*.

**Barnes, Dick and Gale.** Owners of Nordhavn 50, *Ice Dancer*. They have cruised over 70,000 miles including South America and the South Pacific.

**Bass, Don.** Honorary Research Professor of Engineering and Mathematics, Memorial University, Canada. Expert on boat dynamics at sea, including roll-stabilization.

**Bray, Patrick.** Canadian naval architect and yacht designer. First-prize winner for technical innovation in Spanish design competition for his 75-foot long-range trawler, *Trekker 75*. Founder of Bray Yacht Design and Research.

**Briggs, Larry.** First circumnavigator in a trawler yacht. Three round-the-world voyages to his credit.

**Buehler, George.** Yacht designer (including the popular Diesel Duck line of boats). Author of *The Troller Yacht Book: How to Cross Oceans Without Getting Wet or Going Broke, Second Edition* (George Buehler/Booklocker.com, 2011).

**Bulger, Scott.** Owner of Nordhavn 40, *Alanui*.

**Calvert, Brian.** Cruising the South Pacific in Selene 48, *Furthur*. Website: www.furthur.talkspot.com.

**Carver, Hugo.** Partner in Knight & Carver. Trained as a marine engineer. Worked on ships for several years before going into the boatbuilding business. Built a number of Captain Beebe's boats, including *Teka III*.

**Cooper, Dave.** Owns *Swan Song*, a Roughwater 58, with Nancy Terrell.

**D'Antonio, Steve.** Expert on marine mechanical and electrical systems and author of a comprehensive look at boat systems, as yet untitled, from International Marine/McGraw-Hill, forthcoming 2013. Frequent contributor to *PassageMaker Magazine* and other publications.

**Dashew, Steve and Linda.** Steve is the developer of Sundeer and Deerfoot line of sailboats and designer and previous owner of sailboat *Beowulf*. Recently designed the powerboat *Windhorse* and the line of FPB powerboat designs derived from the *Windhorse* experience. With wife Linda, author of *The Offshore Cruising Encyclopedia*, Second Edition (Beowulf, 2002); *Mariner's Weather Handbook* (Beowulf, 1998); and *Surviving the Storm: Coastal and Offshore Tactics* (Beowulf, 1999). Their website is setsail.com.

**Dufour, Marie and Jean Pierre.** Owners of *Domino*, 65' catamaran designed by Malcolm Tennant.

**Eslinger, Phil.** Owner of Nordhavn 50, *Flat Earth*.

**Flanders, Scott and Mary.** Owners of Nordhavn 46 *Egret*. Their article, "*Egret's* Circumnavigation and You" (*PassageMaker Magazine*, July/August 2011) gives details of their adventures with circumnavigation. Numerous other magazine articles also describe their experiences. They share their stories and advice on the voyage of *Egret* website sponsored by Nordhavn (http: www.nordhavn .com/egret/index.php4).

**Freeman, R. M.** Founder of Wood-Freeman Autopilots. Expert on rudder design and modification.

**Gauthier, Joyce.** Owner of Malahide 65, *Ursa Major*, and expert on Romsdals and Malahide boats.

**Gerr, Dave.** Expert in yacht and small-craft design. He is director of the Westlawn Institute of Marine Technology and president of Gerr Marine. He has written more than 400 articles and books, including *Boat Mechanical Systems Handbook: How to Design, Install, and Recognize Proper Systems in Boats* (International Marine/McGraw-Hill, 2008).

**Grab, Christi and Eric.** Completed two-year circumnavigation in their Nordhavn 43, *Kosmos*, in 2009. Christi is author of *The Unexpected Circumnavigation: Unusual Boat, Unusual People Part I: San Diego to Australia* (2010) and *Part II: Australia to Oman* (2011).

**Gray, Ben.** Owner of *Idlewild*. Author of *An Incredible Journey: The Idlewild Expedition* (Smashbooks, 2011) about his unusual route through the rivers of Northern Canada then onward around the world.

**Hass, Heidi and Wolfgang.** Owners of Nordhavn 46, *Kanaloa*, on which they have completed two circumnavigations.

**Isaacs, Jeffery.** Author, along with David Johnson, of *Wilderness and Rescue Medicine* (Jones & Bartlett Publishers, 2012).

**Jones, Braun and Martina.** Owners of Nordhavn 64, *Ocean Pearl*, a replacement for their Nordhavn 62, *Grey Pearl*. They have circled the Pacific from Alaska to Thailand, via Japan. They have also crossed the Atlantic with the Nordhavn Rally.

**Kasten, Michael.** Yacht designer. His firm, Kasten Marine Design, specializes in both sail and powerboats. Publishes numerous helpful articles on his website, www.kastenmarine.com.

**Kessler, Bruce and Joan.** Owners of *Spirit of Zopilote*. Circumnavigators. Founders and organizers of FUBAR. Frequent contributors to boating seminars.

**Kimley, Bill and Stella.** Founders of Seahorse Marine and manufacturers of several lines of Diesel Duck steel boats.

**Klopfer, Benno.** Owner of *Diesel Duck* 41, which he built himself; upon completion he circumnavigated South America.

**Leishman, James F.** Co-author of *Voyaging Under Power*, Third Edition (International Marine/McGraw-Hill, 1994) and a co-owner of Pacific Asian Enterprises (PAE), builder of Nordhavn Yachts.

**Long, Roger.** Senior research vessel design consultant with JMS Naval Architects.

**Lund, Andy.** Owner of N46, *Resolution*.

**Marchaj, C. A.** Author of *Seaworthiness: the Forgotten Factor*. Expert on boat stability. Retired professor of aerodynamics and hydrodynamics of boats at Southhampton University, Great Britain.

**McIntyre, Don.** Owner of Seahorse Marine motorsailer, *Ice*. Accomplished sailor and adventurer. Completed the BOAC Single-Handed Around the World race in 1990. Has made numerous sailing voyages to Antarctica. Author of *Two Below Zero* (Australian Geographic, 1997).

**McFadden, Mike.** Crewmember on Andy Lund's N46, *Resolution*.

**McNett, Roy.** Owner of Beebe design, *Steel Magnolia*. Cruising in the Caribbean.

**Miller, Richard.** Expert on Willard boats and history.

**Neville, Charles.** Yacht designer of power boats and trawlers including several Cape Horn boats. Founder of Charles Neville associates.

**Nunas, Maurice and Louise-Ann.** Owners of Kadey-Krogen 48 Whaleback *Akama*. They have travelled on her throughout southeast Asia, Australia, and New Zealand.

**Othman, Ghanimal.** First Kuwati to circumnavigate.

**Pardey, Lin and Larry.** Authors of *The Capable Cruiser*, 3rd Edition (Lin Pardey Publications, 2010) website: www.landlpardey.com.

**Parlatore, Bill.** Founder of *PassageMaker Magazine*. Author of numerous articles on a wide variety of passagemaking topics.

**Perrine, Don.** Owner of Nordhavn 47, *Jade Explorer*.

**Peterson, Mike and Kim.** Owners of *Chrysalis* (designed by Malcolm Tennant). Kim is author of *Charting the Unknown: Family, Fear, and One Long Boat Ride* (Behler, 2010).

**Quentrall-Thomas, Peter.** Restored Beebe's boat, *Passagemaker*. Cruising the rivers of South America in 2012.

**Reilly, Hugh.** Owner of the historic passagemaker, *Westward*. Circumnavigated the Pacific.

**Roberts-Goodson, Bruce.** Yacht designer and founder of Bruce Roberts Yacht Design.

**Rogers, Jim.** Expert on Romsdals and Malahides, particularly photo history.

**Root, Sheppard.** Accomplished an early voyage from Hong Kong to the United States on a 40-foot Cheoy Lee trawler.

**Salmons, Bob.** Owner of *Veronica*, a Willard 40' full-displacement boat with bilge keels.

**Seaton, Stephen.** Designer of numerous passagemaking and expedition yachts for over forty years. He was one of the founders of Northern Marine and is an active designer for the Seaton Yachts. He is the only yacht designer featured in the first edition of this book.

**Senter, Bob.** Expert on John Deere and Lugger engines. Teaches classes in diesel engines for passagemakers and others.

**Sever, Peter J.** Founder of Cape Horn Trawlers.

**Sink, Jim and Suzy.** Undertook the first circumnavigation by a Nordhavn 46, *Salvation II*, completed in 1995.

**Stabbert, Donald and Sharry.** Owners of *Starr*, a 75-foot Northern Marine passagemaker. They have completed voyages to Europe, the South Pacific, and to Japan via Guam. Don is owner of Salmon Bay Marine in Seattle.

**Tennant, Malcolm.** Designer of catamarans and founder of Malcolm Tennant Multihull Design Co. After Malcolm's untimely death, Tony Stanton became head of the company.

**Terrell, Nancy.** Owner, along with Dave Cooper, of *Swan Song*, a Roughwater 58.

**Torelli, John and Maria.** Owners of several trawlers in San Diego, California. They have written numerous articles related to the lifestyle and true costs associated with owning and living aboard. Their book, *Life Is a Journey: Why Not Live Aboard a Trawler* (2009) is available at www.lulu.com.

**Umstot, Mary.** Author of *Voyaging to the Mediterranean Under Power: Imprints of Ports, People, Sunsets, and Storms* (Booklocker, 2010); and *Passagemaking Under Power Series: The Adventuresome Crew of* Teka III (Mary Umstot, 2011). Mary has authored numerous articles in *PassageMaker Magazine* and other nautical publications.

**Van Dorn, William G.** Author of *Oceanography and Seamanship, Second Edition,* (Cornell Maritime Press, 1993). Professor, University of California, San Diego. Founding director of Center for Coastal Studies.

**Wagner, Alan.** Owner of *Passage of Time*, a 53' Kasten-designed aluminum passagemaker. Moderator of the Passagemaking Under Power (PUP) list.

**Williams, Ken and Roberta.** Previous owner of a Nordhavn 62. In 2012 they are cruising the Mediterranean in Nordhavn 68, *San Souchi*. They organized and led the Great Siberian Sushi Run (GSSR) from Alaska to Japan.

**Wood, Bill.** Owner of *Sea Quest*, a Romsdal 65.

**Zajec, Lucka.** Crewmember on *Furthur*, a Selene 48. Lives in Slovenia.

# Acknowledgments

My wife, Mary, was not only instrumental in getting me to write this revision, she has also read every word and actively contributed a number of sections either as new text or as adaptations from her books or *PassageMaker* articles. Hugo Carver has been with me for every chapter, giving knowledgeable reviews and sometimes even contributing wonderful insights, such as his "Comfort" piece in Chapter 15, Crossing Oceans. Bill Parlatore, one of the true experts on passagemakers, has also read all the chapters and has added some of his own input in several. Steve Dashew was particularly generous with his time and his vast collection of photos. He spent two days with me early in the project answering questions and providing information. Michael Kasten and Stephen Seaton have been particularly helpful in making sure my chapter on seaworthiness is correct and useful. Both shared much information on design that has made the book better. Michael has contributed several sidebars in various chapters and spent a great deal of time clarifying the ISO stability ratings in Appendix B. Dr. Don Bass, Professor at Memorial University, read and critiqued my chapter on roll attenuation strategies. He also helped clarify the section on anti-roll tanks. Bob Jones of Ocean Marine Navigation was kind enough to read my chapter on weather. Dr. Ewin Thompson read the section on lightning and contributed a photo showing his strategy for reducing lightning damage. Bob Senter, a Lugger and John Deere expert, has helped with a number of chapters including systems and maintenance. He and Hugo Carver, a marine engineer and boatbuilder

mentioned above, have been my experts in these technical matters. Jim Leishman, author of the last edition, spent several hours providing insights and approaches to the book. He was also helpful in getting information on the various Nordhavns used as examples in the book. Some of his sections from the previous edition have been repeated and he has added some new insights for this edition.

Information from other cruisers makes this book different from past editions. There were hundreds of people who shared their experiences—I can only name a few, but all are important. You will see their names as you read through the chapters. Milt Baker has been invaluable with his information and help on Nordhavn and other cruisers' experiences. He helped design and execute Appendix C, Real World Fuel Burn. Throughout the book Milt has provided insights that have made the book much richer and more informative. My friends Christi and Eric Grab have also been willing to share their experiences from their circumnavigation. No matter what I asked, they produced. You will find many stories from their voyages. Scott Flanders also shared his very detailed and interesting logs with the readers. One could write a whole book just about his experiences.

The chapter relating to past passagemakers needed information that is not readily available. Joyce Gauthier was very helpful with Romsdals and Malahides, sharing her knowledge and photos generously. Bernie Arthur graciously provided information and drawings for his Skookum line of passagemakers. Richard Miller was particularly helpful with the section on Willards. Larry Polster at Kadey-Krogen was helpful for everything relating to the Krogen boats. Jenny Stern helped find photos of Nordhavns.

*PassageMaker Magazine* has been particularly helpful, making copies available of any back issues I needed for my research. They also freely gave permission to use excerpts and photos from their articles. *Ocean Navigator* has also allowed use of their articles throughout the book. The builders and designers who submitted their work are also greatly appreciated. They shared not only the specifications, but the lines for their designs—information that is not normally available. Some were brave enough to furnish stability curves, but others were reluctant unless everyone could agree on a common method of calculation and reporting. Perhaps the ISO method will eventually be adopted as a U.S. standard.

Finally, my editor, Molly Mulhern, deserves a lot of credit for the final form of the book. When I finished my research, I found much more information and photos for the revision than when it was originally conceived. She was patient and adaptable in integrating these changes and making them work.

# Index

Numbers in **bold** indicate pages with illustrations

high seas, maneuvering in, 343; ideal passagemaker design, 55; improving performance, **75**, **76–77**; *Passagemaker*, 27; size and aspect ratio, 74–**75**; stability and, 69, 74; tillers, emergency, **161**–62; twin rudder, 74, 77, **79**; voyage planning and preparations, 267

Ruffin, Frank and Maude, 251

running lights, 169–**170**, **311**, 314, 349

safe to store valuables, 143

safety: concerns aboard, 366; at the dock, 353; near-shore, 349–353, **350**, **351**, **352**; offshore, 347–**49**

sailing rig and sails: anchoring sails, 364–**65**; expense of, 33; get-home options, **151**, 283; *Passagemaker*, **26**, 28, 33–**34**; *Passagemaker* concept, 19–20, 22, 25; roll and pitch oscillations and, 69; steadying sails and stabilization, **83**, **104**–5

sailing vessels: designs for cruising and long voyages, 17, 19; Fastnet disaster, 61–62; Hawaii, cruising time to, 36; long voyages in, 5–6; motorsailers, 20, 33–34, **119**; night passages, 273–74; pitchpoling and capsizing, survival of, 346; rallies, 373; simplicity of systems aboard, 107; stability data on, 82; watchstanding, 273

SailMail SSB communication system, 172, 336

Salmons, Bob, **103**

saloons: design choices, 134–35; handholds in, 121, **132**, **134**, 143–44; location of and accommodation layouts, 120–24, 129, **131**–35; seating arrangements, **132**, **134**, 144

*Salty Dawg*, 396–97

*Salvation II*, 41–45, **42**, **43**, 253, **254**–55

Sanders, Brian, 191

*Sans Souci*, 255

*Sarah Sarah*, **163**, 396–97

*Sara Reid*, 3

*Saratoga*, USS, **3**, 5

satellite phones, 172, 305

Schuette, Hank, 41–**45**

sea anchors and drogues, 343–44

*Seabird*, 255

seacocks and through-hull fittings, 248, 267, 313, 317, 353

*Seaducktress*, **192**

seagoing motorboats. *See* passagemaking yachts/seagoing motorboats

Sea Grant Program (MIT), 79

*Seahorse*, 396–97

Seahorse Marine, 191, 193, 198, 325. *See also* Diesel Duck boats

Seakeeper gyro, **104**

seakindliness: bulbous bows and, 79–82, **81**; comfort and, 383–84; concept of and vessel characteristics, 61, 83; hull shape and, 69–71, **70**; size of boat and, 113

*Sea Quest*, 238–**39**, 331

*Sea Raven*, 241

*Searcher*, 250–51

*Seascape*, **107**, 121,**297**

seasickness, 82, 84, 113, 272, 288–89, 385

seating arrangements, **134**, **136**–37, **142**–43, 144

Seaton, Stephen: articulated foil rudders, **78**; A/B ratio, opinion about, 54; designs by and background, 224, 235, **245**; hatches and ventilation, 145; Neville, partnership with, 210, 246; self-righting boats, 67. *See also* Cape Scott 54; Werner Bay 50

Seaton 64, 224, **227–29**

seaworthiness: 61–82; of catamarans, 72; concept of and vessel characteristics, 61; interest in and importance of, 61, 384; *Passagemaker* concept, 25; of trawlers, 50, 57

security: boardings and robberies, 13; for dinghies, 128, 357; piracy concerns, 262, 293, 309, 356–58; safe to store valuables, 143

Selene: 76–77, 137 305–7, **306**, **381**

self-righting boats, 67–68

Senter, Bob, 147, 148, 164, 320

Seven Seas Cruising Association (SSCA), 260, 375

Sever, Peter J., 256–58

Seychelles, 309, 357

*Shaka*, 256

sharpies, 2–3

ship lights, 277, 280

shipping services, 255, 310

shop manuals and mechanical references, 319, 326, 386

shop space (workshop), **139**, 317–18

shore power, **168**–69

shower and shower pan, 312

sight gauges, 282

*Silver Spray*, **187**

Singapore: boat building in, 28–30, 249; cruising from and around, 5, 11, 27, 30–**31**, 252, 261, 272–73

singlehanded operation/one-man watch, 19, 25, 33

single-sideband (SSB) nets, 45, 172, 271, 336, 372, 376

single-sideband (SSB) radios: communications with, 42, 45, 336, 376; controls, **167**; monitoring of, 172; uses for, 171–72; voyage planning and preparations, 268; weather information from, 45, 172, 336

Sink, Jim and Susy, 37, **41**–**45**, 253, 254–55, 259

Skookum Marine, 241–43; Skookum 42, 240; Skookum 53, 241, **242**, 396–97

Slorach, Andrew, 221

Smith, Bill and Arlene, **152** 255

social connections. *See* communities and social considerations

Somalia, 309, 357

South America, 16; cruising from and around, 293, 301–5, **302**, **303**, **304**, 321; piracy concerns, 357; wind and weather conditions, 328–29, 330, 331

South Coast Marine, 184

South Pacific islands, 17, 272, 305–7

Spain: pickpockets, 295–96; Rota, Spain-Canary Islands passage, 45, 334–36; wind and weather conditions, 331; wintering in, **376**

spare parts, 311, 314–17, **315**, 398–400

Sparkman & Stephens, 257

*Special Blend*, **184**, **382**, 396–97

speed: fuel burn, 396–97;cost of, **52**–53; cruising speed, 59; fuel burn, 396–97; hull speed, 52, 53, 55, 56–57; prismatic coefficient and efficiency under power, **22–23**, 55–56; range, fuel consumption, and, 20, 28, 43, 53, 56, 387–391, **390** ; top speed, 59; voyaging decisions about, 39

speed/length ratio (S/L): catamarans, 53, 72; concept of and vessel characteristics, 50, 51–53; displacement boats, 53; horsepower requirements and, **52–53**, 59, 149, 387–391, **388**, **389**, **391**; ideal passagemaker design, 55; prismatic coefficient and efficiency under power, **22–23**, 55–56; range and, **52–53**, 58–59; seagoing motorboats, 49; of trawlers, 57